Foundation Engineering

P.C. VARGHESE

Honorary Professor, Anna University, Madras
Formerly, Professor and Head, Department of Civil Engineering
Indian Institute of Technology Madras, Chennai, and
UNESCO Chief Technical Advisor, University of Moratuwa, Sri Lanka

PHI Learning Private Limited

New Delhi-110001

2011

Rs. 425.00

FOUNDATION ENGINEERING
P.C. Varghese

ISBN-978-81-203-2652-1

The export rights of this book are vested solely with the publisher.

Eighth Printing ... ... **February, 2011**

Published by Asoke K. Ghosh, PHI Learning Private Limited, M-97, Connaught Circus, New Delhi-110001 and Printed by Mudrak, 30-A, Patparganj, Delhi-110091.

To

Professor Arthur Casagrande
under whose guidance the author started his studies
in Geotechnical Engineering

Contents

Chapter 9   Load Carrying Capacity of Piles by Static Formulae   173–209

Chapter 10   Load Carrying Capacity of Piles by Dynamic Formulae   210–237

Preface

Two distinct disciplines are involved in the design of foundation structures. The first is the soil mechanics part which is generally dealt with by those specialised in geotechnical engineering. The second is the detailed design of structural elements which is generally carried out by structural engineers. This book deals principally with the geotechnical part which is designated as *Foundation Engineering*. "Foundation Engineering" by R.B. Peck, W.E. Hansen and T.H. Thornburn (New York, Wiley 1974) is considered as a classical book on this subject.

After teaching and practising Design of Concrete Structures and Foundation Engineering for more than four decades, I felt that it may be desirable to present a textbook on Foundation Engineering written from the perspective of structural engineers. This is the background of this book.

Foundation Engineering is too broad to be treated adequately in a single volume. Hence only those topics commonly found necessary by structural engineers have been dealt with in this book. Special topics like foundations of dams, tunnels, airports, dewatering of foundations, which are also of importance to civil engineers, are not included in this text.

Foundation Engineering is both a science and an art. It is different from structural engineering as we are dealing with a natural material and not a manufactured product. Properties of soil vary very much even at the same site. Hence the subject involves the use of a large amount of empiricism (or knowledge derived from experience) as well as theory. Understanding the nature of the basic parameters to be considered in the design is more important in Foundation Engineering than the selection of the exact values of the properties of the soil, which can never be determined. These aspects were always emphasized by Prof. Karl Terzaghi and Prof. Arthur Casagrande of Harvard University under whom I commenced my studies in geotechnical engineering. I have tried to maintain the same emphasis in this book also.

This book is essentially meant as a textbook for undergraduate and postgraduate students in Civil Engineering. Practising engineers will also find this book very valuable in their work. Undergraduate students can get a clear grasp of the fundamentals and need not study all the topics included here. Postgraduate students are expected to have a good knowledge of all the topics discussed in this text.

The aim of the book is to present the fundamentals of the various topics in an easy to understand style. References have been made to the Indian Codes dealing with the various topics.

One of the special features of this book is the **lecture-based presentation.** Each chapter deals only with one lecture topic, followed by a large number of worked-out examples. This presentation has been found to benefit the teachers preparing their lectures and the students to learn the subject at depth. This presentation is also helpful to field engineers for their self-study.

I take the presentation of this book as a great opportunity to pass on to the students and fellow engineers the advice I received from Prof. Casagrande about how to study the subject of Soil Mechanics, and from Prof. Terzaghi about how to practise the art of Foundation Engineering. Their messages are given as Introduction and Appendix E, respectively, in this book.

I fervently hope that the readers will find this book both interesting and useful. Any suggestions for improving the contents will be highly appreciated.

P.C. Varghese

Acknowledgements

I gratefully acknowledge the help I received from a number of my colleagues and other publications in the preparation of this book.

I thank Dr. S.R. Gandhi, Professor, Geotechnical Engineering, Indian Institute of Technology Madras and Dr. K. Ilamparuthi, Professor and Head, Soil Mechanics and Foundation Engineering, College of Engineering, Guindy, Anna University for going through the manuscript and giving me valuable suggestions. I appreciate the help I received from Dr. M. Muttharam of Soil Mechanics and Foundation Engineering Division, College of Engineering Guindy for checking the final proofs. I am thankful to Mrs. Rajeswari Sivaraman in word processing my handwritten manuscript. Mr. R. Ramadas helped me in preparing all the initial drawings.

This book has a number of equations, figures, etc., which would not have been possible without the help of other publications. References have been made to them at the end of each chapter and they are too numerous to be mentioned here. I gratefully acknowledge each of these publications.

Finally, I wish to put on record my sincere appreciation of the excellent cooperation I received from the Publishers, Prentice-Hall of India, New Delhi, both during the editorial and production stages of this book.

P.C. Varghese

Introduction

There can be no better introduction to the subject of Foundation Engineering than the following advice Prof. A. Casagrande used to give to his students at the start of his lectures in Soil Mechanics at Harvard University.

The following are some of the general remarks I would like to make at the beginning of my course in Soil Mechanics. I stress particularly the necessity of critical thinking and of independent judgement. In my experience I have found nothing more stimulating and better suited to the development of the courage that is necessary for independent and critical thinking than a knowledge of the historical development of the subject. Unfortunately, the type of undergraduate instruction offered by many engineering schools and the typical average textbooks show just the opposite trend which, in my opinion, tend to smother any critical instincts which the students may possess. I admit that it is very much easier for students merely to memorize "by heart methods and formulae" for the solution of the problem. It is also better for their peace of mind if they do not hear about all the simplifying assumptions which make up our theories and all the difficulties we encounter in the actual application of the theory to engineering problems. Whether the students will appreciate this kind of training in later years when they begin to discover the shortcomings in their studies is another question.

As an introduction to Soil Mechanics and Foundation Engineering as well as a primer for the development of critical attitude to the subject, I urge my students to study thoroughly the opening address presented by Prof. Terzaghi before one of the conference of building engineers. "I know of no better guide in the development of the right mental attitude towards the practice of Foundation Engineering than a careful study of this masterful expression of the development of this science."

P.C. Varghese

Units

It is customary in Soil Mechanics to use SI units. Stresses are expressed in kN/m^2 and weights in kN/m^3. However, structural engineers in India are more used to strengths in N/mm^2 for concrete and steel. As the strengths of soils are much less than steel and concrete, the traditional MKS system of using kg/cm^2 for strength of soils is still followed by many engineers for foundation design. This is so because a large number of empirical relation in those units are available in foundation engineering. For example, in the classical literature on soil mechanics, the static cone resistance was always expressed in kg/cm^2. In these units the SCPT value of a soil is of the order of magnitude 2 to 10 times the SPT or N values, depending on the nature of the soil. Again, the approximate unconfined strength of clays in kg/cm^2 is traditionally taken as of the order of $N/10$ kg/cm^2. Expressing the strength of soils in kg/cm^2 will also convey to the structural designer an idea of the relative strength of the soil with reference to the concrete and other materials used in foundations.

Accordingly, a deliberate departure has been made in this book in not sticking strictly to using the standard units only. It has also been done because the conversion from one unit to the other is rather easy. The following conversion factors can be used to convert a given unit to any other unit as required:

$1\ kg/cm^2 = 100\ kN/m^2 = 10\ t/m^2 = 1/10\ N/mm^2$
$1\ N/mm^2 = 10\ kg/cm^2$, and $1\ MN/m^2 = 100\ t/m^2$
$1\ ton = 1000\ kg = 10\ kN$
$1\ kg/cm^3 = 10 \times 10^6\ N/m^3$ (Subgrade reaction)
$1\ t/m^2 = 1/10\ kg/cm^2$
$1\ kN/m^2 = 1/100\ kg/cm^2$
$1\ Pascal\ (Pa) = 1\ N/m^2$
$1\ kPa = 1\ kN/m^2 = 1/1000\ N/mm^2$
$1\ t/sqft = 1\ kg/cm^2$ (approx.)

Example 1 **(Unconfined strength of clays)** For a clay with SPT value of N, the unconfined strength will be of the order of $N/10$ kg/cm^2 (see Table 1.6).

Example 2 **(Properties of sand)** For a sand deposit, its static cone penetration in kg/cm^2 will be 2 to 10 times the SPT value, depending on its nature (IS 2911 and Table 1.7). Its ϕ value can be estimated as $\phi = 0.3\ N + 27$ or $\phi = \sqrt{20\ N} + 15$ degrees.

1
Engineering Properties of Soils

1.1 INTRODUCTION

In theoretical soil mechanics, we try to understand the fundamental behaviour of soils and also study the laboratory techniques to estimate the soil properties. On the other hand, in applied soil mechanics we study how to use the above soil parameters to solve practical problems. For this purpose, except in simple cases, we have to make many simplifying assumptions, based on intuition, scientific reasoning and past experience. This is specially true in situations where decisions are to be made on the basis of not very accurate soil investigation reports. In many instances interpretation from geological reports and field tests will give us a better idea of the engineering properties of soils than the results of badly conducted laboratory tests. In this chapter we will make a short review of the laboratory and field methods to arrive at quantitative assessment of the properties of the soil.

1.2 MODELS USED IN DESIGN OF FOUNDATIONS

In general we use one of the following models to solve practical problems in soil mechanics:

1. By using empirical or thumb rules without any calculations based on past experience or local practice. For example we will design a low retaining wall by this method. Similarly for timbering of a shallow excavation up to 3 m height, it is more economical to use local practices.

2. By theoretical calculations using the soil properties and theories of soil mechanics as in the study of the stability of an earth slope.

3. By actual prototype testing under field conditions after theoretical study as in the design of pile foundations.

4. By adopting construction with the observational method of using field indicators to monitor soil behaviour as in soil improvement by pre-loading.

The method of using combination of numerical calculations for initial design combined with prototype testing and field observations is the most commonly used and recommended method for foundation construction in major projects. The pure observational method has the disadvantage that we may come across many surprises during construction so that forward planning becomes difficult unless we have large amount of experience on similar projects. The method of numerical

1

calculation requires the choice of representative parameters which can be obtained only from very accurate field investigation and laboratory reports. It is of utmost importance that representative soil properties are used in our design calculations. An approximate calculation with satisfactory soil properties will give us better results than an exact theoretical analysis with doubtful soil properties. When solving problems by using theoretical calculations we use one or more of the methods shown in Table 1.1 depending on the problem.

TABLE 1.1   CLASSIFICATION OF METHODS USED IN SOIL MECHANICS

Problem	Model
Stress distribution	Boussinesq's elastic half space
Plastic failure	Rankine's plastic state
Consolidation and settlement of cohesive soils	Terzaghi's model — Spring supported piston and dashpot
Strength of soils	Coulomb–Mohr model and Roscoe's critical state model
Earth pressure	Coulomb's wedge or Rankine's plastic failure
Stiffness of soil	Elastic half space or Winkler models
Contact pressure	Elastic half space or Winkler models

1.3   IMPORTANT ENGINEERING PROPERTIES

Soil properties can be divided into two groups namely physical properties (Group I) and, mechanical or engineering properties (Group II). These are indicated below [1], [2]:

Group I—Physical properties.   These properties give us a general indication of the type and state of the soil we are dealing with. They are also known as *index properties*. The important ones are the following:

- Geological origin
- Grain size distribution, unit weight and specific gravity
- Liquid and plastic limits *along with natural water content of fine grained soils*
- Void ratio and relative density of clays and sands respectively
- Shrinkage limit of fine grained soils
- Activity of clays
- Sensitivity of clays
- Swelling index of clays.

Group II—Mechanical (or engineering) properties.   These are the properties we use in our engineering calculations. The important ones are the following:

- Shear strength and stress-strain characteristics
- Modulus of subgrade reaction
- Deformation modulus (modulus of elasticity)
- Consolidation characteristics
- Other special properties like permeability for special problems.

One of the fundamental differences of natural soil deposits from other manufactured civil engineering materials like steel is its non-uniformity. At the same site, soil may vary along its length and depth of the site. Hence what we should aim at is to get a representative general value of the properties. Because of this reason, in soil engineering, we seek to find properties by laboratory tests as well as by special field tests. Much data can be obtained from simple field tests like standard penetration tests or static cone penetration tests. A foundation engineer should necessarily be aware of the empirical relations between simple field tests and the engineering properties of the soil. *Special emphasis is given in this chapter to explain these relationships to enable the designer to make an intelligent guess of the properties of the soil we are dealing with, from field tests and index properties.*

1.4   REVIEW OF PHYSICAL PROPERTIES

The following sections give a brief review of the physical properties and show how they can also be used to get an approximate idea of the general engineering properties of soils.

1.4.1   Geological Origin

Soils from different geological origin behave differently. Soil investigation report should always give a brief geological history of the site and origin of the soil. Soil deposits can have one or more of the following geological origins discussed in more detail in Chapter 27.

- In-situ weathering of rock (the rock type should be specified)
- River or alluvial deposits
- Lake or lacustrine deposits
- Marine (beach and sea) deposits
- Organic deposits (peat, lignite)
- Wind or aeolian deposits (dune sand).

Besides, site deposits of different geological origin can also exist one over the other.

1.4.2   Grain Size Distribution

Before the importance of mineralogy of clays was known, soils were classified only by grain size. The generally accepted modern classification of soil based on grain size is shown in Fig. 1.1

We plot grain size on semilog scale, as we have to represent sizes from 100 mm to 0.001 mm in the same diagram. Plots with values increasing to the right hand side as well as those decreasing to the right are used in practice. It is good to remember that coarser particles of the soils generally consist of single grained quartz mineral whereas clays are made of different clay minerals (kaolinite, illite, montmorillonite etc.) which are active minerals. Whereas mechanical properties of sands depend mostly on grain size and relative density, the properties of clays depend on their mineral compositions and water content.

We may assume that the smallest size that we can see by the naked eye as single grain is about 0.06 mm (0.02–0.06 mm is silt). Particles below this size are called *fines*. Hence we should first examine the soil to find out the percentage of fines with reference to the whole sample. We should also be aware that it is the finest 20 to 25 percent part of the soil that will have the greatest influence on the mechanical behaviour of the soil. It is the finest 10 percent that determines the permeability of the soil. (This will be clear if we imagine that the coarse particles act as inert

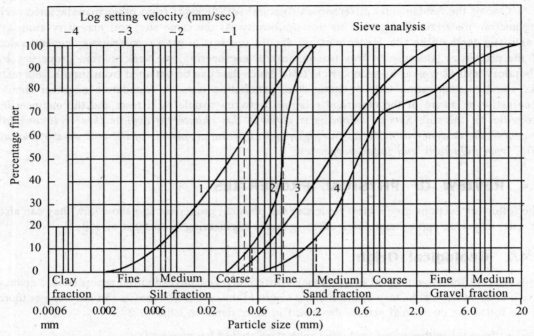

Fig. 1.1 **Grain size distribution chart and classification of soils: 1. Well graded sandy silt; 2. uniform fine sand; 3. well graded sand; 4. poorly graded gravelly sand.**

spheres and if soil has even only 15 percent of clay, all the voids can be filled with clay which will influence the total behaviour of the soil.)

Next we should examine the gradation of the soil. Without good gradation and low relative density, sands are liable to settle down by vibration. Gradation also affects permeability and compaction characteristics of soil. Traditionally the following quantities are of importance:

1. D_{10} = Allan Hazen's effective grain size.

2. $U = D_{60}/D_{10}$ = coefficient of uniformity = slope of the grading curve. To be well graded it should be between 1 and 8 for silts and clays, greater than 4 for gravels and greater than 6 for sands.

3. Coefficient of curvature $C_{cr} = D_{30}^2/(D_{10}D_{60})$

4. *Fineness modulus.* This term is more used in concrete technology than in soil mechanics. It is defined as one hundredth of the sum of cumulative percentages retained on a series of specified sieves in sieve analysis. The larger the fineness modulus the larger will be the particle sizes.

1.4.3 Limits of Consistency

Liquid and plastic limits together with natural water content are the most important property in cohesive soils. We should remember that for testing the limits we take the soil fraction passing 0.425 mm. (The portion used for hydrometer analysis is sieved through 0.075 mm and lowest limit of sand size is 0.06 mm) Thus the sample for limit test contains not only the clay sizes but also the silts and even a portion of fine sand. Hence the limit test should be interpreted with reference to that part of the soil used for the limit test in the total mass.

Note: Instead of using the Casagrande apparatus, in some countries like Russia and China, liquid and plastic limits are determined by a 30° conical penetrometer loaded with a specified weight. Water contents for penetrations of 17 mm and 2 mm are taken as the liquid and plastic limits.

Position of soil on plasticity chart. The plasticity chart (shown in Fig. 1.2) with a line called A-line was developed by Casagrande to determine the plastic properties of soils. He found that soils of the same locality and same geological (mineralogical) origin seem to group together in this plot. Higher the point on this chart the tougher are the clays. The A-line separates the organic soils from inorganic soils and also silts from inorganic clays as shown in Fig. 1.2.

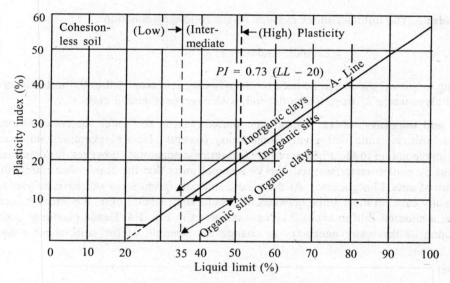

Fig. 1.2 Plasticity chart and A-line.

Comparison of water content (*w*) with limits. If the liquid limit is considered as the water content at which the soil behaves as a semi-liquid and the plastic limit as the point where it behaves as a semi-solid and the shrinkage limit where it behaves as a solid, the comparison of the in-situ water content of plastic soils with these limit values will give us an indication of the undisturbed state of the soil as shown in Fig. 1.3. If the in-situ water content is below but near about the liquid limit, then a normally consolidated soft clay is expected. On the other hand if the water content is very low, near the plastic limit, it will generally be an overconsolidated clay. This is expressed as *consistency index* or *relative consistency*, I_c.

$$I_c = (LL - w)/PI \qquad (1.1)$$

where *LL* and *PI* respectively stand for liquid limit and plastic index.

If $I_c = 0$ then it is a liquid. If $I_c = 1$ soil is at plastic limit (*PL*).

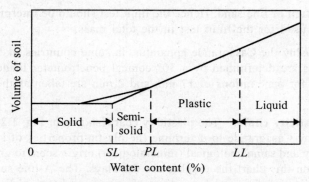

Fig. 1.3   Atterberg limits and consistency.

Liquidity index.   The liquidity index is given by the following equation:

$$\text{Liquidity index } (LI) = \frac{w - PL}{PI} \qquad (1.2)$$

The following empirical guide can be used to classify clays: *LI* from 1.0 to 0.6 implies normally consolidated clays while *LI* from 0.6 to 0.0 indicates overconsolidated clays.

Flow index and toughness index.   Casagrande showed that at the water content corresponding to the liquid limit, all soils will give a fixed shear strength. He had expressed this value as 27 gm/cm^2 corresponding to the 25 blows of the Casagrande apparatus (however, for determination of liquid limit by penetrometer method, the IS assumption is that the above shear strength is of constant value of only 17.6 gm/cm^2). At the plastic limit, different soils will have different shear strengths. In any case, in most soils, between the liquid and plastic limits, the strength increases by more than a hundred fold to about 2 kg/cm^2 as shown in Fig. 1.4. Hence plasticity index can be looked upon as the water necessary to change the strength of the soils about a hundred

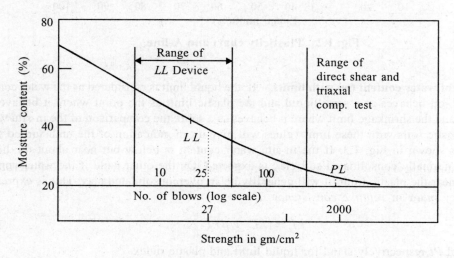

Fig. 1.4   Strength of clays at different consistencies.

fold from the strength at the liquid limit. Also if two clay soils of different *PI* are stressed by the same amount, more water will be squeezed out of the soil with a higher *PI*, thus producing more settlement.

The slope of the flow curve which is the curve drawn with the number of blows (on log scale) on *X* axis and the water content on *Y* axis, is called the *flow index*. We may say that for two soils having the same plastic index values, the soil with a flatter flow curve (lower flow index) will have a larger shear strength at plastic limit. If s_1 is the fixed shear strength at liquid limit (equal to 0.02 kg/cm^2) and s_2 the shear strength at plastic limit (which is variable),

$$(PI/\text{Flow index}) = \log (s_2/s_1) = \text{Toughness index } (T_w) \tag{1.3}$$

Roughly, the one hundred times variation of strength should give a toughness index of 2. In practice toughness index of soils varies from 0 to 3 in most cases though in rare cases it may reach 5. It gives us a measure of the increase of strength with decrease in water content. If toughness index is less than 1, the soil is very friable at plastic limit.

Correlation between plasticity index and shear strength.   There are some correlations between plasticity index and shear strength.

Skempton and others have shown that for normally consolidated clays there is an empirical relation between the ratio of (shear strength/overburden pressure) and the plasticity index. This is shown in Fig. 1.5a, see [1].

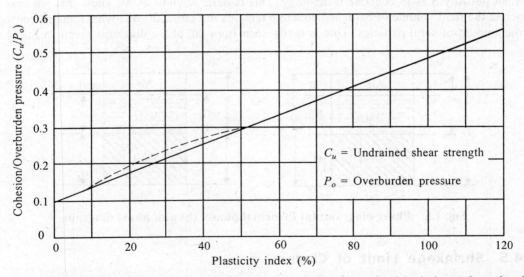

Fig. 1.5a Estimation of cohesion for normally consolidated clays from plasticity index and overburden pressure.

Another relation between plasticity index *PI* and SPT value *N* to give mass shear strength of clays has been published by Stroud [3]. This is shown in Fig. 1.5b, refer [2].

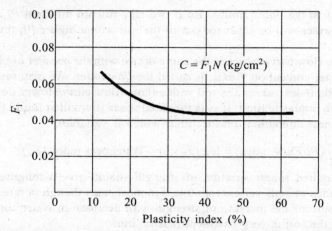

Fig. 1.5b Estimation of cohesion from plasticity index and N value.

1.4.4 Void Ratio

It was Terzaghi who first pointed out that while dealing with problems in soil mechanics (as for instance, while considering the consolidation strength) we should take void ratio e as the base and not porosity n as in concrete technology. This is quite obvious as we know that whereas in concrete the final volume of hardened concrete remains the same, in soils what remains constant is the amount of solid particles. This is easily seen from the phase diagrams given in Fig. 1.6.

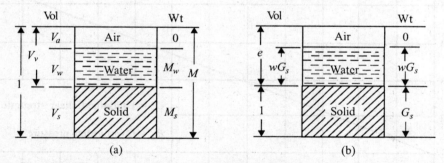

Fig. 1.6 Phase diagram: (a) Principal phase; (b) unit phase diagram.

1.4.5 Shrinkage Limit of Clays

This is a very important test for finding out the expansive nature of clays (this will be described in Chapter 21). It is more meaningful to carry out the test using an undisturbed sample of soil with natural water content and 20 to 30 cc in volume.

1.4.6 Activity of Clays

Another plot commonly used to have a rough idea of the type of clay minerals present in the clay fraction of the soil is the *Activity Chart*. As shown in Fig. 1.7, it is drawn with *PI* on the *Y* axis

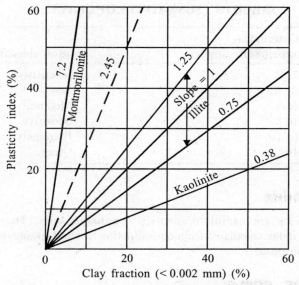

Fig. 1.7   Activity chart and composition of clays.

and percent of clay (particle size less than 0.002 mm) on the *X* axis. Activity is defined as the ratio of the *PI* value to the percentage of clay present. Table 1.2 gives us an indication of the type of clay minerals present in the soil sample. The test is also used for identification of expansive clays. More expensive tests like x-ray diffraction tests and differential thermal analysis can be used in important projects to confirm preliminary findings based on index properties.

$$\text{Activity ratio} = PI/\% \text{ clay}$$

TABLE 1.2   CLAY MINERALS AND ACTIVITY

Activity ratio	Type of clay minerals	Description of activity
Less than 0.38 > 0.38 and < 0.90 > 2.45	Kaolinite Illite Montmorilloinite (Black cotton soils)	
< 0.75 0.75 to 1.25 > 1.25		Inactive Normal Active (Probably expansive type)

1.4.7   Sensitivity of Clays

Sensitivity of clays means the loss of strength with disturbance It is defined as the ratio of the strength of the undisturbed soil sample and the remoulded soil sample both under undrained conditions. Table 1.3 is used for describing such soils. Marine clays are examples of sensitive clays.

TABLE 1.3   SENSITIVITY OF CLAYS

Ratio of strengths Undisturbed/disturbed soil samples	Soil classification
≤ 1	Insensitive
1 to 1.2	Low
2 to 4	Medium
4 to 8	Sensitive
8 to 16	Extremely sensitive
≥ 16	Quick

1.4.8 Swelling Index

Laboratory and field tests are useful to identify expansive soils. They are described in Chapter 21. The swelling index calculated from consolidation test and simple differential free swell tests are used for this purpose.

1.5 STRENGTH OF SOILS

So far we dealt with index properties. Considering engineering properties strength is the most important property. Coulomb was the first to publish (in 1773) about soil friction and earth pressures. He used it for design of earth fortifications. Coulomb's law of shear strength of soil is as follows:

$$\tau = c + \sigma \tan \phi \tag{1.4}$$

where

   τ = shear strength
   c = cohesion (later on called apparent cohesion)
   σ = total compressive stress
   ϕ = angle of internal friction (apparent friction).

It was as late as in 1920 that Terzaghi pointed out the limitations of Coulomb's law and the *importance of pore pressure* in mobilizing friction in soils. He modified the above equation as follows:

$$\tau = c' + (\sigma - u) \tan \phi' = c' + \sigma' \tan \phi'$$

where

   c' = true cohesion
   u = pore water pressure
   σ' = effective pressure
   ϕ' = true friction.

The prime sign was used to indicate that they refer to values with respect to effective stresses. This theory has been used since 1920 and is referred to as the *Classical Theory* of strength of soils. Measurement of shear strength by the direct shear apparatus has been in use for the past nearly 200 years. The first triaxial compression machine to measure shear strength was constructed by Casagrande in 1930 at Massachusetts Institute of Technology [4]. The story of the development of this machine since then to this day to increase its useful for routine tests and research in soils is a fascinating story. Even though many advanced tests can be done on a modern triaxial compression machine, the *routine tests* conducted in most of the laboratories using these machines are only the following:

- Unconfined compression test
- Unconsolidated–undrained triaxial test (Quick or Q test)
- Consolidated undrained triaxial test (Consolidated quick or R test)
- Consolidated drained triaxial test (Slow or S test).

We may also add to this list the special test called the 'Triaxial compression test with pore pressure measurements and volume change'. However this test still remains as a research tool than a routine test. When clays are tested under fully drained condition (with no pore pressures) it is only the 'overconsolidated clays' that give sizable value of cohesion. Normally consolidated clays give only small values of cohesion as shown in Fig. 1.8.

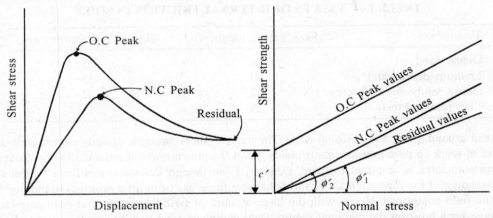

Fig. 1.8a Peak shear strength and residual shear strength from direct shear tests on overconsolidated clays (OC). Normally consolidated clays (NC). (Soft clays do not show a peak value.)

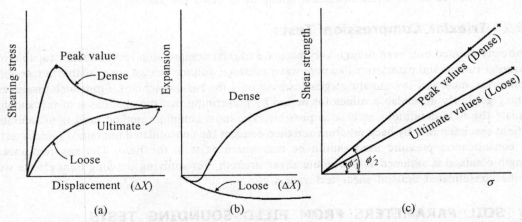

Fig. 1.8b Peak shear strength by direct shear test on sands: (a) Stress–strain curves; (b) change in specimen thickness; (c) peak and ultimate values.

In most of our calculations in foundation design, we use shear strength. *For these shear strengths, the samples should be tested in the laboratory under the same conditions that exist in the field. The recommended speeds for direct shear* (drained tests) are as follows.

1 mm/min for sands, 0.01 mm/min for silts and 0.001 mm/min for clays. These speeds are assumed to dissipate pore pressures completely. Today, triaxial compression tests are more often used for strength tests than the direct shear tests.

1.5.1 Shear Strength of Soils

Figure 1.8b gives the results of drained tests on dense and loose sand specimens. Two curves can be obtained, one by using the data obtained for the peak values and the other by using the ultimate values. Values of ϕ obtained are different as shown in Table 1.4. From these and other types of test, investigators working at Cambridge University (U.K.) under the leadership of Roscoe

TABLE 1.4 VALUES OF INTERNAL FRICTION IN SOILS

Type of soil	Peak values (degrees)	Ultimate values (degrees)
Dense sand	55	35
Medium dense sand	40	32
Dense sandy silt with clay	47	32
Clay (drained test)	25	15

proposed around 1965, the 'Critical State Theory' for shear strength of soils. A similarly large amount of work on pore pressure coefficients A and B were carried out around 1954 by Skempton and his associates in Imperial College, London. Even though these theories have widened our understanding of the fundamentals of soil behaviour there has been little progress in linking these with the field conditions. Hence with the large amount of field/laboratory and field co-relations that have been built on the classical theory, field engineers tend to continue to use the classical theory than its modern variations for routine designs. This conservative practice of using ultimate values is followed in India also.

Note: For values of undrained shear strengths of clays see Table 1.6.

1.5.2 Triaxial Compression Tests

As already pointed out, even though very accurate triaxial compression test machines capable of measuring various soil parameters like pore water pressure, volume change are available in research laboratories, most soil investigating agencies have only the basic machines. From such machines we may get fairly dependable values for design by prescribing that the conditions of test should simulate the field conditions as best as possible. The most common method used is to saturate the field specimen first by back pressure and then conduct the consolidated undrained (quick) test. The consolidation pressure used should be that which exist in the field. The apparent shear strength obtained is assumed as the in-situ shear strength. For studying the long term effects we use the consolidated drained shear test values.

1.6 SOIL PARAMETERS FROM FIELD SOUNDING TESTS

In any soil explorations, field tests like standard penetration test (SPT) should be considered as a very essential component. A number of such inexpensive field tests to study the variation of the soil formation along with a few expensive laboratory test is the ideal method for site exploration. The importance of these tests lie in the fact that in soil mechanics there are a large number of empirical relations between these simple tests and the soil properties which give us a very powerful means to verify laboratory results and arrive at satisfactory soil parameters for design. The three types of field sounding tests commonly used are the following. A review of these tests and their use is also given in the following sections.

- Standard penetration test (SPT and N values) IS 2131.
- Dynamic cone penetration test (DCPT) IS 4968 Parts I and II gives N_{cd} values.
- Static cone penetration test (SCPT and q_c values in kg/cm^2) IS 4968 Part III.

The SPT originated in the U.S.A. while the SCPT was developed in Europe by the Dutch. Hence the latter is also known as the *Dutch Cone Penetrometer test*. In loose and soft deposits SCPT gives us more reliable information than SPT (as SCPT was originally expressed in kg/cm^2 and as 1 kg/cm^2 is roughly equal to 1 ton/sq. ft, we usually express q_c in kg/cm^2 rather than in kN/m^2. For any conversion we can use the equivalence 1 kg/cm^2 = 100 kN/m^2).

1.7 DYNAMIC PENETRATION TESTS

1.7.1 Standard Penetration Test (SPT)

This test is described in all textbooks on soil mechanics. Essentially they are made in 100 mm dia. boreholes shelled out inside steel casings. SPT test is made for every meter advance through the soil. The actual depths should be staggered in different holes so that no strata is missed during the exploration. For this test the special split spoon sampler is driven to penetration of 450 mm, by counting the blow for each 75 mm of penetration (75 × 6 = 450 mm) marked on the drill rod. Otherwise, drive it in three successive 150 mm penetrations, the first 150 mm value being considered as only the seating value. This procedure can assess any disturbed soil present at the bottom of the borehole. The number of blows per foot (300 mm) penetration is the SPT value. Normally, (unless needed to assess the strength of rocks) if the blows per foot of penetration are more than 60, the driving is discontinued and the SPT value is simply recorded as more than 60. Not much significance is given to variations of SPT values that are above 50 to 60, except inferring that the material is hard.

We should always remember that SPT should not be conducted in holes with uplift conditions. Hence holes in sands should be filled with water before conducting the test and the excavated soil in the hole should be carefully removed before conducting the SPT test so that very little disturbed soil is left at the bottom of the hole. We should also correct the SPT values for (1) overburden pressure and (2) for submergence in the case of very fine silty sands as explained.

Correction for overburden pressure. It was only as late as in 1957 that Gibbs and Holtz suggested that corrections should be made for field SPT values for depths. He took the standard pressure as 280 kN/m^2 (corresponding to a depth of 14 m assuming the bulk density as 20 kN/m^2 as standard). Thus the corrected values were to be given by the following formula:

$$N_{\text{(corrected)}} = \left(\frac{350}{70 + \sigma} \right) N = C_N N \qquad (1.5)$$

where σ = the overburden pressure in kN/m^2 and C_N is the correction factor.

As the correction factor came to be considered only after 1957 all empirical data published before 1957 like those by Terzaghi is for uncorrected values of SPT values. Since then a number of investigators have suggested different standards to which the depth corrections are to be made as shown in Fig 1.9a [4]. Thus, for example, in 1963. Thornburn suggested a standard pressure

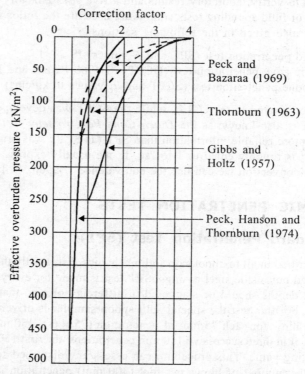

Fig. 1.9a   Correction factors for influence of effective overburden pressure on SPT (N) values suggested by various investigators.

of 138 kN/m² (corresponding to a standard depth of 7 m). Finally, in 1974, Peck, Hanson and Thornburn [5] suggested a standard pressure of 100 kN/m² (1 kg/cm²) corresponding to a depth of 5 m of soil with $\gamma = 20$ kN/m². All field SPT values after 1974 are corrected by the correction factor shown in Fig. 1.9 which can be represented by the following equation:

$$C_N = 0.77 \log_{10}(2000/p) \tag{1.6}$$
$$N_C = (C_N)N$$

where

N_C is the corrected value

p is the overburden pressure in kN/m².

(For $p = 100$ kN/m² or 1 kg/cm², the correction factor N_C will be equal to 0.77 $\log_{10} 20$ which is equal to unity.) We should remember that the standard for values published after 1974 is with reference to this correction. No correction is generally applied to position of water level for sands unless it is fine.

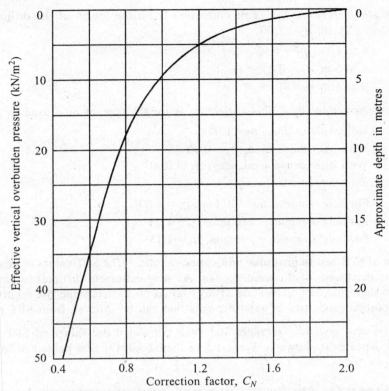

Fig. 1.9b   Correction factors for *N* values [Peak, Hansen and Thornburn (1974)].

Another equation used for adjustment for overburden pressure is

$$C_N = \left(p_0''/p_0'\right)^{1/2} = \left(\frac{95.76}{p}\right)^{1/2} \tag{1.6a}$$

where

p_0' = actual overburden pressure

p_0'' = standard overburden pressure = 95.76 kN/m² or 100 kN/m² (approx.)

Correction for silts and fine sands below water level.   The correction for values of *N* greater than 15 in fine sands below water level is as follows:

$$N_C = 15 + 0.5 \, (N - 15) \tag{1.7}$$

This correction is due to the fact that higher values are liable to be recorded due to pore pressure.

Other corrections.   Some authors like Bowles recommend further corrections as follows.[6]

1. *Hammer efficiency, η_1.*   This depends on the energy ratio or efficiency ratio *E* given by the hammer. It is usually taken as 70% for normal operation. For any other energy ratio we use the expression,

$$E_{r1} \times N_1 = E_{r2} \times N_2, \qquad \eta_1 = \frac{E_r}{E_{70}}$$

where *N* is the SPT value.

2. *Rod length correction,* η_2. This correction is for the length of the drilling rod used. For length > 10 m, $\eta_2 = 1.00$,

$$6 \text{ to } 10 \text{ m } \eta_2 = 0.95$$
$$4 \text{ to } 6 \text{ m } \eta_2 = 0.85$$
$$0 \text{ to } 4 \text{ m } \eta_2 = 0.75.$$

3. *Sampler correction,* η_3. This correction is for the type of hole used.

Hole without liner, $\eta_3 = 1.00$
With liner loose sand, $\eta_3 = 0.90$
With liner dense sand, clay, $\eta_3 = 0.60$

4. *Borehole diameter correction,* η_4

For hole diameter 60–120 mm, $\eta_4 = 1.00$
For hole diameter = 150 mm, $\eta_4 = 1.05$
For hole diameter = 200 mm, $\eta_4 = 1.15$

(A) Application of SPT test to granular and cohesive soils. The SPT values in sand give a good indication of the denseness of the sand deposit. As it is extremely difficult to get undisturbed samples in sand deposits, SPT values are always relied on to determine the relative density of sand. Some important properties of sand deposits that can be inferred from SPT tests.

SPT and relative density. Terzaghi and Peck correlated the values of SPT with relative density of sand deposits as shown in Table 1.5 in their book [7] first published in 1948.

TABLE 1.5   SPT VALUES AND RELATIVE DENSITY OF SAND

SPT value	< 4	4–10	10–30	30–50	> 50
Denseness	Very loose	Loose	Medium	Dense	Very dense
Static cone resistance q_c (kg/cm^2)	< 20	20–40	40–120	120–200	> 200

The frequently used values of ϕ for SPT results on sand is as shown in Fig. 6.3. A much more exact correlation between SPT denseness and angle of friction represented in Fig. 1.10. (As these values were published in 1974, they should refer to corrected SPT value.) The curve marked 2 in Fig. 1.10 gives the average values given in most textbooks. It can be also represented as $\phi = 0.3N + 27$. Another expression used is $\phi = \sqrt{20N} + 15$ degrees.

(B) Application of SPT to cohesive soils (clays). Even though SPT values are not considered as a good measure of the strength of clays, it is used extensively as a measure of the consistency of clays. The consistency is then related to its approximate strength. The commonly used relationships are as given in Fig. 1.11 and Table 1.6.

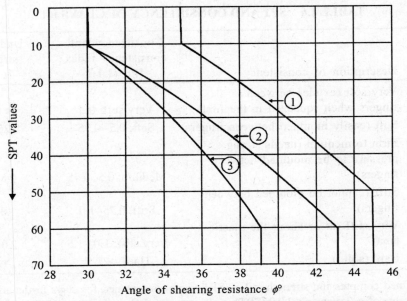

Fig. 1.10 SPT – ϕ relation for granular soils: (1) Well graded sand and gravel; (2) uniform fine sand (average values); (3) silty sand (see also Fig. 6.3).

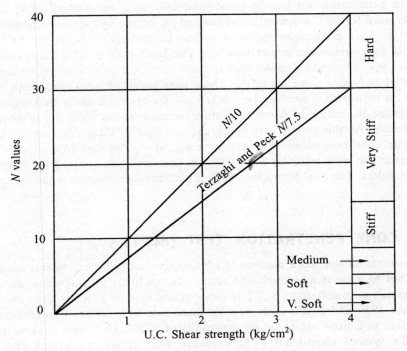

Fig. 1.11 Relation between SPT and unconfined shear strength of clays.

TABLE 1.6   SPT AND CONSISTENCY OF CLAYS [6]

N values	Description of consistency	Consistency and consistency index [Eq. (1.1)]	Undrained strength $q_u = 2c$ (kg/cm^2)
0–2	Very soft (exudes between fingers when squeezed in the first)	Very soft: 0.5	< 0.25
2–4	Soft (easily moulded between fingers)	Soft: 0.5–0.75	0.25–0.5
4–8	Firm to medium (needs strong pressure to be moulded between fingers)		
8–16	Stiff (cannot be moulded between fingers)	Medium: 0.5–0.75	0.5–1.0
16–32	Very stiff (at or about the plastic limit)	Stiff: 0.75–1.0	1.0–2.0
> 32	Hard (solid)	Very stiff: 1.0–1.5	2.0–4.0
		Hard: > 1.5	> 4.0

Note: Unconfined compression strength = 1/8 (SPT value) is assumed for clays in the above table. A conservative value of q_u(kg/cm^2) = 1/10 (SPT) is also taken by others for clays of high *PI* values > 30).

1.7.2   Dynamic Cone Penetration Test (N_{cd})

The dynamic cone penetration test can be considered only as a variation of SPT. Instead of the spoon sampler used for SPT, a special solid cone of 60 degree and 50 mm diameter is used as a penetrometer. This probe can be used either in the borehole as an SPT test or without a borehole as a continuous penetration test. The latter may be of the recoverable type or the expendable type. Experience shows that in most soils, the solid cone penetrometer test *tends to give a slightly higher value than SPT*. These tests are to be used along with SPT tests so that a correlation between the two can be worked out for each site under investigation. It is then used to determine the nature of deposits in other locations at the same site without putting an expensive borehole. As this test is very much cheaper than SPT tests in boreholes, a large number of dynamic cone penetration tests can be made at various locations at nominal cost along with SPT tests. The blow count for every 100 mm penetration due to a 65 kg weight falling through 750 mm is taken. The total blows for one foot (300 mm) penetration is the dynamic cone value, N_{cd}.

1.8   STATIC CONE PENETRATION TEST (SCPT) (q_c)

The static cone penetration test has a number of advantages over SPT. Its greatest advantage is that the test need not be made in a borehole and hence it is less likely to suffer from disturbances due to boring operations. In soft clays SCPT is better suited than SPT. It has been in extensive use in Europe since 1930 and is still more popular there than SPT. Most of the empirical data regarding pile design in Europe are based on the results of SCPT. The value is expressed as q_c in kg/cm^2 and this symbol should not to be confused with q_u the unconfined compression strength.

In brief, the test consists of finding the resistance to penetration in kg/cm^2 of a 60° cone of base diameter 35.7 mm (area 10 cm^2) with special arrangements to eliminate shaft friction. The cone is gradually pushed at a rate of 5 mm/second into the soil for a distance of 10 cm at a time and the maximum pressure required in kg/cm^2 is designated as the SCPT value. The term *friction cone penetrometer* denotes an advanced version of this static cone by which the cone resistance and shaft resistance can be measured separately. It can be seen that the SCPT is specially applicable to places with low SPT values as in clays and loose sands.

Application to sand deposits. The denseness and the angle of shear resistance of sand deposits will be a function of q_c (the static cone resistance). The correlation for ϕ, for given cone resistance and overburden pressure as proposed by Durgonogle and Mitchell in 1975 [8] is given in Fig. 1.12a. The values can be used directly also for estimation of settlements in sands as described later in the chapter on settlement calculations.

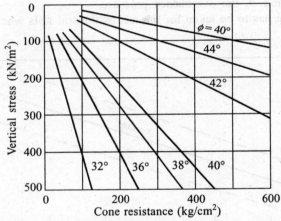

Fig. 1.12a Relation between static cone penetration resistance and friction in sand for varying vertical stresses [Durgonogle and Mitchell].

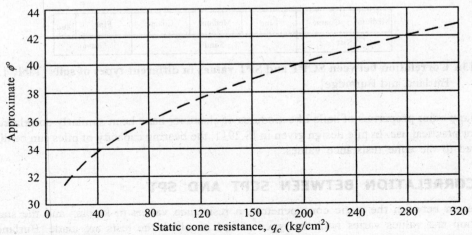

Fig. 1.12b Relation between static cone penetration resistance and approximate friction values in sand.

In sand deposits, if we compare the probe as a pile test, we can show that the cone resistance can be related to the pile end resistances: [9]

$$q_c = (\text{const})N_q\sigma'_o$$

where

q_c = CPT value

N_q = bearing capacity factor (a function of ϕ)

σ'_o = effective overburden pressure (subject to limitations given in Chapter 9).

Application to cohesive soils. The slow pushing of a cone into the clay soil can be also considered as similar to a pile test conducted to final failure. In the case of clay, at the point of failure, the tip resistance has the following value (see Chapter 12).

$$q_c = 9c + \sigma_o \quad \text{or} \quad c = (q_c - \sigma_o)/9 \tag{1.7a}$$

where c is the cohesion and σ_o the overburden pressure.

A conservative value has to be taken for the test as the soil fails when the cone penetrates into the soil.

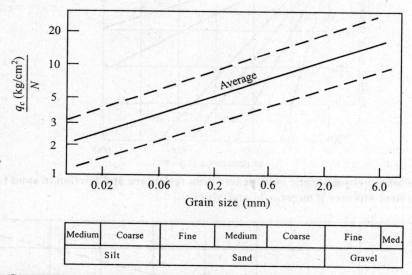

Fig. 1.13a Correlation between SCPT and SPT values in different types of soils [Table 1.7 and Burland and Burbidge].

Many other properties of soils like modulus of elasticity have been similarly correlated with SCPT for practical use. In pile design given in IS 2911, the bearing capacity of piles can be directly correlated to the cone resistance values.

1.9 CORRELATION BETWEEN SCPT AND SPT

The relation between the static cone penetration resistance values in kg/cm² and the standard penetration test values varies with the types of soil in which the tests are made. Burland and Burbidge have shown in 1981 that the correlation between these tests can be represented as shown in Fig. 1.13a, refer [2]. The ratio of q_c/N recommended in IS 2911 in connection with pile foundation is given in Table 1.7, see [10].

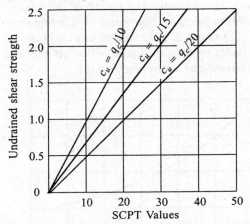

Fig. 1.13b **Relation between static cone penetration test values and undrained shear strength in clays.**

TABLE 1.7   **CORRELATION BETWEEN** N **AND SCPT** q_c [8]
[IS 2911 Appendix A]

Soil type	q_c/N (kg/cm²)	
	IS (2911)	Others
Clays	1.5–2.0	—
Silts, sandy silts and slightly cohesive silt sand mixtures	2.0–2.5	2.0
Clean fine to medium sands and slightly silty sands	3–4.0	3.5
Coarse sands and sands with gravel	5–6.0	5.0
Sandy gravel and gravels	8–10	6.0

Note: For clays we may assume SCPT value q_c (kg/cm²) = 1.5 to 2.0 N.

1.10   IN-SITU VANE SHEAR TEST

This is a very useful test used in the field and also in the laboratory for measurement of the undrained peak shear strength of cohesive soils. This test was developed by the Scandinavian countries to measure the shear strength of soft and sensitive clays, but presently it is used in all types of clays. It is especially useful for very soft clays and also very stiff fissured clays in which it is difficult to extract undisturbed samples for laboratory testing. Details of the test are given in IS 4434 (1967).

For soft clays (SPT less than 8), field vane shear test is the most reliable test. Generally a 50 mm diameter, 100 mm long vane (length/diameter = 2) is used for the test. Other diameters depending on the strength are also used and in the presentation of the results in the report, we should also report the diameter of the vane used for the test. In theory, if s_v and s_h are the shear strength in the vertical and horizontal directions, the total torque for a vane of diameter D will be as follows (we assume that the top of the vane is also inside the soil):

$$T = (\pi D^2/2)[Hs_v + (D/3)s_h] \qquad (1.8)$$

where D and H are respectively the diameter and height of the vane.

Unless we assume s_v and s_h to be equal, two vanes of different diameters are needed to solve the above equation. Bjerrum [11] found in 1972 that in soft clays the vane test field value has to be modified by a correction factor (shown in Fig. 1.14) to get the true value. Correction is for anisotropy and the speed of failure due to testing rate.[2]

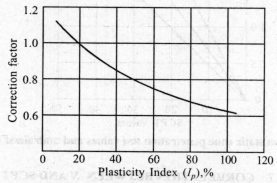

Fig. 1.14   Correction factor for vane shear test [Bjerrum].
(Factor = Field vane value/mobilised value)

1.11 ESTIMATION OF MODULUS OF SUBGRADE REACTION AND MODULUS OF ELASTICITY

Two of the other important engineering properties of the soil we use in design are the *modulus of subgrade reaction* and the *modulus of elasticity*. Generally, the modulus of subgrade reaction is denoted by the symbol k in kN/m^3. If we multiply k by the breadth B, we get kB which is represented by the symbol K in units of kN/m^2. In many literatures k itself will be shown as K and we should look for the units to find out what it represents.

Modulus of subgrade reaction, also called 'soil spring constant', is used to solve problems of beams on elastic foundation using Winkler model. It is defined as follows and expressed in kg/m^3 or kN/m^3. [Symbol k is as used by IS2950 Part I-1981 on raft foundation.]

$$k = \frac{\text{pressure}}{\text{settlement}} \text{ (in units of force per length}^3)$$

Modulus of elasticity or deformation modulus is used for determination of settlement of foundations and is expressed in kg/m^2 or kN/m^2. The settlement s of a rigid plate under a uniform load q is given by the equation, [12]

$$s = \left[\frac{q(1-\mu^2)}{E_s}\right]BI_w \qquad (1.9)$$

where

$\qquad B$ = least dimension of the plate

$\qquad I_w$ = influence factor (0.82 for a square)

E_s = deformation modulus (kg/cm^2)

μ = Poisson's ratio of the soil.

The stress deformation diagram that can be obtained by a plate load test on a soil stratum will be as shown in Fig. 1.15. The value of the initial tangent modulus will be different from the secant modulus.

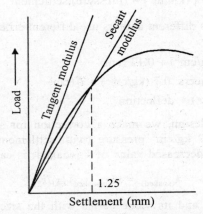

Fig. 1.15   **Load-settlement curve in plate load test.**

Generally the secant modulus corresponding to 25 to 50 per cent of the failure stress is used for all practical applications. The cone penetrometer test can also be used as an indirect method for estimation of the k and E_s values corresponding to the above stress level, especially in sands. We know from elastic theory and field bearing test that k has no unique value but depends on the size of the loaded area, it decreases with increasing size of plate.

The modulus of subgrade reaction that we come across in horizontal deflection of laterally loaded piles is the coefficient (modulus) of horizontal subgrade reaction denoted by k_h.(in kg/cm^3). The value of k_h for an overconsolidated clay is usually assumed to remain constant with depth. On the other hand for most normally consolidated clays and granular soils this soil modulus varies with depth. Accordingly we have the following values for k_h.

1. $k_h = mk_v$ (for overconsolidated clays—$m \geq 1$), and
2. $k_h = n_h y$ (for granular soils)

where, for dimensional uniformity,

n_h = the constant of soil modulus (kg/m^4)

y = depth below the ground level.

For n_h to have the same dimension as k_v, we sometimes write $k_h = n_h y/D$, where n_h is in kg/cm^3 and D is the depth. This subject is further discussed in the section dealing with well foundations and laterally loaded piles. The various methods to determine k and E_s are briefly described below.

1.11.1 Estimation of Modulus of Subgrade Reaction

First we will discuss some methods for the estimation of the modulus of subgrade reaction.

Method 1: *Estimation of k by plate load test (Terzaghi's method)*

Details of the plate load test for k values are given in IS 9214 (1979). A square plate not less than 30 cm (1 ft) in size is loaded to a total settlement of at least 1.8 mm. From the pressure corresponding to a settlement of about 1.25 or 1.3 mm is taken to calculate k.

$$k \text{ (kN/m}^3) = \text{(pressure)/settlement}$$

As pointed out by Bowles different authors use different criterion for determining k values. Some of these are given below:

Road Research Lab: q (kg/cm^2) ÷ 0.13 (cm)

U.S. Corporation of engineers: 0.7 (kg/cm^2) ÷ δ (cm)

Others: (1/2 yield pressure) ÷ deflection

For highway pavement design, we make a correction for soaking. For this purpose, an unsoaked specimen under 0.69 kg/cm^2 pressure (with settlement s_1) is soaked and the new settlement s_2 is recorded. The decreased value of k (soaked) is calculated as follows:

$$k_{\text{(soaked)}} = (k_{\text{unsoaked}})\,(s_1/s_2) \tag{1.10}$$

k value is not a soil property and its value varies with the size of the contact surface. The following are the correction suggested by Terzaghi.

Correction for cohesive soils. k_p value obtained from a square plate of size B_p is corrected for a width B by the following relation to get k (k decreases with increase in size).

$$kB = k_p B_p \tag{1.11}$$

Correction for cohesionless soils.   The value k_1 obtained from 0.30 metre square plate is corrected for a plate of width B metre from the following relation:

$$k = k_1 \left(\frac{B + 0.30}{2B} \right)^2 \tag{1.12}$$

However, this correction seems to give too small a value of k for medium dense to dense sands.

Correction for length/breadth effect.   Terzaghi proposed the following correction also for the $L/B = m$ effect for k derived from square plate:

$$k' = k_{\text{(square)}}[(m + 0.5)/1.5\,m] \tag{1.13}$$

However, this correction is not generally carried out in our routine calculations.

Method 2: *Estimation of k from E_s obtained from triaxial test (Vesic's method)*

This method requires the value of E_s that can be got from a triaxial test on a specimen corresponding to the ground condition and the σ_3 value between $0.5B$ to B beneath the foundation level. The value of k is calculated by using the following equation proposed by Vesic. Details of triaxial test are available in IS 2720 Part (xii) 1981 on testing of soils.

$$k = \frac{0.65}{B} \left[\frac{E_s B^4}{E_c I_c} \right]^{1/12} \left[\frac{E_s}{1 - \mu^2} \right] \tag{1.14}$$

(which may be taken as)

$$= \frac{0.9 \text{ to } 1.5}{B} \left[\frac{E_s}{1 - \mu^2} \right]$$

$$\approx \frac{1.2 E_s}{B(1 - \mu^2)} \text{ or } \frac{E_s}{B(1 - \mu^2)} \text{ (in units of force/length}^3) \tag{1.14a}$$

where

E_s = modulus of soil as obtained from triaxial test

E_c = modulus of material of foundation structure (concrete)

I_c = moment of inertia of foundation

μ = Poisson's ratio (see Table 1.11)

B = breadth of foundation

Note: When $B = 1$ we get $k = E_s/(1 - \mu^2)$ in kN/m^2.

Method 3: *Estimation of k from m_v values for clays—Extrapolation from consolidation test.*

In this method, the value of subgrade modulus is calculated from odometer test on clay samples.

The odometer settlement = $s_0 = (\Delta q)(m_v)(H)$

$$\Delta q/s_0 = 1/(m_v H) = k$$

where

m_v = average coefficient of volume compressibility

H is taken as equal to $0.5B$ to B.

Even though Tschebotarioff does not recommend this method for silts, it is said to give fair results for clays. As we know from theory of consolidation tests, in all cases, the actual experimental curve should be used for the evaluation of k (the use of indirect evaluation of m_v should be avoided).

Method 4: *Estimation of k from E values for clays.*

We assume that the effect of loading extends to a depth of B only. The value of E from unconfined or other pertinent tests are taken and k is calculated as follows:

$$k = E/B \text{ (kg/cm}^3 \text{ units).}$$

Method 5: *Approximate values of k from codes of practice*

Most often for preliminary design we adopt the values usually prescribed in codes of practice. The values given in Table 1.8 are as per IS 2950 code of practice for raft foundations (2nd revision).

TABLE 1.8 VALUES OF MODULUS OF SUBGRADE REACTION k
[IS 2950 – 1981 (Second Revision) Table 1]

(a) Cohesionless soils (values for 30 × 30 cm plate)

SPT value	Relative density	Dry/Moist	k value (kg/cm³)
			Submerged
< 10	Loose	1.5	0.9
10 to 30	Medium	1.5–4.7	0.9–2.9
> 30	Dense	4.7–18.0	2.9–10.8

(b) Cohesive soils (Values for 30 × 30 cm plate)

q_u = Unconfined camp: strength (kg/cm²)	Consistency	k value (kg/cm³)
1 to 2	Stiff	2.7
2 to 4	Very stiff	2.7–5.4
> 4	Hard	5.4–10.8

Note: A value $k = 120\ q_u$ in kN/m³ (where q_u is unconfined strength in kN/m² is commonly used for preliminary estimate in clay soils.)

1.11.2 Estimation of Deformation Modulus (Modulus of Elasticity)

In soils deformation modulus is also called *modulus of elasticity*. As already stated, we use the secant modulus at 25 to 50 per cent of failure stress in most of our calculations. The following are the commonly used methods for its estimation:

Estimation of E of value for cohesionless soils (sands). As it is difficult to take undisturbed samples of sand deposits, the static cone penetration test SCPT or SPT value is generally used to estimate the E_s value of sand.

Schmertman recommends the following values for the secant modulus at 25 per cent stress level for normally consolidated sands q_c = SCPT value in kg/cm².

$E = 4q_c$ when $q_c < 100$ kg/cm²

$E = (2q_c + 20)$ for q_c between 100–500 kg/cm² (Approximate value $2q_c$ is used)

$E = 120q_c$ for $q_c > 500$ kg/cm²

For overconsolidated sands, the recommended values are:

$E = 5q_c$ for $q_c < 500$ kg/cm²

$E = 250q_c$ for $q_c > 500$ kg/cm²

D'Appolonia uses SPT values and gives the following values for normally consolidated (virgin compressed) sand.

$E = 220 + 11(N)$ kg/cm²

For pre-compressed sand, over consolidation ratio (OCR) = $\dfrac{\text{preconsolidation stress}}{\text{present effective stress}}$

$E = 540 + 14(N)$ kg/cm²

Other empirical relations for sand are shown in Figs. 1.16a and 1.16b.

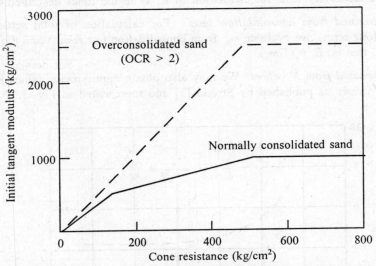

Fig. 1.16a Relation between static cone penetration resistance and initial tangent modulus [Lunne and Christoffersen].

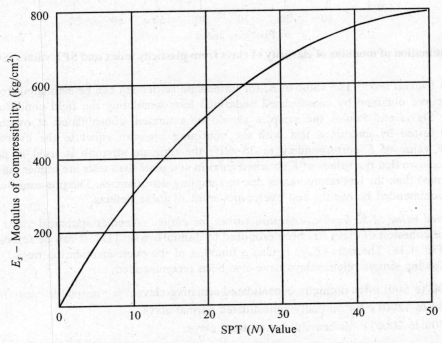

Fig. 1.16b Relation between SPT values and modulus of compressibility (elastic modulus) in sands [Schultze and Muhs].

Estimation of E_s for cohesive soils (clays).   As it is not difficult to take undisturbed samples in clays, we can use laboratory tests for estimation of E_s as in the cases described below.

E_s from m_v obtained from consolidation tests: For calculation of total settlement (i.e. immediate plus the long term), we evaluate m_v from consolidation test results and the reciprocal of m_v is taken as E_s, that is, $E_s = (1/m_v)$.

E_s from m_v estimated from N values: We may also obtain approximate values from index properties and SPT values as published by Stroud [3] and represented in Fig. 1.17 [2]. Here, $E_s = (1/m_v)$.

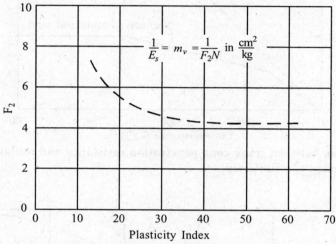

Fig. 1.17   Estimation of modulus of elasticity of clays from plasticity index and SPT values [Stroud].

E_s from triaxial test: The value of E_s for immediate settlement can be estimated from the stress-strain curve obtained by consolidated undrained tests simulating the field condition. As suggested by Davis and Poulos the samples should be saturated, consolidated at overburden pressure and tested by undrained test with the confining pressure equal to the overburden pressure. The value of E corresponding to 25–50% the ultimate strength is used in design. Research has shown that the values of E obtained from in situ plate load tests are higher (as much as 1.8 to 4 times) than the laboratory values due to sampling disturbances. The pre-consolidation procedure recommended before the test overcomes most of these defects.

Undrained value of E_s from c_u cohesion values for clays: Another statistical value of E_s from values of cohesion of clays has been proposed by Jamiolkowski [13]. It can be represented as shown in Fig. 1.18. The ratio (E_s/c) is also a function of the overconsolidation ratio.

The following simple relationships have also been recommended:

E_s = (200 to 500) c for normally consolidated sensitive clays

   = (750 to 1200) c for normally consolidated normal clays

   = (1500 to 2000) c for heavily consolidated clays.

Note: An average value $E = 700 \, c$ is usually taken for normally consolidated clay.

Approximate E_s values from codes of practice.   Average values recommended by codes of

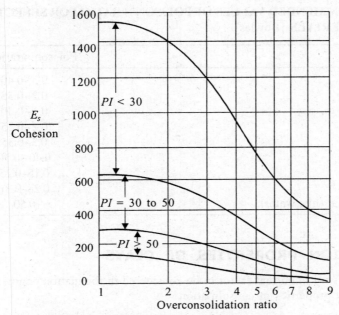

Fig. 1.18   Estimation of modulus of elasticity of clays from cohesion in values [Jamiolkowski].

practices are generally used for routine office design. These are given in Table 1.9 and Table 1.10. Recommended values of Poisson's ratios are given in Table 1.11.

TABLE 1.9   RANGE OF VALUES OF E_s FOR COHESIONLESS SOILS
(Cohesionless soils IS 2950 Part 1 1973 (first revision) Table 1)

Type of cohesionless soil	E_s value (kg/cm^2)
Sand, loose, round	200–500
Sand, loose, angular	400–800
Sand, medium dense, round	500–1000
Sand, medium dense, angular	800–1000
Gravel	1000–2000
Broken stone angular	1500–3000
Silt	20–200

TABLE 1.10   RANGE OF VALUES OF E_s FOR CLAYS

Type of clay	E_s value (kg/cm^2)
Very soft	20–150
Soft	50–250
Medium soft	150–500
Hard	500–1000
Sandy	250–2500

TABLE 1.11   RECOMMENDED VALUES OF POISSON'S RATIO FOR SELECTED MATERIALS [Bowles]

Material	Poisson's ratio (m)
Dense sand	0.3–0.40
Loose sand	0.2–0.35
Wet clay	0.1–0.30
Sandy clay	0.2–0.35
Silt	0.3–0.35
Saturated clay or silt	0.40–0.50
Concrete	0.15–0.25
Steel	0.28–0.31
Incompressible material (like water)	0.50

1.12   CONSOLIDATION PROPERTIES OF CLAYS

Consolidation of clays is a very important factor to be considered in foundation engineering. The following are the important properties in consolidation.

1.12.1   Compression Index C_c

It has relevance only for normally consolidated clays for which the following empirical relations may be used to find the approximate values.

$C_c = 0.009 \, (LL - 20)$ for undisturbed clays of low sensitive

$C'_c = 0.007 \, (LL - 20)$ for re-moulded samples

$C_c = 1.3 \times C'_c$

Exact values should be found by tests. We use the following formula to find settlement of normally consolidated clays.

$$\Delta H = C'_c \left(\frac{H}{1 + e_0} \right) \log_{10} \left(\frac{\sigma_0 + \Delta\sigma}{\sigma_0} \right) \qquad (1.15)$$

Some of the other equations proposed for C_c in terms of initial void ratio e_0 or the percentage water content w are the following:

$$C_c = 1.15 \, (e_0 - 0.35) \qquad \text{for all clays}$$
$$= 0.30 \, (e_0 - 0.27) \qquad \text{for silty clays}$$
$$= 0.75 \, (e_0 - 0.50) \qquad \text{for soils of low plasticity}$$
$$= (1.15 \times 10^{-2}) \times (\% \text{ water content}) \qquad \text{for organic clays.}$$

The values of C_c for medium sensitive normally consolidated clays lie between 0.2 and 0.5. For high compressible peats it can be as large as 10 to 15. C_c for normally consolidated clays is a constant value. For overconsolidated clays it varies with pressure.

1.12.2 Coefficient of Compressibility, a_v and Coefficient of Volume Compressibility or Coefficient of Volume Change, m_v

a_v is defined as

$$\frac{\Delta e}{\Delta \sigma} = a_v \text{ (in m}^2/\text{kg)}$$

m_v is defined as

$$\frac{a_v}{1 + e_0} = m_v \text{ (in m}^2/\text{kg)}$$

But

$$\Delta H = \frac{\Delta e}{1 + e_0} H_0$$

Hence,

$$\Delta H = \frac{a_v H_0 \Delta \sigma}{1 + e_0} = m_v H_0 \Delta \sigma \tag{1.16}$$

m_v can be considered as the inverse of E_s. *It can also be looked upon as the height of water expelled in a unit height of soil under unit pressure.*

With increase in pressure, values of a_v and m_v decrease rapidly. Figure 1.17 gives the empirical relationship between m_v and SPT values for clays for average conditions of pressure.

1.12.3 Coefficient of Secondary Consolidation, C_∞

To find the amount of secondary consolidation, we plot void ratio versus $\log_{10} t$. Creep settlement depends on the coefficient of secondary consolidation. Creep or secondary consolidation settlement is given by the formula

$$\Delta s = C_\infty \left(\frac{H}{1 + e_f} \right) \log_{10} \left(\frac{t_2}{t_1} \right) \tag{1.17}$$

where

H = thickness of clay layer

C_∞ = coefficient of secondary consolidation

e_f = void ratio at the end of primary consolidation

t_1 and t_2 = beginning and end of secondary consolidation.

The value of C_∞ has been found to vary with initial moisture content. It varies from 0.01 for 50% water content to 0.03 for 100% water content. (see also section 4.5.)

1.12.4 Permeability of Soils

In natural stratified deposits, horizontal permeability will be larger than the vertical permeability. The following are the range of values met with:

- Fine gravel to fine sand: 1.0 to 10^{-3} cm/sec
- Fine sand to silts: 10^{-2} to 10^{-6} cm/sec
- Homogeneous clays: less than 10^{-6} cm/sec

1.12.5 Coefficient of Consolidation, C_v

This coefficient determines the rate at which consolidation will take place. For reliable results it is always advisable to use actual test results as empirical values are deceptive.

$$C_v = \frac{T_v H^2}{t} = \frac{T_{50} H^2}{t_{50}} = \frac{0.197 H^2}{t_{50}} \tag{1.18}$$

where

t_{50} = time for 50% consolidation (determined by Casagrande method)

H = one-half height of specimen with double drainage

The reported values of C_v range from 1×10^{-4} to 1×10^{-8} m²/s.

1.13 SETTLEMENT OF OVERCONSOLIDATED CLAYS

In normally consolidated clays we can use C_c values in Eq. (1.15) to find settlement. However, in overconsolidated clays, one alternative is to use Eq. (1.15) in two stages as follows (see also Fig. 1.19):

$$\Delta H = C_r \left(\frac{H_0}{1+e_o} \right) \log_{10} \frac{\sigma_c}{\sigma_o} + C_c \left(\frac{H_0}{1+e_c} \right) \log_{10} \frac{\sigma_c + \Delta\sigma}{\sigma_c} \tag{1.19}$$

where

C_r = recompression index

σ_o, σ_c = overburden and pre-consolidation pressures.

Alternatively, we can compute the settlement in overconsolidated clays by using Eq. (1.16), where the corresponding m_v values are used. The principles of determination of pre-consolidation pressure by Casagrande construction and Sehmertmann's procedure to construct the field consolidation curve from the laboratory consolidation test curve are shown in Fig. 1.19. (See also Fig. 4.5.)

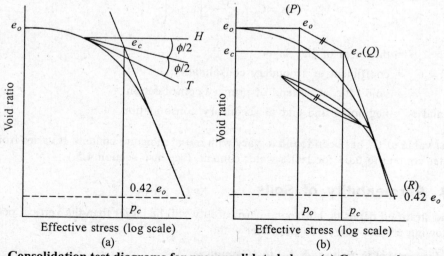

Fig. 1.19 Consolidation test diagrams for preconsolidated clays: (a) Casagrande procedure for preconsolidation pressure p_c from laboratory test curve; (b) Schmertmann's procedure to construct field consolidation curve from laboratory test curve (p_o = existing overburden pressure, *see also* Fig. 4.5).

We may also assume that the immediate settlement in clay foundations will be 0.1 time the oedometer settlement in normally consolidated clays and 0.5 to 0.6 times the oedometer value in overconsolidated clays.

Table 1.12 can be used to estimate the unit weight, void ratio and water content of commonly occurring soils for preliminary calculations. For final calculations, these should be found out by actual tests.

TABLE 1.12   PRELIMINARY ESTIMATE OF SOIL PROPERTIES

Soils	Unit weight saturated	Unit weight dry	Void ratio e	Water content w (%)
Uniform sand loose	18.9 kN/m^3	14.3 kN/m^3	0.85	32
Uniform sand	20.9 kN/m^3	17.5 kN/m^3	0.51	19
Dense soft clay	17.7 kN/m^3	—	1.20	45
Stiff clay	20.7 kN/m^3	—	0.60	22
Organic clay	15.8 kN/m^3	—	1.90	70

EXAMPLE 1.1   (Corrected SPT value)

A standard penetration test in dense sand gave the following values in a hole with liner. $N = 25$, overburden pressure is 200 kN/m^2; hammer efficiency = 80; length of hole = 14 m and diameter of hole = 100 mm.

(a) Estimate the corrected N value.
(b) Estimate the probable E value of the deposit.
(c) Estimate its angle of internal friction.

Ref.	Step	Calculations
Sec. 1.7 Eq. (1.6)	1	*Estimate C_N* C_N = 0.77 log 10 (2000/p) = 0.77 log 10 (2000/200) = 0.77
Eq. (1.6a)		Alternatively, $C_N = (95.76/200)^{1/2} = 0.69$
	2	*Corrections for other data*
		$\eta_1 = \dfrac{80}{70} = 1.14$
Sec. 1.7.1 (other corrections)		η_2 = length > 14 m = 1.0 η_3 = with liner dense sand = 0.6 η_4 = dia. of hole 100 mm = 1.0
	3	*Final correction* $C_N = C_N \times \eta_1 \times \eta_2 \times \eta_3 \times \eta_4$ $= 0.69 \times 1.14 \times 1.0 \times 0.8 \times 1.0 = 0.63$ (Generally, η_1 to η_2 corrections are not carried out as SPT values are not to be viewed as a very accurate test) Corrected $N_{70} = 25 \times 0.63 = 16$
	4	*Estimate E values from SPT test*
Sec. 1.11.2 Fig. 1.16(b)		(a) D'Appolonia $E = 220 + 11(N) = 396$ kg/cm^2 (b) Schultze and Muhs $E = 400$ kg/cm^2 Adopt $E = 400$ kg/cm^2

EXAMPLE 1.2

The following N values were obtained in two field tests. Comment on the in-situ nature of the soil:

Test No. 1—Sand deposit N value 10
Test No. 2—Clay deposit N value 10.

Ref.	Step	Calculations
Table 1.5 Fig. 1.10 Sec. 1.7.1	1	*Estimate the properties of sand, SPT = 10* The sand can be considered as loose to medium. The ϕ value = 30 degrees $\qquad$ = 0.3N + 27 = 30 degrees
Sec. 1.7.1 Table 1.6 Fig. 1.11	2	*Estimate the properties of clay SPT = 10* (a) The clay can be classified as fairly stiff clay (cannot be moulded between fingers)—Unconf. Comp: strength = 1 to 2 kg/cm^2 (N/8) (b) Consistency index $I_c = [(LL - w)/PI]$.
Table 1.6		For this clay, I_c will be 0.75 to 1.0, which means the water content will be near the plastic limit. The clay will be 'medium' to 'stiff' in consistency.

EXAMPLE 1.3   (Estimation of E value of sand)

Estimate ϕ and E value of a sand deposit with SPT value 10.

Ref.	Step	Calculations
Sec. 1.7.1 Fig. 1.10	1	*Estimate the ϕ value* $\phi = \sqrt{2N} + 15 = \sqrt{200} + 15 = $ about 30° $\phi = 0.3\,N + 27 = 3 + 27 = 30°$ ϕ from Fig. 1.10 = 30°
Fig. 1.16b	2	*Estimate E value* E_s from Fig. 1.16b = 300 kg/cm^2 = 30 MN/m^2

EXAMPLE 1.4   (Activity of clays)

A soil is found to have 20% of its portion below particle size of 0.002. Limit tests gave the following values LL = 60% and PL = 25%. Comment on the type of the soil.

Ref.	Step	Calculations
Fig. 1.7	1	*Calculate PI* $PI = LL - PL = 60 - 25 = 35\%$
	2	*Find activity* Activity ratio = PI/ % clay $= \dfrac{35}{20} = 1.75 > 1.25$
Table 1.2	3	The clay may be expansive type

EXAMPLE 1.5   (Estimation of properties of clay sample)

The average SPT value of a clay sample with the index properties given below was 20

$$LL = 45\%, \qquad PL = 25\%, \qquad N = 20, \qquad PI = 20,\%$$

Estimate its various properties for preliminary designs.

Ref.	Step	Calculations
Fig. 1.2	1	*Identification* Sample $LL = 45\%$. $PI = 45 - 25 = 20\%$ Inorganic clay of intermediate plasticity
Fig. 1.5b	2	*Estimate shear strength from N value* (a) Method 1. From Fig. 1.5b $N = 20$; $PI = 20$; $F_1 = 0.055$ $c = F_1 N = 0.055 \times 20 = 1.1$ kg/cm^2
Table 1.6		(b) Method 2. Direct from N value $N = 20$; $q_c = 20/8 = 2.5$ kg/cm^2 (approx.) $c = 1.25$ kg/cm^2 (approx.)
Table 1.6 Sec. 1.4.3	3	*Estimate the consistency* For $N = 16$ to 32, consistency index = 1.0 to 1.5 $(LL - w)/PI = 1$; Hence, $w = 25\%$ approx. (This should be checked with field data.)

REFERENCES

[1] Leonards, G.A., Engineering Properties of Soils, in *Foundation Engineering*, McGraw Hill, New York, 1962.

[2] Tomlinson, M.J., Foundation Design and Construction, ELBS, Longman Edition, Singapore, 1995.

[3] Stroud, M.A., The Standard Penetration Test for Insensitive Clays and Soft Rocks, *Proceedings of the European Symposium on Penetration Tests*, 1975.

[4] Simons, N.E. and Menzies, B.K., *A Short Course in Foundation Engineering*, Butterworth, London, 1977.

[5] Peck, R.B., Hanson, W.E. and Thornburn, T.H., *Foundation Engineering*, 2nd ed., John Wiley & Sons, New York, 1974.

[6] Bowles, J.E, *Foundation Analysis and Design* (International Edition), McGraw Hill, Singapore, 1988.

[7] Terzaghi, Karl and Peck, R.B., *Soil Mechanics in Engineering Practice*, John Wiley & Sons, New York, 1948 (1967).

[8] Durgonoglu, H.T. and Mitchell, J.K., Static Penetration Resistance of Soils, *Proc. Conf. in-situ Measurement of Soil Properties, Am. Soc. of Civil Eng.*, Raleigh, North Carolina, 1975.

[9] Singlert, G., *The Penetrometer and Soil Exploration*, Elsevier Publishing Co., Amsterdam, 1972.

[10] IS 2911–Part 1, Sec. 3, COP for Design and Construction of Pile Foundations Precast Driven Concrete Piles. Appendix B, BIS, New Delhi.

[11] Bjerrum, L. and Simon, N.E., Comparison of Shear Strength Characteristics of Normally Consolidated Clays, *Proceedings of Research Conference on Shear Strength of Cohesive Soils*, Boulder, Colorado, 1960.

[12] Joseph E. Bowles, *Analytical and Computer Methods in Foundation Engineering*, McGraw Hill New York, 1974.

[13] Jamiolkowski, M., Design Parameter for Soft Clays, *Proceedings of the 7th European Conference on Soil Mechanics and Foundation Engineering*, U.K., 1979.

[14] IS 2131–1981, *Method of Standard Penetration Test*, BIS, New Delhi.

[15] IS 4968 1968, *Method of Subsurface Sounding for Soils—Part 1: Dynamic Method Using 50 mm Cone without Bentonite Slurry; Part 2: Dynamic method using Cone and Bentonite Slurry; Part 3: Static Cone Penetration Test*, BIS, New Delhi.

[16] IS 2720—Part XI, 1971, *Determination of Shear Strength Parameters of Specimen Tested in Unconsolidated Undrained Triaxial Compression without the Measurement of Pore Pressure* Part XII: 1981, *Test for Measurement of Pore Pressure*, BIS, New Delhi.

[17] IS 2950–1992, *Code of Practice for Design and Construction of Raft Foundations*, Second Revision, BIS, New Delhi.

[18] IS 9214 – 1979, *Method for Determination of Subgrade Reaction (k-value) of Soils in the Field*, BIS, New Delhi.

2

Contact Pressures on Base of Footings

2.1 INTRODUCTION

Engineers are interested in the following two types of stresses produced in the soil by structural foundations.

1. *Contact pressures*. The stresses produced in the soil which is in direct contact with the base of the foundation are called *contact* or *base pressures*. They are of importance in designing for calculating the bending moments and shear forces experienced by foundation structures like footings.

2. *Stresses inside the soil mass*. These are stresses produced inside the mass of the soil below the foundation horizon. They are used for calculation of settlements and stability of foundations.

In this chapter, we will deal with the basic nature of contact pressures under different types of foundations and look at the approximations we make in our designs. Chapter 3 deals with stresses inside the soil mass.

2.2 RIGID AND FLEXIBLE FOUNDATIONS

Let us assume that a steel water tank (with a thin steel plate at its bottom) is placed on a soil bed. In this case, the plate carries a uniformly distributed load and the plate can take the shape of the deflection of the foundation. Such foundations where distribution of contact pressure will be same as the foundation loading itself, are called *flexible foundations*.

A second case is also possible. Imagine a thick reinforced concrete footing with a concentrated load acting on it. In this case, the block settles as a unit, i.e., the settlement is uniform and the pressure distribution under the footing will not be the same as the load on top of it. Such foundations, which settle as a block, are called *rigid foundations*.

2.3 CONTACT PRESSURES UNDER RIGID AND FLEXIBLE FOOTINGS

Clay soils are considered as homogeneous, elastic and isotropic and simple theory of elasticity is applicable to them. However in sand, strength increases with confinement. Hence we have different types of distribution of contact pressures for clays and sands as explained below.

Case 1: Rigid strip footing in clay with a line load P per meter. Contact pressure along breadth.

The settlement of the footing is uniform but the contact pressure need not be uniform. The elastic stress distribution is given by the following formula, which can be derived from theory of elasticity, applicable to clay [1].

$$p = \frac{W}{\pi a \sqrt{1 - \left(\dfrac{x}{a}\right)^2}} \tag{2.1}$$

where

p = contact stress
a = one-half breadth of footing = $B/2$
W = line load per meter length
x = distance outwards from centre of footing.

This distribution will be as shown in Fig. 2.1a. The contact pressure at the edges will be very large and it decreases towards the centre.

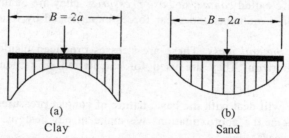

(a)   (b)
Clay   Sand

Fig. 2.1   Contact pressure distribution under a rigid strip footings. (In sand, the edge pressure will depend on the depth of the footing.)

Case 2: Rigid strip on sand with line load W per meter length. Contact pressure along breadth.

Here also the settlement is uniform and we have to estimate the pressure distribution. In the case of sand of a footing at ground level, the soil at the exterior ends of the footing cannot develop any strength without confinement so that the pressure will be convex as shown in Fig. 2.1b. However, with increasing depth of foundation the distribution changes as shown in the figure with some pressure at the edges.

Case 3: Settlement of flexible footings in clay under uniform load.

In flexible footings, as already explained, the foundation pressures will be the same as the applied pressure. Hence the foundation pressures are known. It is the settlement that we are now concerned. As shown in Chapter 4 on settlement, using theory of elasticity to a flexible foundation on clay, we can show that the settlement for the centre part will be more than that for the edges and the distribution of settlement will be as shown in Fig 2.2a. This is described as a dish like settlement.

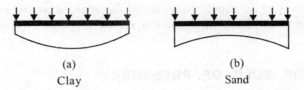

| (a) | (b) |
| Clay | Sand |

Fig. 2.2 Settlement of flexible strip footings.

Case 4. Settlement of flexible footing in sand under uniform load.

As already explained, sand at ground level has no confinement at the edges and the settlement distribution will be as in Fig. 2.2b. We should remember that the elastic distribution of contact pressure, which we described above, will change as the load is progressively increased to failure. The more stressed parts will go into plastic stage. However, with a suitable factor of safety applied to the ultimate failure load, the actual distribution in practical cases will be intermediate between the elastic and the ultimate plastic distribution. This aspect is described in Appendix A.

2.4 CONCEPT OF MODULUS OF SUBGRADE REACTION

From the above discussions we find that the calculation of contact pressures is not quite simple. For practical applications we have to simplify the concepts and use it with enough factor of safety. We assume that in the elastic stage, for a foundation the pressure exerted at the base (contact pressure) is proportional to the settlement. Or,

$$p = ks \text{ or } k = \frac{p}{s}$$

where
  p = pressure (k is in kN/m^3).
  The fictitious pressure that satisfies the above equation for unit settlement is k, the *coefficient* of *subgrade reaction*. This theory is called *theory of subgrade reaction*.

  Note: k is used as the symbol for the coefficient of subgrade reaction as proposed in IS 2950, 1981 on raft to undation [3].

2.4.1 Subgrade Reaction on Rigid Foundation

If we assume that a rigid footing remains plane when it settles under a load, the reaction from below must be linear. Accordingly, the contact pressure can be easily determined by statics if we assume the contact pressure is proportional to the deflection.

2.4.2 Subgrade Reaction on Flexible Footings

In flexible footings we cannot assume that the settlement is planar. But we can assume that the vertical pressure is proportional to the settlement and use the theory of elastic beams on continuous elastic supports for design of flexible raft foundations. We should always remember that k is a fictitious quantity and depends on many factors as already pointed out in Chapter 1. It serves as a convenient device to derive, at least roughly, the contact pressure distribution in flexible footings and rafts. However, we should be aware of the approximations made when we use the results in our practice. The theory of beams on elastic foundation is dealt with in detail in Appendix A.

2.5 CONCEPT OF BULB OF PRESSURE

The second aspect to be studied when considering foundation is the distribution of stresses inside the soil mass due to loads on the foundation. An approximate representation of the effect of the load is a bulb of pressure as shown in Fig. 2.3. Detailed discussions on this topic are given in Chapter 3. The bulb of the significantly stressed zone is taken to extend to a depth of 1.5 to 2 times the breadth of the footing. Below this level, the stress produced is less than about 20% of the stress due to overburden pressure.

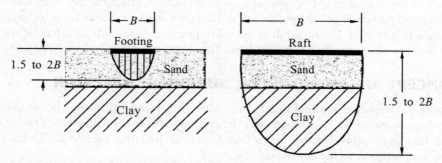

Fig. 2.3   Effect of breadth of foundations on the depth to which significant stress is transmitted in small footings and large rafts.

It is important to note that the depth to which the effect of footing will be felt depends on the breadth B and also that closely spaced footings can extend their effect to greater depths as shown in Fig. 2.3. A raft foundation of large width will stress the soil to larger depths whereas small individual footings placed far apart will only stress the upper layers of the soil. This is a very important concept to remember in foundation engineering.

2.6 EFFECT OF RIGIDITY ON SETTLEMENT CALCULATIONS

In settlement analysis there are two aspects to be considered, namely total settlement and differential settlement. The settlement that is obtained by simple analysis generally refer to flexible foundations. Differential settlement is usually taken as a function of the maximum settlement. In a real structure the stiffness of the structure tends to reduce the differential settlement. Hence in real structures we base our design for differential settlement and assume that the differential settlement will be a certain percentage of total settlement depending on the type of foundation. For example, with a large number of simple footings on a uniform deposit, the probable differential settlement between footings will be 3/4 of the maximum settlement of the footings. This aspect is described in detail in Chapter 6.

2.7 ASSUMPTIONS FOR PROPORTIONING OF RIGID FOOTINGS

The concept that a concentrated load placed at the centre of gravity of a rigid footing will be distributed uniformly at foundation level is used in designing rigid footings. Footings can be any of the following types [2]:

1. Spread footings (also called individual footings)
2. Combined footings
3. Cantilever or strap footings
4. Continuous or strip footings

Short descriptions of these are given below.

2.7.1 Spread Footings

These footings carry a single column load and can be square or rectangular in plan. It is common practice to use a linear distribution of contact pressure beneath these rigid footings. These pressures can be calculated by the following formula (also refer to Fig. 2.4)

$$p = \frac{W}{A} \pm \frac{M}{I} y \tag{2.2}$$

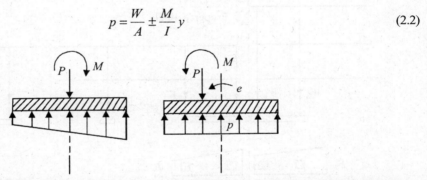

Fig. 2.4 Method of positioning of load in a footing subjected to moments for uniform foundation pressure.

If $M = We$, then for a rectangular footing ($B \times L$) with load eccentricity along B, the pressure due to W will be as follows:

$$p = \frac{W}{BL}\left[1 \pm \frac{6e}{L}\right] \tag{2.3}$$

We should ensure that e is less than $L/6$ so that there is no tension at the base of the footing.

Theoretically we can place the centre of gravity of the footings eccentric to the line of action of the load and moments so that the ground pressure will be uniform as shown in Fig. 2.4. If the eccentricity acts in X and Y, we use the following formula to find pressures at various salient points x, y in the footing. These stresses should be within allowable values.

$$q = \frac{W}{A} \pm \frac{M_x Y}{I_x} \pm \frac{M_y X}{I_y} \tag{2.4}$$

2.7.2 Combined Footings

When the footing supports a line of two or more columns it is called *combined footings*. It can be rectangular or trapezoidal in shape. When two column footings are connected by a narrow rigid beam, it is called a *cantilever* or *strap footing*. Combined footings can be designed as simple slabs or as a slab with a longitudinal spine beam.

Even though in the strict sense combined footings should be designed as beams on elastic foundations, in many cases they can be assumed to be a rigid foundation. We try to bring about uniform base pressure by making the centre of gravity of the loads to coincide with the center of gravity of the loaded area. The necessity for a combined footings can arise under the following situations:

- When the individual footings planned for a site overlap or come very near each other in plan, we combine then into a combined footing.

- If there is a space restriction and the exterior column is coming close to the boundary of the site, we cannot provide centrally loaded exterior column foundation (see Fig. 2.5).

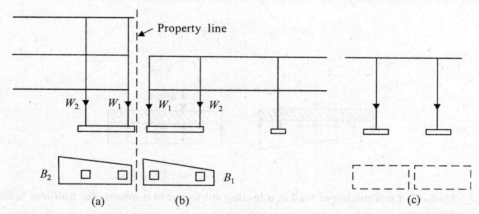

Fig. 2.5 **Combined footings: (a) Load on inner footing more than that of outer; (b) load on inner footing less then that of outer; (c) interior footings.**

Under the above circumstances, we combine the exterior column with the interior column so that their combined center of gravity is well inside the property line.

The principle of proportioning combined footings is to bring the centroid of the area of the foundation in line with the center of gravity of the loads or at least as close to it as possible. Under these conditions we assume the footing to be rigid and develop linear contact pressure. These footings can be rectangular or in general, trapezoidal in shape. If there are restrictions on where the outer extremities of the footings can be from the position of the columns, these are also taken into account and the length L of the footings is fixed. As shown in Fig. 2.6, the dimensions B_1 and B_2 of the footings can be determined from the following equation:

A = bearing area from allowable soil pressure W/q

$$A = \left[\frac{B_1 + B_2}{2}\right] L \tag{2.5}$$

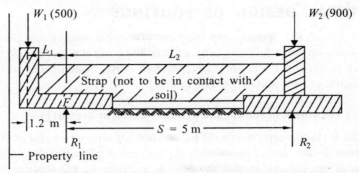

Fig. 2.6   Strap and cantilever footing balancing the outer footing near the property line.

$$\overline{x} = \frac{L}{3}\left[\frac{2B_1 + B_2}{B_1 + B_2}\right], \qquad B_2 > B_1 \tag{2.6}$$

where

$\overline{x}$ = CG of the loads W_1 and W_2 from side B_2 adjacent to the larger load.

2.7.3   Cantilever or Strap Footings (Balanced Footings)

Cantilever footings are also applicable, when it is impossible to place a foundation centrally beneath a column due to adjacent buildings or due to the soil stresses going beyond admissible values. The principle in its layout is shown in Fig. 2.6. It can assume different shapes depending on the assumed fulcrum point (see also Fig. 5.1). The load W_1 on the outer columns is to be balanced by load W_2, from the inner column. Taking F as the fulcrum, for safety W_2l_2 should be greater than W_1l_1 to give a factor of safety of not less than 1.5 for rotation. Instead of W_2 as a footing we may use a mass concrete block or tension pile to produce W_2. The beam connecting W_1 and W_2 is called the strap beam and it is cast monolithically with the footing. For structural design the whole system is taken as a unit (as shown in Example 2.3).

2.7.4   Strip Footings

Strip footings or wall footings are continuous footings built as foundations for walls. They can be of plain or reinforced concrete. Brick walls can be directly built on RC continuous footings thus eliminating the need of corbelling of bricks from foundation level as is necessary for plain concrete footings.

As a rough rule, the width of the strip footing is made at least three times the thickness of the wall. For plain footings, its depth is usually made on the basis of distribution of the load at 45 degrees through the base concrete.

In the construction of low rise buildings with closely spaced columns and brick walls, a beam and slab construction of the strip footing (i.e. T-beam) can be used with good results. The walls can be built directly on top of the beams. This will give better rigidity to the foundation than in the case of a simple continuous slab construction. The rigidity of these foundations can be further increased as described in Chapter 21. They resist differential settlements better than simple continuous slab construction.

2.8 STRUCTURAL DESIGN OF FOOTINGS

In the design of spread RC footing, the location of critical section for bending is based on Richart's experiments on these footings conducted in 1948 and the location of critical section for shear on the work of Moe in 1961. They are specified in RC design codes like IS 456:2000 and are available in textbooks on reinforced concrete [4].

EXAMPLE 2.1 **(Alignment of footings to produce uniform pressure)**

A footing 2.6×2.6 m has to carry a vertical load of 600 kN with a moment of 100 kNm along one of its axes. Determine the contact pressure if the column is placed at the centre of the footing. Plan the position of the column so that the bearing pressure on the footing will be uniform.

Ref.	Step	Calculations
	1	*Determine the eccentricity of the load* $e = \dfrac{M}{W} = \dfrac{100}{600} = 0.167$ m This should not exceed $\dfrac{L}{6} = \dfrac{2.6}{6} = 0.43$ m $0.167 < 0.43$ m, which implies, all pressures are positive,
Eq. (2.3)	2	*Determine the pressures* $p = \dfrac{W}{B^2}\left[1 \pm \dfrac{6e}{L}\right] = \dfrac{600}{(2.6)^2}\left[1 \pm \dfrac{6 \times 0.167}{2.6}\right]$ $= 88.75 + 34.2 = 122.95$ kN/m^2 (*p* max) $= 88.75 - 34.2 = 54.55$ kN/m^2 (*p* min) Check average pressure $= \dfrac{122.95 + 54.55}{2} = 88.75$ Total pressure $= 88.75 \times (2.6)^2 = 600$ t
	3	*Determine eccentricity of load to produce uniform pressure* Place the column with eccentricity of 0.167 m towards the lower pressure side so as to produce a moment equal and opposite to that of the column moment. The resultant pressure will be uniform.

EXAMPLE 2.2 **(Layout of combined footing)**

Two columns, one carrying 180 kN and the other 360 kN are spaced 2.1 m apart and are to be placed on a combined footing. If the safe bearing capacity of the soil is 100 kN/m^2, give a layout of the footing.

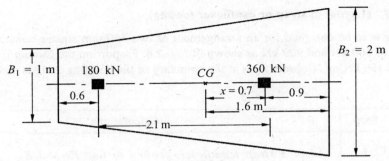

Fig. E.2.2

Ref.	Step	Calculations
	1	*Find the total length of the footing* Spacing of column = 2.1 Allow 0.6 m beyond the *CG* of the smaller load and 0.9 m beyond the *CG* of the larger load. $L = 2.1 + 0.6 + 0.9 = 3.6$ m and $\dfrac{L}{3} = 1.2$ (*L* is fixed)
	2	*Find total area required for the footing* $A = \dfrac{W_1 + W_2}{q} = \dfrac{540}{100} = 5.4 \text{ m}^2$
	3	*Find the position of the CG of the load from the larger load* Taking moments about the 360 kN load, $(360 + 180)\, x = 180 \times 2.1$ $x = \dfrac{180 \times 2.1}{540} = 0.7$ m from 360 kN
	4	*Find x_2 the distance from B_2 (side of larger load)* $x_2 = x + 0.9 = 0.7 + 0.9 = 1.6$ m
	5	*Find B_1 and B_2*
Eq. (2.5)		$(B_1 + B_2) = \dfrac{2A}{L} = \dfrac{2 \times 5.4}{3.6} = 3 \text{ m}$ Eq. (1)
Eq. (2.6)		$x_2 = 1.6 = \left(\dfrac{2B_1 + B_2}{B_1 + B_2}\right)1.2$, where $x_2 = CG$ from B_2 $1.6B_1 + 1.6B_2 = 2.4B_1 + 1.2B_2$ Solving the equation $B_2 = 2B_1$, From Eq. (1) above, we get $B_1 = 1$ m; $B_2 = 2$ m.
	6	*Find the final dimension of combined footing* A trapezoidal footing $B_1 = 1$ m; $B_2 = 2$ m and $L = 3.6$ m The *CG* of the load and that of the area coincide to give uniform pressure.

EXAMPLE 2.3 (Layout of strap or cantilever footing)

A strap footing is to be designed for an arrangement of two 400 mm square columns W_1 and W_2 carrying loads of 500 kN and 900 kN as shown in Fig. 2.6. Proportion the footing if the allowable soil pressure is 150 kN/m². Column P_1 is at the boundary of the building and the distance between loads is 6.2 m.

Ref.	Step	Calculations
Fig. 2.6	1	*Adopt a strap (cantilever) footing to find R_1 and R_2* Distance between loads = 6.2 m Column load near property line = 500 kN = W_1 *Assume fulcrum at 1.2 m from W_1 (to get enough factor of safety, against rotation)* Reaction at fulcrum = R_1 Distance of R_1 from R_2 = 6.2 − 1.2 = 5 m = S Taking moments about load (W_2 = 900 kN) $5R_1 = 6.2 \times 500$ given $R_1 = 620$ kN Hence, $R_2 = W_1 + W_2 - R_1 = 500 + 900 - 620 = 780$ kN (As $R_1 > W_1$, we will have $R_2 < W_2$)
	2	*Calculate FS against rotation* $$FS = \frac{W_2 L_2}{W_1 L_1} = \frac{900 \times 5}{500 \times 1.2} \approx 7.5$$ 7.5 > 1.5, which is admissible.
	3	*Find dimension of footing under column W_1* Length of footing = 2(1.2 + 0.5 × col. size) = 2(1.2 + 0.2) = 2.8 m B required = $\dfrac{R_1}{L_1 \times q_a} = \dfrac{620}{2.8 \times 150} = 1.47$ m; Adopt 1.5 m. Footing adopted is 2.8 m × 1.5 m.
	4	*Find dimensions of footing under W_2* Assume square footing $R_2 = 730$; $B = \sqrt{\dfrac{730}{150}} = 2.2$ m.
	5	*Sketch the SF and BM of the combined footing* Assuming the whole foundation to work as one unit and assuming uniform pressure under the footing due to R_1 and R_2, draw the SF and BM diagrams. The strap beams are to be designed for the corresponding shear and bending moments. (*Note:* As the soil pressure under the footings are uniform, the CG of footings and loads will coincide. This can also be checked).

REFERENCES

[1] Bowles, J.E., *Foundation Analysis and Design*, McGraw-Hill International Edition, Singapore, 1988.

[2] IS 1080-1985, *Code of Practice for Design and Construction of Shallow Foundations*, Bureau of Indian Standards, New Delhi.

[3] IS 2950 (part 1) 1981, *Code of Practice for Design and Construction of Raft Foundations*, Bureau of Indian Standards, New Delhi.

[4] Varghese, P.C., *Limit State Design of Reinforced Concrete,* 2nd ed., Prentice-Hall of India, New Delhi, 2002.

3

Stress Distribution in Soils

3.1 INTRODUCTION

This chapter deals with the calculation of stresses in soils at different depths due to surface loadings. *This is covered in IS 8009 (Part I) Code of Practice for Calculation of Settlement of Foundation* [1]. These stresses are mostly used for calculating settlements and also for determining how far the soils are stressed beneath the foundation. For detailed tables and charts, reference should be made to the above code or to handbooks on the subject [2], [3]. We use the theory of elasticity for solving these problems and it is assumed that the soil is not loaded beyond its elastic limits.

3.2 SOIL CONSIDERED AS AN ELASTIC MATERIAL

If a soil medium is uniform everywhere, it is called *homogeneous*. If its physical properties are identical in all directions (independent of orientation) it is called *isotropic*. If the material recovers its original shape after the load is removed it is called *elastic*. If the stress-strain relation of the material is linear, it is said to obey Hook's law. An isotropic material has two elastic constants, namely, modulus of elasticity E and Poisson's ratio μ. When $\mu = 0.5$, we can assume that the material undergoes deformation with constant volume. Even though in triaxial test on clays we may assume deformation under constant volume, for most soils the real value of μ is about 0.3 so that in effect they do not undergo deformation under constant volume. They are not homogeneous also. If $\mu = 0$, we have a substance like water which is incompressible. Many deposits are stratified with modulus of elasticity E differing in the vertical as well as the horizontal directions.

3.3 BOUSSINESQ'S EQUATION

In 1885 Boussinesq published his derivation of the stresses inside a homogeneous isotropic elastic mass due to a point load on the surface. The formulae obtained by Boussinesq for the stresses can be stated as follows with reference to Fig. 3.1. The derivations of these formulae can be obtained in books on theory of elasticity.

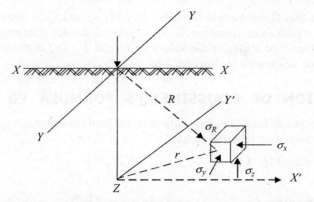

Fig. 3.1   Stresses in soil due to a point load at surface in cylindrical coordinates.

3.3.1 Formulae for Point Load

The formula for point load Q can be expressed in simple form as follows (see Fig. 3.1):

$$\sigma_z = \left(\frac{3Q}{2\pi}\right)\left(\frac{z^3}{R^5}\right) \tag{3.1}$$

which is a function of (R/z) only and is independent of E and μ.

$$\sigma_R = \frac{Q}{\pi R^2}\left[(2 - \mu)\cos 0 - \left(\frac{1 - 2\mu}{2}\right)\right] \text{ along the radius } R.$$

This is dependent on μ. For a material deforming at constant volume $\mu = 0.5$.

$$\sigma_R = \frac{3Q}{2\pi}\left(\frac{\cos\theta}{R^2}\right) \tag{3.2}$$

The tangential stress acting on planes normal to r and z is given by the following equation:

$$\tau_{rz} = \left(\frac{3Q}{2\pi}\right)\left(\frac{rz^2}{R^5}\right) \tag{3.3}$$

This expression of stress is also independent of E and μ.

Similar expressions can also be found for σ_y, σ_x, τ_{xy}. The sum of the principal stresses at any point is known as the first invariant and is equal to

$$I = \sigma_x + \sigma_y + \sigma_z = \frac{Qz(1 + \mu)}{\pi R^3} \tag{3.4}$$

A *point of great significance is that σ_z and τ_{rz} are independent of the Poisson's ratio μ and all the formulae are independent of E. Only deformations are influenced by E. Hence,*

Terzaghi pointed out that Boussinesq's formulae [Eqs. (3.1) and (3.3) above] can be freely used for all types of soil media even though soils as a material do not conform to Boussinesq's half-space material. Neither E or μ affects the values of σ_z and τ_{rz}. The distributions of these vertical and shear stresses are dealt with in Section 3.8.

3.4 APPLICATION OF BOUSSINESQ'S FORMULA TO OTHER CASES

The effects of other types of loads can be easily derived from Boussinesq's formula. The following cases are generally treated in most textbooks.

Case 1: Line load (see Fig. 3.2)

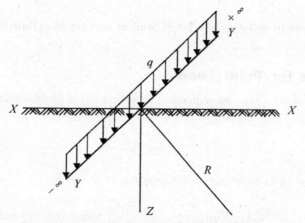

Fig. 3.2   Stresses in soil due to a line load.

This is a plane strain problem as the strain and stresses at all sections normal to the plane of loading are the same. If the line load is in the Y direction, the following value can be obtained by integration of the effects of point load q from $y = -\infty$ to $+\infty$

$$\sigma_z = \frac{2q}{\pi z \left[1 + (x/z)^2\right]^2} = \frac{2q}{\pi R}\cos^3\theta$$

$$\sigma_R = (2q/\pi R)\cos\theta$$
$$\sigma_y = (\sigma_R/\mu)$$
$$\sigma_x = \sigma_R \sin^2\theta$$
$$q \ = \text{line load per unit length.}$$

$$(3.5)$$

Case 2: Triangular and uniform strip loadings

For the stresses at various depths for a triangular load of infinite length (strip load) as shown in Fig. 3.3a, the distances are measured from the point where $q = 0$ as origin. Distance x is taken as positive in the direction where q increases and negative in the opposite direction. The coefficients for stresses at various depth to width ratios (z/B) are shown in Table 3.1 for a triangular strip. The coefficients for stresses due to a uniform strip loading as shown in Fig. 3.3b can be tabulated as

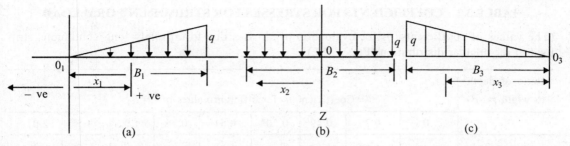

Fig. 3.3 **Stresses under triangular and uniform loads showing positive values of *x* for the three cases of loadings.**

TABLE 3.1   COEFFICIENTS FOR STRESSES FOR STRIP OF TRIANGULAR LOADING

(The values of coefficient η_1 or η_3 for evaluation of stresses due to infinitely long continuous strip load of triangular distribution (Figs. 3.3a and 3.3c).)

Ratio of depth z to width z:B	Coefficient η_1 or η_3 for different values of $x_1 : B_2$ (or $x_3 : B_3$)												
	−1.5	−1.0	−0.5	0.0	0.25	0.50	0.75	0.99	1.00	1.01	1.5	2.0	2.5
0.00	0.00	0.00	0.00	0.00	0.25	0.50	0.75	0.99	0.50	0.00	0.00	0.00	0.00
0.10	0.00	0.00	0.00	0.05	0.25	0.49	0.73	0.53	0.47	0.46	0.00	0.00	0.00
0.25	0.00	0.00	0.00	0.08	0.26	0.48	0.64	0.37	0.42	0.40	0.02	0.00	0.00
0.50	0.00	0.00	0.02	0.13	0.26	0.41	0.48	0.37	0.35	0.33	0.06	0.02	0.00
0.75	0.01	0.02	0.04	0.15	0.25	0.34	0.36	0.31	0.29	0.29	0.11	0.02	0.01
1.00	0.01	0.03	0.06	0.16	0.22	0.28	0.28	0.25	0.25	0.25	0.13	0.05	0.01
1.50	0.02	0.05	0.08	0.15	0.18	0.20	0.20	0.19	0.19	0.18	0.12	0.06	0.04
2.00	0.03	0.06	0.09	0.13	0.15	0.16	0.16	0.15	0.15	0.15	0.11	0.07	0.05
3.00	0.05	0.06	0.08	0.10	0.10	0.10	0.11	0.10	0.10	0.10	0.09	0.07	0.05
4.00	0.05	0.06	0.07	0.08	0.08	0.09	0.08	0.08	0.08	0.08	0.08	0.06	0.05
5.00	0.05	0.05	0.06	0.06	0.06	0.06	0.06	0.06	0.06	0.06	0.06	0.05	0.04
6.00	0.04	0.04	0.05	0.05	0.05	0.05	0.05	0.05	0.05	0.05	0.05	0.05	0.04

[*Note:* x is the distance of the point considered from a point at which $q = 0$ as in Fig. 3.3 (x is taken as positive in the direction in which q increases). Strip B is equal to the width of the strip loading.]

in Table 3.2. In this case, the origin is taken as the midpoint of the width B. The vertical pressure σ_z is given by the following formula:

$$\sigma_z = q\eta \quad (see \text{ Table 3.1})$$

where q = the maximum vertical load equal to γh the unit weight for an embankment. The application of the above tables to an embankment load is illustrated in Example 3.1.

TABLE 3.2 COEFFICIENTS FOR STRESSES FOR STRIP OF UNIFORM LOAD

(The values of coefficients η_2 for evaluation of stresses due to infinitely long continuous strip load of rectangular distribution (Fig. 3.3b).)

Ratio of depth to width $z_2 : B_2$	Coefficient η_2 for different values of $x_2 : B_2$								
	0	0.25	0.49	0.50	0.51	0.75	1.0	1.5	2.0
0.00	1.00	1.00	1.00	0.50	0.00	0.00	0.00	0.00	0.00
0.10	0.99	0.98	0.56	0.50	0.44	0.04	0.00	0.00	0.00
0.25	0.96	0.90	0.52	0.50	0.48	0.31	0.02	0.00	0.00
0.50	0.82	0.74	0.50	0.48	0.46	0.34	0.08	0.02	0.00
0.75	0.67	0.61	0.46	0.45	0.40	0.35	0.15	0.04	0.02
1.00	0.55	0.51	0.42	0.41	0.40	0.34	0.19	0.07	0.03
1.25	0.46	0.44	0.38	0.37	0.37	0.32	0.20	0.10	0.045
1.50	0.40	0.38	0.34	0.34	0.33	0.30	0.21	0.115	0.06
1.75	0.35	0.34	0.31	0.31	0.31	0.27	0.22	0.13	0.07
2.00	0.31	0.31	0.29	0.28	0.28	0.25	0.21	0.14	0.08
3.00	0.21	0.21	0.20	0.20	0.19	0.18	0.17	0.135	0.10
4.00	0.16	0.16	0.15	0.15	0.14	0.14	0.14	0.12	0.10
5.00	0.13	0.13	0.12	0.12	0.12	0.12	0.12	0.11	0.09
6.00	0.11	0.11	0.10	0.10	0.10	0.10	0.10	0.10	0.09
10.00	0.064	0.064	0.062	0.062	0.062	0.062	0.062	0.062	0.059

[*Note*: x is the distance of point considered from *CG* of load.]

Case 3: Pressure below the corner and centre points of a uniformly loaded rectangular area (Steinbrenner's method)

This is a very important case for many applications. Solutions leading to the same final results have been proposed by many investigators. Love solved the problem in 1928 and Steinbrenner derived one chart for the calculation of pressure beneath the corners and another chart for the computation of pressure under the centre point in 1934. However the most commonly used chart is that by Fadam [1] developed at Harvard University in 1941 and published in 1948.[4] Fadam's chart and method of calculation of pressure σ_z is shown in Fig. 3.4[1]. The following formula is used:

$$\sigma_z = q \times K \tag{3.6}$$

where K is read from Chart 3.4.

Case 4: Modification of Fadam's chart for pressures at any point due to a uniform rectangular loaded area

Fadam's chart which gives the coefficients for stress under the corner of a rectangular footing is a very convenient chart for finding pressures at any point due to a uniformly loaded rectangular

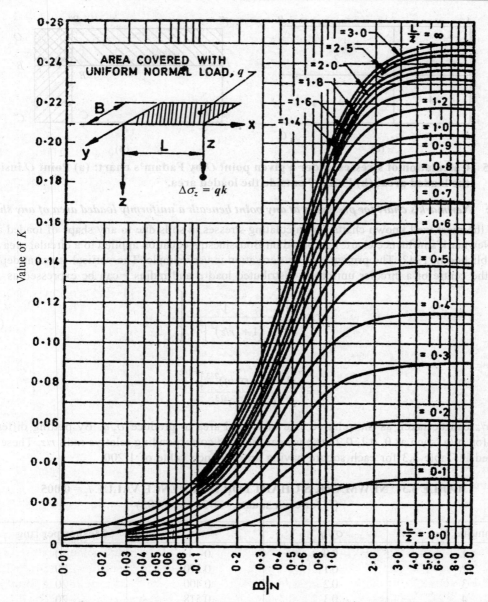

Fig. 3.4 Influence factors for vertical stress beneath a corner of a uniformly loaded area (After Fadum 1941, IS 8009 Part I, Fig. 18).

area by centering rectangular areas around the point and summing up the pressures of stresses under the corners as shown in Fig. 3.5.

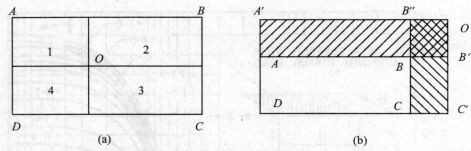

Fig. 3.5 **Calculation of stresses under a given point** O **by Fadam's chart: (a) Point** O **inside the loaded area; (b) Point** O **outside the loaded area.**

Case 5: **Newmark's chart for pressures at any point beneath a uniformly loaded area of any shape**

One of the most well known charts for calculating stresses in soils due to any shape of loaded area is the Newmark's influence chart. It is based on Boussinesq's equation applied to a circular area and was published in 1942. The principle of its derivation is very simple. The vertical stress at depth z below the centre of a circular uniformly distributed load q and radius r can be expressed as

$$\sigma_z = q \left[1 - \frac{1}{\left\{ 1 + (r/z)^2 \right\}^{3/2}} \right] \tag{3.7}$$

Hence,

$$\frac{r}{z} = \left[\frac{\left\{ 1 - (1 - \sigma_z/q)^{2/3} \right\}}{(1 - \sigma_z/q)^{2/3}} \right]^{1/2}$$

Thus, r/z can be taken as the relative size of loaded area to produce σ_z/q. By putting different values for σ_z/q (such as 0, 0.1, 0.2 etc.) we can find the corresponding relative radii r/z. These are tabulated in Table 3.3 for each square having an influence value of 1/200.

TABLE 3.3   NEWMARK'S CHART FOR INFLUENCE VALUE $I_z = 0.005$
(I_z for each square = 1/200 = 0.005)

Annulus No. i	σ_z/q	r/z	Meshes per ring
1	0.0	0	20
2	0.1	0.270	20
3	0.2	0.400	20
4	0.3	0.518	20
5	0.4	0.637	20
6	0.5	0.766	20
7	0.6	0.918	20
8	0.7	1.110	20
9	0.8	1.387	20
10	0.9	1.908	20
11	1.0	∞	
		Total	200

With regard to Table 3.3, if we draw radial lines of 20 in number as adopted by Newmark and draw circles for r/z corresponding to each σ_z/q value in Table 3.3 with suitable scale, we get a diagram as shown in Fig. 3.6. There will be 200 divisions, each of influence factor 0.005.

8.6 cm

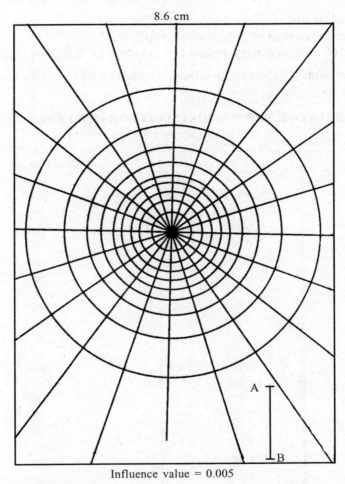

A

B

Influence value = 0.005

Fig. 3.6 Newmark's influence chart for increase in vertical stress due to a uniformly loaded flexible footing (IS 8009 part 1 1976, Fig. 17).

Here, the first inner circle gives an area which when drawn to the scale shown for z on the chart will give an increase of $\sigma_z/q = 0.1$. As there are twenty sectors, each sector covered will have an influence value of 0.1/20 or 1/200. This is applicable to each succeeding circle. (In Fig. 3.6, $AB = 2$ cm.)

To use the diagram to find the value of σ_z at 10 m depth, we assume the scale for AB as 2 cm = 10 m, i.e. the scale of plan is 1 cm = 5 m. The building for which the chart is to be used is then drawn on tracing paper with a scale 1 cm = 5 m and superposed on the chart with the point for which σ_z is required positioned over the centre of the chart. The number of squares (influence areas) enclosed by the loaded area is counted. The vertical pressure at the point is given by the equation,

$$\sigma_z = qI_zN \tag{3.8}$$

where

q = uniformly distributed load
I_z = influence value marked at bottom of chart
N = number of influence areas enclosed in the chart by the given loaded area.

If we need an influence chart for an influence value of 0.001, then the corresponding values will be as in Table 3.4.

TABLE 3.4   DATA FOR NEWMARK'S CHART FOR INFLUENCE VALUE $I_z = 0.001$
(I_z for each square = 1/1000 = 0.001)

Circle no.	r/z	No of subdivisions for the annulus
1	0.073	8
2	0.128	16
3	0.183	24
4	0.226	24
5	0.264	24
6	0.330	48
7	0.391	48
8	0.448	48
9	0.504	48
10	0.560	48
11	0.617	48
12	0.677	48
13	0.739	48
14	0.806	48
15	0.879	48
16	0.959	48
17	1.050	48
18	1.156	48
19	1.284	48
20	1.446	48
21	1.668	48
22	2.014	48
23	2.415	32
24	3.315	32
25	4.899	16
	∞	8
	Total	1000

The procedure to determine the pressure by Newmark's chart is as follows:

Step 1: Compute the ratio D/z where D is the depth of the point in the problem and z is the length indicated on the chart as influence value.

Step 2: Draw on tracing paper, the plan of the foundation using the scale 1 to D/z.

Step 3: Place the plan over the chart so that the point at which the stress is to be computed is at the centre of the diagram as in Fig. 3.6.

Step 4: Two possibilities are addressed in this step; (a) for uniform loading and (b) for random loading.

(a) For uniform loading count the number of influence areas enclosed by the plan of the loaded area as N. In case of uniform loading, the increase in vertical pressure is as follows:

$$\sigma_z = q I_B N \tag{3.9}$$

(b) For random loading over the area, determine the average pressure on each of the squares covered.

$$\sigma_z = \sum_1^n q_1 I_B n_1 \tag{3.9a}$$

where
$\quad I_B$ = influence value
$\quad q_1$ = average pressure or loading on the area
$\quad n_1$ = number of influence areas covered by q_1.

3.5 WESTERGARD'S SOLUTION [IS 8009 (PART I) 1976]

Boussinesq assumed soil as an ideal material. Only normally consolidated clays can be considered as such a material. In overconsolidated clays and in laminated clays with thin soil layers of infinite rigidity in between the strata, the lateral strain is restricted by the rigidity of these layers. Hence the ratio of the modulus (E_h/E_v) is very large in fact, equal to infinity. Westergard [5] gave a solution for such problems in 1938. Later in 1948 Taylor evolved a chart for use of the above theory for practical purposes as shown in Fig. 3.7. This chart is used in the same manner as Newmark's chart [1].

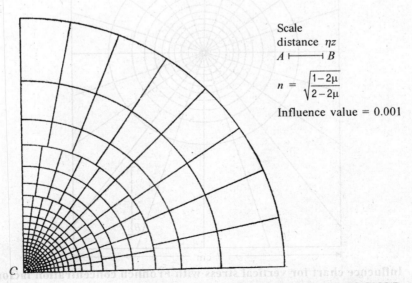

Scale
distance ηz
$A \longmapsto\longmapsto B$

$n = \sqrt{\dfrac{1-2\mu}{2-2\mu}}$

Influence value = 0.001

Fig. 3.7 **Influence chart for vertical stress according to Westergard's theory (IS 8009 Part 1, Fig. 19).**

The unit distance AB marked in the chart is ηz, where $\eta = [(1 - 2\mu)/(2 - 2\mu)]^{1/2}$ and μ is the Poisson's ratio for the soil.

3.6   METHODS FOR SPECIAL CASES [1]

Stress distribution for much more complex conditions is available. Three such methods are stated below.

3.6.1   Fröhlich's Concentration Factor Method [IS 8009 (Part I) 1976]

In the case of sands, experimental evidence indicates that (E_h/E_v) is considerably less than 1. Published experimental evidence suggests that σ_z for a rectangular loaded area can be computed from the semi-empirical equation that Frohlich worked out in 1934 for a material with elastic anisotropy and poor tensile strength. For this purpose, a concentration factor is used. For the case where the modulus of elasticity increases linearly with depth, a concentration factor of 4 is recommended. Charts similar to Newmark's chart, as shown in Fig. 3.8, are available for the application of this theory.

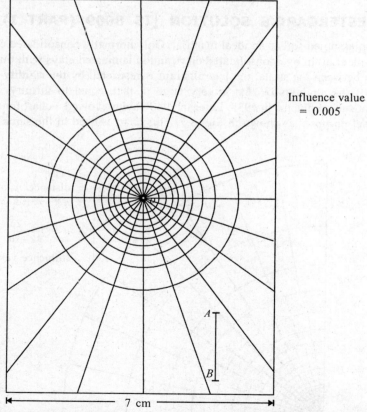

Influence value
= 0.005

A

B

|← ———————— 7 cm ———————— →|

Fig. 3.8   Influence chart for vertical stress with Fröhlich concentration factor $m' = 4$ (IS 8009, Part 1—1976, Fig. 20).

3.6.2 Burmister's Method for Layered Soils

Many natural soil deposits occur in layers. In 1943 Burmister [6] derived expressions for stresses and displacements for two- and three-layered elastic systems. These are available in reference books for application to such cases [2].

3.6.3 Stress Distribution below Embankments

It has been found from field measurements that the stress distribution below the foundation of earth embankment, as calculated by assuming the embankment, to be a trapezoidal loading made of a rectangle and a triangle, gives higher pressures than the actual values. However, the fact that such application of Boussinesq's solution (as a plane strain problem) does not lead to a correct assessment was shown by Perloff [2]. It is well known that shear distortions occur at the interface between the embankment and underlying soil. (Embankments have been strengthened by reinforcing mats at fill foundation surfaces.) Whereas the vertical stress in Boussinesq's solution is independent of E and μ. In the field, the values have been found to depend on μ also. Charts for correct estimation of these pressures are available in many references [2].

3.7 STRESS DISTRIBUTION FOR LOAD APPLIED BELOW THE SURFACE

When vertical loads are applied below the surface, on excavating a depth of soil, the stresses at a corresponding depth D are reduced due to two reasons. Firstly, the overburden is removed and secondly, the application of load below the base alters its distribution. (In both cases, the vertical stresses at a point z below the load will be less than that for the loading at the surface.) This problem of excavation analysis has been dealt with by many investigators and solutions in the form of tables and charts are also available for easy calculation of stresses [2].

Another problem of importance is the distribution of stresses due to loaded piles. The Boussinesq's equation cannot be used for this case since it assumes that the load acts on the boundary of the half space only. Piles transfer the loads in the interior of the elastic half space. The solution was published by Mindlin in 1936 [7]. On the basis of Mindlin, Poulos and Davis [8] developed charts for influence factors for calculating settlements of piles and piers.

3.8 PRESSURE DISTRIBUTION AT BASE OF STRIP FOOTINGS

Figure 3.9 shows the distribution of vertical normal stresses and Fig. 3.10, the distribution of shear stresses under a uniformly distributed strip load. For a strip load, the *principal stresses* at the centre line below the strip can be expressed as follows.

$$\sigma_1 = (q/\pi)(\theta + \sin \theta)$$
$$\sigma_2 = (q/\pi)(\theta - \sin \theta)$$
$$\tau = (1/2)(\sigma_1 - \sigma_2) = (q/\pi) \sin \theta; \quad \text{max. value} = q/\pi \qquad (3.10)$$

where

q = load per unit area
θ = central angle as shown in Fig. 3.10.

3.8.1 Summary of Findings

As shown in Fig. 3.10, shear stresses increase to a maximum when $\theta = 90°$ at a depth of about $B/2$. *At this point, its value will be* (q/π) or $0.32q$. Subsequently, it decreases with depth. On the

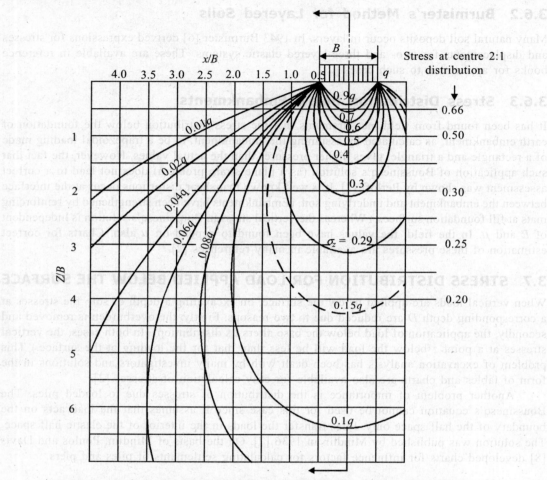

Fig. 3.9   Isobars for vertical (normal) stresses under a strip load.

other hand, the vertical stress decreases steadily with depth as shown in Fig. 3.9. The vertical stress reduces to one-third its surface value at $2B$, which can be considered as the zone of major influence of footings.

3.9   HEAVE IN CLAY DUE TO EXCAVATION

The decrease of load due to excavation and the consequent heave in clay soils is an important problem for soil engineers. As already mentioned in Section 3.7, this can be carried out by the "excavation analysis" developed by Baladi in 1968, which takes into account the effect of the material surrounding the excavation on the stresses and deformation [2]. An approximate method is to consider excavation as an unloading with E value greater than for loading. However, heave due to excavation in clays when given access to water should be estimated on the basis of oedometer rebound curves.

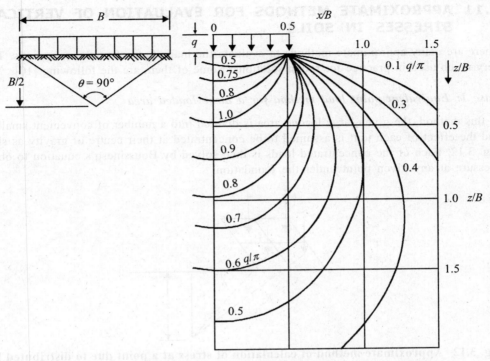

Fig. 3.10   Shear stress distribution under a strip load as a function of q/π.

3.10   STRESSES ON RETAINING WALLS DUE TO LOADS BEHIND THE WALLS

There are many situations where the effect of loads behind walls are to be evaluated. We may use Boussinesq's equation for their solution. An empirical method given by Terzaghi and Peck [9] for a line load (like a railway line or water tank behind a wall) is shown in Fig. 3.11. This problem will be dealt with in more detail in Chapter 17 on retaining walls.

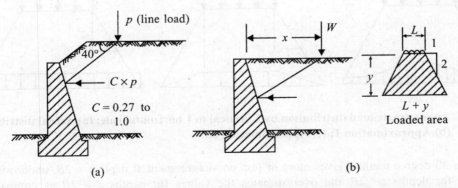

Fig. 3.11   Loads behind retaining walls: (a) Line load; (b) concentrated load.

3.11 APPROXIMATE METHODS FOR EVALUATION OF VERTICAL STRESSES IN SOILS

There are many approximate methods to evaluate the magnitude of pressures in soils. They are very much used in practice for rough solutions. Some of them are the following [10].

Case 1: Equivalent point load method for a large loaded area

In this method, the given large loaded area is divided into a number of convenient smaller units and the effect of each unit is assumed to be concentrated at their centre of gravity as shown in Fig. 3.12. Each of the concentrated loads is then solved by Boussinesq's equation to obtain the pressure at any given point under the foundation.

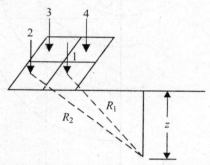

Fig. 3.12 Approximate method of calculation of stress at a point due to distributed load by Boussinesq's formula.

Case 2: Dispersion method for a uniformly loaded area

In these methods, a uniform load is distributed at various angles. In one method, the load is assumed to be distributed at an angle of 30° to the vertical or 60° to the horizontal. Another assumes a distribution of 2 vertical to 1 horizontal corresponding to 26.5° to the vertical as indicated in Fig. 3.13. This distribution is usually approximated to 30 degrees.

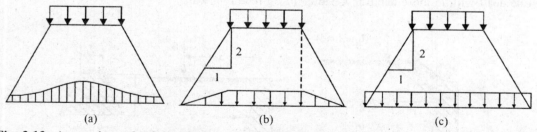

Fig. 3.13 Approximate load distribution by 2 vertical to 1 horizontal rule: (a) Actual distribution; (b) Approximation 1; (c) Approximation 2.

[The 30 degree method gives more or less good agreement at depth $z = 2B$, underestimates the value for depths $z < 2B$ and overestimates the values for depths $z > 2B$ as compared to Boussinesq's distribution (see Fig 3.9).]

Case 3: Distribution of loads from group of piles (Fig. 3.14), refer [11]

It has been found from experience that for calculation of settlements the stress distribution in soils due to a group of piles can be assumed as follows for the three types of cases that usually occur in practice:

Type 1: Friction piles in clay. Figure 3.14a. We replace the pile group by an equivalent raft placed at 2/3 the pile length *below the ground level*. Some assume the dimension of the equivalent raft as the same as the outer dimension of the pile cap and that all the loads on the foundation are distributed on that raft. The load is distributed from the raft to the soil below at 1 horizontal to 2 vertical. The assumption that top soil does not take load is logical only when the top layers of the soil at the site are weak. On the other hand, if the top soil is not weak, we may assume a load distribution of 1 horizontal to 4 vertical from the pile cap to the raft placed at 2/3*L*, as shown in Fig. 3.14a.

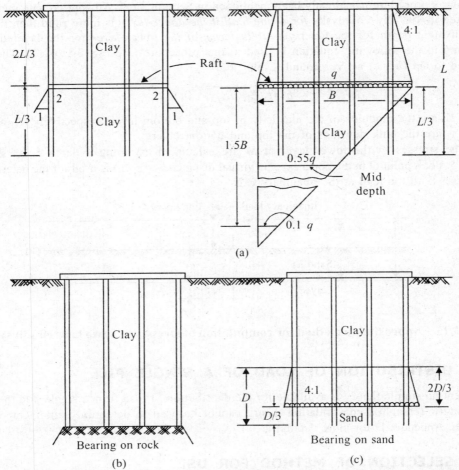

Fig. 3.14 Assumed distribution of load by a group of piles for calculation of settlements: (a) Friction piles in clay as a raft at 2/3 length of pile; (b) bearing piles in rock; (c) piles through clay in a sand layer.

For a quick estimation of the settlement we may also assume that the settlement is due to the consolidation of a clay layer of height 1.5B (where B is the breadth of the raft) with an average pressure of 0.55q as shown in Fig. 3.14b using the following formula (see Example 4.7);

$$\Delta = m_v \times 0.55q \times 1.5B \qquad (3.11)$$

Type 2: End bearing piles bearing on rock. See Fig. 3.14b. In this case a distribution of 1 horizontal to 2 vertical at the end of the pile can be assumed.

Type 3: Piles driven through clay into a strong strata (sand). See Fig. 3.14c. If the pile penetrates for a length into the strong layer the distribution can be assumed (as in Case 1) to be only in the strong layer. In this case, the negative skin friction from the top clay layer will also have to be considered.

Case 4. Loads on stratified soils

Burmister's procedure has already been mentioned in Section 3.6.2. An approximate method was suggested in 1937 by Pokrovsky *for a line load if the upper layer* is more rigid than the lower. An equivalent depth for the top layer 't' *in terms of the lower layer* for the layered system, according to the following equation is used in this procedure (see Fig. 3.15) [12]. The load is assumed to act $(h - t)$ above ground level.

$$h = t\sqrt{E_1\gamma_2/E_2\gamma_1} \, , \, (h > t)$$

E_1 and E_2 are the modulus of the elasticity of top and bottom layers respectively $(E_1 > E_2)$ and γ_1 and γ_2 are the bulk densities of the top and bottom layers.

The stresses in the lower layer at M are calculated assuming a depth z_2 as shown in Fig. 3.15. For a point Q in the upper layer, a virtual distance $z_1 = z(h/t)$ is used for the determination of stresses with the load at the imaginary G.L.

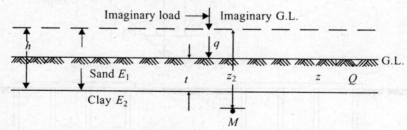

Fig. 3.15 Approximate method for computation of stresses in a two layered soil system.

3.12 DISTRIBUTION OF LOAD OF A SINGLE PILE

At present no simple theory is available for the distribution of load from a single pile to the soil. Accordingly Terzaghi's consolidation theory cannot be used to determine settlement of single piles (see Appendix D for more details).

3.13 SELECTION OF METHOD FOR USE

Appendix B of IS 8009 (Part I) 1976 gives us a guide on the selection of the method to be used for the computation of pressure increment in soil deposits. These are given in Table 3.5.

TABLE 3.5   SELECTION OF METHOD [IS 8009 (Part I) 1976]

Description of strata	Applicable method
Normally consolidated clays	Boussinesq's
Overconsolidated and laminated clays	Westergard's
Sand deposits	Fröhlich's
Variable deposits	Boussinesq's
Layered deposits	Burmister's

3.14   SUMMARY

We should be aware that most of the solutions for calculation of pressures in soils described above are for uniform loads on flexible foundations. We found in Chapter 2 that the contact pressures in rigid foundations need not be uniform. Hence the pressures we calculate by assuming uniform pressures under footings are not strictly applicable for practical cases. Solution for parabolic and other distribution of loadings applied on top of the soil are available but they are more complex in nature. However, as in the case of many other problems, in soil mechanics a fair estimate of values is all what is wanted and the standard methods can be used with confidence for most of the practical cases. We use separate theory for calculation of contact pressures. *Stress distribution is mainly used for calculating the probable settlement of foundations under elastic state of stress. Hence the applied loads should not produce stresses beyond the elastic limits.* We should always be aware of the limitations of the theory, and its application while using these methods.

EXAMPLE 3.1   **(Stress due to an embankment load)**

An embankment 4 m in height is as shown in Fig. E.3.1. If the unit weight of the material is 18 kN/m³ find the vertical stress at a point P 4 m inside the left hand toe at a depth 3 m.

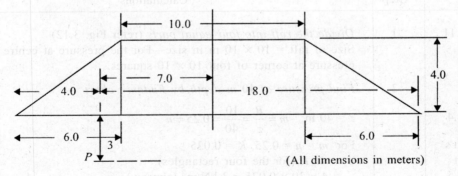

(All dimensions in meters)

Fig. E.3.1

Ref.	Step	Calculations
Sec. 3.4	1	*Find ratios from Tables* 3.1 *and* 3.2 $x_1/B_1 = 4/6 = 0.67$ $x_2/B_2 = 7/10 = 0.70$ $x_3/B_3 = 18/6 = 3.0$ $z/B_1 = 3/6 = 0.5$ $z/B_2 = 3/10 = 0.3$ $z/B_3 = 3/6 = 0.5$
Table 3.1 Table 3.2	2	*Read off values of* η_1, η_2 *and* η_3 η_1(for $z/B_1 = 0.5$ and $x_1/B_1 = 0.67$) $= 0.44$ η_3(for $z/B_3 = 0.5$ and $x_3/B_3 = 3.0 = 0$ (no effect) η_2(for $z/B_2 = 0.3$ and $x_2/B_2 = 0.70$) $= 0.30$
	3	*Calculate increase in pressure* $\Delta\sigma_z = rh(\eta_1 + \eta_2 + \eta_3)$ $= 18 \times 4(0.44 + 0.30 + 0) = 52.2 \text{ kN/m}^2$ *Note*: As remarked in Sec. 3.6.3, these calculations are not absolutely valid. Separate methods are available to compute more accurate values under embankments [2].

EXAMPLE 3.2 (Approximate methods of calculation of stresses)

A raft 20×20 m has an intensity of loading of 30 kN/m^2. Determine the vertical pressure at the centre of the raft at a depth of 40 m by Fadam's chart. Calculate the same by equivalent point load method using Boussinesq's formula and also by approximate 2 to 1 distribution.

Ref.	Step	Calculations
Sec. 3.11	1	*Divide the raft into four equal parts* (refer Fig. 3.12) Size of raft = 10×10 m in size—For the pressure at centre find the pressure at corner of four 10×10 squares.
	2	*Find pressure at 40 m depth by Fadam's chart*
Fig. 3.4		$z = 40$ m; $\quad m = \dfrac{B}{z} = \dfrac{10}{40} = 0.25 = n$
Fadam's chart Fig. 3.5		For $m = n = 0.25$, $K = 0.025$ $\sigma_z = 4q\,K$ (for the four rectangles) $\quad = 4 \times 30 \times 0.025 = 3 \text{ kN/m}^2$ (approx.)
Fig. 3.12 Sec. 3.11	3	*Find pressure at 40 m depth* (by Boussinesq's formula) Consider four squares 10×10 m $= 30 \times 100 = 3000$ kN $R = \sqrt{5^2 + 40^2} = 40.3 \text{ m}$

Case 1 Eq. (3.1) Sec. 3.11 Case 2	4	$\sigma_z = \dfrac{3Q}{2\pi} \times \dfrac{z^3}{R^5} = \dfrac{3 \times 3000}{2 \times 3.14} \times \dfrac{(40)^3}{(40.3)^5}$ $\quad = \dfrac{3 \times 3000}{2 \times 3.14}\left(6.02 \times 10^{-4}\right) = 0.86$ Total σ_3 due to four squares $= 4 \times 0.86 = 3.44 \text{ kN/m}^2$ *Find pressure by* 2 : 1 *distribution* Total load $= 20 \times 20 \times 30 = 1200$ kN; area $= 400$ sqm Distributed area at 40 m depth on 2:1 dispersion $(20 + 20 + 20)^2 = 60 \times 60$ sqm Intensity of load $= \dfrac{12000}{60 \times 60} = 3.33 \text{ kN/m}^2$ *Conclusion*: In many soil mechanics problem we can find the approximate vertical stress by simple 2 : 1 dispersion method.

EXAMPLE 3.3   (Use of Newmark's chart)

A rectangular foundation *ABCD* 6 m in length and 3 m in width is loaded with a UDL of 200 kN/m² at ground level. Determine the vertical stress at a point 3 meters below the point *O* located 1.5 m in front of the centre of the long edge of the foundation (use Fig. 17 IS 8009—Part I).

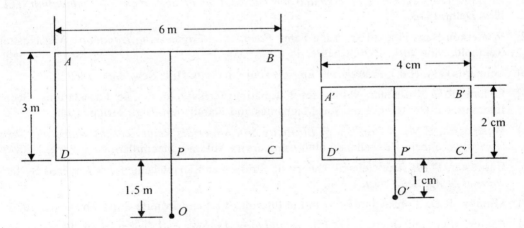

Fig. E.3.3

Ref.	Step	Calculations
Step Fig. 3.6	1	*Compute D/z* Refer Fig. 3.6 $AB = z = 2$ cm; depth $= 300$ cm Scale $= D/z = \dfrac{300}{2} = 150$
Sec. 3.4	2	*Draw the loaded area on tracing paper with* 1:150 *scale*
Case 5		$AB = \dfrac{600}{150} = 4$ cm; $BC = \dfrac{300}{150} = 2$ cm; $OP = \dfrac{150}{150} = 1$ cm
	3	*Place the plan over chart 3.6 so that point O at which stress is required is at the centre of chart*
	4	*Count the number of influence areas enclosed by the plan* $N = 30$ (approx.)
	5	*Calculate the pressure*
Eq. (3.8)		$\sigma_z = qI_z N = 200 \times 0.005 \times 30 = 30 \text{ kN/m}^2$

REFERENCES

[1] IS 8009 (Part I), *Code of Practice for Calculation of Settlement of Foundation*, B.I.S. New Delhi, 1976.

[2] Winterkon Hans F. and Hsai Yang Fang, *Foundation Engineering Handbook*, Van Nostrand Reinhold, New York, 1970, Chapter 4.

[3] Leonards G.A. (Ed.), *Foundation Engineering*, McGraw-Hill, New York, 1962.

[4] Fadum, R.E., Influence Values for Estimating Stresses in Elastic Foundations, Second International Conference on Soil Mechanics and Foundation Engineering, 1948.

[5] Westergard, H.M., *A Problem of Elasticity Soft Materials Reinforced by Numerous Strong Horizontal Sheets*, Timoshenko 60th Anniversary Volume, Macmillan, New York, 1938.

[6] Burmister, D.M., The General Theory of Stresses and Displacements in Layered Systems, *Journal of Applied Physics*, Vol. 89, 1945.

[7] Mindlin, R.D., Forces at a Point in the Interior of a Semi Infinite Solid Physics 7, 1936.

[8] Poulos, H.G. and Davis, E.H., Pile *Foundation Analysis and Design*, John Wiley & Sons, New York, 1980.

[9] Terzaghi, Karl and Peck, R.B., *Soil Mechanics in Engineering Practice*, John Wiley & Sons, New York, 1948.

[10] Blakes, L.S., *Civil Engineering Reference Book*, Section 8, Newnes Butterworth, London, 1975.

[11] Tomlinson, M.J., *Pile Design and Construction Practice*, A Viewpoint Publication, London, 1980.

[12] Szechy, K. and Varga, L., *Foundation Engineering, Soil Exploration and Spread Foundations*, Akademiai Kiado, Budapest, 1978.

4

Settlement of Foundations

4.1 INTRODUCTION

The total settlement of a foundation can be divided into the following three components:

1. The immediate settlement Δ which takes place due to elastic deformation of soil without change in water content.
2. The consolidation settlement ΔH which takes place in clayey soil mainly due to the expulsion of the pore water in the soil.
3. Secondary (creep) settlement ΔS which takes place over long periods due to viscous resistance of soil under constant compression.

IS 8009 (Part I) 1976 [1] deals with settlement of shallow foundations and Part II (1980) with settlement of deep foundations. In this chapter we will deal with the following commonly used methods of calculation of settlement of foundations.

1. Methods using elastic theory for all types of soils. (Section 4.2)
2. By Teng's formula based on SPT values for granular soils. (Section 4.3.1)
3. Meyerhof's formula based on SPT values for granular soils. (Section 4.3.2)
4. De Beer's method based on SCPT values for granular soils. (Section 4.3.3)
5. Schmertmann's method based on SCPT values for granular soils. (Section 4.3.3)
6. Terzaghi's consolidation theory for clays. (Section 4.4)
7. Equivalent raft approach for pile group in clays. (Section 4.8).

4.2 ELASTIC SETTLEMENT OF FOOTINGS

Elastic or immediate settlement of a rectangular flexible shallow footings is given by the following equation [1]:

$$\Delta = \left[\frac{qB(1-\mu^2)}{E_s} \right] I_w \tag{4.1}$$

where

q = intensity of pressure
B = least lateral dimension = width
μ = Poisson's ratio
E_s = modulus of elasticity of soil assumed to be constant with depth
I_w = influence factor depending on shape of footing and its rigidity as given in Table 4.1 for various points.

TABLE 4.1   INFLUENCE FACTOR I_w [IS 8009 (Part I) 1976, Table 2]

Shape	I_w for flexible foundation			I_R for rigid foundation
	Centre	Corner	Average	
Circle (dia = B)	1.00	0.64	0.85	0.86
Square	1.12	0.56	0.95	0.82
Rectangle (L/B)				
1.5	1.36	0.68	1.20	1.06
2.0	1.53	0.77	1.31	1.20
5.0	2.10	1.05	1.83	1.70
10.0	2.52	1.26	2.25	2.10
100.0	3.38	1.69	2.96	3.40

Note: I_R can be taken as $0.8I_w$ centre.

In the above expression we assumed the depth of soil below the foundation to be infinite or very large. If it is limited less than 10 times B, the value of I_w should be determined from *Steinbrenner's Influence factor* given in Fig. 4.1 [1].

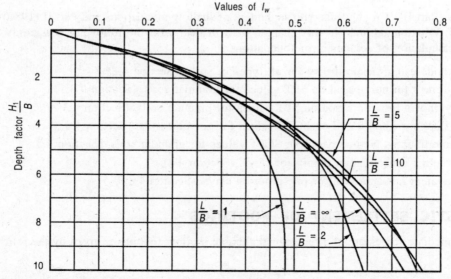

Fig. 4.1   Steinbrenner's influence factor for settlement of the corner of a flexible loaded area $L \times B$ on compressible stratum of $\mu = 0.5$ and thickness H_1 (IS 8009 Part I, Fig. 11).

Equation (4.1) can be obtained by similarity of deformation of an elastic rod.

$$\Delta = \frac{PL}{AE_s} = \frac{pL}{E_s} \qquad (4.2)$$

If we assume that the depth of influence of loading is of the order of B only, then $L = B(1 - \mu^2)$. The E_s value may be found as discussed in Section 1.9, the most common method being, to use SPT values. If the strength and elastic modulus of the soil increases with depth the above equation is not valid as the actual settlement will be much less than that calculated from the E value at foundation level.

The *settlement of a rigid plate* on a semi-infinite homogeneous elastic medium has been worked out by complex calculations involving distribution of pressures and is as follows:

$$\Delta = \frac{qB(1 - \mu^2)I_R}{E_s}$$

where $I_R = 0.82$ for a square plate.

It is approximately equal to the average settlement of a flexible circular plate (see Table 4.1).

4.2.1 Correction for Depth of Foundation

Footings are always placed (at least 1.5 m) below ground level. In 1948, Fox proposed a correction, which is given as Fig. 12 of IS 8009 (Part I). Bowles has modified these as shown in Fig. 4.2a, which gives the reduction factor to be used for correction for the depth of foundation [2].

$$\Delta_D = \Delta \times F$$

Here, Δ is the value of the settlement of a footing at the surface and F is the reduction factor. Fox's correction factors for depth are given in Fig. 4.2b.

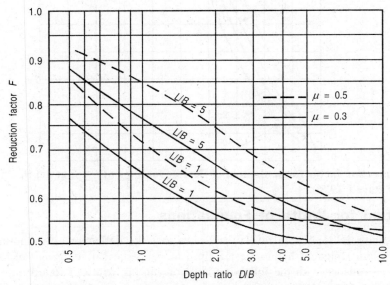

Fig. 4.2a   Reduction factor for settlement of footing of width B located at depth D below ground level (Bowles).

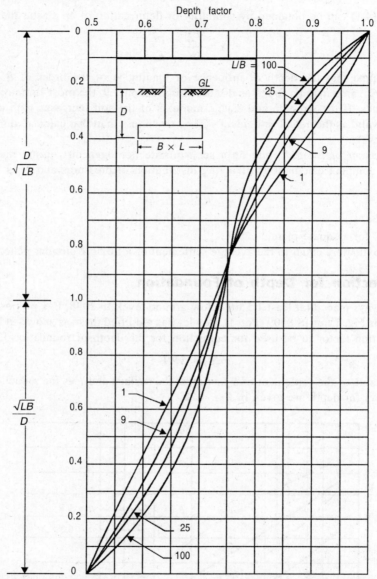

Fig. 4.2b Fox's correction factor for settlement of flexible footings of $L \times B$ at depth D for $\mu = 0.5$ (IS 8009 Part I 1976).

4.2.2 Correction for Width of Foundations

The theory of elasticity as applicable to clay indicates that the deflection of a footing will be proportional to its width. Terzaghi has suggested from model tests that *settlement of foundations in sands* occurs in accordance with the following law, for varying width of foundation:

$$\Delta_B = \Delta_1 \left[\frac{2B}{B + 0.3} \right]^2 \tag{4.3}$$

where,

Δ_1 = settlement of a 0.3 m square plate

Δ_B = settlement of a plate of width B.

4.3 SETTLEMENT OF FOUNDATION ON COHESIONLESS SOIL

As it is difficult to take undisturbed samples in cohesionless soils, we depend on the results of in-situ tests (SPT or SCPT tests) to estimate the total settlement. Moreover as the allowable soil pressure in these soils is governed more by considerations of settlement than bearing failure, it is desirable to predict them to a fair degree of accuracy.

The SPT corrected values at foundation level N_1, at depth $1.5B(N_2)$ and at depth $2B(N_3)$ are used as follows to find the average value of N to be used in our assessment of settlements and bearing capacity:

$$N = \frac{3N_1 + 2N_2 + N_3}{6}$$

4.3.1 Terzaghi and Peck's Correlation

From Terzaghi and Peck's [3] correlation of settlement with SPT values, Teng [4] proposed the following expression for the load for a given settlement of a footing of breadth B in a sand deposit with SPT value of N:

$$\text{(For } \Delta = 25 \text{ mm), } p = 34.6(N-3)\left(\frac{B+0.3}{2B}\right)^2 \text{ kN/m}^2$$

$$\text{(For } \Delta = 1 \text{ mm), } p_1 = 1.385(N-3)\left(\frac{B+0.3}{2B}\right)^2 \text{ kN/m}^2$$

Hence the settlement in mm for a load q in kN/m^2 is as follows:

$$\Delta = \left(\frac{0.722q}{N-3}\right)\left(\frac{2B}{B+0.3}\right)^2 \text{ mm} \tag{4.4}$$

where q is in kN/m^2 and B in meters.

IS 8009 (Part I) 1976 gives readymade curves from which the settlements can be read off for a given width of footing and SPT values (see Fig. 4.3). Corrections are also usually made for level of the ground water table and for depth of the foundation. However, the standard water table correction is too severe. As it was found that Eq. (4.4) (or Fig. 4.3) gives high values of settlements, Meyerhof in 1965 proposed the following:

$$\text{Actual settlement} = \frac{\text{settlement by Eq. (4.4)}}{1.5} \tag{4.5}$$

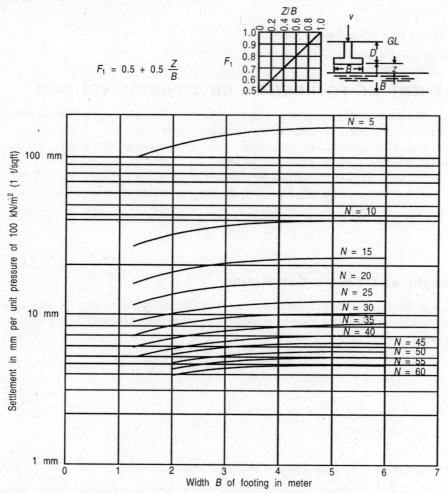

Fig. 4.3 Settlement in mm of a footing of width B loaded with 100 kN/m^2 resting on dry cohesionless soil of given SPT (N). [IS 8009 Part I 1976]

4.3.2 Meyerhof's Formula Based on SPT Values for Cohesionless Soils

Meyerhof noted that the Terzaghi and Peck's correction overestimates the actual settlement considerably. He proposed the following formula based on SPT tests for settlement in mm for q in kN/m^2 and B in meters

$$\Delta = \frac{1.6q}{N} \qquad\qquad \text{for } B < 1.25 \text{ m} \qquad\qquad (4.6a)$$

$$\Delta = \frac{2.84q}{N}\left[\frac{B}{B + 0.3}\right]^2 \qquad \text{for } B > 1.25 \text{ m} \qquad\qquad (4.6b)$$

$$\Delta = \frac{2.84q}{N} \qquad\qquad \text{for large rafts} \qquad\qquad (4.6c)$$

4.3.3 Settlement from Static Cone Penetration Tests for Cohesionless Soils

In this test, a standard 60° cone with 10 cm^2 cross-section is to be used. There are two methods that could be used. These are now described.

Method 1: By De Beer [IS 8009 (Part I) 1976 Sec. 9.1.2]: The settlement of every layer can be calculated by this method [5].

The compressibility coefficient C is given by

$$C = \frac{1.5 q_c}{p_0} \tag{4.7}$$

where

q_c = cone resistance in kN/m^2

p_0 = existing effective pressure in the stratum in kN/m^2 (settlement is calculated by Eq. (4.9) below.)

In practice, a diagram showing variation of q_c with depth is first prepared. It is then broken up into different parts each having almost equal q_c. For each layer, p_0 and Δp are calculated and the total settlement is the sum of the settlement of each layer. As it has been found that the above method generally overestimates the observed settlement (about twice as much) Meyerhof has suggested the calculation of C as follows [1965].

$$C = \frac{1.9 q_c}{p_0} \tag{4.8}$$

The settlement Δ of each layer is calculated from the following equation:

$$\Delta = 2.303 \frac{H}{C} \log_{10} \left(\frac{p_0 + \Delta p}{p_0} \right) \tag{4.9}$$

Method 2: Settlement from cone penetrometer by Schmertmann's strain influence factor. In 1970 Schmertmann [6] proposed a different approach to estimate settlement from q_c values for sandy soils. This method is very much used in practice. He assumed the following distribution of vertical strain under the centre of a footing. The greatest strain for a square footing occurs at a depth of about $0.5B$ as depicted in Fig. 4.4a and for a strip footing $L/B > 10$ at a depth B as shown in Fig. 4.4b. He gave the following equation for settlement in which the upper limit will be $2B$ for $L/B = 1$ and $4B$ for $L/B > 10$ as illustrated in Fig. 4.4b.

$$\text{For a square footing, } \Delta = C_1 C_2 \Delta p \sum_0^{2B} \frac{I_z}{E}(\Delta z) \tag{4.10}$$

[C_1 and C_2 are different from C in Eqs. (4.7) and (4.8)]

(The upper limit is $2B$ for square footing and $4B$ for strip footings)

where

$E = n q_c$ (deformation modulus, $n = 2.5$ for square and 3.5 for long foundations corresponding to 25% failure stress level)

p_0 = initial effective pressure at foundation level

$$C_1 = 1 - 0.5 \left(\frac{p_0}{\Delta p} \right) \text{(depth correction factor)}$$

C_2 = empirical creep factor = $1 + 0.2 \log_{10} \left(\dfrac{t}{0.1} \right)$ (observations show that there is creep settlement in sand also).

Δp = *net increase* in pressure at foundation level

t = period in years for which settlement is needed

I_z = vertical strain influence factor from Eq. (4.10)

The fomula for peak $I_z = 0.5 + 0.1 \sqrt{\dfrac{\Delta p}{p_v}}$ (4.10a)

where

p_v = effective overburden pressure at depth $B/2$ for square and at B for a long strip foundation.

For all practical purposes, the diagram shown in Fig. 4.4 can be used for calculating I_z. In order to apply the method, the cone resistance diagram is to be drawn as shown in Fig. 4.4 to scale and the settlement calculated for each layer (see Example 4.6). *Care should be taken when splitting the diagram into Δz layers.* For example, for $L/B = 1$, the parts above $B/2$ and those below $B/2$ should be split into separate Δz layers. Similarly, for $L/B > 10$, the separation should be made at B as shown in Fig. 4.4.

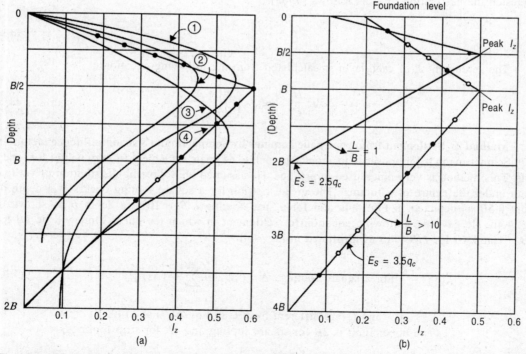

Fig. 4.4   Estimation of settlement in sand by Schmertmann's method: (a) Basis of the method for $L/B = 1$ ① I_z by elastic theory, ② ③ Results of field tests, ④ Schmertmann's assumption for $L/B = 1$; (b) I_z for $L/B = 1$ and $L/B > 10$.

4.4 ESTIMATION OF TOTAL SETTLEMENT OF FOUNDATIONS ON COHESIVE SOILS

In the case of cohesive soils, the total settlement can be expressed as follows:

$$S_t = \Delta + \Delta H + \Delta S$$

where

Δ = immediate settlement

ΔH = consolidation settlement

ΔS = creep or secondary consolidation settlement.

However, as the settlements of cohesive soils are computed by actual oedometer (consolidation) tests in the laboratory, the first two parts are not separated, but combined into one. Also, if immediate settlement needs to be separately calculated, it can be carried out by the same theoretical method described in Section 4.2 with a probable value of E_s. Although initial, primary and secondary consolidation settlements are often calculated separately, all of them occur simultaneously in the flield. The following relationship is usually found to be true in the field.

For normally consolidated clays, oedometer settlement is ten times the immediate settlement and the final settlement is 1.1 times the oedometer settlement. In overconsolidated clays, the immediate settlement is 0.5 to 0.6 times the oedometer settlement.

For calculating the consolidation settlement in fine grained soils IS 1904 recommends the full dead load, and all the fixed equipment load and onehalf the design live load. Alternately we may use the same loads given in Section 6.2.1 for bearing capacity calculations.

4.4.1 Settlement Calculation in Normally Consolidated and Lightly Overconsolidated Clays

As the compression curve in the laboratory and in the field follows the virgin curve, the total settlement can be calculated from the value of the compression index of the soil obtained from oedometer tests. In general, the settlements of clays can be computed from any one of the following equations. Taking the depth of compressible layer as H, the consolidation settlement as ΔH and the oedometer sample with e_0 as the initial void ratio, we have the following relations.

1. $\dfrac{\Delta H}{H} = \dfrac{\Delta e}{(1 + e_0)}$; hence $\Delta H = H\left(\dfrac{\Delta e}{1 + e_0}\right)$ for the same conditions $\qquad$ (4.11)

2. Coefficient of compressibility a_v is defined as follows:

$$a_v = \frac{\Delta e}{\Delta p}; \ \text{hence} \ \ \Delta H = \left(\frac{a_v}{1 + e_0}\right) H \Delta p \qquad (4.12)$$

$\dfrac{a_v}{1 + e_0}$ is called coefficient of volume compressibility and represented as m_v. Thus,

$$\Delta H = m_v H \Delta p \qquad (4.13)$$

Also, note that

$$m_v = \left(\frac{\Delta e}{1 + e_0}\right)\left(\frac{1}{\Delta p}\right) = \frac{\text{strain}}{\text{stress}} \ \text{(which is the inverse of } E_s)$$

Thus, m_v is also associated with $1/E_s$ value of the soil. The unit of m_v will be m^2/kN. E_s is also equal to the bulk modulus when deformation is only in one direction.

3. Normally, consolidated clays can be identified from their consolidation test e-log p curves as shown in Fig. 4.5a. If we plot the consolidation data of a *normally consolidated* clay as e versus $\log_{10} p$ curve, we get a straight line with constant slope, from the points of overburden pressure as in Fig. 4.5a. Hence,

$$\frac{\Delta e}{\log_{10}\left(\dfrac{p_0 + \Delta p}{p_0}\right)} = \text{constant} = C_c \text{ compression index.}$$

Therefore,

$$\Delta H = H\left(\frac{\Delta e}{1 + e_0}\right) = C_c\left(\frac{H}{1 + e_0}\right)\log_{10}\left(\frac{p_0 + \Delta p}{p_0}\right) \tag{4.14}$$

It should be noted that a_v and m_v are not constants, but vary with the stress in the soils, the values obtained for a given stress range to be used for accurate results.

For normally consolidated soils, C_c is a constant and generally we use Eq. (4.14) for the calculation of settlements. The following are three of the main empirical formulae recommended for C_c values for low sensitive clays. (Section 1.12.1).

$$
\begin{aligned}
C_c &= 0.009\,(LL - 10) &&\text{for undisturbed soil in terms of } LL \\
C_c &= 0.30\,(e_0 - 0.27) &&\text{for undisturbed soil in terms of } e_0 \\
C_c &= 0.007\,(LL - 7) &&\text{for remoulded or disturbed soil}
\end{aligned}
\tag{4.15}
$$

4.4.2 Settlement of Overconsolidated Clays

Overconsolidated clays can be easily identified from the e versus log p curve got from consolidation tests Fig. 4.5b. In such soils, if the loading happens to be less than the pre-consolidation pressure, the compressibility will be considerably lower than that for a normally consolidated clay. The settlement in such cases should be computed from.

$$\Delta H = \Delta_p m_v H \tag{4.16}$$

It is very important to note that the value of m_v should be from consolidation test results *for the range of loading that will happen in the field.* The procedure for extrapolation of the field consolidation curve from laboratory tests using Schmertmann's procedure is as shown in Fig. 4.5

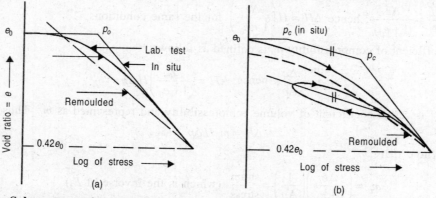

Fig. 4.5 **Schmertmann's method for reconstruction of virgin field compression curve for clays:** **(a) Normally, consolidated clays; (b) Overconsolidated clays.** (p_o = in situ pressure; p_c = pre-consolidation pressure. See also **Fig. 1.19**.)

and is explained in books on soil mechanics. The pre-consolidation pressure can be determined by Casagrande's construction. This procedure is described in Appendix C of IS 8009 Part I (1976).

Alternately in overconsolidated clays, the consolidation is calculated in two parts; first part is up to the pre-consolidation pressure, and the second part is along the virgin compression curve.

Let

p_c = pre-consolidation pressure
p_0 = existing pressure
Δp = increase in pressure assumed to be larger than $(p_c - p_0)$

In pre-consolidated clays, the settlement is calculated by the following equation in two stages:

$$\Delta H = C_r\left(\frac{H}{1+e_0}\right)\log_{10}\frac{p_c}{p_0} + C_c\left(\frac{H}{1+e_0}\right)\log_{10}\frac{p_c+\Delta p'}{p_c} \qquad (4.17)$$

where $\Delta p = (p_c - p_0) + \Delta p'$ and C_r and C_c are compression indices for each stage (C_r is also called recompression index and will be very much less than C_c).

4.4.3 Correction Factor for Clay Layer Resting on Cohesionless Soil Layer or on Rock

In 1957 Skempton and Bjerrum pointed out that the one dimensional consolidation theory assumed by Terzaghi is correct only when a clay layer is sandwiched between two sand layers [1]. When a clay layer starting from ground surface rests on rock or sand layer, the consolidation is three dimensional and a correction factor λ depending on the pore water coefficient as explained in IS 8009 (Part I) Section 9.2.3 should be applied.

$$\Delta H = \lambda \times (\text{settlements derived from oedometer test})$$

where the factor λ is related to the pore pressure parameter A and the ratio H/B, is as shown in Fig. 4.6. In the absence of pore pressure data, λ values are taken from Table 4.2.

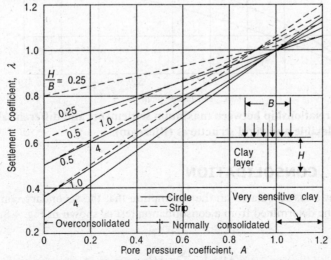

Fig. 4.6 **Settlement correction coefficients for footings on clay layers resting on rock or sand (IS 8009 Part I 1976, Fig. 10).**

TABLE 4.2   VALUES OF COEFFICIENT λ FOR CLAY OVER SAND OR ROCK
[IS 8009 Table 1]

Type of clay	λ Values
Very sensitive clays (soft alluvial and marine clays	1 to 1.2
Normally consolidated clays	0.7 to 1.0
Overconsolidated clays	0.5 to 0.7
Heavily overconsolidated clays	0.2 to 0.5

Note: An average value of 0.75 is taken for normally consolidated clays.

4.4.4 Correction Factor for Rigidity of Foundation

As already pointed out in Table 4.1, a *rigidity factor equal to 0.8 is generally recommended* by IS 8009 Clause 9.5.2 for rigid footings.

$$\Delta \text{ (rigid)} = 0.8 \times \Delta \text{ at centre of flexible foundation.} \tag{4.18}$$

From theory of elasticity, the settlement of a perfectly rigid foundation $= \pi/4 \times$ maximum settlement of perfectly flexible foundation. In all buildings we have both, foundation rigidity and structural rigidity. Rigid columns increase the rigidity by 20 to 30%. Continuous load bearing walls increase the rigidity by 80% or more. The observed differences in differential settlements are shown in Fig. 4.7 [7]. The figure also shows that differential settlement can be taken as a function of maximum settlement.

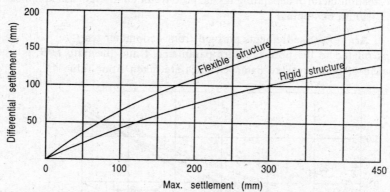

Fig. 4.7   Approximate relationship between maximum settlements and differential settlements as observed on flexible and rigid structures (Bjerram).

4.5 SECONDARY CONSOLIDATION

The secondary consolidation is calculated on the assumption that the secondary compression index C_∞ is a constant and can be determined from a consolidation test as shown in Fig. 4.8. It is calculated as follows:

$$\Delta S = \left(\frac{\Delta e}{1 + e_0}\right) H$$

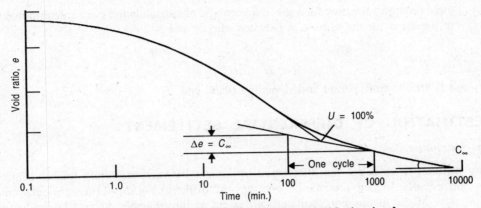

Fig. 4.8   Determination of secondary consolidation in clays.

when $\Delta \log t$ is one log cycle,

$$C_\infty = \frac{\Delta e}{(\Delta \log t)} = \Delta e' \text{ (change of } e \text{ for one log cycle)}$$

$$\Delta S = \left(\frac{\Delta e'}{1+e_f}\right)H = \frac{C_\infty (\Delta \log t)H}{1+e_f} \qquad (4.19)$$

where e_f is the void ratio at the end of consolidation [see Eq. (1.24)]. Δt is the time of secondary consolidation, for example, if it is required for a period from 25 to 100 years, is $\Delta \log t = \log_{10} 100/25$).

4.6   DETERMINATION OF RATE OF SETTLEMENT

The rate of primary consolidation is governed by the coefficient of consolidation C_v (in m^2/s):

$$C_v = \frac{K}{m_v \gamma_w} \qquad (4.20)$$

where K is the permeability (in m/s).

The value of C_v can be found out (a) as calculated from K and m_v values or (b) by Casagrande's "logarithm of time" fitting method or (c) by Taylor's "square root of time" fitting method.

For a given degree of consolidation U_s, the time factor T_v has a definite value depending on the boundary condition. The relationships are as follows:

$$U = \frac{\text{settlement in time } t}{\text{final settlement}}$$

$$T_v = \frac{C_v t}{H^2} \qquad (4.21)$$

where

t = time for $U\%$ consolidation.

From these relations, the time for a given percentage of consolidation can be determined when T_v and C_v are the same for the same $U\%$ between sample and site.

$$\frac{t_1}{H_1^2} = \frac{t_2}{H_2^2}$$

(4.22)

where t_1 and t_2 are the time period corresponding to H_1 and H_2.

4.7 ESTIMATION OF DIFFERENTIAL SETTLEMENT

Footing foundations

It is very difficult to calculate the differential settlement between uniformly loaded continuous footings and equally loaded rectangular footings of different *rigidity*. Terzaghi recommends a value of 50% of the maximum calculated settlement as the probable differential settlement of footings of equal size and equal loading in a building. Differences in size of footings can introduce further differential settlement of 25%. Accordingly, Terzaghi recommends the following relation for probable differential settlement for footing foundations in buildings. [3]

$$\begin{bmatrix} \text{differential settlement} \\ \text{in footings} \end{bmatrix} \not> \begin{bmatrix} 3/4^{\text{th}} \text{ the maximum calculated} \\ \text{settlement of footings} \end{bmatrix}$$

(4.23)

Thus for a maximum settlement of 1 inch in footings, the expected differential settlement will be 3/4 inch. The well-known design curves for allowable bearing capacity based on SPT value of N and breadth B of footing assume that footings can accommodate a differential settlement of 3/4 inch so that the total settlement can be equal to 1 inch or 25 mm. This aspect is discussed in Section 6.8.

Raft foundations

On account of the ability of the raft to bridge over the random distribution of soft spots in soil strata and also because of the rigidity of the raft itself, the differential settlement of practical rafts will not be more than 50% of the differential settlement calculated for footings. Hence the differential settlement in rafts can be calculated as follows:

$$\begin{bmatrix} \text{diffential settlement} \\ \text{in raft foundations} \end{bmatrix} \not> \begin{bmatrix} 3/8^{\text{th}} \text{ the maximum} \\ \text{calculated settlement} \end{bmatrix}$$

(4.24)

It should also be noted that in sands the settlement of an area will be fairly uniform only if it is located at a depth of about 2.5 m below the ground level. If the depth is shallow the outer parts of the loaded area will not be confined and are likely to settle more than the central part, which is confined.

4.8 SETTLEMENT OF A GROUP OF PILES USED AS FOUNDATION (DEEP FOUNDATIONS)

It is difficult to calculate accurately the settlement of a group of piles from the load settlement data of a single pile. Generally, the settlement for a group of piles will be more than that for a single pile carrying the same load per pile. The method of calculation of stresses in the foundation for determination of settlement of a group of piles is given in Section 3.11 **Case 3**.

Calculation of settlement of group of piles from m_v value of soil.

As explained in Section 3.11, if the soil layer is uniform, we can use the approximation shown in Fig. 3.14a. We assume the effect is only for a depth $1.5B$ and that the average pressure is $0.55q$. Then, the settlement will be as follows: (see Example 4.7)

$$\Delta H = m_v \times 0.55q \times 1.5B$$

Approximate evaluation of settlement of a group of piles in sand from tests on single piles

In sands, data from a single pile test may be used for the approximate settlement of a group of piles by using the formula recommended by Skempton in 1953 [8]. Taking S_g for group settlement and S_i for single pile settlement,

$$K = \frac{S_g}{S_i} = \left[\frac{4B + 2.7}{B + 3.6}\right]^2 \text{ or } \left[\frac{4B + 3}{B + 4}\right]^2 \not> 16 \tag{4.25}$$

where B is the width of pile group (centre to centre of piles) in meters.

Meyerhof (1959) also has given the following similar formula for the estimation of a settlement of a group of piles from results of test on a single pile.

$$K = \frac{S_g}{S_i} = \frac{s(5 - s/3)}{(1 + 1/r)^2} \tag{4.26}$$

where
s = ratio of pile spacing to pile diameter
r = number of rows in the pile group

In general, the settlement of a pile group in sand will be much more than that of a single pile under the same load [9].

4.9 SETTLEMENT OF PIER FOUNDATIONS

Terzaghi [3] has stated that if the depth of the shaft of a pier foundation exceeds four or five times its diameter, the state of stress in the sand near the bottom is practically independent of the depth of the shaft. Hence the effect of the depth of foundation on settlement of piers is relatively small compared to its ultimate bearing capacity. Allowable settlement will control the safe load on pier foundations. Accordingly, Terzaghi suggests that *the settlement of pier foundations in sand at any depth will not be less than about one half the settlement of an equally loaded area of footing at shallow depth*. Hence, settlement of pier = 1/2 × (settlement of footing at shallow depth).

4.10 ALLOWABLE DIFFERENTIAL SETTLEMENTS

When considering the settlement of structures like buildings we are interested in the quantities *deflection ratio* (Δ/L) and *angular distortion* ($h/L = \omega$), which are illustrated in Fig. 4.9. Both these quantities are important and specification has been laid down for their allowable limits.

IS 1904 (1986) "Code of practice for design of foundation in soils—general requirements" gives guidelines for limiting angular distortion in building designs. The studies of Skempton and McDonald on existing buildings have shown that it is the angular distortion h/L (where L is the

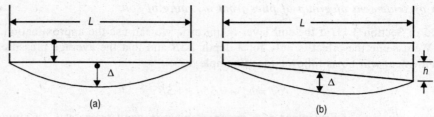

(a)   (b)

Fig. 4.9   Angular distortion and settlements.

length over which the differential settlement is measured) that is more important than the total differential settlement. The allowable values according to IS 1904 are given in Table 4.3.

TABLE 4.3   ALLOWABLE MAXIMUM AND DIFFERENTIAL SETTLEMENT OF BUILDINGS
[IS – 1904 Table 1]

C. No.	Type of structure	Steel	Reinforced concrete	Plain brick walls multistoreyed $L/H \leq 3$	$L/H > 3$	Water towers/ silos
1	**Isolated foundations**					
	1. *Sand and hard clay*					
	Maximum (mm)	50	50	60	60	50
	Differential (mm)	0.0033L	0.0015L	0.00025L	0.0033L	0.0015L
	Angular distortion	1/300	1/666	1/4000	1/3000	1/666
	2. *Statics*					
	Maximum (mm)	50	75	80	80	75
	Differential (mm)	0.0033L	0.0015L	0.00025L	0.0033L	0.0015L
	Angular distortion	1/300	1/666	1/4000	1/3000	1/666
2.	**Raft foundations**					
	1. *Sand and hard clay*					
	Maximum (mm)	75	75	—	—	100
	Differential (mm)	0.0033L	0.002L	—	—	0.0025L
	Angular distortion	1/300	1/500	—	—	1/400
	2. *Plastic clay*					
	Maximum (mm)	100	100	—	—	125
	Differential (mm)	0.0033L	0.002L	—	—	0.00025L
	Angular distortion	1/300	1/500	—	—	1/400

Note: Here, *L* is the length of deflected part (centre to centre of columns) and *H* is the height of wall from foundation/footing.

In general, IS 1904 allows a maximum settlement of not more than the following for individual footings: 65 mm on clay and 40 mm on sand. For rafts, the values are 65 to 100 mm for clays and 45 to 65 mm for sand. The permissible values for differential settlement are 40 mm for clay and

25 mm for sand. The permissible angular distortion in framed structures should be only 1/500 to 1/1000 depending on their use and importance. Angular distortions of more than 1/150 produce considerable cracking in brick and panel walls.

4.11 METHODS TO REDUCE SETTLEMENT IN BUILDINGS

The following are some of the methods that can be used to reduce settlement in buildings.

1. Reduce the load on the soil by removing soil and adopting basement floor (i.e. adopt a floating or compensated foundation)
2. Reduce the load on soil by using lighter building materials like ribbed floors, light weight wall panels.
3. Adopt a pile foundation properly designed to reduce settlement
4. Adopt pre-loading of the site to attain necessary pre-consolidation stage by heaping of sand and also by providing sand drains for quick dissipation of pressure
5. Extend construction period to reduce damage on building
6. Design the structure so that the differential settlement is small. This is achieved by providing rigidity to the structure so that the whole structure settles uniformly. This will even out the settlement.
7. Prevent lateral strain in soft clays (if they are present underneath the foundation) by providing lateral confinement by suitable constructions like sheet pile walls.
8. Provide construction joints and time schedule for the construction of various parts to take care of settlements.
9. Provide jacking arrangements under columns so that the settlements can be adjusted by jacking and providing additional extensions to the column to the foundation.

4.12 ROTATION OF FOOTINGS SUBJECTED TO MOMENTS

Footings of columns in soil subjected to moments will rotate and the amount of rotation that can take place is important in structural analysis. It is easier to work out the problem if we assume that the footing is supported on a bed of springs and the modulus of subgrade reaction theory is used. We can assume that for all practical purposes, the modulus of subgrade reaction can be expressed as follows as a constant k (see Section 1.11). Consider a footing $B \times L$ $(B > L)$.

$$k = \frac{E_s}{B(1-\mu^2)} \text{ (kN/m}^3) \text{ [see Eq. (1.14a)]}$$

As shown in Fig. 4.10, considering a footing $B \times L$ the rotation about breadth B will be as follows:

$$M = 2 \int_0^{B/2} L(Kx\theta)x\, dx = \frac{LB^3 K\theta}{12}$$

Replacing K in terms of E_s, we get θ in the following form:

$$\theta = \frac{12M}{LB^3 K} = \frac{12M(1-\mu^2)}{LB^2 E_s} = \frac{(1-\mu^2)}{E_s} \frac{M}{B^2 L} I_\Theta \tag{4.27}$$

where

I_Θ = influence factor to compute rotation of footings.

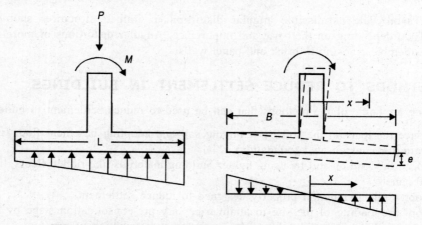

Fig. 4.10   Rotation of footings under the action of a moment.

Taylor and others have investigated this problem in more detail and their recommended values are much less than that obtained by factor 12 in the above equation. It is found to vary with L/B ratio and also the rigidity of the foundation. Hence we introduce a factor I_Θ. Some of the values recommended by Bowles for I_Θ are shown in Table 4.4 [2].

TABLE 4.4   RECOMMENDED VALUES FOR I_Θ

L/B	Flexible	Rigid
0.1	1.04	1.59
1	3.15	4.17
2	3.57	4.59
5	3.77	4.87
10	3.81	4.98
100	3.82	5.06

Another method suggested is to calculate the settlements at the most stressed end and the least stressed end and estimate the rotation from these values. The magnitude of the moment produced at the column end fixed to the foundation (due to the above, rotation of the foundation) is given by the formula:

$$M_1 = \left[\frac{4E_c I}{L} \right] \theta \qquad\qquad (4.28)$$

where $E_c I$ is the flexural rigidity of the column.

The direction of M_1 will be opposite to the direction of the original moment M so that there will be a release in the moment due to the rotation. *In the limiting case, the net moment can reduce to zero.* There will be also corresponding changes in the far end of the column. In effect, the bottom becomes a hinged support depending on the modulus of rigidity of the foundation material.

4.13 SUMMARY

Settlement of structures is a very import topic in foundation engineering. In theory, we compute the settlement of flexible structures. In practice all structures have rigidity. Similarly, although we assume homogenous conditions, soil deposits are very much varying both in vertical and horizontal directions. Hence the history of the performance of structures already built are of great importance. There are a large number of case studies reported in foundation engineering literature [8]. A study of these cases will enable us to make good judgement in the cases we have to deal with.

EXAMPLE 4.1   (Immediate settlement of footings)

Calculate the immediate average settlement of a flexible footing 2.4×1.2 m in clay loaded at 300 kN/m^2 assuming $E = 5000$ kN/m^2 and $\mu = 0.25$.

Ref.	Step	Calculations
	1	*Data*
Sec. 4.2		$q = 300$ kN/m^2; $B = 1.2$ m; $\mu = 0.25$ $E_s = 5000$ kN/m^2
Eq. (4.1)		$\Delta = \dfrac{qB(1-\mu^2)I_w}{E_s}$; $L/B = 2.4/1.2 = 2.0$
Table 4.1		$I_w\left(\text{for } \dfrac{L}{B} = 2\right) = 1.31$ (average value)
	2	*Calculate elastic settlement* $\Delta = \dfrac{300 \times 1.2 \times (1 - 0.062) \times 1.31}{5000} = 0.0884 = 88$ mm

EXAMPLE 4.2   (Settlement in sand and correction for depth)

A column footing 5×5 m is founded at 3 m at depth in a stratum of medium dense sand giving SPT = 20. Determine the immediate settlement at the surface of the centre point if the column load is 100 tons and then apply correction for depth of footing.

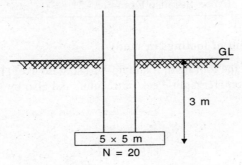

Ref.	Step	Calculations
Sec. 1.10		*Settlement from theory of elasticity*
Fig. 1.16b	1	*Determine E_s value from SPT value*
Table 1.10		$N = 20$ (find E_s from SPT value)
		$E_s = 220 + 11N = 220 + 220 = 440$ kg/cm^2 = 44000 kN/m
		$\mu = 0.3$
	2	*Calculate settlement if loaded at the surface*
Eq. (4.1)		$\Delta = \dfrac{qB(1 - \mu^2)I_w}{E_s}$ from theory of elasticity
Table 4.1		For square $I_w = 0.95$ (average for flexible footing),
		$q = \dfrac{1000}{5 \times 5} = 40$ kN/m^2
		$\Delta = \dfrac{40 \times 5 \times (1 - 0.3^2) \times 0.95}{44000} = 0.0039 = 3.9$ mm
	3	*Find correction for depth of footing for $\mu = 0.5$ (Method 1)*
		$D/B = \dfrac{3.0}{5} = 0.6$ and $\mu = 0.5$; $L/B = 1$
Fig. 4.2a		Depth factor $F = 0.82$
	4	*Calculate settlement of footing*
		$\Delta_D = \Delta \times F = 3.9 \times 0.82 = 3.2$ mm
		Corrected settlement = 3.2 mm
	4(a)	*Alternatively, use Fox's correction factor I_s given $\mu = 0.5$ (Method 2)*
Fig. 4.2b		Use $\dfrac{D}{\sqrt{L_B}} = \dfrac{3.0}{\sqrt{5 \times 5}} = 0.6$
		For $L/B = 1$, depth factor = 0.82.
		$\Delta_1 = 3.9 \times 0.82 = 3.2$ mm
		(*Note*: See also Example 4.3)

EXAMPLE 4.3 (Settlement of footings in sand)

Determine the settlement of the footing in Example 4.2 using Eq. (6.11) for settlement calculation of footing from SPT values from Terzaghi–Peck correlation and also by using Fig. 4.3.

Ref.	Step	Calculations
Eq. (4.4)	1	*Equation for setttlement of footings in sand proposed by Teng* $$s = \left[\frac{0.722q}{N-3}\right]\left[\frac{2B}{B+0.3}\right]^2 \text{ at ground level}$$ where s is in mm and q in kN/m^2 $q = 40$ kN/m^2; $B = 5$ m and $N = 20$ $$s = \left[\frac{0.722 \times 40}{17}\right]\left[\frac{2 \times 5}{5+0.3}\right]^2 = 6.1 \text{ mm}$$ = 6.1 mm (as against 3.9 mm in Example 4.2)
Fig. 4.3	2	*Calculate settlement of footing using Fig.* 4.3 For $N = 20$ width of footing 5 m, Δ for 100 kN/m^2 = 17 mm Hence, Δ for 40 kN/m^2 = 17 × 0.4 = 6.8 mm Teng's formula and Fig. 4.3 give the same results.

EXAMPLE 4.4 **(Calculation of settlement in sands from SPT–values)**

Determine the settlement of a 10 m square area loaded at 100 kN/m^2, placed at 1 m below the ground level in a bed of sand. Ground water level is just below the footing. The SPT values are as follows:

Depth	Average SPT
1 m to $B/2$ (5 m)	$20(N_1)$
5 m to B (10 m)	$25(N_2)$
10 m to $2B$ (20 m)	$30(N_3)$

Ref.	Step	Calculations
Text Sec. 4.3	1	*Find average value of SPT N* $$N = \frac{3N_1 + 2N_2 + N_3}{6} = \frac{60+50+30}{6} = 23$$
Eq. (4.4)	2	*Settlement by Terzaghi–Peck correlation* (*Assume SPT values are the corrected values*) given $q = 100$ kN/m^2 $$\Delta = \frac{0.722}{(N-3)}\left(\frac{2B}{B+0.3}\right)^2 \text{ mm}$$ $$= \frac{0.722 \times 100}{20}\left[\frac{20}{10.3}\right]^2 = 13.7 \text{ mm}$$ Correction for ground water level is not generally applied to settlements but only for bearing capacities.

Ref.		Calculations
	3	*Apply Meyerhof's recommendation*
Sec. 4.3.1		Actual settlement $= \dfrac{\Delta}{1.5} = \dfrac{13.6}{1.5} = 9$ mm
Fig. 4.3	4	*Calculation of settlement using IS 8009 Chart* For $q = 100$ kN/m^2 and $B = 10$ m (> 6 m); $N = 23$ $\Delta = 14$ mm (without correction) (It will be the same as the value in step 2 as both are based on the same principle.)
	5	*Settlement using Meyerhof's formula* Average N over $B = \dfrac{(5 \times 20) + (5 \times 25)}{10} = 22.5$
Sec. 4.3.2		$\Delta = \dfrac{2.84q}{N}\left[\dfrac{B}{B+0.3}\right]^2$, where N is the SPT value
Eq. (4.6b)		$\Delta = \dfrac{2.84 \times 100}{22.5}\left[\dfrac{10}{10.33}\right]^2 = 11.8$ mm

EXAMPLE 4.5 (Settlement by De Beer's method)

Estimate the settlement of a 10 m square area loaded 1 m at 100 kN/m^2 placed 1 m below ground level with ground water at the level of the footing. The static cone resistance q_c values for the sand deposit are as follows: G.L. to 6 m = 8000 kN/m^2; 6–11 mm = 10,000 kN/m^2; below 11 m = 12,000 kN/m^2.

Ref.	Step	Calculations
	1	*Assume* $\gamma_{\text{sat}} = 20$ kN/m^3. *Then,* $\gamma_{\text{sub}} = 10$ kN/m^3
Sec. 4.3.3		$C = 1.5\dfrac{q_c}{p_0}$ (De Beer and Martin)
		Assume seat of settlement is within $2B$ (i.e.) $2 \times 10 = 20$ m
Eq. (4.9)		Total settlement $\Delta = \sum 2.303\dfrac{H}{C}\log_{10}\left(\dfrac{p_0 + \Delta P}{p_0}\right)$
	2	(Assume three layers 5 m, 5 m and 10 m below the foundation level consider middepth of each layer and find p_o and Δ_p *Find p_0 and Δ_p at midpoint of each layer* *Layer 1*: $p_0 = (20 \times 1) + (10 \times 2.5) = 45$ kN/m^2 Assume 2 to 1 distribution (for exact values, use Fig. 3.6 of Chapter 3) $\Delta p = \dfrac{100 \times 10 \times 10}{12.5 \times 12.5} = 64$ kN/m^2 *Layer 2*: $p_0 = 20 + 10 \times 7.5$ m $= 95$ kN/m^2 $\Delta p = \dfrac{100 \times 10 \times 10}{17.5 \times 17.5} = 32.65$ kN/m^2

Layer 3: $p_0 = 20 + 10 \times 15 = 170$ kN/m^2

$$\Delta p = \frac{100 \times 10 \times 10}{25 \times 25} = 16 \text{ kN/m}^2$$

(Increase in pressure is only about 10% of pressure.)

Find C values

$$C = \frac{1.5 q_c}{p_0}$$

For *Layer 1,* $C = \dfrac{1.5 \times 8000}{45} = 267$

For *Layer 2,* $C = \dfrac{1.5 \times 10,000}{95} = 157$

For *Layer 3,* $C = \dfrac{1.5 \times 12,000}{170} = 106$

Add the values for each layer from tabulation

Total settlement $\Delta = 0.034$ m $= 34$ mm

Final tabulation (From steps 2, 3 and 4)

Layer No.	H (m)	P_0 kN/m^3	Δp (kN/m^2)	C	Δ (m)
1	5	45	64.0	267	0.01655
2	5	95	32.65	157	0.00940
3	10	170	16.0	106	0.00813
				Total	0.03408

The left margin contains: "3", "4", and "Table given in Step 1".

EXAMPLE 4.6 **(Schmertmann's method for settlement in sand** [11]**)**

Calculate the settlement of the footing 10 m square loaded with 120 kN/m^2 using Schmertmann's method.

q_c values 0 to 5 m = 8000 kN/m^2; 5 to 10 m; = 10000 kN/m^2; 10 to 23 m = 12000 kN/m^2

Assume depth of foundation as 1 m.

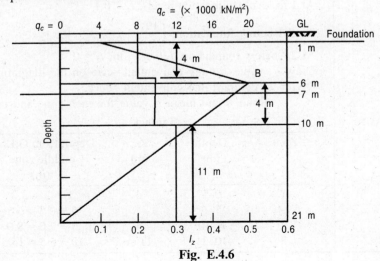

Fig. E.4.6

Ref.	Step	Calculations
Fig. E4.6	1	*Determine Δz in mm. q_c values are as below:* $B = 10$ m (foundation depth 1 m) Start from 1 m depth (foundation level). Divide into suitable layers. *Layer 1:* 1 m to 5 m (Δz) = 4 m *Layer 2A:* 5 m to 6 m (Δz) = 1 m *Layer 2B:* 6 m to 10 m (Δz) = 4 m *Layer 3:* 10 m to 21 m (Δz) = 11 m Total = 20 m (= $2B$) For convenience, plot q_c as shown in the diagram.
Sec. 1.11.2	2	*Find E_s. Assume $E = 2q_c$ for each layer* (*see tabulation* steps 5 and 6) (Fig. 4.4 gives $E = 2.5q_c$ for $L/B = 1$ and $E = 3.5q_c$ for $L/B > 10$)
	3	*Find p_0 and C_1 and C_2* Depth of foundation = 1 m $p_0 = 1 \times 20 = 20$ kN/m^2 (at foundation level) Applied load = 120 kN/m^2. Deduct excavation load. Net applied load = $\Delta p = 120 - 20 = 100$ kN/m^2 (a)
Sec. 4.3.3		$$C_1 = 1 - 0.5\left(\frac{p_0}{\Delta p}\right) = 1 - 0.5\left(\frac{20}{100}\right) = 0.9 \cdot$$ (b) C_2 = (creep factor for 5 years) $$= 1 + 0.2\log_{10}\left(\frac{t}{0.1}\right) = 1 + 0.2\log_{10}\left(\frac{5}{0.1}\right) = 1.34$$
	4	*Draw Schmertmann diagram for $B/L = 1$ (Fig. E. 4.6)* Theoretical peak $I_z = 0.5 + 0.1\sqrt{\Delta p/p_v}$ $\Delta p = 100$ kN/m^2; $p_v = 120$ kN/m^2; $I_z = 0.6$ Let us approximate I_z to 0.5 (Fig. 4.6) Draw Schmertmann diagram to scale. At 1 m level (foundation level); $I_z = 0.1$ At $B/2$ below foundation, $\left(\dfrac{10}{2} + 1\right)$ m, $I_z = 0.5$ At $2B$ below foundation, $(20 + 1)$ m; $I_z = 0$ Draw q_c values to any convenient scale on the diagram. Divide q_c diagram into convenient zones. Read η and mean I_z value for each zone and tabulate.
Eq. (4.10a)		
	5	**Table 1**

Table 1

Zone	Depth (m)	Δz (m)	Depth from G.L. to middle zone (m)	I_z
1	0–5	4	1 + 2 = 3.0	0.35
2A	5–6	1	5 + 0.5 = 5.5	0.40
2B	6–10	4	6 + 2.0 = 8.0	0.40
3	10–21	11 m	10 + 5.5 = 15.5	0.20

	6	*Compute settlement*

$$\Delta = C_1 C_2 (\Delta p) \sum_0^{2B} \frac{I_z}{E}(\Delta z)$$

(When Δp and E are in kN/m², Δz is in mm and Δ will be in mm.)
Read off I_z from Fig. E4.6 (value at mid-height)

Tabulate $\dfrac{I_z \Delta z}{E}$ as follows: (q_c = static cone value)

Table 2

Layer	Δz (mm)	q_c (kN/m²)	$E = 2q_c$ (kN/m²)	I_z	$\dfrac{I_z \Delta_z}{E}$
1	4000	8000	16,000	0.35	0.088
2A	1000	10,000	20,000	0.4	0.020
2B	4000	10,000	20,000	0.4	0.080
3	11,000	12,000	24,000	0.20	0.092
				Total	0.280

Eq. (4.10) (a, b c above)	7	*Calculate* $\Delta = C_1 C_2 \Delta p \, \Sigma \, (I_z D_z / E)$ $\Delta = 0.9 \times 1.34 \times 100 \times 0.280 = 33.8$ mm (*Note*: This value is comparable to that obtained in Example 4.5 solved by De Beer and Martin's method.)

EXAMPLE 4.7 (Settlement of pile foundation in clay)

A group of nine friction piles of 200 mm diameter spaced at 0.5 m transfer a load of 400 kN into a 10 m thick clay layer with sand below. It penetrates to a depth of 6 m in the clay layer. If the clay is normallly consolidated with a liquid limit of 40%, estimate the probable settlement of the pile group. Assume saturated water content is 39%; $G = 2.7$ and the water level is at ground level. Let $\gamma = 20$ kN/m³.

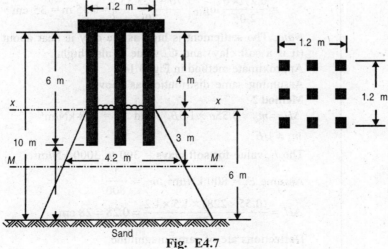

Fig. E4.7

Ref.	Step	Calculations
Fig. E.4.7	1	*Determine characteristics of soil* $C_c = 0.009(L.L. - 10) = 0.009 \times 30 = 0.27$ $e_0 = wG = 0.39 \times 2.7 = 1.05$
	2	*Calculate 2/3 depth XX* $2/3L = \dfrac{2 \times 6}{3} = 4$ m from top of pile = level of assumed mat. $H = 6$ m and mid depth of consolidating layer 3 m from raft level or 7 m from G.L.
	3	*Estimate pressure at mid depth, i.e.* 3 m *from XX* Area of mat at 2/3 $L = (0.5 \times 2) + 0.2 = 1.2$ m Assuming 2 to 1 dispersion from XX (assume no distribution from top to 4 m level). $p_0 = (20 - 10) \times 7 = 70$ kN/m^2 (assuming submerged). Width of equivalent raft 3 m below transfer raft, assuming 2 to 1 distribution load length at *M.M.* = 1.2 + 3 = 4.2 m Area = 4.2 × 4.2 m $\Delta p = \dfrac{400}{(4.2)^2} = 22.7$ kN/m^2 ; Δp at top $= \dfrac{400}{(1.2)^2} = 228$ kN/m^2 Average $\Delta p = \dfrac{22.7 + 228}{2} = 125.35$ kN/m^2
Chapter 3 Sec. 3.11 Sec. 4.8 Fig. 3.14	4	*Estimate settlement* **Method 1** $\Delta H = \dfrac{C_c H}{1 + e_0} \log_{10}\left(\dfrac{p_0 + \Delta_p}{p_0}\right)$ $= \dfrac{0.27 \times 6}{2.05} \log_{10}\left(\dfrac{70 + 125.35}{70}\right) = 0.35$ m $= 35$ cm *Note:* The settlement is high as the clay is near about its liquid limit (it is a soft clay) and C_c value is also high. Approximate method in Fig. 3.14a Assuming same distribution as above: **Method 2** $\Delta H = m_v \times 0.55q \times 1.5B$ and $q = 228$ kN/m^2 $m_v = 1/E_s$ The E_s value for soft clays = 300 to 3000 kN/m^2. Assume $E_s = 800$ kN/m^2; $m_v = \dfrac{1}{800}$ $\Delta H = \dfrac{(0.55 \times 228) \times 1.5 \times 1.2}{800} = 0.28 = 28$ cm Deflections are of same magnitude.

EXAMPLE 4.8   (Rotation of foundation due to moments)

A rectangular footing 3×2 m with 0.5 m thickness is under a column 420×420 mm. It is subjected to a moment of 90 kNm. Estimate its rotation if $E_{soil} = 21 \times 10^3$ kN/m^2 and $\mu = 0.3$. Assume the axial load is 500 kN.

Ref.	Step	Calculations
	1	Find $\quad e = \dfrac{M}{P}$ $e = \dfrac{90}{500} = 0.18 < B/6$, hence no tension in foundation is likely to occur.
	2	*Calculate the rotation,* $\boldsymbol{\theta}$
Eq. (4.27)		$\theta = \dfrac{12M(1-\mu^2)}{LB^2 E_s} = \dfrac{12 \times 90 \times 0.91}{2 \times 9 \times 21000} = 2.6 \times 10^{-3}$ radians
		(This value will be much less if we use Table 4.4)
	3	Let us calculate the rotation necessary to produce a moment of 90 kNm at the foundation. From structural analysis, the moment produced by a rotation θ in a beam with far end fixed is given by the following expression:
Eq. (4.28)		$M = \left(\dfrac{4E_c I}{L}\right)\theta$, where E_c is for concrete
		I of column $= \dfrac{(0.42)^4}{12} = 2.6 \times 10^{-3}$ m^4 $E_c = 25 \times 10^6$ kN/m^2. Let $L = 3$ m θ to produce moment of 90 kNm at the column end.
		$\theta = \dfrac{ML}{4E_c I} = \dfrac{90 \times 3}{4 \times 25 \times 10^6 \times 2.6 \times 10^{-3}} = 1.04 \times 10^{-3}$ radians only
		Hence, the structure will re-adjust to a new equilibrium with rotation of the foundation to behave as a hinged end at foundation.

EXAMPLE 4.9   (Settlement due to consolidation of clay)

A circular rigid tower of 6 m diameter and loaded at 200 kN/m^2 is constructed on a site where the top layer is 5 m of sand, the second layer is 1.8 m clay and below that there is impervious bedrock. If the ground water level is 1.5 m below ground level, estimate the average "consolidation settlement" of the foundation. Assume weight of sand above water level as 19 kN/m^3, saturated density of sand as 20 kN/m^3 and that of clay as 19.5 kN/m^3.

Laboratory test on undisturbed clay samples gave the following results.

Pressure, p (kN/m^2)	50	100	200	300
Void ratio, e	0.70	0.63	0.58	0.56

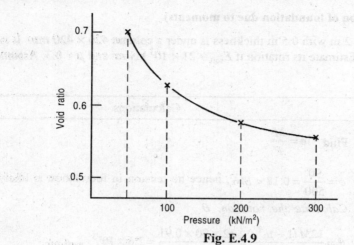

Fig. E.4.9

Ref.	Step	Calculations
Sec. 4.4	1	*Find pressure at mid depth of clay layer (of only 1.8 m thick)* (a) For 1.5 m of dry sand = $1.5 \times 19 = 28.5$ kN/m² (b) For 3.5 m of wet sand = $3.5 \times 20 = 70.0$ kN/m² (c) For 0.9 m of clay = $0.9 \times 19.5 = 18.0$ kN/m² (d) *Less* 4.4 m (i.e 3.5 + 0.9) of water = 44 kN/m² Effective pressure $p_0 = (a + b + c - d) = 72.5$ kN/m²
	2	*Find the increase in pressure assuming 2:1 distribution* with 2:1 distribution, $$\Delta_p = \frac{200 \times \pi \times 6^2}{\pi(6 + 5.9)^2} = 50.8 \text{ kN/m}^2$$ $p + \Delta_p = 72.5 + 50.8 = 123.3$ kN/m² (Note the increase in pressure)
Fig. E.4.9	3	*Find e_0 and e_1 from laboratory test values* Draw e–p curve and obtain values from the curve. e_0 at 72.5 kg/m² = 0.67 e_1 at 123.5 kg/m² = 0.62
Eq. (4.11)	4	*Calculate consolidation settlement of foundation* $$\frac{\Delta H}{H} = \left(\frac{\Delta e}{1 + e_0}\right) \text{ or } \Delta H = \left(\frac{\Delta e}{1 + e_0}\right)H$$ H = thickness of clay = 1800 mm $$\Delta H = \left[\frac{0.67 - 0.62}{1.67}\right]1800 = 53.8 \text{ mm}$$

EXAMPLE 4.10 (Calculate the rate of consolidation)

In the laboratory oedometer test on 20 mm sample, consolidation was reached under a certain increase in pressure in 90 minutes. How long will it take to reach consolidation under the same increase in pressure for a 2 m clay layer if it is sandwitched between a sand layer on top and an impervious rock at the bottom.

Ref.	Step	Calculations
Sec. 4.6	1	*Describe laboratory condition* Sample length = 20 mm (drainage on top and bottom). Hence $h_1 = 10$ mm and $t_1 = 90$ min
	2	*Describe field condition* $H = 2000$ mm (drainage one side)
	3	*Calculate time for consolidation*
Eq. (4.22)		$$\frac{t_1}{(H_1)^2} = \frac{t_2}{(H_2)^2} \text{ or } t_2 = \frac{(H_2)^2}{(H_1)^2} \times t_1$$ $$t_2 = \frac{90 \times (2000)^2}{(10)^2 \times 60 \times 24 \times 365} = 6.8 \text{ years}$$

EXAMPLE 4.11 (Consolidation of normally consolidated clays)

In a normally consolidated clay of *L.L.* = 65.5% and 5 m thickness, the overburden pressure is increased from 250 kN/m^2 by 120 kN/m^2. Estimate the settlement that can take place. Assume saturated water content of 45%.

Ref.	Step	Calculations
Sec. 4.4.3	1	*Estimate compression index,* C_c, p_0, Δp *and* e_0 $C_c = 0.009(L.L. - 10) = 0.009 \times 55.5 = 0.50$ $p_0 = 250$ kN/m^2; $\Delta_p = 120$ kN/m^2; $p_0 + \Delta p = 370$ kN/m^2 given $w = 45\%$ $e_0 = wG$; assuming $G = 2.7$ $e_0 = 0.45 \times 2.7 = 1.215$
Eq. (4.14)	2	*Estimate consolidation settlement* (ΔH) $$\Delta H = \frac{C_c H}{(1 + e_0)} \log_{10}\left(\frac{p_0 + \Delta p}{p_0}\right)$$ given $H = 5$ m = 5000 mm $$\Delta = \left(\frac{0.5 \times 5000}{2.215}\right) \log_{10}\left(\frac{370}{250}\right) = 192 \text{ mm}$$

REFERENCES

[1] IS 8009 Part I (1976). *Code of Practice for Calculation of Settlements of Foundations, Shallow Foundations;* Part II (1980): *Deep Foundations*, Bureau of Indian Standards, New Delhi.

[2] Bowles, J.E., *Foundation Analysis and Design*, McGraw-Hill, Singapore, 1988.

[3] Terzaghi, K. and Peck, R.B., *Soil Mechanics in Engineering Practice*, John Wiley & Sons, New York, 1967.

[4] Teng, W.C., *Foundation Design*, Prentice-Hall of India, New Delhi, 1965.

[5] De Beer, E.E., Bearing Capacity and Settlement of Shallow Foundations on Sand. Proceedings, *Symposium on Bearing Capacity and Settlement of Foundations,* Duke University, Durham (North Carolina), 1965.

[6] Schmertann, J.H., Static Cone to Compute Static Settlement over Sand, *American Society of Civil Engineers*, Vol. 8.8, SM, 1970.

[7] Szechy, K. and Varga, L., *Foundation Engineering*, Akademiai Kiado, Budapest, 1978.

[8] Skempton, A.W., *Discussions on Pile and Pile Foundation*, 3rd ICSMFE, Zurich, Vol. 3, 1953.

[9] Poulos, H.G. and Davis, E.H., *Pile Foundation Analysis and Design*, John Wiley & Sons, New York, 1980.

[10] IS 1904 (1986), *Code of Practice for Design and Construction in Soils, General Requirements*, Bureau of Indian Standards, New Delhi.

[11] Settlement of Structures, *Proceedings of Conference by British Geotechnical Society*, Pentech Press, London, 1974.

5

General Requirements of Shallow and Deep Foundations

5.1 INTRODUCTION

Foundations with depth/breadth ratio equal to or less than one are normally called *shallow foundations*. Those with this ratio greater than 5 are considered as *deep foundations*. The intermediate types are said to be moderately deep. In many situations when prefabricated steel columns are used in construction, we place a pedestal between the steel columns and the footing foundation [1]. These pedestals are generally considered as only an extension of the footing. Spread footings can be classified as follows as shown in Fig. 5.1 (see also Section 5.10).

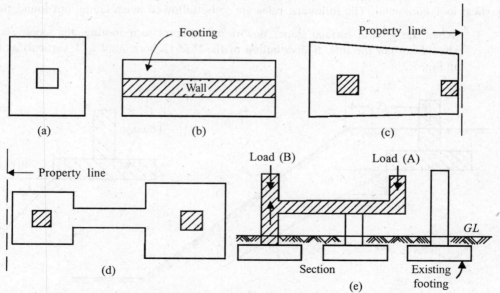

Fig. 5.1 Types of footings: (a) Simple square footing; (b) strip footing; (c) combined trapezoidal footing; (d) strap footing; (e) strap footing for a new column load (A).

1. Simple (square, circular or rectangular) footings with flat or sloping top surface
2. Strip footings
3. Combined footings (rectangular, trapezoidal, or other shapes)
4. Strap footings (balanced base type and cantilever type)

The choice of any of these particular type depends on factors like the intensity of load, nature of subsoil, nature of super structure and location of load to property line. We must remember that in most cases simple footings are the most economical foundations.

In this chapter we shall explain some of the basic principles pertaining to shallow and deep foundations.

5.2 DEPTH OF FOUNDATIONS

The minimum depth of foundations prescribed by IS 1904 [2] is 0.5 m. In clayey soils and especially in case of expansive clays, the depth should be below a level where there is no variation of moisture with change of seasons. As the external walls have to act as a protection against insects and rodents, the depth should be sufficient so as to prevent their access through burrows made under the foundation. Generally, a minimum depth of 1 m is adopted for foundations. In general, even though in sandy soils and silty clays the depth can be 0.5 to 0.7 m in clay soils, where the variation of moisture content causes shrinkage, the depth should vary from 1.5 to 3 m depending on the region. Some structural factors that influence the depth of foundations are discussed in the following sections.

Depth between adjacent footings of new constructions.   In general, the load can be assumed to spread into the soil from the edge of footing at 30° to the horizontal in soil and 60° in rock. (Some take this distribution as 1 vertical to 2 horizontal or 26.6° to 30° to the horizontal in clay and 1 to 1.2 or 40° to 45° in sand.) For estimation of stresses for calculating the settlement of piles, we assume 2 vertical to 1 horizontal. The following rules are to be followed when laying out foundations:

1. When the ground surface slopes downward adjacent to a footing, the sloping surface should not cut the line of distribution of the load (2 horizontal to 1 vertical) as shown in Fig. 5.2.

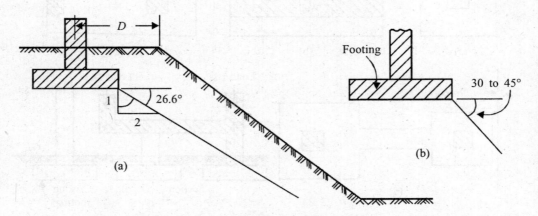

Fig. 5.2   Action of footing near slopes.

2. In granular soils, the line joining the *lower adjacent edges* of the upper and lower footings shall not have a slope steeper than two horizontal to one vertical (Fig. 5.3).

3. In clayey soil, the line joining the *lower adjacent edge* of the upper footing and the *upper adjacent edge* of the lower footing should not be steeper than 2 horizontal to 1 vertical.

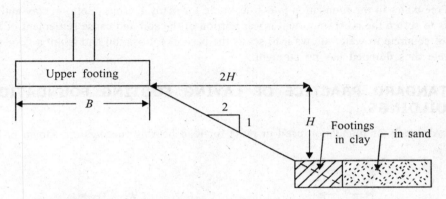

Fig. 5.3   Rules for location of adjacent footings at different levels.

Constructing a new footing near the footing of an old building.   A footing significantly affects the stresses to a depth equal to twice its width. In order to avoid damage to the existing structure, the areas of stress distribution should not significantly interfere with each other.

Accordingly, we should adhere to the following rules:

1. Minimum horizontal distance between the two footings should not be less than the width of the larger footings to avoid damage to the existing structure.

2. If the distance is limited, the principle of 2 horizontal to 1 vertical dispersion should be used so that the foundation of the old building is not very much affected by the new construction.

In any case, extreme care should be taken for supporting the sides of the excavations if the new footings have to go deeper than the old foundation.

Footings on surface rocks and sloping rock faces.   In places where solid rock is available near the ground level (less than 90 cm in depth), the rock should be chipped and the concrete of the foundation should be properly keyed into the rock. In places where the rock surface is on a shallow slope, it is advisable to provide dowel rods 16 mm dia dowelled to a minimum depth of 225 mm at a spacing of not more than 1 metre and adequately grouted. In such places, we can also bench the rock surface to provide a better key to the foundation.

5.3 IMPORTANCE OF SOIL IMMEDIATELY BELOW FOUNDATION SHALLOW

In cohesionless soils it is the settlement that governs *the safe bearing capacity*. In cohesive soils, both settlement and strength of foundations are important.

However we know from the theory of stress distribution that a depth of soil immediately below the footing equal to 1.5 to 2 times the breadth of footing only has considerable effect on the strength and settlement of footings. Hence, care should be taken that the excavations should not loosen the material in this region.

Similarly, during construction of the foundation, the base of the excavation should be definitely kept dry. Free water in the foundation is not desirable for many reasons. Both, in clay and in sand, water tends to soften the most important upper portion of the soil and cause settlement of footings. Dumping of concrete in water allows it to set as the base of foundation and is not a good practice. The concrete thus dumped has no strength.

5.4 STANDARD PRACTICE OF LAYING FOOTING FOUNDATION OF BUILDINGS

The standard details of foundation used in India for load bearing footings are shown in Fig. 5.4.

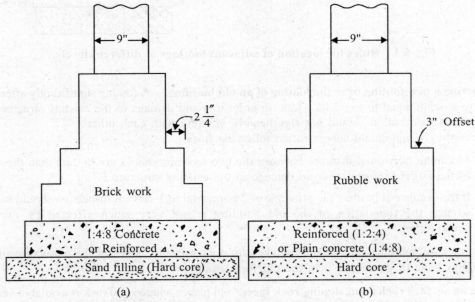

Fig. 5.4 Conventional footings: (a) Brick work; (b) rubble work.

To start with, if the foundation soil is clayey, it is preferable to have a 150 mm to 300 mm thick hardcore or sand filling, greater thickness is to be provided for the more clayey soil. Over this, a block of 1:2:6 lime, brick jelly concrete (preferred for clay soils) or plain cement concrete 1:4:8 with large size (50 mm) aggregate is laid. The thickness of this layer should be 150 to 450 mm depending on the site. Construction of brickwork or reinforced concrete footing is commenced only after this levelling course has properly set. (It is very import to note that excavations after construction of the foundation should not go below these sand layers.)

Brick walls using 9 inch bricks (bricks are still manufactured to this size) and stepped footings can be built over plain cement concrete using $2^1/_4$ inches offset, each successive course being one half brick that is, $4^1/_2$ inches larger in width. Each course consists of 2 or 3 brickwork in height.

For such walls, reinforced concrete foundations are not needed. (Thus, a 9 inch wall is carried through $13^1/_2$ inches, 18 inches and $22^1/_2$ inches in steps, each step being 2 or 3 course brickwork depending on depth and width of the foundation needed.) In places where the ground water is high or the subsoil and ground water are saline, it is advisable to adopt rubble masonry for foundations. In such places the submerged brickwork tends to deteriorate with time. The minimum thickness of these stone (rubble) walls is 375 mm with total offset of 150 mm (6 inches) as against 115 mm ($4^1/_2$ inches) in brick construction.

When properly designed reinforced concrete strip footings are used as foundation the brickwork can be constructed with less or no offsets, straight from the R.C. continuous footing. In waterlogged areas it is advisable to use rubble masonry up to the plinth level to reduce effects of submergence. Foundations with R.C. stub columns (given in Fig. 21.9 of Chapter 21) are also used in such cases.

5.5 CONSTRUCTION OF FOOTINGS FOR BASEMENTS

When continuous wall footings are used in the construction of basements after excavation, care should be taken to *see that the footings are not founded on back fill.* A stepped continuous footing with walls over the footing as shown in Fig. 5.5a is a better solution to the problem. Walls retaining earth should also be checked for stability against failure [3].

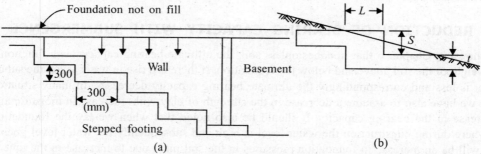

Fig. 5.5 Construction of foundations: (a) For basements; (b) along a slope.
(t = trench fill depth)

When continuous footings are built along slopes, it is advisable to build as stepped footings as shown in Fig. 5.5b. For conventional strip foundation, we make S equal or less than t and L equal to t or 25 or 300 m whichever is greater. [4].

5.6 FOUNDATIONS ON FILLS

Foundations on fills that have been built under controlled conditions with proper compaction can be designed as normal foundation. Uncontrolled fills should be excavated and they should be either refilled with controlled fill or the foundation should commence from the original ground level. Raft foundations can bridge over stray loose pockets in an otherwise good refill. They can also be used in some situations where the fill is otherwise uniform and stable.

5.7 FOUNDATIONS ON SOFT DEPOSITS

One of the following methods are generally adopted for foundations on soft deposits:

- Adopt shallow foundation after applying soil improving techniques like preloading.
- Adopt a floating or compensated foundation by using basement raft after excavation of calculated weight of foundation soil.

- Use soil replacement, that is, excavate the soft deposit and replace it with controlled good fill.
- Adopt pile foundation.

5.8 SAFE BEARING CAPACITY FOR SIMPLE CASES

In many situations, the safe bearing capacity of soils can be taken from those specified in codes of practices. These basic values are allowed under the following conditions:

- The soil is uniform to a depth at least three times the footing width.
- The resultant of external forces passes through the middle third of the footing area.
- Most of the external forces are not dynamic in nature.
- The ground water level is at a depth of at least equal to the footing width in granular soils and twice the width in cohesive soils.

If the bottom of the footing is at least 2.0 m below the ground level, then only the allowable bearing capacity should be increased by the weight of the soil between the footing bottom and the surface as any subsequent excavation near the footing will reduce the bearing capacity.

5.9 REDUCTION OF BEARING CAPACITY WITH SUBMERGENCE

It is shown in Chapter 6 that in cohesionless soil, the ultimate bearing capacity is a function of the unit weight of the soil above and below the foundation. If there is a rise in water level, the submerged weight is less and correspondingly the ultimate bearing capacity decreases. In many situations for clays, we have also to assume a decrease in the strength of clay with increase in moisture and thus a decrease in the bearing capacity. It should be also noted that when we lay the foundation at a site where during construction the water level is high and subsequently the water level goes down, there will be an increase in foundation pressures in the soil mass due to increase in the unit weight of the soil. This can cause additional settlement of the ground under the footing. This is specially true in clayey soil. Thus lowering of water table can cause cracking in buildings. One of the classical cases of such occurrence was seen in Mexico City, where during the development of the city, the lowering of water table caused by extraction of ground water led to large scale settlement and consequent damages to buildings and structures founded on volcanic soil.

5.10 TYPES OF FOUNDATIONS AND THEIR USES

The common types of shallow and deep foundations and their use can be summarized as follows:

Isolated footings (Fig. 5.1). These are used for column loadings and can be of brick work, mass concrete or reinforced concrete. It is ideal when column load is axial and not very large compared to the bearing capacity of the soil.

Strip footings. These are generally used for wall footings where the loading is not very large. The width of footing is to be based on the bearing capacity or the thumb rule that it should be not less than three times thickness of wall or two times thickness of wall plus 30 cm.

Combined footings. When two adjacent columns of different loads have to be accommodated together, we use a combined footing.

Balanced footings or cantilever footings. These are commonly used when one column which exist too near the property line has to be balanced by an adjacent column.

Raft foundation. These are used when the foundation soil offers poor bearing capacity and particularly when it has weak patches. With isolated footings, they come too close to each other and differential settlements tend to be very large. Different types of slabs offering different rigidities can be used depending on the nature of the soil and the pattern of loading.

Pile foundation. When the top strata is very poor and reasonably good soil strata exist below the top soil, a pile foundation becomes more reliable and economic than others. Also in certain situations where settlements cannot be tolerated, we have to use piles. For large rigid frame structures like tall buildings, chimneys and where settlements are dangerous and very high lateral loads are to be transmitted through the foundations, pile foundations are the obvious choice. In the ideal pile foundation, all the loads are assumed to be taken by piles and the number of piles necessary are calculated accordingly.

Piled raft. When the bearing capacity of a raft is satisfactory but the settlement is not satisfactory, a combination of raft on piles will provide the advantages of both, rafts and piles. As a means of reducing settlements, piles are called upon only to take a small percentage of the load and the rest is designed to be carried by the raft.

Compensated or floating foundations. The method used in this type is to excavate considerable amount of soil, as nearly equal to the weight of the building as possible, from the bottom of the structure and build basement floors, so that the load carried by the soil is considerably reduced. In fully compensated foundation, the weight of the soil excavated will be equal to the weight to be carried by the foundation.

Pier or well foundations. Large diameter piles, piers, and deep-well foundations are usually used for bridges and other structures to carry heavy loads. Deep-well foundations are specially useful for bridges across large rivers with deep scouring of the river bed.

EXAMPLE 5.1 (Footing near a slope)

A footing 2×2 m is to be founded at a depth of 1 m near a $40°$ slope 5 m in height. Find the minimum distance the centre of the footing should be placed so that the stability of the footing is not affected by the slope.

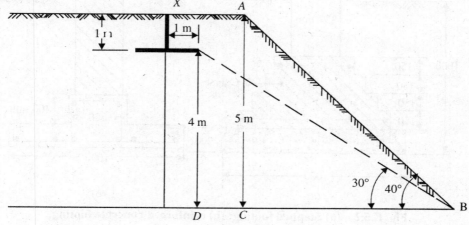

Fig. E.5.1

Ref.	Step	Calculations
Fig. E.5.1	1	*Find the height of the base of footing from toe of slope* (*Principle:* A 30° line from the base of the footing should not cut the slope) Depth of footing = 1 m Height of slope = 6 m Height of footing above toe = 6 − 1 = 5 m
	2	*Find horizontal distance for safe foundation* The 30° line from the edge of the foundation should meet the toe. $$BC = \frac{AC}{\tan 40} = \frac{5}{0.83} = 6.02 \text{ m}$$ $$BD = \frac{ED}{\tan 30} = \frac{4}{0.58} = 6.90 \text{ m}$$ CD = BD − BC = 0.88 m
	3.	*Determine position of centre of footing* AX = CD + 1/2 width = 1.88 m (say 2 m) The centre of footing should be 2 m from edge of slope.

EXAMPLE 5.2   (Design of conventional brick footings)

The load bearing brick wall for a building has to carry 120 kN per metre length. The soil has a safe bearing capacity of 150 kN/m². Design (a) a conventional stepped brick footing and (b) a suitable continuous reinforced strip footing for the above conditions.

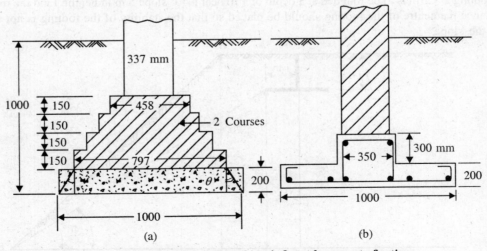

Fig. E.5.2   (a) Stepped footing; (b) reinforced concrete footing.

Ref.	Step	Calculations
E.5.2a	1	*Find thickness of wall required (adopt plain footing)*
		Load = 120 kN
		Assume compressive strength of brick = 4 m/mm^2.
		Allowable compression = 0.4 N/mm^2 [1/10th strength]
		Thickness required $= \dfrac{120 \times 1000}{0.4 \times 1000} = 300$ mm
		Adopt a 337 mm ($1^1/_2$ brick wall)
	2	*Find width of footing required*
		Bearing capacity = 150 kN/m^2
		Assume excavation compensates weight of brick work.
		Breadth required $= \dfrac{120}{150} = 0.8$ m = 800 mm
		Minimum required (by thumb rule)
		3 × thickness of wall = 3 × 300 = 900 mm
		Adopt 1 m width.
	3	*Find the width of footing from field practice*
		Thumb rule = (2 × thickness of wall) + 30 cm
		$\qquad\qquad$ = 2 × 337 + 300 = 974 mm
		Adopt B = 1 m (as in step 2)
	4	*Detail the footing*
Sec. 5.4		Assume levelling course of plain cement concrete 1:4:8 over
		150 mm (6") of hard core (sand filling).
		Adopt four offsets of 115 mm ($4^1/_2$") of 2 bricks high.
		Width of offsets = 4 × 115 = 460 mm
		Total width = 460 + 337 = 797 mm (say 800 mm)
		Thickness of concrete required for 45° dispersion
		Through P.C.C. = 1000 – 800 = 200 mm
		Provide 200 mm (8") plain cement concrete.
		Summary
		150 mm hard core (sand filling)
		200 mm × 1000 mm plain concrete footing
		$1^1/_2''$ brick wall with 4 offsets ($4^1/_2''$) each two brick in height.

IS 456 Fig. E.5.2b	5	*Alternate design (R.C. footing)*

Adopt a strip footing of reinforced concrete slab and beam under the wall width = 1000 mm.

Minimum depth of slab = 150 mm, adopt 200 mm

Breadth > wall thickness. Say 350 mm.

Assume depth over slab = 300 mm

Design slab as cantilever slab as per IS 456

Span of cantilever = (1000 − 350)/2 = 325 mm

IS 456	6	*Design of beam under wall*

Total depth of beam = 300 + 200 = 500 mm

Theoretically the beam must be designed as a beam on elastic foundation carrying a U.D.L. (Uniformly Distributed Load.)

Approximate design is made by assuming that the beam has to bridge a gap of 1 to 2 m without support. In any case provide longitudinal steel on both faces so that the total steel will not be less than 0.3 per cent.

REFERENCES

[1]   Varghese, P.C., *Limit State Design of Reinforced Concrete*, 2nd ed., Prentice-Hall of India, New Delhi, 2002.

[2]   IS 1904 (1986), *COP for Design and Construction of Foundations in Soils, General Requirements*, Bureau of Indian Standards, New Delhi.

[3]   Teng, W.C., *Foundation Design*, Prentice-Hall of India, New Delhi, 1965.

[4]   Tomlinson, M.J., *Foundation Design and Construction*, ELBS with Longman, Singapore, 1995.

6

Bearing Capacity of Shallow Foundations

6.1 INTRODUCTION

Even though Boussinesq's formulae to calculate the normal stresses and shear stresses were published as early as in 1885, these could not be used for design of foundations, as exceeding shear strength of a soil at a local point cannot lead to the general failure of the foundation. It was only after 1943, when Terzaghi published his well known theoretical methods to calculate the ultimate bearing capacity of footings and the settlement of foundations from soil properties, that engineers could get a clear picture of the theory for estimation of bearing capacity from soil properties.

In general, foundations are classified as shallow or deep depending on the ratio of the depth to width of the foundation. If the depth of the foundation is more than five times its width (shorter dimension) it is called a deep foundation (CP 2004 uses an arbitrary depth of at least 3 m to differentiate the two types). Terzaghi dealt with the bearing capacity of shallow foundations. Later research workers like Meyerhof modified Terzaghi's theory for its application to deep foundations like pile foundations. In this chapter we will deal with the historical development of the formulae for bearing capacity of shallow foundations. The general formula for bearing capacity will be dealt with in Chapter 7. The examples in this chapter have references to the contents of Chapter 7 also.

6.2 SOME DEFINITIONS

Before discussing bearing capacity we should clearly understand the following definitions.

- *Ultimate bearing capacity* is the value of the loading intensity the ground can support just before total failure. Generally the term denotes the gross ultimate bearing capacity. *The net ultimate bearing* capacity is the gross ultimate bearing capacity minus weight of the soil above the foundation to which no factor of safety need to be assigned. These are represented by the symbols q_{ult} and q_{net} respectively.

- *Safe bearing capacity* is the net ultimate bearing capacity divided by the factor of safety plus the surcharge γD, where γ is the unit weight of soil and D is the depth of foundation. This is represented by the symbol q_{safe}.

- *Soil pressure for settlement* is the value of the net pressure that can be applied on the foundation for a specified settlement, say 25 mm or 40 mm as may be prescribed.

- *Allowable soil pressure or allowable bearing pressure* is the maximum loading intensity at which the soil will not fail in shear, with the specified factor of safety and also will not undergo more than the specified maximum allowable settlement.

- *Presumed bearing capacity* is the net loading intensity prescribed as appropriate to the particular type of ground for preliminary design by Code of Practice.

- *Factor of safety.* The factor of safety to be used is as follows:

  (a) For structures where maximum loads are likely to occur often—like railway bridges and water tanks—the FS (factor of safety) should be 3 to 4.

  (b) Where maximum loads occur occasionally as in highway bridges, the FS should be 2.5 to 3.5.

  (c) When maximum loads are not likely to occur as in residential buildings, the FS should be 2 to 3.

In general, foundations in clays should be given a larger factor of safety against shear failure than foundations in sands.

6.2.1 Loads for Foundation Design

In multistorey building the design load for foundations should be the same as used for structural design of columns IS 875 (Part 2) 1987 on loads on buildings and BS 6399 recommend design to be made for full dead load together with *the live load reduced as follows:*

No. of floors (including roof) supported by column	Percentage reduction of live load
1	0
2	10
3	20
4	30
5 to 10	40
over 10	50

(*Note:* No reduction is to be made for ground floor to basement.)

6.3 TERZAGHI'S THEORY

We can imagine two critical states to happen as we increase the load on a footing. At the first critical load, the maximum shear stress in the soil reaches the shear strength according to the elastic theory. However, this does not lead to general failure of the foundation. Further increase of load leads to the ultimate critical load at which plastic failure occurs in the foundation material. Design based on ultimate state condition with suitable factor of safety was thus foreseen as a method for design in foundation engineering even before it was thought of in structural design.

In 1943 Terzaghi published his theory of ultimate bearing capacity of footings [1]. His theory was a modification of Prandel's concept for resistance to penetration of a punch into metals published

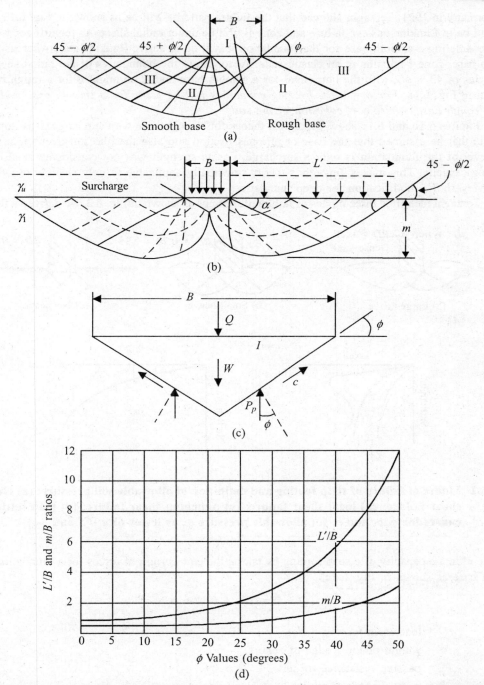

Fig. 6.1 Terzaghi's theory for ultimate bearing capacity of a footing: (a) Failure patterns with smooth and rough bases; (b) failure of rough base with surcharge; (c) forces acting on the base; (d) length and depth of shear zone depending on ϕ values (after Meyerhof).

in Germany in 1921. Terzaghi showed that the failure patterns will be as shown in Fig. 6.1a. Zone III will be in Rankine passive failure and zone II will be under radial shear. As regards zone I if we are considering a smooth base for the foundation it will be in active Rankine state whereas with a rough base, zone I remains in an elastic state. Accordingly the boundaries of the radial shear rise at angles of $45 + \phi/2$ with the horizontal for a smooth base and at an angle ϕ for a rough base as shown in Fig. 6.1a. *For $\phi = 0$ the bearing capacities will be 5.14c for a smooth base and 5.70c for a rough base, where c = cohesion of the soil.*

Figures 6.1b and 6.1c show Terzaghi's theory for a rough base with surcharge. It is important to note that he assumed that the base or pile has friction and also that the soil overburden above the level of the foundation is only a surcharge, i.e. its strength was not considered at all in the bearing capacity. This makes Terzaghi's theory principally applicable to only shallow foundations (see Meyerhof's modification for deep foundation).

Terzaghi identified three modes of failure of footings as shown in Fig. 6.2. He derived a formula

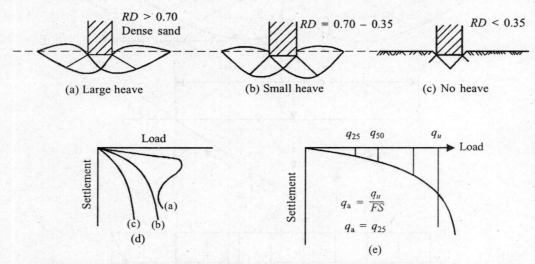

Fig. 6.2 **Modes of failure of strip footing and definition of allowable soil pressure: (a) General shear failure; (b) local shear failure; (c) punching shear failure; (d) load settlement curves for *a*, *b*, and *c*; (e) allowable pressure q_a as lesser of q_u/FS and q_{25}.**

for the ultimate capacity of a strip footing by taking the equilibrium of forces for a foundation with rough base as shown in Fig. 6.1c.

$$Q + W = 2P_p + Bc \tan \phi$$

where

$\qquad Q$ = load from footing = Bq_u

$\qquad W$ = weight of the wedge of zone I

$\qquad P_p$ = passive resistance of soil

$\qquad B$ = width of strip footing

$\qquad c$ and ϕ = cohesion and friction of soil.

From these, Terzaghi's ultimate bearing capacity equation for a strip footing corresponding to general shear failure can be derived. The formula is as follows:

$$q_{ult} = cN_c + \gamma_0 DN_q + 0.5B\gamma_1 N_\gamma \tag{6.1}$$

N_c, N_q and N_γ are known as *bearing capacity factors*. The formula has the following three components:

1. Cohesion c and its dimensionless factor N_c (cohesion plays a part at the bottom of the wedge as well as on the magnitude of the passive pressure).

2. Unit weight of the surcharge γ_0 and its depth D with its dimensionless factor N_q.

3. Unit weight of soil below the foundation γ_1 and its dimensionless factor N_γ. The factor B also comes into effect as the depth of failure zone depends on its value.

The net ultimate bearing capacity and safe bearing capacities will be as follows: (Deducting $\gamma_0 D$ from q_{ult} we get q_{net})

$$q_{net} = cN_c + \gamma_0 D(N_q - 1) + 0.5B\gamma_1 N_\gamma \tag{6.2}$$

$$q_{safe} = q_{net}/FS + \gamma_0 D \tag{6.3}$$

No factor of safety need to be allowed for the surcharge.

6.4 BEARING CAPACITY FACTORS

The values of Terzaghi's bearing capacity factors for given values of ϕ are given in Table 6.1[2]. Bearing capacity factors for practical use can also be obtained from plots of these values against SPT values as shown in Fig. 6.3[3].

TABLE 6.1 TERZAGHI'S BEARING CAPACITY FACTORS
(Rough base)

Angle $\phi°$	N_c	N_q	N_γ
0	5.7	1.0	0.0
5	7.0	1.6	0.14
10	9.5	2.7	0.70
15	13.0	4.5	2.0
20	17.0	7.5	4.8
25	24.0	13.0	9.8
30	37.0	23.0	20.0
35	58.0	42.0	43.0
40	98.0	77.0	98.0
45	172.0	173.3	297.5

Note: Up to 30° the value of N_q is greater than N_γ.

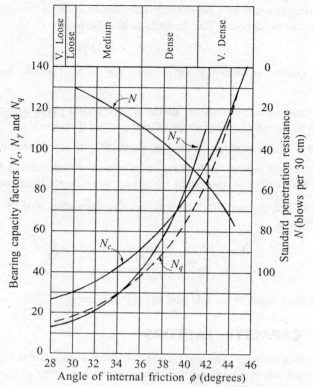

Fig. 6.3 **Values of ϕ, N_c, N_r and N_q from SPT (N) values in cohesionless soils** (after Peck, Hansen and Thornburn).

6.4.1 Points to be Noted in the Derivation

The following points are to be noted in the derivation of the above equations:

- The depth of soil below the level of the foundation and the horizontal distance in the plastic failure zone depends on the nature of the failure surface assumed as well as the angle of internal friction of the soil. As shown in Fig. 6.1d up to $\phi = 30°$ (loose soils), the depth m involved is equal to or less than the width of the foundation and for $\phi = 45°$ (dense), the depth involved is upto twice the width. Hence Terzaghi recommends [2] that for a footing, the strength of the soil or SPT value below the foundation should be evaluated for every 75 cm for a depth equal to twice the largest width of the footing and the average value for this depth should be used for estimating the allowable soil pressure. (The significant depth for settlement is also taken generally as 2B. [see Section 4.3.3].

- When $\phi = 0$ the value of $N_c = 5.14$, $N_q = 1.0$ and $N_\gamma = 0$. This forms the basis of Skempton's equation for bearing capacity of clays described in Section 6.5.

- A more general equation for the net bearing capacity of a rectangular foundation of breadth B and length L as suggested by Schulze in 1940 is as follows.

$$q_{\text{net (ult)}} = (1 + 0.3B/L)(cN_c) + \gamma_0 D(N_q - 1) + 0.5B\gamma_1 N_\gamma(1 - 0.2B/L) \qquad (6.4)$$

Usually a factor of safety is applied to this load and $\gamma_0 D$ is added to it to get the allowable bearing capacity.

$$q_{safe} = (q_{net}/FS) + \gamma_0 D$$

The shape of the footing has an effect on the bearing capacity factors as explained in Chapter 7. For example, the values of the first and last terms in Eq. (6.4) vary as follows:

— For a strip footing, the first and last terms within brackets are equal to 1.
— For a square footing, the first term in brackets is 1.3 and the last term in brackets is 0.8.

6.4.2 Local and General Failures

The relation between intensity of load and settlement of footings in dense and stiff soils are shown in Fig. 6.2. Sand with SPT below 10 is loose and that with SPT values more than 30 is dense. The failure in dense soils are referred to as general failures and those in loose soils as local failures. Terzaghi suggested that the decreased local failure capacity can be calculated by using the following values:

$$c' = \left(\frac{2}{3}\right)c$$

$$\phi' = \tan^{-1}\left(\frac{2}{3}\tan\phi\right) \tag{6.5}$$

The corresponding bearing capacity factors are denoted by N_c', N_q' and N_γ'. Table 6.2 gives the type of failure corresponding to void ratio of the soil.

TABLE 6.2   TABLE FOR SELECTION OF GENERAL AND LOCAL FAILURE [4]

Void ratio e	Soil condition	Recommended method of analysis
> 0.75	Loose	Local shear
< 0.55	Dense	General shear
0.55 to 0.75	Medium	Interpolate between 1 and 2 (mixed shear)

6.5   BEARING CAPACITY OF SHALLOW FOOTINGS IN CLAYS

For a continuous footing in clay, the net ultimate bearing capacity may be expressed in terms of q_u, the unconfined compression strength given by Eq. (6.2), is as follows:

$$q_{net} = 5.7c = 2.85q_u$$

Using a factor of safety of 3 (least value needed for clays) *for a strip foundation,* we get the equations

$$(q_{net}/F.S) = 0.95q_u \approx q_u$$

$$q_{safe} = q_u + \gamma D \text{ (approx.)} \tag{6.6}$$

Thus we arrive at the simple thumb rule that the safe bearing capacity of a shallow strip foundation in clay is approximately equal to the unconfined strength of the clay plus the overburden pressure. We can also relate it to SPT values as shown in Table 1.6. (If we assume that for clays q_u in kg/cm^2 = 1/10 SPT value, *then* q_{safe} (in t/m^2) *will be equal to the SPT value*.

For a square or circular footing, from Eq. 6.4,

$$q_{safe} = 1.3 q_u + \gamma D \qquad (6.6a)$$

6.5.1 Skempton's Recommendations for Bearing Capacity in Clays [5]

The general expression for the ultimate bearing capacity of a strip footing in clay derived from Eq. (6.1) and as given by Skempton is:

$$q_{ult} = c N_c$$

where

c = Average cohesion for a depth equal to two-thirds the width of footing

N_c = Bearing capacity factor which varies with D/B ratio and B/L ratios as shown in Fig. 6.4.

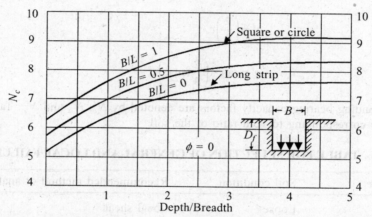

Fig. 6.4   Skempton's values for bearing capacity factor N_c for cohesive soils varying with depth/ breadth ratios [IS 6403–1981].

In 1951, the following modifications were suggested by Skempton for a rectangle $B \times L$ to incorporate Meyerhof's theory for strength of overburden pressure:

When $D/B < 2.5$,

$$N_c = 5(1 + 0.2B/L)(1 + 0.2D/B) \le 9 \qquad (6.7)$$

When $D/B \ge 2.5$,

$$N_c = 7.5(1 + 0.2B/L) \qquad (6.8)$$

Accordingly, for a square or round foundation with D/B ratio greater than 2.5 (i.e. for deep foundations), $N_c = 7.5 \times 1.2 = 9$, as shown in Fig. 6.4.

6.6 EFFECT OF WATER TABLE ON ULTIMATE BEARING CAPACITY

In Eq. (6.1) the unit weights above the foundation γ_0 and that beneath foundation γ_1 have to be adjusted when these soils are submerged. In the case of sands, we may assume that submerged weight is only one half the saturated weight. Accordingly the weights are adjusted with regard to reduction factors as follows (refer to Fig. 6.5 and Eq. (6.10).

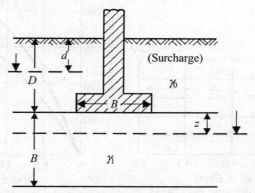

Fig. 6.5   Reduction factor for bearing capacity due to position of water table.

$$R_q = 0.5(1 + d/D) \not> \text{(correction for } N_q) \tag{6.9a}$$

$$R_\gamma = 0.5(1 + z/B) \not> \text{(correction for } N_\gamma) \tag{6.9b}$$

The bearing capacity equation is thus reduced to the following:

$$q_{\text{ult}} = cN_c + \gamma_0 D N_q R_q + 0.5B\gamma_1 N_\gamma R_\gamma \tag{6.10}$$

6.7 ALLOWABLE BEARING CAPACITY

The allowable bearing capacity is the lesser of the value obtained from considerations of ultimate failure with the specified factor of safety as well as allowable settlement. This is true for foundations in clays and sands. In clays we find settlement from consolidation theory. In sands we have to determine it from empirical relations involving SPT values as shown in Chapter 4.

6.8 SETTLEMENT OF FOOTINGS IN SAND DEPOSITS FROM SPT VALUES

Settlement of foundations in sand was discussed in Sec. 4.3. From test results, we know that in cohesionless soil, for the same intensity of load, the settlement of a footing increases with its width according to the following formula. (The settlement beyond $B = 4$ m can be taken as more or less constant.)

$$s = s_1[2B/(B + 0.3)]^2$$

where B is the breadth in meters and s_1 is the settlement of a 0.3 m square plate.

Another *important empirical relation* that Terzaghi [2] established from his observation is that in both strip and also in individual footings *of equal size and equally loaded* the differential settlement that can be expected in all types of soil is about 50 per cent of the maximum expected settlement of these footings. In actual practice, the sizes of the footings can also be different. Hence in real field situations we may assume that the maximum expected differential settlement will be roughly 75 per cent of the expected maximum settlement. Accordingly, if we assume an allowable

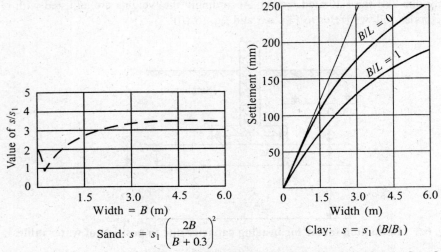

$$\text{Sand:} \quad s = s_1 \left(\frac{2B}{B+0.3}\right)^2 \qquad\qquad \text{Clay:} \quad s = s_1 \,(B/B_1)$$

Fig. 6.6   Increase in settlements of footings with width of footings in sand and in clay.

differential settlement of 18 mm (3/4 inch) the maximum settlement we can allow in the footing will be 25 mm (1 inch).

In 1969, Teng [6] proposed the following important relation between settlement of a footing in sand and its SPT value N. [See Eq. (4.4)]

$$s = \left[\frac{0.722q}{N-3}\right]\left[\frac{2B}{B+0.3}\right]^2 \text{ mm} \tag{6.11}$$

where

s = settlement in mm

q = intensity of load in kN/m^2

B = breadth of footing in metres.

From the above, the net load required for 1 mm settlement will be as follows:

$$q_1 = 1.385(N-3)\left[\frac{B+0.3}{2B}\right]^2 \text{ (in kN/m}^2 \text{ per mm settlement)} \tag{6.12a}$$

where

q_1 = bearing pressure for 1 mm settlement in kN/m^2

N = corrected SPT value

B = width of the footing in metres.

For 25 mm settlement, we get the following equation as the net allowable bearing pressure in kN/m^2.

$$q_{\text{net}} = q_{25} = 34.6(N-3)\left(\frac{B+0.3}{2B}\right)^2 = 8.6(N-3)\left(\frac{B+0.3}{B}\right)^2 \tag{6.12b}$$

Taking $B = 4$ m,

$$q_{net} = 10(N - 3) \text{ (approx.)} \tag{6.12c}$$

To this, we can add the effect of depth as given in Section 6.8.2.

Peck, Hanson and Thornburn [3] used this relation in 1974 to plot the graph for safe bearing capacity in sands for N values. The value of $\left(\dfrac{B + 0.3}{2B}\right)^2$ decreases rapidly with B as shown in Fig. 6.7, so that the empirical value of q_a for cohesionless soils with a variation of B can be expressed in kN/m^2 as follows:

$$\begin{aligned}
\text{Net} \quad q_a &= 10.5NB && \text{for } B < 1 \text{ m for 25 mm settlement} \\
q_a &= 10.5N \text{ for } B > 1 \text{ m} && \text{for 25 mm settlement} \\
q_a &= 0.42N \text{ (kN/m}^2\text{) (approx.)} && \text{for 1 mm settlement for } B > 1 \text{ m.}
\end{aligned} \tag{6.13}$$

An average value of N for a depth B below the footing is taken as the N value for calculation of bearing capacity.

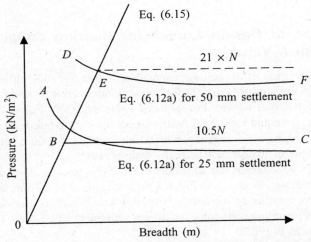

Fig. 6.7 Variation of safe soil pressure with width based on shear failure [Eq. (6.15)] and with soil pressure for 25 mm settlement [Eq. (6.12a)].

6.8.1 Correction for Ground Water Level for Bearing Capacity Based on *N* Values

Opinions differ whether further corrections are needed on bearing capacity calculated on corrected N values. Meyerhof [7] has suggested that no corrections need be applied to such results. He even recommended a 50% increase in bearing capacity of sand deposits based on settlement analysis. These proposals were confirmed by D'Appolonia et al. in 1968 [8]. However, some textbooks recommend correction for water level based on Eq. (6.9) as follows:

$$R_\gamma = 0.5 \,(1 + z/B) \le 1 \text{ as in Eq. (6.9b)}$$

6.8.2 Correction for Depth of Foundation

Different investigators have suggested different expressions for correction for depth of foundation in sand deposits.

Meyerhof's correction is as follows:

$$R_d = (1 + D/B) \leq 2 \tag{6.14}$$

Brinch Hansen has derived another set of depth factors for bearing capacity (d_γ, d_q and d_c) which are also used. The values recommended by IS 6403 are given in Table 7.1. Its value is given by $1 + 0.2(D/B) \tan (45 + \phi/2)$.

6.8.3 Ultimate Bearing Capacity in Sands from *N* Values

Instead of using N values directly as above, we may estimate ϕ values or N_c, N_q and N_γ values from Fig. 6.3 and arrive at the safe net bearing capacity as:

$$q_{\text{safe}} = \frac{1}{F.S}\left[\left(N_q - 1\right)\gamma_0 D + 0.5B\gamma_1 N_\gamma\right] \tag{6.15}$$

6.8.4 Derivation of Design Curves for Bearing Capacity of Granular Soils from *N* Values

We will examine the variation of the bearing capacities in granular soils obtained with respect to a fixed settlement, say 25 mm and also the bearing capacity obtained from shear failure. The safe load is to be the lesser of the two values. For a given value of (D/B) Eq. (6.12a) (with respect to settlement) will give a curve and Eq. (6.15) (with respect to bearing failure) will give a straight line (see Fig. 6.7). The bearing capacity increases with width from shear failure considerations, but from considerations of settlement it does not increase with bredth.

The lesser of the two values is the allowable bearing pressure. In 1948, Terzaghi and Peck [2] gave a set of curves for design as shown in Fig. 6.8 for a settlement of 40 mm. In 1974, Peck, Hansen and Thornburn [3] gave another set of curves, Fig. 6.9 which can be used for design of footings from SPT values in cohesionless soils for a maximum settlement of 25 mm. These curves have the general shape as given in Fig. 6.7.

We can observe with regard to Fig. 6.9 that for (D/B) > 0.5 for breadth of footing equal to or more than 1 meter (for all practical purposes) the allowable bearing pressure is controlled by settlement. For a maximum allowable settlement of 25 mm in footings and for width greater than 1 m and D/B > 0.5, we have the following:

$$q(\text{allowable}) = 10.5N \ (\text{kN/m}^2) = 1.05N \ (\text{t/m}^2) \ (\text{approx.})$$

Thus we obtain a simple rule that a rough approximate allowable *bearing capacity in tons per square meter equals N, the SPT value, for an allowable settlement of 25 mm.*

In Fig. 6.9 the differential settlement expected is 3/4 of 25 mm ≈ 18 mm. If settlement beyond this is allowable, we can correspondingly increase the pressure to higher values. Thus for $\Delta = 50$ mm, $q_a = 21(N)$ expressed in kN/m^2 represented by DEF in Fig. 6.7.

Special mention should be made about footings in saturated sands with N equal to 5 or less than that. Such soils show rapid subsidence with change of water level when loaded. In such cases, either the sand deposit should be compacted or the footing should be founded on piles. *All sands with N less than 10 are to be considered as loose (ϕ values are 30° or less).*

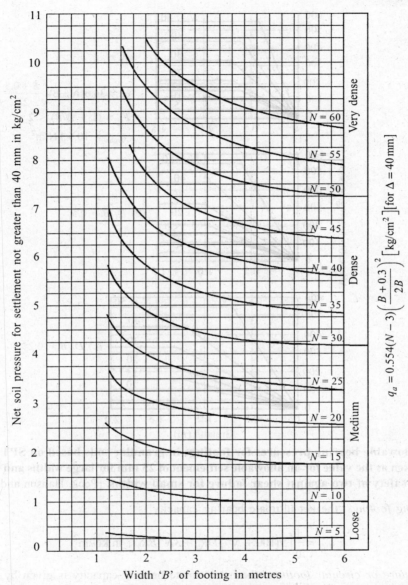

Fig. 6.8 **Net soil pressure corresponding to 40 mm settlement of footings in sand [IS 6403–1971].**

6.8.5 Bearing Capacity against Shear Failure in Sands from *N* Values

Using the concepts developed by Peck, Hansen and Thornburn (illustrated in Fig. 6.3), Teng [4] has given the following empirical and conservative formula based on Eq. 6.15 *for the net ultimate bearing capacity for sands* in terms of the SPT value *N*. These can be directly used to get N_q and N_γ values from *N* values.

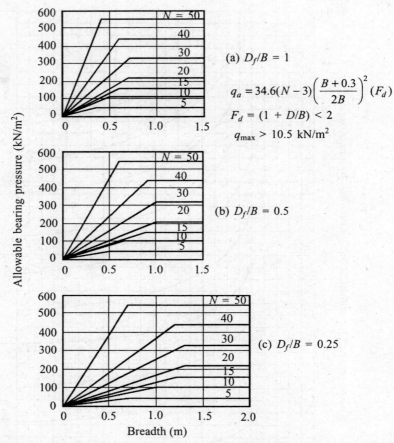

Fig. 6.9 **Allowable bearing pressures for footings in granular soils based on SPT values. It is taken as the value for an allowable settlement of 25 mm for large widths and with a factor of safety of two against shear failure for small widths. [Peck, Hansen and Thornburn].**

For long footings, the net ultimate bearing capacity is

$$q_{ult} = \frac{1}{6}\left[5\left(100 + N^2\right)DR_q + 3N^2BR_\gamma\right] \text{ in kN/m}^2 \qquad (6.16a)$$

For square or circular footings, the net ultimate bearing capacity is given by

$$q_{ult} = \frac{1}{6}\left[6\left(100 + N^2\right)DR_q + 2N^2BR_\gamma\right] \text{ in kN/m}^2 \qquad (6.16b)$$

(q_{ult} is equal to the net ultimate bearing pressure, i.e. pressure at the bottom of the footing *in excess of the pressure* at the same level due to the weight of the soil immediately surrounding the footing [4].)

Applying a factor of safety of 3 *for long footings*, we get

$$q_{safe} = \frac{1}{18}\left[5\left(100 + N^2\right)DR_q + 3N^2BR_\gamma\right] \text{ in kN/m}^2 \qquad (6.16c)$$

where

R_q = correction for water level for γ_0 [(Eq. 6.9a)]

R_γ = correction for water level for γ_0 [(Eq. 6.9b)]

D = depth of footing in metres

B = breadth of footing in metres.

6.9 SAFE BEARING CAPACITY IN CLAYS

Based on our discussion in Section 6.5, the following methods can be used to find the safe bearing capacity of cohesive soils.

Method 1: It is easier to determine the value of cohesion of clay deposits by undisturbed sampling or by in-situ shear test. Hence we can use Skempton's formula [(Eq. 6.6)] to determine the ultimate bearing capacity. We find out the safe bearing capacity by using an *F.S* of 3

$$q_{\text{safe}} = (q_{\text{net}}/3) + \gamma D = \text{unconfined compression strength} + \gamma D$$

Method 2: The second empirical method to make a rough estimate of the bearing capacity is to relate the unconfined compression strength to SPT tests. Terzaghi and Peck have given us from experience conservative values of unconfined compressive strength of clays based on the SPT values which are shown in Table 1.6. The method described herein should be applied only to unimportant jobs as it is purely empirical. SPT tests are not generally applicable to clay soils. (Similar formulae can be derived for the static cone penetration test also.)

From Table 1.6 it can be seen that the unconfined compressive strength (in kg/cm^2) of soft clay can be taken as $N/10$. Noting that footing should not be founded on clays with SPT values less than 4, we may use the following relationship (given by Eq. (6.17)) between safe bearing capacity and the SPT value given by Eq. (6.6) when an *F.S* of about 3 is used.

From Eq. (6.6), we have

$$q_{\text{safe}} = q_u + \gamma D = N/10 + \gamma D \text{ (in kg/cm}^2\text{)}$$

At 1 kg/cm^2 (10 t/m^2) for all practical purposes, the above equation may be written as

$$q_{\text{safe}} \text{ (for clays)} = N + \gamma D \text{ (in tons/m}^2\text{)} \tag{6.17}$$

6.9.1 Important Thumb Rule

The following thumb rule is easy to remember. From considerations of maximum settlement of 25 mm in sand and from considerations of shear failure in clays, *the safe bearing capacity in tons per square metre* is approximately equal to the corresponding SPT value N for practical footings above one metre in breadth.

6.10 GENERAL REMARKS

For computing the bearing capacity of footings in clays, we should investigate the strength to a depth below the footing at least equal to B for square and $2B$ for continuous footings. The unconfined compressive strength is determined if possible at every 15 to 30 cm interval for these depths. The average value of unconfined strength is estimated for each of the bearing and the smallest of the average values is taken for design [2].

In many tropical clay deposits, the top layers are strong because of their drying in summer. The clays below this layer may be soft. If such clays are not expansive, they require detailed investigations as to what depth the footings should be placed. It is better to place these footings at minimum depth considering also the depth of backfill that will be placed in the place. The probable settlement that can take place should be calculated for all footings founded on clays from actual consolidation test values.

Soils intermediate between sand and clay which are silts with N less than 10 are loose. Loose silt is very bad as a foundation material because of settlements. Medium to dense silts, if non-plastic, behave like fine sands and if plastic, behave like clays.

6.11 BEARING CAPACITY OF STRATIFIED SOILS

Stress distribution in layered soils is dealt with in Section 3.11. Analysis of the bearing capacity factor N_c by Button [9] for a *two layered clay system* is reported in most textbooks [6]. It is represented in Fig. 6.10. He found out that N_c value varies with the ratio of cohesions as well as the depth of the top layer with reference to the width of the footing. With a weak lower layer ($c_2/c_1 = 0.3$), a depth of $1.5B$ of the stronger layer was required for $N_c = 5.4$. When $c_2/c_1 = 0.6$, the depth of the stronger layer required is only B. However with an upper soft layer with more than $0.5B$ deep (towards the right hand side of diagram), the bearing capacity depends entirely on the top soft layer.

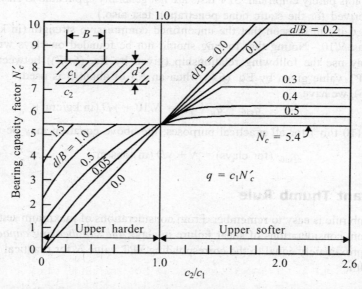

Fig. 6.10 Ultimate bearing capacity for a two-layer system of clay, $q_{ult} = c_1 N'_c$ [Button].

In granular soils also the same trend is found to be true. As a rule, if the weak layer is immediately below the foundation, for a depth of 2/3 to full width of the foundation, the average strength of the weak soil will control the design of the footing. If the stronger layer is immediately beneath the foundation we can assume that it will act as a footing and transfer the load to the weaker soil. This distribution can be estimated by exact theory or by using the 2:1 approximate distribution. However reports on small-scale tests indicate that the bearing capacities were noticeably reduced when the depth of the stronger upper layer was less than 2*B*. In cases where the thickness was less than *B*/2, the bearing capacity was governed entirely by the lower weak layer. As a rule, as long as the thickness of the top stronger layer is only equal or less than the width of the foundation we should not depend on the strength of the top layer at all.

6.12 PRECAUTIONS TO BE TAKEN IN FOUNDATION PREPARATION FOR FOOTINGS

We have already seen that the depth of soil that materially affects the strength of a square footing is about *B* and for a strip footing, it is around 2*B*. Accordingly if a footing rests on a thin layer of weak soil (as happens during foundation construction when rainfall, ground water, or external watering softens the top layers of a footing or when the loose soil from the excavation is not removed before laying the foundation) an initial rapid downward movement which stabilizes itself later will be noticed on loading the foundation. This is due to the failure of the topsoil. Such a situation can be avoided by compacting the excavation and also providing an *additional compact sand layer with a well compacted mat layer of mass concrete of 50 to 75 mm thickness (1:4:8) over the sand layer.* This is the standard practice in India and should be followed in all cases to prevent the loosening of the topsoil immediately below the footings.

6.13 LOAD TESTS FOR BEARING CAPACITY

Even though load tests were used very frequently in the past (before Terzaghi's theory was published) to find bearing capacity we now know that such tests do not reflect the properties of the soil up to a significant depth of the foundation [10] [11]. They can be used only if soil is uniform along the depth. The recommended practice is to load a square plate of 300 mm size till a settlement of 25 mm or 50 mm as required is obtained. A load settlement curve is plotted on log-log scale by which the yield stress can be easily identified by the break in the shape of the plots. Alternatively, the load for a given settlement can be read off from the plot. In many cases load tests have been made on real size footings to evaluate the safe bearing capacity [12].

6.14 DESIGN PRACTICE

The design procedure should be based on IS Codes of practice [13][14]. For an important or major project, thorough soil investigation should be made and the design should be based on data obtained from field and laboratory results. However, for routine jobs, safe bearing capacity recommended by the above code (given in Table 6.3) can be used. These values are based on experience and are considered as very safe for most cases. Note that, in all cases we should ensure that there are no soft layers beneath the foundation for a depth equal to about twice the breadth of foundation.

TABLE 6.3   SAFE BEARING CAPACITY OF FOUNDATIONS
[IS 1904: 1978, Table 2]
(This table has been discontinued in the revised code.)

Type of rock/soil	S.B.C in t/m^2
(a) Rock	
Solid rock	324
Laminated rock	162
Residual-broken bed rock	88
Soft rock	44
(b) Non-cohesive soils	
Gravel and coarse sand (dry)	44
Medium dry sand, gravel mixture	24
Fine sand (dry)	10
(c) Cohesive soils	
Stiff clay (dry)	44
Medium clay (indented by thumb)	24
Medium clay (moist)	15
Soft clay (indented by moderate thumb pressure)	10
Very soft clay (can be penetrated several inches by thumb)	5

(*Note:* 1 t/m^2 = 1/100 N/mm^2; S.B.C. of solid rock $\approx$ 3 N/mm^2 only)

6.15 SUMMARY OF FORMULAE FOR BEARING CAPACITY OF SOILS

(1)   General bearing capacity formula IS 6403 (1981). (See also Chapter 7.):

$$q_{\text{ult}} = cN_c s_c d_c + (\gamma_0 D)N_q s_q d_q + 0.5 B \gamma_1 N_\gamma s_\gamma d_\gamma$$

$$q_{\text{safe}} = \frac{1}{F.S}[q_{\text{ult}} - \gamma_0 D] + \gamma_0 D$$

(2)   Skempton's modification for N_c (Eq. 6.7):

$$N_c = 5(1 + 0.2B/L)(1 + 0.2D/B)$$

(3)   Water level corrections for γ_0 and γ_1 in (1) above [Fig. 6.5]:

$$R_q = 0.5[1 + d/D] \not> 1 \qquad (6.9\text{a})$$

$$R_\gamma = 0.5 (1 + z/B) \not> 1 \qquad (6.9\text{b})$$

(4)   Teng's equation for settlement from N value in sands [(Eq. 6.12)]:

$$\text{for 1 mm settlement,} \quad q_1 = 1.385(N-3)\left[\frac{B+0.3}{2B}\right]^2 \quad (\text{kN/m}^2) \qquad (6.12\text{a})$$

$$\text{for 25 mm settlement,} \quad q_{25} = 34.63(N-3)\left[\frac{B+0.3}{2B}\right]^2 \quad (\text{kN/m}^2) \qquad (6.12\text{b})$$

where B is in meters.

In practical footings, the bearing pressure for given settlement, as related to N values, are as follows:

$$q_{25} = 10.5N \ (kN/m^2)$$
$$q_1 = 0.42N \ (kN/m^2)$$
$$q_{25} = N \ (t/m^2), \text{ and}$$

(5) Teng's equation for ultimate bearing capacity *in shear failure* from N value in sands [Eqs. (6.16a,b)] (Use $F.S = 3$ to get q_{safe}.)

For long footings, the net bearing capacity is given by

$$q_{ult} = \frac{1}{6}\left[5(100 + N^2)DR_q + 3N^2 BR_\gamma\right] \ (kN/m^2) \tag{6.16a}$$

For square or circular footings, the net bearing capacity is given by

$$q_{ult} = \frac{1}{6}\left[6(100 + N^2)DR_q + 2N^2 BR_\gamma\right] \ (kN/m^2) \tag{6.16b}$$

(6) Safe bearing capacity in clays (Section 6.9)

$$q_{safe} = \frac{1}{F.S}(2.85 \times \text{Unconfined compression strength}) + \gamma_0 D$$

$$\approx \text{Unconfined compression strength} + \gamma_0 D$$

$$\approx 10N + \gamma_0 D \ (kN/m^2)$$

or

$$q_{safe} = N + \gamma_0 D \ (tons/m^2, \text{approx.}) \tag{6.17}$$

(7) Thumb rule. From consideration of allowable settlement of 25 mm in granular soils and from consideration of shear failures in clays, the net safe bearing capacity in tons/m^2 is *approximately equal to the SPT value in these materials.*

EXAMPLE 6.1 (Bearing capacity from elastic theory)

Determine the maximum intensity of load that can be allowed on a strip footing in clay if the shear stress under the footing should not exceed shear strength. Use elastic theory.

Ref.	Step	Calculations
Sec. 3.8	1	*Find the maximum shear stress under a strip footing.* Maximum shear stress occurs at $B/2$ below the footing and its magnitude is equal to q/π.
Eq. (3.10)	2	*Find maximum allowable load from elastic theory* $q/\pi \not> \text{shear strength} = c$ $q \not> 3.14c$ *Note:* Terzaghi's theory of failure of footings is derived from ultimate failure theory. It gives a value of $q \not> 5.14c$ for a smooth base and $q \not> 5.7c$, for a rough base. These are higher than $3.14c$ as above. In soil mechanics, we generally use ultimate load theories and apply the necessary factor of safety to get the safe conditions.

Note: The following examples are to be read after a study of Chapter 7 also.

EXAMPLE 6.2   (Estimation of bearing capacity from general bearing capacity equation)

Estimate the gross and net safe bearing capacities of a 2.5 × 3.5 m footing placed at a depth of 1.7 m on a strata of soil of unit weight 20 kN/m³. Assume the following soil properties and condition of water level.

Case 1. $c = 65$ kN/m² and $\phi = 0$ with water level at 5 m below the level of foundation.

Case 2. $c = 3$ kN/m² and $\phi = 27°$ with depth of water level at 1.2 m from the ground level.

Ref	Step	Calculations
		Case 1
		$\phi = 0$; $c = 65$ kN/m² (clay foundation)
Chap. 7	1	*Find B.C factors (smooth base)*
Fig. 7.2		$N_c = 5.14$; $N_q = 1$; $N_\gamma = 0$; $\gamma_0 D = 20 \times 1.7 = 34$ kN/m²
Eq. (7.3)		Net ultimate $B.C = cN_c s_c d_c + \gamma_0 D N_q s_q d_q$
Table 7.1		Shape factor $s_c = \left(1 + \dfrac{0.2B}{L}\right) = 1 + \dfrac{0.2 \times 2.5}{3.5} = 1.14$
		$s_q = \left(1 + \dfrac{0.2B}{L}\right) = 1.14$
		Depth factor $d_c = \left(1 + \dfrac{0.2D}{B}\right) = \left(1 + \dfrac{0.2 \times 1.7}{2.5}\right) = 1.14$
		d_q for $\phi < 10° = 1$
		No effect of water level as W.L. $> B$ below foundation
	2	*Calculate safe bearing capacity*
Eq. (6.3)		$q_{ult} = (65 \times 5.14 \times 1.14 \times 1.14) + (34 \times 1.14)$
Eq. (a)		$= 434 + 39 = 434.2 + 39 = 473$ kN/m²
		$\dfrac{q_{net}}{F.S} = \dfrac{473 - 34}{3} = 146.3$ kN/m²
		$q_{safe} = 146 + 34 = 180$ kN/m² [No factor of safety for surcharge]
		Case 2
		$\phi = 27$; $c = 3$ kN/m²
Table 6.1	1	*Find B.C factors* $\phi = 27$ degrees; $c = 3$ kN/m²
		Assume general shear failure.
		$N_c = 27$; $N_q = 13.2$; $N_\gamma = 9.3$;
		$\gamma_0 D = 1.7 \times 20 = 34$ kN/m²

Ref.	Step	Calculations
Table 7.1		Gross $q_u = cN_cs_cd_c + (\gamma_0 D)N_qs_qd_q + \dfrac{1}{2}B\gamma N_\gamma s_\gamma q_\gamma$
		$s_c = 1.14; \quad s_q = 1.14; \quad s_\gamma = \left(1 - \dfrac{0.4B}{L}\right) = 0.71$
		$d_c = \left(1 + \dfrac{0.2B}{L}\right)(\tan 45 + \phi/2) = 1.14 \times 1.63 = 1.89$
		$d_q = d_\gamma = \left(1 + \dfrac{0.1D}{B}\right)(\tan 45 + \phi/2) = 1.068 \times 1.63 = 1.74$
	2	*Find the effect of water level reduction*
Eq. (6.9)		$R_q = 0.5(1 + d/D) = 0.5(1 + 1.2/1.7) = 0.85$
Eq. (6.10) Fig. 6.5		$R_r = 0.5(1 + z/D) = 0.5(1 + 0) = 0.50$
	3	*Tabulate factors* (kN units)

$c = 3$	$\gamma_0 D = 34$	$0.5B\gamma_1 = 25$
$N_c = 27$	$N_q = 13.2$	$N_r = 9.3$
$s_c = 1.14$	$s_q = 1.14$	$s_r = 0.71$
$d_c = 1.89$	$d_q = 1.74$	$d_r = 1.74$
	$R_q = 0.85$	$R_r = 0.50$

Ref.	Step	Calculations
Eq. (7.3)	4	*Calculate the bearing capacity*
		$q_u = (3 \times 27 \times 1.14 \times 1.89) + (34 \times 13.2 \times 1.14 \times 1.74 \times 0.85)$
		$\quad + (25 \times 9.3 \times 0.71 \times 1.74 \times 0.50)$
		$\quad = 1075 \text{ kN/m}^2$
		$q_{\text{safe}} = \dfrac{1075 - 34}{3} + 34 = 381 \text{ kN/m}^2$

EXAMPLE 6.3   (Bearing capacity of footing in clay)

Estimate the safe bearing capacity of a 1.5 m square footing in saturated clay deposit with SPT value of 20. The depth of the foundation is 2 m and unit weight of soil is 20 kN/m^3. Assume a suitable factor of safety.

Ref.	Step	Calculations
	1	*Assume required F.S* Minimum factor of safety of clay = 3
	2	*Estimate cohesion from N value* $q_U(\text{kg/cm}^2) = N/8 = 20/8 = 2.5 \text{ kg/cm}^2 = 250 \text{ kN/m}^2$ $c = q_U/2 = 125 \text{ kN/m}^2$
	3	*Determine q_{ult} from the bearing capacity formula* $q_{\text{ult}} = cN_cs_cd_c + \gamma_0 DN_qs_qd_q + 0.5\gamma_1 BN_\gamma s_\gamma d_\gamma$

Table 7.1		$N_c = 5.7$ (rough base); $\qquad N_q = 1; \qquad\qquad N_\gamma = 0$

$c = 125$ kN/m$^2 \qquad\qquad \gamma_0 D = 40$ kN/m$^2 \qquad (\phi = 0)$

$s_c = 1.3$ for square $\qquad\qquad s_q = 1.2$ for square

$d_c = (1 + 0.2D/B) = 1.27 \qquad d_q = 1$

$q_{ult} = (125 \times 5.7 \times 1.3 \times 1.27) + (40 \times 1.0 \times 1.2 \times 1.0)$

$\qquad = 1176 + 48 = 1224$ kN

$$q_{safe} = \frac{q_{ult} - \gamma_0 D}{3} + \gamma_0 D = \frac{1224 - 40}{3} + 40 = 435 \text{ kN/m}^2$$

Sec. 6.5 — 4 — *Determine q_{ult} without the shape and depth factor*

Eq. (6.7)

$$q_{safe} = \frac{cN_c}{3} + \gamma_0 D = \frac{125 \times 5.7}{3} + 40 = 237.5 + 40$$

$$= 277 \text{ kN/m}^2$$

5 — *Estimate q_{safe} from empirical formula in kN/m^2*

Eq. (6.17)

$q_{safe} = 10N + \gamma_0 D = 250 + 40 = 290$ kN/m^2

(The empirical formula gives the value without corrections for shape and depth.)

Note: The settlement should be separately worked out by theory of consolidation.

Example 6.4   (Design of a footing in sand)

Estimate the size of a square footing of a column carrying a load of 1500 kN in a sand deposit with average N value of 15. Assume an allowable settlement of 25 mm depth of foundation, 2 m. Water level is also at foundation level and unit weight of soil is 18 kN/m^3.

Ref.	Step	Calculations
	1	**Method 1.** *Limiting settlement to 25* mm *from empirical curves* Let $D/B > 1$
Fig. 6.9		For $N = 15$; $q_{safe} = 170$ kN/m^2 Size of footing $\left(\dfrac{1500}{170}\right)^{1/2} = 2.97$ m (say 3 m)
	2	Assume $B = 3$ m **Method 2.** *Limiting settlement to 25* mm *by formula 6.12a* $$q_{25} = 34.6(N-3)\left(\frac{B+0.3}{2B}\right)^2$$ $$= 34.6 \times 12 \times (3.3/6)^2 = 125 \text{ kN/m}^2$$ $q_{safe} = 125 + (2 \times 18) = 161$ kN/m^2 (This can be considered same as in *Method 1.*)

Ref.	Step	Calculations
Sec 1.7.1A Fig. 6.3	3	*Method 3. From ultimate bearing capacity formula.* *Estimate ϕ value from N = 15* $\phi = \sqrt{20N} + 15 = 32°$ ϕ from Fig. 6.3 = 32° Assume B = 3 m $q_{ult} = \gamma_0 D N_q s_q d_q + 0.5 \gamma_1 B N_\gamma s_\gamma d_\gamma$ (a) $\gamma_0 = 18, \gamma_1 = (18 - 10) = 8$ (kN/m³) $N_q = 30, N_\gamma = 41$ $s_q = 1.2, s_\gamma = 0.8$ $d_q = d_\gamma = (1 + 0.1D/B) \tan(45 + \phi/2)$ $\qquad = (1 + 0.1 \times 2/3)(\tan 45 + 16) = 2.01$ $q_{ult} = (18 \times 2 \times 30 \times 1.2 \times 2.01) + (4 \times 2 \times 41 \times 0.8 \times 2.01)$ $\qquad = 3132$ kN/m² $q_{safe} = \dfrac{3132 - 36}{3} + 36 = 1068$ kN/m² This value is too high as against those settlement consideration. Settlement controls the design *Method 4. By thumb rule* $q_{25} = N = 15$ t/m² (approx.) Assume size of footing as 3 m × 3 m.

EXAMPLE 6.5   **(Determination of allowable bearing capacity)**

Determine the allowable bearing capacity of a 2 m square footing placed at a depth of 1.5 m in a sand deposit of unit weight 20 kN/m³ with an average corrected SPT value of 27. Water table is at 2 m from ground level. Assume a factor of safety of 3 against shear failure and maximum allowable settlement of 40 mm. Check the value from IS 6403-(1971) design curves.

Ref.	Step	Calculations
Eq. (6.9)	1	*Calculate from Eq. (6.16b) with F.S = 3 and reduction factors* $q_{safe} = \dfrac{1}{18}\left[6(100 + N^2)DR_q + 2N^2 BR_\gamma\right]$ for shear failure. $R_q = 1$ as water table is below foundation $R_\gamma = 0.5(1 + z/B) = 0.5(1 + 0.5/2) = 0.625$ $q_{safe} = \dfrac{1}{18}\left[6(100 + 27^2) \times 1.5 \times 1 + (2 \times 27^2 \times 2 \times 0.625)\right]$ $\qquad = 516$ kN/m² (Apply depth factor = weight of soil above = $1.5 \times 20 = 30$ kN/m² which can be neglected.)

	2	*Find the bearing capacity for 25 mm settlement*
Eq. (6.12a)		$$q_{25} = 34.6(N - 3)\left(\frac{B + 0.3}{2B}\right)^2 \text{ kN/m}^2$$
		$$= 34.6 \times 24 \times (2.3/4)^2 = 274 \text{ kN/m}^2$$
		$q_{40} = 274(40/25) = 438 \text{ kN/m}^2 \text{ (say } 440 \text{ kN/m}^2\text{)}$
Fig. 6.8	3	*Check value from IS 6403 (Terzaghi and Peck diagrams (see Fig. 6.8)* $q_{40} = 440 \text{ kN/m}^2$ for $B = 2$ m and $N = 27$ (The diagram is derived from the formula in step 2)
	4	*Apply Meyerhof's depth correction (we may also use Table 7.1)* $R_d = (1 + D/B) = (1 + 1.5/2) = 1.75 \not> 2$ $q_{40} = 440 \times 1.75 = 770 \text{ kN/m}^2$ (Generally, this correction is not used.)
	5	*Find allowable bearing capacity (least among the values in steps 1, 2 and 3)* $q_{\text{allowable}} = 440 \text{ kN/m}^2$
		Conclusion. Empirical design methods based on SPT values give us easy and rapid procedures for estimation of safe bearing capacity both in sand and clay soils.

REFERENCES

[1] Terzaghi, Karl, *Theoretical Soil Mechanics*, John Wiley & Sons, New York, 1943.

[2] Terzaghi, Karl and Peck, R.B., *Soil Mechanics in Engineering Practice*, John Wiley & Sons, New York, 1948.

[3] Peck, R.B., Hanson, W.E., and Thornburn, T.H., *Foundation Engineering*, 2nd ed., Wiley Eastern, New Delhi, 1980.

[4] IS 6403 (1981), *COP for Determination of Bearing Capacity of Shallow Foundations*, BIS, New Delhi.

[5] Skempton, A.W., The Bearing Capacity of Clays, *Proceedings Building Research Congress*, Vol. I, London, 1951.

[6] Teng, W.C., *Foundation Design*, Prentice-Hall of India, New Delhi, 1965.

[7] Meyerhof, G.G., Shallow Foundations, J.S.M.F.D., Vol. 91, SM2, ASCE, New York, 1965.

[8] D'Appolonia, D.J., D'Appolonia, E., and Brisette, R.F., Settlement of Spread Footings in Sand, J.S.M.F.D., SM3, ASCE, New York, 1968.

[9] Buttons, S.J., The Bearing Capacity of Footings on a Two-Layer Cohesive Subsoil, *Proc. 3rd Intern. Conf. on Soil Mechanics and Foundation Engineering*, 1953.

[10] Leonards, G.A. (Ed.), *Foundation Engineering*, McGraw-Hill, New York, 1962.

[11] Tomlinson, M.J., *Foundation Design and Construction*, 6th ed., ELBS, Longman, Singapore, 1995.

[12] Varghese, P.C. and Raju, V.S., Safe Bearing Pressures in Loose Sand Deposits, *Seventh Annual General Meeting of Indian Geotechnical Society,* Bangalore, 1975.

[13] IS 1904 (1978), *COP for Structural Safety of Buildings Shallow Foundations* (Second revision), BIS, New Delhi.

[14] IS 1080 (1980), *COP for Design and Construction of Simple Spread Foundation* (First revision), BIS, New Delhi.

7

Factors Affecting Bearing Capacity of Shallow Foundations

7.1 INTRODUCTION

In Chapter 6, we dealt with the classical theory of bearing capacity of centrally loaded footings. However, there are many other factors like size and shape of the foundation that affect the bearing capacity of footings. A few of these important factors are dealt with in this chapter.

7.2 MAJOR FACTORS AFFECTING BEARING CAPACITY

The major factors that affect bearing capacity of footings are [1]:

1. Size of the foundation
2. Shape of the foundation
3. Depth of the foundation
4. Inclination of the load
5. Inclination of the foundation base
6. Inclination of the ground
7. Position of ground water table.

These are dealt with in the following sections.

7.3 EFFECT OF SIZE OF FOUNDATION

Terzaghi's equation for a strip foundation derived in Chapter 6 is as follows:

$$q_{ult} = cN_c + \gamma_0 DN_q + 0.5\gamma_1 N_\gamma B \tag{7.1}$$

N_c, N_q and N_γ are called Terzaghi's bearing capacity factors as clarified in Chapter 6. The first term represents the contribution of cohesion, the second the contribution due to surcharge of unit weight γ_0 and the third, the contribution by the shear strength of soil below foundation level with friction and self-weight γ_1 of soil below the foundation level.

In 1940 Schultze extended the bearing capacity theory to a rectangular foundation $B \times L$ by introducing *shape factors* as follows:

$$q_{ult} = \left(1 + 0.3\frac{B}{L}\right)cN_c + \gamma_0 DN_q + \left(1 - 0.2\frac{B}{L}\right)\frac{\gamma_1 B}{2}N_\gamma \qquad (7.2)$$

In 1955 Brinch Hansen proposed the general theory taking many other factors also into account. It can be seen that ultimate bearing capacity increases with the B/L ratio according to the above formula. IS 6403 recommendation regarding shape factor is given in Section 7.4.

7.4 EFFECT OF SHAPE, DEPTH AND INCLINATION OF LOAD ON BEARING CAPACITY OF FOOTINGS

Effects of these three important factors finally proposed by Brinch Hansen are described below [1]:

1. *Shape:* In a long strip footing the shear planes develop only along the width of the foundation (plane strain condition). In a rectangular footing, shear planes may develop along breadth and length, thus mobilizing a larger soil mass than in a strip footing. Thus the shape of the footing affects its bearing capacity.

2. *Foundation depth:* The influence of the depth of foundation is very complex on the bearing capacity. It even determines the mode of failure. It is very evident that with increasing depth the bearing capacity increases not only because of the overburden pressure but also due to the failure pattern of deep foundations. As we have already seen, the effect of depth of foundation of less than 2 m is not generally taken into account in considering bearing capacity. The depth of foundation to be considered in various types of situations is shown in Fig. 7.1. The effect of overburden is the main consideration in deciding the depth of shallow foundation.

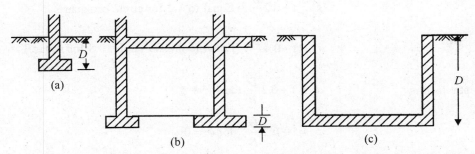

Fig 7.1 Surcharge effects for bearing capacity: (a) For an ordinary footing; (b) for a footing in the basement; (c) for a raft foundation.

3. *Inclination of the load:* The bearing capacity decreases rapidly with larger inclination of the load from the vertical and this reduction is more pronounced for horizontal bases than for inclined bases so that with inclined loads there is some advantage in adopting inclined bases. This topic is described in Section 7.5.

7.4.1 IS Code Recommendations

Both Hansen and Meyerhof have given their equations for the various effects given above. Based on these values, IS 6403–1981 [2] has recommended the following equations for the calculation of the ultimate bearing capacity of shallow footings.

$$q_{\text{ult}} = cN_c s_c d_c i_c + q_0 N_q s_q d_q i_q + 0.5\gamma_1 BN_\gamma s_\gamma d_\gamma i_\gamma W' \qquad (7.3)$$

where

B = width of foundation

c = undrained cohesion of soil

q_0 = effective overburden pressure at foundation level = $\gamma_0 D$

γ_0 = effective unit weight of soil above foundation level

γ_1 = effective unit weight of soil below foundation level

N_c, N_q and N_γ are the bearing capacity factors

s_c, s_q and s_γ are shape factors

d_c, d_q and d_γ are depth factors

i_c, i_q and i_γ are inclination factors which depend on inclination α of load to the vertical

W' is a factor for effect of water table which is 1 if water table is at a depth B below the foundation level and linearly varies to 0.5 if it is at the base of foundation.

The values of these modifying factors as recommended in IS 6403-1981 are given in Table 7.1.

TABLE 7.1   SHAPE, DEPTH AND INCLINATION FACTORS FOR MEYERHOF'S BEARING CAPACITY EQUATION [IS 6403 (1981)]

Factors	Value
Shape factors	$s_c = 1 + 0.2\dfrac{B}{L}$. (Equal to 1.3 for circle or square)
	$s_q = 1 + 0.2\dfrac{B}{L}$. (Equal to 1.2 for circle or square)
	$s_\gamma = 1 - 0.4\dfrac{B}{L}$. (Equal to 0.6 for circle; 0.8 for square)
Depth factors	$d_c = 1 + 0.2\dfrac{D}{B} \tan (45 + \phi/2)$
	$d_c = 1 + 0.2\dfrac{D}{B}$ for $\phi = 0$
	$d_q = d_\gamma = 1 + 0.1\dfrac{D}{B} \tan (45 + \phi/2)$ for $\phi > 10°$
	$d_\gamma = d_q = 1$ for $\phi < 10°$
	$i_c = i_q = \left(1 - \dfrac{\alpha}{90}\right)^2$
Load inclination factors (Load inclined at α to normal to surface)	$i_\gamma = \left(1 - \dfrac{\alpha}{\phi}\right)^2$, where α and ϕ are in degrees.

According to IS 6403 the value of N_c, N_q and N_γ is to be taken as those derived by Vesic. They may be also calculated from the following equations (Vesic's equations).

$$N_c = (N_q - 1) \cot \phi$$

$$N_q = [\exp(\pi \tan \phi)] \tan^2 (45 + \phi/2)$$

$$N_\gamma = 2(N_q + 1) \tan \phi$$

These are tabulated for ϕ values in Table 7.2.

TABLE 7.2 VESIC'S BEARING CAPACITY FACTORS [IS 6403]

ϕ°	N_c	N_q	N_γ (Vesic)	N_γ (Hansen)
0	5.14	1.0	0	0
5	6.50	1.6	0.4	0.1
10	8.30	2.5	1.2	0.4
15	11.00	3.9	2.6	1.2
20	14.83	6.4	5.4	2.9
25	20.7	10.7	10.9	6.8
26	22.25	11.8	12.5	7.9
30	30.13	18.4	22.4	15.1
36	50.55	37.7	56.2	40.0
40	75.25	64.1	109.3	79.4
45	133.73	134.7	271.3	200.5

Note: Vesic's N_c and N_q factors are identical and N_γ factors are larger than that of Meyerhof and Hansen. See Table 6.1 for Terzaghi's bearing capacity factors.

7.5 STABILITY UNDER INCLINED LOADS

Inclined loads which have vertical and horizontal components can be treated by one of the following methods.

Method 1: Conventional method (B.S. method): When foundations (like base slab of cantilever retaining walls) are subjected to horizontal and vertical loads with resultant eccentricity, the common practice is to check for the safety of the vertical loads and horizontal loads separately. The resistance to the horizontal load is provided by friction and the passive resistance of soil in front. B.S code of practice CP 2004 suggests a simple empirical procedure for design of column foundations under inclined loads on horizontal base (Fig. 7.2). The inclined loads are resolved into vertical and horizontal components as shown in Fig. 7.2 (horizontal loads can be due to wind or other causes). If the following interaction condition, Eq. (7.4), is satisfied, the design is assumed to be safe [3]. It is very important that when we take the passive earth pressures as resisting horizontal forces, the fill on top of footing should be specially compacted. Also, as large movements are necessary to develop maximum passive pressures, the full value should not be taken for designs.

$$\frac{Q_v}{Q_{v\,all}} + \frac{Q_H}{Q_{H\,all}} < 1 \qquad (7.4)$$

where

$\quad Q_v$ = vertical component of inclined load

$\quad Q_H$ = horizontal component of inclined load

$\quad Q_{v\,all}$ = allowable vertical load

$\quad Q_{H\,all}$ = allowable horizontal load.

$\quad N$ = total vertical force on base.

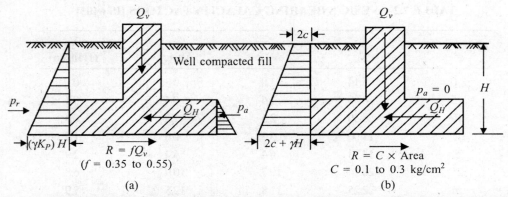

Fig. 7.2   Simple empirical method for stability check of footings subjected to inclined loads: (a) Cohesionless soils; (b) cohesive soils.

The value of the passive pressures should be calculated conservatively. However, for small projects, instead of deriving them, the following conservative values can be used:

1. *Passive resistance in granular soils shown in the table below:* $(p_r = \gamma K_p)$, refer [1]

Sand and or gravel with	p_p in t/m^2		Friction coefficient f
	Under water	Dry	
< 5% silt	3.36	5.60	0.55
5–30% silt	2.89	4.00	0.45
> 30% silt	1.92	2.40	0.35

2. *Value of cohesion (given in the table below) to calculate passive resistance for cohesive soils, see* [1]

Type of clay	Cohesion in kg/cm^2	Unit weight γ (t/m^3)
Very soft	0.10	1.76
Soft	0.20	1.92
Medium to hard	0.30	2.00

Method 2: *Use of load inclination factors:* The second method that can be used to estimate bearing capacity of footings under inclined loads is to use Brinch Hansen's inclination factors given in Table 7.1.

7.6 EFFECT OF ECCENTRICITY OF LOAD

In many cases, the loads are applied to a footing with eccentricity. For these cases the AREA method (recommended by American Railroad Engineers Association) described below gives a simple solution. Theoretical and experimental investigations show that the following approximation can be made to determine bearing capacity under eccentric loading. The given foundation $B \times L$ with eccentricities of e_B and e_L along the B and L directions respectively is replaced by a fictitious foundation with dimensions as shown in Fig. 7.3; see ref. [3]

$$B' = B - 2e_B, \qquad L' = L - 2e_L \qquad (7.4)$$

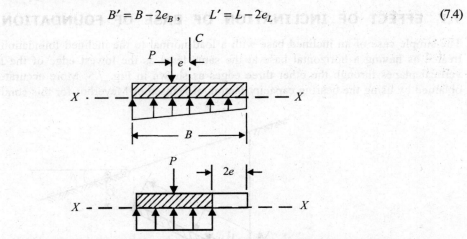

Fig. 7.3   Design of eccentrically loaded footings by conversion to equivalent uniformly loaded footings.

This method can be justified by the fact that if $e < B/6$ (no tension) the load can be considered as a central load on breadth $2(B/2 - e_B) = B - 2e_B$ as shown in Fig. 7.4. (It is called AREA method.)

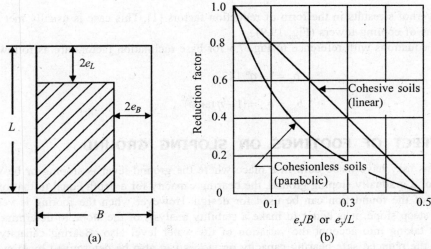

(a)

(b)

Fig. 7.4   Eccentric loads on footings: (a) Eccentricity in both x and y axes; (b) reduction factors for eccentricity of loads [1]. (AREA method)

This simple method implies that the bearing capacity of the footing decreases linearly with eccentricity of load as shown in Fig. 7.4(b). However in granular soils, according to Meyerhof, the relation is more parabolic. Reduction factor as in Fig 7.4b is recommended.

When the eccentric load is only on one side of a column (or significantly greater than the other) the most economical construction can be obtained by offsetting the centre of gravity of the footing itself relative to the column in the direction of the eccentricity so that the resulting pressure from below the foundation will be uniform. [Fig. 2.4 in Chapter 2]

7.7 EFFECT OF INCLINATION OF BASE OF FOUNDATION

The simple case of an inclined base with a load normal to the inclined foundation surface can be treated as having a horizontal base at the same level as the lowest edge of the foundation with vertical planes through the other three edges as shown in Fig. 7.5. More accurate results can be obtained by using the bearing capacity factors of Hansen or Meyerhof for this condition. Teng also

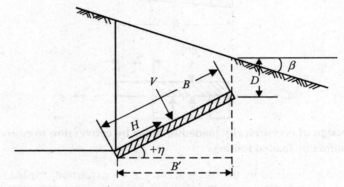

Fig. 7.5 Inclined base.

gives Meyerhof's results in the form of reduction factors [1]. This case is usually met with in the foundations of cooling towers (Fig. 19.9).

The equations with reference to Fig. 7.5 for base inclination factors are as follows [4], [5]:

$$b_c = 1 - \eta°/147°$$

$$b_{qv} = b_{rv} = (1 - \eta \tan \phi)^2$$

7.8 EFFECT OF FOOTINGS ON SLOPING GROUND

Foundations may have to be built in a place where the ground level is sloping or be very nearly a slope. For a gradually sloping ground, the bearing capacity for a depth equal to that of the centre of gravity of the foundation can be used for design. However when the footing is very near the edge of a steep slope, it is better to make a stability analysis of the slope to determine the safety conditions taking into account the variation of the water level also. Bearing capacity factors to determine the reduced safe bearing capacity on slopes can also be determined by Bowles method [4]. While building near slopes, we may observe the rule explained in Section 5.2.

7.9 EFFECT OF SHAPE OF BASE OF FOUNDATION

Experiments show that, in cohesionless soils, the bearing capacity is greater under concave foundation (looking from below) than under convex shapes. The increase can be as much as 20% depending on the relative density of the soil and curvature of the foundation.

7.10 FOOTINGS ON STRATIFIED SOILS

Section 6.11 deals with this aspect. More details can be obtained from Reference [4] given at the end of this chapter.

7.11 GENERAL EQUATIONS FOR BEARING CAPACITY

Hansen, Meyerhof and many others also have given their general equations like Eq. (7.3) for bearing capacity of footings taking into account the shape factors, depth factors, load inclination factors, base inclination factors and ground surface inclination factors. Of these, Meyerhof's method is more popular in North America and Hansen's factors in European countries [6]. IS 6403 recommendation (Hansen's values) as given in Table 7.1 of this chapter can be safely used for all practical designs.

The following procedures can be used for calculation of bearing capacity of footings:

Description of situation	Method to be used
Eccentrically loaded horizontal footings (and to get a quick estimate to compare with other methods).	Conventional or AREA method.
Base tilted, or footing on a slope, or when applied loads are inclined.	Hansen's methods

7.12 SUMMARY

Many factors as given in Section 7.2 affect the bearing capacity of footings. Of these, the load inclination factor and the eccentricity of the load on the base are the most important factors that tend to reduce bearing capacity. It is very important that the horizontal force that acts on the footing is adequately resisted by base friction and reliable passive resistance of soil.

EXAMPLE 7.1 **(Eccentrically loaded footings using AREA method)**

A footing 2×2 m has to carry an axial load of 600 kN with $M_x = 180$ kNm and $M_y = 60$ kNm. The soil has cohesion $c = 0.15$ kg/cm^2, $\phi = 25°$ and depth of foundation = 1.5 m. Assuming the weight of soil as 20 kN/m^3, find the safety of the footing, if the ground water level can be assumed to rise up to the foundation level. (Use AREA method together with shape and depth factors.)

Ref.	Step	Calculations
Sec. 7.4.1 Eq. (7.3)	1	*Write down the formula (assume no inclination of load)* $q_{net} = cN_c s_c d_c + q_0(N_q - 1) s_q d_q + 0.5\gamma B N_\gamma s_\gamma d_\gamma W'$ $c = 15 \text{ kN/m}^2, \quad \phi = 25°$
Fig. 6.2a	2	*Find the bearing capacity factors (assume general shear condition)* $N_c = 20.7, \quad N_q = 10.7$ and $N_\gamma = 10.9$ $\gamma = 20 \text{ kN/m}^3 = \gamma_0$ $q_0 = \text{effective pressure} = 20 \times 1.5 = 30 \text{ kN/m}^2$ $W' = 0.5$
Sec. 7.6	3	*Find the eccentricities and equivalent size of footing* $e_x = \dfrac{180}{600} = 0.3 \text{ m (less than 2/6)}$ $e_y = \dfrac{60}{600} = 0.1 \text{ m}$ Effective width $B' = B - 2e_x = 2 - 0.6 = 1.4 \text{ m}$ Effective length $L' = L - 2e_y = 2 - 0.2 = 1.8 \text{ m}$
Table 7.1	4	*Calculate the shape and depth factors* $\therefore s_c = s_q = 1 + 0.2\dfrac{B'}{L'} = 1 + \dfrac{0.2 \times 1.4}{1.8} = 1.16$ $s_\gamma = 1 - 0.4\dfrac{B'}{L'} = 0.69$ $d_c = 1 + 0.2\left(\dfrac{D}{B'}\right)\tan(45 + \phi/2)$ $= 1 + 0.2\left(\dfrac{1.5}{1.4}\right)\tan(45 + \phi/2) = 1.34$ $d_q = d_\gamma = 1 + 0.1\left(\dfrac{D}{B'}\right)\tan(45 + \phi/2) = 1.17$
Step 1	5	*Calculate the bearing capacity* $q_{net} = (15 \times 20.7 \times 1.16 \times 1.34) + (30 \times 9.7 \times 1.16 \times 1.17)$ $\quad + (0.5 \times 20 \times 1.4 \times 10.9 \times 0.69 \times 1.17 \times 0.5)$ $\quad = 482.6 + 394.9 + 61.6 = 940 \text{ kN/m}^2$
	6	*Find FS of net capacity to actual load* $FS = \dfrac{940 \times 1.4 \times 1.8}{600} = 3.9$ is greater than 3. (*Notes*: 1. We have not considered increased *B.C* due to strength of top soil. 2. These calculations refer only to bearing capacity against shear failure and do not take into consideration the settlement of the footing.)

EXAMPLE 7.2 **(Eccentrically loaded footings—use of inclination factors and B.S. method)**

Determine the factor of safety of the 1.4 m × 1.8 m footing in Example 7.1 if the inclination of the load is 15° from the vertical.

Ref.	Step	Calculations
		1. Inclination factor method
	1	*Determine the load inclination factors*
Table 7.1		$i_c = i_q = \left(1 - \dfrac{\alpha}{90}\right)^2 = \left(1 - \dfrac{15}{90}\right)^2 = 0.69$
		$i_\gamma = \left(1 - \dfrac{\alpha}{\phi}\right)^2 = \left(1 - \dfrac{15}{25}\right)^2 = 0.16$
	2	*Calculate* q_{net} *with these factors*
Eq. (7.3)		$q_{net} = 482.6 \times 0.69 + 394.9 \times 0.69 + 61.6 \times 0.16$
		$= 333.0 + 272.5 + 9.8 = 615 \text{ kN/m}^2$
		(Inclination has decreased the capacity by 35%)
	3	*Determine the factor of safety*
		$FS = \dfrac{615 \times 1.4 \times 1.8}{600} = 2.58$
		Inclination of load has reduced the factor of safety from 3.9 to 2.58
		2. B.S. Method
	4	*Calculate horizontal and vertical components of the load*
		$Q_v = 600 \cos 15° = 580 \text{ kN}; \ Q_H = 600 \sin 15° = 155 \text{ kN}$
		Assume friction = tan 25 ≈ 0.5 (assume cohesion = 0)
		Base friction = 0.5 × 580 = 290 (assume $\delta = \phi$)
		Passive resistance from 1.5 m thick, well compacted soil.
		$P_p = \dfrac{\gamma h^2}{2} \tan^2 (45 + \phi/2); \ \tan (57.5)° = 2.46$
		$= \left[\dfrac{20 \times 1.5 \times 1.5 \times 2.46}{2}\right] = 55 \text{ kN/m}$
		Total horizontal resistance = 290 + 55 = 345 kN
	5	*Use interaction formula*
		$Q_v = 580 \text{ kN};$ assume $F.S = 2$
Example 7.1		$Q_{v \, all} = \dfrac{940 \times 1.4 \times 1.8}{2.0} = 1184 \text{ kN}$
Step 3		$Q_H = 155 \text{ kN} \qquad Q_{H \, all} = 345 \text{ kN}$
Eq. (7.4)		$\dfrac{Q_v}{Q_{v all}} + \dfrac{Q_H}{Q_{H \, all}} = \dfrac{580}{1184} + \dfrac{155}{345}$
		$= 0.48 + 0.45 = 0.93 < 1.$ Hence safe.

EXAMPLE 7.3   (Simple analysis of eccentrically loaded footings)

The base slab *AB* of a cantilever retaining wall 3.9 m in breadth subjected per meter run of the wall to a horizontal force of 144 kN and a vertical load of 433 kN, the resultant acting at 1.75 m from the toe *A*. If the allowable soil pressure is 200 kN/m^2 and the coefficient of friction between the soil and the concrete wall is 26°, check the safety of the foundation.

Ref.	Step	Calculations
	1	*Data: Consider* 1 m *length of foundation* $H = 144$ kN AB = width = 3.9 m $P = 433$ kN Position of loading = 1.75 from A [toe] Friction = tan 26 ≈ 0.5 (approx.)
	2	*Calculate eccentricity* $e = \dfrac{3.9}{2} - 1.75 = 0.20$ m; as $e < \dfrac{3.9}{6} = 0.65$ m Hence there is no tension and eccentricity is small.
	3	*Calculate maximum soil pressure per unit length* $p = \dfrac{P}{B} \pm \dfrac{Pe}{(I/y)}$ $I/y = Z = \dfrac{1 \times B^3}{12}\left(\dfrac{2}{B}\right) = \dfrac{B^2}{6}$ $p = \dfrac{433}{3.9} \pm \dfrac{433 \times 0.20 \times 6}{3.9 \times 3.9} = 111 \pm 34 = 144$ and 77 kN/m^2 Max pressure at toe = 144 kN/m^2 < 200 kN/m^2 (allowable)
Fig. 7.2	4	*Determine factor of safety against sliding* Max sliding resistance = μP = 0.5 × 433 = 216 kN F.S. against sliding $= \dfrac{216}{144} = 1.5$ (This type of analysis is more conventional for the above case than that of combining the horizontal and vertical loads as an inclined load and reducing the bearing capacity using inclination factors as is done in Example 7.4.)

EXAMPLE 7.4   (AREA method for eccentrically loaded footings)

A reinforced concrete column footing is acted on by a vertical load of 300 kN and moment of 150 kNm due to beam moments. It has a foundation on a 3.3 × 3.3 m square footing. The underlying soil is clay with an unconfined compressive strength of 0.6 kg/cm^2 and unit weight of 0.6 kg/cm^2. Determine the safety of the foundation if it is founded 1 m below ground level.

Ref.	Step	Calculations
	1	*Determine eccentricity of load and check < B/6*
		$$e_x = \frac{M}{P} = \frac{150}{300} = 0.5 \text{ m}$$
		$\frac{B}{6} = \frac{3.3}{6} = 0.55$ m. Hence, $e < \frac{B}{6}$. There is, thus, no tension.
	2	*Find reduced dimensions L′ and B′*
Sec. 7.6		$B' = B - 2e_x = 3.3 - 1 = 2.3 \text{ m}$
		$L' = L = 3.3$ m (Eccentricity on one side only).
	3	*Find the bearing capacity factors*
		$q_0 = 1 \times 20 = 20 \text{ kN/m}^2$
Table 6.1		$\phi = 0$; $N_c = 5.14$; $N_q = 1$ and $N_\gamma = 0$
Table 7.1		Shape factors $s_c = s_q = 1 + \dfrac{0.2B'}{L'}$
		$$= 1 + \frac{0.2 \times 2.3}{3.3} = 1.14$$
		Depth factor $d_c = 1 + \dfrac{0.2D}{B'} = 1 + \dfrac{0.2}{2.3} = 1.09$
		$d_q = 1.0$
	4	*Determine the ultimate bearing capacity*
Eq. (7.3)		$q_{ult} = cN_c s_c d_c + q_0 N_q s_q d_q$
		Unconfined strength, q_u
		$q_u = 0.6 \text{ kg/cm}^2 = 60 \text{ kN/m}^2$; $c = \dfrac{60}{2} = 30 \text{ kN/m}^2$
		$q_{ult} = 30 \times 5.14 \times 1.14 \times 1.09 + 20 \times 1 \times 1.14 \times 1.0$
		$= 191.6 + 21.8 = 213.4 \text{ kN/m}^2$
		$q_{net} = q_{ult} - \gamma D = 213.4 - 21.8 = 191.6 \text{ kN/m}^2$
		$q_{safe} = \dfrac{191.6}{3} + 21.8 = 85.7 \text{ kN/m}^2$
	5	*Determine the safe load*
		$Q_{safe} = 85.7 \times 2.3 \times 3.3 = 453 \text{ kN} > 300 \text{ kN}$
		Hence it is safe.

EXAMPLE 7.5 (Conventional analysis of eccentrically loaded footings)

In Example 7.4, if the moment of 150 kNm is produced by a horizontal force of 150 kN. Examine the safety of the footing, neglecting depth factor.

Ref.	Step	Calculations
	1	*Data* As in Example 7.4; Vertical load $P = 300$ kN Horizontal force = 150 kN; Moment = 150 kNm;
	2	*Assuming the footing under P and M find I/y* $$Z = \frac{I}{y} = \frac{3.3 \times 3.3^3 \times 2}{12 \times 3.3} = \frac{3.3^3}{6}$$
Eq. (7.3)	3	*Find safe bearing pressure without all the factors* $$q_{\text{ult}} = cN_c + q_0 N_q = 30 \times 5.14 + 20 \times 1 = 174 \text{ kN/m}^2$$ Allowable pressure $= \dfrac{174}{2.5} = 70 \text{ kN/m}^2$
	4	***Method 1: Conventional method*** *Calculate max. and min. base pressures* $P = 300$ kN; $M = 150$ kNm $$e = \frac{M}{P} = \frac{150}{300} = 0.5 \text{ m} < \frac{3.3}{6} \text{ (no tension)}$$
Step 2		Max. pressure $= \dfrac{P}{A} \pm \dfrac{M}{Z} = \dfrac{300}{3.3 \times 3.3} \pm \dfrac{150 \times 6}{(3.3)^3}$ $= 27.5 \pm 25 \text{ kN/m}^2$ $= 52.5$ and 2.5 kN/m^2 less than 70 kN/m^2 (safe) Maximum pressure is less than allowable. Hence safe
	5	*Determine F.S against base friction with coefficient 0.5* $H = 0.5 \times 300 = 150$ kN (total base friction) Factor of safety $= \dfrac{150}{150} = 1$ only Hence, the passive resistance of soil has also to be assumed for safety.
	6	***Method 2: Using inclination factors*** *Using load inclination which has maximum effect to check safe bearing capacity* Find inclination of load with the vertical. $$\tan \theta = \frac{H}{P} = \frac{150}{300} = 0.5; \quad \alpha = 26.6°$$
Table 7.1		$$i_c = i_q = \left(1 - \frac{\alpha}{90}\right)^2 = (0.70)^2 = 0.49$$

	7	Find ultimate bearing capacity
		$q_0 = cN_ci_c + p_0N_qi_q$
		$= 174 \times 0.49 = 85.3 \text{ kN/m}^2$
		Allowable pressure $= \dfrac{85.3}{2.5} = 34 \text{ kN/m}^2$
		Allowable load $= 34 \times 3.3 \times 3.3 = 370 \text{ kN}$
		Load $= 300 \text{ kN} < 370 \text{ kN}$. Hence safe.

EXAMPLE 7.6   (Layout of footings for uniform pressure)

A column has to carry a vertical dead load of 600 kN and live load 400 kN. The dead load moment of 230 kNm and live load moment of 270 kNm along one of its axes. Assuming the *safe bearing capacity* (S.B.C.) of 150 kN/m², layout the footing such that the soil pressure under it will be approximately uniform under maximum loading.

Ref.	Step	Calculations
	1	*Determine maximum loading and eccentricity*
		$P = 600 + 400 = 1000 \text{ kN}; \ M = 230 + 270 = 500 \text{ kNm}$
		$e = \dfrac{M}{P} = \dfrac{500}{1000} = 0.5 \text{ m}$
	2	*Determine dimension of footing*
		Assuming square footing with S.B.C = 150 kN/m²
		$B = \sqrt{\dfrac{1000}{150}} = 2.58 \text{ m. Assume 3.3 m.}$
	3	*Determine layout for uniform pressure*
		Plan the footing so that the centre line of column is 0.5 m from C.G. of the footing along the XX axis as shown in Fig. 7.4
	4	*Determine uniform pressure*
Sec. 7.6		Effective breadth $B = B - 2e = 3.3 - 1.0 = 2.3 \text{ m}$
		Uniform base pressure $= \dfrac{1000}{2.3 \times 3.3} = 131 \text{ kN/m}^2 < 150$ (safe)

EXAMPLE 7.7   (Design of inclined bases by base inclination factors)

A strip footing 2 m × 2 m has a tilted base inclined at 10° to the horizontal as shown in Fig. 7.5. Estimate its ultimate bearing capacity assuming unit weight of soil as 18 kN/m³. Cohesion 25 kN/m² and $\phi = 25°$. Assume $H = 200$ kN, $V = 600$ kN and the average depth of footing in 0.3 m. [3].

Ref.	Step	Calculations
		Note: This problem can be theoretically solved by using Hansen's method with modifying factors for depth, load inclination and base inclination. (As an approximation for small base inclinations we can equate inclined base area equal to the projected area without the base inclination factor.)
		Method 1: With bearing capacity factors *Find Hansen's bearing capacity factors for general shear*
Table 7.2	1	$\phi = 25°$ $N_c = 20.7$; $N_q = 10.7$ and $N_\gamma = 6.8$
	2	*Find α for H = 200 kN and V = 600 kN* $\alpha = \tan^{-1}\dfrac{200}{600} = 18.43$
	3	*Find equilibrium for H (due to friction and cohesion)* Capacity for friction $= 600 \times \tan 25° + (25 \times 4)$ $= 379$ kN > 200 kN [value of *H*]
Table 7.1	4	*Find depth factors (use I.S values)* For conservative values take $d = 0.3$ m $d_c = 1 + (0.2 \times 0.3)/2(\tan 57.5) = 1.03$ $d_\gamma = d_q = 1 + (0.1 \times 0.3)/2(\tan 57.5) = 1.02$
Table 7.1	5	*Load inclination factors* $i_q = i_c = (1 - 18.43/90)^2 = 0.63$ $i_\gamma = (1 - 18.43/25)^2 = 0.07$
Sec. 7.7	6	*Base inclination factors for $\eta = 10°$* $\eta = 10° = (3.14 \times 10)/180 = 0.175$ radians $b_c = 1 - 10/147 = 0.93$ $b_{q_v} = b_{\gamma_v} = (1 - \eta \tan \phi)^2$ $= (1 - 0.175 \tan 25)^2 = 0.85$ (Note that these are nearly equal to $\eta = 0.98$.)
	7	*Ultimate bearing capacity with all factors* $q_{ult} = 25 \times 20.7(1.03 \times 0.63 \times 0.93)$ $+ 0.3 \times 18 \times 10.7(1.02 \times 0.63 \times 0.85)$ $+ 0.5 \times 18 \times 2.0 \times 6.8(1.02 \times 0.07 \times 0.85)$ $= 350$ kN/unit area
Eq. (7.3)		$V_v = 350 \times 2 \times 2 = 1400$ kN (Based on actual area)

8	**Method 2: Approximation on projected area** *Approximate calculation on horizontal base without base inclination factor* $q_{ult} = 25 \times 20.7(1.03 \times 0.63)$ $\quad\quad + 0.3 \times 18 \times 10.7(1.02 \times 0.63)$ $\quad\quad + 0.5 \times 18 \times 2 \times 6.8(1.02 \times 0.07) = 381$ kN/unit area
Sec. 7.7	Capacity on projected area $= 381 \times 2 \times 2 \cos 10 = 1500$ kN Deleting factors 0.93 and 0.62 in step $= 281$ kN *Note*: The major reduction in bearing capacity is due to inclination of the load.

REFERENCES

[1] Brinch Hansen, J., A Revised and Extended Formula for Bearing Capacity. *Bulletin No. 28*. Danish Geotechnical Institute, 1968.

[2] IS 6403, 1981, *Code of Practice for Determination of Bearing Capacity of Shallow Foundations*, B.I.S., New Delhi, 1990.

[3] Teng, W.C., *Foundation Design*, Prentice-Hall of India, New Delhi, 1965.

[4] Bowles, J.E., *Foundation Analysis and Design*, (International Students Edition), McGraw-Hill, Singapore, 1988.

[5] Winterkon, H.F. and Fang, H.Y., *Foundation Engineering Handbook,* Van Nostrand Reinhold, New York, 1975.

[6] Tomlinson, M.J., *Foundation Design and Construction*, ELBS with Longman, Singapore, 1995.

8

Design of Raft Foundations

8.1 INTRODUCTION

A raft or mat foundation consists of a *large concrete slab* or *a slab and beam system* resting on soil or rock and supporting all the loads through a number of columns or walls. When the raft is supported on piles it is called a *piled raft*. In this chapter we will deal only with rafts resting directly on soil. Chapter 15 deals with piled rafts and Chapter 18 with floating foundations. IS 2950 (Part I) 1981 Second Revision is the Indian Code of Practice for design and construction of raft foundations [1].

8.1.1 Situations where Rafts are Used

Rafts are used under the following conditions:

1. In structures like chimneys, silos, cooling towers, buildings with basements where continuous water proofing is needed and in floating foundations where a rigid structure is needed to reduce settlements.

2. Where differential settlements in structure are to be reduced. As observed by Terzaghi and Peck, the differential settlement in rafts is only one half that of footings of the same intensity of loading due to the random distribution of compressible zones and also due to stiffening effect of the raft and building frame [2]. Due to continuity and negative moments the bending moments produced in rafts tend to be less. *Thus an allowable maximum settlement of 50 mm is usually specified for rafts, whereas for footings only 25 mm is specified for the same allowable differential settlement of 18 mm (3/4 inch) for both cases.* (see Sec. 4.7)

3. Mats are specified to bridge over pockets of weak spots in moderately weak soil.

4. In situations where individual footings may touch or overlap each other and it is advisable to excavate the full site instead of the ground under individual footings. (In such situations, careful analysis should be made as to whether individual footings or rafts are more economical. In general, where settlements expected are small, individual strips and footings tend to be cheaper than rafts, which will require much more steel to carry increased shear and bending moments due to continuity.)

5. It is very important that when we adopt a raft foundation we should carefully check whether there are any weak spots below the foundation. As the influence of the foundation is felt to a depth 1 to 2 times its breadth below it, we must be aware that the bulb of pressure of wide rafts extends to deeper layers than in footings. In situations where there are soft deposits below hard layers, individual footings should be preferred over rafts.

6. It is also a usual practice these days to use mat foundation over piles to reduce settlements. For this purpose only part of the load is taken by piles. These are called piled rafts.

8.2 TYPES OF RAFTS AND THEIR USE

Rafts can be classified as follows (shown in Fig. 8.1):

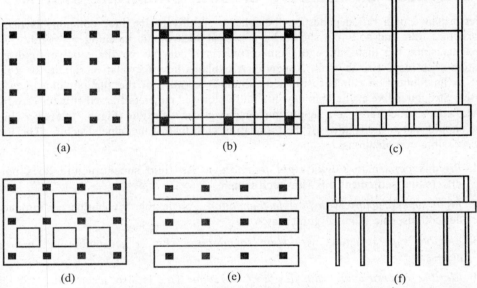

    (a)   (b)   (c)

    (d)   (e)   (f)

Fig. 8.1 Types of raft foundations: (a) Flat plate; (b) beam and slab; (c) cellular raft; (d) grid foundation; (e) strip raft; (f) piled raft.

1. Plain slab rafts, are flat concrete slabs with or without pedestals.

2. Beam and slab rafts are those with downstanding beams or upstanding beams. (Due to difficulties and hazards in construction the upstand beams with compacted granular materials between beams covered with mass concrete is more popular than downstand beams.) A stiffened edge raft with the peripheral downstand or stepped down beam can also be used as a cut off against ingress of water to the ground floor and is very popular in practice.

3. Cellular rafts (rigid buoyancy rafts) for compensated foundations are necessary to avoid differential settlements. Such procedures are used mainly for very weak soils.

4. Piled rafts are rafts supported on piles. This sharing of loads is a means to reduce settlement in buildings.

5. Strip rafts and grid foundations are also generally designed on the same principles as rafts.

8.3 LOADS ON RAFTS

Rafts can be subjected to vertical loads, horizontal loads and also to moments from column members. The total loading from a block of flats of R.C frame and brick infill and plastered finishes will be about 12.5 kN/m^2 (1.25 t/m^2) per storey compared to a live load of 2 kN/m^2 assumed for the design of floors. Thus, for a four-storey apartment (ground + three) the ground pressure will be only about 50 kN/m^2 (5 t/m^2). (In general, the column loads of a four-storey residential flat will vary from 20 to 80 tons, with the mean column load of 40 to 50 tons). We may also take a higher load of 25 kN/m^2 for the ground floor. Horizontal forces like wind and earthquake increase the vertical loads in one part and reduce them in other parts. They may also produce moments at the base of columns, which in turn, will influence the raft pressures.

8.4 STIFFNESS OR RIGIDITY OF SOIL STRUCTURE SYSTEM

The performance of a raft depends on the relative rigidity of its three components namely the superstructure, raft and soil. We should have a clear idea of the meaning of 'rigidity' of these components since the distribution of contact pressures depends on the relative rigidity of the foundation with respect to the soil. Appendix A explains how the relative rigidity of a raft with respect to its foundation can be estimated. Similarly rigidity of the superstructure can also be estimated. Structures like a silo, chimney or a multi-storeyed concrete framed structure are rigid. On the other hand, a structural system supporting a gantry girder is flexible (Fig. 8.2). It is very important that we should match the rigidity of the foundation with that of the superstructure. The following are the possible combinations:

1. *Rigid superstructure with rigid foundation:* As rigid superstructure does not allow differential settlement this is a good match.

2. *Rigid superstructure with flexible foundation:* As flexible foundation can produce large deflections, this is not a good match.

3. *Flexible superstructure with rigid foundation:* This is acceptable but may not be necessary.

4. *Flexible superstructure with flexible foundation:* This is also acceptable.

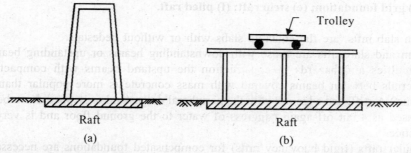

Fig. 8.2   Examples of rigid and flexible superstructure: (a) Chimney; (b) gantry girder.

There are many case histories where mismatching of foundation and superstructure has led to failures. For example, a rigid silo supported on large size columns on a flexible foundation can crack badly due to mismatch, as the differential settlement in the flexible raft cannot be tolerated by the rigid columns. This will lead to excessive cracking of the columns. There are also many cases of failure of steel oil tanks installed on rigid concrete rafts on soft soils due to mismatch with the foundation. (see Sec. 8.14).

8.5 ALLOWABLE SOIL PRESSURES FOR RAFTS IN COHESIONLESS SOILS

The following are some of the considerations in the selection of allowable soil pressures in cohesionless soils. [2]

The denseness of a sand deposit is reflected by the SPT value. $N \approx 15$ corresponds to the critical void ratio so that SPT value range 10 to 30 corresponds to medium dense sand. A value below 10 indicates that the sand is loose.

The settlement of footings in sand as related to SPT (N) value is discussed in Section 6.8 and is valid for rafts also. Because of the large size of rafts, the bearing capacity against shear failure in unyielding sand is very large. Hence bearing capacity will be decided on allowable settlement. Terzaghi has shown from field observations that in sands, the *differential settlement of rafts* is only one half of that of a footing foundation for the same pressure. We have seen that if a set of footings in a building is designed for a maximum settlement of the footing of 25 mm (one inch) the differential settlement will be 18 mm (3/4 inch). Hence if we design a raft for 25 mm the differential settlement will be only 9 mm only. The maximum settlement of a raft and a large footing will be the same as can be seen from Fig. 6.9. Hence, *larger pressures of the order of twice that are assigned for footings are allowed for rafts in sands for the same differential settlement. Experience in the field has also confirmed the validity* of this assumption. Accordingly, we can assume the following empirical rule for safe bearing capacity of rafts in sands.

Assuming Terzaghi's expression for bearing capacities and settlements based on SPT values, we get the following expressions for *allowable pressures for rafts in sands* in kN/m^2 for a given value of settlement. (Note: These settlement rules are not applicable to clays.)

1. Using Eq. (6.13) for $B > 4$ m and for settlement of 1 mm, we get the allowable pressure for footings as:

$$q_1 = 0.42 \, NR_q R_d \ (\text{kN/m}^2)$$

The pressure for any given settlement can be worked out. For example, if 50 mm settlement is specified, then

$$q_{50} = 21 NR_q R_d \ (\text{kN/m}^2) \tag{8.1a}$$

2. Based on shear failure and assuming $FS = 3$ from Eq. (6.16b), the *safe bearing capacity* will be as follows:

$$q_{\text{safe}} = \frac{1}{18}\left[6(100 + N^2)DR_q + 2N^2 BR_\gamma\right] \tag{8.1b}$$

Here, R_q, R_γ, R_d are the correction factors for *water level, for unit weight* and for *depth of foundation,* respectively. The value of the depth D should not be more than 4 m.

The following points need special mention:

(i) Correction factors are given in Chapter 6 for depth of ground water table and depth of foundation.

(ii) If SPT value (after correction) is 5 or less than 5, than the sand will be loose and needs consolidation. Special care should be taken when constructing in such sites.

(iii) Load on the foundation is equal to the sum of dead load and live load. (Sec. 6.2.1)

Net pressure (q_{net}) in excess of the pressure at base in an excavated raft bed of depth D_f is given by:

$$q_{net} = \frac{W}{A} - \gamma D_f \qquad (8.2)$$

where

W = total load
A = area of raft
D_f = depth of foundation
γ = unit weight of soil.

The following thumb rule can be used in practice, see Eq. (6.12b), for allowable bearing pressure in sands with reference to settlement. For differential settlement of 18 mm safe BC in kN/m^2 is as follows:

For footings $= 10.5N(\Delta = 25$ mm and $\delta\Delta = 18$ mm)
For rafts $= 21.0N(\Delta = 50$ mm and $\delta\Delta = 18$ mm) \qquad (8.3)

where

Δ = settlement and $\delta\Delta$ = differential settlement.

8.6 ALLOWABLE PRESSURES FOR RAFTS IN COHESIVE SOILS

Allowable pressure based on settlement. The design of rafts in clays based on settlement is by no means a routine procedure. From the following derivation we can note that designs in clay cannot be based on calculation of stresses only but should be based on settlement forecast and the estimated maximum curvature to which the raft will be subjected to. The selection of the thickness of the slab and the amount of reinforcements to be used should be carefully made so that the raft does not crack up during the deformations due to settlement. The curvature in which the slab will bend consequent to settlement as well as the bending moment produced can be estimated with reference to Fig. 8.3.

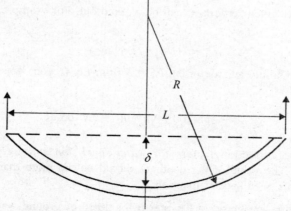

Fig. 8.3   Settlement and stresses in raft foundations.

Let δ be the deflection in a beam of length L bent in radius R. Then,

$$(2R - \delta)\delta = \frac{L^2}{4} \quad \text{(where } L = \text{total span)}$$

Assuming that δ is small,

$$2R\delta = \frac{L^2}{4} \quad \text{or} \quad \frac{1}{R} = \frac{8\delta}{L^2}$$

As in bending,

$$\frac{M}{I} = \frac{E}{R} = \frac{f}{y}, \quad M = \frac{EI}{R} = \frac{8EI\delta}{L^2}.$$

The stress (f) is as follows:

$$f = \frac{M}{Z} = \left(\frac{8EI\delta}{L^2}\right)\left(\frac{t}{2I}\right), \quad \text{where } t = \text{thickness}$$

Thus,

$$f = \frac{4E\delta t}{L^2} = \frac{Et}{2R} \quad \text{as} \quad \delta = L^2/8R \tag{8.4}$$

We should note that if the settlement is of the same order as the thickness of the plate, the thin plate theory will not be adequate. (In the classical theory of bending of plates, plates are divided into four groups: (i) thin plate with small deflection; (ii) thin plates with large deflections; (iii) membranes; and (iv) thick plates). In large deflection of thin plates (deflection more than half of its thickness) appreciable tensile stresses due to membrane action will be present in the plate. This can cause extensive cracking in concrete.

Allowable pressures based on strength in cohesive soils. As there is no contribution from the friction component of the soil, the safe bearing can be calculated for cohesive soils as follows:

$$q_{\text{ult}} = cN_c + qN_q \quad \text{and} \quad (N_\gamma = 0) \tag{8.5}$$

If D/B ratios are large, we can apply Skempton's value for N_c as shown in Fig. 6.4 and Eq. (6.8) of Chapter 6. (Normally, D/B of raft foundation is not very large as in the case of pile foundations where we can assume $N_c = 9$.) An alternative method is to use bearing capacity factors given in Table 7.1. As $N_q = 1$ for clays and qN_q is the overburden pressure, which is a positive quantity that does not require a factor of safety to be applied, the safe load q_a can be also calculated from the following equation:

$$FS = \frac{cN_c}{q_a - \gamma D_f} \tag{8.6}$$

where q_a is the gross load to be applied on the foundation.

The following points need special mention:

(i) When $q_a = \gamma D_f$ in the above equation, as in a compensated raft FS is very large,

(ii) In the case of *rafts on weak soils,* the dead load and the probable live loads should be very accurately estimated as the total loads have a great influence on a weak soil as compared to soils with good bearing capacity.

(iii) *For practical purposes, it is more pertinent to assume that the allowable bearing capacity in rafts in clay soil is the same as for footings and then give correction for D_f/B the depth ratio.*

8.7 STRUCTURAL DESIGN OF RAFT FOUNDATIONS

For a successful design, the layout of rafts should be carried out with due consideration of both settlements and bearing capacity. For example, the flat slab analogy which has been very successfully used in many cases has also led to structural failures in many other cases due to lack of understanding of the basics. It is very evident that the flat slab analogy based on small deflection is valid only where the differential settlement between columns is small. In situations where the differential settlements are large, flat slab analysis will never give us satisfactory results. Basically the following two approaches have been used for design of rafts: [3]

1. Rigid foundation approach (empirical approach without considering nature of the soil)
2. Flexible foundation approach (considering the nature of the soil by its modulus of subgrade reaction or its modulus of elasticity).

In the rigid foundation approach, the raft is assumed to be rigid and the pressure distribution is assumed to be either uniform or varying linearly. The rigid raft is designed either as a floor system, (flat slab or two-way slab) or as a series of combined footings in X and Y directions. Only the bearing capacity of the soil (but not its flexibility) is taken into consideration. [4]

In the flexible foundation approach, we have the two models namely the Winkler model and the elastic half space model. Here also we may design the whole raft as a single system using sophisticated software programs like finite element method or analyze them as a series of beams on elastic foundations in the X and Y directions by elemental analysis (Theory of analysis of beams on Winkler foundation is described in Appendices A, B and C). In any case, we give about 1.5 m extension of the raft (or an edge beam) at edges, to take care of the uplift and other edge conditions.

8.7.1 Relative Stiffness Factor of Raft Foundations

According to ACI 336 (1988) whether a raft as a whole behaves as a rigid or a flexible structure depends on the relative stiffness of the structure and the foundation soil. This relation can be expressed by the *stiffness factor K_r* given below [1]. This also applies to single units like a footing. (see IS 2950 (Part 1) 1981 Clause C_2)

$$\text{For the whole structure, } K_r = \frac{EI}{E_s B^3 A} \tag{8.7a}$$

$$\text{For rectangular beams or rafts, } K_r = \frac{E}{12E_s}\left(\frac{D}{B}\right)^3 \tag{8.7b}$$

$$\text{For circular rafts } K_r = \frac{E}{12E_s}\left(\frac{D}{2R}\right)^3 \tag{8.7c}$$

where

EI = flexural rigidity of the superstructure and foundation per unit length at right angles to B in kg/cm^2

E_s = modulus of compressibility (or elasticity) of foundation soil in kg/cm^2

B = length of section in the bending axis in cm

A = length perpendicular to B

D = thickness of raft or beam in cm

R = radius of raft in cm

Also, for a raft with beams and shear walls,

$$EI = E\left(I_F + \sum I_b + \sum ah^3/12\right)$$

where

EI_F = rigidity of foundation
EI_b = rigidity of beams
a = shear wall thickness
h = shear wall height.

When $K_r > 0.5$, the foundation can be considered as rigid with the ratio of differential settlement to total settlement being equal to 0. For $K_r = 0.5$, the ratio of differential settlement to total settlement is 0.1 and, if $K_r = 0$, then this ratio is equal to 0.35 for square mats and 0.5 for long foundations.

8.7.2 Characteristic Coefficient λ (Characteristic Length Parameter)

When the foundation is considered as a beam on elastic foundation, it is more convenient to use the characteristics coefficient λ to estimate its behaviour as a rigid or flexible member. In Appendix A, it is explained that the performance of a beam on elastic foundation (using Winkler model) is given by its characteristic coefficient, λ as: (IS 2950 Clause C-3)

$$\lambda = \left(\frac{kB}{4E_c I} \right)^{1/4}$$

(8.8)

where

k = modulus of subgrade reaction corrected for width B in kN/m^3
B = breadth of raft in m
E_c = modulus of elasticity of concrete = $5\sqrt{fck} \times 10^6$ kN/m^2
I = moment of inertia of raft in m^4
L_B = length of the beam in m

(*Note:* The unit of λ is $1/m$ so that λL_B will be a number with no units.)

The column spacing in terms of λ affects the performance of the beam on elastic foundation loaded with column loads. Vesic's classification of single beams on elastic foundation is shown in Fig. 8.4. [3] [see Appendix A for more details].

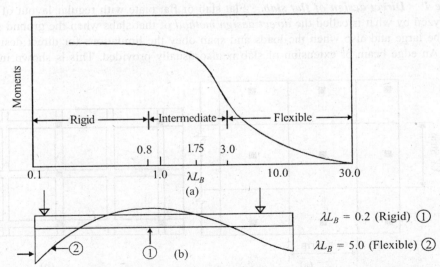

Fig. 8.4 Flexible and rigid foundations: (a) Classification according to Vesic based on λL_B; (b) variation of contact pressures depending on rigidity.

8.7.3   Methods of Design of Raft Foundations

The following are some of the recommended methods used for analysis of raft foundations for buildings on columns [5]. (The method to be used depends on the relative rigidity of the raft with respect to the foundation soil.)

1. Rigid beam analysis (conventional method)
2. Winkler model analysis as plates or beams on elastic foundations
3. As plates on beams on elastic half space (elastic continum)
4. Readymade closed form solutions by elastic theory
5. ACI simplified method of beams on elastic foundation. (Appendix B)
6. ACI method of plates on elastic foundation (Appendix C).

The above methods and their limitations are briefly dealt with in the following sections. However, the following practical details are very important. The detailing of steel should comply with standard practice with both faces perioded with equal steel to compensate for the lack of knowledge of the signs of the bending moment in a real raft foundation due to variation of foundation conditions. A simple rule is to use a slabdepth 50 mm in excess of the greater effective depths obtained from punching shear and bending moment considerations. A minimum steel of 0.5 percent is to be provided on both faces (totalling 1%) in each direction of the slab. A large external cover of 75 mm and a similar internal cover of 45 mm at least should be also adopted.

8.8   RIGID BEAM ANALYSIS (CONVENTIONAL METHOD)

This method can be used when the settlements are small as is assumed in a floor system. According to IS 2950 (1981), this method may be used with the condition, $\lambda L < 1.75$, where L is the column spacing and λ is the characteristic parameter. [3]

8.8.1   Details of Conventional (Rigid) Method

Case 1:   Direct design of flat slab.   Flat slab or flat plate with regular layout of column can be analyzed by what is called the *direct design method* of that slabs when the ground settlements will not be large and also when the loads and span obey the limitations for direct design of flat slabs [4]. An edge beam or extension of slab is also usually provided. This is shown in Fig. 8.5a.

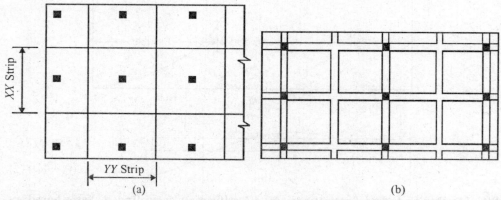

Fig. 8.5   Design of raft foundations: (a) Flat slab analysis; (b) ACI two-way slab analysis or IS beam and slab analysis.

Case 2: *Equivalent frame analysis of flat slabs.* Direct design of flat slabs is not applicable where adjacent spans differ more than 15% of the greater span or where the length to width ratio exceeds two or where there are less than three rows of panels in the two directions. For such conditions, *equivalent frame analysis* should be used. It takes into account the stiffness of members based on gross cross section of concrete alone. The stiffness effects of drop panels and splays may be ignored. If the dead load far exceeds the live load, a single analysis by total load will give satisfactory results. Variation of vertical loads due to horizontal forces should be also taken into account. (The difference between the first and the second methods shown above is only in the structural calculations to be made.)

Case 3: *Beam and slab construction.* See Fig. 8.5b. This construction is used when the thickness of slab becomes excessive for providing for rigidity when designed as a slab or when the load and span variations are large or when the expected differential settlements is large (more than one half of the thickness of plate contemplated). In such cases it is better to plan for a stiffer foundation by adopting beam and slab construction. The slabs and beams are designed assuming uniform, or in case of eccentricity of resultant load, uniformly varying foundation pressure. The slabs (200 to 600 mm in depth) span between beams. Generally beams are provided in both directions to give rigidity to the system. The secondary beams may be placed at one third the span of the main beams. Main beams are 1 to 1.8 m in depth and the cross beams 0.5 to 0.7 m in depth. The slab is given an overhang all around the main structure for better structural performance and also for resisting any floatation due to ground water.

For analyzing the system, we cut the foundation into its elements, slabs and beams the procedure being called, *elemental analysis.* Slabs can be designed as two-way slabs in accordance with the table of coefficients for slabs. Beams are designed as T beams. For analysis, moment distribution method or any other method can be used. Arbitrary values $\pm wL^2/10$ for positive and negative moments give us very conservative results for beam design.

Case 4: *Deep cellular raft construction.* Buoyant raft or cellular raft consists of a hollow box construction of structural walls, beams and raft slab. The raft usually replaces the existing in-situ soil to a specified depth. For simple elemental design, the slab in contact with the ground is divided into a number of two-way slabs continuous over cross walls. The soil pressures are the uniformly distributed load due to the total dead and live loads. (The UDL due to dead load of the foundation slab is usually neglected as it acts opposite to the soil loading.) The cross walls can be designed as ordinary concrete walls with nominal 0.5% reinforcement. The wall will also act as beams between columns with a net loading from soil pressure less self weight of the wall beam and slabs. Simple coefficients of $\pm wL^2/10$ usually give good results [5]. Alternatively, the whole cross section may be considered to be an I or box section in two directions. The elemental design given above usually gives very safe and conservative results. This method is generally used as a preliminary design for determining the total steel required.

8.9 WINKLER MODEL ANALYSIS

The second method of analysis is based on the Winkler model. In the rigid analysis, we do not take into consideration the nature of the soil and its elastic characteristics. The first method to take into account the soil characteristic was the Winkler model which considered the raft as a beam on elastic foundation. The Winkler model is based on the value of the modulus of subgrade reaction. Later the method of considering foundation as "Elastic Half Space Model" which is based on the modulus of elasticity of the soil was evolved. A simple parameter used to test the behaviour of a raft as rigid or flexible is the parameter λ called the 'characteristic length parameter' given in Section 8.7.2. The characteristic coefficient λ can be used as a measure of the rigidity of rafts as shown in Fig. 8.5. If the column spacing L is such that $\lambda L < 1.75$ then rafts can be designed by conventional or rigid design. If $\lambda L > 1.75$ the foundation characteristics also need to be considered in our design. Of the two models namely, the Winkler and the elastic half space models, the first is more amenable to easy solution and hence is more popular. We will deal with Winkler method in more detail.

Solution by Winkler model. As distinct from the rigid foundation approach, the flexible foundation approach tries to take into account the rigidities of both structure and soil. The following two approaches are popularly used.

Procedure 1: By considering the whole raft as a slab or beam, the slab system is modelled for analysis by computer programs. Figure 8.6a shows a finite element analysis of a raft using SAP IV computer program. This requires the use of a computer and a computer program.

Procedure 2: The raft is cut into a series of structural elements into which we can divide the system (elemental method) as we do in ordinary reinforced structural design (Fig. 8.6b). Example 8.10 illustrates how the mat is divided *for elemental analysis*. The beam elements are then analyzed as beams on elastic foundation by Winkler theory.

The first method of modelling is a specialized subject and advanced books on that subject should be consulted. It also needs a powerful computer and specialized software for solution.

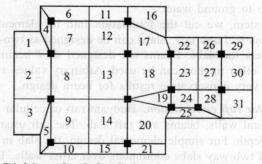

Fig. 8.6a   Division of raft for finite element analysis as a full slab.

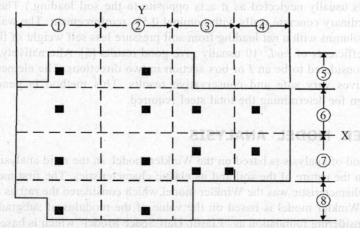

Fig. 8.6b   Elemental analysis by cutting the raft into beams in X and Y directions.

8.9.1 Procedure for Elemental Analysis of Mats by Winkler Model

The procedure for the second method is as follows. We proceed as follows for elemental analysis by Winkler model [5].

Step 1: Find depth required from punching shear consideration.

Step 2: Consider the whole raft as a single beam on elastic foundation in the X direction with all column loads perpendicular to the length coupled together. Determine the moments and moments per unit width as beam on elastic foundation. Determine roughly the total reinforcements required in each region. (As explained in Appendix A, calculations can be made by using a computer or published tables.)

Step 3: Repeat the analysis in the Y direction also.

Step 4: For a more refined analysis cut the raft into convenient strips in X direction and analyse each strip as beams on elastic foundation and design the strip. Check depth got in step 1.

Step 5: Cut the raft into strips in Y direction and repeat the design.

Step 6: Compare steel required from steps 2 and 4 and steps 3 and 5 and then adopt a suitable distribution of steel.

Step 7: Check for minimum steel. In general not less than 0.5% steel at top and an equal amount at bottom is usually provided in both the directions as explained in Section 8.7.3.

8.9.2 Influence of Parameters on the Results of Winkler Analysis

The two important parameters involved in Winkler analysis are the modulus of subgrade reaction and the rigidity of the raft. It will be interesting to study how these parameters affect the results of the analysis. λ is a function of fourth root of K/I. Larger values of K make a given raft foundation act more flexible and larger values of I with same K values make the foundation more rigid. The more the rigidity of the foundation the more uniform is the pressure distribution as shown in Fig. 8.4. with increasing value of bending moments. With more flexible foundation the pressures will be higher only near the loads and hence *lesser the bending moments*.

In general, we may say that rigid analysis gives us more conservative values of bending moments than flexible analysis. Thus, rigid analysis results in bigger sections and more steel.

8.10 SOLUTION AS PLATES OR BEAMS ON ELASTIC HALF-SPACE (ELASTIC CONTINUUM)

In the third method, we assume the raft is supported on an elastic half-space on elastic continuum. It is the most accurate method to analyse the raft.

For using this method, the vertical displacement of the raft and the continuum at various common points across the interface are equated. For regular surfaces like a circular tank base, the elastic layer surface displacements can be based on the analytical solution given by Burmister in 1956. For building foundations, however, difficulties arise as the rafts are irregular in plan and subjected to non-symmetric loads. The general method of raft analysis uses the finite element method called the *surface element method*. It is based on the principle of coupling of a finite element raft structure to a ground continuum by a basic technique developed by Cheung and Zienkiewicz. For details of the method, reference is made to advanced books on the subject [6].

8.11 CLOSED FORM SOLUTIONS BASED ON ELASTIC THEORY

The fourth method for design of rafts is the large amount of tables and charts available in literature for rafts of regular shape. These can be used for design of regular shapes like circular shapes [6].

8.12 ACI METHODS FOR ANALYSIS OF BEAMS AND GRIDS ON ELASTIC FOUNDATION

The fifth and sixth methods mentioned in Sec 8.7.3 are the ACI methods. The ACI Committee 436, as well as IS 2950 Part I (1981), recommended the use of a simplified method [7] for analysis of beams on elastic foundations using Winkler model for limited cases. This method is explained in Appendix B. The method of analysis of flexible plates on elastic foundation is given Appendix C.

8.13 RAFT-SUPERSTRUCTURE INTERACTION

The performance of the raft along with the rigidity of the superstructure will depend on the *type of connection between* the raft and the superstructure. Hence in structures like silos and oil tanks, the wall rigidity plays an important part. However in buildings it has been observed that a 'rudimentary approach' is generally adequate to take care of the rigidity of the superstructure. For flexible structures with widely spaced columns and few building walls between raft and superstructure the effect of superstructure can be ignored or added on to the raft slab arbitrarily [5]. The expression to calculate *EI* of foundation was described in Section 8.7.1.

8.14 TANK FOUNDATIONS

Terzaghi has described the case study of two steel tanks of 30 m in diameter and 10 m in height (built in Germany for storing molasses) over a bed of soft clay of 4 m over stiff clay [2]. The load has a uniform pressure of 162 kN/m^2. A dish shaped settlement with a maximum differential settlement of 0.1 m at the centre of the tank was expected.

In the first tank that was constructed a flexible design was adopted by placing the steel tank over a thin reinforced slab of 10 cm thick. In this case the bending moments were small. For the second tank a somewhat rigid construction was used. A beam and slab raft with 50 cm thick slab and 1 m × 0.5 m size beam was adopted below the steel plate. Whereas the flexible raft performed well, the rigid raft tried to even out the settlement and in that process produced large bending moments. As it was not strong enough to withstand these moments, large cracks were produced in the concrete. The rivets of the bottom plate of the steel tank gave way. Thus, the cause of the failure was the adoption of the more expensive rigid raft. This shows that if a decision to construct a more rigid foundation is taken, the corresponding bending moments should be determined and the raft should be designed for these larger moments and shears. In a flexible structure, the moments produced will be smaller but deflections will be larger than in rigid rafts. Tank foundations are generally designed to be flexible. An accurate assessment of the short and long term settlements due to external load is the most important requirement. We assume that in most parts, the contact pressure is the same as that of the liquid. But the walls produce moments and vertical loading at the periphery. The contact stresses near the circumference is also quite high due to rigidity of edges. In order to counteract these effects tanks are generally provided with a reinforced concrete ring beam 0.45 m to 1 m in depth and 0.45 m to 0.6 m in width. The width of the edge beam is adjusted to iron out the edge stresses. One method is to have a foundation of compacted granular fill of about 0.3 m above the ground level extending 1 m all around the tank, and a 50 mm asphalt paving extending to 0.7 m beyond the tank. This can act as a flexible foundation for these tanks (Fig. 8.7). Alternatively a thin concrete slab may be used above the ground fill. In order to reduce settlement due to working loads these tanks can be preloaded with water before they are commissioned.

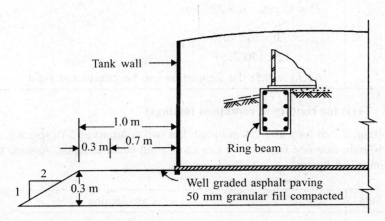

Fig. 8.7 Typical flexible foundation for liquid storage tanks.

8.15 SUMMARY

Analysis of raft foundation is a very complex soil–structure interaction problem as it is very difficult to estimate the soil parameters involved. Any practical method should consider not only the contact pressures but also the long and short term settlements that can be produced in the structure [8]. In important cases, trial must be made for a range of values rather than one single soil characteristic. The exact points of maximum and minimum moments and points of contraflexure are impossible to predict. It is therefore very important that the detailing of steel we use should conform to the standard practice of detailing of reinforcements recommended for rafts. In general, reinforcements are provided both at the top and bottom layers in both directions and the amount should not be less than 0.5 percent of the section in each layer.

EXAMPLE 8.1 (Test for rigidity of footings)

A square isolated footing is 2.25 m in size and its depth is 400 mm. Check whether it will act as a rigid footing in a soil with $E_s = 150$ kg/cm^2. Assume $E_c = 20 \times 10^4$ kg/cm^2.

Ref.	Step	Calculations
Sec. 8.7.1	1	*Determine rigidity factor K_r* $$K_r = \frac{E_c D^3}{12 E_s B^3}$$ $E_c = 20 \times 10^4$ kg/cm^2; $E_s = 150$ kg/cm^2; $\dfrac{E_c}{E_s} = 1333$ $D = 40$ cm; $B = 225$ cm $$K_r = \frac{20 \times 10^4 (40)^3}{12 \times 150 (225)^3} = 0.62$$ As $K_r > 0.5$; the foundation can be considered rigid.

EXAMPLE 8.2 (Test for rigidity of combined footings)

A combined footing, 5.7 m long and 2.4 m broad, has two columns at 5 m spacing. If the depth of the footing is 750 mm, examine whether we can adopt rigid beam analysis. Assume the modulus of subgrade reaction is 2.5 kg/cm^3.

Ref.	Step	Calculations
Sec. 8.7.2	1	*Calculate the elastic length* $L_e = \left(\dfrac{1}{\lambda} \right)$ $\dfrac{1}{\lambda} = L_e = \left[\dfrac{4EI}{KB} \right]^{1/4}$ (elastic length); Column spacing = 5 m $E_c = 20 \times 10^4$ kg/cm^2; $\dfrac{I}{B} = \dfrac{1 \times (75)^3}{12} = 3.52 \times 10^4$ per unit width $k = 2.5$ kg/cm^3 $L_e = \left(\dfrac{4 \times 20 \times 10^4 \times 3.52 \times 10^4}{2.5} \right)^{1/4} = 325$ cm $= 3.25$ m $= 1/\lambda$ $\lambda L_B = L_B / L_e$ $\dfrac{L_B}{L_e} = \dfrac{5.0}{3.25} = 1.53$
Fig. 8.4		As $\lambda L_B = 1.53 < 1.75$, the combined footing can be designed by rigid beam theory.

EXAMPLE 8.3 **(Estimation of bearing capacity of raft in sand from SPT values)**

Determine the safe bearing capacity of a raft in sand of unit weight 20 kN/m³ with an average corrected SPT value of 18. Assume the depth of the foundation is 1.5 m and the breadth is 6 m. A maximum settlement of 40 mm can be allowed for the raft. Assume water level is at 3 m below ground level.

Ref.	Step	Calculations
	1	**Method 1**
		From chart for bearing capacity for footings
		Find bearing capacity for footing for 25 mm settlement
		$$\frac{D_f}{B} = \frac{1.5}{6} = 0.25$$
		For $N = 18$, Settlement = 25 mm
		Allowable pressure = 200 kN/m²
	2	*Interpolate for* 40 mm *settlement for footing*
		$$q_{40} = q_{25}\left(\frac{40}{25}\right) = \frac{200 \times 40}{25} = 320 \text{ kN/m}^2$$
		Method 2
	1	*Use formula directly for B.C. of footing*
		Safe bearing pressure
Eq. (6.12a)		(a) For settlement of 1 mm = $q_1 = 0.42$ N
		Hence for 40 mm, $q_{40} = 0.42 \times 40 \times 18 = 320$ kN/m²
		(b) From shear failure $(FS = 3)$
Eq. (8.1b)		(1) $q_{\text{safe}} = \dfrac{1}{18}\left[6(100 + N^2)DR_q + 2N^2 BR_r\right]$
		(Refer to Fig. 6.5.)
Eq. (6.14a)		$R_q = 1$ and $R_\gamma = 0.5\ (1 + z/B) = 0.5(1 + 1.5/6) = 0.625$
		$$q_{\text{safe}} = \frac{1}{18}\left[6(100 + 18^2) \times 1.5 + 2 \times 18^2 \times 6 \times 0.625\right]$$
		$$= 347 \text{ kN/m}^2$$
	2	*Bearing capacity can be also obtained from I.S. modified bearing capacity factors*
Sec. 1.7.1		Assumed ϕ corresponding to N values $[\phi = 20\ N + 15]$ degrees
Fig. 1.10		$F.S. = 3$; $N = 18$; $\phi = 33°$; $N_q = 17$; $N_r = 13$
Fig. 6.3		$\dfrac{q_{\text{ult}}}{3} = \dfrac{1}{3}\left[\gamma_0 D_1 N_q R_q + 0.5\gamma_1 BN_r R_r\right]$
		$$= \frac{1}{3}[20 \times 1.5 \times 13 \times 1 + 0.5 \times 20 \times 6 \times 13 \times 0.625]$$
		$$= 300 \text{ kN/m}^2 \text{ (approx.)}$$

Step 2 q_{40}	4	*Recommendations* Adopt allowable $q_a = 320$ kN/m² Expected settlement = 40 mm Expected differential settlement = 1/2 that of footing $$= \frac{1}{2} \times \frac{18 \times 40}{25} = 14.4 \text{ mm}$$ *Note:* If we are given another value, say δ mm as *allowable differential settlement* of a raft, then the corresponding expected maximum settlement of the raft footing will be $2 \times \left[\dfrac{25 \times \delta}{18}\right]$ mm.

EXAMPLE 8.4   (Estimation of bearing capacity of raft in clay from SPT value)

Estimate the allowable bearing capacity of a 12 m × 16 m raft in clay, the loading on the raft due to dead and live loads being 50 kN/m². The raft is located at 1.5 m below G.L and the depth of clay extends to a depth of 16 m below the foundation; the material below that depth being dense sand.

The average SPT value of the clay is 6 and the ground water level is at the level of the foundation. Assuming unit weight of soil as 18 kN/m² and that $c_c/(1 + e_0) = 0.03$, estimate the safe bearing capacity and the expected settlement of the raft.

Ref.	Step	Calculations
	1	*Estimate net loading on the raft* Net load = Gross load $- r_0 D$ $= 50 - (18 \times 1.5) = 23$ kN/m²
	2	*Estimate safe bearing capacity from N value* By thumb rule, the safe bearing capacity in tons/sqft = SPT value $q_{safe} = 10N = 10 \times 6 = 60$ kN/m²
Eq. (6.7)	3	*Calculate safe bearing capacity by formulae* $q_{ult} = cN_c s_c d_c + r_0 D N_q s_q d_q$ (general formula) or $q_{ult} = cN_c + r_0 D$ (Skempton's formula) Let us adopt Skempton's N_c $N_c = 5(1 + 0.2 B/L)(1 + 0.2(D/B))$ $\quad = 5(1 + 0.2 \times 14/18)(1 + 0.2 \times 15/14) = 5.8$ Assume unconfined strength = $N/10 = 0.6$ kg/cm² $= q_u$ $q_u = 60$ kN/m²; cohesion = $60/2 = 30$ kN/m Net $q_{ult} = cN_c = 30 \times 5.8 = 174$ kN/m² $q_{safe} = (F.S = 3) = 174/3 = 58$ kN/m² (nearly equal to step 2) (To this we may add the weight of soil excavated.)

	4	*Estimate the expected total settlement*
Chapter 1		$$\Delta = \frac{c_c}{1 + e_0} H \log \frac{p_0 + \Delta p}{p_0}$$
		p_0 at mid depth (8 m below foundation):
Step 1		$p_0 = (18 \times 1.5) + (18 - 10) \times 8 = 91 \text{ kN/m}^2$
		ΔP at mid, depth with 1:2 dispersion ($q = 23 \text{ kN/m}^2$)
		$$\Delta P = \frac{23 \times 12 \times 16}{(12 + 8)(16 + 8)} = 9.2 \text{ kN/m}^2$$
		$$\Delta = \left[0.03 \times 16 \times \log \frac{91 + 9.2}{91} \right] 1000 = 45 \text{ mm}$$
IS 8009		IS 8009 correction factor for rigidity = 0.8 (Sec. 4.4.4)
		IS 8009 correction factor for depth = 1.0 (Sec. 4.2.1)
		IS 8009 correction for pore pressure = 9.7 (Sec. 4.4.3)
		Corrected $\Delta_1 = 45 \times 0.8 \times 0.7 = 25.2 \text{ mm} \simeq 25 \text{ mm}$

EXAMPLE 8.5   (Estimation of bearing capacity of raft in sand from N values)

Estimate the allowable bearing capacity of a raft foundation 13.5 × 9 m in size over a sand deposit with average SPT value of 10. Assume depth of foundation is 1.8 m unit weight soil is 20 kN/m³ and allowable settlement is 25 mm. What is the expected differential settlement?

Note: SPT = 15 corresponds to sand at critical void ratio. Hence sand with SPT 10 to 30 to medium dense sand)

Ref.	Step	Calculations
	1	*Estimate safe bearing capacity from SPT N value*
		Lesser value will be for a square $R_q = 1$; $R_r = 1$
Eq. (6.16c)		$$q_{safe} = \frac{1}{18} \left[5(100 + N^2)D + 3N^2 B \right]$$
		$$= \frac{1}{18}[5(100 + 100)1.8 + 3 \times 100 \times 9]$$
		$$= 250 \text{ kN/m}^2$$
		(Note that the first term is the surcharge effect.)
	2	*Estimate allowable B.C. for 25 mm settlement*
Eq. (6.12a)		$$q_{25} = 34.6(N - 3)\left(\frac{B + 0.3}{2B} \right)^2 \text{ kN/m}^2$$
		$$= 34.6(10 - 3)\left(\frac{9 + 0.3}{18} \right)^2 = 64.7 \text{ kN/m}^2$$
		$q_{gross} = 64.7 + 1.8 \times 20 = 100 \text{ kN/m}^2$

Ref.	Step	
	3	*Select lesser of the two* Allowable bearing capacity = 100 kN/m^2
Eq. (6.13) Fig. 6.9	4	*Check with empirical values* (a) *From formula* Allowable B.C = q_{25} = 10.5 N for width > 1 m $\qquad\qquad$ = 10.5 × 10 = 105 kN/m^2 (b) *Peck, Hansen, Thornburn graph* $\dfrac{D}{B} = \dfrac{1.8}{9} = 0.2$; For N = 10; q_a = 110 kN/m^2 The empirical values are in agreement.
	5	*Estimate the differential settlement* For a footing, differential settlement = 18 mm Expected raft differential settlement = 1/2 of footing = 9 mm

EXAMPLE 8.6   (Bearing capacity of raft in sand based on allowable settlement in sand)

A reinforced concrete raft is to be constructed as a sand deposit. The intensity of loading of total load is 190 kN/m^2 and the raft is placed 1.5 m below ground level. Assuming the unit weight of sand is 20 kN/m^3 estimate the minimum SPT value necessary to support the above loading so that the differential *settlement does not exceed 9 mm.* Assume breadth of raft as 6 m.

Ref.	Step	Calculations
Sec. 8.1.1	1	*Find allowable equivalent total settlement for a footing* Footing differential settlement = 2 × raft settlement $\qquad\qquad\qquad\qquad$ = 2 × 9 = 18 mm For ($\delta\Delta$) = 18 mm; Δ = 25 mm (for a footing) Hence find N for 25 mm on footings.
	2	*Find load on raft level* Net load = 190 – 30 = 160 kN/m^2
Fig. 6.9	3	*Find from Fig. 6.9 required N for 160 kN/m^2 and Δ = 25* mm With D/B = $\dfrac{1.5}{6}$ = 0.25, required N = 15 (SPT)
	4	*Find N required from empirical formula for Δ = 25* mm q_a = 10.5 N for B > 1 m For 160 = 10.5 N, value of N = 15 (SPT)
	5	*Recommendation* The minimum SPT N value required = 15 (However, in an actual case study of this problem, the immediate settlement for the above conditions was only 30% of the theoretically calculated settlement for the N value and the settlement continued over a long period.) [8].

EXAMPLE 8.7   (Bearing capacity of raft in $C - \phi$ soils)

Find the allowable bearing capacity of a raft in saturated clay with its base at a depth of 1.5 m below ground level. The clay has a unit weight of 20 kN/m³. In the drained test $c' = 10$ kN/m² and $\phi' = 20$ and in the undrained test $q_u = 80$ kN/m² and $\phi = 0$. The water level is 1 m below the ground level, and $B = 4$ m.

Ref.	Step	Calculations
		Procedure 1. The bearing capacity in clays of rafts is the same as that of footings (effects of large size and allowable larger settlements do not affect the results). We use the bearing capacity factors.
		Separate calculations should be made for settlement due to consolidation to limit the settlement. Hence the following calculations are made on the assumption that the total settlement will be less than
		2. Bearing capacity based on drained conditions will be always higher than that in undrained conditions. Hence we need usually consider only the undrained condition. In the following procedure both are considered.
	1	*Calculate B.C under undrained condition*
		Undrained $q_{ult} = N_c c + \gamma D$
		$= (5.14 \times 40) + (20 \text{ kN for 1 m } + 10 \text{ kN for next 0.5 m})$
		$= 5.14 \times 40 + 25 = (206 + 25) \text{ kN/m}^2$
	2	*Calculate BC for drained state*
		Drained q_{ult} = Find factors for $\phi' = 20°$ and $c' = 10$ kN/m²
		$q_{ult} = c'N_c + qN_q + 0.5\gamma BN_\gamma$
		$= (10 \times 14.8) + (25 \times 6.4) + (0.5 \times 10 \times 4 \times 5.4)$
		$= 416$ kN/m² This being very high, adopter lower value.
	3	*Assuming undrained condition, find BC with FS = 2*
		No *FS* need to be applied for surcharge.
		$q_{safe} = \dfrac{206}{2} + 25 = 128 \text{ kN/m}^2$

EXAMPLE 8.8   (Stresses in concrete rafts under storage tanks)

A 12.2 m diameter oil tank is supported on a thick bed of clay by a concrete slab 10 cm thick. It has been found that under a full tank load, the differential settlement between centre and edge will be approximately 0.10 m. Estimate the stress produced in the concrete on account of differential settlement due to consolidation of the clay assuming a dish like settlement.

Ref.	Step	Calculations
Eq. (8.4)	1	*Find the stress created by the curvature produced by differential settlement (assume as a plate)* $$f = \frac{4E\delta t}{L^2}$$ Assume $E = 20 \times 10^4$ kg/cm^2 = 20×10^6 kN/m^2 $\delta = 0.10$ m; $t = 0.10$ m $$f = \frac{4 \times 20 \times 10^6 \times 0.1 \times 0.1}{(12.2)^2} = 5375 \text{ kN/m}^2 = 54 \text{ kg/cm}^2$$ (In the above calculation, plate action has not been taken into account.) A tension of 54 kg/cm^2 is too high for concrete unless the section is reinforced. Also the differential settlement is of the same order as the thickness of the slab so that membrane tension will be also present.
Eq. (8.4)	2	*Find radius of curvature of bending in one plane* $$R = \frac{L^2}{8\delta} = \frac{(12.2)^2}{8 \times 0.1} = 186 \text{ m}$$ $$\frac{t}{R} = \frac{0.1 \times 100}{186} = 0.054\%$$ Thickness = 0.054% radius (plate can be considered as thin) Generally, tension in concrete slabs should not exceed the maximum allowable value to avoid excessive cracking.

EXAMPLE 8.9 (Elemental design of rafts)

For the design of a raft 80 cm thick in clay soil, it is divided into strips. One of the strips is 3.3 m wide and 22 m in length with a number of columns at equal spacings. Determine (a) conditions under which this strip can be designed as a rigid strip; (b) conditions where ACI method can be used. The allowable net bearing capacity of the soil is assumed to be 5 t/m^2 (50 kN/m^2). (Assume $q_u = 2.4 \times$ net bearing capacity.)

Ref.	Step	Calculations
Sec. 1.11.1 Table 1.8	1	*Estimate value of modulus of subgrade reaction (clay soil)* $q_u = 2.4 \times 50 = 120$ kN/m^2 $k = 120\, q_u = 120 \times 50 = 6000$ kN/m^2; $I = Bd^3/12$
	2	*Find elastic length $(1/\lambda)$ of strip $(E_c = 20 \times 10^6$ kN/m$^2)$,* $$\left(\frac{1}{\lambda}\right) = L_e = \left(\frac{4EI}{Bk}\right)^{1/4} = \left[\frac{4EB \times (0.8)^3}{12 \times B \times k}\right]^{1/4} = \left[\frac{4E \times (0.8)^3}{12 \times k}\right]^{1/4}$$

	3	$L_e = \left(\dfrac{4 \times 20 \times 10^6 \, (0.8)^3}{12 \times 6 \times 10^3} \right)^{1/4} = 4.8 \text{ m}$; Column spacing $= L$ *(a) Condition for strip to be classified as rigid* $\lambda_L \not> 1.75$ Spacing of column $L \not> 1.75 L_e \not> 8.4$ m
Appendix B	4	*(b) Conditions for ACI method to be used* $L \not< 1.75 L_e$ and $\not> 3.5 L_e = 3.5 \times 4.8 = 16.8$ m Spacing not less than 8.4 m and not more than 16.8 m, we can use ACI approximate method. If the mat is considered as very flexible, we use Hetenyi's curves (given in Appendix C).

EXAMPLE 8.10 **(Design of mat foundation of uniform thickness)**

A mat of uniform thickness for an eight storey residential block has a column layout as shown in Fig. 8.6. Explain suitable design methods for the raft foundation [5].

Ref.	Step	Calculations
		The mat should be first planned so that *CG* of loads and that of mat should more or less coincide. **Method 1: Considering raft as a whole** Ideally the raft should be first designed as a flexible plate supported on elastic foundation. However due to limitation of data regarding soil properties as well as computational facilities next best solution can be obtained by assuming Winkler model. If a programme like SAP IV is available a finite element solution can be obtained. For this purpose the raft can be divided into convenient elements as shown in Fig. 8.6a. **Method 2: Elemental analysis** The design can be further simplified by considering the raft as a plate, split into a number of *beams on elastic foundation*. As explained in Section 8.9.1 the "elemental analysis" is made as follows. Refer Fig. 8.6b.
Sec. 8.9.1	1	*Find depth by punching shear consideration*
	2	*Consider the whole raft as a beam with columns lumped together on elastic foundation in the X-direction—find roughly steel required*
	3	*Repeat analysis in the Y-direction*
	4	*Cut the raft in the X-direction into convenient strips. In the given case it can be divided into four strips as shown in Fig. 8.6b*
	5	*Repeat step 4 in the Y-direction. The raft is divided into five convenient strips as shown in Fig. 8.6b*
	6	*Compare the quantities of steel required in steps 2 and 4 and also in steps 3 and 5 and arrive at a suitable distribution of steel*
	7	*Check for minimum steel. There should be at least 0.5% steel at top and bottom in both directions in each strip.*

EXAMPLE 8.11 (Design of beam and slab rafts)

A beam and slab raft has to be designed for an office building. Explain how the *elemental design* of the raft can be made.

Ref.	Step	Calculations
Sec. 8.8		**Method 1: Elemental analysis by IS456 – 2002** Here, the CG of loads and raft should coincide. *Conventional analysis* is to first design the slab *assuming uniform distribution of load.* [Check by method of coefficients whether the beams are rigid or flexible.] Then design the beams as T beams on rigid or on elastic foundation as the case may be.
		Method 2: Two-way slab analysis by ACI method for flat slabs Divide the raft into strips consisting of slabs with beams in X and Y directions. Check the rigidity of these beams. If they are rigid use conventional method of flat slab analysis. If they are flexible, use the Winkler model solution. Distribute steel as per convention. A more refined solution will be to consider the whole raft based on the Winkler model foundation and use computer program based on the finite element method.
		Method 3: More advanced methods The most refined method is to treat the whole raft as on an elastic half-space. (However, the effort, time and cost may not yield better results than the approximate methods above except in special situations).

REFERENCES

[1] IS 2950 (Part I) 1981, *Code of Practices for Design and Construction of Raft Foundation* (Second revision), Bureau of Indian Standards, New Delhi.

[2] Terzaghi, K. and Peck, R.B., *Soil Mechanics in Engineering Practice*, John Wiley & Sons, 1950.

[3] Winterkorn, H.F. and Fang, H.Y., *Foundation Engineering Handbook* (Chapter on Mat Foundation), Van Nostrand Reinhold, New York, 1970.

[4] Varghese, P.C., *Advanced Reinforced Concrete Design*, Prentice-Hall of India, New Delhi, 2001.

[5] Chandra Gupta, S., *Raft Foundations—Design and Analysis with Practical Approach*, New Age International, New Delhi, 1997.

[6] Hemsley, J.A., *Elastic Analysis of Raft Foundations*, Thomas Telford, London, 1998.

[7] Bowles, T.E., *Foundation Analysis and Design* (International Edition), McGraw-Hill, Singapore, 1988.

[8] *Proceedings of Conference on Settlement of Structures.* British Geotechnical Society, Pentech Press, London, 1975.

9

Load Carrying Capacity of Piles by Static Formulae

9.1 INTRODUCTION

Piles are structural members used to transmit surface loads to deeper layers. These foundations are classified as deep foundations and are used for one or more of the following purposes:

1. To carry loads which are too heavy to be supported by a shallow foundation. The loads are to be transferred to deeper, stronger and less compressible strata or over a larger depth of the foundation soil as in foundations of tall buildings.
2. To carry part of the load to deeper soil for reducing the settlement as in piled raft foundations.
3. To carry horizontal loads as in bridge abutments or retaining walls and also to increase the stability of tall buildings. Inclined piles are also used to carry inclined loads with horizontal force components.
4. To withstand uplift forces in foundations as in expansive soils and floating foundations.
5. To avoid loss of support by scour as in bridges.
6. To produce large differential settlement in situations where there are large variations of column loads.
7. To compact foundation material such as loose sands.

This chapter is devoted to the theoretical estimation of the ultimate capacity of piles from properties of the soil strata where the piles are installed. However field loading tests should be always carried out whenever possible especially in large projects to check these theoretical values against actual field capacities.

9.2 TYPES OF PILES

Concrete piles are most commonly used in India while steel piles are popular in the U.S.A. Concrete piles are commonly classified on the basis of various criteria as follows.

Piles may be classified on the basis of their size (diameter). Piles larger than 600 mm in diameter are called *large diameter piles*. In India, piles larger than one meter in diameter are commonly used for bridges. Sizes 300 to 600 mm are called normal or small diameter piles. Piles of 150 to 250 mm in diameter are called mini piles while those below 150 mm diameter are classified as micro piles.

On the basis of the method of installation, piles can also classified as driven cast in-situ, bored cast in-situ, precast driven or as precast piles driven in pre-bored holes.

Piles are classified as follows depending on their action (that is, the purpose they are intended to serve).

- Displacement piles (driven piles)
- Non-displacement piles (bored piles)
- Small displacement piles (driven steel *H* pile)

9.3 COMMONLY USED SIZES — STRUCTURAL CAPACITY

The more commonly used pile sizes are the following:

- The bored cast in-situ piles are of 400, 450, 500, 600, 750, 800, 900, 1000, 1100, 1200 up to 2000 mm diameters.
- R.C piles less than 500 mm in diameter and up to 16 m in length are commonly used as precast piles. For large length special piles like prestressed concrete piles or segmental piles, special driving equipment are necessary. Cast in-place piles are usually circular while precast piles can be circular, square or hexagonal in shape.

A rough idea of the size of the concrete pile to carry a given load can be obtained from the rule that its maximum working *structural capacity is calculated at* $0.25 f_{ck}$ (say, 5N/mm^2) on the area of the pile. Thus, a 350 mm solid concrete pile of area 960 cm^2 can allow a working load up to 96000 × 5(N), that is, 480 kN. In prestressed concrete piles with M50 concrete, stress up to 11 N/mm^2 can be allowed under working load conditions. Hence, a hollow spun prestressed concrete pile of 350 external and 220 mm internal diameters with area 582 cm^2 can take a load up to 58200 × 11(N) = 640 kN.

9.4 BARRETTE FOUNDATIONS

Where diaphragm wall machines are available, wall-like under ground structures, which can be of T, H. or cruciform in shape can be formed to carry loads instead of the classical piles. These structures are called Barrette foundations (Fig. 9.1). They can also be considered as bored piles. Such constructions are nowadays used extensively, especially in crowded cities.

Fig. 9.1   Barrette foundations made by diaphragm walling machine.

9.5 IS CODES ON PILES

The specification for the four types of commonly used concrete piles are covered by Indian Standard IS 2911 (Second revision) [1] under the following heads:

1. Driven cast in-place (displacement) piles—Section 1
2. Bored cast in-situ (non-displacement) piles—Section 2

3. Pre-cast driven (displacement) piles—Section 3

4. Pre-cast piles driven in pre-bored (non-displacement) piles—Section 4.

In addition, the following Indian Standards also pertain to pile design and construction:

IS 2911 Part II—Timber piles

IS 2911 Part III—Under reamed piles

IS 2911 Part IV—Load tests on piles.

9.6 FACTORS AFFECTING CHOICE OF TYPE OF PILE

The following are some of the important factors that affect the choice between precast driven, driven cast in-situ, and bored cast in-situ piles:

1. **Disturbance of nearby old structures.** Vibrations are caused during pile driving.

2. **Ground heave and pile heave.** Both of these can happen as described in Section 9.6.1 below.

3. **Sensitivity of soil strata.** If soil is sensitive, it breaks up during pile driving. Under these conditions, steel H bearing piles have been found to be preferable.

4. **Length and size of pile.** Precast R.C driven piles are small in size and are usually of length up to 16 m and size less than 550 mm. Bored piles can be taken very deep provided they are reasonably large. They can also be of large diameters.

5. **Ground surface condition before operations.** For any pile driving operation, the equipment should be able to move freely to and fro at the site.

6. **Ground surface condition after piling.** The finishing level of bored cast in-place piles can be easily controlled even below ground level. With precast driven piles (with varying depth of driving) piles will be projecting above the ground after the set is reached.

7. **Time taken for piling.** This is a very important factor in many projects. Driven precast and cast in-situ piles, if properly organised, can be more quickly executed than bored cast in-place piles. However if ground heave is expected, *driven cast in-place piles* will pose problems involving the integrity of the pile.

8. **Loss of ground and over-break.** With sandy fills and very soft silty clay layers, loss of ground should be expected with driven piles due to consolidation.

9. **Loss of bearing at pile tip.** In bored cast in-place piles, the success in washing the base of the pile depends on the availability of good equipment, workmen and experienced contractors.

10. **Surface water currents.** In sandy areas near large water bodies (like rivers and estuaries where tides are present) subsurface flow channels may exist. In such cases, the concrete in cast in-place piles can be washed out before it sets, thus causing local weakness.

11. **Difficulty in pulling out casing.** In pure sand deposits while using driven cast in-place piles it will be difficult to pull out the casing after concreting. Defects like necking occur in such cases.

12. **Quality of concrete and its capacity to withstand deterioration.** In bad environmental conditions with chlorides and sulphates precast driven piles are superior to cast in-place concrete which needs very good care and supervision in its placement. Many authorities feel that the dumping of concrete especially in driven cast in piles from large height and with the pile reinforcement in place, segregation of concrete cannot be avoided. They discourage the use of driven cast in-situ piles.

skin friction. It is claimed that this can be reduced in precast piles ... However it may also be said that because of larger disturbances ... driven piles produce more negative friction.

... during driving. If the driving is hard, precast driven piles tend ... dy due to driving stresses and at head due to inadequacy of ... gth at the top. These should be carefully looked into.

... or bearing piles *in weathered rock*, bored cast in-place piles ... , socketing of piles can also be carried out. This will increase ... considerably in soft and weathered rock formations. When good rock is ... able at reasonable depths, bored piles taken to rock present the best solution.

16. **Size of pile.** For large diameter piles (1 to 2 m in dia.), bored piles are invariably used today for bridges in India. Bored cast in-place piles are the obvious choice under such situations.

9.6.1 Ground Heave and Pile Heave in Displacement Piles

Driven piles are displacement piles and bored piles are replacement piles. When precast driven piles or driven cast in-place piles are installed in groups in soft clays (which can occur near about the ground level to shallow depths) a volume of soil equal to the volume of the penetration of the pile has to be displaced by the pile. In situations where the pore pressure developed cannot be dissipated quickly there will be no volume change in the clay. This makes the soil to heave up. (This is called ground heave.) This, in turn exerts an upward force on those piles that have already been installed a little earlier than the pile being driven causing them to rise up. (This is called pile heave.) Even though the order of driving and spacing of the group can to some extent mitigate the above effects it is difficult to prevent it completely. Selection of bored cast in-situ piles that do not produce such heave or use of small displacement steel piles are suitable in such cases. All precast piles that come up due to heave have to be re-driven after the group is completed to get the final set. Bored cast in-place piles do not pose this problem.

As the above heaving can also cause lateral displacement, this upward heaving and lateral displacements can considerably damage the freshly placed green concrete in driven cast in-situ piles. The method to predict the above situation should be based on past experience and an examination of the soil conditions at site. Saturated soft clays with very low permeability of the order of 10^{-6} cm/sec and low shear strength that are found not far from the ground level should be carefully analysed for this phenomenon when driven piles are contemplated for the site. A number of projects in which driven cast in-place piles were used without taking the above facts into account have incurred large expenses for repair of the damaged piles and also considerable delay in the execution of the projects.

9.7 LOAD CARRYING CAPACITY

At present, the following three methods are used to estimate the load bearing capacity of piles:

1. The *static method* based on soil properties for all types of piles.
2. The *dynamic method* using pile-driving formulae based on the resistance observed in the field in driving the piles for driven piles.
3. The *wave equation method* for driven piles. (Both the theoretical method and case method using field values are used.) IS 2911 incorporates only the first two methods and in this chapter we will deal with the static method. The dynamic methods are discussed in

Chapter 10. It is also to be noted that piles are generally considered and designed as a short column even if it is of very long length when they are embedded in soils with undrained shear strength of not less than 0.1 kg/cm². The points of inflection for calculation of effective length is given by IS 2911 as follows.

9.8 EFFECTIVE LENGTH—POINT OF INFLECTION

If the pile is projecting free above the ground level, the following criteria can be used to fund the point of inflection or contraflexure to find effective length [IS 2911 part I/sec 1 1999 cl 6.5.1]:

1. If the ground is firm, the depth of PI is taken as 1/10 the projecting pile length or 1m subject to a minimum of 3D (B.S. Code CP 2004 recommends it as 1.5 m).

2. If the top embedded stratum is soft below 0.1 kg/cm² in undrained shear strength, the depth of point of inflection is to be taken as one-half the, depth of penetration but not more than 10D. or 3 m, whichever is less.

3. If the stratum is liquid, mud is to be treated as water.

4. If the top end is fixed, both in position and in direction, the upper point of inflection may be taken as one-fourth the exposed length below the top of the pile.

9.9 HISTORIC DEVELOPMENT OF STATIC METHOD

The static method to determine the load carrying capacity of piles uses the simple principle that the ultimate carrying capacity of the pile is the sum of the ultimate bearing capacity of the base or toe (undergoing base failure) and the carrying capacity of the stem in friction in sands or adhesion in clays. The theory for calculation of both these quantities were developed over a period of time in various stages as follows:

Calculation of base resistance. It was only as late as 1943 that Terzaghi derived his dimensionless bearing capacity factors N_c, N_γ and N_q representing the effects of cohesion, the soil weight and the surcharge respectively for shallow foundations of depth less than 4 to 5 times the breadth of the foundations as shown in Fig. 9.2. The failure plane meets the surface of the ground away from the edge of the foundation in footings. However, Terzaghi's theory was found to grossly underestimate the strength of deep foundations.

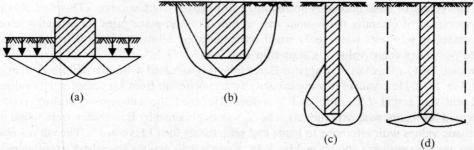

Fig. 9.2 **Modes of failure of foundations: (a) Terzaghi's theory for shallow foundations; (b) Meyerhof's theory for intermediate depths; (c) Meyerhof's theory for deep foundations (piles); (d) Berezantev's assumptions for pile foundations.**

Around 1954 Meyerhof pointed out the deficiencies in the assumptions of Terzaghi's theory for application to deep foundation in cohesionless soils. With increase in depth of foundation, the failure surface tends to change as shown in Fig. 9.2. For deep foundations (depth greater than 10B) Meyerhof assumed a failure surface which curves back with increasing L/D ratio of piles and meets the pile surface as shown in Fig. 9.2e. Consequently, the quantity of soil that affects N_q value is much more than in footings and Meyerhof's N_q values are much larger than those of Terzaghi's.

Settlement of piles. For analysis of settlement of piles we should examine the plots of settlement with base resistance and also settlement with shaft resistance separately which can be obtained by cyclic load tests (see Appendix D).

The shape of the two separate diagrams for base and shaft resistance for long and short piles are shown in Fig. 9.3. We notice that whereas the full mobilisation of shaft resistance takes place with a pile settlement of only 0.5 to 1 per cent of the pile diameter, it requires as much as 5 to 20% of the pile diameter to mobilise the full base capacity of the pile. (This factor depends also on the type of soil. In overconsolidated brittle clays even though a movement of 10 to 20 mm is normally sufficient to produce peak adhesion, this adhesion rapidly decreases with further movement of the pile. Only 35% of the peak value will be available if it is moved to five to ten times the deformation for development of peak resistance.

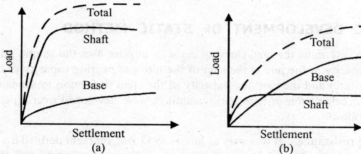

Fig. 9.3   Load-settlement curves for piles in stiff clays: (a) Long piles with long shafts; (b) short underreamed piles.

However, many field tests demonstrated that the settlements at working loads calculated from the ultimate pile capacity using Meyerhof's bearing capacity factors and factor of safety 2 to 3 was much larger than what are usually allowed for piles in practice. This is principally due to the fact that the movement of base necessary to mobilize full capacity is too large. (This fact also points to the importance of cleaning the bottom part of bored cast in-place piles for attaining necessary base resistance in pile tests where only small settlements are allowed.) Various investigators have suggested N_q values for ϕ values as shown in Fig. 9.4a.

Around 1961, a Russian investigator Berezantev [2] assumed a simpler failure mechanism as shown in Fig. 9.2d. He assumed bearing capacity factors different from Meyerhof's. His values take into account the actual L/D ratio and ϕ values. He used the concept of sliding zones and supplemented his theory with experiments. The N_q values obtained by Berezantev were found to give more realistic values with reference to loads and settlements than Meyerhof's. The curves obtained by various investigators are shown in Fig. 9.4a. Berezantev's values have been recommended by many codes. IS 2911 Second Revision uses Berezantev's values for driven piles. For bored piles IS 2911, uses the same values for L/D of 20 up to $\phi = 35°$ while Vesic's curves are used for values greater than $\phi = 35°$. These curves are given in Fig. 9.4b.

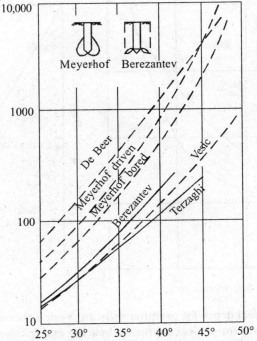

Fig. 9.4a   Bearing capacity factor N_q according to various investigators.

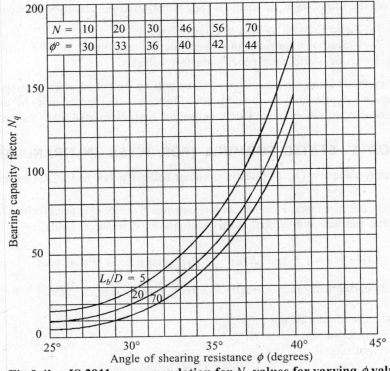

Fig 9.4b   IS 2911 recommendation for N_q values for varying ϕ values.

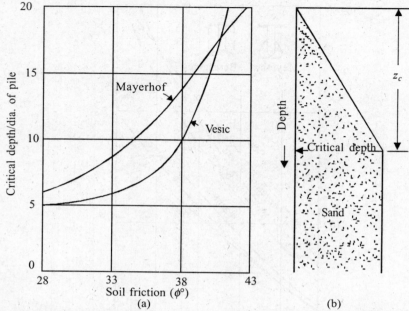

Fig. 9.4c Concept of critical depth for granular soils: (a) Vesic's recommendations; (b) IS 2911 recommendations for critical depths for bearing and friction $15d$ **for** $\phi \le 30°$ **and** $20d$ **for** $\phi \ge 40°$.

IS 2911 gives the following three methods for estimation of pile capacity from soil properties:

1. Method 1—Static formula using c–f values of soil
2. Method 2—Meyerhof's formula for driven piles in sand based on SPT values
3. Method 3—Using static cone penetration test values

The above three methods as applied to different cases will be described under various headings in the following sections. A pile analysis should proceed by computing the capacity by all these three methods. If a reasonable agreement is not found, judgement must be used to select the probable value.

9.10 METHOD 1—STATIC FORMULA (FOR PILES IN GRANULAR SOILS)

The ultimate bearing capacity, Q_u, of piles in granular soils is given in IS 2911 by the following formula:

Q_u = End bearing resistance + skin friction resistance (Symbol Q is used for pile capacity got by static formula and symbol R for those got by dynamic formula.)

$$Q_u = A_P(0.5D\gamma N_\gamma) + A_p(P_D N_q) + \sum_{1}^{n} K_1 P_{D1}\, \tan\delta\, A_{s1} - \text{Wt. of pile} \qquad (9.1)$$

End bearing resistance = small (N_γ effect) + very large (N_q effect) + friction

where

A_P = cross-sectional area of the pile
D = stem diameter of pile
γ = unit weight of soil

N_γ = bearing capacity factor taken for general shear—(IS 6403) Fig. 9.4

N_q = berezantsev's bearing capacity factor—Fig. 9.4 (IS 2911)

P_D = effective overburden pressure (critical depth taken as 15D for $\phi \le 30°$ and 20D for $\phi > 40°$—Indian Railways recommend only 6D for $\phi = 26°$

K_1 = coefficient of earth pressure (Tables 9.1, 9.2 and 9.2A can be used)

P_{D1} = effective overburden pressure of corresponding layer (This effect is controlled by prescribing limiting friction).

δ = angle of wall friction usually taken as $3/4\phi$ of soil.

A_s = surface area of pile.

The first term and the last term are usually small and can be neglected in Eq. (9.1).

$$Q_{ult} = A_p P_D N_q + \sum_1^n K_1 P_{D1} \tan \delta \tag{9.1a}$$

Notes: We should bear in mind certain important points while using the above formula. These are:

1. The zone affecting the base bearing capacity is usually taken as a zone 8D above and 4D below the pile tip. Hence value of ϕ should correspond to that region. The major contribution will by the large value of N_q due to strength of soil near the pile point.

2. Research by Vesic [3] has shown that the *base resistance as well as shaft resistance of* piles in sand first increases rapidly with depth due to the weight of overburden but after a depth called the *critical depth*—of 10 to 20 times the pile diameter depending on the denseness of sand—further increase in capacity is very small. Hence, IS 2911 specifies that P_D should not exceed critical depth as represented by the following conditions.

   (a) critical depth 15D for $\phi \le 30°$

   (b) critical depth 20 D for $\phi \ge 40°$

The values for critical depth got by Vesic and Meyerhof are shown in Fig. 9.4c.

Interpolation may be used for obtaining the intermediate value. Specifications like those of Indian Railways have stipulated critical depth as only 6D in loose sands, 8D in medium sand and 15D in dense sands.

3. Tomlinson [4] recommends that friction in sands should not exceed 110 kN/m^2 (11t/m^2) in straight piles. Taper on pile shaft can increase the friction to a slightly higher value. *A conservative value of* 60 kN/m^2 *is generally recommended as ultimate value in sands* (see Table 9.2).

4. IS 2911 gives the same formula for calculation of the side friction and end bearing of bored cast in-situ, precast driven as well as for the driven cast in-situ piles. However, special mention should be made for the effect of the method of installation on bearing capacity of piles. The following method is commonly used by many designers. The basis of the method is that in the case of medium and loose sands (with SPT values less than 8 to 15) it is known that there will be considerable increase in friction and bearing capacity due to densification when pre-cast piles are driven into such stratum. Accordingly corrections are recommended seperately for end resistance and side friction as described next.

5. The following correction for end resistance in cohesionless soils (N_q values) for types of installation is recommended. If internal friction prior to installation of pile of the soil is ϕ, the following corrections, are to be made in ϕ for calculation of N_q.

(a) For driven cast in-situ piles, value of φ is kept unchanged.

(b) For driven precast piles the value φ is changed to (φ + 40)/2 to take care of compaction due to pile driving. (Thus, if for φ = 30°, φ is taken as 35° for driven piles).

(c) For bored cast in-situ piles where the bottom of the hole is cleaned thoroughly by continuous mud circulation, value φ is assumed as unchanged.

(d) For bored cast in-situ piles where continuous mud circulation is not used for cleaning the base, the value of is reduced by 3 to 5 degrees.

6. A correction is recommended for values for K in view of skin friction. $KP_D \tan \delta$ gives the friction component along the shaft. The value of the friction coefficient K for driven and cast in-situ piles can be taken as given in Tables 9.1, 9.2 and 9.2A. In general, K for driven piles is larger than for bored piles as IS recommends a value between 1 and 2 for driven piles and 1 to 1.5 for bored piles. Others assume that $K_0 = (1 - \sin \phi)$ and use the relation K/K_0 in Table 9.2A to find the value of K. The variation of K values with the method of construction of piles is shown in Fig. 9.5. For $\tan \delta$, value of δ is usually taken as 0.75ϕ.

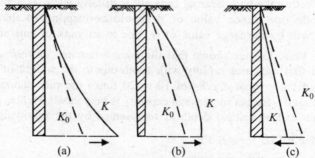

Fig 9.5 Probable values of K with method of installation: (a) Driven circular piles producing outward displacement of soil; (b) driven conical piles producing marked outward displacement; (c) bored piles producing inward displacement of soil.

7. For an end bearing pile in dense sand, a minimum *penetration of 5 times the diameter of the pile into the dense sand* is necessary to develop the full capacity in bearing if that layer is well below the ground level and has ample confining pressure. Meyerhof's formula assumes that full bearing capacity is developed when $L/D = 10$, i.e penetration is ten times the diameter.

8. It is also interesting to note that according to Berezantev, the N_q value depends on the L/D value. N_q alues are larger for $L/D = 5$ than $L/D = 20$ (see Fig. 9.4b).

TABLE 9.1 BROMS VALUES FOR K AND δ FOR DIFFERENT PILE MATERIALS IN GRANULAR SOILS

Types of piles	K for driven piles		Angle of wall friction
	Dense; $\phi \geq 40°$	Loose; $\phi \leq 25°$	δ
Concrete	2.0	1.0	0.75ϕ
Steel	1.0	0.5	20°
Timber	2.5	1.5	0.75ϕ

See also Table 9.2 for values for types of installation.

TABLE 9.2 VARIATION OF BASE AND SHAFT RESISTANCE OF CONCRETE PILES WITH METHOD OF INSTALLATION IN GRANULAR SOILS

Soil density (IS 2911)	Critical depth ratio of driven pile	K Values		N_q Values	
		Pre-cast driven pile	Cast in-situ piles	Pre-cast driven pile	Cast in-situ piles
Dense ($\phi > 40°$)	20	2.0	1.5		
Medium	(Intermediate)	1.5	1.3	As mentioned in Sec. 9.10 item 5	
Loose $\phi \leq 25$ to $30°$	15	1.0	1.0		

Notes: The following points are important and may be borne in mind:

1. A conservative value of $K = 1$ can be assumed for all piles except for piles with steel liners, where $K = 0.7$ can be assumed. *The ultimate frictional resistance should preferably be restricted to 6 t/m^2 in sands.*
2. IS 2911—Part 1 Sec. 2 states that for bored piles in loose to medium sands, K value of 1 to 1.5 can be used.
3. IS 2911 also states that the ultimate base resistance in sand should be restricted to a maximum value of 150 kg/cm^2 (1500 t/m^2) for precast driven piles and 100 to 110 kg/cm^2 (1000 to 1100 t/m^2) for cast in-situ piles.

TABLE 9.2A DETERMINATION OF K FOR DIFFERENT METHODS OF INSTALLATION OF PILES [Ref. 4]

Method of installation	K/K_0*
Driven large displacement piles (Concrete piles)	1 to 2
Driven small displacement piles (Steel H piles)	0.75 to 1.75
Bored cast in-situ piles	0.7 to 1
Jetted piles	0.5 to 0.7

*$K_0 = (1 - \sin \phi)$ = coefficient of earth pressure at rest.

9.10.1 Structural Capacity of Piles

As discussed in Sec. 11.6.1 the working load on the pile should not exceed its structural capacity given by the following formula:

$$Q_{st} = (0.25 f_{ck}) A_c$$

where

f_{ck} = cube strength of concrete
A_c = area of cross section of concrete pile

9.11 METHOD 1—STATIC FORMULA (FOR COHESIVE SOILS)

The ultimate bearing capacity, Q_u of piles in cohesive soils is given by the following formula (IS 2911 part 1 Sec. 3):

$$Q_u = \text{end bearing resistance } Q_p + \text{skin friction resistance } Q_s.$$

$$Q_u = A_P N_c c_p + \sum_{i=1}^{n} \alpha_i c_i A_{si}$$ (9.2)

where

N_c = bearing capacity factor in clays which is taken as 9 (see Skempton's curve in Chapter 6)

c_p = average cohesion at pile toe

α_i = adhesion factor

c_i = average cohesion of the ith layer on the side of the pile

A_{si} = surface area of pile stem in the ith layer.

$\alpha_i c_i$ = adhesion between shaft of pile and clay.

It should be remembered that the average cohesion at pile toe can be different from the values of cohesion along the length of the pile. According to IS 2911, the differences between precast driven and cast in-situ piles can be accounted for by multiplying α value by a factor equal to 0.8 for cast in-situ piles. The adhesion factor recommended by some of the other investigators is shown in Fig. 9.6. Field observations show that for concrete piles the ultimate adhesion in clay does not exceed 7 t/m². Very stiff clay has cohesion of the order of 15 t/m² but very small α values of the order of 0.25 so that the ultimate adhesion can be as low as 3.75 t/m².

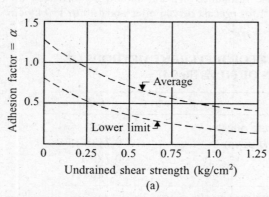

(a)

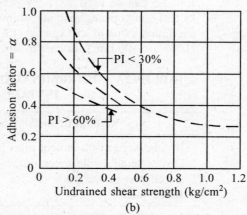

(b)

Fig. 9.6   Adhesion factors for clays for driven piles: (a) According to Tomlinson; (b) according to Flaate.

9.11.1   Adhesion Factor α

Bowles has given three methods (α, β and γ methods) to estimate skin friction. As it is difficult to estimate the various quantities involved, simple methods of estimation are considered good enough for a fair estimation of skin friction.

The shaft resistance of piles in clay depends on the cohesion of the clay and its adhesion factor α, the adhesion being αc. Soft clays have a better adhesion factor than hard or brittle clays. IS recommends the following methods to estimate the adhesion factor α for driven piles.

Method 1: *From empirical value of α*

The values of α recommended by IS 2911 Part I Section 3 Clause B2 for driven piles for various soils are given in Table 9.3.

TABLE 9.3 ADHESION FACTOR FOR CLAYS, FOR PRECAST DRIVEN PILES IN CLAYS

SPT values of clays N	Consistency	Range of cohesion		Adhesion factor α	
		(kN/m^2)	(kg/cm^2)	Driven	Bored
< 4	Soft to very soft	1 to 25	0.01–0.25	> 1.0	Reduce the
4 to 8	Medium stiff	25 to 50	0.25–0.5	0.7–0.4	driven
8 to 15	Stiff	50 to 100	0.5–1.0	0.4–0.3	values by
≥ 15	Stiff to hard	≥ 100	> 1.0	0.3–0.25	factor 0.8

Notes: 1. The value of c for clays is $N/16$ to $N/20$ kg/cm^2 (approximately) as derived from N values.
2. The value of α shall be limited to 0.5 for sensitive clays.
3. The value of α may be more than 0.7 in clays overlain by sand.

Method 2: *From field c/σ_v values* (IS 2911 Part 1 Sec. 2 Bored piles).

IS 2911 has introduced Tomlinson's recommendations for adhesion factor to be computed from field values of c/σ_v (cohesion–vertical pressure ratio, represented as ψ) as follows [4]. For normally consolidated clays, the value of c/σ_v can be assumed to range from 0.2 to 0.3, so that $(c/\sigma_v)^{1/2}$ can be assumed to have a mean value of 0.5. If the value of c/σ_v ($= \psi$) is greater than 0.5, the clay can be assumed to be overconsolidated.

On the basis of the above assumption, the following α values are recommended by IS 2911 (Sec. 2)

If $\psi \le 1$, then
$$\alpha = \frac{0.5}{(c/\sigma_v)^{1/2}} = 0.5\,\psi^{-0.5}, \text{ but } \not> 1. \tag{9.3}$$

If $\psi > 1$, then
$$\alpha = 0.5\,\psi^{-0.25}, \text{ but } \not< 0.5 \text{ and } \not> 1. \tag{9.4}$$

For bored piles the value of α as obtained above is to be multiplied by 0.8.

9.11.2 Correction for Pile Length as Affecting Adhesion in Clays (F)

Tomlinson [4] has explained that research in offshore piles has shown that the two important factors that influence adhesion in heavily loaded piles driven to deep penetration in clays are the following:

1. The overconsolidation ratio of the soil as already explained.

2. The slenderness or aspect ratio (also called length L/B ratio)

The effect of the length factor F has been found to be as follows:

$$F = 1 \quad \text{for} \quad L/B \le 50$$
$$F = 0.7 \quad \text{for} \quad L/B \ge 120$$

Intermediate values can be assumed to be linear. The following formula will give the adhesion between shaft of pile and clay in terms of the two factors, α and F.

$$Q_i = (\alpha F c) A_{si} \tag{9.5}$$

9.12 CAPACITY OF PILES IN $c-\phi$ SOILS BY STATIC FORMULA

IS 2911 does not recommend any specific static formula for the load carrying capacity of piles in soils with $c - \phi$ values. Using the fundamental soil properties with such soils, it is customary to use one of the following methods.

Method 1: If the soil has small value of ϕ treat it as a purely cohesive soil. Similarly if the cohesion is small and ϕ is large than treat the soil as being cohesionless.

Method 2: Where the soil has large values of both c and ϕ (as for a true $c - \phi$ soil), we should use the conservative Terzaghi's bearing capacity factors to determine the load carrying capacity. This formula is expressed as follows.

$$Q_b = A_P \left[cN_c + \sigma_{vb}N_q + 0.5\gamma DN_\gamma \right] + \sum A_s (\alpha c + K\sigma_v \tan \phi) \tag{9.6}$$

where

N_c, N_q, N_γ = Terzaghi's bearing capacity factors

σ_{vb}, σ_v = effective overburden pressure of base and pile shaft, irrespective of the critical depth.

9.12.1 Quick Estimation of Capacity of Individual Piles

A quick estimation of capacity of pile can be made from SPT values using Meyerhof's method described in Section 9.15.

9.13 FACTOR OF SAFETY FOR STATIC FORMULA BASED ON SOIL PROPERTIES

The factor of safety to be used in the static formula should depend on many factors such as the following:

1. Reliability of soil parameters used for calculations
2. The manner in which load is transferred to the soil
3. The importance of the structure
4. Allowable total and differential settlement tolerated by the structure.

IS 2911 recommends a minimum factor of safety of 2.5 for piles founded in soil using reliable soil parameters in static formula. (Factors of safety of 3 are to be used for socketed piles in rock. The factor of safety recommended by IS 2911 when using dynamic formula for estimation of pile capacity is given in Table 10.1 in Chapter 10. When using load tests, a factor of safety of 1.5 to 2.0 is generally specified with respect to the load at allowable deformation.) It may also be noted that there is a practice of giving a smaller factor of safety of 1.5 or even 1 for shaft resistance and a larger factor of safety of say, 3 for end bearing resistance due to the way they are harnessed on loading as shown in Fig. 9.3. The values are shown in Table 9.4.

TABLE 9.4   FACTORS OF SAFETY FOR STATIC FORMULA FOR PILES

Case	Factor of safety
1. On total capacity	2.5
2. On shaft resistance	1.5
3. On base resistance	3.0

Note: For dynamic formula, $FS = 2.5$ for soils and 1.5 for rocks is commonly used.

9.14 LIMITING CAPACITY OF PILES

Safe structural capacity of piles as a structural element. The minimum percentage of steel specified in most cast in-situ piles is less than 0.8 per cent, which is the minimum in R.C. columns. The maximum load carrying capacity as a structural member should therefore be calculated only on the area of concrete. The general I.S specification for allowable average compressive stress in concrete *under working load* of such piles is that it should not exceed 25% of the specified cube strength (subject to a maximum of 5N/mm^2 according to B.S). Where the pile has a permanent steel lining of adequate thickness, the allowable stress in concrete can be suitably increased (In Indian Railways, bored cast in-situ piles for bridges are specified to have steel lining for the full depth below ground level.)

Limiting end bearing resistance in cohesionless soils [4]. As given in Table 9.2 generally a limiting value is prescribed for the base resistance depending on the material at the base. For sands Tomlinson (based on the work of Kamp) recommends it as 1000 t/m^2 to 1500 t/m^2 as shown in Fig. 9.7. IS 2911 specifies that the base resistance of bored piles should not exceed 1100t/m^2 (IS 2911 Part I Sec. 2. Second Revision, Clause C_1)

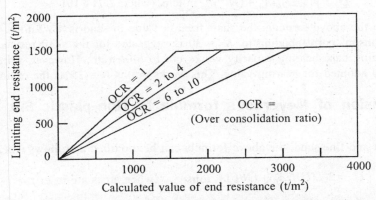

Fig. 9.7 **Limiting values for end resistance in sands. (End resistance calculated from static cone penetrometer tends to be larger than real values.)**

Limiting value of side friction in sand for straight-sided piles. As already stated in Section 9.10, Tomlinson [4] recommends a value of 11 t/m^2 as the maximum value of side friction that can develop in sand with straight-sided piles. But a value of 6 t/m^2 can be taken as a realistic maximum value (see Table 9.2).

Limiting value of adhesion in clays. The limiting values as given in Section 9.11 of 7 t/m^2 can be taken for clays.

9.15 METHOD 2—MEYERHOF'S FORMULA FOR DRIVEN PILES IN SAND BASED ON SPT VALUES

Meyerhof's formula is given in IS 2911 for driven piles in sands. The capacity of piles in sand is to be calculated from results of SPT values of the soil. In 1959, Meyerhof [5] proposed the following formula for the ultimate bearing capacity of driven piles in cohesionless soils. (In this formula the value of N used should be the corrected SPT values.)

$$Q_u = 4N_P A_P + \frac{\bar{N}A_s}{50} \quad \text{(U.S. tons with areas expressed in sq. ft.)}$$

where N_p = SPT value of tip and $\bar{N}$ = average SPT on the region of the shaft.

When A_p and A_s are expressed in square metres, we get the *approximate value in metric tons* (Assume 1 sqm = 10 sq.ft.)

$$Q_u = 4N(10A_p) + \frac{\bar{N}}{50}(10A_s)$$

$$Q_u = 40NA_p + (\bar{N}/5)A_s \text{ tons (where areas } A_p \text{ and } A_s \text{ are in m}^2) \tag{9.7}$$

This formula is valid for piles with L/D equal to or greater than 10. In order to take the effect of lower L/D values also into account, the formula is also expressed (with A_p and A_s in m^2) as follows (IS 2911 – Part I Sec. 1).

$$Q_u = 4(L/D)NA_p + (\bar{N}/5)A_s \text{ in tons (where } L/D \not> 10) \tag{9.7a}$$

According to the above formula, the shaft friction value in sand is $(\bar{N}/5)$t/m^2. However an upper limit of 6 tons/m^2 corresponding to $\bar{N}$ = 30 is suggested for the shaft resistance in sand. Similarly, the limiting base bearing capacity works out to $(40N)$t/m^2. However, a limiting value 1000t/m^2 is usually adopted for bearing value. This works out as N = 25 as the critical value.

9.15.1 Extension of Meyerhof's formula to Non-plastic Silt and Fine Sand

For non-plastic silt and fine sand, the above formula can be modified as follows (IS 2911)

$$Q_u = 3(L/D)NA_p + (\bar{N}/6)A_s \text{ tons} \quad \text{(when areas are in m}^2) \tag{9.8}$$

$$Q_u = 30NA_p + (\bar{N}/6)A_s \text{ tons} \quad \text{for } L/D > 10 \tag{9.8a}$$

where A_p and A_s are in m^2. (This means that bearing is taken as 30 N and friction as $\bar{N}/6$ in silt.)

9.15.2 Meyerhof's Approach Extended to Clay

It should be remembered that Meyerhof proposed his formula for bearing capacity of piles in cohesionless soils only. However, we may assume SPT value N as a measure of the consistency of clays and thus indirectly its cohesion values as $c = N/20$ kg/cm^2 or $N/2$ t/m^2 (see Table 9.3).

Using the relationship 1 kg/cm^2 = 10 t/m^2, we have the following

$$Q_u = 9cA_p + \alpha cA_s = 9\left(\frac{N}{20}\right)(10)A_p + \alpha\left(\frac{\bar{N}}{20}\right)(10)A_s \text{ (tons)}$$

$$= 4.5NA_p + (\bar{N}/2)A_s \text{ metric tons (assuming } \alpha = 1). \tag{9.9}$$

where A_p and A_s are in m^2.

Thus, we may redefine the formula as follows (in metric tons):

(a) *End bearing in:*
   Sand = $40N$ t/m^2 ($\ngtr 1000$ t/m^2)
   Silt = $30N$ t/m^2
   Clay = $4.5N$ t/m^2

(b) *Side friction in:*
   Sand = $\bar{N}/5$ ($\ngtr 6$ t/m^2)
   (For steel H piles in sand $N/10$)
   Silt = $\bar{N}/6$ t/m^2
   Clay = $\bar{N}/6$ ($\ngtr 7$ t/m^2)

Even though IS 2911 has included this formula for design of piles in saturated sand only, many designers use it for a preliminary estimate of pile capacity in all types of soil as shown above.

9.16 METHOD 3 — LOAD CARRYING CAPACITY FROM STATIC CONE PENETRATION TESTS

Static cone penetration test is a miniature pile test to failure. For a long time this method was used in Europe for the analysis of pile capacity. IS 2911 recommends this method when static cone resistance data is available, for the full depth of the soil profile. The end bearing and side friction are calculated separately as follows.

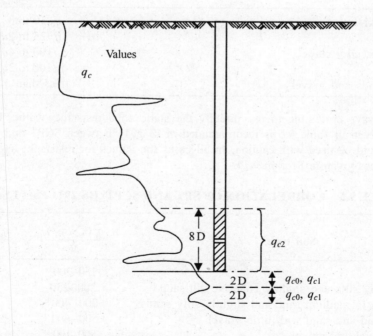

Fig 9.8 IS 2911 specification for detaining ultimate base resistance of piles in sand from static cone penetration test.

Unit end bearing. The ultimate end bearing resistance q_u according to IS 2911 can be taken as follows. (The units will be the same as used for SCPT q_c measured in the field.)

$$q_u = [(q_{c0} + q_{c1})/2 + q_{c2}]/2 \qquad (9.10)$$

where

q_{c0} = average SCPT value for $2D$ below pile toe

q_{c1} = minimum SCPT value for $2D$ below pile toe

q_{c2} = average of the envelope of minimum SCPT value over $8D$ above the toe of the pile.

(The method used in Netherlands is to take the average cone resistance q_{c1} over the depth of four diameters below the pile toe and the average q_{c2} eight pile diameters above the toe and then take average of q_{c1} and q_{c2} as the ultimate base resistance.)

Ultimate skin friction resistance. The approximate values of skin friction can be got from Table 9.5. The units will be the same as the SCPT values are.

Ultimate load carrying capacity. The sum of the ultimate end bearing and side friction values gives us the ultimate capacity of the pile.

TABLE 9.5 ULTIMATE SKIN FRICTION RESISTANCE FROM STATIC CONE TEST VALUES (IS 2911 Part I Sec. 1)

(q_c = Static cone resistance in kN/m^2)

Type of soil	Local side friction
$q_c < 1000$ kN/m^2	$q_c/30$ to $3q_c/30$
Clays	$q_c/25$ to $2q_c/25$
Silty sands, silty clays	$q_c/100$ to $4q_c/100$
Sands	$q_c/100$ to $2q_c/100$
Coarse sands and gravel	less than $q_c/150$

Note: It is always preferable to use directly the static cone resistance value. However rough correlation as given in Table 9.6 is recommended in IS 2911 between SCPT and N values. Such correlations should be used with caution. In all cases the values for resistance should not exceed the limiting values given in Section 9.14.

TABLE 9.6 CORRELATION OF SPT AND SCPT [IS 2911 Part I Sec. 1]

Soil type	$\dfrac{q_c \text{(kN/m}^2)}{N}$	$\dfrac{q_c \text{(kg/cm}^2)}{N}$
Clays	150–200	1.5–2.0
Silts, sandy silts and slightly cohesive silt-sand	200–250	2.0–2.5
Clean fine to medium sand and slightly silty sands	300–400	3.0–4.0
Coarse sand and sand with little gravel	500–600	5.0–6.0
Sandy gravel and gravel	800–100	8.0–10.0

Note: q_c in kg/cm^2 = 1.5 to 10 times N value depending on soil type.

9.17 NEGATIVE SKIN FRICTION

In conditions where the soil can move down relative to the pile, instead of the pile going down because of the loading, the soil tends to 'hang on to the pile' and transfer its load also on to the pile. Here the skin friction between soil and pile increases the load on the pile and hence this type of friction is called *negative skin friction*.

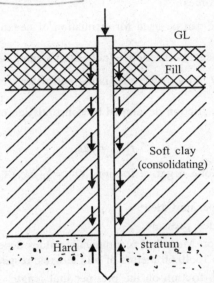

Fig. 9.9   Negative skin friction in piles.

Some of the site conditions where negative skin friction can occur are given below. Refer also IS 2911 [Part I, Sec. 3]

1. When the pile is installed in a fill, which will undergo consolidation (Fig. 9.9)
2. In a soil which will be disturbed or remoulded thoroughly during the pile installation
3. In piles installed in soft clay with surcharge loading on it
4. In soils where lowering or variation of ground water can occur, thus leading to significant settlement of soil strata around the pile
5. In cases where piles are driven through a strata of soft clay into firmer soils and the soft clay tends to settle relative to the pile
6. In piles in a clay stratum which undergoes shrinkage settlement.

As negative skin friction is due to consolidation, it takes place slowly and increasing with time. Hence its effects are not felt in pile load tests.

9.17.1 Estimation of Negative Skin Friction

It appears that even a small relative movement between pile and soil around the pile (of the order of 10 mm), mobilises full negative skin friction. However we should realize the difference between the following two conditions that can occur in the field.

Case 1. In the first case, the pile may rest on a hard stratum without any possible downward movement of the pile but the soil around it settles. Here full negative friction acts.

Case 2. In the second case, the pile rests on a comparatively compressible strata so that the pile settles to the same extent with the surrounding soil. In this case if the settlement of the pile is large, the soil around the pile will have to pull the pile up in 'positive friction'. Hence judgement must be used when estimating these forces.

The following procedure can be used for estimation of negative friction in single piles.

Method 1: Maximum negative friction = (cohesion) × (area of pile shaft).

$$N_f = cA_p, \text{ where } A_p \text{ is the perimeter area.} \tag{9.11}$$

Method 2: For negative friction developed by consolidation of soil with piles, the following expression is applicable [1].

$$f_{s-ve} = \beta\mu_0$$

$$\text{Total negative friction, } Q_N = \Sigma(\beta\mu_0)A_{si} \tag{9.11a}$$

where

f_{s-ve} = negative friction per unit area

μ_0 = effective overburden pressure

β = the reduction factor. Meyerhof recommends values depending on length of piles, 0.3, 0.2, 0.2 for length 15,40,60 metres of pile lengths, respectively.

Q_N = total negative skin friction on the pile per unit length

A_{si} = perimeter area

In places where we expect negative skin friction, the usual practice is to design piles for the following condition depending on the severity of the negative skin friction.

Condition 1: Q_u (required) = *FS* (working load + negative skin friction)

This approach is very conservative as in the calculation of negative skin friction we are calculating the maximum negative friction and putting a safety factor for it.

Condition 2: Q_u (required) = *FS* (working load) + negative skin friction

This second procedure is the one generally used. It should be used after a careful assessment of the soil conditions and the importance of the structure.

9.17.2 Methods of Mitigating Negative Skin Friction

The following methods are used to mitigate skin friction in piles:

1. Coat the surface of the precast pile with thick coat of special bituminous paint which have been proved to reduce skin friction as much as 90 per cent of the theoretical value.

2. Drive the piles inside a casing. In the top negative friction height, the space between pile and casing is filled with a viscous material and the casing is withdrawn after installing the pile.

3. In Holland they have successfully experimented with precast concrete piles with shafts of smaller cross sectional area along its length as compared with the base. This solution is possible with bearing piles only where we do not depend on the shaft resistance.

9.18 COMPARISON OF CAPACITIES OF DRIVEN AND BORED PILES

When the total capacity of a pile is due to both bearing and side resistance, driven piles can be expected to give a much higher capacity than bored piles, especially in cohesionless soils. However where there are bearing piles to bear on a very firm strata like rock or very dense sand at great depths, bored piles can be expected to have better load resistance than driven piles. However it is very important that in bored piles the base should be very carefully cleaned before concreting. Otherwise debris collected at the bottom will enable only the frictional part of the resistance of the pile to be mobilized at the allowable settlement stipulated in the pile test.

9.19 CAPACITY OF PILES FOUNDED ON SOLID ROCK

Many bored piles are founded on rock or weathered rock. In most cases they can be loaded to the structured capacity. The bearing capacity of piles founded on rock also depends on the type of rock met with at the tip of the pile and also the method of installation of the piles at its base. Piles can be driven piles or bored and cast in-situ piles. Rocks are classified as solid or weathered depending on core recovery while drilling. Steel H piles are generally recommended for piles driven *to refusal on rock*. If the rock is irregular (as noticed from the depth of refusal in different piles) the piles are fitted with a rock point to enable the pile to 'wedge' itself to the rock.

9.19.1 Driven Piles Resting on Rock

Small or medium diameter piles are installed by driving. When driving piles to good rock, it is the general practice to provide the piles with special shoes and drive the piles to refusal (i.e. less than 10 mm penetration for ten blows with a heavy pile hammer). In such cases the pile capacity is taken as its structural capacity considering it as a concrete column as described in Section 9.14. We should remember that in order to design the shaft as a reinforced concrete column (with strength of steel also taken into account) the minimum steel necessary as per codes is 0.8 per cent. In bored piles however the specification require as little steel as 0.4 per cent. In driven piles we have more steel to take care of handling stresses. For the pile to act as reinforced concrete column the base of the pile should develop the strength required without deformation. Similarly the fixity condition at the top should comply with the structural requirements of a column. Tomlinson [4] recommends the strength of piles driven into soft rock to be estimated from the following equation derived along the lines of finding the minimum depth of foundation by Rankine's theory.

$$\text{Base resistance} = q_u = 2q_{uc}N_\phi$$

where

q_{uc} = uniaxial compression strength of rock

$N_\phi = \tan^2 (45 + \phi/2)$

ϕ = friction value. It is taken as 30 to 40° for high friction rocks like basalt and granites, 25–35° for medium friction rock such as sandstone, and 20–25 for low friction, rocks, e.g. as mica schist.

As given in Section 14.6 when large diameter piles are driven for offshore structures, special PDA equipment is used to assess their capacity. However when the rock surface is sloping or covered with a good depth of weathered rock (as happens in the tropics) special considerations in construction should be made. The I.S method of calculating strength of socketed piles is described in Section 9.20.

9.19.2 Bored Piles in Solid Rock

Core recovery is the ideal test for identifying the type of rock below. Data on rate of chiselling is also used to identify the rock. A stratum is considered as rock when the rate of penetration of chiseling with a winch operated 3t chisel falling through 1.2 m height is less than 100 mm per hour. The corresponding rate of penetration with a 2t chisel and a fall of 1 m will be 55.6 mm per hour (got by equating energies). Large diameter piles are usually installed as bored cast in-situ piles. *When piles end in rock, bored piles are much superior than driven piles.* The bored piles need to penetrate only a small distance say 150 mm for small piles and 300 mm (1/2D) for large piles to develop its full structural capacity in solid rock. With small penetration, good care should be taken to get a good contact between the concrete at end of pile and rock. *Extreme care should be taken to wash the base of bore hole clean before depositing concrete.* There are many field cases where large settlement of pile occurred on test load because of lack of supervision in cleaning the loose deposits from the bottom of the hole before pouring the concrete.

With fractured or weak rocks also, it is possible to develop the full structural capacity of the pile by providing greater penetration into such rocks in order to carry some of the load in shear between concrete and the rock. This is known as *socketing*.

9.20 SOCKETING OF BORED PILES IN WEATHERED AND SOFT ROCK

In rock formations, weathered rock should be distinguished from solid rock by tests such as core recovery ratio. *According to IS 2911 Part I Sec. 2 Appendix C—Clause C2, piles that can be rested on sound rock may be loaded to their safe structural capacity after a keying into rock 150 mm for small diameter piles and 300 mm for large diameter piles. However for piles founded in weathered rock we take a different approach called socketing.*

In many Indian specifications socketing in solid rock is usually specified. Even though socketing in solid rock may be desirable if the piles were to rest directly on sloping solid rock with very little overburden above the rock, it may not be necessary when there is enough overburden to resist lateral displacement of the pile. Hence the necessity of socketing in solid rock should be decided with reference to the local conditions. A blanket specification that all piles in rock should be socketed is rather wasteful.

In the design of socketing for weathered rock, an empirical approach is made to arrive at the necessary socket length for loading the pile to its full structural capacity. It should be clearly noted that the aim is to load the pile to its capacity with enough factor of safety. As it is difficult to obtain cores in weathered rock, the method suggested by Cole and Stroud by using N values is widely used for identifying the various grades of rock. Accordingly the bearing strengths of rock and weathered rock are estimated as shown in Table 9.7 [7] [1]. Some agencies specify that when the piles are subjected to uplift, the depth of overburden is less than 15 m and we meet weathered rock, piles should be always socketed. Horizontal forces founded on sloping weathered rock are also socketed.

As the Cole and Stroud method needs separate SPT tests, another approach by counting the energy for advancing the hole by the chisel for advancing the bore has been proposed for the Bombay region. However, the results show that this method gives very conservative results.

TABLE 9.7 SCALE OF STRENGTH AND *N* VALUES SPT FOR ROCKS
[Cole and Stroud]

Value of N	Shear strength (kg/cm^2)	Strength	Grade	Breakability	Penetration	Scratch
400	400	Strong	A	Difficult to break against solid object with hammer		Cannot be scratched with knife
600	200	Moderately strong	B	Broken against solid object by hammer		Can just be scratched with knife
	100					
	80					
	60					
400		Moderately weak	C	Broken in hand by hitting with hammer		Can be just scratched by thumb nail
	40					
200	20		D	Broken by leaning on sample with hammer	No penetration with knife	Can be scratched by thumb nail
		weak				
	10					
	8		E	Broken by hand	2 mm with knife	
100						
80	6					
60	4	Hard or very weak	F	Easily broken by hand	5 mm with knife	
		(N less than 60 are considered as soil)				

9.20.1 Strength of Socketed Piles by Cole and Stroud Approach

Total bearing resistance = (end bearing resistance) + (socket bond strength between rock and pile)

$$Q_{ap} = \left[c_u N_c \frac{\pi D^2}{4} \right] \frac{1}{FS} + \frac{\alpha \tau_a \pi DL}{FS} \qquad (9.12)$$

where

c_u = shear strength of rock below base of pile (Table 9.5)
N_c = bearing capacity factor
D = diameter of pile
α = reduction factor
τ_a = average shear strength of socketed length
L = length of socket
FS = factor of safety (recommended = 3)
$\alpha\tau_u$ = adhesion for which the lesser value of 0.05 times cylinder strength of concrete and 0.05 times unconfined compression strength of rock has been recommended [7].

It may seem strange that according to the present practice the length of penetration required in dense sand with SPT value of 100 to 200 will be less than the socket length needed in weathered rock of similar SPT values. This is due to the fact that the full side friction of piles in sand can develop with less movement than that required for the development of the full base capacity. Also in the calculation of the bearing capacity of socketed piles, we depend more on the base bearing and socket friction than on side soil friction along the length of the pile.

With $N_c = 9$; $F.S = 3$, we have the end bearing capacity as follows:

$$q_a = \frac{c_u N_c}{3} = \frac{c_u \times 9}{3} = 3c_u \, (\text{kN/m}^2) \text{ when factor of safety is 3.} \tag{9.13}$$

where c_u = average shear strength of rock at base of pile.

To find length of socket from the design stress of the pile and strength of weathered rock, we proceed as follows. Let

$$Q_{ap} = q_m \left(\frac{\pi D^2}{4} \right) = \text{structural capacity of pile}$$

where q_m = *average stress in pile due to applied load* Q_{ap} (which is limited to $0.25 f_{ck}$).

Taking $\alpha\tau_a$ as the average safe shear strength of socketed rock and q_a from Eq. (9.13) above, we have the following equation:

$$q_m \frac{\pi D^2}{4} = q_a \frac{\pi D^2}{4} + \alpha\tau_a \, (\pi DL)$$

where $\alpha\tau_a$ *average safe shear strength of rock* along the socket length (assume $\alpha = 0.3$) and, safe strength of concrete in punching shear is $0.16 \sqrt{f_{ck}} > \alpha\tau_a$).

Now, the required L/D of the socket length works out to the following:

$$\frac{L}{D} = \frac{1 - q_a/q_m}{4(\alpha\tau_a/q_m)} \tag{9.14}$$

The value of shear strength of rock is to be interpolated from the N values for weathered rock. (see Table 9.7). The procedure is illustrated by Example 9.7.

The following points are important with regard to this method and should be noted.

1. This method assumes that there is no contribution from side friction above the socketed length. This is a very conservative assumption.

2. High values of end bearing resistance in bored cast in-situ piles should be adopted only when the necessary means and supervision are available to clear the bottom of the hole from all debris and to provide proper end bearing for the pile.

3. A fuller treatment of strength of socketed piles in rock is given in Reference 9 which can be consulted for detailed design.

9.21 BUCKLING OF SLENDER PILES

This subject has already been mentioned in Section 9.8 and IS 2911 Part I Sec. 3 on precast driven piles discusses about the probability of buckling of piles. This has to be taken into account only if the pile projects above the ground level in air or water without any lateral support or it is embedded in very weak soils (c less than 0.1 kg/cm^2).

Bjerrum's theoretical studies of buckling of *steel piles* has shown that buckling needs to be considered only if:

$$\left[EI/A^2 \right] < \left(f_{yp} \right)^2 / 4kB$$

where

  I and A are respectively the moment of inertia and area of pile

  f_{yp} = yield stress in steel
  E = young's modulus of steel
  k = horizontal subgrade reaction kg/cm^3
  B = width of pile.

Taking typical value of kB as 5 kg/cm^2 this will work out to $I/A^2 < 0.30$ for steel piles. However, investigations show that for concrete piles that are generally used in practice, buckling will not take place unless the soil is extremely soft. Chapter 14 of the book *Pile Foundation Analysis and Design* by Poulos and Devis [8] gives a good treatment of the subject based on subgrade reaction theory. Buckling of fully and partially embedded piles and poles are dealt with by Bowles [6] also. As already stated in Section 9.8 and given in IS 2911, R.C piles installed in soils of undrained shear strength at least 10 kN/m^2 will not undergo buckling on loading.

9.22 UPLIFT RESISTANCE (TENSION CAPACITY) OF PILES

Piles which are used in large towers and chimneys or in dry docks can go in tension under uplift loads and overturning moments. This subject is fully described by Tomlinson [9]. Similarly, expansion of top layers of expansive soils like black cotton soils can produce uplift of piles. The uplift resistance of straight sided friction piles are calculated in the same way as explained for compression piles when the L/d ratio is greater than 5. (Bearing resistance of the pile is absent when the pile is in pure tension.) In the case of shorter lengths (when $L/d < 5$) there is a likelihood of reduction of the frictional resistance. A factor of safety of 3 is recommended for tensile strength. It should also be noted that generally the movement necessary to mobilise the skin friction and hence tension in piles is small.

Tension piles for towers can be constructed with enlargement of the base in which case the strength of a part of the soil above the base of the pile can also be made to resist the uplift forces as in the case of under reamed piles. Drilled in rock anchors are also commonly used to resist tension forces and details of their design are explained in reference 9. Past experience shows that in sands the resistance in tension is only 2/3 that of skin friction value in compression. In clays they develop more or less the same skin friction as in compression. As a rule we may assume that the ultimate tension capacity of a friction pile is two-thirds its ultimate skin friction capacity in compression.

9.23 TAPERED PILES

Driven tapered piles with larger dimension at the top are found to be very effective as friction piles and compaction piles when installed *in sand deposits*. Their action can be visualized as shown in Fig. 9.10.

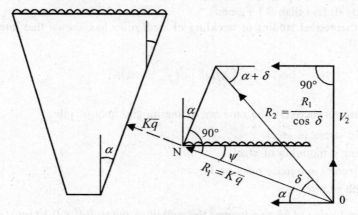

Fig. 9.10   Action of tapered piles.

Assuming a taper of α, soil friction of ϕ, friction between pile and soil as δ and that the lateral soil pressure acts normal to the surface of pile, we get the following expressions from Fig. 9.10.

R_1 = pressure normal to pile surface = $K\overline{q}$

R_2 = resultant force at angle δ = $R_1/\cos \delta$

F = friction along surface of pile = $\Sigma A_s K\overline{q} \tan \delta$

V_1 = vertical component of F = $F \cos \alpha$ (α is usually small)

V_2 = vertical force due to bearing of pile along its length = $\Sigma A_s K\overline{q} \dfrac{\sin (\alpha + \delta)}{\cos \delta}$

V_b = vertical resistance at the tip of the pile

$k \overline{q}$ = earth pressure normal to pile surface

Field tests have shown an increased capacity for these piles which at present is attributed to the increase in the values of K and δ. A value of $K = 1.7 K_0$ to $2.2 K_0$ is recommended for these piles, compared to 1 to 2 for straight piles. Another explanation for the increased capacity is that there is an increase in the friction value of these piles as shown in Fig. 9.11. These piles do not have much advantage in clay soils.

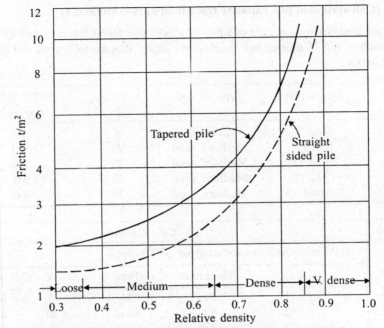

Fig 9.11 Increased friction capacity of tapered piles.

9.24 BEARING AREAS OF DRIVEN HOLLOW AND 'H' PILES

The performance of driven open-ended pipes is described in Section 11.8 under pile shoes. The bearing areas for ultimate point capacity compared to solid piles are given in Fig. 9.12.

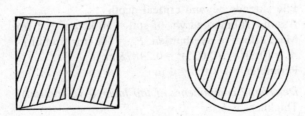

Fig 9.12 Bearing areas of driven steel and hollow piles.

9.25 SUMMARY

The bearing capacities arrived at by the static formulae should be always verified by field tests. The formulae used for piles resting in soils is different from the formulae used for bearing piles resting on rock or weathered rock. As modern large diameter piles are mostly bored piles taken to bed rock, their capacities should be calculated carefully so as to take full advantage of their large strength. Structural capacity of bored piles with minimum steel of 0.4% should be calculated only on the strength of concrete. However, if they are to be treated as columns, the end conditions and steel detailing should also satisfy the conditions of a column.

EXAMPLE 9.1 (Calculation of pile capacity from field data—Method 1)

Estimate the ultimate load bearing capacity of a precast driven pile 500×500 mm with 25 mm *chamfer at the corners* in section and 15 m long can develop in a strata with the following soil data. (Assume submerged conditions.)

Layer	Depth (m)	Type of soil	N values	SCPT Value (kg/cm^2)
1	0 to 5	Clay fill	4	16
2	5 to 11	Medium sand	20	120
3	11 to 13	Medium sand	25	150
4	13 to 15	Medium sand	35	200
5	Beyond 15	Medium sand	50	300

Ref.	Step	Calculations
	1	*Determine soil properties from SPT values*
	2	*Find properties of pile section*
Sec. 9.10		$\dfrac{L}{D} = \dfrac{15}{0.5} = 30$; $>$ critical depth $20D = 10$ m
Note (2)		Pile extends beyond critical depth
		Assume submerged wt. of soil = 10 kN/m^3 = 1 t/m^3
		Max. effective overburden, $P_D = 10$t (for friction)
		$A_p = (0.5)^2 - 2(0.025)^2 = 0.24875$ m^2
		Perimeter = $4 \times 0.5 = 2$ m
	3	*Determine components of top layer* (–ve friction)
		Thickness = 5 m;
		$q_{si} = -A_i c = -(2 \times 5) \times 2 = -20$ tons (–ve friction)
		As the layer is at the top and as the pile is
		precast we can reduce this drag by brituminous coatings
	4	*Estimate friction from 2nd to 4th layer*
Eq. (9.1a)		$Q_s = \Sigma\, KP_D \tan \delta A_p$;
		$A_p = $ Perimeter = 2 m
		For piles driven in medium sand, $\phi = 40°$ (assumed)
Tables 9.1 and 9.2		$K = 1.5$; Assume $\delta = (3/4)\phi$
		The following values can be used.
		(*Note*: K for driven piles is assumed $> K$ for bored piles.)

Step 1 sub-table:

Layer	Thickness	Type	N	c, ϕ values
1	5 m	Clay	4	$c = 0.2$ kg/cm^2
2	6 m	Sand	20	$\phi = 33°$
3	2 m	Sand	25	$\phi = 35°$
4	2 m	Sand	35	$\phi = 37°$
5	–	Sand	50	$\phi = 41°$

Layer	Thickness (m)	Mean Depth (P_D)	$\phi°$	$\delta = 3/4\ \phi$
2	6	8	33°	25
3	2	12	35°	26
4	2	14	37°	27
5			41	

Table 9.24

Calculate frictional resistance of each layer
(Assume $K = 1.5$ and $\gamma = 1$ t/m^2

$q_{s1} = 1.5 \times 8 \times \tan 25° = 5.59$ t/m^2

$q_{s2} = 1.5 \times 12 \times \tan 26° = 8.77$ t/m^2

$q_{s3} = 1.5 \times 14 \times \tan 27° = 10.77$ t/m^2

Table 9.2
Note 3

Allowable maximum $= 11$ t/m^2 (All values < 11 t/m^2)
$= Q_s = 5.59(2 \times 6) + 8.77(2 \times 2) + (10.77 \times 2 \times 2)$
$= 145$ t

(*Note:* Some authorities restrict maximum friction to 6t/m^2, Sec. 9.10, Note 3)

5 *Calculate bearing strength*

Eq. (9.1)
$Q_b = A_p (0.5\ D\gamma\ N_\gamma + P_D N_q) -$ Wt. of pile (W)
$\phi = 41°\ N_\gamma = 142$; Assume $\gamma = 1$ t/m^3
$Q_b = P_D N_q$
For N_q, we use Berezantev's curves (IS 2911)

Sec. 9.10(2)
For N_q; $\phi = \left(\dfrac{37+41}{2}\right) = 39°$

Fig. 9.4
$N_q = 120$ and $P_D N_q = 1200$
($Q_b = 0.249\ [(0.5 \times 0.5 \times 1 \times 142) + (10 \times 120)] - $ W
$= 0.249\ (35.5 + 1200) \approx 1200$ t/m^2 (see below)

Sec. 9.14
and
Table 9.2
(Notes)
(First term $= 8.8$ t; and the wt. of pile $= (0.5)^2 \times 15 \times 2.5 = 9.3$ t
—neglect first and last term)
Limiting $P_D N_q$ to 1100 tons/m^2, which is < 1200 t/m^2,
$Q_b = 0.249 \times 1100 = 273$ tons (approx.)

6 *Total bearing capacity*

Steps 4
and 5
$Q_u = Q_b + Q_s = 273 + 145 = 418$ tons

$Q_{allowable} = \dfrac{Q_u}{F.S} -$ Negative skin friction

$= \dfrac{418}{2.5} - 20 = 147$ tons

7 *Check on structural capacity*
Based on concrete only; $f_c = 0.25 f_{ck}$

Sec. 9.10.1
Assuming $f_{ck} = 20$ N/mm^2
$Q_{st} = 0.25 \times 20 \times 500 \times 500 = 125$ tons
Assume safe load $= 125$ tons only

EXAMPLE 9.2 **(Calculation of pile capacity from Meyerhof's formula—Method 2)**

Estimate the ultimate bearing capacity of pile in Example 9.1 by Meyerhof's formula based on SPT values.

Ref.	Step	Calculations
IS 2911 Sec. 9.15 Eq. (9.7a)	1	*Meyerhof's formula for concrete piles* Friction in sand $= N/5$ (in t/m^2) Friction in clay $= N/2$ (in t/m^2) End bearing in sand $= 40\ N$ (in t/m^2) for $\dfrac{L}{D} > 10$ $Q_u = 40NA_p + \Sigma \dfrac{N}{5} A_s = Q_p + Q_s$ (ultimate in tons)
Table 9.2	2	*Determine frictional capacity* First strata clay negative skin friction $= 20$ tons Second strata sand N $= 20$ ($q_s = 20/5 = 4$t/m^2) Third strata sand N $= 25$ ($q_s = 25/5 = 5$t/m^2) Fourth strata sand N $= 35$ ($q_s = 35/5 = 7$t/m^2) (as maximum allowed is 11t/m^2 use above value) Perimeter of pile $= 4 \times 0.5 = 2$ m $Q_s = (4 \times 6 \times 2) + (5 \times 2 \times 2) + (7 \times 2 \times 2) = 96$ tons
Step 1 Table 9.2 (Notes)	3	*Determine capacity in bearing* N = Assume mean value $= 39$ $\dfrac{L}{D} = \dfrac{15}{0.5} = 30 > 10$ (pile depth > critical depth) $q_b = 40 \times 39 = 1560$ t/m^2 Max. allowed end bearing for driven piles $= 1500$ t/m^2 $Q_b = A_p \times 1500 = 0.24875 \times 1500 = 370$ tons (approx.)
	4	*Calculate the total capacity* $Q_u = Q_b + Q_s = 370 + 96 = 466$ tons $Q_{allowable} = \dfrac{466}{2.5} - 20 = 166$ tons
Example 9.1 Step 7	5	*Calculate the structural capacity* $Q_{st} = 125$ tons only. Hence safe capacity $= 125$ tons

EXAMPLE 9.3 **(Calculation of pile capacity from SCP test data—Method 3)**

Determine the ultimate capacity of the pile in Example 9.1 from static cone penetration test data

Ref.	Step	Calculations
Sec. 9.16	1	*Calculate end bearing capacity* q (end resistance) $= \left[\left(\dfrac{q_{co} + q_{c1}}{2}\right) + q_{c2}\right] \times \dfrac{1}{2}$ Assume q_{co} = average over $2D$ below tip = 300 kg/cm^2 q_{c1} = Minimum over $2D$ below tip = 300 kg/cm^2 q_{c2} = Average over $8D$ = 4 m above tip = 250 kg/cm^2 $q = (300 + 250)/2 = 275$ kg/cm^2 = 2750 t/m^2
Table 9.2 (Notes)		Limiting base resistance for driven pile = 1500 t/m^2 $Q_b = 1500 \times A_p = 370$ tons
	2	*Calculate frictional bearing capacity* $Q_s = \Sigma Q_s A_s$ Expressing in q_c in t/m^2 (10 kg/cm^2 = 1 t/m^2) Top layer negative skin friction – 20 tons (from Example 1) Expressing values in t/m^2,
Table 9.5		Layer 2 (6 m, sand) q_c – 1200, (friction = $\dfrac{q_c}{100}$ = 12 t/m^2) Layer 3 (2 m, sand) q_c = 1500, (friction = $\dfrac{q_c}{100}$ = 15 t/m^2) Layer 4 (2 m, sand) q_c = 2000, (friction = $\dfrac{q_c}{100}$ = 20 t/m^2)
Sec. 9.14		Friction has to be limited to 6 to 11 t/m^2 $A_s = 2[6 + 2 + 2]$ m^2 $Q_s = 2 \times (11)(6 + 2 + 2) = 220$ tons
	3	*Estimate total pile capacity* $Q_u = Q_b + Q_s = 370 + 220 = 590$ tons $Q_{\text{allowable}} = \dfrac{590}{2.5} - 20 = 236 - 20 = 216$ tons
Example 9.1 Step 7	4	*Calculate structural capacity* $Q_{str} = 125$ tons. Hence safe capacity = 125 tons.

EXAMPLE 9.4 **(Differences between driven and cast in-place piles)**

The point resistance and side friction resistance of bored piles in clayey and sandy soils are considered to be less than that of the driven piles. How do you take account of this aspect in calculation of the capacity of piles by static method.

Ref.	Step	Calculations
	1	*Correction for side friction* (a) *Clay soils* $Q_s = \Sigma \, \alpha_i c_i A_i$ where α is the adhesion factor IS 2911 part I gives the adhesion factor for driven piles (see Table 9.3 of text) For bored piles these values are usually *reduced by a factor* 0.8 (IS 2911 part I Sec. 2. Bored cast in-situ piles-Appendix C) (b) *Sandy soils* $Q_s = \Sigma \, KP_D \tan \delta A_{si}$ (1) The factor that change are K and δ K and δ can be taken as shown in Tables 9.1 and 9.2 for driven and bored piles (2) Another method used by Tomlinson [4] is given in Table 9.2A. $K_0 = 1 - \sin \phi$ and $\dfrac{K}{K_0}$ is taken from Table 9.2A. Value of δ is taken as for 0.75ϕ concrete.
	2	*Correction for end resistance* (a) *Clayey soils* $Q_c = A_p N_p c_p$ where c_p is the average cohesion at the toe. In bored piles, it is absolutely essential that the base should be fully cleaned of debris before concrete is placed. Otherwise a suitable reduction factor depending on the quality work has to be assumed. (b) *Sandy soils* $Q_c = A_p \left(\dfrac{1}{2} D\gamma Nq + P_D N_q \right) = A_p P_D N_q$ (neglecting first term) Here value of is modified as described in notes under Table 9.2. In sand the limiting value of end bearing is taken as 1500 t/m^2 for driven piles, IS 2911 states that for bored piles it should not exceed 1100 t/m^2 (A safe value of 1100 t/m^2 may be accepted for both cases).

EXAMPLE 9.5   (Design of bored piles from soil properties—Method 1)

The soil profile at a site for a multistorey building is as follows. Determine the capacities of 400 mm, 760 mm and 900 mm diameter bored piles extending to a depth of 29 m. Assume the unit weight of soil as 1800 kg/cm^3 and that submergence can occur.

Depth (m)	Type of soil	Cohesion (kg/cm^2)	Angle of friction
0–5	Stiff clay	0.5	–
5–21	Soft clay	0.1	–
21–25	Stiff clay	0.5	–
25–29	Medium sand	–	30°
Below 29	Weathered rock	–	38°

Ref.	Step	Calculations
		(*Note:* We will calculate friction and bearing for a pile of diameter D)
Sec. 9.10	1	*Method of calculation of end resistance*
		$Q_b = A_p(0.5\ D\gamma N_{\bar{\gamma}} + P_D N_q)$ – Wt. of pile
		Neglecting first and last term, we get
		$Q_b = A_p(P_D N_q)$ where P_D = effective overburden pressure
Fig. 9.4b		Submerged weight of soil $\gamma = 0.8$ t/m^3
Sec. 9.14		Assume critical depth = $20D = h_c$
		Assume for end $N_q = 100$ for 38°
		Assuming maximum allowable end resistance of 1100 t/m^2 for
		Bored piles critical diameter of pile be D.; $N_q = 100$
		$q_b = (20D \times 0.8 \times 100) = 1100$ t/m^2
		Critical $D = 0.688$ or 688 mm dia.
		For dia. above 700 mm, limit $q_b = 1100$ t/m^2
	2	*Calculate skin resistance (for different values of P_D)*
		$Q_s = \Sigma\ \alpha c A_s$ and $\Sigma\ K P_D \tan\delta A_s$
		1. *Clay* (0–5 m). It can produce negative skin friction.
		$\quad Q_{s1} = 0.5 \times 5 = 2.5$ t/m^2
		$\quad Q_{s1} = (\pi D \times 5)2.5 = -39.25D$ tons
		2. *Clay* (5–21). It can produce negative skin friction
		$\quad q_{s2} = 1 \times 1 = 1$ t/m^2
		$\quad Q_{s2} = (\pi D \times 16)1 = -50D$ tons
		3. *Clay* (21–25)—no further consolidation (no drag)
		$\quad q_{s3} = 0.5 \times 5 = 2.5$ k/m^2
		$\quad Q_{s3} = (\pi D \times 4)2.5 = 31.4D$ tons
		4. (Sand (24 – 29) m sand; $\phi = 30°$ at 27 m depth.
		For K use Table 9.2; IS 2911 value = 1.0
		$\delta = 0.75 \times 30 = 22.5°$ (wall friction)
		$\tan\delta = 0.41$; mean depth = 27 m; use $K/K_0 = 1$
		$K P_D \tan\delta = 1 \times (0.8 \times 27)\ 0.41 = 8.8$ t/m^2
		(8.8 is less than 11 t/m^2, max. allowed)
		$Q_{s4} = (\pi D \times 4)\ 8.8 = 110D$
		Alternate method for K in 4 above
		$K_0 = 1 - \sin\phi = 1 - \sin 30 = 0.5$
		$K/K_0 = 0.71$ to 1 for bored piles
		$K = 1 \times 0.5 = 0.5$ only
	3	*Determine total skin resistance*
Table 9.2A		$(110D + 31.4D) = 141D + $ ve
Steps 2.1 to		$(-39D - 50D) = -89D + $ ve
2.4	4	*Calculate end bearings for different diameters*
		(a) *Diameter of pile is* 400 mm
		$20D = 8$ m depth of tip pile 29 m, $L/D = 20$,
		Hence $N_q = 100$
		$P_D = 8 \times 0.8 = 6.4$ t/m^2; $q_b = 6.4 \times 100 = 640$ t/m^2
		$640 <$ max. allowable 1100 t/m^2

$$Q_b = \frac{\pi(0.4)^2}{4} \times 640 = 80.3 \text{ tons}$$

$$+ Q_s = 141D = 141 \times 0.4 = 56 \text{ t and } (Q_b + Q_s = 136 \text{ t})$$
$$- Q_s = -89D = -89 \times 0.4 = -35t$$

Q_b = 136 t and −35 t (negative friction)

Calculate structural capacity

Q structural $(\pi D^2/4)(0.25 f_{ck})$

$Q_{st} = (\pi(400)2/4) \times 0.25 \times 20 = 62 \text{ tons}$

(b) *Diameter of pile is 760 mm*

$20D = 20 \times 0.76 = 15.2 \text{ m} < 29 \text{ m (depth)}$

$P_D = 15.2 \times 0.8 = 12; q_b = 12 \times 100 = 1200$

As it is > 1100, the allowable value, use 1100 only

$$Q_b = \frac{\pi(0.76)^2}{4} \times 1100 = 498 \text{ tons}$$

$$+Q_s = 141 \times 0.76 = 107 \text{ t}$$
$$-Q_s = -89 \times 0.76 = -67 \text{ t}$$

$Q_u = 498 + 107 = +605 \text{ t and } -67 \text{ t (negative friction)}$

$Q_{st} = 226 \text{ tons}$

(c) Diameter of pile is 900 mm

Similar calculation will yield.

$Q_u = +826 \text{ and } -80 \text{ tons (negative drag)}$

$Q_{st} = 317 \text{ tons (Structural capacity)}$

5.   *Tabulate the results (all values in tons)*

Pile dia.	Q_{st}	Q_u	$Q_u/2.5$	Q_{-ve}	Q_{safe}
400	62	136	54	−35	19
760	226	605	242	−67	159
900	317	826	330	−80	237

Example: For 400 mm pile $(Q_u/2.5 - Q_s) = 19$ tons.

6   *Find efficiency of the piles*

If we calculate ton carried per cubic metre of pile, we get the following:

(a) For 400 mm dia. pile,

$$\text{Tonnage per m}^3 = \frac{19 \times 4}{\pi(0.4)^2 \times 29} = 5.21 \text{ t/c.m}$$

(b) For 760 mm dia. pile,

$$\text{Tonnage per m}^3 = \frac{159 \times 4}{\pi(0.76)^2 \times 29} = 12.0 \text{ t/c.m}$$

(c) For 900 mm dia. pile,

$$\text{Tonnage per m}^3 = \frac{237 \times 4}{\pi(0.9)^2 \times 29} = 12.8 \text{ t/c.m}$$

Thus, larger diameter piles becomes more economical and an optimum diameter can be found for use.

(*Note:* In Aroor (Kerala), for the railway bridge over Vembanad lake, the negative skin friction was estimated as very high. With 550 mm dia. bored pile with M20 concrete, the structural capacity is only 120 tons and the negative skin friction was 143 tons with no capacity to carry the load. Hence 800 mm dia. piles were adopted, which have structural capacity of 251 tons, negative skin friction 200 tons, and carrying capacity of 50 tons).

EXAMPLE 9.6 (Ultimate capacity of pile from SCPT data—Method 3)

In a site the soil profile consists of loose sand of static cone penetration test value of (SCPT) 40 kg/cm^2 to a depth of 11 metres, which is underlain by a deposit of dense–fine to coarse sand. In this layer, the value of CPT gradually increases from 130 kg/cm^2 at 11 m to 250 kg/cm^2 at a depth of 17 metres. Design a 400 mm dia pile to carry a load of 50t in compression.

Ref.	Step	Calculations
IS2911	1	*Formula for Q_u from SCPT data*
Eq. (9.16)		$$Q_u = \left[\left(\frac{q_{co} + q_{c1}}{2}\right) + q_{c2}\right] \times 0.5 \, A_c = \text{End bearing capacity}$$
	2	*Required resistance* $Q_t = 50 \times 2.5 = 125$ tons Assuming a fully bearing pile of 400 mm diameter (0.1256 m^2) the bearing pressure required will be: $$\frac{125 \times 4}{\pi \times 0.4 \times 0.4} = 995 \text{ t/m}^2 = 99.5 \text{ kg/cm}^2$$ Accordingly, the pile cannot be founded on the top sand deposit with the given SCPT value of only 40 kg/cm^2. Hence it should penetrate the dense sand deposit.
	3	*Value of SCPT at different layers* Value up to 11 m = 40 kg/cm^2 Value at 11 m = 130 kg/cm^2 Value at 17 m = 250 kg/cm^2 Assume the pile penetrates 2.0 m in dense sand so that its total length is 13 m. Assuming a steady increase of in (250 − 130) = 120 kg/cm^2 in 6 m. (i.e. an increase of 20 kg/cm^2 per metre depth) q at pile toe = 130 + (2 × 20) = 170 kg/cm^2 = q_{cq} q at 2D = 170 + (0.8 × 20) = 186 kg/cm^2 below pile toe q_0 = average value within 2D below pile toe = (170 + 186) 0.5 = 178 q_{c2} = average over 8D (3.2 m) above pile toe

Sec. 9.14	4	
Table 9.5	5	
	6	

$$(2 \text{ m in dense sand}) = \frac{(40 \times 1.2) + (150 \times 2)}{3.2} = 108 \text{ k/cm}^2$$

Find the ultimate end bearing resistance

$$q = \left[\frac{170 + 178}{2} + 108 \right] \times 0.5 = 141 \text{ kg/cm}^2$$

$$= 1410 \text{ t/m}^2 > 1000 \text{ t/m}^2$$

(limiting value of bearing in sand = 1000 t/m^2)

$$Q_u = qA_c = 1000 \times 0.1256 = 125 \text{ tons}$$

Capacity in friction

Layer 1: loose sand 0 to 11 m (SCPT = 40 kg/cm^2)

Assume $Q_c/100 = 0.4$ kg/cm^2 = 4 t/m^2

$$Q_{s1} = \pi \times 0.4 \times 11 \times 4 = 55 \text{ tons}$$

Layer 2: Dense sand 11 m to 13 m (2 m depth)

Average q value = 150 – Assume friction = $q_c/100$

Friction $\dfrac{150}{100} = 1.5$ kg/cm^2 = 15 t/m^2

Assume limiting value = 11 t/m^2 (Many limit it to 6 t/m^2)

$$Q_{s2} = \pi \times 0.4 \times 2 \times 11 = 27.6 \text{ t}$$

Total friction = 55 + 27.6 = 83 tons

Ultimate capacity of pile

$$Q_u + Q_s = 125 + 83 = 208 \text{ tons}$$

$$Q_{allowable} = \frac{208}{2.5} = 83 \text{ tons}$$

FS for 50 T load $\dfrac{208}{2.5} = 4.16$

A 400 mm dia. pile extending to 13 m below ground level, penetrating 2 m into the dense sand will very safely carry 50 t in compression.

REFERENCES

[1]　IS 2911, *Code of Practice for Design and Construction of Pile Foundation* (Second Revision), Sections 1 to 4, Bureau of Indian Standards, New Delhi, 1999.

[2]　Berezantsev, U.G., Load Bearing Capacity and Deformation of Piled Foundations, 5th International Conference in Soil Mech. and Foundation Engineering, 1961.

[3]　Vesic, A.S., *A Study of Bearing Capacity of Deep Foundations*, Final Report Georgia Institute of Tech., Atlanta, USA 1967.

[4]　Tomlinson, M.J., *Foundation Design and Construction*, E.L.B.S. Edition, Pitman Publishing Company, 1995.

[5]　Meyerhof, Penetration Tests and Bearing Capacity of Piles, *Journal of Soil Mechanics and Foundation Division*, American Soc. of Civil Engineers, Volume 82, S.M.I., 1956.

[6]   Bowles, J.E., *Foundation Analysis and Design*, International Student Edition, McGraw-Hill, Singapore, 1982.

[7]   Cole, K.M. and Stroud, M.A., *Rock Socket Piles at Coventry Point—Piles in Weak Rocks*, Proc. Inst. of Civil Engineers, London, 1977.

[8]   Poulos, H.G. and Davis, E.H., *Pile Foundation Analysis and Design*, John Wiley & Sons, New York, 1940.

[9]   Tomlinson, M.J., *Pile Design and Construction Practice*, A View Point Publication, London, 1977.

10

Load Carrying Capacity of Piles by Dynamic Formulae

10.1 INTRODUCTION

This chapter explains the use of pile driving formulae to estimate ultimate capacity of piles. It is useful to remember its limitations. Except for the wave equation analysis, dynamic formulae are normally applicable only for point bearing piles in cohesionless soils. These formulae are not applicable to clay soils as its strength is time dependent. In clays we may use the set condition to check only the quality of driving. Terzaghi has pointed out that when we base our design on pile driving formulae, we run the risk of driving much more piles than necessary. Otherwise we should go for an expensive load test to determine the true capacity of the piles and base our design.

In this chapter we will describe the Hiley, Simplex and Janbu formulae (the three dynamic formulae given in IS 2911) and also briefly examine the modern method of wave equation analysis, generally used for offshore pile installations.

10.1.1 Pile Driving Equipment

The components of a pre-cast pile driving system consist of four items which are now briefly described:

1. *Pile frame:* This is a frame mounted on crawlers, trucks or sledges with arrangements for lifting, aligning and driving the piles.

2. *Pile hammer:* Consists of the ram and anvil. These are made of cast iron or cast steel and are used to drive the pile. Hammer may be any one of the following:

   — Drop hammer
   — Single acting hammer (steam or pneumatic)
   — Double acting hammer (steam or pneumatic)
   — Diesel hammer
   — Vibratory hammer.

Each of these has its particular use and literature on construction equipment must be consulted for proper selection. In drop hammers, the falling weight has to be guided along its fall. But modern double acting and diesel hammers are generally mounted on the pile top itself and only the alignment of the piles has to be kept up during driving. The falling weights strike on the anvil.

3. *Helmet:* This assembly consists of the dolly, steel cap and cushion as shown in Fig. 10.1. Helmets are placed over concrete piles to hold the resilient dolly and packing as shown in the figure. Only driving caps are used for steel piles instead of helmets. They are specially

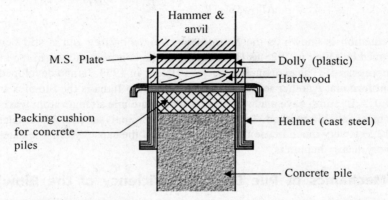

Fig 10.1   Details of pile head with cast steel helmet dolly and packing cushion.

shaped to receive the particular shape of the pile and are also fitted with an access for the hard wood dolly. Steel wedges are used to keep the caps tight on the pile, as loose caps will lead to damage of the piles. It should be noted that lack of resilience of these materials could lead to excessive damage of the piles. Concrete piles are always driven with a soft packing on top of the pile which is not necessary for steel piles.

4. *Follower:*   Follower is an extension, which transmits hammer blow to the pile when the pile head is out of reach of the hammer, when it is acting below the ground level or near the ground level.

The final penetration per blow for which the pile has to be driven is called the set. It is measured for the last 10 blows. As it is difficult to cast circular piles at sites, small diameter piles are usually made square with chamfered corners. However, when the side dimensions are greater than 500 mm an octagonal section is to be preferred as it closely follows a circle. For very long length piles, factory made pre-stressed concrete circular spun piles are extensively used in practice.

10.2 PILE DRIVING FORMULAE

The method to determine the ultimate capacity of piles by equating the energy imparted by the falling weight and the resistance to penetration of the pile during the last few blows (termed set) was first attempted by Sanders who published his formula in 1850 as follows:

$$WH = RS$$

where

W = weight of hammer

H = height of fall

R = the pile capacity (We use symbol R for pile resistance obtained by dynamic formula)

S = pile penetration for the last blow or set

In 1898, Wellington pointed out that the equation does not take the energy losses into account. He modified it as follows:

$$WH = R(S + C)$$

From field measurements he observed $C = 1$ inch for drop hammers on wooden piles and $= 0.1$ inch for steam hammers. Using a factor of safety 6, the formula with H in feet, it becomes:

$$\text{Allowable } R_a = \frac{1}{6}\left[\frac{12WH}{S + C}\right] = \frac{2WH}{S + C}$$

This equation is known as the *Engineering News Formula* and is still being used by some. It was improved by Hiley in 1925 as Hiley formula. His contribution was in the identification of the various components of C as explained in Section 10.2.3. In 1953, Jambu developed a similar formula called Jambu formula. Another formula commonly used in India is the Simplex formula.

In 1960, A.L. Smith gave a new approach to estimate pile strength from wave equation analysis. This is the most reliable method. Today wave equation analysis with PDA machine (described in section 10.12.5) is very much in use for the estimation of the capacity of large diameter offshore piles driven by very heavy hammers.

10.2.1 Mechanics of Pile Driving (Efficiency of the Blow)

The fundamental relationship between the weight of the pile and the hammer to be used for driving the pile can be derived from Newton's law of conservation of momentum. As there is loss of energy, we should use the momentum principle to find the velocities of the hammer before impact v_1 and the pile after impact v_2. Taking the weight of hammer as W and weight of pile as P and assuming coefficient of restitution to be zero (i.e. hammer travels with the pile), we get

$$Wv_1 = (W + P)v_2$$

$$v_2 = \left(\frac{W}{W + P}\right)v_1$$

Therefore,

$$v_1 = \left(\frac{W + P}{W}\right)v_2$$

Denoting the ratio of energies after impact to the energy before impact as η, we have

$$\text{Efficiency, } \eta = \frac{\dfrac{1}{2}\left(\dfrac{W + P}{g}\right)v_2^2}{\dfrac{1}{2}\left(\dfrac{W}{g}\right)\left(\dfrac{W + P}{W}\right)^2 v_2^2} = \frac{W}{W + P}$$

If

$$W = 0.1P, \quad \eta = 9\% \text{ [low]}$$
$$W = 0.3P, \quad \eta = 23\%$$
$$W = 0.5P, \quad \eta = 33\%$$
$$W = P, \quad\quad \eta = 50\%$$
$$W = 2P, \quad\quad \eta = 67\% \text{ [good]}$$

[These equations will be modified when the coefficient of restitution $e > 0$, as shown in Eqs. (10.2) and (10.3) in the following sections.]

It is clear from the above derivation that to get a good *efficiency of the operation, the weight of hammer should be comparable with the weight of the pile*. It also can be seen that with a given hammer, the lighter pile can be more efficiently driven than a heavier pile of the same length. Hence, on comparing a steel pile and a concrete pile to carry the same load, the steel pile will be much lighter and can be more efficiently driven by most of the available hammers.

10.2.2 Hiley Formula for End Bearing Piles

The modified Hiley formula given below may be considered more appropriate when the pile derives its capacity mainly from the end bearing. The resistance offered to the final penetration of the pile is used to estimate the ultimate capacity. The formula is derived as follows:

Energy of blow = (resistance of pile; distance travelled)
Distance travelled = penetration + function of elastic compression

$$(\alpha Wh)\, \eta = R(S + C/2)$$

$$R = \frac{(\alpha Wh)\, \eta}{(S + C/2)} \tag{10.1}$$

where

R = ultimate driving resistance

W = weight of hammer ram

h = height of fall in cm

α = hammer fall efficiency (0.8 to 1)

η = efficiency of blow as obtained from Section 10.2

S = final set in cm per blow

C = sum of elastic compression given in section 10.3 in cm.

(We may also substitute h, S and $C/2$ 10.3 in mm.)

The factor of safety to be used as recommended by IS 2911 is given in Table 10.1. As already stated, the *dynamic formulae are not applicable to soft clays*, which tend to develop pore pressure on driving. Strictly speaking, the Hiley formula is applicable to point resistant piles in sand, when hammer drop is in the range 1.3 to 1.8 m and final set is less than 5 mm per blow. However they are used in all cases in practice.

The hammer efficiency α given in IS 2911 (99) Part I Sec. 3. [1] for Hiley formula with respect to height of fall of hammer is as follows:

Drop hammers winch operated $\alpha = 0.8$

Drop hammers trigger release $\alpha = 1.0$

Single acting hammer $\alpha = 0.9$

Double acting hammer $\alpha = 1.0$

For special hammers the manufacturer will give the efficiency of their hammers. The factor of safety to be used with Hiley formula is given in Table 10.1.

TABLE 10.1   FACTOR OF SAFETY RECOMMENDED BY IS 2911 (99) Part I Sec. 3

Type of ground From load tests	Hiley's Formula	
	Resistance not reduced on re-driving	Resistance reduced on re-driving
Rock	1.5	–
Non-cohesive soils	2.0	2.5
Hard cohesion soils 1.5 to 2.0	2.0	2.5
Soft cohesive soils	Not applicable	

[*Note:* Minimum *FS* for results of static formula on reliable data = 2.5]

10.2.3 Efficiency of Blow

We have already seen in Section 10.2 that the efficiency of blow depends on the relative weight of the hammer and the pile. Its modification when there is the factor *e* called the *coefficient of restitution* can be easily derived and is as follows: Let

$$W = \text{weight of hammer}; \quad P = \text{weight of pile}$$

When $W > P$,
$$\eta = \frac{W + Pe^2}{W + P} \tag{10.2}$$

When $W < P$,
$$\eta = \left[\frac{W + Pe^2}{W + P}\right] - \left[\frac{W - Pe}{W + P}\right]^2 \tag{10.3}$$

Neglecting the second term, we get

$$\eta = \left[\frac{W + Pe^2}{W + P}\right]$$

where
  P = weight of pile
  W = weight of the hammer
  e = coefficient of restitution of the material under impact (refer to Table 10.2).

This shows an increase in efficiency with heavier hammers and larger *e* values. It can be theoretically shown that heavy hammers with shorter heights of falls give us better driving than light hammers with high falls. There will be lesser loss of energy with the former case.

TABLE 10.2   VALUES OF COEFFICIENT OF RESTITUTION
[IS 2911 Part I Sec. 3 – 1979]

Material	e
Steel ram of double acting hammer on steel anvil driving R.C. pile.	0.50
Cast iron ram of single acting drop hammer striking on R.C. pile.	0.40
Single acting or drop hammer with cap, helmet hard wood dolly in R.C. piles or directly on timber piles.	0.25
For deteriorated condition of head of pile or dolly.	0

10.3 DETERMINATION OF TEMPORARY ELASTIC COMPRESSION DURING DRIVING

The contribution made by Hiley was the identification of the components of C the temporary compression due to the hammer blow to be used in piledriving formulae. It may be represented as: $C = C_1 + C_2 + C_3$. The terms constituting it are:

1. Temporary compression of helmet and dolly (three cases), C_1
2. Temporary compression of pile, C_2
3. Temporary compression of ground, C_3.

The recommendation of British Steel Piling Company, as given in BSP pocket book (1969) [2], has been adopted by IS 2911 also for Indian practice. They can be expressed as follows. However, it is important to remember that every effort should be made to find field values of C_2 and C_3 when we use this formula on projects.

10.3.1 Temporary Compression of Dolly [C_1]

The following empirical expressions taken from BSP pocket book [2] are given in IS 2911 for finding C_1 for the three cases. Let R be the ultimate driving resistance in tons and A the overall cross section area of the pile in square centimetres.

Case (a). Driving without helmet or dolly but only a cushion or pad of 25 mm thick on head. We may consider R/A as the equivalent of stress in t/cm^2.

$$C_1 = 1.761(R/A) \text{ cm (with } R \text{ in tons and } A \text{ in cm}^2). \tag{10.4}$$

Case (b). Driving of concrete or steel piles with helmet and short dolly up to 40 mm, but without cushion.

$$C_1 = 3.726 (R/A) \text{ cm (with } R \text{ in tons and } A \text{ in cm}^2) \tag{10.5}$$

Case (c). Concrete piles driven with only 75 mm packing under helmet and without dolly.

$$C_1 = 5.509(R/A) \text{ cm (with } R \text{ in tons and } A \text{ in cm}^2) \tag{10.6}$$

When packing on top of piles and dolly are used together we can combine a and b or b and c to get the required value. Even though it is difficult to measure C_1 directly in the field, assumed values should be roughly checked by field observations.

The values specified by Chellis are recommended for C_1 in the book, *Foundation Engineering* edited by G.A. Leonards and *Foundation Analysis and Design* by Poulos and Davis are given in Table 10.3.

TABLE 10.3   VALUES OF TEMPORARY COMPRESSION [C_1]

Material under blow	Type of driving (C_1 in mm)			
	Easy (mm)	Medium (mm)	Hard (mm)	Very hard (mm)
Concrete piles with 75–100 m packing inside cap placed on head of pile	(1.25 + 1.75)*	(2.5 + 3.75)*	(3.75 + 5.5)*	(5.0 + 7.5)*
Concrete piles with 12.5 to 25 mm mat pad only on head	0.63	1.25	1.88	2.5

*The first value is for cap and wood dolly above the cap. The second values are for the packing between the cap and pile head.

10.3.2 Temporary Compression of Pile [C_2]

This represents the compression of the pile itself. The value of C_2 is given by the following expression in IS 2911:

$$C_2 = \frac{100RL}{AE} \text{ cm} \tag{10.7}$$

where R is in kN, L in metres, A in m^2 and E in kN/m^2, corresponding to wood, concrete, steel, as the case may be. (Usually, E for concrete is taken as 25×10^6 kN/m^2 and for steel 200×10^6 kN/m^2.)

For concrete piles, taking $E = 25 \times 10^6$ kN/m^2 and with R in tons, L in metres, and A in cm^2, Eq. (10.7) reduces to

$$C_2 = \frac{0.4RL}{A} \text{ (cm)} \quad R \text{ is in tons, } L \text{ in m, and } A \text{ in } cm^2. \tag{10.7a}$$

If we take $E = 15 \times 10^6$ kN/m^2 for concrete, it reduces to

$$C_2 = \frac{0.657RL}{A} \text{ (cm)} \text{ when } R \text{ is in tons, } L \text{ in m, and } A \text{ in } cm^2. \tag{10.7b}$$

For steel piles, use $C_2 = \dfrac{0.05RL}{A}$ (cm) when R is in tons, L in m, and A in cm^2. $\qquad$ (10.7c)

10.3.3 Temporary Compression of Ground [C_3]

This temporary compression called quake of the ground is due to stress in the ground and its modulus. The formula given in IS 2911 Part I Sec. 3 is the following:

Let A_p = overall cross-section area of pile at toe in cm^2

$$C_3 = 0.073 + 2.806 \frac{R}{A_p} \text{ (cm)} \text{ when } R \text{ is in tons and } A_p \text{ is in } cm^2. \tag{10.8}$$

Its nominal value is around 2.5 mm and it may vary from 0 to 5 mm. A rough analysis of the expressions will show that for a long pile, say above 15 m, the major component of temporary compression will be the deformation of the pile itself. There will be only little penetration unless larger weight and higher height of hammer drops are used to get the required set.

As stated in IS 2911, the assumed values of $C_2 + C_3$ *for the given conditions should be always measured in the field especially when the specified set is small.* This fact should be specially noted by all field engineers (see Section 10.9).

10.4 SELECTION OF PILE HAMMERS

The simplest of the hammers is the drop hammer, and its energy is on account of the falling weight. However more or less the same arrangement as in Fig. 10.1 on the pile head is used to receive the hammer blow irrespective of the type of hammer. The following types of modern pile hammers are more efficient than the drop hammers, their energy delivery depending on the data of the manufacturers.

1. Single acting steam or compressed air hammers
2. Double acting steam or compressed air hammers for sheet pile driving
3. Diesel hammers

Of these, the diesel hammers need special mention. They are mostly used where hard driving is required and are *generally not very effective in soft soils*. In soft soils, the rebound of the hammer will not be enough to compress the diesel engine and make it work. The working of a diesel hammer can be briefly described as follows. The falling ram compresses a mixture of diesel and air in the cylinder to a very high value and ignites it so that the energy imported to the pile is not only due to the falling weight but also the explosion of the mixture. As the pile is driven in a three-step operation of air compression, ram impact and explosive force, there is less damage to the pile, when it needs hard driving. As the cycle is to be repeated by the upward rebound of the hammer, it is not easy to operate this hammer in soft soils, which do not produce enough rebound. The recommended pile driving formula to be used in these diesel hammers is of the following form [2].

$$R_u = \left(\frac{E}{S + C} \right) \left(\frac{W}{W + P} \right) \tag{10.9}$$

The value of energy E depends on the rating of the hammer. For the Japanese Kobelco hammers, $E = 2WH$ where W is the weight of the hammer and H is the drop. Thus, these hammers deliver twice as much energy as a drop hammer.

To select a hammer required for pile driving, we first estimate the depth to which the pile should penetrate to get the required capacity by using the static bearing capacity formula like Meyerhof's formula. Then we choose a hammer for the desired set. Alternately, determine the necessary set for the available hammer. Such a procedure will save a lot of expense in pile foundations. Otherwise we tend to drive down the piles much in excess of the required capacity and length or tend to drive a pile with a hammer unsuitable for its weight. The above procedure is very important.

10.5 DRIVING STRESSES IN PILES

IS 2911 Part I Sec. 3 (second revision) Clause 6.11.5.1 gives the following method to determine the dynamic stresses created in the pile while driving. An approximate value can be obtained by multiplying the static value, R/A (where R is got from a pile driving formula and A is the equivalent area of pile including the steel) by a multiplying factor. With reference to the static values R/A in N/mm^2 driving can be classified as follows [4]:

Easy driving	3 to 5 N/mm^2
Medium	7.0 N/mm^2
Hard	10.0 N/mm^2
Very hard	$\geq 14.0\ N/mm^2$

The multiplying factor suggested by IS 299 for estimation of actual dynamic stresses is $(2/\sqrt{\eta}) - 1$, where η is the efficiency of the blow (Section 10.2.1). This procedure gives a rough idea of the driving stresses in the pile. The wave analysis method (Section 10.12) is the second method to estimate these stresses.

Bowles [3] recommends that driving stresses as obtained above from R/A should not be greater than 0.4 to 0.5 cube strength (0.5 to 0.6 the cylinder strength) of the concrete. *Stresses in the range of* $0.68 f_{ck}$ *may result in pile fracture beneath the ground level*. In all cases driving stresses for different sets can be calculated and a diagram showing driving stress against set can be drawn as explained in Example 10.2. This diagram can be used to select the hammer and set for a given field conditions.

Another problem that causes anxiety in pile driving is the settlement or heave in adjacent structures due to pile driving. Heave is observed in clays and settlement in sands. The magnitude of the effect decreases with the distance of the structure from the pile. For ordinary drop hammers the average the effect has been felt only for a distance of about 30 m (100 ft). from the pile being driven. For other high energy hammers the effect will be felt farther.

10.6 JETTING OF PRE-CAST PILES

In sandy deposits jetting can be adopted for easy penetration. This has been used in many places along canal banks for revetment and it is easy in operation. For this purpose, usually a central jet pipe (50–75 mm) in size is cast in the pile terminating into a tapered nozzle emerging at the sides. The piles are jetted to about one metre above the founding depth and then driven down by a hammer to the final depth. Adequate quantity of water at the required pressure should be pumped for successful jetting down of the pile [4]. This principle of jetting down piles have been very successively used for installing sheet piles in sand deposits for making cofferdams and for construction of bridge piers also. IS 2911 Part 1–Sec.3, Clause 8.5.6 under "Control of Pile Driving" gives very good information regarding jetting of piles, estimation of water required for jetting and other matters. In practice, jetting pressures of 5 to 10 kg/cm^2 and up to 2 litres of water per minute per square centimetre of pile cross-section are used in sands.

10.7 EXAMINATION OF SUITABILITY OF HAMMER FOR DRIVING

Pile specifications state that piles should be installed for a given set. However the temporary compression can be looked upon as a fixed amount of energy for a given value of R to be expended before the rest of the energy of the blow can be transferred to the pile to move it downwards. Hence too light hammers with low energy cannot be efficient. Also, falls of over 1.5 m for continuous periods will be very harmful to piles and piling equipment. Another problem that faces the piling engineer is the stresses created in continuous hard driving through hard ground or a serious of hard beds that have to be penetrated. Continuous amount of energy delivered at the top without penetration is returned as rebound, which can result in producing tensile stresses in the pile, fatigue and collapse of the piles, especially in places where such damages may not be visible. In such situations, the piles should be made stronger as a rule, especially by using larger amount of laterals (stirrups) and also special precautions should be taken in driving the pile.

As a thumb rule, hammers are selected with respect to the weight of pile, to have an efficiency of not less than 30%. As timber piles are light, the weight of the hammer usually tends to be as much as the weight of the pile itself. For concrete piles, the weight of hammer should not be less than one half the weight of the pile and in no case, less than one third the weight of the pile. The fall to be adopted should not be more than 1.3 m for drop hammers. In the field, we should select as heavy a hammer as possible. The height of the fall should then be selected to give a reasonable good set.

10.8 LIFTING AND PITCHING OF PILES

The usual diameters and maximum lengths of precast R.C driven piles are as follows:

> 250 mm square or dia. — 12 metres in length
> 300 mm square or dia. — 15 metres in length
> 350 mm square or dia. — 18 metres in length
> 400 mm square or dia. — 21 metres in length
> 450 mm square or dia. — 25 metres in length

Piles are first lifted and then pitched from the various points for driving. The maximum bending moments created for various types of lifting and pitching operations are as in Table 10.4.

TABLE 10.4   COEFFICIENTS FOR SHEAR AND BEARING

Operation	Shear	Bending moment
*Lifting $1/5$ th points–(2 points)	0.20 W	$WL/40$
Lifting $1/4$ th points–(2 points)	0.25 W	$WL/32$
Pitching from $1/3$ th points–(1 point)	0.66 W	$WL/22$
Pitching from $1/5$ th points–(1 point)	0.80 W	$WL/14$
Pitching from $1/4$ th points–(1 point)	0.75 W	$WL/18$
Pitching from one end	0.50 W	$WL/8$

*Means lifting at two points each $1/5$th length from the ends.

Note: During hoisting, the pile will be *suspended* at one point near the head. The bending moment will be the least when it is pulled at $0.23 L$ when the value of the bending moment will be $WL/23.5$ (IS 2911) Part I/Sec. 3)

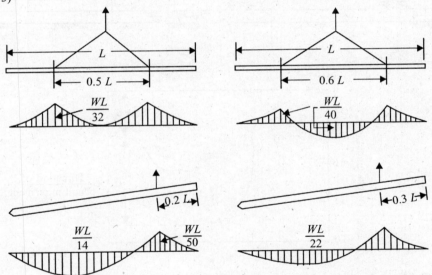

Fig 10.2   Maximum moments induced in pre-cast piles during handling.

10.9   FIELD MEASUREMENT OF SET OF PILES

Set is defined as the distance through which the pile (or casing in driven cast in-situ piles) travel in the final stages of driving for say, the last 10 blows. Piles are to be driven till the final required set is obtained. For example it may be specified as 25 mm in 10 blows (or set of 2.5 mm per blow) with a 3 ton hammer. A set of 1 to 2 mm for 10 blows is taken as refusal. However sets less than 0.5 mm per blow are not generally used in the field as the driving operation can be too slow and the piles can get damaged with heavy hammers. The measurement of set in the field is to be carried out as specified in IS 2911. In brief the set as well as the temporary compression of the pile and the ground can be measured in the field by fastening a sheet of paper to the pile with a pencil on a horizontal support and moving the pencil horizontally along the paper as the pile is driven. The trace thus obtained will give the set and the temporary compression caused by driving the pile. The profile will be somewhat as shown in Fig. 10.3c.

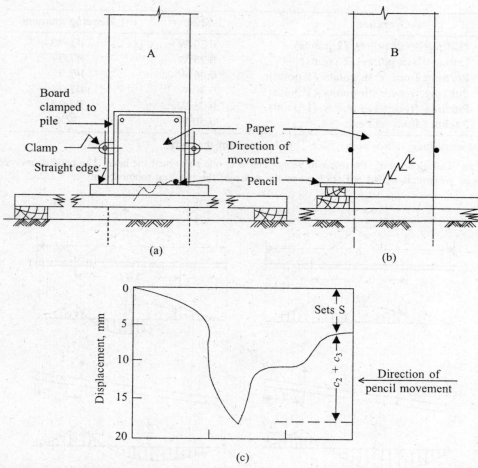

Fig 10.3   Field measurement of temporary compression: (a) Typical method pencil in front; (b) alternate method pencil on side; (c) typical graph.

One of the most important points that should be remembered in pile driving (but unfortunately not practised very much in the field) is that value of $C_2 + C_3$ assumed in our preliminary calculations should be verified as far as possible in the field by site measurement. This is especially true when we have to specify the set required. For *an economical design* all driven piles in all soil formations need not be driven to refusal with a heavy hammer. Piles have to be driven only to such depth as needed to develop the required resistance with safety or to develop enough anchorage to withstand the uplift forces. In practice most pile driving contractors insist that the client drives the piles to refusal, to depths greater than required. Hence a lot of money and time can be saved by a proper study of the problem as explained in Example 10.6 and making field measurement of $C_2 + C_3$. It is advisable to draw the "set-pile capacity" and "set pile stress" diagrams before prescribing the required set. This must be made compulsory as a field practice.

10.10 FIELD RECORD OF PILE DRIVING

It is very important and mandatory that careful records of driving of each pile should be kept as specified by IS 2911 Part I Sec. 3—Pile Casting and Installation Record. Any discrepancy in the set or depth for the required set should be immediately brought to the notice of the engineer in charge.

10.11 OTHER PILE DRIVING FORMULAE

The following two formulae have also been currently used in India for estimating the ultimate load capacity of driven piles.

10.11.1 Simplex Formula for Friction Piles

The skin friction component also of the pile capacity is brought into an empirical expression in the *simplex formula* by measuring the total hammer blows for the full driving of the pile. In this case, it is necessary to maintain a uniform fall of the hammer throughout the driving of the pile. The formula is expressed as

$$R = \left(\frac{N_p}{L}\right) \times \frac{WH}{2.54 + s} \times \sqrt{\frac{L}{2.36}} \text{ (kN)} \tag{10.10}$$

where

R = ultimate driving resistance in kN

N_p = total number of blows to drive the pile

L = length of pile in metres

W = weight of hammer in kN

H = height of free fall in metres

s = average set i.e. penetration in cm for the last blow being the average of last four blows.

10.11.2 Janbu Formula [6]

Another formula recommended by IS 2911 for estimating ultimate capacity R_U of driven piles is the Janbu formula. In this formula, the units to be used are kN and m with $FS = 3$ to 6.

$$R_U = \frac{1}{k_U} \times \frac{\alpha W H \eta}{S} \tag{10.11}$$

where

R_U = ultimate capacity (FS to be used, 2.5)

η = efficiency factor (0.70 for good, 0.55 for average and 0.40 for difficult or bad driving conditions)

$k_U = C_d \left(1 + \sqrt{1 + \lambda_c / C_d}\right)$

$C_d = 0.75 + 0.15 \, P/W$

W = weight of hammer/ram

P = weight of pile

$\lambda_c = \alpha WH/AES^2$

H = height of fall of hammer in metres (α as mentioned in Sec. 10.2.2)

A = area of pile or area of casing for cast in site pile.

E = elastic modulus of pile or casing tube in cast-in-situ pile.

S = set per blow (average of last four blows)

L = length of pile

10.12   WAVE EQUATION ANALYSIS OF PILES [WAP]

In offshore oil industry, situations arise where a small number of very large diameter piles up to 1.8 to 2 m in diameters have to be driven by very heavy hammers (as heavy as 200 tons) to develop bearing capacities as high as 3000 tons. For economy and smooth progress of work in such cases considerable time and effort should be spent during the planning and design stage itself to select proper pile driving equipment so that piles can be driven with the available hammers and for the required penetration to develop the ultimate resistance. The wave equation analysis is principally used for the following cases:

1. Evaluating drivability with a given hammer.
2. Relating pile capacity per specified blow with the given hammer.
3. Investigating pile driving stresses and field control of driving to prevent damages in piles. It can predict also tension that may occur in piles during driving.
4. Testing the capacity and integrity of piles already installed at the site.

Unlike the pile driving formulae, the wave equation *analysis is suitable for piles in all types of soils.*

10.12.1   Review and Basic Assumptions

It was around 1950 that E.A.L. Smith, a mechanical engineer working with Raymond Pile Co., first suggested the use of wave equation analysis to analyse problems in pile and he published his findings in 1960 [5]. Later due to the work of a large number of investigators this method has been refined to its present form. Whereas the old dynamic formula like Hiley formula use Newton's law of motion relating to impact for the analysis of piles, the new wave equation method of analysis examines the dissipation of the energy of the impact wave with time as it travels down the pile to its tip and is reflected back to the pile head. The energy given by the hammer generates a compression wave in the pile, which travels down at a speed equal to the velocity of sound in the pile material, given by the following formula

$$v = (E/\rho)^{1/2}$$

where

v = velocity of sound

E = modulus of elasticity of the material of the pile

ρ = density of the material of the pile.

This wave energy given to the pile by the hammer down is dissipated by the side resistance of the soil, as it travels down. If there is any energy left as it travels to the tip, it works against the tip resistance causing penetration of the pile into the soil. In doing so it starts a reflected compression stresses wave back to the head of the pile. In long piles with little or no soil resistance at the point, the reflected wave can cause critical tensile stresses and cracking near the bottom or middle of the pile.

10.12.2 Computer Program

It is very difficult to workout wave equation analysis by hand calculations. Bowles in his book on Analytical and computer methods in foundation engineering [6] gives a small programme illustrating the basic problem of wave analysis. More refined general-purpose programmes, which can handle many more variables are also available in the market. In the following sections, the basic theory of PDA (pile driving analyzer) is presented.

This method of analysis got a boost when CAPWAP (case analysis of piles by wave analysis of piles) was developed (Section 10.12.6). Today it is considered as the most reliable method for estimating the capacity and integrity of pile foundations by direct measurement.

10.12.3 Differential Equation for the Longitudinal Transmission of Stress in a Rod

The stress wave produced by a hammer blow on top of a rod travels down the rod. Its velocity, (denoted by U) at any point on the forces on the element as shown in Fig. 10.4 can be expressed as follows [5]: Let R be the resistance force,

$$\text{Force, } F_r = AE \times \text{strain} = AE\frac{\partial u}{\partial y}$$

$$\text{Force, } F_B = AE\left[\frac{\partial u}{\partial y} + \frac{\partial^2 u}{\partial y^2}dy\right]$$

$$\text{Balance force, } \Delta F = F_B - F_r = AE\left[\frac{\partial^2 u}{\partial y^2}\right]dy \pm R\,dy \tag{a}$$

However,

$$\Delta F = \text{mass} \times \text{acceleration} = Ma$$

$$= (\text{area} \times \text{density} \times dy)(\text{acceleration})$$

$$= A\rho\,dy\frac{\partial^2 u}{\partial t^2} \tag{b}$$

Equating relations (a) and (b) above, we get

$$\frac{\partial^2 u}{\partial y^2} = \frac{E}{\rho}\frac{\partial^2 u}{\partial y^2} \pm \frac{R}{A_p} \tag{10.12}$$

But $E/\rho = v^2$, where v = velocity of the stress wave. Thus, we get the basic equation of propagation of wave as follows, which is similar to Eq. 10.12.

$$\frac{\partial^2 u}{\partial t^2} = v^2\frac{\partial^2 u}{\partial y^2} \pm \frac{R}{A_p} \tag{10.12a}$$

The components of the hammer-pile-soil model as shown in Fig. 10.4 are used in practice to solve the above equation.

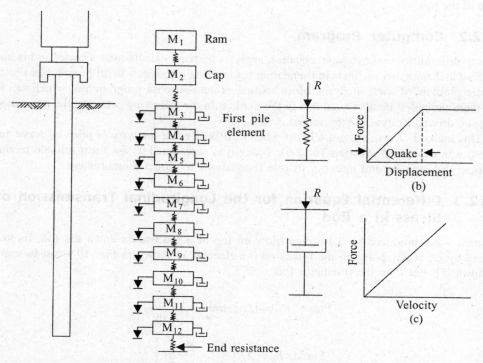

Fig 10.4   Smith idealization for wave equation analysis of pile during driving.

(a) The ram, cap block, pile cap, and cushion block are represented by a system of discrete weight and springs.

(b) The pile is divided into a number of segments along its length as discrete lengths, area and elasticity (spring stiffness).

(c) The frictional soil resistance on the side of the pile is represented as a series of side resistance R_U. This can be positive or negative. In addition soil is represented as an elastoplastic spring with quake and damping constants.

(d) The point resistance is represented by a simple spring and dashpot under the point of the pile.

A wave equation computer programme can be written for calculating the various elements in the above system for the velocities, displacements and forces generated by the impact of the blow for definite time increments [3], [6]. The following items are important in this context.

1. *Selection of time interval.* It is obvious that the time interval to be selected for the propagation of the waves is important in this study. *It should be short and should be such that the distance travelled by the wave in the time interval must be much less than the length of the segment of the pile chosen.* Thus for example, for a segmental length of 2.0 m and assuming it should be one half the travel time,

$$\Delta t = \left(\frac{2.0}{v}\right)\left(\frac{1}{2}\right) \text{ (say)}$$

Assuming $v = 5000$ m/s,

$$\Delta t = \frac{0.5 \times 2}{5000} = 0.2 \times 10^{-3} \text{ seconds}$$

It can be shown [6] that if the pile is divided into independent segments, the accuracy of the solution will depend more on the choice of the period Δt than the number of segments to which the pile is cut. This principle is very important in wave equation analysis.

2. *Spring constant of pile.* The spring stiffness of each of the elements ΔL of the pile is the force required for unit deformation of the element.

$$\left(\frac{F}{A}\right)\left(\frac{\Delta L}{1}\right) = E \quad \text{or} \quad F = \frac{FA}{\Delta L}$$

3. *Soil quake.* The maximum amount of elastic soil deformation or movement that should take place before the soil reaches plastic failure is defined as the *soil quake*. We have two types of quakes namely, the loading quake and the unloading quake. The unloading quake can be estimated as the total rebound of the pile head minus the elastic compression of the pile. From the results of a large amount of field and theoretical work, the values recommended for loading soil quakes for the sides and the pile points are given in Table 10.5.

TABLE 10.5   RECOMMENDED VALUES OF SOIL QUAKE

Soil	Desai and Christian [7]		Bowles [6]
	Side quake (mm)	Point quake (mm)	Quake (mm)
Sand	5.08	10.16	1.3–5.1
Clay	2.54	2.54	1.3–7.6
	(Unloading quake of 2.54 mm for both sands and clay)		

4. *Soil damping parameters (J).* The viscosity of the soil is represented by dashpots in which the force is proportional to the velocity. Different values of soil damping parameters have been recommended by various authors as shown in Table 10.6.

TABLE 10.6   RECOMMENDED VALUES OF SOIL DAMPING PARAMETERS

Soil	Desai and Christian [7]		Bowles [3]
	Friction damping, J Sec/m	Point damping (J') Sec/m	Damping constant, J Sec/m
Sand	1.65	0.55	0.33–0.66
Clay	0.66	0.003	1.31–3.3

5. *Soil resistance.* Smith expressed the instantaneous side soil resistance force acting on the rigid pile mass as R_d. It consists of the static soil resistance and the resistance due to velocity of penetration and is expressed as:

$$R_d = R_s(1 + JV)$$

where

R_d = total soil resistance

R_s = static soil resistance

J = damping constant

V = instantaneous velocity of soil

The soil resistances on the sides and tip have to be determined by the analysis.

10.12.4 Effect of Soil Parameters

As regards pile forces, Bowles [6] state that soil parameters are not very critical in wave equation analysis. Thus for the range of quake values 1 to 3 mm, the variation of computed pile forces vary only 2 to 3%. However, soil parameters are necessary for the equations to give results. The characteristics of the hammer (weight and efficiency) and the nature of cushion play a much more important part in the analysis than the soil parameters.

The sum of side resistance (R_d) and point resistance (R_p) gives the ultimate pile resistance, that is, $R_U = (R_d + R_P)$.

By wave analysis of a given pile and hammer, we can construct the following graphs (see Section 10.2):

1. Driving resistance (kN) against set (blows for 300 mm) for different hammers for assessing equipment suitability for pile and soil conditions.

2. Driving resistance against set for the chosen hammer and pile capacity.

3. Driving stresses against set (top and bottom compression stresses, tension stresses in concrete piles) for checking their values.

4. Driving resistance against pile length for determining the length of pile for the necessary resistance (i.e. resistance distribution along the length of pile.)

10.12.5 Case Method Analysis and Pile Driving Analyser [CAPWAP]

In 1964, research at Case Western University under Gobble led to the development of an easy to use technique to predict pile capacity under dynamic loading by direct measurement [8]. The procedure is shown in Fig. 10.5. Reusable transducers measuring strain and acceleration are attached with bolts or anchors to the pile head and the output produced during driving of piles are directly measured. Alternately they can be directly entered a computer to perform instant wave equation analysis. This method of analysis is known as the Case Method of Analysis of Piles (CAP). Equipment known as Pile Driving Analyzer (PDA) machines are available for use in the field that give the predicted pile bearing capacity for each hammer blow. This method is known as CAPWAP method (Case Analysis of Piles by Wave Analysis of Piles). The capacity predicted by this method is known as the Soil Resistance at time of Driving (SRD). The transferred energy, the maximum tensile and compressive stresses, the maximum pile top movement, velocities and accelerations and also an indication of pile integrity can be obtained. The equipment can also be used for testing the integrity of cast in-situ piles as described in Chapter 14 on Field Testing of Piles. Table 10.7 shows the results of WAP tests as reported from Singapore [9] [10]. They agree quite well with field load tests.

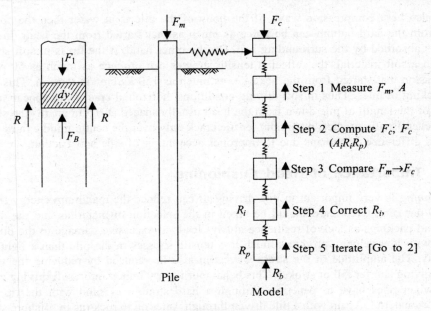

Fig 10.5   CAPWAP method of analysis.

TABLE 10.7   RESULTS FROM WAP ANALYSIS USING CASE METHOD [9][10]

S. no.	Material of pile	Capacity by WAP analysis (tons)			Damping constant (J), s/m		Quake (mm)		Ultimate load from tests (tons)
		Total	Skin	Toe	Skin	Toe	Skin	Toe	
1	Concrete	272	262	10	0.6	0.5	6	2	268
2	Concrete	360	260	100	0.3	0.95	2	5	380
3	(Steel)	372	352	20	0.5	0.3	2	3	330
4	(Steel)	310	300	10	0.28	2.5	5	5	390
5	(Steel)	250	240	10	0.43	2.16	4.5	4.5	283
6	(Steel)	400	305	95	0.1	0.7	7.5	20	390

10.13 TENSION CRACKING OF PILES DURING DRIVING

Apart from damages by compression due to overdriving, cracks can also appear due to tension. The stress wave theory can explain many of the observed phenomena of tension cracking of piles during driving. When a concrete pile is struck by a hammer at its top, the impact lasts only for 4 to 8×10^{-3} seconds. The compression wave travels at about 4000 m/second. The wavelength of the stresswave depends on the duration of the impact and is of the order of 16 to 50 m. The maximum compressive stress at the pile head can be generally 70 to 240 kg/cm^2. In some cases it may be as high as 300 kg/cm^2. If this compression wave travelling to the tip meets a hard bottom, the reflected wave will also be a compression wave. If the body of the pile is in water then the compression produced from the hard bottom can be twice as much as that started from the head. In practice a large part is absorbed by the surrounding soil. On the other hand, if the tip is in soft soil and the driving is in a soft material, the reflected tensile stresses can produce as much as 50 per cent of the compression that started from the head i.e. as much as 150 kg/cm^2 in tension. This can cause serious cracking of piles. Thus in soft driving conditions, horizontal cracks can appear suddenly at about 1/3 of the length of pile down from the head usually spaced at 0.5 m apart. The stress wave theory however usually predicts maximum tensile crack only over the centre middle third of the pile length. This difference is perhaps due to improper accounting of side soil friction.

10.13.1 Importance of Head Cushioning

Head cushioning is very important in pile driving. It can reduce the maximum energy transfer as much as 50 per cent. Great care should be taken in the selection of materials and the dimensions of dollies and packings as lack of resilience always leads to excessive damage to the pile head. A heavy ram with low velocity produces much less tensile stresses in the pile than a light ram with high velocity. The amplitude of the stress wave can also be reduced by reducing the velocity of impact (by giving shorter fall or stroke). This behaviour is very important in soft driving conditions, especially when piles have to penetrate through a hard stratum of sand with the tip travelling through a soft material. Again with a pile driven through water on to rock (as in offshore structures), a high compressive stress can reflect from the tip and travel to the head. If there is no ram, as it reaches the head to produce compression, it can theoretically reflect back from the free head as a tensile wave. However, in practice, this is very rare mainly due to damping and skin friction acting in the system.

10.14 SUMMARY

The classical method of estimation of the ultimate bearing capacity of piles by dynamic formulae is more accurate for granular soils than for saturated soft clays which develop pore pressures during pile driving. The modern wave analysis gives a better prediction of pile capacity in all types of soils. The use of pile Driving Analyser equipment has considerably helped to predict the capacities of piles more accurately by field observation during the installation of the pile. PDA equipment can also be used for integrity testing of piles that have been already installed at site.

The best way to choose the hammer and the required set with conventional pile driving is by drawing the load-set and stress-blows diagrams (as explained in Example 10.2). For large projects, decisions regarding pile capacity, hammer to be used and set to be specified should be made only after preliminary pile driving and field load tests. For small projects, the assessments have to be made from experience and from calculations based on static formula as well as the performance of a few working piles driven in the beginning of the project.

EXAMPLE 10.1 (Application of Hiley formula)

A reinforced concrete pile 500 × 500 mm and 15 m long is to be driven in a cohesionless soil by a 5 ton hammer with a fall of 2 m. Determine the set to be specified if it is to have a safe capacity of 120 tons. Assume it is driven finally with a follower of weight 0.2 tons. Driving is without dolly or helmet, but with cushion on top of pile. Assume f_{ck} = 20 N/mm^2.

Ref.	Step	Calculations
	1	*Check required ultimate bearing capacity with structural capacity*
Sec. 11.6.1		Structural capacity = $0.25 \times 20 \times 500 \times 500 = 125$ t (120 t acceptable)
		$R_U = 120 \times 2.5 = 300$ t (assume $F.S = 2.5$)
	2	*Data*
Sec. 10.2.2		Effective drop = $0.8 \times 2 = 1.6$ m; Wt. of hammer = 5 t
		Wt. of pile $= \left[(0.5 \times 0.5 \times 15) + \left(\dfrac{0.5 \times 0.5 \times 0.5}{3} \right) \right] 2.5 = 9.5\,\text{t}$
		(pile) (shoe)
		$P = 9.5$ t + Wt. of follower (0.2 t) $= 9.7$ t
Table 10.2		$e = 0.25$
	3	*Calculate efficiency*
Eq. (10.3)		$\eta = \dfrac{W + Pe^2}{W + P} = \dfrac{5 + 9.7(0.25)^2}{5 + 9.7} = 0.381$
	4	*Calculate value of C*
		$C = C_1 + C_2 + C_3$
Sec. 10.3.1		C_1 = temporary compression of dolly and packing
		$C_1 = \dfrac{1.761R}{A} = \dfrac{1.761 \times 300}{50 \times 50} = 0.212$ cm
Sec. 10.3.2		$C_2 = \dfrac{0.657RL}{A} = \dfrac{0.657 \times 300 \times 15.5}{50 \times 50} = 1.222$ cm
Sec. 10.3.3		$C_3 = 0.073 + 2.806\,\dfrac{R}{A}$
		$= 0.073 + \left(\dfrac{2.806 \times 300}{50 \times 50} \right) = 0.409$ cm
		$C = 0.212 + 1.222 + 0.409 = 1.843$ cm
		$C/2 = 0.921$ cm $= 9.21$ mm
	5	*Calculate required set*
Eq. (10.1)		$R = \dfrac{(WH\eta)}{S + C/2}$
		Effective fall $H = 0.8 \times 2 = 1.6$ m = 1600 mm
		$300 = \dfrac{5 \times 160 \times 0.381}{S + 0.921}$ (Using tons and mm units)
		$\therefore S = 0.095$ cm $= 0.95$ mm per blow
		Set penetration for 10 blows = 9.5 mm (or 10.5 blows for 100 mm.)
		The pile has to be driven by the specified hammer and fall to a set of 9.5 mm for 10 blows. This is practically driving to refusal.
		Note: In actual practice, values of $C_2 + C_3$ should be verified in the field while driving the piles.

EXAMPLE 10.2

Taking Example 10.1 draw the resistance–set and stress–set curves. Comment on the results assuming $f_{ck} = 25$ N/mm^2.

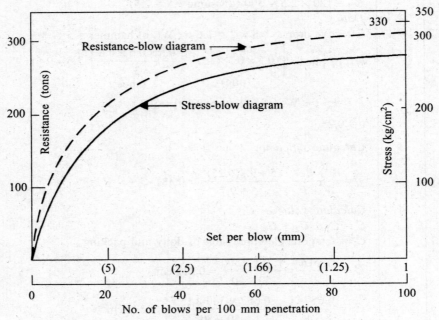

Fig. E.10.2

Ref.	Step	Calculations
Step 5	1	*Write down Hiley's pile driving formula*
Example 10.1		$R_U = \dfrac{5 \times 1600 \times 0.381}{S + 9.21}$ (in ton, mm units)
Eq. (10.1)		R_U for $S = 0$; $= 331$ tons.
	2	*Determine sets and stresses for different R_U values and tabulate.* (Stresses are calculated as shown in step 3)

R_U (t)	S (mm)	Stress (kg/cm^2)	Blows for 100 mm penetration
330	0	296	∞
300	0.95	269	105
250	2.98	224	33.5
200	6.03	179	16.5
150	11.10	134	9.0
100	21.27	90	4.7

Note: We assume C = constant which is not theoretically right.

Sec. 10.5	3	*Estimate driving stress or pile head* Multiplying factor $= \left(\dfrac{2}{\sqrt{\eta}} - 1\right)$ $= \left(\dfrac{2}{\sqrt{0.381}} - 1\right) = 2.24;\ A = 50 \times 50\ \text{cm}^2$
Example 10.1		Stress $= (R_U/A) \times 2.24$ $= \dfrac{R_U \times 1000 \times 2.24}{50 \times 50} = R_U \times 0.896\ \text{kg/cm}^2$ Tabulate and draw graph.
Sec. 10.5 Fig. E.10.2	4	*Comment on results* Max allowable stress $= 0.6 \times 250 = 150\ \text{kg/cm}^2$ (assumed) Stress for the required 10.5 blows per 100 mm penetration is 125 kg/cm^2. Hence driving can be considered as hard. It is near the maximum allowable stress.

EXAMPLE 10.3 (Calculation of set for piles)

Determine the set needed for the following piles, all driven by a 5 ton hammer falling through the height as shown in the table.

S. No.	Size of pile (mm)	Length of pile (m)	Fall of hammer (metres)	Pile capacity expected (tons)
1.	500 × 500	15	2	120
2.	400 × 400	15	1.5	90
3.	400 × 400	10	0.5	50
4.	300 × 300	15	1.0	60
5.	300 × 300	10	0.5	30
6.	225 × 225	10	0.5	25

Ref.	Step	Calculations
	1	Repeat the calculation as in Example 1 for the different piles. For 500 × 500 pile, from example, the set required is 9.5 mm for 10 blows.
	2.	*Set for* 400 × 400 *pile at* 15 m *with* 1.5 *fall* $R = 90 \times 2.5 = 225\ \text{t}$ $(\therefore F.S = 2.5)$ $h = 0.8 \times 1.5 = 1.2\ \text{m}$ $P_1 = 6.1\text{t};$ Wt. of follower $= 1.5$ (say) Wt. of pile $P = 6.1 + 1.5 = 6.25\ \text{t}$ Let $e = 0.25$ $\eta = \dfrac{W + Pe^2}{W + P} = 0.48$ $C = C_1 + C_2 + C_3 = 2.17;\ C/2 = 1.08\ \text{cm}$

$$225 = \frac{5 \times 120 \times 0.48}{S + 1.08}; \ S = 0.20 \text{ cm per blow}$$

$S = 20.0$ mm for 10 blows.

3   *Calculate the set required for* 400×400 mm—10 m *long pile for 50 ton capacity* Similar calculations give:

$S = 43.5$ mm for 10 blows

(*Note:* The resistance requirement is much lower and can be easily obtained by a 5t hammer)

4   *Calculate the set required for* 300×300 mm, 15 m *long pile for 60 ton capacity*
$S = 35.5$ mm for 10 blows

5   *Calculate the set required for* 300×300 mm—10 m *long pile for 30 ton capacity*
$S = 135.0$ mm for 10 blows

6   *Calculate the set required for* 225×225 mm—10 m *long pile for 25 ton capacity*
$S = 180.0$ mm for 10 blows

Tabulate the values as follows:

TABLE DATA FOR DRIVING WITH A 5 t HAMMER

Sl. No.	Pile size	Wt. of pile (tons)	Capacity tons	Efficiency η	Hight of fall of 5 t hammer (m)	Required set for 10 blows (mm)
1	500×500 (15 m)	9.5	120	0.38	2	9.6
2	400×400 (15 m)	6.1	90	0.48	1.5	20.0
3	400×400 (10 m)	4.1	50	0.57	0.5	43.5
4	300×300 (15 m)	3.4	60	0.61	1.0	35.5
5	300×300 (10 m)	2.3	30	0.70	0.5	135.0
6	225×225 (10 m)	1.3	25	0.80	0.5	180.0

This example is to show that as the weight of pile reduces in comparison to the weight of the hammer (3rd column), the efficiency of the blow increases (5th column). Efficiency analysis helps us in the selection of a proper pile hammer for driving the pile. Examine also the set required for lower pile capacities.

EXAMPLE 10.4   (Use of Janbu formula)

A 400×400 mm R.C. pile 20 m long weighing 74 kN is driven as a bearing pile with a set of 30 mm for last blows using a drop hammer 30 kN in weight falling through 1.5 m. Determine the capacity of the pile assuming a weight of dolly, helmet, packing is 4 kN. Use Janbu formula.

Ref.	Step	Calculations
Sec. 10.11.2	1.	**Data** Wt. of pile + dolly = 74 + 4 = 78 kN Wt. of hammer = 30 kN P/W = 78/30 = 2.6 (assume η = 0.44) Hammer more than 1/3 wt. of pile. Hence acceptable Assume hammer is single acting and hammer efficiency α = 0.9 Effective height of fall = 0.9 × 1.5 = 1.35 m Set $\dfrac{30}{10}$ = 3 mm = 0.003 m per blow
Eq. (10.11)	2	**Compute R_U by Janbu's formula** $R_U = \dfrac{1}{K_U}\dfrac{\eta WH}{S}$ $K_U = C_d\left(1 + \sqrt{1 + \lambda_C/C_d}\right)$ $C_d = 0.75 + 0.15\,P/W$ $\quad = 0.75 + (0.15 + 2.6) = 1.14$ $K_C = \dfrac{\eta WHL}{AES^2} = \dfrac{0.44 \times 30 \times 1.35 \times 20}{0.16 \times 15 \times 10^6 \times 9 \times 10^{-6}} = 16.5$ $K_U = 1.14\left[1 + \left(\dfrac{17.5}{1.14}\right)^{1/2}\right] = 5.60$ $R_U = \dfrac{0.44 \times 30 \times 1.35}{5.60 \times 0.003} = 1060\ \text{kN}$ With *F.S* = 2.0 $\quad Q = 530\ \text{kN} = 53t$
Eq. (10.1)	3.	**Compare with Hiley's formula** $R_U = \dfrac{WH\eta}{S + C/2}$ *H* and (*S* + *C*/2) in mm units (assume *C* = 19 mm) $R_U = \dfrac{30 \times 1350 \times 0.44}{(3 + 9.5)} = 1425\ \text{kN}$ $Q = 712\ \text{kN}$ (*F.S* = 2)
Sec. 9.3 and Sec. 11.6.1	4	**Check structural capacity** For f_{ck} = 20; working stress = 0.25 × 20 = 5 N/mm^2 $Q = 400 \times 400 \times 5 = 800\ \text{kN}$ Hence capacity = 80 tons Structural capacity exceeds soil capacity. Soil capacity controls.

EXAMPLE 10.5 (Simplex formula for friction piles)

A 300 mm dia. 20 m long pile is driven by a 3.75 ton hammer with a drop of 1 metre. The total number of blows for 20 m penetration is 550 and the last penetration reading was 60 blows for 1 m penetration. Estimate the capacity of the pile.

Ref.	Step	Calculations
Sec. 10.11.1	1	*Data for simplex formula* $N = 550$; $L = 20$ m; $W = 37.5$ kN. $\alpha H = 0.8 \times 1 = 0.8$ m; $S = \dfrac{1000}{60} = 1.67$ cm
Eq. (10.10)		$R_U = \dfrac{N}{L} \dfrac{WH}{(S + 2.54)} \left(\dfrac{L}{2.36}\right)^{1/2}$ L in m; H in m; S in cm; W in kN where $= \dfrac{550}{20} \times \dfrac{37.5 \times 0.8}{(2.54 + 1.67)} \left(\dfrac{20}{2.36}\right)^{1/2}$ $= 570$ kN $= 57$ tons *Note:* If the pile is to be considered as only an end bearing pile as worked by Hiley formula with $S = 1.67$ cm $= 16.7$ mm, and $C/2 = 24.45$ mm
Eq. (10.1)		$R_U = \dfrac{0.8 \times 3.75 \times 1000 \times 0.68}{(16.70 + 24.45)} = 49.0$ tons In end bearing, we assume all the energy is transferred to the tip of the pile.

EXAMPLE 10.6

Driven cast in-situ concrete piles 350 mm dia. are to be installed at a site by first driving a hollow steel tube into the ground by a winch operated hammer 3.75 tons in weight, falling through one metre and then pouring concrete into the hole. Total weight of the steel tube and dolly on top is 2 tons. Calculations by the static formula based on soil properties showed that the length of pile required is 15 metres for developing a carrying capacity of 40 tons. Field measurement of elastic compression $(C_2 + C_3)$ according to IS 2911 gave it as 10 mm. Estimate the set that will be required to develop the above capacity. Find the capacity of the pile if it is driven to a set of 50 mm in 10 blows.

Ref.	Step	Calculations
Sec. 9.3 and Sec. 11.6.1	1	*Check structural capacity (working load)* Assume $f_{ck} = 20$; allowable stress $= 0.25 \times 20 = 5$ N/mm^2 $Q = \dfrac{\pi(350)^2}{4} \times 5 = 480$ kN $= 48$ tons > 40t $R = 2 \times 40 = 80$ tons (ultimate with F.S $= 2$)

	2	*Find efficiency of blow*
Eq. (10.3)		$W > P$; then $\eta = \dfrac{W + Pe^2}{W + P}$ (assume $e = 0.3$)

$$\eta = \frac{3.75 + 0.18}{3.75 + 2.0} = 0.68$$

α for winch operated drop hammer = 0.8

	3	*Find elastic compression C*

$C_1 = 3.276 \times R$

Sec. 10.3.1

$$A = \left(\frac{\pi \times 35^2}{4} \right) / 4 = 962 \text{ cm}^2$$

$$C_1 = \frac{3.726 \times 80}{962} = 3 \text{ mm}$$

$(C_2 + C_3)(\text{measured}) = 10$ mm
$C = 3 + 10 = 13$ mm; $C/2 = 6.5$ mm

	4	*Estimate set required*
Eq. (10.1)		$R = \dfrac{\alpha WH\eta}{S + C/2} = \dfrac{0.8 \times 3.75 \times 1000 \times 0.68}{S + 6.5} = 80$ tons

Set $S = 19$ mm per blow or 190 mm for 10 blows

	5	*Capacity of pile for a set of 50 mm in 10 blows*

Note: For a study of the problem let us find R_U for different sets and tabulate the values.

R_U for set of 5 mm

$$R_U = \frac{0.8 \times 3.75 \times 1000 \times 0.68}{5 + 6.5} = 177 \text{ tons}$$

Calculate for different sets and tabulate as follows:

Set per blow (mm)	R_U	No of blows per 10 cm penetration
0	313	∞
2	240	50
5	170	20
10	123	10
15	95	6.7
20	77	5.0
25	64	4.0
30	56	3.4
40	44	2.3

6	*Plot the diagram R_U set and find set required* From diagram (Fig. E.10.6), set required = 19 mm for R_U = 80 tons. *Conclusion:* (1) As only 80 tons ultimate load is required, it is not necessary to drive the pile to refusal. (2) It is ideal to first estimate the length of pile by static formula and drive the pile to the required depth. Use dynamic formula to check the driving resistance in the field. Use load test to confirm the results. (3) As stated in IS 2911 it is always preferable to make field observation of $(C_2 + C_3)$ and substitute in Hiley's formula. It will give more accurate results, than the results got from book values.

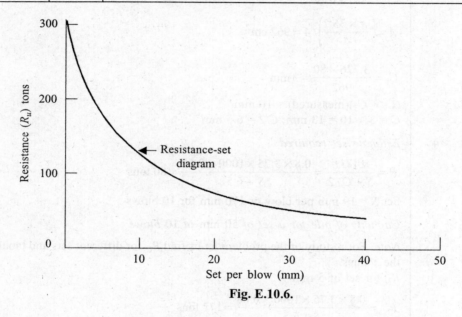

Fig. E.10.6.

REFERENCES

[1]   IS 2911 (1999), (Part 1, Sec. 3: *Precast Concrete Driven Piles* (Second Revision), Bureau of Indian Standards, New Delhi.

[2]   British Steel Piling Company Ltd., *the BSP Pocket Book*, London, 1969.

[3]   Bowles, J.E., *Foundation Analysis and Design*, International Edition, McGraw-Hill, Singapore, 1982.

[4]   Tomlinson, M.J., *Foundation Design and Construction*, E.L.B.S. Longman, Singapore, 1995.

[5]   Smith, E.A.L., Pile Driving Analysis by the Wave Equation, *Journal of Soil Mechanics and Foundation Division*, ASCE, Vol. 86(4), 1960.

[6]   Bowles, J.E., *Analytical and Computation Methods in Foundation Engineering*, McGraw-Hill, New York, 1974.

[7] Desai C.S. and Christian, *Numerical Methods in Geotechnical Engineering*, McGraw-Hill, New York, 1977.

[8] Gobble, G.G., Likins, G.E., and Rausche, F., Bearing Capacity of Piles from Dynamic Measurements, Final Report, Department of Civil Engineering, Case Western Reserve University, 1975.

[9] Chow, Y.K. and Smith I.M., *A Numerical Model for Analysis of Pile Drivability*, Proceedings of International Conference on the Application of Stress Waves on Piles, Sweden, 1984.

[10] Tan, S.B., et al., *Dynamic Pile Testing in Singapore,* 9th S.E. Asian Geotechnical Conference, Thailand, Dec. 1987.

[11] Chellis, R.D., *Pile Foundations,* McGraw-Hill, New York. 1961

[12] Janbu, N., An Energy Analysis of Pile Driving with the Use of Dimensionless Parameters. Norwegian Geotechnical Institute, Oslo Publication No. 3, 1953.

11

Structural Design of Concrete Piles

11.1 INTRODUCTION

In this chapter, we will deal briefly with the specifications for structural detailing of reinforced and pre-stressed concrete piles. The specifications for reinforced concrete piles are those specified in IS 2911 [1].

11.2 COVER TO BE USED

Nominal cover is defined as the design depth of concrete to all steel including links. The minimum nominal cover for piles as specified in IS 2911 are as follows. [1]

Cast in-situ piles—50 mm (normal) to 75 mm (aggressive) conditions. Pre-cast piles—40 mm (normal) to 50 mm (aggressive) conditions.

11.3 REQUIREMENTS OF CONCRETE FOR PILE WORKS

As concrete is fed in cast in-situ concrete piles by pouring it from the top, it is important that the pile holes are completely filled without external compaction and hence self compacting concrete is to be used. The mix should not also segregate during the fall. In bored cast in-place piles, concrete should be placed by tremie if it is placed under water or bentonite. In pre-cast piles, the pile is cast above the ground. The requirements of concrete for these different types of placements are given in Table 11.1.

TABLE 11.1 REQUIREMENTS OF CONCRETE IN PILES

Type of pile	Slump and cover (mm)	Required cement content, grade, water cement ratio
Driven cast in-situ (Type A piling; concrete poured in water free hole)	(a) Slump 100 (min.) to 150 (max.) (b) Cover 50 to 70	In normal conditions minimum cement content should be 400 kg/m³ and max *w/c* ratio 0.5 (Type and amount to comply with IS 2911 part I, Sec. 1. Annex E when sulphates are present and min. grade M25 to be used.)
Bored cast in-situ piles (Type B piling. Concrete placed under water)	(a) Slump 150 (min.) to 200 (max.) (b) Cover 50 to 70	Minimum 400 kg/m², max. w/c ratio 0.5. Tremie method to be used. (Mix to be altered when sulphates are present. Min. M25 grade to be used with plasticizers if necessary.)
Pre-cast driven piles of reinforced concrete (Type C)	(b) Cover 40 to 50	Minimum 330 kg/m³: max: w/c ratio 0.50; min. grade, M20
Pre-stressed concrete; pre-cast and spun piles	(b) Cover 40 to 50	Minimum grade, M40 to M60

11.4 DETAILING OF STEEL IN CAST IN-SITU PILES

Even though before the advent of IS 2911, many bored cast in-situ piles were constructed with reinforcements only on the top part of the pile, after the introduction of IS 2911 it is mandatory to provide minimum steel of 0.4% of the sectional area of the pile (calculated on the outside area of the casing if casings or shaft is used) for the full length of the pile. (Extra reinforcements as many be necessary for lateral load and moments on piles is also necessary.) The maximum percentage longitudinal steel reinforcement should be limited to 1.5 to is 2% to allow easy placement of concrete. The distance between bars in cast in-situ piles should be at least 100 mm for the full depth of the cage for easy flow of concrete. As the minimum reinforcement necessary for column action is 0.8% (many other codes specify it as 1%) the provision of 0.4% steel is not considered as giving any strength in such piles. The safe structural carrying capacity (design load) is calculated assuming the pile is unreinforced and the maximum allowable stress in concrete is $0.25f_{ck}$ which can be derived as follows.

$$P = \frac{P_U}{F.S} = \left(\frac{0.4f_{ck}}{1.6}\right) A_c = 0.25 f_{ck} A_c = \text{(maximum working load)}$$

Accordingly most codes specify that the average compressive stress under *working load shall not exceed* 25% of the specified cube strength at 28 days calculated on the total cross-sectional area of the pile (IS 2911 Part I/Sec. 1 1999. Clause 7.3.5).

The lateral steel of the reinforcing cage are to be in the form of links or spirals. The minimum diameter of the links should be 6 mm and if free of concrete the *spacing shall not be less than* 150 mm (IS 2911 Part I Sec. 2. 1999, Clause 6.11.3). These ties should be so spaced as to make the cage rigid. However, spacing of main steel and laterals should not hinder the free flow of concrete and the concrete should undergo self compaction since they are not subjected to any external compacting methods. Typical examples are given in Table 11.2.

TABLE 11.2   TYPICAL EXAMPLES OF PROVISION OF STEEL IN CAST IN-SITU PILES

Capacity (tons)	Dia. of pile (mm)	Longitudinal steel (Fe415)		Laterals
		No./dia	Percentage	
40	300	4 of 12 mm	0.64	6 mm @ 150 mm
60	400	6 of 12 mm	0.54	6 mm @ 150 mm
70	425	6 of 12 mm	0.48	6 mm @ 150 mm
120	550	6 of 12 mm	0.50	6 mm @ 150 mm
150	650	8 of 16 mm	0.48	6 mm @ 150 mm
200	750	10 of 16 mm	0.45	6 mm @ 150 mm

Note: Spacing of laterals should not be less than 150 mm.

11.5 DETAILING OF LONGITUDINAL STEEL IN PRE-CAST PILES

The longitudinal and transverse steel provided in piles should enable the pile to:

- Withstand handling stresses (see Chapter 10)
- Endure driving stresses (see Chapter 10)
- Provide the necessary structural capacity.

The maximum bending moment is produced while handling if the pile is pitched at the head. Its value is equal to $WL/8$. To prevent 'whipping' during handling, the L/D ratio of the pile should never exceed 50. Otherwise, segmental piling should be used. The percentage of longitudinal steel usually used for precast piles are as follows: (In all cases its adequacy for handling stresses should be checked.)

L/D ratio of pile	Per cent of longitudinal steel
< 30	1.2
30–40	1.5
> 40	2.0

As the percentage of longitudinal steel used is always more than 0.8% in pre-cast piles, it is allowed to design these piles as short columns *where the piles are wholly embedded in stable soils* or rock. The end conditions for a column should also be satisfied.

11.6 LINKS IN PRE-CAST DRIVEN PILES (IS 2911 PART I SEC. 3)

The laterals in pre-cast piles are of importance in resisting driving stresses, especially at the two ends. IS 2911 Part I (Sec. 3) 1999 Sec. 6.11.6 gives the following special emphasis on layout of *lateral reinforcements in pre-cast R.C piles*. In addition to the following, the spacing of links or hoops should also satisfy the conditions for a short column if it is so required. These conditions are:

1. The minimum diameter and spacing of links or hoops should allow free flow of concrete and at the same time give enough rigidity to the cage.
2. At each end of the pile, for a distance of about 3 to 4 times the least width, it should not be less than 0.6% of the gross volume of the concrete in that section.
3. In the body of the pile the links should not be less than 0.2% of the gross volume of the pile. (Generally, they are spaced not more than 150 mm or width of the pile.)
4. The transition should be gradual over a length of 3 times the least width of the pile.

While casting pre-cast piles, the longitudinal steel should be held apart by temporary or permanent spacer forks, at 1.5 m or less centred along its length. Field observations show that for square piles it is better to adopt a square layout of longitudinal steel with square laterals than a circular arrangement with circular loops. With the latter system, piles tend to crack up more easily on driving than with the former type.

11.6.1 Structural Capacity

With only nominal steel, the allowable structural capacity of piles is taken as $0.25 f_{ck} A_c$. Indian code IS 2911 Part I (Sec. 3) 1999 Sec. 6.5.1 state that the axial capacity of pre-cast piles after installation can be considered as its strength as a short column when the pile is wholly embedded in stable soil. When embedded in very soft soil or water or when it is free in air, it should be designed as a short or long column depending on its free length. The point of inflection at the embedded end is taken as 1 m or a minimum of 3 times the diameter in good soil and 3 m or 10 diameter in very soft soils above the ground (See Section 9.8). The details of reinforced concrete pre-cast pile are shown in Fig. 11.1.

11.7 PRE-STRESSED CONCRETE PILES [2]

The high strength of concrete and the initial compression of concrete help prevent micro cracking of concrete while handling and driving if the piles are pre-stressed. This compression also gives these piles good durability and resistance to corrosion in marine works. Even though solid pre-stressed piles have been used in India in many marine works, spun hollow pre-stressed concrete piles which are light and hence easy to drive and easy to connect together as segmental piles are yet to become popular in India. The advantage of pre-stressing can be explained as follows.

For M 35 concrete, static modulus of rupture is $0.7 f_{ck}$ that is, equal to 4.1 N/mm^2 while the dynamic value is 0.8 times the static value. Thus the dynamic value = $0.8 \times 4.1 = 3.5$ N/mm^2 (approx.). With a pre-stress of 5 N/mm^2, the rupture tension is $(5 + 3.5) = 8$ N/mm^2, which means greater resistance to cracking during driving of piles.

Gerwick [2] recommends a minimum steel ratio of 0.5% pre-stress steel of Fe 1500 N/mm^2 in these piles. Comparing it with Fe 415 steel it will correspond to the following percentage of steel.

$$\text{Equivalent Fe 415 steel} = \frac{0.5 \times 1500}{415} = 1.8\%$$

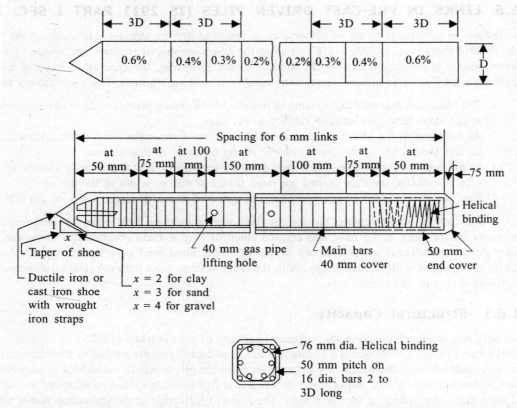

Fig 11.1 Arrangement of reinforcements in pre-cast driven R.C. piles. Distribution of laterals along the length of the pile as percentage of volume of pile.

In practice, an initial pre-stress of only 4.5 to 6.5 N/mm² is given to the concrete in the pile. As the pile has to act as a compression member too much pre-stress reduces the structural capacity. Where increased durability is required and where pile driving has to be avoided, pre-cast piles can be used in pre-bored holes as described in IS 2911 Part I, Sec. 4 (1999) with the annular space grouted. Pre-stressed concrete piles are being increasingly used to resist uplift (tension), bending and dynamic loads. Solid piles or filled-in hollow piles can be used as fenders to resist ship impact.

Structural capacity of pre-stressed piles. We can estimate the structural capacity of pre-stressed piles by the following methods:

1. From the ultimate load capacity
2. Using working load concept
3. By empirical method

From the ultimate load capacity

As a short pre-stressed column, the design load can be derived as follows:

$$P = \frac{P_U}{FS} = \frac{0.4 f_{ck} A_c - 0.6 f_e A_s}{FS}$$

where

FS = factor of safety 1.5 to 2

f_e = effective pre-stress after losses in steel

Using working load concept. Gerwick recommends the following formula:

$$\text{Load capacity} = \left[\frac{f_{ck}}{3.65} - \text{pre-stress after loss in concrete} \right] A_c$$

$$= [0.27 f_{ck} - f'_e] A_c$$

where f'_e = effective pre-stress in concrete (4.5 to 6.5 N/mm^2).

Hence for pre-stressed concrete piles, it is absolutely necessary that the value of f_{ck} should be very high. Spun concrete has the advantage that concrete up to M60 and M80 grades can be easily produced by the spinning process.

By empirical method. Based on field studies, Gerwick has recommended the following formula for working load on pre-stressed piles based on allowable stress and area [2].

$$P = 0.275 \times \text{cylinder strength} \times \text{area of concrete}$$

Hence we may adopt the same rule as used for reinforced concrete piles (i.e. the allowable stress in concrete should not exceed $0.25 f_{ck}$) for pre-stressed concrete piles also.

$$P = 0.25 f_{ck} \times A_c$$

11.7.1 Provision of Longitudinal Steel

In solid pre-tensioned pre-stressed concrete piles, strands (like 7 wire 12.5 mm size strands) are more suitable than rods for developing bond. Extra bars of ordinary steel, Fe 415 or Fe 250, may be provided for bonding with the pile cap at the head. In cylindrical spun piles, pre-stressed concrete wires are placed at mid-thickness along the periphery of the pile. In many cases button heads are also provided at the ends for anchorage.

11.7.2 Laterals in Pre-stressed Solid and Hollow Concrete Piles

As regards laterals, the general rules for solid R.C. piles should be followed for solid pre-tensioned piles also. There is to be an increase corresponding to the increased f_{ck}. However as longitudinal cracking has been noticed in hollow and cylindrical piles during driving, the Concrete Society, U.S.A. recommends a greater area of spirals to be provided for hollow concrete piles than for solid piles. It is better to provide laterals as spirals than hoops in cylindrical pile as the ends of pre-stressed piles are subjected to tensile bursting stresses due to pre-stress as well as radial bursting pressures from hammer blows. Hence, more binders are necessary at the top and bottom of these piles. The British Pre-stressed Concrete Development Group recommends 0.6% of the volume in the pile for solid piles. In USSR, they increase the steel area at the head by placing 5 layers of mesh spaced at 5 cm. In any case it will be advisable to provide steel area of at least one per cent as a *solid band around the pile* on the walls for a distance of 30 cm at pile head to withstand the impact stresses at the top. We also provide spirals of 6 mm dia. as close as possible at the bottom ends of the pile [2].

To withstand driving stresses Gerwick [2] recommends "hoops of *mild steel* placed as close as possible to the outside of the wall". As cover for durability is not of importance for this special steel its nearness to surface is of no concern. The absolute minimum steel of 0.8% up to 1% as laterals (0.4% for pre-stress bursting and 0.4% for radial bursting) should be provided in the top, for a length of at least one diameter or 30 cm, whichever is larger. Detailing of this top part is very important in hollow piles as otherwise they tend to break up during driving. Hollow pre-stressed spun concrete piles are provided with end plates and also with a steel band covering the sides as described above and as shown in Fig. 11.2. They are very helpful for extending the pile to large lengths by welding. Driving is possible immediately after completion of the welded joint, which takes hardly about 20–30 minutes. Such piles are extensively used in the far easte countries. As these hollow piles are less heavy than R.C. solid piles, lighter hammers can be used for driving these piles.

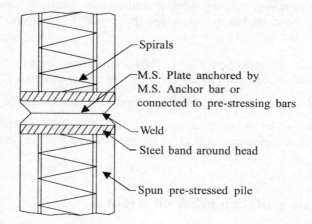

—Spirals

—M.S. Plate anchored by M.S. Anchor bar or connected to pre-stressing bars

—Weld

—Steel band around head

—Spun pre-stressed pile

Fig. 11.2 Details of the ends of pre-stressed concrete spun piles and method of joining the piles.

11.8 PILE SHOES

Pencil type pile shoes were once very popular for all pre-cast solid piles. Tests have demonstrated that pile shoes are unnecessary for a great majority of cases. For driving in sands, silts and clay, a square tip is satisfactory. Pile tips are generally given additional links or special reinforcements. Figures 11.1 and 11.3 show details of pile tips used for solid reinforced concrete piles. (Nozzle holes can be placed at the tips of piles, which are installed by water jetting. This may be a single nozzle at the tip or for easier penetration, one in the tip and four on the sides.)

Open and closed tips are used for spun piles in Japan. With open ended tips, as driving proceeds, skin friction develops at both exterior and interior surfaces up to a stage when plugging of the interior starts. After the formation of the plug (with soil inside) the pile behaves like a solid

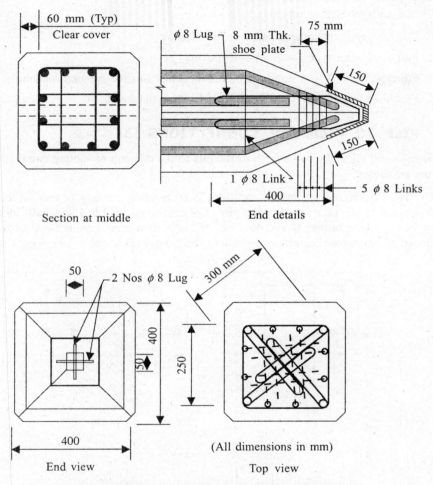

Fig. 11.3   Details of a pre-cast reinforced concrete pile.

pile. (In a test case, a plug of 2.6 m was formed inside a hollow driven pile of 15 m length). Thus there will not be much difference between driving a solid and a hollow pile of moderate length.

In Japan, where pre-stressed hollow piles are very popular, the following tips are used:

Open end shoes in spun piles:

1. *Standard type (outer taper)* commonly used. An outer taper of 30° is given to shoe and the cutting edge is reinforced by a round steel bar ring.

2. *Standard type (inner taper)* is the same as above, but with inner taper.

3. *Steel pipe type* where a steel pipe is attached to the end plate of the pile.

4. *Finned steel pipe type* in which fins are attached to the pipe to help to penetrate hard ground layers.

Closed end shoes in spun piles:

1. Standard type of concrete with no metal shoe

2. Full steel shoe type for sand and gravels

3. Fin type (with 3 to 4 numbers of fins attached to shoe for hard driving)

4. Flat head type where the tip is tapered into a flat head.

11.9 PILE TO PILE CAP CONNECTIONS [3]

Considering solid piles, the connection of the pile to the pile cap or footing can be divided into the following two cases:

Case 1: The load is mainly vertical and there is no bending moment or tension load (as exists in expansive soils) to be transmitted to the pile. The horizontal load is also small. In such cases, the concrete in the pile is broken out to the level of the bottom reinforcement mat of the pile cap and the exposed reinforcement continues to satisfy the *compression anchorage length* as in Fig. 11.4.

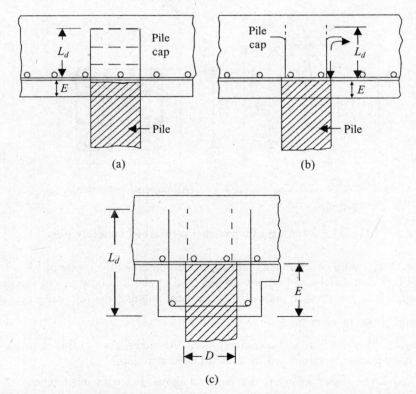

Fig. 11.4   Pile cap connection details of solid reinforced concrete pile: (a) Detailing anchorage to carry only compression; (b) and (c) detailing of anchorage length to carry compression and bending.

(*Note:* In case (c), cap extended to length E when bearing area is required to carry any horizontal load.)

Case 2: In this case, we have in addition to vertical compression load, horizontal, bending or tension loads. For solid piles, the exposed reinforcement should have enough bond length take the tension and bending by providing full tension on charge length. For punching shear detailing can be made as shown in Fig. 11.5.

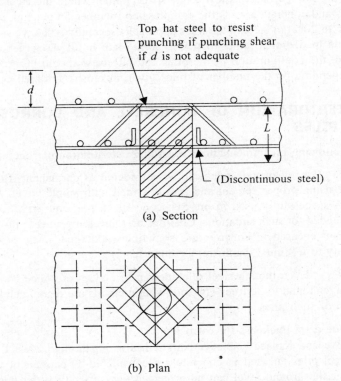

Top hat steel to resist punching if punching shear if d is not adequate

d

L

(Discontinuous steel)

(a) Section

(b) Plan

Fig. 11.5 Pile to foundation connection in pre-stressed piles: (a) Top hat reinforcement to resist vertical reaction if punching shear is exceeded; (b) diagonal bars provided to replace continuity of bottom steel.

In the case of hollow or pre-stressed piles, the pile to foundation connection can be detailed as follows. For the case of simple compression piles, the pile is cut down to the under side of the reinforcement mat of the foundation. In cases where moments are to be transferred, the piles are projected into the pile cap for a distance equal to the diameter of the pile. The connection should satisfy punching shear and bearing stress requirements also. In all cases, the horizontal load is taken by the bearing of the embedded length of pile so that the following condition is satisfied.

$$\text{Bearing stress} = \frac{\text{ultimate horizontal load}}{\text{dia. of pile} \times \text{embedment length}} = \frac{H}{DL} \not> 0.6 f_{ck}$$

Spun piles can be provided with end plates and the necessary reinforcement can be welded to this steel. Alternatively connection between the hollow pile cap and the pile can be also made by reinforced concrete cast into the top part of the hollow pile.

11.10 DESIGN OF PILE CAPS

There are two approaches for the design of pile caps involving two or more piles. In the first approach we consider the pile caps as a beam spanning between the piles. In the second approach we assume that the pile cap acts as a truss or space frame, where the steel reinforcements act as tension members and concrete acts as the compression member. In general, we find that there is a small saving (0.5 to 20%) of steel in the truss approach especially when we assume that the column load is acting in a loaded area rather than as a point load. In all cases, depending on the number of piles involved, the configuration of the piles and pile caps should be arranged in the standard configuration depending on the number of piles given in most reinforced concrete books [4].

11.11 DETERIORATION OF CONCRETE AND CORROSION OF STEEL IN PILES

Teng gives the following recommendations regarding deterioration of concrete and steel piles [5].

1. *Concrete piles:* Concrete piles can be considered as permanent if made of good quality concrete using proper cement and also provided with ample cover. Asphalt impregnation has been successfully used in pre-cast concrete in sea front structures and is sometimes recommended for such situations. Coatings on reinforcing steel to protect it from corrosion even when encased in concrete are sometimes specified. (Atmospheric corrosion takes place only to a limited depth from ground load.)

2. *Steel piles:* Even though steel piles driven in clays were once considered permanent it is no longer found to be true. The following methods are recommended for increasing the life span of such piles.

   — Provide extra thickness for corrosion
   — Remove and replace corrosive soils it has to go through at shallow depths
   — As steel piles encased in concrete are considered as permanent, the portions of steel piles near the ground level can be protected very effectively by encasing the piles with concrete.
   — Other methods of corrosion protection like cathodic protection can also be used.

   This subject has also been dealt with by Tomlinson [6]. He remarks that "provided that the chloride content of materials used for mixing the concrete are within limits, that admixtures containing chlorides are not used and the cover to the steel is appropriate, there should be little risk of corrosion damage in R.C. piles". It is essential that the concrete is dense and well compacted.

3. *Precautions to be taken in water containing sulphates:* The precautions recommended for concrete exposed to water containing sulphates as given IS 456-2000 should be always followed.

11.12 SUMMARY

Structural detailing of driven piles is very important as the piles have to withstand a large amount of driving stresses. It is also necessary that the detailing of piles to pile caps are carried out properly. The detailing to be used for the piles that are under direct loads and moments is different from the detailing to be used for the piles which are only under direct load with no moments.

EXAMPLE 11.1 (Detailing of pre-cast driven piles)

The available driving equipment can comfortably drive a pre-cast pile of 300 mm square in size for length of 10 m required at site. Detail the reinforcement assuming that the full structural capacity in compression of the pile can be mobilized by the bearing stratum. Assume pile passes through clay with cohesion more than 10 kN/m².

Ref.	Step	Calculations
Sec. 11.5	1	*Check size to length of pile* Max. *L/D* allowed for driven piles = 50 Max. length for 300 mm square = 15 m > 10 m
Sec. 11.5	2	*Find percentage of steel to be used and check* $$\frac{L}{D} = \frac{10 \times 1000}{300} = 33 > 30, \text{ use } 1.5\%$$ Assume normal cover = 40 mm (normal condition) (Using 8 mm laterals 20 mm dia. rods, distance to centre of steel = 40 + 8 + 10 = say 60 mm = cover to centre of steel.) (Cover O.K.)
	3	*Find area of steel* Required $A_s = \dfrac{1.5 \times 300 \times 300}{100} = 1350$ mm² Usually available bars are 20–25 mm: Using 4 bars of 20 mm gives 1257 mm² % of $A_s = \dfrac{1257 \times 100}{300 \times 300} = 1.4\% < 6\%$ (max. allowed) (Minimum steel for design as a column = 0.8%)
IS 456 Cl. 39.3	4	*Determine load capacity as a short column* With Fe 415 steel and $f_{ck} = 20$ N/mm² $P_U = 0.4 f_{ck}(A_c - A_s) + 0.67 f_y A_s$ $\qquad = 0.4 \times 20 \times (300 \times 300) + 0.67 \times 415 \times 1257$ (approx.) $\qquad = 1069$ kN $P \text{ (allowable)} = \dfrac{1069}{1.5} = 712$ kN say 70 tons
	5	*Check for hoisting and handling moments and shear:* Max. moments on handling occurs when the pile is picked up at one end $M = \dfrac{WL}{8}$ W = 0.3 × 0.3 × 25 × 10 = 22.5 kN $M_U = \dfrac{1.5 \times 22.5 \times 10}{8} = 42.2$ kNm (required) Moment of resistance on steel beam theory (neglecting concrete) $\qquad = \dfrac{1350}{2} \times 0.87 \times 415 \times (300 - 2 \times 60) = 44$ kNm > 42.2 kNm

		Hence, safe in worst handling moment (*Note:* If the pile is picked up at 0.293L, the bending moment will be least and then the *BM* = *WL*/23.3)
Sec. 11.6	6	*Detail links over length of pile* Distribute links as follows: 3*D* from ends 0.6% of volume of concrete 3*D* (transition) 03% of volume of concrete Balance at centre 0.2% Links for 3*D* at ends = 3 × 300 = 900 mm should be 0.6%
	6(a)	*Calculate for* 0.6% Volume $= \dfrac{0.6 \times 300 \times 300 \times 900}{100} = 486 \times 10^3$ mm^3 Cover to centre of link = 88 mm; area of 8 mm ϕ = 50.3 mm^2 Vol. of each lateral = (300 – 88) × 4 × 50.3 = 42.65 × 10^3 mm^3 Number of laterals required $= \dfrac{486}{42.65} = 11.39$ (say, 12)
Sec. 11.4		Spacing $\dfrac{900}{12}$ = 75 mm As spacing is less than 150 mm, we may use 12 mm dia. bar. (Maximum spacing allowed is width of pile = 300 mm)
Table 11.2		Area of 12 mm bar = 113 mm^2 Vol. of lateral = 95.8 mm^3 Number required $= \dfrac{486}{95.8} = 5.07$ Spacing $= \dfrac{900}{5} = 180$ mm > 150 mm Adopt 12 mm @ 180 mm for the ends (Similarly, work out for the others.)

EXAMPLE 11.2 (Structural strength of piles in tension)

Calculate the structural capacity of the pile in Example 11.1 if the pile is under tension due to uplift using M20 concrete and Fe 415 steel.

Ref.	Step	Calculations
	1	*Uplift capacity of piles (IS 2911– part I/Sec. 3. Clause 6.5.3)* Uplift capacity is the sum of frictional resistance and the buoyant or total weight of pile, as applicable with an *FS* = 1.5 (least *FS* can be 1.25) The tension capacity of the pile as a structural member should be more than its uplift capacity as a pile. Required to calculate structural capacity only.

	2	Find minimum steel as tension member (Fe 415 steel) (Minimum steel = 0.4% of total sectional area; we use working stress method for design) Steel in pile = 1.4% > 0.4% O.K. (i.e. A_s = 1257 mm^2)
Example 11.1 step 3		As = 1257 mm^2 (minimum required)
	3	Calculate capacity assuming all tension is taken by steel. Cracking is restricted with allowable tension in steel $T = A_s$ (permissible stress) = $A_s f_s$ B.S. allow the following stresses for Fe 415 bars, f_s = 100 (exposure A); 130 (exposure B) and 140 (exposure C) in N/mm^2 Assume f_s = 140 N/mm^2; A_s = 1257 N/mm^2 $T = 1257 \times 140 = 176$ kN (with limited cracking) f_s = allowable = 230 N/mm^2 (unlimited cracking) $T = 1257 \times 230 = 289$ kN (a)
	4	Calculate tension allowing no cracking of concrete $f_t = \dfrac{f_{ck}}{20}$ by limiting tension in concrete $A_e = A_c + (m - 1)A_s$; $m = \dfrac{280}{3\sigma_{cb}} = \dfrac{280}{3 \times 7} = 13$ (approx.) $A_e = 300 \times 300 + 12 \times 1257 = 105{,}084$ mm^2 [Equivalent area] $f_t = 20/20 = 1$ N/mm^2 $T = 105{,}084 \times 1 = 105$ kN (no cracking) (b)
*	5	Calculate capacity allowing cracking in concrete with no steel $f_t = \dfrac{0.7\sqrt{f_{ck}}}{(FS = 1.5)} = 2.08$ N/mm^2 $0.7 f_{ck}/FS\,(1.5) = 2.08$ N/mm^2 $T = 105{,}084 \times 2.08 = 214$ kN Note: As the steel area is more than the nominal, we can take the area of steel also into account in calculating tension capacity.
Step 4 Step 3	6	Summary of results of allowable tension in pile including its weight (a) No cracking allowed, $T = 105 + 22 = 127$ kN (b) No restriction on cracking, $T = 289 + 22 = 311$ kN Note: We have also to consider the tension capacity of the piles from considerations of the strength of soils, which is the side resistance.

EXAMPLE 11.3 (Design of bored cast in-situ piles)

Design the size and steel for a bored cast in-situ pile of structural capacity of 75 tons, using M25 concrete and Fe 415 steel.

Ref.	Step	Calculations
IS 2911 Sec. 2. part 2	1	*Estimate allowable concrete stress* Minimum grade of concrete shall be M25. $f_c = \dfrac{f_{ck}}{4} = \dfrac{25}{4} = 6.25$ N/mm^2 (allowable)
	2	*Determine diameter required for 75* t *capacity* $A = \dfrac{75 \times 10000}{6.25} = \dfrac{\pi D^2}{4}$ gives $D = 390$ mm Nearest commercial size = 400 mm
IS 2911 Sec. 2. Part 2 Cl. 6.11	3	*Estimate steel to be provided* Min: longitudinal steel =0.4% $A_s = \dfrac{\pi \times 400 \times 400 \times 0.4}{4 \times 100} = 502$ mm^2 Providing 6 rods of 12 mm dia. gives an area 678 mm^2, which is > 502 mm^2
Table 11.2	4	*Estimate laterals required* Provide laterals 6 mm @ 150 mm centre (laterals should not be placed at less than 150 mm)
	5	*Specify mix proportion* Minimum cement content is 400 kg/m^3 for bored pile. Use plasticizer to get necessary slump with min. *w/c* ratio, max. *w/c* ratio = 0.5. (*Note:* Even though the pile will have a structural capacity of 75 tons with enough *F.S.* the actual ultimate load as a pile will depend on the nature of the end bearing material and surrounding soil.)

REFERENCES

[1] IS 2911 (1999), *Code of Practice for Design and Construction of Pile Foundations, Part 1, Concrete Piles* (Second Revision), Bureau of Indian Standards, New Delhi.

[2] Gerwick, B.C., Pre-stressed Concrete Piles, *Journal of Pre-stressed Concrete Institute*, Detroit, October, 1968.

[3] Ray S.S., *Reinforced Concrete Analysis and Design,* Blackwell Science, London. 1995.

[4] Varghese, P.C., *Limit State Design of Reinforced Concrete*, 2nd ed., Prentice-Hall of India, New Delhi, 2002.

[5] Teng, W.C., *Foundation Design*, Prentice-Hall of India, New Delhi, 1965.

[6] Tomlinson, M.J., *Foundation Design and Construction*, ELBS Longman, Singapore, 1995.

12

Construction of Cast in-situ Piles

12.1 INTRODUCTION

Cast in-situ piles can be *driven cast-in-situ* or *bored cast in-situ*. The first type should be designed as a displacement pile and the second as a replacement type of pile. One of the advantages of these piles is that as there are no handling stresses in these piles, the steel reinforcements necessary is only minimal. The advantage of bored cast in situ piles is the least disturbance it causes to adjacent structures. In this chapter, we will briefly deal with driven cast in-place piles and in more detail with bored cast in-place piles.

12.2 CONSTRUCTION OF DRIVEN CAST IN-PLACE PILES

These piles are installed by first driving a heavy steel casing of 250 to 600 mm diameter depending on the diameter of pile required in segments of tubes each of 3 m length secured together with the lower end closed by an expendable shoe. The tube is driven into the ground by a hammer. In a successfully conducted job there should be no water in the tube before concreting these piles. This assures concreting to be carried out in dry conditions. Tremie method of placement of concrete cannot be used in these piles as it may interfere with the pulling out of the driven pipes.

Hence after the hole is formed by displacements of the soil, the reinforcement cage is lowered within the tube. The tube is then filled with high slump concrete through a funnel at the top up. Concrete is poured to a height more than one full length of one drive pipe at a time. One length of pipe is then pulled up keeping the level of the concrete always above the bottom of the remaining string of pipes. Some compaction of the concrete can take place by successively pulling up the pipe for a small distance and then pushing it down. Concrete is placed in sections so that sections of pipe can be pulled out. This type of placement of concrete is one of the disadvantages of this method. Some authorities do not recommend these piles for the following reasons.

- Pile driving causes disturbances in surrounding structures.
- As the concrete is poured from the top it tends to fall on the reinforcement cage before it reaches the bottom. Hence segregation can take place unless special care is taken in the mix design.

- Under certain circumstances this type of displacement piles can cause tension failure of the adjacent piles in which the concrete is still fresh and has not set. This is a very serious draw back. A number of such failures have been reported especially where the top-soil is clay. *This factor should also be examined in detail at all sites where driven cast in piles are planned.*

Studies regarding strength and segregation of concrete consequent to free fall up to 15 m show that we can reduce the ill effects if the concrete used is well designed with addition of super plastisers. Even though concrete hitting reinforcement bars produce rebounding of aggregates, movement of bars and complete coating of rebars with cement paste, special high slump mix of slump 100–125 using water reducers (super plastisers) can be specially designed for this type of placement [1].

12.3 BORED CAST IN-SITU PILES

These piles (also called as cast in-place piles) are very much preferred in cities as they do not cause any disturbance to surroundings. In bored cast in-place piles, the holes are first bored with a temporary or permanent steel casing or by using bentonite slurry to stabilize the sides of the bore. Holes can also be formed by augers. A prefabricated steel cage is then lowered into the hole and concreting is carried by the *tremie method* as described in IS 2911 and Sec. 12.9 below. Boring holes by using bentonite mud is much more popular than using casing pipes. One of the great advantage of this method is that large diameter piles (up to 5 m in diameter) can be installed by this method. Hence, these piles are very much used for bridges and other heavy structures. As these are very popular in India, we will deal with these in a little more detail. However, it should be clearly remembered that *bored piles smaller than* 400 mm *in diameter are not recommended for use in practice.* The sides of cast in-situ small diameter piles are liable to cave in. In such cases, there will be no continuity in the length of piles.

12.4 PROPERTIES OF BENTONITE TO BE USED

The specific gravity of most clays is about 2.7 so that suspensions of clay in water can be made up to a bulk density of 1.04 to 1.10 g/cc easily. As this density is higher than that of water, the technique of using drilling mud to stabilize deep holes for oil wells has been in practice from very early days in oil drilling industry. In addition bentonite clays have wetting properties which hold the particles in suspension for a very long time. Thus bentonite clay is the ideal material for the above use in normal conditions. However, bentonite tends to flocculate in salt water or water containing chemicals so that in such situations Altapulgite clay or Altapulgite mixed with illite is preferred. Alternately, in such situations, bentonite clay is mixed in fresh water for a minimum period of 24 hours and allowed to age before it is used in the bore hole. It is theoretically possible to use even ordinary clay and prepare a slurry by mixing and agitating it to keep the clay in suspension. Such a bore is called a *self-puddle hole*. The advantage of bentonite as compared to ordinary clays is that bentonite keeps itself in dispersed condition for a very long time and in course of time it forms a gel instead of flocculating and settling down like ordinary clays. In case of granular soils, the bentonite suspension penetrates into the sides under pressure and forms an impervious layer. In clays, it forms only a thin coating. The positive pressure inside the hole stabilizes the soil.

The bentonite to be used for bore holes should be of good quality and must be tested frequently to meet the requirements given in Table 12.1

TABLE 12.1   TEST FOR PROPERTIES OF BENTONITE, see [2]
(IS 2911 Part I Sec. 2)

Property	Result	Test
Density g/cc	1.03–1.10 ≯ 1.12	Mud density balance method
Viscosity	30–60 s (90*)	Marsh cone method
Shear strength (10 min gel)	1.4 to 10.0 N/m^2	Shear meter method
pH	9.0–11.5	pH indicator or paper strip
Liquid limit	> 450%	Casagrande apparatus.

(*Only under special circumstances)

Test for Bentonite. The preliminary tests for suitability of bentonite before its purchase for the purpose of pile construction are the following [2]:

1. Liquid limit—It should be 450% or more.
2. Swelling index (differential swell after 12 hours in abundant quantity of water > 540%)
3. Gel test—A 4% bentonite solution in water should form a gel, after the suspension is left standing undisturbed for some time
4. Sand content should be less than 7%.

The expected properties of the bentonite slurry are as follows.

— Heavy enough to stabilize the sides
— Viscous enough to hold the stones, gravel sand etc. in suspension
— Fluid enough to allow easy operation of tools and displaced by the concrete placed by tremie.

It is very important to note that the cutting action on soil is improved by the bentonite slurry of very good quality because of its higher density and higher viscosity. The power to lift up soil particles depends a lot on the qualities of the slurry. The concentration of good bentonite and the densities that can be obtained are as follows

Bentonite concentration %	3	4	5	6	7	8
Density obtained (g/cc)	1.017	1.023	1.028	1.034	1.040	1.046

We should also bear in mind that when using bentonite with estuarine clays of very low shear strength, it may not be possible to stabilize the walls of boring by bentonite suspension only. In such cases, casing pipes or liners which are left in place may have to be used. The SPT values of soil will give us an idea of in-situ soil conditions for such cases.

Consumption of bentonite.   Theoretically 50 kg (one bag) of bentonite is enough for every 4 to 5 m depth of a bore hole of one metre diameter. In actual practice, it works out to one bag for every one metre depth in clayey soils and 2.5 to 3 bags of bentonite for every one metre depth of 1 m diameter hole in sandy soils.

Preparation of suspension. Bentonite suspension for circulation methods is prepared as follows. A 4 to 8% suspension is prepared using fresh water and sodium bentonite. After mixing properly in a suitable mixer, it is stored for at least 24 hours for aging. Normally, bentonite is reused 3 to 4 times by using a settling tank and close circuit circulation. However, in soft clays it may be possible to use it only once.

12.5 METHODS OF ADVANCING THE HOLE

There are various methods of advancing bore holes with the circulation of bentonite. Some of these methods are now discussed.

Method 1: Piles installed by bailer and cutting tools. This is a crude but the simplest method of advancing the hole when using the chisel and bailer bucket to advance the hole. The slurry is formed by simply adding the bentonite into the hole and mixing it in the hole, with the level of the suspension inside the bore hole always kept about 1 m above the ground water level, or if necessary to the top of the level of the casing. When meeting cohesionless materials, the slurry may be thickened. The aim is to help the stabilization of hole by forming an impermeable thin film around the bore hole. The bentonite suspension is assumed to penetrate into the sides under positive pressure. After a while it forms a jelly, thus making the sides impervious by producing a plastering effect. This is described as a crude method of installing bored piles because adding bentonite in the hole as in this method does not give us the full benefit of piling. The up and down movement of the bailer causes the soil from the sides and bottom to flow in. It is also very difficult to remove all the loose materials that collect at the bottom in the end. Hence as far as possible, the bailer method should not be used on important works.

Method 2: Continuous mud circulation (CMC) method (Fig. 12.1). This method is a more refined one than the above method. In this case, bentonite of sufficient viscosity and velocity (as delivered

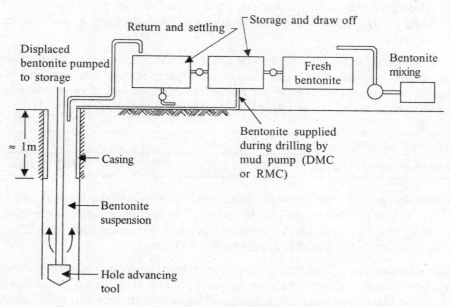

Fig. 12.1 Layout of equipment for boring using bentonite suspension.

by a mud pump) is maintained in continuous circulation so that particles are suspended in the mud and brought to the surface by the flow of bentonite. The level of the bentonite suspension is kept constant. For this purpose, a mud pump of sufficient capacity (depending on diameter and depth of hole) is employed for continuous circulation. Material in the bore hole is loosened (spoil formed) by means of a suitably designed chopper or reamer or drilling bit. The bentonite solution is circulated by pumping. It serves the two purposes of (i) stabilizing the bore hole and (ii) conveying the spoil from bottom of the hole to the top. The mud pump capacity should be able to maintain the volume and velocity to lift up the spoil from the bore hole. It will depend on the diameter and depth of the hole to be bored. The mud pump may be used in the following four different ways:

1. *Direct mud circulation (DMC):* In this method, the bentonite suspension is pumped into the bottom of the hole through the drill rods and it overflows at the top of the casing. The mud pump should have the capacity to maintain a velocity of 0.41 to 0.76 metres per second to float the cuttings.

2. *Reverse mud circulation (RMC):* For large diameter holes, the pump is more efficient if the bentonite suspension is fed directly at the top of the hole and it is pumped out from bottom of the hole with suitable rotary pump fitted at the bottom of the drill rods. This method is called the *reverse mud circulation method*. Whereas borehole sizes in direct circulation are limited by the mud pump capacity, in reverse circulation method even a medium sized pump can create enough bailing velocity to bring cuttings up and the inner diameter of the drill pipe need not be large.

3. *Rapid direct mud circulation (R-DMC):* This is an improved version of the DMC where a tube carrying compressed air is also sent to the bottom of the bore. The air helps in mixing up the loosened soil with the bentonite slurry more effectively so that even heavy particles are forced out of the bore suspended in the bentonite. However, in all cases where rapid excavation of the bore is planned, the tendency of sides to cave in should be carefully examined.

4. *Air lift reverse mud circulation drilling (A-RMC):* This method of drilling is used for large diameter holes. Compressed air is used in this method to circulate the drilling fluid and cuttings to the surface.

It has also been observed in the field that with bentonite clay there is more caving in during the time there is no work than during the working period. This may perhaps be due to thickening of the bentonite into a gel when not in agitation. This gel may exert less lateral pressure than bentonite in liquid mud form. Hence concreting of holes should be planned immediately after circulation of bentonite and never in a hole, in which work was suspended over night.

12.6 CHOICE OF TOOLS

The boring tools that are used depend on the type of the soil. Some of the tools used are:

- Percussion tools, e.g. sludge pump
- Augers including continuous flight spiral auger
- Buckets, with bottom opening flap
- Grabs.

12.7 LIMITATIONS OF BENTONITE METHOD

The bentonite method has some limitations. A brief list of these is as follows:

1. Pile diameters should not be small. Normally, they should be 400 mm to 5 m in diameter.
2. It will have potential danger if used in artesian conditions.
3. It is difficult to use this method in soils with permeability greater than 1 m per second or in soft clays with shear strength less than 20 kN/m^2 (0.2 kg/cm^2).
4. It is difficult to clean the bottom of the hole when boring ends in coarse materials, disintegrated rocks, etc. which do not come up easily along with the suspension.
5. It is difficult to install raker piles by this method.
6. In non-cohesive soils or fine sands, the rate of progress of work should be slow enough for the bentonite to penetrate into the soil and produce the plastering effect. The rate of progress should be suitably adjusted. Otherwise side collapse may occur.
7. If subsoil or ground water contains salts, it will adversely affect the action of bentonite. Protection of sides from caving in may be found to be difficult.

12.8 ACTION TO BE TAKEN BEFORE CONCRETING

The following precautions are very important for success in the construction by bentonite stabilization:

- The specific gravity of bentonite should be checked at intervals by taking samples from the bottom. If it exceeds 1.25, replacement of bentonite at the bottom may be necessary without decreasing the level of bentonite in the hole. The density should be brought down to about 1.12 by flushing before concreting.

- As the tendency of caving in is more, when the bentonite is not in circulation, operations for final concreting should always start as soon as the hole is completed and cleaned.

- Before the steel cage is lowered, the hole should be flushed with fresh bentonite slurry for at least 15 minutes (in direct circulation by the mud circulation chisel resting at the bottom) so that it is completely cleared. Accumulated debris at the bottom can considerably increase the settlement when the piles are loaded. This aspect is very important in construction of bored cast in-situ piles. Many load tests (especially in bearing piles) have produced inconsistent results due to carelessness in cleaning the bottom of the hole before concreting.

12.9 CONCRETING OF PILES

The precautions to be taken in the use of treime concrete in piles are described in IS 2911 part I. Section 2.

After cleaning the holes, the reinforcement cage is lowered into the hole. The bore is once again flushed and concrete poured through a tremie pipe of 200 mm in diameter. Concrete of slump 150 m, cement content not less than 400 kg/m^2, water cement ratio $\not> 0.5$, maximum size of aggregate 20 to 25 mm with suitable plasticiser is recommended for use. The procedure is as follows:

First, a guide casing, if not already provided, is placed over the hole for proper seating of the tremie funnel. The tremie is lowered to the bottom of the hole. To start with, the bottom of concreting funnel is closed with a steel plate. After filling the funnel to its full capacity the steel plate is removed and concrete discharged. The bottom of the tremie should always be at least 2 m within the concrete so that the *bentonite is replaced from bottom upwards*. Only the initially poured concrete is in contact with the bentonite as shown in Fig. 12.2. Concreting is carried out to at least 60–90 cm above the cut off level. If the cut off level is at the ground level the top concrete is allowed to spill over till good concrete is visible.

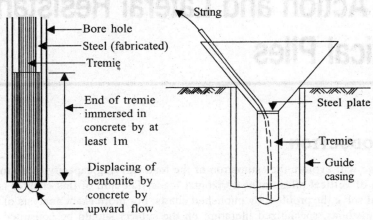

Fig. 12.2 Concreting by tremie.

When bentonite piling was introduced before its final adoption, much doubt was raised about the strength of concrete placed in bentonite (which is a suspension of clay) as well as about the bond characteristics of steel that have been coated with bentonite. However, tests have shown that *placing concrete by displacing bentonite suspension from bottom* (in contrast to pouring concrete into bentonite suspension) does not affect concrete strength. Similarly the bond between steel and concrete is also not very much reduced in this process. Hence the importance of properly placing concrete by tremie by displacement of bentonite from bottom up should be strictly followed in the field.

12.10 SUMMARY

Cast-in-situ piles can be of two types: The driven cast in situ and the bored cast in situ piles. Of these, the bored cast in situ piles are very popular in India in crowded towns and cities as they do not disturb the surround soil or structures during their installation. In India most large diameter piles used for bridges are bored cast in situ piles installed by bentonite slurry method. However, great care, as described in this chapter, should be taken for a successful completion of their installation.

REFERENCE

[1] IS 2911 (1999), Part I Section 2: *Code of Practice for Design and Construction of Pile Foundation, Bored Piles*, BIS, New Delhi.

13

Group Action and Lateral Resistance of Vertical Piles

13.1 INTRODUCTION

In this chapter, we will explore the estimation of the load carrying capacity of a group of piles and also the strength of vertical piles under horizontal loads. The aim of this chapter is to explain the fundamentals and solve the problem by published charts. For more exact analysis of these problems using computer methods, specialized literature on the subject should be consulted [1] [2].

13.2 MINIMUM SPACING OF PILES

IS 2911 Part I Sec. 2 (1979) Clause 5.6 [3] gives the following as the minimum spacing of piles to be adopted in practice in terms of d, the diameter of the pile.

1. Bearing piles (general) $2.5d$
2. Bearing piles on rock $2.0d$
3. Friction piles $3.0d$

The Norwegian Code of Practice recommends the following values for spacing of piles.

Length of piles	Friction piles		Bearing piles
	in sand	in clay	
Less than 12 m	$3d$	$4d$	$3d$
12–24 m	$4d$	$5d$	$4d$
More than 24 m	$5d$	$6d$	$5d$

13.3 ESTIMATION OF GROUP BEARING CAPACITY

IS 2911 recommends the following values:

Case 1: Pile cap above ground level. The capacity of the group is lesser of the following two following (values).

(a) Group capacity as the capacity of a single pile multiplied by the number of piles. (This is true mostly for bearing piles only.)

(b) For friction piles in soft clay, the group capacity will be the frictional capacity along the perimeter of the column of soil enclosed by the pile group together with the end bearing of the above column of soils as shown in Fig. 13.1.

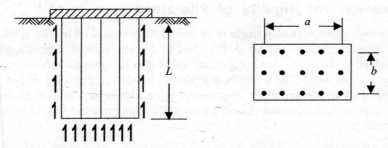

Fig. 13.1   Strength calculation for a group of piles by block failure.

Taking *a* and *b* as the sides of the column, the value of the ultimate bearing capacity will be as follows:

$$Q_c = Q_b + [2(a+b)L]s \qquad (13.1)$$

Q_b = bearing capacity of the base ($a \times b$) as deep foundation in clay
L = friction length in load carrying strata
s = average ultimate shear value of strata

However, for large spacings, the surface area of the block increases and the individual pile failure capacity multiplied by the number of piles may control the capacity.

Case 2:   Pile cap cast directly on reasonably firm strata.   In this case, the additional capacity of the pile cap on the ground is added to the capacity worked out as in Case 1. Deductions in the pile-cap bearing area are also to be made for the area occupied by the piles in the pile cap.

Case 3:   Presence of weak clay layer under the bearing stratum.   The strength of the foundation at the base with a spread of 60° at 2/3*L* (where *L* is the length of the pile) in the case of piles in clay and at the end of the piles in case of sand as shown in Fig. 13.2 should be examined to ensure the safety in bearing of the foundation.

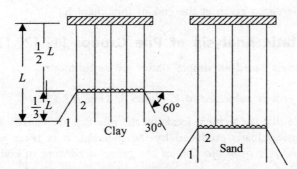

Fig. 13.2   Testing for strength of foundation at the base of a group of piles in clay and sand.

13.3.1 Use of Group Efficiency Factors for Piles in Sand

A number of group efficiency equations are also in use for determining the bearing capacity of pile groups. A simple rule is to take an efficiency ratio of 0.7 for spacing of piles of $2d$ increasing to unity at spacing of $8d$. However this method has not been found very valid for all situations.

13.3.2 Necessity for Rigidity of Pile Head

IS 2911 Part I specifies that normally single piles in buildings should be tied by grade beams in two *right-angled directions*. "Two pile" caps shall be tied by a grade beam in a direction at right angles to the line of the piles. It is only for bridges and other special circumstances that we can design without the above constraints. The grade beams should be always provided at the pile cap level.

In the case of structures on single or group of piles with large variation in number of piles, the consequent differential settlement should be carefully examined and should be taken care of if it is found necessary.

13.4 EFFECT OF PILE ARRANGEMENT

Tests and theory show that friction piles in rectangular or circular groups give better performance than a square group. Also, there will be more cost savings by using lesser number of longer piles than an increased number of shorter piles. It is important that length should not vary in the same group but separate footings can have different pile tip elevations.

13.5 GENERAL ANALYSIS OF PILE GROUPS

Pile groups may contain battered piles and the group may be subjected to axial, as well as lateral loads with moments. Methods to analyse this problem are of much importance in structural design. The following three methods (in increasing order of refinement) are used for the analysis [1] [2] [3]:

1. Simple *statical methods* omitting the presence of soil and considering the pile group as an assembly of structural members only.
2. The *equivalent bent method* in which the effect of soil is taken into account for determining the equivalent free standing length of piles by modulus of subgrade reaction analysis.
3. The *elastic continuum method* where the interaction between piles and soil is considered.

Of these, only the simple statical approach is dealt with in this chapter. The other methods can be got from the references given at the end of this chapter.

13.5.1 Simple Static Analysis of Pile Groups [1] [2] [3]

Two of the simple methods based on simple statics are as follows:

Method 1: *Piles groups subjected to V, H and M [Fig. 13.3.]*

1. First we assume that the vertical loads on the pile cap are equally taken by the piles. As regards the vertical loads produced by the moment, it is taken as proportional to the *distance x of the pile from the C.G of the group according* to conventional rule.

Thus, the total vertical load in each pile due to V and M will be

$$V_i = \frac{V}{n} \pm \frac{Mx_i}{\Sigma(x_i)^2} \qquad (13.2)$$

2. The effect due to H is taken care of in the following way:

$$H_i = V_i \cos\theta \text{ (for each pile)}$$

where θ is the inclination of the pile with the horizontal. Then the total horizontal force from all the pile $= \Sigma H_i$

3. The unbalanced horizontal force H_{Ub} is calculated as

$$H_{Ub} = H - \Sigma H_i$$

This is equally distributed as active horizontal forces on the pile. Alternately, the inclination of the piles can be adjusted so that the residual horizontal force is zero so that each pile is only axially loaded along its length.

A graphical method of the above solution is given in Fig. 13.3.

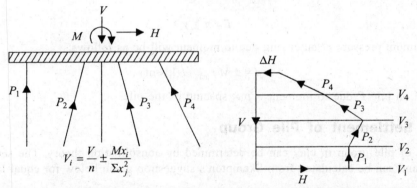

Fig. 13.3 Analysis of a pile group for vertical and horizontal loads with moment.

Method 2: *Pile group subjected to inclined loads.* In groups of piles closely spaced at not more than $3d$ or with single piles in three directions subjected to an inclined load can be easily analysed by the graphical method (as shown in Fig. 13.4 for a simple layout). Inclined loading on group of closely spaced vertical piles should be examined for bearing capacity by taking closely spaced piles as an equivalent single pile. Tension piles are not to be included in these methods [2].

Examples of computer based solutions for very complex pile systems are given by Bowles [4].

Method 3: *Pile groups in circular arrangement.* Pile groups under concrete industrial chimney foundation or piles driven in concentric circles under foundations of towers are analysed by treating each circular ring of piles as an annular ring with an assumed thickness t based on the total area of the piles.

$$\text{M.I. of annulus} = \sum \frac{\pi}{4}\left[(\gamma+t)^4 - (\gamma^4)\right]$$

where r = radius of the ring.

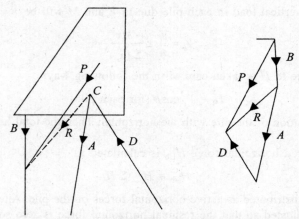

Fig. 13.4   Analysis of a pile group under inclined loads.

Neglecting second order quantities, this reduces to

$$I = \pi \sum \gamma^3 t$$

Maximum pressure at outer ring due to moment will be as follows:

$$p = \pm M \gamma_{\max} / I \,(\text{kN/m})$$

Load on pile P due to moment $= p \times$ spacing of the pile.

13.5.2   Settlement of Pile Group

Settlement of pile group in clay can be determined by consolidation theory. The settlement of a group in sand can be calculated from Skempton's suggestion given below for equal loads on piles

$$\frac{\partial_B}{\partial_S} = \left(\frac{4B + 2.7}{B + 3.6} \right)^2 \text{ or } \approx \left(\frac{4B + 3}{B + 4} \right)^2 \tag{13.3}$$

where

δ_B = settlement of pile group of width B in metres

δs = settlement of single pile at the same load intensity

B = breadth of pile group in metres.

13.6   LATERAL RESISTANCE OF SINGLE PILE

In pile foundations for taking lateral loads, we either provide batter piles or we have to depend on the lateral strength of vertical piles. In the latter case, the following conditions should be satisfied:

1. The pile must have the necessary load and moment capacity.
2. The soil surrounding the pile should have the capacity to support the reaction from the pile.
3. The lateral deflection should be that which is allowable according to the situation.

Values given in Tables 13.1 and 13.2 are recommended by the Norwegian Geo-technical Institute as a guidance for concrete piles for lateral loading in different types of soils.

TABLE 13.1 LONG TERM LATERAL LOAD ON PILES

Pile area (m^2)	Max. bending moment (kNm)	Allowable long term load (kN)		
		Clay $\phi' = 26°$	Silt $\phi' = 35°$	Sand $\phi' = 40°$
0.04	4.5	5	6	7
0.06	8.5	8	10	12
0.09	15.0	13	16	19

TABLE 13.2 SHORT TERM LATERAL LOADS ON PILE IN CLAYS

Pile area (m^2)	Allowable short term lateral loads (kN)		
	$c = 10$ kN/m^2	$c = 25$ kN/m^2	$c = 50$ kN/m^2
0.04	7	15	20
0.06	10	20	30
0.09	15	30	40

13.6.1 Methods to Determine Lateral Strength of Piles

Some of the theoretical and empirical methods used to determine the lateral capacity of piles are given below.

Method 1: *Use of active and passive earth pressure theories.* It is applicable only to short piles undergoing rigid rotation. Also as the movement necessary for mobilizing full passive pressures is large, the results should be used with sufficient safety factor. This method gives ultimate values.

Method 2: *Use of modulus of horizontal subgrade reaction theory.* We can either form closed form solutions or solve each problem by computer methods as described by Bowles [4]. However as coefficient of subgrade reaction of the soil is not a fundamental property of the soil, the results should be used with judgement. This method gives elastic analysis.

Method 3: *Use of elastic continuum theory applied to soils.* Because of the complexity of the problem, it can be solved satisfactory only by computer. Due to the difficulty of determining the exact soil properties results of this method should be verified by field tests.

Method 4: *Empirical methods.* These methods combine the results of method 2 and also the experimental data obtained from laboratory/field tests to obtain readymade charts for design. Charts published by IS and Broms belong to this category.

In this chapter, we will deal briefly with IS and the empirical methods by Broms.

13.7 IS 2911 METHOD FOR LATERAL RESISTANCE OF PILES

Reese and Matlock [5] were the first to recommend, in 1956, non-dimensional analysis for lateral resistance of vertical piles. As in beams on elastic foundations they adopted a non-dimensional quantity called *Relative Stiffness Factor* to predict the behaviour of piles. Based on the above work and also that of Davisson [6] [7], the ACI Committee 336 [8] recommended in 1972 the quantities R and T to determine the *relative stiffness* factor for the following cases:

Case 1: Where the modulus of horizontal subgrade reaction is constant along the depth as in over consolidated clays they recommended factor R (see Sec.13.7.2).

Case 2: Where the modulus of horizontal subgrade reaction increases with depth as in sand deposits and in normally consolidated clays, they recommended factor T (R_2 in ACI report).

The ACI publication (8) gives us readymade charts for solving these problems based on the above quantities. If computer programmes are available, they can be generated for each problem climinating the need for these readymade charts. These charts are available in other Indian publications also [9]. However, we shall concentrate more on the charts made by Broms since they are more often used nowadays. Before we examine Broms chart, we will examine the IS method in more detail.

13.7.1 Basis of IS Method [10]

Based on the principles described above and also depending on the constraints at the top of the piles, IS 2911 Part I /Sec. 3 —Appendix D classifies piles as follows (This is similar to Broms method described in later sections.):

- Free headed piles (piles unrestrained at the top)
- Fixed headed piles or restrained piles connected to pile caps at the top.

Each of these piles can be again classified as long piles and short piles depending on their relative stiffness factors. The failure mechanisms of these piles due to horizontal loads are different and are shown in Figs. 13.5 and 13.6.

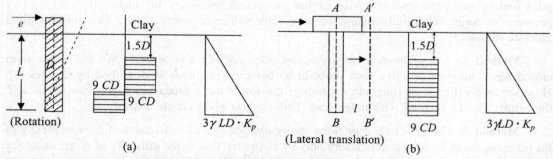

Fig. 13.5 Failure mechanisms of short piles in cohesive and granular soils: (a) Unrestrained piles; (b) restrained piles (Broms).

While the short piles unrestrained at top fail by rotation as a rigid body about a centre of rotation, the same pile, when restrained at the top is assumed to fail by translation (Fig. 13.5). As regards long piles, both restrained and unrestrained piles behave as an elastic beam member as the

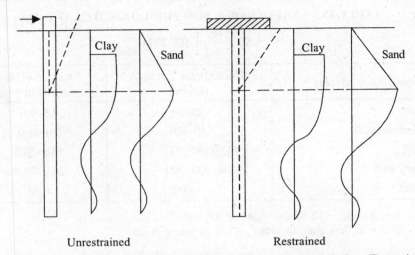

Fig. 13.6   Failure mechanisms of long piles in sand and clay (Broms).

lower end cannot rotate but is fixed in position (Fig. 13.6). Hence in the case of long piles the failure will be by fracture of the pile at the point of maximum moment or by shear. However, while the free end of an unrestrained long pile acts as a cantilever, the fixed end long pile acts as a fixed beam, with both ends fixed, developing moments both at top and bottom. Accordingly, the maximum moment developed in the long restrained pile will be only one half that of the cantilever.

13.7.2   Assumptions in IS 2911 Method (*see also* Section 20.8)

We must note that IS 2911 Part I Sec. 3 Appendix D makes the following assumptions. (As given in IS 2911, we will use the symbol K for the modulus of subgrade reaction for piles and k_1 for modulus got for a 30 cm square plate.)

1. *Modulus of horizontal subgrade reaction, K:* We assume the following values of K:
    (a) For preloaded clays (type 1 soils), this modulus is assumed to be constant. It is related to k_1 (Terzaghi's modulus for a 30 cm square plate) as follows for a pile of width B:

$$K = \frac{k_1}{1.5} \, (\text{kN/m}^3), \qquad p = Ky \tag{13.4}$$

where p is the pressure and y the deformation.
    (b) For sands and normally consolidated clays, modulus varies with depth (type 2 soils)

$$K = (\eta_h)(z/B), \qquad p = \eta_h \, (z/B)y \tag{13.5}$$

where

η_h = coefficient of horizontal modulus variation (kN/m³)

z = depth below G.L.

B = width of shaft in metres.

The range of values of k_1 and η_h are given in Tables 13.3 and 13.4.

TABLE 13.3   VALUES OF k_1 FOR PRE-LOADED CLAYS

$$\left(K_B = \frac{k_1}{1.5} \right) \text{ [IS 2911]}$$

Consistency of clay	Unconfined strength (kN/m²)	Range of k_1 (MN/m³)
Soft	25–50	4.5–9.0
Medium stiff	50–100	9.0–18.0
Stiff	100–200	18.0–36.0
Very stiff	200–400	36.0–72.0
Hard	> 400	> 72

Note: 1. 1 kg/cm³ = 10 MN/m³ = 10 × 10³ kN/m³
2. For q_u less than 20 kN/m², K_1 is be taken as zero.

TABLE 13.4   VALUES OF η_h FOR SANDS $K_h = \eta_h [z/B]$
(Modulus varying with depth) [IS 2911] [3]

Description of soil	η_h (MN/m³)	
	Dry	Submerged (Terzaghi)
Loose sand	2.5	1.4
Medium sand	7.5	5.0
Dense sand	20.0	12.0
Very loose sand & normally consolidated clays	–	0.4

2. *Stiffness factors R and T:*   As explained in Section 13.7. Reese and Matlock introduced the quantities R and T, called stiffness factors to predict whether the piles act as long or short piles. [5]. They are in units of length.

For pre-loaded clays with constant K; R in metres = $\left[\dfrac{EI}{KB} \right]^{1/4}$ (13.6)

For sands with η_h values; T in metres = $\left[\dfrac{EI}{\eta_h} \right]^{1/5}$ (13.7)

where

E = young's modulus of pile material

I = moment of inertia of pile cross section

B = width or diameter of pile shaft

K and η_h are as explained above.

3. *Criteria for classification of piles into short rigid piles or long elastic piles:*   Having calculated the stiffness factors R and T from Eqs. (13.6) and (13.7) the criteria for behaviour as a short rigid pile or as a long elastic pile are related to the total embedded length L as follows: (L/T and L/R will be numbers)

If $L \leq 2T$ or $\leq 2R$, the pile is short and rigid; (L/T or $L/R \leq 2$).   (13.8)

If $L \geq 4T$ or $\geq 3.5R$, the pile is long and elastic; ($L/T \geq 4$ or $L/R \geq 3.5$).   (13.9)

If $L > 5T$ or $> 4.5R$, the pile is definitely long; ($L/T > 5$ or $L/R > 4.5$).   (13.9a)

The intermediate cases indicate the behaviour between the two. It can be seen that generally the ultimate lateral load of a long pile is much higher than that for a short pile. The following lengths are considered sufficient to *develop the maximum resistance in the soil* and there will not be much benefit in taking piles deeper than these values.

For constant soil modulus, free head $L = 3.5R$ and fixed head $L = 2R$

For linearly increasing soil modulus, free head $L = 4T$ and fixed head $L = 2T$

The method described in IS 2911 is applicable for long piles only.

4. *Defletion and moments in a long elastic pile by simple cantilever approach (IS 2911 method):*   The IS method is suitable only for relatively small lateral loads acting on long piles. The depth of fixity of the long piles along the embedded length L can be estimated by using of Fig. 13.7 for free headed and fixed headed piles.

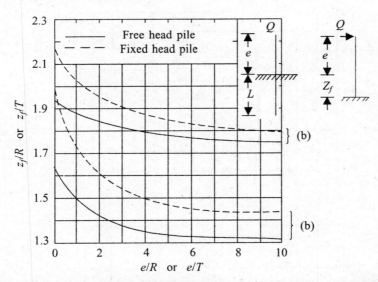

Fig. 13.7   Method recommended by IS 2911 to determine depth of fixcity of piles under lateral loads: (a) For piles in preloaded clays; (b) for piles in sands and normally loaded clays.

Taking e as the length above ground level, we enter e/R or e/T and read off z_f/R or z_f/T from the diagram. It gives the value z_f the depth of fixity.

(a) *Calculation of ultimate value of H:* The ultimate value of the lateral load H should be either the maximum resistance that can be offered by the soil or the ultimate moment of resistance of the pile, whichever is the lesser of the two.

In most cases of short piles, the lateral load will be determined by the soil capacity and IS 2911 does not give a suitable method to calculate the resistance of short piles. (Broms method given in Section 13.8 can be used for this purpose.) However for long piles in IS 2911 method the ultimate value of H is taken as the load at which the moment of the pile is equal to its ultimate moment capacity.

(b) *Calculation of moment:* As we know from the depth of fixity z, the value of moments in long piles due to a lateral force H can be calculated as

$$M = H(e + z) \qquad \text{(free head pile as a cantilever)}$$

$$M = \frac{H(e + z)}{2} \qquad \text{(fixed head pile as a fixed beam)}$$

Accordingly, the ultimate lateral loads will be as follows [2]:

$$H_U = \left(\frac{M_U}{e + z}\right) \qquad \text{for free head piles} \tag{13.10}$$

$$= \left(\frac{2M_U}{e + z}\right) \qquad \text{for fixed head piles} \tag{13.11}$$

IS 2911 part I Sec. 1. Appendix D.4.2 recommends a correction factor for the moments as calculated above. [Tomlinson does not take this factor into consideration in the calculation of H_U [2].] These are shown in Fig. 13.8.

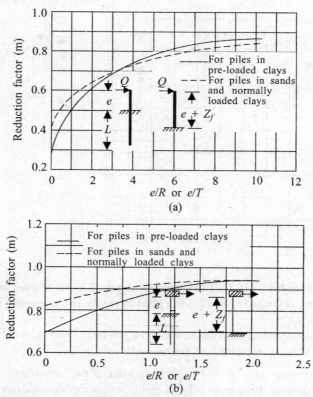

Fig. 13.8 Reduction factors recommended by IS 2911 for maximum moments calculated by IS method: (a) For free head piles; (b) for fixed head piles.

(c) *Deflection of pile at ground level:* We are also interested in the magnitude of deflection due to the lateral load H acting at the ground level and at the top end. It will be the greater of: the deflection produced due to stressing of the soil below ground level and the deflection produced in the pile due to the application of the load as a structural member.

Broms chart described in Section 13.8 can be used to estimate the first value while the second value can be evaluated from the formulae for deflection of cantilever and beams. For long piles in which the lateral resistance is high, it will be as follows as given in IS 2911.

$$y = H(e + z)^3/3EI \quad \text{for free head pile as a cantilever} \tag{13.12}$$

$$= H(e + z)^3/12EI \quad \text{for fixed head pile} \tag{13.13}$$

13.8 BROMS CHARTS FOR LATERAL LOAD ANALYSIS ON SINGLE PILES [11] [12] [13]

The most commonly used method these days for the analysis of lateral loads in piles is the Broms charts. Broms recommends the following values for K_h derived from K_1 (the modulus of subgrade reaction applicable to a square plate 1m in size). Assuming B to be the ratio of the width to the diameter of pile,

$$\text{For long piles,} \quad K = \frac{0.4k_1}{B}$$

$$\text{For short piles,} \quad K = \left(\frac{2L + 2B}{5L}\right)\frac{k_1}{B} \approx 0.4\left(\frac{L + B}{LB}\right)k_1 \tag{13.14}$$

where

L = length of the pile
B = breadth or diameter of the pile
K_1 = modulus of subgrade reaction for 1 m square plate.

13.8.1 Details of Broms Method

The Broms method is more rigorous than the IS method and it is based on the readymade charts published by him in 1965. His charts are based on theory and experimental observations. The following dimensionless quantities are used in these charts when deflections are considered. They are similar to the quantities R and T described in Section 13.7.2.

$$\beta = \left(\frac{KB}{4EI}\right)^{1/4} \quad \text{for type 1 soils}$$

$$\eta = \left[\frac{\eta_h}{EI}\right]^{1/5} \quad \text{for type 2 soils}$$

where

K = modulus of subgrade reaction in MN/m^3
η_h = constant of modulus of subgrade reaction MN/m^3

[*Notes:* 1. $\beta = \left[\dfrac{1}{1.4R}\right]$ and $\eta = \dfrac{1}{T}$ as against in Eqs. (13.6) and (13.7)

(2) (η should not be confused with η_h).

(3) Type 1 soils are cohesive soils and type 2 soils are cohesionless soils.

We should note that in his investigation Broms calculated the resisting forces at ultimate or Rankine failure conditions and hence the modulus of subgrade reaction does not appear in his equations. However, when calculating deflections, the modulus of subgrade reaction also has been considered since we are making an elastic analysis.

Let us describe the Broms charts that are used for analysis of ultimate lateral resistance and deflection. In these charts H represents the ultimate lateral resistance value and y_0 the deflection due to H at ground level.

Case Charts for piles in cohesive soils (Type 1 soils). K is constant with depth, c_u = cohesion and B = dia. of pile.

1. *For short piles for type 1 soils:* The ultimate lateral resistance is related to embedded length.

$$\left[\frac{H}{c_u B^2} \text{ for } \frac{L}{B} \text{ for various } e/B \text{ values} \right], \text{ where } H = \text{horizontal force, see Fig. 13.9.}$$

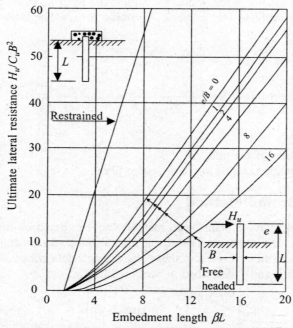

Fig. 13.9   Chart for estimating the ultimate lateral resistance of short piles in Type 1 (clay) soils (Broms).

2. *Fog long piles in type 1 soils:* The ultimate lateral resistance is related to the ultimate resistance moment of the pile, whose ultimate moment of resistance is M_U.

$$\left[\frac{H}{c_u B^2} \text{ for } \frac{M_U}{c_u B^3} \text{ for various } e/B \text{ values} \right] \text{ are given in Fig. 13.10.}$$

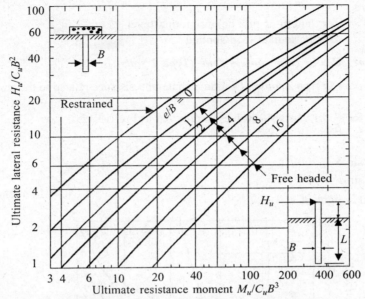

Fig. 13.10 **Chart for estimating the ultimate lateral resistance of long piles on Type 1 (clay) soils** (Broms).

3. *Lateral deflection:* This is the deflection y_0 at *ground surface* of horizontally loaded pile. (As this will be an elastic analysis, the modulus also has to be considered.)

$$\left[\frac{y_0 KBL}{H} \text{ for } \beta L \text{ for various } \frac{e}{L} \text{ values} \right] \text{ are given in Fig. 13.11.}$$

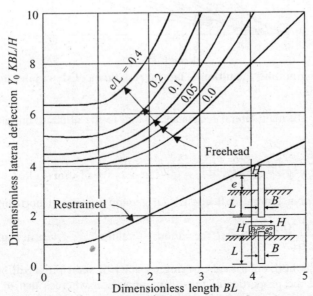

Fig. 13.11 **Chart for estimating the lateral deflection at ground level for piles in Type 1 (clay) soils under working loads** (Broms).

In these charts,

$$L = \text{length of pile below ground level}$$
$$H = \text{horizontal load applied}$$

Case 2. Charts for piles in cohesionless soils (Type 2 soils).

1. *For short piles in type 2 soils:* The ultimate lateral resistance related to the embedded length.

2. $\left[\dfrac{H}{K_P B^3 \gamma} \text{ for } \dfrac{L}{B} \text{ for various } \dfrac{e}{L} \text{ values} \right]$ are given in Fig. 13.12.

where

$$K_P = \frac{1 + \sin \phi}{1 - \sin \phi}$$

$\gamma = $ unit weight of soil.

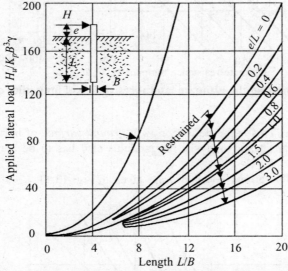

Fig. 13.12 **Chart for estimating the ultimate lateral resistance of short piles in Type 2 (granular) soils** (Broms).

2. *For long piles:* Ultimate lateral resistance related to the ultimate moment of resistance of piles.

$$\left[\frac{H_U}{K_P B^3 \gamma} \text{ for } \frac{M_U}{B^4 \gamma K_P} \text{ for various } \frac{e}{B} \text{ values} \right], \text{ see Fig. 13.13.}$$

3. *Lateral deflection:* Lateral deflection y_o *at ground surface* of horizontally loaded pile.

$$\left[\frac{y_0 (EI)^{3/5} (n_h)^{2/5}}{HL} \text{ for } \eta L \text{ for various } \frac{e}{L} \text{ values} \right] \text{ are given in Fig. 13.14.}$$

It is obvious that the horizontal load carrying capacity of short piles will be a function of the depth of penetration and the properties of the surrounding soil whereas that of the long pile will be independent of the penetration depth; but will depend on the ultimate capacity of the pile and

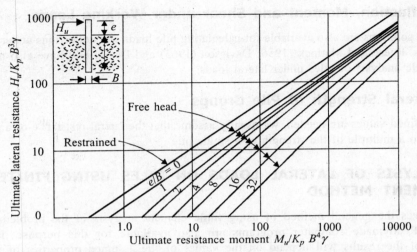

Fig. 13.13 **Chart for estimating the ultimate lateral resistance of long piles in Type 2 (granular) soils** (Broms).

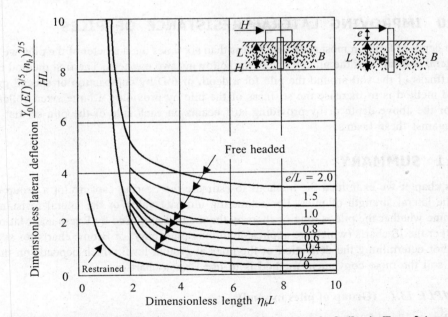

Fig. 13.14 **Chart for estimating the lateral deflection at ground level of piles in Type 2 (granular) soils under working loads** (Broms).

the properties of the soil. Similarly, the lateral deflection at ground surface for short and long piles will mainly depend on the length of the pile, the horizontal load, the size of the pile and the modulus of subgrade reaction of the soil. Generally, as in bearing capacity, we check the safety under ultimate load conditions. The use of Broms charts is shown in Example 13.3.

13.8.2 Deflection, Moment and Shear under Working Loads

Winkler model solutions are also available for calculating pile loads and deflections under working load conditions. Reese and Matlock (1956) Davisson (1963) and Das (1998) have also published charts for elastic analysis of piles under lateral loads.

13.8.3 Lateral Strength of Pile Groups

Unless very refined values are needed, we usually assume that the lateral resistance of a group of piles is equal to a multiple of the strength of a single pile.

13.9 ANALYSIS OF LATERAL LOADS ON PILES USING FINITE ELEMENT METHOD

Bowles [4] gives the general method of using finite element analysis of the problem by use of computer. Readymade computer programs are also available for this purpose. However the accuracy of the results will depend on the values of the assumed properties of the soil. Computer analysis combined with field tests should be used where large loads and accurate results are needed for major engineering projects.

13.10 IMPROVING LATERAL RESISTANCE OF PILES

As the depth of fixity in most soils will be less than six times the diameter of the pile, we can increase the lateral resistance of the pile by one of the following two methods. The first method is to increase the stiffness of the soil around the pile for a depth of 6 D by compaction or special grouting. The second method is to increase the stiffness of the pile by providing a large sized collar around the pile for the above depth or by providing stiff beams on each side of the pile so that the pile can bear against these beams.

13.11 SUMMARY

In this chapter we examined the methods to estimate the bearing capacity of a group of piles and also the lateral strength of piles. For estimating ultimate value of the lateral resistance, we first determine whether the pile is long or short by the method proposed by Reese and Matlock and then use either the IS charts (which are applicable to long piles only) or Broms charts for short and long piles. For determining the deflection of the piles at ground level which depends on the properties of the soil the most convenient method is to use Broms charts.

EXAMPLE 13.1 (Group of piles in sand)

Nine driven piles of 300 mm dia. and 10 m length are formed into a group, square in plan with a spacing of $3d$ between them. Assuming the foundation is loose to medium sand of $\phi = 20°$ and its unit weight is 18kN/m^3, determine the carrying capacity of the group. Assuming that the settlement at the carrying capacity of the pile as a single pile is 2.5 mm, estimate the settlement of the pile group. Assume ultimate capacity of single pile as 396 kN.

Ref.	Step	Calculations
Sec. 13.3		*Method:* Strength of group is lesser of the following:
		(a) $(N) \times$ (Strength of one pile) $\times$ efficiency (b) Strength as a column equal to size of group.
	1	*Determine strength of the group from strength of one pile* $Q_{ult} = 396$ kN Assume efficiency = 1 $Q_u = 396 \times 9 = 3564$ kN; $Q_{safe} = \dfrac{3564}{2.5} = 1426$ kN Average load on each pile $= \dfrac{1426}{9} = 160$ kN (approx.)
	2	*Calculate group settlement* Let the group be $3 \times 3 = 9$ piles; $\delta_s = 2.5$ mm Width of block $= B = 2 \times 0.9 + 0.3 = 2.1$ m
Sec. 13.5.2		$\dfrac{S_g}{S_i} = \left[\dfrac{4B + 2.7}{B + 3.6}\right]^2 = \left[\dfrac{4 \times 2.1 + 2.7}{2.1 + 3.6}\right]^2 = 3.66$ $S_g = 3.66 \times 2.5 = 9.15$ mm
	3.	*Capacity as a footing at depth* 10 m *as a deep foundation* (Neglect skin friction on sides) $Q_U = p_d N_q A_c;\ \dfrac{L}{B} = \dfrac{10}{2.1} = 4.8 <$ critical depth
B.C. Factors		(Critical depth $= 18B = 18 \times 2.1 = 37.8$ m) $\phi = 32°$; $N_q = 35$; bearing capacity $= q_u$ $q_u = 18 \times 10 \times 35 = 6300$ kN/m^2
Step 1		Let ultimate load of foundation be denoted as Q_u; then $Q_u = 6300 \times (2.1 \times 2.1) = 27700$ kN > 1426 kN (For sands, bearing capacity values are not critical)
	4	*Find bearing capacity of group* Group capacity = 1426 kN (step 1) Probable settlement = 9.15 mm (step 2)

EXAMPLE 13.2   (Group of piles in clay)

A group of friction piles in clay consists of 15 piles of 500 mm dia. (grouped as 5×3) spaced at 1 m apart. If the undrained shear strength c of the clay is 0.3 kg/cm^2 and the piles are 20 m in length estimate the *group capacity and its efficiency*. [Note: The pile cap will extend 25 cm around the piles and the pile cap will touch the soil but as the soil is clay the strength of the pile cap resting on the ground need not be considered.]

Ref.	Step	Calculations
Chapter 9	1	Calculate capacity of each pile and that of the group $$Q_{ult} = Q_u = 9cA_p + \alpha_c \Sigma A_s \left(\text{where } \frac{L}{D} = \frac{20}{0.4} = 50; N_c = 9 \right)$$ $c = 30$ kN/m^2; $\alpha = 0.9$ $$A_p = \frac{\pi(0.4)^2}{4} = 0.13 \text{ m}^2; A_s = \pi \times 0.4 \times 20 = 25 \text{ m}^2$$ $Q_u = (9 \times 30 \times 0.13) + (0.9 \times 30 \times 25) = 710$ kN Capacity of 15 piles = $15 \times 710 = 10650$ kN
Chapter 9	2	Calculate strength along group perimeter Dimension of group: perimeter. (5 piles) $(4 \times 1) + (0.50) = 4.5$ m (3 piles) $(2 \times 1) + (0.50) = 2.5$ m Find N_c from Skempton curve $$\frac{L}{D} = \frac{20}{2.5} = 8 > 4; N_c = 9$$ $Q_u = cN_cA_p + \Sigma K_cA_c$; Let $K = 0.9$ $A_p = 2.5 \times 4.5$ and $A_c = 20 \times 2(4.5 + 2.5) = 280$ m^2 $Q_u = 9 \times 30 \times 2.5 \times 4.5 + 0.9 \times 30 \times 280 = 10598$ kN
	3	Find lesser of the values for capacity and hence efficiency The capacity values are nearly equal $$\text{Efficiency} = \frac{\text{capacity by block failure}}{\text{capacity as } (n \times \text{capacity of one pile})} = 1.00$$ [*Note:* Settlement has to be separately calculated as in Chapter 4]

EXAMPLE 13.3 (Laterally loaded piles in clays IS 2911 Method)

A 300 mm square wooden pile is driven 5 m below ground level in pre-loaded clay. The load to be applied is 1 m above the ground. Determine the ultimate load that can be applied on a pile with $M_U = 100$ kNm. Assume $K_h = 15$ MN/m^2, $E = 10 \times 10^2$ MN/m^2, and cohesion of clay = 1 kg/cm^2.

Ref.	Step	Calculations
Sec. 13.7	1.	(Note: Soil is clay. Hence we use factor R.) Calculate R in metres as in IS 2911 (Type 1 soil) $$R = \left[\frac{EI}{K_hB} \right]^{1/4}, \quad I = \frac{\pi D^4}{64} = 4 \times 10^{-4} \text{m}^4$$
Eq. (13.6)		$$R = \left[\frac{(10 \times 10^2)(4 \times 10^{-4})}{15 \times 0.3} \right]^{1/4} = 0.546 \text{ m}$$

	2	*Check whether pile is long or short*
Eq. 13.9		$$\frac{L}{R} = \frac{5}{0.546} = 9.16 > 3.5R$$
		Pile acts as a long pile and, therefore, the IS method is applicable

Method 1: Analysis by IS2911 charts

3   *Determine depth of fixity from chart (free headed pile)*

$$\frac{e}{R} = \frac{1.0}{0.546} = 1.83; \quad \frac{z}{R} = 1.42$$

Fig. 13.7 $z_1 = 0.546 \times 1.42 = 0.775$ m

(*Note:* $\frac{0.775}{0.300} = 2.58$ nearly three times dia. of pile is depth of fixity)

4   *Estimate bending moment in the pile*

Sec. 13.7.2   As the pile is a long pile, the pile acts as a cantilever fixed in the soil at depth z. The maximum moment induced is M_u.

Sec. 4(b) $M_u = H(e + z)$ where M_u = moment on pile

If $M_u = 100$; $H = \frac{100}{(1 + 0.78)} = 56$ kN [Without correction]

5   *Find H applying reduction factor; find M_u given in IS 2911*

The actual BM will be less than the cantilever moment calculated from Fig. 13.7.

Fig. 13.8   With $e/R = 1.83$, we have reduction factor $m = 0.62$

Actual $M_u = 0.62(H)(e + z)$ (corrected value)

6   *Maximum lateral load capacity*

$$H = \frac{M_u}{(0.62)(e + z)}$$

In this method, the strength of soil is not considered and is assumed to be safe.

For a pile with $M_u = 100$ kNm,

$$H = \frac{100}{(0.62)(1 + 0.78)} = 90.6 \text{ kN}$$

Method 2: Analysis by using Broms charts (long pile in clay).

Let = $M_u = 100$ kNm (as above)

7   *Find parameters for Broms chart Long pile—Type 1 soil*

Fig. 13.10 $$\frac{M_u}{cD^3} = \frac{100}{100(0.3)^3} = 37 \quad (c = 100 \text{ kN/m}^2)[B = D]$$

$$\frac{e}{D} = \frac{1}{0.3} = 3.3, \text{ which gives } \frac{H_u}{cD^2} = 7 \text{ (approx.)}$$

$H_u = 7 \times 100(0.3)^2 = 63$ kN

Comment: The two methods do not yield the same result. The value got by IS 2911 method without correction factor is nearer the Broms value.

EXAMPLE 13.4 (Laterally loaded piles in sand IS 2911 Method)

A concrete pile 450 mm dia. And 15 m length is installed in a deposit of sand. Its coefficient of subgrade reaction $n_h = 10 \times 106$ N/m³. Find the deflection of the pile head considering it as a free head pile under a horizontal force of 30 kN. Assume E value of concrete as 20 kN/mm².

Ref.	Step	Calculations
Sec. 13.7	1	[Note: Soil is sand. Hence we use factor T.] *Find whether pile is long or short* $I = \dfrac{\pi D^4}{64} = \dfrac{3.14 \times (0.45)^4}{64} = 2.01 \times 10^{-3}$ $E = 20$ kN/mm² $= 20 \times 10^9$ N/m² $EI = 20 \times 10^9 \times 2.01 \times 10^{-3} = 40 \times 10^6$ Nm²
Eq. (13.7)	2	*Calculate T. Check pile is short or long* $T = \left(\dfrac{EI}{\eta_h}\right)^{1/5} = \left(\dfrac{40 \times 10^6}{10 \times 10^6}\right)^{1/5} = (4)^{1/5} = 1.32$
Eq. (13.9a)		Length of pile $L = 15$ m Length $> 5 \times 1.32 = 6.6$ m. Pile is long. Hence, IS method is applicable .
	3	*Find length of fixity z_f (free head pile)*
Fig. 13.7		$\dfrac{e}{T} = 0; \dfrac{Z_1}{T} = 1.92$ (free head pile) $z_f = 1.92 \times 1.32 = 2.53$ m
	4	*Calculate deflection as a cantilever fixed at 2.53 m* $\Delta = \dfrac{HL^3}{3EI} = \dfrac{30(2.53)^3}{3 \times 40 \times 10^3}$ (kN and m) $= 4 \times 10^{-3}$ m Deflection = 4 mm

EXAMPLE 13.5 (Lateral resistance of short pile from Broms chart)

A concrete pile 900 mm diameter and 6 m long is installed in a clay soil with cohesion, 1.2 kg/cm² (N value 12). Estimate the ultimate lateral resistance if the load is applied at a point situated at 4 m above the ground level. Assume $K_1 = 25.0$ MN/m³ and $E_c = 26$ kN/mm². If the allowable deflection at ground level is only 25 mm, estimate the load that it can take.

Ref.	Step	Calculations
	1	[*Note:* As soil is clay we use factor R.] *Calculate R in metres* $I = \dfrac{\pi D^4}{64} = \dfrac{\pi (0.9)^4}{64} = 3.2 \times 10^{-2}$ m⁴ $K_h = \dfrac{K_1}{1.5} = \dfrac{25}{1.5} = 16.66$ MN/m³

Eq. (13.6)

$$E_c = 26 \text{ kN/mm}^2 = 26 \times 103 \text{ MN/m}^2$$

$$R = \left[\frac{E_c I}{KB}\right]^{1/4} = \left[\frac{26 \times 10^3 \times 3.2 \times 10^{-2}}{16.66 \times 0.9}\right]^{1/4} = 2.7 \text{ m}$$

2   *Check whether pile is long or short*

Eq. (13.8)

$$\frac{L}{R} = \frac{6}{2.7} = 2.22 \text{ (just over 2)}$$

The pile should be considered as short.
(IS method is not applicable for short piles)

3   *Find ultimate lateral resistance from Broms chart*
Type of pile – Free headed pile; short pile in Type 1 soil.

Fig. 13.9

$$\frac{e}{D} = \frac{4}{0.9} = 4.44, \qquad \frac{L}{B} = \frac{6.0}{0.9} = 6.7$$

Fig. 13.9 gives $\dfrac{H}{c_u B^2} = 8.0$. We have $c_u = 120 \text{ kN/m}^2$

$$H = 8.0 \times 120(0.9)^2 = 778 \text{ kN} = 77.8 \text{ tons (ultimate load value)}$$

4   *Find horizontal force when displacement at ground level is* 25 **mm**

$$\beta = \left[\frac{KB}{4EI}\right]^{1/4}$$

$$= \left[\frac{25 \times 0.9 \times 10^2}{4 \times 26 \times 10^3 \times 3.2}\right]^{1/4} = 0.286; \quad \left[\text{also} \approx \frac{1}{1.4R}\right]$$

Fig. 13.11

$$\beta L = 0.286 \times 6 = 1.71; \quad e/L = \frac{4}{6} = 0.67$$

$$\frac{yKBL}{H} = 10 \text{ (extra plated)}$$

$$H = yKBL/10; \text{ given } y = 0.025 \text{ m}$$

$$H = \frac{0.025(25 \times 10^3) \times 0.9 \times 6}{10} = 337.5 \text{ kN}$$

5   *Determine FS against ultimate strength*

$$FS = \frac{778}{337} = 2.3$$

(*Note*: Ref. 2 gives analysis with c and ϕ values by Brinch Hansen's coefficient which gives safer values.)

EXAMPLE 13.6 (Deflection of cantilever)

A long pile has the depth of fixity, $z = 1.0$ m and $e = 4$ m (the load is applied 4 m above the ground level). Determine the deflection at the top when the deflection at ground level is 25 mm assuming it acts as a cantilever.

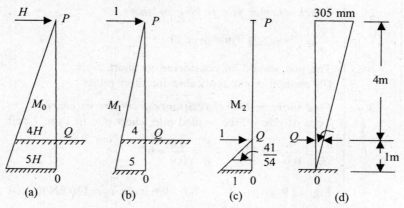

Fig. E.13.6

Ref.	Step	Calculations
		Method: This is a problem in theory of structures. We will use the unit load method. Let a load H at top end of the pile produce a bending moment, $BM = M$ BM with unit load where the deflection is required $= m$ Deflection $y = \int \dfrac{Mm\,dx}{EI}$ which may be geometrically evaluated as: $\qquad = \dfrac{[\text{Area of } M_0 \text{ diagram}]\,[\text{Ordinate of } m \text{ diagram at C.G. of } M_0]}{EI}$ Integration is to be made only between points of discontinuity in slopes. To find deflection at end, proceed as follows:
	1	*Find area of M_0 diagram with H at top of pile.* Max BM $= 5H$; Area of $M_0 = \dfrac{1}{2} \times 5 \times 5H = 12.5H$
	2	*Find ordinate of m_1 produced by unit load at end at C.G. of M_0* $m_1 = \dfrac{2 \times 5}{3} = 3.33$
	3	*Find deflection at end of cantilever.* $\int \dfrac{M_0 m_1}{EI} = \dfrac{12.5H \times 3.33}{EI} = \dfrac{41.7H}{EI}$

	Check deflection of cantilever due to load at end by formula $$\delta \text{ (deflection at end)} = \frac{HL^3}{3EI} = \frac{125H}{3EI} = \frac{41.7H}{EI}$$
4	*Find deflection at* 1m *from the point of fixity (at G.L.)* Apply unit load at 1 m from point of fixity. Take M_0 diagram between ground and 1 m height due to load H $$\text{Area } M_0 = \left[\frac{5+4}{2}\right] H \times 1 = 4.5H$$ $$CG \text{ of } M_0 \text{ from } 0 = \frac{1}{6}\frac{[5+8]}{(5+4)} = \frac{1}{6}\left(\frac{13}{9}\right) = \frac{13}{54} \text{ m}$$ $$m_2 \text{ due to unit load at CG of } M_0 = \frac{1 \times 41}{54} = \frac{41}{54}$$ $$\delta_2 = \frac{M_0 m_2}{EI} = \frac{4.5H \times 41}{54} = \frac{3.41H}{EI}$$
5	*Find* δ_1 *when* δ_2 *is* 25 mm Ratio of δ_1/δ_2 = 41.7/3.41 = 12.22 Value of δ_1 when δ_2 = 25 mm $= 25 \times 12.22 = 3.5 \text{ mm}$ We must note that the deflection is not proportional to the distance from the point of fixity.

REFERENCES

[1] Poulos, H.G. and Davis, E.H., *Pile Foundation Analysis and Design*, John Wiley & Sons, New York, 1980.

[2] Tomlinson, M.J., *Pile Design and Construction Practice*, F.N. Spon, London, 1977.

[3] IS 2911 (1979), Part I Sec. 1: *Code of Practice for Design and Construction of Pile Foundations* (First Revision), Bureau of Indian Standards, New Delhi.

[4] Bowles, J.E., *Analytical and Computer Methods in Foundation Engineering*, McGraw-Hill, New York, 1974.

[5] Reese, L.C. and Matlock, H., *Non dimensional, Solutions for Laterally Loaded Piles with Soil Modulus Assumed Proportional to Depth*, 8th Texas Conference on Soil Mechanics and Foundation Engineering, Special Publication No. 29, University of Texas at Austin, 1956.

[6] Davisson, M.T. and Prakash, S.A., *Review of Soil-Pile Behavior*, Highway Research Record, No. 39, Highway Research Board, USA, 1963.

[7] Davisson, M.T., Design of Deep Foundations for Tall Buildings under Lateral Loads, *University of Illinois Bulletin*, Volume 66, No. 76, Feb. 1969.

[8] ACI Committee 336, *Suggested Design and Construction Procedures for Pier Foundations*, ACI Manual of Concrete Practice, Part 4, 1972.

[9] Kurien, N.P., *Design of Foundations Systems*, Narosa Publishing House, New Delhi, 1972.

[10] IS 2911 (1999) Part I Sec. 3: 1999, *Code of Practice for Design and Construction of Pile Foundations,* (Second revision): (*Pre-cast Driven Piles*), Bureau of Indian Standards, New Delhi.

[11] Broms, B.B., Lateral Resistance of Piles in Cohesive Soils, *Proc. A.S.C.E., Journal of SMFD*, New York, 1964.

[12] Broms, B.B., *Lateral Resistance of Piles in Cohesionless Soils, Proc. A.S.C.E., Journal of SMFD*, New York, 1964.

[13] Broms, B.B., Design of Laterally Loaded Piles, Proc. A.S.C.E., *Journal of SMFD,* New York, (1964a), (1964b), and 1965.

[14] Broms, B.B., Methods of Calculating the Ultimate Bearing Capacity of Piles, A Summary, *Soils and Soils,* Volume 5, 1965.

14

Field Tests on Piles

14.1 INTRODUCTION

IS 2911 (Part 4) [1] gives details of testing piles in the field. The terms used in pile testing are the following:

Ultimate load capacity: It is the maximum load that a pile can carry before failure of the ground or the structural failure of the pile.

Safe load: It is the load derived from the ultimate load capacity obtained by pile load test by applying a suitable or prescribed factor of safety. A factor of safety of 2 is usually taken for results got from field tests on piles.

Working load of a pile: It is the load adopted for design of the pile in the foundation with reference to both its capacity and settlement.

Pile displacements: The total displacement that the pile undergoes under a given load is the gross displacement. The rebound at the top of the pile on removal of the load is the total elastic rebound, which has two parts namely, that due to the elastic deformation of the soil, and that due to the elastic deformation of the pile. The gross settlement minus the elastic rebound gives the net settlement.

Initial tests on piles are the tests usually carried at the start of the project with a view to:

1. Determine the ultimate load capacity and safe load capacity of the pile
2. Provide guidelines for acceptance of routine tests
3. Study the effect of piling on adjacent existing structures and take decision on suitability of type of piles to be used by observing the effects.

These piles are tested to failure or at least twice the design (working) load. Generally such piles are not included in the construction.

Routine or proof tests on piles: IS specifies that 0.5 to 2 per cent of total piles required on the project (depending on the nature of the site and project) should be proof-tested for the following purpose:

1. To determine the safe load on piles
2. To check the safe load and extent of safety for the specific functional requirement of the pile at working load (to estimate settlement expected).
3. To detect any unusual performance contrary to the findings of the initial test if carried out.
4. To check on the quality of the contractor's work at the site.

According to IS, in these tests, the piles should be loaded to at least one and half times the working load and the maximum settlement of the test should not exceed 12 mm. These piles are allowed to be used in the works.

In this chapter we will examine various important considerations for load tests on piles.

14.2 TYPES OF LOAD TESTS ON PILES

The following types of loading tests are generally carried out:

- Vertical load tests to determine the carrying capacity of vertical loads
- Pull-out tests to evaluate the tension capacity
- Lateral load test to determine lateral strength of the pile.

Of these, the vertical load tests are the most important and commonly used tests.

14.3 LOADING ARRANGEMENTS FOR VERTICAL LOAD TEST

In the vertical load test, the load is generally applied by a hydraulic jack and proving ring assembly of sufficient capacity is used to measure the load. The reaction is transferred to a kentledge of capacity 25% more than test load or to anchor piles or to rock anchors. The weight from the kentledge is to be transmitted to the ground at a safe distance from the pile and the minimum distance of anchor piles from the test pile should be 3d or 2 m. In the case rock anchors, they should be at least 2d or 1.5 m from the test pile (d being the diameter of the pile or the circumscribing circle for non-circular piles). The settlement is measured by dial gauges of 0.01 mm sensitivity. There should be at least two numbers of gauges for a single pile and four numbers for a group of piles. These measurements are to be measured from a datum at least 3d or 1.5 m away from the edge of the pile.

14.3.1 Installation of Driven Pile for Initial Pile Test

All details regarding the piles (as to its weight, length, reinforcements) should be reported. Similarly, for driven piles, all details regarding the weight of hammer used, its drop and other details of driving should be recorded. The temporary compressions obtained by site measurement and the set in millimetres per blow in the final stages of recording are also to be noted very carefully.

14.3.2 Preparation of Pile Head

According to IS 2911 (Part 4) Clause 6.1.1, the head of the pile should be carefully prepared to receive the load by chipping of the pile head to a suitable level and finishing the top with a thin coating of plaster of paris or similar synthetic material. A suitable thick bearing plate with a centre depression for the jack to rest at level is placed on top of the pile.

14.4 TYPES OF VERTICAL LOAD TESTS ON A SINGLE PILE

The three types of vertical load tests commonly used are the following:

1. The maintained load test (ML test)
2. The constant rate of penetration test (CRP test)
3. The cyclic load test.

These are briefly described below. IS 2911 (Part 4) gives details of these tests.

14.4.1 The Maintained Load Test

This test is used as an initial as well as a routine test. The loads are applied in increments of about 20% of the estimated safe load, so that the failure load will be applied in about eight to ten equal increments. Readings of settlements are usually taken immediately on loading and then gradually extended to ten-minute intervals till the rate of settlement is less than 0.1 mm per hour. It is always desirable to unload the pile after reaching the estimated design working load and wait till the rebound ceases and then once again reload the pile to the working load in one step and continue incremental of loading the pile to its ultimate stage or proof load. The ultimate load may be said to be reached when the final settlement is more than 10% of the diameter of the pile or when the settlement goes on increasing without increasing the load. In proof load test, the loading is generally taken to 1.5 times working load or till the final settlement is 12 mm. After reaching the final load, the load should be released in decrements of about one-sixth of the total load and the recovery measured. Each step of unloading is done only after the full rebound at each stage has been stabilised. After full unloading, the measurements are continued for 24 hours to determine the full elastic recovery. When conducting a routine test, pile is loaded to the proof load, which is usually taken as 1.5 times the working load. A limiting value is usually specified for the settlement and recovery after complete unloading. These loading and unloading data are represented on a load settlement diagram as shown in Fig. 14.1 using a suitable scale. The shape of the load settlement curve will depend on the type of the pile.

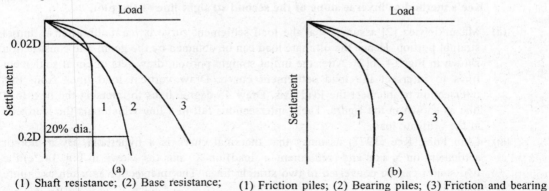

(a)
(1) Shaft resistance; (2) Base resistance;
(3) Total resistance

(b)
(1) Friction piles; (2) Bearing piles; (3) Friction and bearing piles.

Fig. 14.1 **Load settlement relationship for friction and bearing piles: (a) Development of shaft and base resistance; (b) load settlement curves for different types of piles.**

Determination of failure load. The load settlement part of the curves can be of different shapes as shown in Fig. 14.1. Some of the criteria proposed to obtain the ultimate or failure load from the load settlement curve are as follows:

(i) According to De Beer (1968), the load settlement curve is plotted in log–log plot and the point of intersection of the two straight lines thus obtained is the failure load (see Fig. 14.2a).

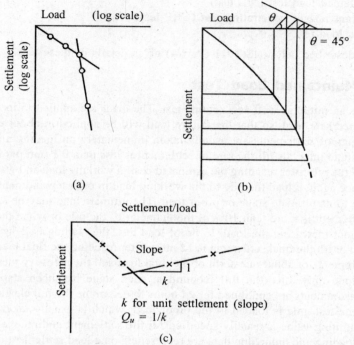

(a)

(b)

(c)

Fig. 14.2 **Determination of failure load of piles from load test diagram: (a) De Beer's method by log-log plot; (b) Mazurkiewicz method assuming parabolic shape; (c) Chin Fung Kee's method as inverse slope of the second straight line of the plot.**

(ii) Mazurkiewicz [2] assumes that the load settlement curve is parabolic after an initial straight portion. Hence the ultimate load can be obtained by the geometric construction shown in Fig. 14.2b[2]. After the initial straight portion, draw sets of equal settlement lines to intersect the load settlement curve. Draw vertical load lines from this intersection to intersect the load axis. Draw 45 degree lines to intersect the next load line as shown in the figure. These intersections fall in a line which cuts the load axis at the ultimate load.

(iii) Chin Fung Kee (1977) assumes that the final curve is a hyperbola. By a plot of settlement on Y axis and (settlement ÷ load) on X axis (as shown in Fig. 14.2c) the two stages can be converted to two straight lines. The intersection is taken as failure load [3].

(iv) Piles can be predominantly friction or bearing piles (Fig. 14.1). For friction pile, the load settlement curve will be a linear portion followed by a steep downward curve. The peak load point is very obvious and it is taken as the ultimate load. This occurs also at small settlement values, about 0.2 to 0.5% diameter of piles. For a predominantly end bearing pile there may not be definite peak. For such piles a *settlement of* 10% *diameter of pile* (or any other specified value) is taken as the ultimate load capacity.

(v) IS criterion for *safe load* or *working load* on single pile is given in IS 2911 (Part 4) (1985). It specifies the safe load of a single pile as the *lesser of the following two values*:

1. Two-thirds of the load where the total settlement attains 12 mm (or other specified value).
2. 50% of the final load at which the total displacement is equal to 10% of the pile diameter (7.5% of bulb diameter for under-reamed piles). This also implies that the ultimate capacity of the pile (failure load) occurs at 10% displacement.

Generally speaking, the 12 mm settlement criterion for working load gives higher values than the value got from ultimate load with a factor of safety equal to 2.

Among the various methods described above, to determine the ultimate loads the log–log plot gives conservative results. The parabolic and hyperbolic assumptions give more realistic values. For example the following values were obtained for a test on a 400-mm diameter pile by various methods. For a pile group the test load at 25 mm or half load at 40 mm is taken as the safe load.

1. Max. test load at settlement 10% dia = 180 tons and settlement = 40 mm (10% dia.)
2. 50% load at settlement of 10% dia. = 90 tons
3. From log–log plot, ultimate load = 130 tons and settlement = 16 mm
4. From parabolic plot, ultimate load = 180 tons
5. From hyperbolic plot, ultimate load = 175 tons
6. 2/3 of load for 12 mm settlement = 64 tons (safe load)

From the above data we have the following safe load:

Safe load, according to IS = 64 tons (lesser of 2 and 6)

$$\text{Ultimate/FS based (on log–log plot)} = \frac{130}{2} = 65 \text{ tons}$$

It is also very important to note that the load settlement curve should be drawn on a suitable scale as illustrated in Fig. 14.3. Otherwise, it can give wrong values for failure loads.

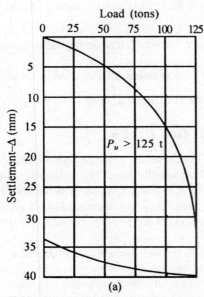
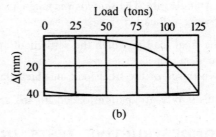

Fig. 14.3 **Importance of choosing proper scale for load settlement curve for proper interpretation. The ultimate load is clearly indicated in Fig. 14.3a.**

14.4.2 The Constant Rate of Penetration Test

This test has only limited use. It is used as an initial test to determine rapidly the ultimate bearing capacity of the pile, but the load-deflection curve obtained by the test cannot be taken to predict the settlement under the working load conditions. This method *should not be included as a routine test* for construction when piles are designed by limiting deflections. It may be used as an investigation tool when the design of the pile is based on ultimate load with a *factor of safety* as against the method of *limiting deflections*.

The CRP method consists of jacking the pile into the soil at a constant rate of penetration of approximately 0.75 mm per minute for friction piles to 1.5 mm per minute for predominantly end bearing piles. It may be noted that a rate of penetration as much as twice the above values do not very much affect the results of the test. The test is continued till the field penetration is as much as 10% of the diameter of the pile or till the deflection increases very fast without addition of further loads. The load corresponding to a penetration of 10 per cent of the diameter of the pile is taken as the ultimate load capacity.

14.4.3 The Cyclic Load Test

This test is used as an initial test to determine separately the skin friction and point bearing load on single piles of uniform diameter. IS Code 2911 (Part 4)—Appendix D should be consulted when this type of test is contemplated [1]. This test and instrumented piles were once used extensively for research purposes. However, they are seldom used nowadays on projects. The test procedure is described in Appendix D of this book.

14.5 VERTICAL LOAD TEST ON PILE GROUP

For testing a group of piles, a pile cap is first cast and the loading is carried on the pile cap as in the case of a single pile. The *safe load* is taken according to IS 2911 (Part 4) Clause 6.16 as the lesser of the following values [1]:

1. The final load at which the settlement attains a value of 25 mm or the value specified by the designer
2. Two-thirds of the final load at which the total displacement attains a value of 40 mm.

In routine tests, pile groups are loaded till the settlement is at least 25 mm.

14.6 NONDESTRUCTIVE TESTS (NDTs) ON PILES

In many situations as in piles for offshore structures, load tests as described above are difficult. There are no easy facilities for producing reactions especially when the piles are large. Oil installations use small number of very large piles (up to 1.8 m dia.) driven with extremely large hammers (up to 200 tons) to provide loads up to 3000 tons. They are also usually installed out in the sea. These are very expensive piles. They are proof-tested by nondestructive tests which are specially suited for such piles.

Another reason for the development of such tests is the widespread use of bored piles. The set attained by driven piles gives us a good indication of the strength of the piles. However, when installing bored cast in-situ piles, overbreak and other defects arising from collapsing soils or poor workmanship should be identified for the proper performance of the piles. Here also, NDTs are the most suitable to test their integrity. Yet another use of such tests (like those using Pile Driving Analysis machine) is that it can assess the capacity of driven piles at the same time as it is driven in the field. Because of these and other necessities, new and quick methods of assessing the *pile integrity* (the soundness of the pile all along its length) as well as the *pile capacity* have been evolved and are used widely in practice. Some of them are briefly described in this section.

14.6.1 Types on Nondestructive Tests

Nondestructive tests on piles can be basically categorised into two types namely the low and high energy methods.

Low energy methods. The low energy methods essentially test the integrity or soundness of the pile. The following tests come in this category.

- Acoustic tests consist of tracing sonic pulses through concrete by using a single hole or two holes drilled in the body of the pile.
- Dynamic response tests (shock tests) consist of using an electrodynamic constant amplitude stress wave at the pile top and measuring the travel of the wave at the pile head. It is also carried out by using a hammer blow to produce a shock and its travel is traced from the top of the pile.
- Sonic echo test is the same as the shock test except that the method looks at only the velocity response in the pile.

High energy methods (use of wave equation analysis). At present Pile Driving Analysis (PDA) equipments using as the CASE method developed at the Case Western Reserve University by Goble and others around 1964 are available in the market. The basic principle of the method is to measure the force and velocity of stress wave produced at the pile top by proper instruments and then using these as inputs for wave equation analysis. This has reduced the driving process to one involving only interaction between the pile and the soil.

The basic concepts of the *wave equation analysis of piles* [WEAP] and its use for prediction of pile capacity and effectiveness of hammer in driving the pile are described in Chapter 10. The Pile Driving Analysis (PDA) machine uses CAP-WEAP method to give the following:

- Soil resistance distribution and ultimate bearing capacity
- Compressive and tensile stresses in the piles
- Pile integrity (extent as well as location of pile damage, if any)
- Hammer efficiency and malfunction of cushions, hammers, if any
- Top movement velocity and acceleration.

The following conditions are needed to assure good correlation of PDA with static testing of piles for pile capacity:

- We must activate all resistance so that a minimum of 2 mm set per blow is obtained.
- We must allow the strength changes to occur before actual testing.
- We must have high quality measurements in all cases.

14.7 OTHER FIELD TESTS ON PILES

Two other important tests on piles are the following:

- Lateral load tests on piles
- Dynamic load tests on piles:

14.7.1 Lateral Load Tests on Piles

These tests are described in IS 2911 (Part 4) (1985)—Section 7 [1]. They are carried out to determine the safe lateral load of the pile. It is conducted by jacking between two piles as described in IS 2911.

14.7.2 Dynamic Load Tests on Piles

These tests are to be conducted according to IS 9716 (1981) [5] and IS 5249 (1977) [6]. The results of the tests are useful for design of foundations or piles subjected to dynamic loads or earthquake loads. The following are the tests to be conducted for determining the *natural frequency* and *damping coefficients* for each of the following four conditions:

1. Free horizontal vibration tests
2. Free vertical vibration tests
3. Forced horizontal vibration tests
4. Forced vertical vibration tests.

In conjunction with these tests, the following tests are also conducted:

- Wave propagation test (Hammer test and steady state vibration test). This test gives the velocity of compression and shear waves.
- Cross hole test at depth corresponding to bottom level of the pile cap. This test gives the velocity of shear waves.

Details of the necessary special equipment and procedures to be followed can be obtained from specialised literature on the subject [7, 8].

EXAMPLE 14.1 **(Analysis of static load tests on piles)**

The following are the results of a maintained load test as a 400 mm diameter pile:

Load (tons)	20	50	100	130	150	160	170
Settlement (mm)	2	4	8	14	22	30	50

Determine the ultimate load and also the safe load according to IS 2911 (Part IV).

Ref.	Step	Calculations
	1	*Draw the load—settlement curve* See Fig. E.14.1
Fig. 14.2	2	*Determine ultimate load Q_U from initial curve by Mazurkiewicz's method.* Mazurkiewicz's method and also inspection of failure point in the diagram gives ultimate load as 170 tons
Sec.14.4.1	3	*Find safe load from I.S 2911 (Part IV)* Least of the following: (a) One half $Q_U = \dfrac{Q_U}{2} = \dfrac{170}{2} = 85$ tons

(b) 50% load at settlement equal to 10% dia. of pile (i.e. 40 mm)

$$= \frac{165}{2} = 87.5 \text{ tons}$$

(c) 2/3 load at 12 mm settlement $= \frac{2 \times 125}{3} = 83$ tons

∴ Safe load = 83 tons

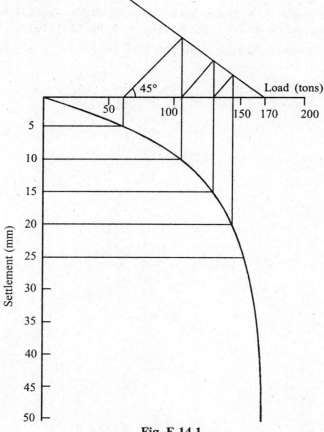

Fig. E.14.1.

REFERENCES

[1] IS 2911 (1985) Part 4: *Indian Standard Code of Practice for Design and Construction of Pile Foundations, Load Tests on Piles*, Bureau of Indian Standards, New Delhi.

[2] Mazurkiewicz, B.K., Test Loading of Piles According to Polish Regulations, Preliminary Report No. 35, Commission on Pile Research, Royal Swedish Academy of Engineering Services, Stockholm, 1972.

[3] Chin Fung Kee, *Proc. Piles in Weak Rock*, Institution of Civil Engineers, London, 1977, Contributions to Discussion Session.

[4] Smith, E.A.L., Pile Driving Analysis by the Wave Equation, *Journal of Soil Mechanics and Foundation Division ASCI*, Volume 86 (4), 1960.

[5] IS 9716 (1981)., *Guide for Lateral Dynamic Tests on Piles*, Bureau of Indian Standards, New Delhi.

[6] IS 5249 (1977), *Methods of Test for Determination of Dynamic Properties of Soil*, Bureau of Indian Standards, New Delhi.

[7] Stoke, K.H. and Woods, R.D., In-situ Shear Wave Velocity by Cross Hole Method, *Journal of Soil Mechanics and Foundation, ASCE*, Volume 98, No SM5, 1972.

[8] Prakash, S., *Soil Dynamics*, McGraw-Hill, New York, 1981.

15

Piled Raft Foundations

15.1 INTRODUCTION

The load on a footing or raft affects the foundation soil for a depth only approximately equal to 1 to 2 times its breadth. A pile foundation transfers its load to deeper layers. If we combine a pile and a raft, the interaction between the two types of structures is very complex. It depends on the rigidity of the raft, the nature of soil below and also the nature and the number of piles below the raft. Tomlinson in his book on Foundation Design and Construction [1] has considered the action of the following cases of piled rafts (shown in Fig. 15.1):

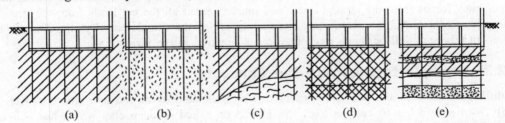

Fig. 15.1 Piled basements: (a) Piles in clay; (b) piles in sand; (c) piles through clay to rocks; (d) piles through soft clay to hard clay; (e) piles in layers of clay and sand.

Case A: Piled raft with piles wholly in compressible clay.

Case B: Piled raft with piles driven into loose sand which otherwise would have resulted in excessive settlement.

Case C: Piled raft with piles installed through compressible soils into hard rock.

Case D: Piled raft with piles installed through soft clay to stiff clay.

Case E: Piled raft with piles installed in alternate layers of soft clay and sand.

Most interactions fall under in Case A, where there is load sharing between piles and raft. In the other cases, all the load has to be taken by the piles and the raft acts as a medium to transfer the load from the columns to the piles and also to withstand any upward hydraulic pressure that may act at the bottom of the raft. Instead of attempting a general solution to the problem in this chapter, we will distinguish between the two types of piled rafts and understand the principles to be used in their design.

15.2 TYPES OF PILED RAFTS

We may classify piled rafts into two types:

Type 1. Piled raft for settlement reduction

Type 2. Piled raft for load transfer.

These two types are described below:

15.2.1 Piled Raft for Settlement Reduction

When we adopt a raft foundation, we may find that the raft is safe from bearing capacity considerations but it may suffer from excessive settlement. The traditional solution of this problem is to provide a basement and basement raft, so that the effective load is reduced. If in any situation this is not possible, the alternative solution will be to provide a few piles under the raft so that the piles relieve the raft of a part of the total load. As the piles do not have to take all the loads, the number of piles required will be much smaller than the traditional piled foundation. Because of some relief of the load, the raft settlement will also fall within allowable limits.

15.2.2 Piled Raft for Load Transfer

The second type of piled rafts are the conventional type which are used in situations where the subsoil is very weak with high water level and rafts have to be adopted. These rafts should resist the buoyancy forces from the ground water and must transmit all the net loads from the structure to the piles to be carried to deeper and stronger layers of the foundation. The number of piles required in this case will be much more than those required in the former case.

15.2.3 Example to Illustrate the Concepts

The difference between the two above cases can be illustrated by an example given in Ref. [1] A raft 15 m square has to carry a load 150 kN/m^2 on a bed of deep clay which has cohesion of 70 kN/m^2.

The *FS* against bearing $\dfrac{N_c c}{w} = \dfrac{5.69 \times 70}{150} = 2.65$ (safe)

Assuming $E_s = 90 \times$ cohesion; $E_s = 90 \times 70 = 6300$ kN/m^2

Elastic settlement of raft $\Delta H = \dfrac{0.95(qB)(1-\mu^2)}{E_s}$

$$= \frac{0.95 \times 150 \times 15 \left(1 - 0.35^2\right)}{6300} = 0.29 \text{ m} = 290 \text{ mm}$$

This settlement is large and has to be reduced. Calculations (as given in Reference 2) show that if we adopt 16 piles of 300 mm dia. and 30 m long, then we can reduce the settlement of the 'piled load sharing raft' to about 150 mm. On the other hand, if we design the piles to take all the loads and the raft to act only as a transfer mechanism we will require 68 piles and the settlement will be also of the order of 120 mm, the reduction of settlement being only 30 mm. The first system will be much cheaper and the settlement will also be within allowable limits.

15.3 TRANSFER OF LOAD TO PILES IN A PILED RAFT

When a single pile is loaded from the top, the load is first resisted by side friction which is fully mobilised with a settlement as little as 0.5 per cent of the pile diameter. It is only after the full friction is mobilised that the full bearing resistance comes into play. In a pile with a slab attached to its top and the slab being in contact with the ground, more load will be transferred to the tip than in the case of loading of a single pile even in the initial stages of loading. This method of transfer of load is an important consideration in piled raft design. Because of this type of load transfer, many designers assume that the raft action comes into effect only after the ultimate load carrying capacity of the piles is exhausted.

15.4 DESIGN OF PILED RAFT FOR SETTLEMENT REDUCTION (TYPE 1 PILED RAFTS)

In this problem we have arrived at two answers:

- First, we have to find the number, dimensions and disposition of piles required to reduce the settlement to an allowable value.
- Second, we have to find the bending moments produced in a raft which has to carry part of the super load directly to the soil and has also to transmit the rest of the load to the piles.

The second problem is a structural engineering problem where the soil supports and pile supports are represented suitably for analysis. Some of the methods used to solve the first problem to find the number and disposition of piles are as follows.

Method 1: *Theoretical method.* Poulos and Davis in Chapter 10 of Ref. [1] lists a number of approaches to analyse this situation. In brief, an elastic solution is attempted. First the load settlement characteristics of a group of piles of given size and spacing attached to a slab resting on the ground is obtained by using values obtained from field tests on single piles. The computer methods recommended have the advantage that distribution of settlement, pile load and raft bending moment can be obtained by the analysis.

Method 2: *Simplified method of analysis by obtaining the load settlement curve to failure of piles. This method is discussed by Poulose and Davis* in Ref. [2]. It is applicable only where a relatively few piles are added to the raft. If they are closely spaced, failure will take place by block failure than by failure of individual piles. In general, it assumes that loading under undrained condition can be considered as purely elastic up to the load at *which the pile would fail if no pile cap was present.* Further loading will be taken by the raft. Hence, the additional settlement will be that due to load on the raft only. Thus the undrained load settlement curve will consist of two linear sections shown in Fig. 15.2. However, if the piles are sufficiently close for a block failure, the ultimate failure of the group should be considered and not its individual capacity.

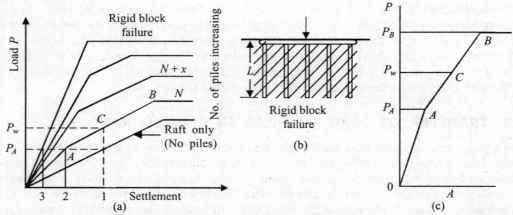

Fig. 15.2   Concept of piled raft foundation: (a) Decrease in settlement under a given load with increasing number of piles; (b) rigid block failure; (c) load settlement curve for a specified number of piles.

In Fig 15.2a for the curve *OACB* for *N* piles, from *O* to *A*, only the piles act while from *A* to *B* the raft comes into action. Thus the total settlement for a working load P_w corresponding to point *C* in Fig. 15.2 can be expressed as follows:

$$s = P_A s_1 + (P_w - P_A)s_2$$

where

P_A = load up to ultimate value of pile system
s_1 = settlement of pile due *to unit load* on pile system
P_w = working load
s_2 = settlement of raft due *to unit load* on raft

Calculations are made on elastic basis and the number of piles required to reduce the settlement to the required value is determined. As can be seen from Fig. 15.2, the settlement decreases with increasing number of piles.

Method 3: *Strip method.* The raft is divided into strips, which are analysed considering them as supported on elastic springs. The piles are analysed considering them as springs of different stiffness. The pile parameters are derived from load test on piles or assumed load settlement curves. The number of piles required to keep the settlement within limits is arrived by trial and error.

Method 4: *By assuming arbitrary sharing of loads.* In this method, the piles and rafts are allowed arbitrary amount of loads and the settlements due to these loads are worked and added together to get the resultant of the piled raft system. This is a very approximate method as the real behaviour of the system may be different from what we have assumed. If the failure of a piled raft system can be a block failure, the system is checked for such failure and the settlement as a block will be as shown in Fig. 15.2. The method is empirical and should be based on field experience.

In a building constructed in stiff clay, measurements showed that about 30 per cent of the building load was carried by piles and 60 per cent by the raft. Other measurements have shown that the overall distribution of load between pile and raft does not change very much with consolidation even though there was some transfer of load from centre piles to edge piles accompanied by a transfer of soil pressure from the edge of the raft to the centre of the raft.

15.5 APPROXIMATE DESIGN OF PILED RAFT FOR LOAD TRANSMISSION [TYPE 2 PILED RAFTS]

In this analysis we assume that all the loads are taken by the piles. Exact analysis of this system can be made by computer methods using finite element analysis. The approximate methods used are the same as for ordinary raft analysis. Piles are assumed to be of uniform strength and are closely spaced. We assume the raft as being supported on an equivalent soil with uniform pressure from below. The following routine methods used for ordinary rafts can be used for approximate analysis [4]:

1. *Conventional rigid beam method:* With closely spaced piles—with spacing nearly equal to the raft thickness—we may assume the raft as resting on a bed of equivalent soil strata. The raft as a whole is considered as a rigid beam both in X and Y directions with all the loads on it. The resultant moment is divided corresponding to the loading and the width of the section. In addition, the analysis is repeated for individual strips with relevant column loads as continuous beams as given below. This approach gives oversafe values of raft thickness and steel required.

2. *Continuous beam method:* In this method, the raft is considered as an inverted floor with uniform pressure below and the column points are considered as rigid supports of an inverted floor. The raft is cut into strips in X and Y directions as these continuous beams are analysed. The maximum positive and negative possible moments are limited to $\pm wL^2/10$.

3. *Continuous beam on elastic foundation method:* In this method, the raft is analysed as beams on elastic foundation.

15.6 EFFECT OF VARIOUS PARAMETERS ON RESULTS OF ANALYSIS

Parametric studies indicate the following trends:

1. The effect of superstructure rigidity on the rigidity of the raft is only of the order of about 20% for a framed building of ten-storey height.

2. If we consider the rigidity of the piles also, we usually take it as $2AE/L$ for friction piles and AE/L for bearing piles. Accordingly, moments in rafts supported on end bearing piles tend to be more than the moments in rafts on friction piles.

3. Variation of the thickness of slab affects the load on the piles. With less stiffness, there is more variation in the loads carried by the pile in different locations. Our aim is to adopt a slab thickness which will make the pile loads uniform. Increasing thickness of raft tends to increase uniformity of loading on the piles.

4. One of the thumb rules adopted to determine the initial thickness of raft is first to find the thickness required from punching shear and then adopt a thickness equal to 2 to 2.2 times that value.

5. In earthquake-prone regions, a separate study should be made for the effects of earthquake forces.

REFERENCES

[1] Poulos, H.G. and Davis, E.H., *Pile Foundation Analysis and Design*, John Wiley & Sons, New York, 1980.

[2] Tomlinson, M.J., *Foundation Design and Construction,* Longman with ELBS, Singapore, 1995.

[3] Naylor, D.J. and Hooper, J.A., *An Effective Stress Finite Element Analysis to Predict Short Term and Long Term Behaviour of a Piled Raft Foundation in Harder Clay*, Conference on Settlement of Structures, Proceedings Pentech Press, London, 1975.

[4] Gupta, S.C., *Raft Foundations: Design and Analysis with a Practical Approach*, New Age International, New Delhi, 1997.

16

Lateral Earth Pressures on Rigid Walls

16.1 INTRODUCTION

Earth pressure theories generally refer to pressures on rigid or unyielding walls. The classical theories due to Coulomb (1776) and Rankine (1857) are used to calculate the lateral pressures on rigid walls due to backfill and uniform surcharge loads. On the other hand, elastic theory based on Boussinesq's (1885) equation is used to determine the lateral pressure produced by line loads and concentrated loads behind the walls on the backfill. These theories of lateral pressures on rigid walls can be extended also to flexible walls like cantilever sheet pile walls as well as to anchored sheet pile walls with some modifications. Data on model studies as well as field measurement have shown that the pressures on flexible walls differ from those predicted by the theory on rigid walls, the greater the flexibility of the wall, the greater being the difference. In this chapter, we will however, restrict our discussion to earth pressure on rigid walls which are back-filled after their construction. They are also different from sloped walls and revetments we build along existing slopes for slope stability as in railway cutting.

16.2 HISTORICAL DEVELOPMENT

Coulomb published his method for calculation of earth pressures on walls (for design of earth fortification for military use) based on friction model as early as in 1776. It was much later in 1857 that Rankine published his theory based on plastic equilibrium. However, it was only as late as in 1934 that Terzaghi pointed out the validity and the limitations of the above two theories. It was he who explained the fundamental principles of action of earth pressures. His observations were based on a series of tests conducted at M.I.T. around 1929 and published in the Engineering News Record in 1934. A good account of these developments is given in Reference [1], listed at the end of this chapter. A summary of his findings is as follows.

Both Coulomb and Rankine did not give any reference to the state of stress in soil *in the natural state* (which is now known as the earth pressure at rest), as well as the importance of the lateral movements required in the earth mass to produce active and passive earth pressures. Coulomb dealt with a classical problem in friction in soils and he considered a wall with friction. He focussed on the stability of the wedge of soil at the point of failure of backfill i.e., at limiting equilibrium and provided an elementary solution of the problem by equilibrium of forces. He also arbitrarily assumed that the pressure variation is hydrostatic.

Rankine dealt with an earth support without friction and considered the soil in the two Rankine states of plastic equilibrium, when shear failure occurs throughout the soil mass.

Before Terzaghi's work, engineers used Coulomb and Rankine's formulae and ensured that hydrostatic pressure distribution existed regardless of whether the necessary condition for such distribution was present or not. The theory was thus applied to retaining walls as well as for timbering of excavation. Many failures of timbering in subway construction work were reported in such cases as early as in 1920. In this chapter, we will briefly deal with the basic principles that govern the magnitude and distribution of earth pressures. All textbooks in soil mechanics give the derivation of the formulae for calculation of these pressures.

16.3 NATURE AND MAGNITUDES OF EARTH PRESSURES

Terzaghi demonstrated experimentally that three types of earth pressure coefficients can be identified when we consider three states of equilibrium of earth behind retaining walls. They are the following:

1. Coefficient of earth pressure at rest, K_0
2. Coefficient of active earth pressure, K_A
3. Coefficient of passive earth pressure, K_P.

Coefficient of earth pressure at rest. In nature, soil is formed in many ways. In soil deposits also, as in a liquid, a horizontal pressure exists with depth, and Terzaghi named it as the *earth pressure at rest*. The pressure at any depth h is given by

$$p_h = K_0 \gamma h$$

where 'K_0' is the coefficient of earth pressure at rest. It has been suggested that for sands and normally consolidated clays, it can be expressed by the effective stress parameter ϕ' by the following formula

$$K_0 = 1 - \sin \phi'$$

For overconsolidated clays and sands, the value of K_0 depends on the stress history of the soil and can also be greater than unity. The magnitude can be as given in Table 16.1.

TABLE 16.1   RECOMMENDED VALUES OF K_0

Type of soil	K_0
Loose sand	0.45–0.50
Dense sand	0.40–0.45
Sand compacted by machines	0.80–1.50
Normally consolidated clays	0.50–0.60
Overconsolidated clays	1.0–4.0

The at-rest condition does not involve failure of the soil, but represents a state of elastic equilibrium. The coefficient of earth pressure at rest with respect to others is shown in Fig. 16.1.

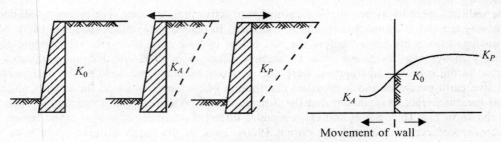

Fig. 16.1   Three types of earth pressure.

Coefficient of active earth pressure. If the wall is to move away from the backfill as shown in Fig. 16.1, a part of the soil mass behind the wall tends to fail, and this mass will exert pressure on the wall. The coefficient of the earth pressure corresponding to the minimum pressure on the wall is the coefficient of the active earth pressure. Here the soil mass is active in exerting pressure on the wall and hence the term 'active earth pressure'.

Coefficient of passive earth pressure. If we press the wall into the soil mass as shown in Fig. 16.1, a larger mass of earth than in the active state exerts resistance to the movement. It is in a passive state and the earth has to be pushed up at failure. The pressure required for a failure to happen is called passive earth pressure. The term 'passive pressure' is used as the soil is in a passive state. The corresponding coefficient of earth pressure is called the passive pressure coefficient. The active and passive cases are the two extreme cases brought about by the proper movement of the retaining structure. If the necessary movement does not take place, the pressure can have intermediate values.

Experiments show that in sand as little as 0.1 to 0.3% of horizontal strain only is required to bring about the active state whereas a strain as large as 2 to 3 per cent is required for the passive state to occur. In loose sands, a much larger movement (of 15%) may be required for the passive state. It is also evident from Fig. 16.2 that for a wedge type of failure, a rotation of the wall at its base will satisfy the required movements. A deflection at the top of the order of 0.001H to 0.05H (where H is the height of the wall) is usually taken as necessary to develop active pressure. It should also be noted that in soils with friction the mass of soil involved in passive state is more than that in the active state.

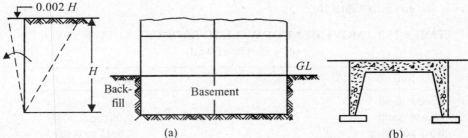

Fig. 16.2   Earth pressures developed with various types of walls: (a) Basement walls; (b) bridge abutments.

However, if we take the case of filling in of a back of basement walls or bridge abutment walls built after the deck is completed (which cannot move or rotate as in the case in Fig. 16.2) the pressure on the wall will more likely be "at-rest pressure" than active pressure state. The pressure will depend on the way the soil is compacted around it. Similarly, in braced excavations (see Fig. 16.3), where the bracings on top are placed before the soil below is excavated, the walls cannot undergo the necessary movements for active state to happen. Terzaghi pointed out that many failures that occurred in the subway constructions were due to wrong assumptions made by the designers that the active earth pressures and hydrostatic distribution of pressures acted on these timbering also. Actual measurements have shown that the distribution of pressures against bracing of open cuts is as shown in Fig. 16.3. Sands and clays produce different pressures as shown in the figure. Had the subway contractors known these during 1920s, most of the costly failures could have been avoided.

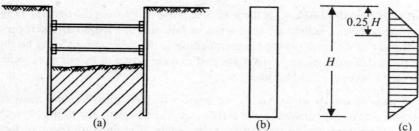

Fig. 16.3 **Earth pressures on timbering of excavations: (a) Order of struting used; (b) distribution earth pressure recommended for design of struts in sand; (c) distribution recommended in clay (*see also* Figs. 22.12 and 22.13).**

Laboratory experiments have proved the effects of movement of walls on earth pressures. As already pointed out, the effect of rotation about the base and lateral movement of walls were carried out by Terzaghi in 1929. With the wall in lateral movement, he found that initially the resultant pressure was found at a level higher than the middle third (i.e., there was tendency for parabolic distribution) until yielding was sufficient to produce the slip, when the resultant acted at $H/3$. In 1939, Taylor carried out model tests to study the effect of rotation of the wall around its top as happens in timbering of excavations. In such cases, the pressure was found to be larger than the active pressure and the resultant also did not act at $H/3$. These experiments fully explained the importance of wall movement and the field observations. These studies were later continued by Taylor to arrive at the modern recommendations for calculating pressures on timbering of excavations. The approximate amounts of movement required to produce active state in various types of soils are given in Table 16.2.

TABLE 16.2   MOVEMENT OF WALL TO PRODUCE ACTIVE STATE
(H = Height of wall)

Soil	Movement at top
Loose sand	0.002 to 0.004H
Dense sand	0.001 to 0.002H
Stiff cohesive	0.01 to 0.02H

16.4 PRESSURES ON RETAINING STRUCTURES

Having understood the basic mechanics of earth pressures, it is easy to investigate the pressures exerted on different types of retaining structures. These structures are divided into the following categories.

1. *Rigid structures:* Rigid type of retaining walls can be one of the following:

   (a) *Gravity walls.* These are generally made of masonry in which tension is not allowed. The stability of the walls is purely due to gravity. Such walls are not generally good as high walls. They are used for heights up to 6 m. Generally 30 to 50 per cent of the height is provided as base width. Sloping from heel upwards adds to the stability of the wall.

   (b) *Reinforced concrete walls.* They can be one of the three types: cantilever walls (used up to 7 to 8 m), counterfort (for above 7 m) and buttress type (similar to counterfort where the vertical walls are built on the opposite side of the backfill).

   (c) *Semi-gravity walls.* These are concrete walls whose action is in between the above two and only small amount of steel is used to reduce the mass of concrete.

   (d) *Crib walls.* These are used for moderate heights (up to 7 m) and are made of cribs, which are filled with granular materials or stones. No surcharge other than earth fills should be placed behind the walls.

2. *Sheet pile walls:* These are flexible walls and are widely used for waterfront structures. The two types that are commonly used are the following (see Chapter 22).

   (a) Cantilever sheet pile walls (sheet piles simply driven into soil).

   (b) Anchored sheet pile walls (sheet piles driven in and anchored at top).

3. *Cellular cofferdams:* These are used for river diversion work as retaining walls, the retained material being water. The soilfill inside the cell and the sheet pile provide the stability. More complex forces like tension capacity of steel interlocks are involved in addition to lateral pressures in their designs. The three main types of cellular cofferdams are the following:

   (a) Circular coffer dams for deep cells

   (b) Diaphragm type for quiet waters

   (c) Clover leaf type used as a corner or anchor cell along with cellular walls.

4. *Reinforced earth retaining walls:* These are explained in Chapter 26. A detailed treatment of the subject of commonly used retaining walls can be found in Chapters 11, 12 and 13 of Reference [2] listed at the end of this chapter.

In this chapter we shall mainly deal with lateral pressure calculation on rigid type of retaining walls.

16.5 COULOMB'S THEORY OF EARTH PRESSURE

Coulomb was the first person to work on friction in soils. His law of shear strength is well known (Section 16.7). He also worked on the theory of earth pressures on rigid walls from his friction theory. He considered the equilibrium of a wedge of soil behind a wall under the action of three forces that act on the wedge; the reaction from the wall, the weight of the soil mass and the reaction on the sliding surface. In the active pressure case, the wedge tends to slide down and exert active pressure. In the passive case, the wall is pushed into the backfill and the wedge tends to slide up. The corresponding pressures on the wall are the active and passive pressures. In both cases, the frictional resistance between soil surfaces act opposite to the movement of the wall. The maximum pressure exerted by the sliding down wedge on the wall is the active pressure and the minimum force necessary to push up the sliding wedge is the passive pressure.

It should be noted that Coulomb simplified the problem by assuming the failure surface to be a plane. For the active case, the error involved in this assumption is small, but for the passive case, the failure plane in reality is curved. It should also be noted that the method cannot be considered as an exact solution since only force equilibrium is satisfied while moment equilibrium is not considered at all. (However, many problems we adopt this approach to get an easy solution.)

16.5.1 Shape of Failure Surface

The shape of the sliding surface to a very large extent depends on the amount of wall friction and also whether the failure is active or passive. In the active case in cohesionless soils, the sliding surface is very close to being planar on the upper part and is only slightly curved on the lower apart due to friction of the wall. If there is no friction on the wall (as we will see in Rankine's theory) the failure surface can be assumed as being fully planar. However, in the passive case, the mechanism of failure becomes more complex. The more the wall friction, the more curved is the failure surface, which has been approximated to circles and logarithmic spirals as shown in Fig. 16.4. Accordingly, with a wall having friction, the passive pressure obtained by assuming plane surface is less than the real value. We should also note that large movements are also needed to fully mobilize passive pressures.

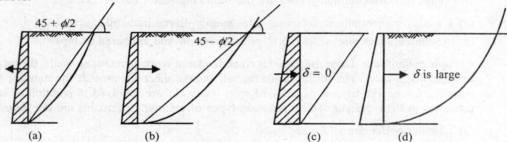

Fig. 16.4 **Shapes of failure surface in fills behind retaining walls: (a) Active pressure; (b) passive pressure; (c) failure with no wall friction; (d) failure with wall friction.**

16.5.2 Derivation of Coulomb's Earth Pressure Formula [3]

Coulomb gave his theory of earth pressure in 1776 from simple statics of frictional forces as shown in Fig. 16.5.

Let

Height of wall = H

Inclination of earth face of wall = α (with the horizontal at the base)

Friction between wall and soil = δ

Slope of backfill = β (with horizontal)

Friction of backfill material = ϕ

Angle of trial wedge = θ (with horizontal)

Take a failure plane inclined at θ as shown in Fig. 16.5. The weight of soil $W = (\gamma) \times$ (Area of the wedge ABC).

$$W = \frac{\gamma H^2}{2 \sin^2 \alpha} \sin(\theta + \alpha) \frac{\sin(\alpha + \beta)}{\sin(\theta - \beta)} \tag{16.1}$$

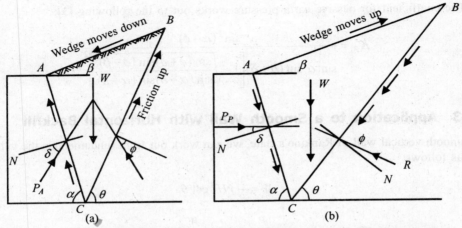

Fig. 16.5   Coulomb's wedge theory: (a) Active pressure; (b) passive pressure.

Note: Size of wedge in passive pressure is larger than that in active pressure.

From the triangle law of forces, taking P as the active pressure acting at an inclination δ to the normal to the back face of the wall,

$$\frac{P}{\sin(\theta-\phi)} = \frac{W}{\sin(180-\psi-\theta+\phi)} \quad (\psi = \alpha-\delta)$$

which gives

$$P = \frac{\gamma H^2}{2\sin^2\alpha}\left[\frac{\sin(\theta-\phi)\sin(\theta+\alpha)\sin(\alpha+\beta)}{\sin(180-\psi-\theta+\phi)\sin(\theta-\beta)}\right]$$

To find the maximum value of P with varying θ, we find $dP/d\theta = 0$ and the corresponding value of θ. The value of P_A acting at an angle δ from normal to the wall reduces to the following values:

$$P_A = \frac{1}{2}\gamma H^2 K_A$$

The coefficient for active earth pressure K_A is given by the following formula [3]:

$$K_A = \frac{\sin^2(\alpha+\phi)}{\sin^2\alpha\,\sin(\alpha-\delta)\left[1+\sqrt{\dfrac{\sin(\phi+\delta)\sin(\phi-\beta)}{\sin(\alpha-\delta)\sin(\alpha+\beta)}}\right]^2} \qquad (16.3)$$

When $\alpha = 90°$, and $\beta = 0$ and $\delta = \phi$, we have

$$K_A = \frac{\cos\phi}{\left(1+\sqrt{2}\,\sin\phi\right)^2}$$

When $\alpha = 90°$ and $\beta = \delta = 0$, we get

$$K_A = \left(\frac{1-\sin\phi}{1+\sin\phi}\right) = \tan^2(45-\phi/2) \qquad (16.3a)$$

which is the Rankine equation for active pressure.

The coefficient for passive earth pressure works out to the following [3]:

$$K_P = \frac{\sin^2(\alpha - \phi)}{\sin^2\alpha \, \sin(\alpha + \delta)\left[1 - \sqrt{\dfrac{\sin(\phi + \delta)\sin(\phi + \beta)}{\sin(\alpha + \delta)\sin(\alpha + \beta)}}\,\right]^2}$$ (16.4)

16.5.3 Application to a Smooth Wall with Horizontal Backfill

For a smooth vertical wall of Rankine's state, we can work out from fundamentals the value of K_A and θ as follows:

$$W = \frac{1}{2}\gamma H^2 \cot\theta$$

$$\frac{P}{\sin(\theta - \phi)} = \frac{W}{\cos(\theta - \phi)}$$

$$P = \frac{1}{2}\gamma H^2 \cot\theta \tan(\theta - \phi)$$

Hence,

$$\frac{dP}{d\theta} = \frac{1}{2}\gamma H^2\left[\frac{\tan(\theta - \phi)}{\sin^2\theta} + \frac{\cot\theta}{\cos^2(\theta - \phi)}\right] = 0$$

$$\frac{\sin(\theta - \phi)\cos(\theta - \phi) + \sin\theta\cos\theta}{\sin^2\theta\cos^2(\theta - \phi)} = 0$$

or, $\sin\phi\,\cos(2\theta - \phi) = 0$.

If $\cos(2\theta - \phi) = 0$, then $\theta = 45 + \phi/2$,

which means that the failure surfaces makes an angle of $(45 + \phi/2)$ with the horizontal.

$$K_A = \cot(45 + \phi/2)\tan(45 - \phi/2)$$

$$K_A = \tan^2(45 - \phi/2) = \frac{1 - \sin\phi}{1 + \sin\phi}$$ (16.5)

The same values of θ and K_A as obtained by Coulomb have also been derived by Rankine from an entirely different approach for wall with no friction (see Section 16.7).

16.5.4 Point of Application of Earth Pressure

Coulomb assumed that for a horizontal backfill carrying no surcharge, the point of application of the active pressure is at $H/3$ from the base of the wall. As will be seen from Rankine's theory, this is a good assumption for a frictionless wall. When the backfill is irregular or when it carries an irregular surcharge or concentrated load, we use Culmann's construction (which is described in Section 16.6) to determine the earth pressure. We also assume that the *point of application* of the resultant pressure is the point (on the wall) where a line from the centre of gravity of the failure wedge drawn *parallel to the surface of sliding* meets the wall.

16.5.5 Effect of Various Parameters

The effect of various parameters on K_A and K_P may be summarized as follows:

Effect of soil friction ϕ: With increasing values of ϕ and for the same α and δ, the value of K_A reduces while that of K_P increases.

Effect of wall friction δ: With increasing values of δ and for the same α and ϕ, the value of K_A decreases while that of K_P increases.

Effect of slope of earth face α: With increasing values of α and for the same ϕ and δ, K_A decreases while that of K_P increases.

16.6 CULMANN'S GRAPHICAL CONSTRUCTION FOR ACTIVE PRESSURE

There are many graphical methods to determine the earth pressures. The more important ones are the following:

1. Culmann's graphical method developed in 1866
2. Rebhann's method (1871) using the Poncelot rule (1840).

16.6.1 Culmann's Graphical Method

As Culmann's method is more widely used to determine earth pressure under various conditions, we will discuss it in more detail. The construction, shown in Fig. 16.6, is another way to represent the triangle of forces.

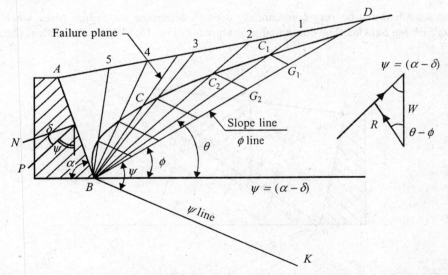

Fig. 16.6 **Culmann's graphical method for determination of active pressure without superloads.**

The various steps in the construction (Fig. 16.6) are as follows:

Step 1. Traces *slope line BD*, which passes through the base of the wall at an angle ϕ from the horizontal into the backfill. This line is also called the *weight line*.

Step 2. Trace the *earth pressure line BK* below the slope line at an angle ψ from the slope line. (ψ is the angle the resultant pressure makes with the vertical so that $\psi = \alpha - \delta$, where α is the slope of the back of the wall with the horizontal. This is called the ψ line.)

Step 3. Take a trial wedge, say along $B1$ and determine its weight (proportional to the area $BA1$) and lay it along the slope line to get point G_1. Any line load or super load is also included in the weight W.

Step 4. Draw a line C_1G_1 parallel to the ψ line and find the point where it meets the assumed failure plane at point C_1. Since the triangle thus obtained is similar to the force polygon, the distance G_1C_1 represents the earth pressure due to the wedge of failure.

Step 5. Assume different trial wedges (planes of failure) to obtain the locus of point C_1 called the *Culmann line*. The maximum pressure obtained is the required pressure and the corresponding failure plane is the plane of failure.

The following are the important points to be noted:

1. If there are any concentrated loads, they are also taken into account in the weight of the wedge considered.
2. *The point of action of P_A is taken as the point where a line from the C.G of the critical wedge, parallel to the failure plane or surface of sliding meets the wall. The line of action will be at δ to the normal to the wall.*

16.6.2 Rebhann's Method Using Poncelot Rule to Find the Critical Plane of Failure

Rebhann's method can be very conveniently used to determine the failure plane *when there is no surcharge on the backfill*. The construction is shown in Fig. 16.7. When the critical plane of failure

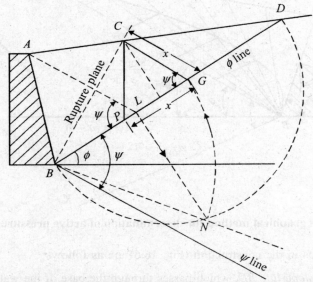

Fig. 16.7 **Rebhann's graphical method based on Poncelet rule for location of failure plane for active pressure; ground slope less than ϕ).**

is to be found this method can conveniently be used. The construction is based on the following principle demonstrated by Poncelot. The construction starts by drawing the ϕ line, and the ψ line. Line AL is drawn at angle ψ. The rest of the construction is self explanatory from Fig. 16.7. BC is the required rupture line and the active pressure is equal to the weight of soil in the triangle CPG. The value of x in the figure is a maximum when $BN^2 = BL \times BD$.

16.7 PLASTIC EQUILIBRIUM OF SOILS — ACTIVE AND PASSIVE RANKINE STATES

While Coulomb investigated only the equilibrium of a sliding wedge behind walls using elementary statics, Rankine was the first to investigate *the state of stress* in a semi-infinite mass of homogeneous, elastic and isotropic soil mass under the influence of its own weight at failure. His work was done in 1857 (much later than Coulomb's), he assumed the Coulomb's failure law for strength of soils, that is, $\tau = c + p \tan \phi$.

Rankine identified two states of stress namely active and passive failure-states which can be represented by the Mohr circle of failure shown in Fig. 16.8. The friction between the wall and soil

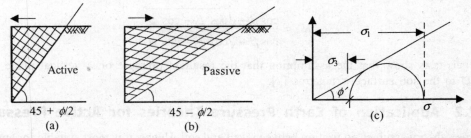

Fig. 16.8 **Rankine's active and passive states: (a) Active state; (b) passive state; (c) principal stresses at failure.**

is not considered at all. The active state is produced when the soil mass moves away from the sand mass and the passive pressure when the wall is pushed into the sand mass. The patterns of failure will be as shown in Fig. 16.8 and the magnitudes of earth pressures can be obtained from the Mohr circle of failure as:

$$\sigma_3 = \sigma_1 \tan^2(45 - \phi/2) = K_A \sigma_1$$

$$\sigma_1 = \sigma_3 \tan^2(45 + \phi/2) = K_P \sigma_3$$

Hence,

$$K_{Active} = \tan^2(45 - \phi/2) = \frac{1 - \sin \phi}{1 + \sin \phi} \tag{16.6}$$

$$K_{Passive} = \tan^2(45 + \phi/2) = \frac{1 + \sin \phi}{1 - \sin \phi} \tag{16.7}$$

16.7.1 Rankine's Pressure on a Sloping Backfill

We take an element of soil with two vertical faces and the other faces parallel to the sloping surface. The vertical and the lateral pressure are assumed as *conjugate stresses* (direction of action of one force is parallel to the plane on which the other force acts) as in Fig. 16.9.

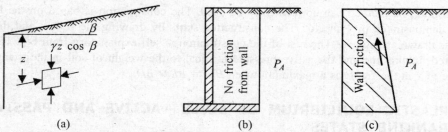

Fig. 16.9 **Earth pressures on retaining walls: (a) Conjugate stress theory for sloping fills; (b) Rankine's theory for cantilever retaining walls; (c) Coulomb's theory for gravity walls with fraction.**

$$\text{Vertical stress} = \gamma z \cos \beta$$
$$\text{Lateral stress} = K_A \gamma z \cos \beta$$

The latter, by theory of conjugate stresses, should *act parallel to the sloping surface;* so also the resultant. The value of K_A is given by

$$K_A = \frac{\cos \beta - \sqrt{\cos^2 \beta - \cos^2 \phi}}{\cos \beta + \sqrt{\cos^2 \beta - \cos^2 \phi}} \tag{16.8}$$

However, tests show that the assumption that the resultant pressure on a vertical plane must be parallel to the soil surface is not true [2].

16.7.2 Application of Earth Pressure Theories for Active Pressure

Rankine's theory assumes no friction between wall and soil. Hence, it is most suitable for application to cantilever retaining walls to calculate the lateral pressure on a vertical plane passing through the heel of the wall as shown in Fig. 16.9. Coulomb's approach is generally used for walls with friction, walls with inclined back or irregular backfill surfaces with or without surcharge loads. Usually the peak value of ϕ is used to calculate the earth pressure.

16.7.3 Calculation of Passive Earth Pressure

We have already seen that for the full development of passive pressure, there should be sufficient movement of the rigid wall. In many cases, all that movement may not be available or permitted because of the limit state of deflection. In such cases, we must be conservative and estimate only a part of the full passive resistance that can develop in the structure. This is specially true in cases where we depend on passive pressures in determining the stability of a structure.

16.8 EFFECT OF SUBMERGENCE AND BROKEN BACK

There are many situations where special considerations are necessary.

16.8.1 Effect of Submergence

Submergence of soil behind retaining walls has the following two effects:

1. The unit weight of soil is reduced to the submerged weight which reduces the pressure on the wall.

2. There is additional pressure due to the pressure of water which considerably increases the net pressure.

These effects are shown in Fig. 16.10 for active pressure for sands.

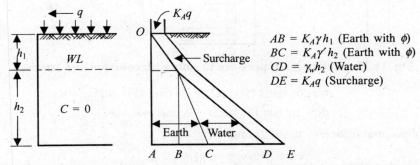

$$AB = K_A \gamma h_1 \text{ (Earth with } \phi)$$
$$BC = K_A \gamma' h_2 \text{ (Earth with } \phi)$$
$$CD = \gamma_w h_2 \text{ (Water)}$$
$$DE = K_A q \text{ (Surcharge)}$$

Fig. 16.10   The effect of submergence and surcharge on active pressure in granular soils.

16.8.2   Pressures on the Wall with Broken Back

The back of the wall is divided into two parts, the top part ending at the point of break and the bottom part. The two parts are treated separately. The pressure on the top part can be determined easily. For the bottom part we can use (a) the graphical method of finding the worst wedge of failure or (b) we may consider the bottom part as a separate part with a surcharge from the top part of the fill above the point of break of the wall as shown in Fig. 16.11.

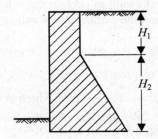

Fig. 16.11   Earth pressure on walls with broken back.

In the first procedure, we assume that the point of application of the resultant pressure on the wall is at the place where a line drawn from the centre of gravity of the wedge of failure parallel to the failure wedge line meets the back of the wall. When we consider the wall as two parts the resultant from the two pressures is taken as the final pressure.

16.9   PRESSURES DUE TO SOILS WITH COHESION

Coulomb's and Rankine's methods are not applicable to cohesive soil. In 1915, Bell suggested the use of the expression derived from Mohr's circle of failure (as used by Rankine) for the evaluation of pressures in cohesive soils with $c - \phi$ values as shown in Fig. 16.12.

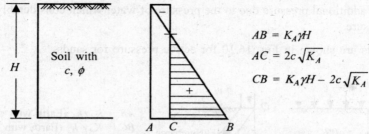

$$AB = K_A \gamma H$$
$$AC = 2c\sqrt{K_A}$$
$$CB = K_A \gamma H - 2c\sqrt{K_A}$$

Fig. 16.12 Active earth pressure in soils with cohesion and friction.

$$\sigma_1 = \sigma_3 \tan^2(45 + \phi/2) + 2c\tan(45 + \phi/2)$$
$$\sigma_3 = \sigma_1 \tan^2(5 - \phi/2) - 2c\tan(45 - \phi/2)$$

These equations reduce to the following:

$$\text{Active pressure} = \gamma H K_A - 2c\sqrt{K_A} \qquad (16.9)$$

It can be seen that the pressure is zero at a height given by the following equation,

$$H = \frac{2c}{\gamma\sqrt{K_A}} \qquad (16.10)$$

Tension can act to this depth and cause cracking of clay. These tension cracks can be filled with water. This can produce water pressures which acts on the retaining wall. Hence if tension in clay is neglected, the second term in Eq. (16.9) is also neglected.

It should, however, be remembered that clay is not recommended as a filling behind the retaining walls as the properties of such fills cannot be predicted even approximately. Volumetric changes of the clay due to drying or swelling can be expected in such a condition. Hence the above theory can be applied to retaining walls built to contain the sides of cuts for in-situ deposits whose $c - \phi$ values can be evaluated. Unless the critical $c - \phi$ values are known, it is difficult to apply this theory to real soils.

Similarly, the passive pressures in $c - \phi$ soils will be given by the following formula:

$$\text{Passive pressure} = \gamma H K_P + 2c\sqrt{K_P} \qquad (16.11)$$

When $\phi = 0$, $K_A = 1$ and $K_P = 1$. Hence, for soils for which $\phi = 0$,

$$\text{Active pressure} = \gamma H - 2c$$
$$\text{Passive pressure} = \gamma H + 2c \qquad (16.11a)$$

The effect of submergence and surcharge on earth pressures in $c - \phi$ soils is shown in Fig. 16.13.

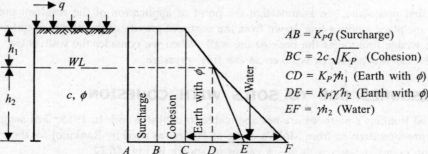

$$AB = K_P q \text{ (Surcharge)}$$
$$BC = 2c\sqrt{K_P} \text{ (Cohesion)}$$
$$CD = K_P \gamma h_1 \text{ (Earth with } \phi)$$
$$DE = K_P \gamma h_2 \text{ (Earth with } \phi)$$
$$EF = \gamma h_2 \text{ (Water)}$$

Fig. 16.13 Effect of submergence on active earth pressure in soils with friction and cohesion.

16.9.1 Critical Depth of Excavation in Clay

As the clay in the top part is in tension, we assume that the clay can be excavated vertically to a depth where the tension is balanced by the lateral pressure. As the pressure variation is linear, this depth is given by the following equation:

$$\text{Tension} = 2c\sqrt{K_A} \quad \text{at} \quad H = 0$$

$$\text{Pressure at depth } H_c = \gamma H K_A - 2c\gamma\sqrt{K_A}$$

For critical depth, these should be equal, i.e.,

$$\gamma H K_A - 2c\sqrt{K_A} = 2c\sqrt{K_A}$$

Therefore,

$$H = \frac{4c}{\gamma\sqrt{K_A}}$$

When $\phi = 0$,

$$H = \frac{4c}{\gamma} \tag{16.12}$$

This gives the height to which excavations in clay can stand without support.

16.10 ECONOMICAL DESIGN OF HIGH RETAINING WALLS

Simple gravity walls and reinforced concrete walls will be found very expensive for very high walls (say) above 10 m and also in situations where high distributed loads will be applied on the back, fill. In these cases, the pressures on the retaining walls will be very high and a configuration of the wall similar to gravity dams or a wall with a tie back as in anchored bulkheads (described in Chapter 22) can be useful. Yet another solution is the provision of a relieving platform.

If we adopt buttress walls (say at 3m, centres) the relieving platforms can be built in the form of simple or tied arches in between these buttress walls. These platforms can also be built without form work after backfilling the wall to the level of these platforms. If we use straight relieving platforms, they may have to be supported at the far end on columns or piles. Use of relieving platforms is quite common in construction of quay walls and high retaining walls. The pressure diagram will be discontinuous at the level of the platform as shown in Fig. 16.14 (see Section 17.9.1 for Gabion walls).

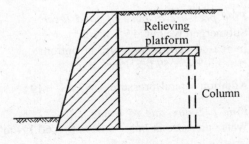

Fig. 16.14 Retaining walls with relieving platforms.

EXAMPLE 16.1 (Calculation of earth pressures)

A retaining wall 8 m height with a smooth vertical back retains the following materials:

Top 2 m: Clay. $\gamma_s = 1.75$ (=17.5 kN/m³); $\phi = 0$ and $c = 10$ kN/m²
Bottom 6 m: saturated sand of $\gamma_s = 1.95$ and $\phi = 30°$

If the water level is on top of the sand layer, draw the diagram of lateral pressure on the wall assuming that no tension crack develops on the top layer.

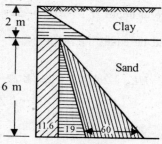

Fig. E.16.1.

Ref.	Step	Calculations
	1	*Calculate pressure at bottom of clay layer*
		$\sigma = \gamma H = 17.5 \times 2 = 35.0$ kN/m²
		$K_A = \tan^2 (45 - \phi/2) = 1$ when $\phi = 0$
Eq. (16.9)		Pressure $= \gamma H K_A - 2c \sqrt{K_A}$
		If we neglect tension, the second term vanishes, then
		$p = \gamma H = 35.0$ kN/m²
	2	*Find pressure on top of the sand layer*
		σ on top of sand $= \gamma H = 35$ kN/m²
Eq. (16.3a)		$K_A = \tan^2 \left(45 - \dfrac{30}{2}\right) = \dfrac{1}{3}$
		$p = K_A \gamma H = \dfrac{35}{3} = 11.6$ kN/m²
	3	*Find pressure at base of sand layer*
		Submerged weight = 9.5 kN/m²
		Increased vertical pressure at bottom
		$\sigma = 9.5 \times 6 = 57.0$ kN/m²
		Addition lateral pressure $= 57 \times \dfrac{1}{3} = 19$ kN/m²
	4	*Find pressure due to water*
		Water pressure at base $= 10 \times 6 = 60$ kN/m²
	5	*Draw the pressure diagram*

EXAMPLE 16.2 (Calculation of earth pressure with surcharge)

Determine the additional pressure in Example 16.1 if there is a surcharge pressure of 20 kN/m² over the clay layer.

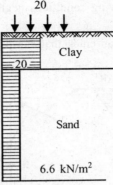

Fig. E.16.2

Ref.	Step	Calculations
Eq. (16.9)	1	*Find additional pressure on clay layer* $\phi = 0$; $K_A = 1$ Horizontal pressure = Vertical pressure $p_h = 20$ kN/m² Total pressure = 35 + 20 = 55 kN/m²
	2	*Find additional pressure on top of sand layer* $$p_h = K_A \sigma_z = \frac{1}{3} \times 20 = \frac{20}{3} \text{ kN/m}^2$$ $$= 6.66 \text{ kN/m}^2$$
	3	*Find additional pressure at bottom of sand layer* The additional effect due to surcharge remains the same (constant) p_h at bottom = 6.66 kN/m²

EXAMPLE 16.3 (Stability of vertical cut is saturated clay)

A vertical cut is made in saturated clay with $c = 30$ kN/m², $\phi = 0$, and $\gamma_m = 20$ kN/m³. What is the theoretical depth to which the clay can be excavated without side collapse?

Ref.	Step	Calculations
Eq. (16.12)	1	*Determine height for which tension being balanced by positive pressure in clay* $$H = \frac{4c}{\gamma} = \frac{4 \times 30}{20} = 6 \text{ m}$$

EXAMPLE 16.4 (Wedge theory in $c - \phi$ soils)

A vertical wall with vertical back is 9 m high. The backfill has the following properties: $\gamma_m = 16$ kN/m³; $c = 12$ kN/m²; $\phi = 30°$; $\delta = 20°$. Assuming a sliding plane 60° to the horizontal, find the thrust on the wall under the following conditions neglecting cohesion along the wall:

1. Neglecting any tension cracks
2. Assuming the depth of tension crack that can develop in the fill is 2 m only.

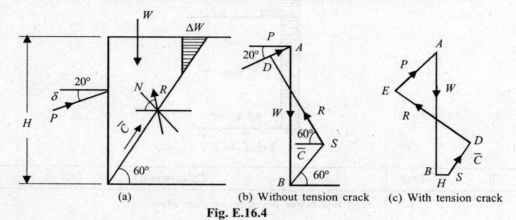

(a) (b) Without tension crack (c) With tension crack

Fig. E.16.4

Ref.	Step	Calculations
		Case 1: Neglect tension in fill [Fig. E.16.4b]
	1	*Consider forces acting on wedge (Fig. E.16.4a and E.16.4b)* (a) Weight of soil = W (b) Cohesion along sliding plane = $\overline{C}$ (c) Friction at 30° to normal to the plane = R Active lateral pressure acting at 20° to normal to the wall = P
	2	*Calculate W and C per unit length* $W = \dfrac{1}{2} \times \dfrac{9 \times 9 \times 1 \times 16}{\sqrt{3}} = 374$ kN $\overline{C} = 12 \times \dfrac{9 \times 2}{\sqrt{3}} = 125$ kN
Fig. 16.4(b)	3	*Determine direction of action of force* W acts vertical C @ 60° with vertical R @ 30 + 30 = 60° with horizontal P @ 20° with horizontal
	4	*Draw the force diagram or resolve the forces (Fig. E.16.4b).* Measure $AD = P = 78$ kN

Ref.	Step	Calculations
	1	**Case 2: With water in tension crack** *Calculate W and C and water pressure* Reduced weight $= \dfrac{1}{2} \times 2 \times \dfrac{2 \times 1}{\sqrt{3}} \times 16 = 18.5$ kN $W = 374 - 18.5 = 355.5$ kN New cohesion on reduced length of sliding $C = \dfrac{12 \times 7 \times 2}{\sqrt{3}} = 97$ kN (for $9 - 2 = 7$ m) Water pressure, $H = \dfrac{1}{2} \times 10 \times 2 = 10$ kN
	2	*Find direction of action forces* W acts vertical H acts horizontal C @ 60° with vertical R @ 60° with horizontal P @ 20° with horizontal
	3	*Draw the force diagram or resolve forces (Fig. E.16.4c).* Measure, $AE = P = 110$ kN

REFERENCES

[1] Terzaghi, K. and Peck, R.B., *Soil Mechanics in Engineering Practice*, John Wiley & Sons, New York, 1948.

[2] Leonards, G.A. (Ed.), *Foundation Engineering* (Chapter on Retaining Wall by G.P. Tschebotarioff), McGraw-Hill, New York, 1962.

[3] Bowles, J.E., *Foundation Analysis and Design*, McGraw-Hill, Singapore, 1988.

17

Effect of Superimposed Loads on Backfill and Empirical Design of Retaining Walls

17.1 INTRODUCTION

One of the important problems we come across while designing retaining walls is the effect of loads behind the walls as shown in Fig. 17.1. A railway line, strip footing (line loads) or an oil tank (concentrated load) can come behind retaining walls. We saw in Culmann's graphical method for earth pressures how the effect can be found graphically. However, many of these problems can be solved by the theory of elasticity and in this chapter we will deal with the standard solutions recommended for the five cases shown in Fig. 17.1.

17.2 CASE 1: EFFECT OF UNIFORM SURCHARGE (q/m^2)

As uniform surcharge is the most common case we will deal with it as the first case. The effect of uniform surcharge (q/m^2) as shown in Fig. 17.1e. is an addition of a constant pressure to the standard earth pressure diagram. The constant pressures to be added are as follows.

For at-rest condition = $K_0 q$
For active condition = $K_A q$
For passive condition = $K_P q$

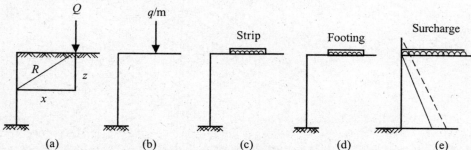

Fig. 17.1 Five types of surcharge loads behind retaining walls: (a) Concertrated load; (b) line load;
(c) strip load; (d) footing load (area load); (e) surcharge (*see also* Fig. 3.11).

17.3 CASE 2: EFFECT OF A CONCENTRATED LOAD (POINT LOAD)

In 1936, Spangler published the results of his laboratory tests on concentrated loads on sand backfills and showed that the effects of concentrated loads behind retaining walls can be predicted by Boussinesq's equation. His observations also showed that the pressure on rigid walls like concrete walls (not flexible sheet pile walls) can be almost double the calculated value by the elastic theory. This observation has been explained by pointing out that the elastic theory assumes that there can be strains and deformations. Rigid walls, however, prevent such deformations, and effect will be the application of a mirror image as load which doubles the lateral load pressure in the case of rigid unyielding walls. Bowles [1] however attributes this effect to the effect of Poisson's ratio and advocates the estimation of pressure by computer analysis (see Fig. 17.2a).

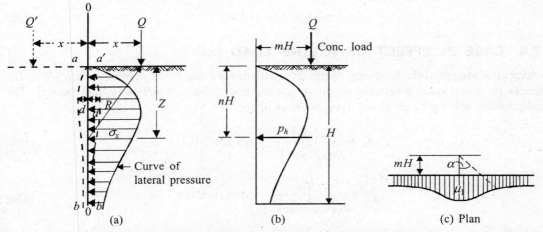

Fig. 17.2 Effect of concentrated load behind retaining walls: (a) Lateral pressure on rigid walls doubled due to mirror image effect; (b) distribution of pressure along the height of the wall; (c) distribution of pressure along the length of the wall.

Boussinesq's equation for horizontal stress σ_x (refer Chapter 4) gives the maximum value when $\mu = 0.5$ (which represents material deforming at constant volume) and is as follows (see Fig. 17.2):

$$\sigma_x = \frac{Q}{2\pi}\left[\frac{3x^2 z}{R^5} - \frac{1-2\mu}{R(R+z)}\right] \tag{17.1}$$

$$= \frac{3Q}{2\pi}\left[\frac{x^2 z}{R^5}\right] \text{ when } \mu = 0.5 \tag{17.1a}$$

Here, Q is the total load. As stated above its value should be doubled for rigid walls [2],[3]. With reference to Fig. 17.2b (where m and n are defined) Terzaghi proposed [2.3] the following equations based on theory of elasticity (with $\mu = 0.5$) for the maximum pressure distribution on the plane of the concentrated load (No doubling is required when using these empirical formulae.) The *maximum horizontal pressure* occurs along the vertical line closest to the load is given by the following formula (see Fig. 17.2b):

$$p_h = \frac{1.77Q}{H^2} \frac{m^2 n^2}{\left(m^2 + n^2\right)^3} \qquad (m > 0.4) \tag{17.2}$$

When $m < 0.4$, the value $m = 0.4$ may be used so that the pressure is given by

$$p_h = \frac{0.28Q}{H^2} \frac{n^2}{\left(0.16 + n^2\right)^3} \qquad (m \le 0.4) \tag{17.2a}$$

The variation of pressure horizontally along the length of the wall is given by the following equation (see Fig. 17.2c):

$$p_0 = p_1 \cos^2 (1.1\alpha) \tag{17.2b}$$

17.4   CASE 3: EFFECT OF A LINE LOAD (q/m)

Terzaghi has suggested the following empirical equations for a line load (q/metre) with $\mu = 0.5$. The formula gives horizontal pressure distribution at a depth nH for a load mH away from the wall. The total pressure will be given by the integration of p_h:

$$p_h = \frac{1.27 q m^2 n}{H \left(m^2 + n^2\right)^2} \qquad \text{when } m > 0.4 \tag{17.3}$$

$$p_h = \frac{0.203 q n}{H \left(0.16 + n^2\right)^2} \qquad \text{when } m \le 0.4 \tag{17.3a}$$

17.4.1   Empirical Method for Line Load

Another empirical method suggested by Terzaghi [4] is to take the effects of a line load on cantilever walls as shown in Fig. 17.3. A line inclined at 40° to the horizontal is drawn to find the location of

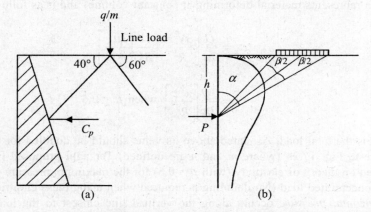

Fig. 17.3   Loads behind retaining walls: (a) Line load; (b) strip load.

the equivalent total force on the wall. The magnitude of the *resultant pressure* for a given load q' is given by the following equation:

$$P' = Cq' \qquad (17.4)$$

where C is 0.27 for coarse sands, 0.29, for sand with silt, 0.39 for residual soils and 1.0 for clays. Also, K_A, which is equal to $\tan^2(45 - \phi/2)$ may be used instead of C. The line of action will be where the 40° line meets the wall. The load may be assumed to be distributed to the lower layers of the soil at an angle of 60° to the horizontal.

17.5 CASE 4: EFFECT OF STRIP LOAD

The following empirical formula is recommended for finding the effect of a strip load of finite width running parallel to the rigid wall. The already doubled value for rigid walls is as follows with reference to Fig. 17.3 [4], [5]. α is the angle the centre of the load makes with the point P.

$$p_h = \frac{2q}{\pi}(\beta + \sin\beta)\sin^2\alpha + \frac{2q}{\pi}(\beta - \sin\alpha)\cos^2\alpha \qquad (17.5)$$

It is also expressed as

$$p_h = \frac{2q}{\pi}(\beta - \sin\beta\cos 2\alpha) \qquad (17.5a)$$

17.6 CASE 5: LATERAL PRESSURE FROM LOADED AREA—NEWMARK'S INFLUENCE CHART

Newmark made use of Eq. (17.1) in 1942 to construct an influence chart to determine the lateral pressure due to a UDL acting on a small area behind the wall for $\mu = 0.5$. The chart is shown in Fig. 17.4 [6], [7]. [This chart can be constructed using the same principles as used for Newmarks charts for vertical stresses.]

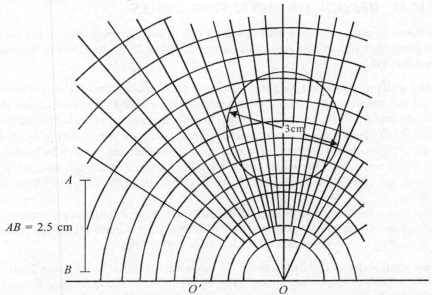

Fig. 17.4 Newmark's influence chart for lateral pressure on retaining walls with influence value 0.001. [Example 17.1]

In this chart (Fig. 17.4) the influence value for each block is 0.001 of the surcharge load and the scale to be used for drawing the loaded area and distance from wall should be such that AB is equal to the depth at which lateral pressures is to be found. The method to use this chart is as follows.

Step 1. Draw, on a tracing paper, the plan of the loaded area of surcharge using a scale AB (which is shown in the chart) equal to the depth below ground level at which pressure is to be found. For example, if the lateral pressure is to be found at 10 m depth, then scale for drawing the loaded area is AB = 10 m.

Step 2. Draw also, in plan, the face of the wall at the given distance from the loaded area using the same scale. Mark point O, the intersection of the centre line of load with the wall line.

Step 3. Superimpose the tracing paper on the Newmark chart so that the face of the wall coincides with the base line of the diagram and the point where σ_x is to be computed coincides with point O of the diagram. (Point O can be placed along the wall to find variation of lateral pressure along the length of the wall.)

Step 4. Count the number of blocks covered by the area of surcharge. Then the pressure P is given by the following formula:

$$P = IMq \qquad (17.6)$$

where

$\quad I$ = 0.001 (influence factor)
$\quad M$ = number of blocks counted
$\quad q$ = U.D.L on the given area.

For rigid walls, the obtained values should be doubled.

17.7 EMPIRICAL DESIGN OF RETAINING WALLS

Theoretical calculations of earth pressures require knowledge of the soil properties of the backfill. Hence, for routine practical design of retaining walls moderate height, Terzaghi and Peck recommend the following procedure [4].

Design of retaining walls of moderate height. Those walls, which we backfill only with broad category of material and not with select backfill, are customarily designed empirically using thumb rules or readymade diagrams. For this purpose Terzaghi broadly classified the backfill material into five different types and assigned empirical coefficient for earth pressure for each type as given in Table 17.1 and Fig. 17.5. As these estimated pressures should be safe, they tend to be higher than the actual values. Design curves for different slopes of backfill of infinite extent and those of limited distance from the wall are available in Reference [4] given at the end of this chapter. These can be used for routine design.

The earth pressure behind walls with sloping backfills will have a horizontal component K_h and a vertical component K_v for the pressure as shown in Fig. 17.5. Charts for slopes ending at limited distances behind walls are also available in Reference [4].

Design of high retaining walls as in abutments. For economic reasons, backfills for high walls should be selected from soils of known properties. They are designed by the theoretical calculations already explained in Chapter 16.

TABLE 17.1 EMPIRICAL DESIGN OF RETAINING WALLS WITH HORIZONTAL BACKFILLS [Fig. 17.5]

Description of soil backfill	Value of $(K_A \gamma) = K_h^*$ kN/m^2 per m
Coarse-grained soils without fines very permeable like lean sand or gravel	4.8
Coarse-grained soil of low permeability	5.6
Residual soils with stones such as fine silty sands, and granular materials with clay content	7.6
Very soft clays, organic silts, silty clays	16.0
Medium or stiff clay deposited in chunks in such a way that during floods and heavy rains negligible water enters through the spaces contained in them	20.0

*These are values of the chart for $\beta = 0$.).

Notes: 1. For pressures on walls with sloping backfills of soil types 1 to 5, refer Fig. 17.5.
   2. See Example 17.5 for method of design.

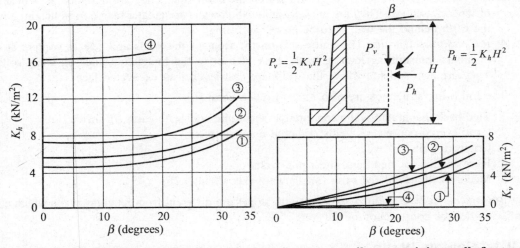

Fig. 17.5 Terzaghi's design charts for active pressures on cantilever retaining walls for typical backfills. (Coefficients for calculation of pressures per metre length of wall K_h and K_v include weight of backfill also.)

17.8 IMPORTANCE OF DRAINAGE OF BACKFILL

As rise of water level behind retaining walls increases the lateral pressures, it is very important that drainage arrangements with *weep holes* are provided for these walls. Usually they are provided at 0.9 m to 1.5 m spacing along the length and are connected to a permeable back drain, continuous on the back of the wall as shown in Fig. 17.6. In addition, the top layer of the fill should be a low permeability layer provided with a gutter to drain away the rain water.

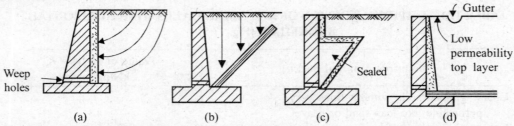

Fig. 17.6 Drainage of retaining walls: (a) Vertical drains; (b) inclined drains; (c) horizontal drain and seal with inclined drainage for clay backfill; (d) drains for clay backfills (In all cases, weep holes and gutters to drain water away from back of the wall should be provided).

17.9 TYPES OF RETAINING WALLS

Conventional retaining walls can be one of the following types as shown in Fig. 17.7:

1. *Simple gravity walls* (free standing suitable when 2 to 3 m high) made of masonry, plain concrete (which can be also semi-gravity type with very little steel) incorporated in the wall.
2. *R.C. cantilever walls* used up to 6 m height.
3. *R.C. counterfort walls.* Counterforts are on the earth side. They are designed as *T* beams of tapering section. They are more suitable when walls are greater than 6 m in height. And the earth behind the wall is to be raised by filling.
4. *R.C. buttressed walls.* The buttress is on the front of the walls and acts as compression members transmitting loading to the base slab or to the foundation piles on weak soils. They are also suitable where the walls are cast against an excavated face.

The following structures are also used to retain earth [6]:

1. Tied back diaphragm walls and circular sheet pile wall with earth fill inside
2. Cantilevered continuous walls of bored concrete piles
3. Cribwork walls
4. Free standing or tied back sheet pile walls
5. Mechanically stabilized earth (MSE) walls (see Chapter 26).

Revetments built to stabilize existing earth slopes are different from retaining walls which are backfilled after the construction of the wall.

17.9.1 Gabion Walls

These are dry rubble walls similar to crib walls. They are made by stone-filled boxes arranged suitably to form a wall. The boxes 1 m in height are made of special mild steel wire mesh with zinc and PVC coating. These boxes are then filled with stones and the boxes are arranged to form the walls. Thermally bonded non-woven geotextile membrane is provided on the earth face for drainage and separation of soil to avoid leaching of fines from the backfill. Proper drainage from the base is also provided at suitable intervals. Recently such walls were extensively used for retaining earth (up to 6 m height) in the Mumbai–Pune expressway [9]. Walls arranged in steps with decreasing width improve the overall stability of such walls. The main advantages of such walls are their suitability in low bearing capacity soils for foundations and their ability to withstand large deformations. They are specially useful in inaccessible mountain slopes where stones are in plenty and reinforced construction is costly.

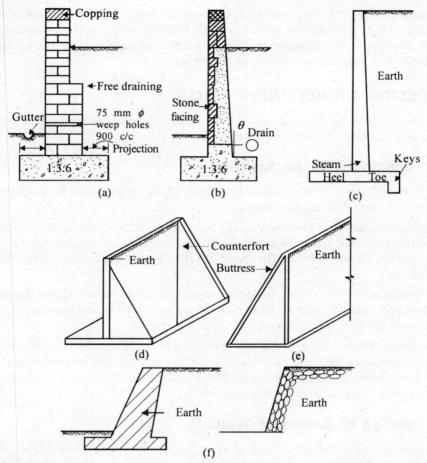

Fig. 17.7   **Types of retaining structures: (a) and (b) Gravity walls; (c) cantilever retaining walls; (d) R.C. counterfort walls; (e) buttress walls; (f) wall and revetment to stabilise slopes.**

17.10 INITIAL PROPORTIONING OF ORDINARY RETAINING WALLS

The usual base width B, for a trial section for a plain concrete with temperature steel gravity walls up to 6 m in height is taken as 30 to 40 per cent of height, the larger ratio being used for weaker foundation soil or for increasing slope of backfill. For masonry gravity walls larger base width of 50 to 70 percent height may be needed. A slope at the back as in Fig. 17.3 helps part of soil also to act towards or stability.

For a reinforced cantilever retaining wall, the following dimensions are usually adopted [4]

1. Thickness of base slab B adopted is usually between 1/8 and 1/12 the height of wall
2. Minimum stem width adopted at top is 150 mm for slabs with a single layer reinforcement and 230 mm for slabs with front and back reinforcement (generally 300 mm is preferable)
3. Rate of increase of stem width is 20 to 60 mm per m height of wall
4. Projection of toe from the centre of stem adopted is usually $L/3$.
5. Base width L is taken as 2/5 to 2/3 the height of the wall depending on soil type.

Although theoretically, the economy of concrete can result from a reduction of thickness of slab from base to top, in counterfort walls a uniform thickness will give the lowest overall cost for walls up to 6 m in height. In R.C. retaining walls, contraction joint at 5 to 10 m spacing and expansion joints at about 30 m spacings should be also provided.

17.11 DESIGN OF RETAINING WALLS

In this chapter we have so far dealt only with the calculation of earth pressures. Actual design should be made by using the following principles.

17.11.1 Conditions to be Satisfied

Having proportioned the wall as described in Section 17.10, we calculate the earth pressures and check the wall for the following conditions:

1. *Structural stability.* The wall should be checked for stability against overturning and sliding. The recommended factors of safety used for overturning are, respectively, 1.5 for granular backfill and 2.0 for clayey backfills. The factor of safety against sliding should be atleast 1.5 (see Section 17.12 also).

2. *Foundation stability.* There should be enough factor of safety against bearing capacity failure. (One of the disadvantages of retaining walls as compared to sheet-pile walls for retaining earth is the need for good foundation soil for retaining walls.)

3. *Structural design.* Simple masonry gravity walls are designed so that the resultant of all the loads falls within the middle third of the base so that there will be no tension in the structure. Reinforced concrete walls are designed using IS456. Mass concrete walls with nominial steel are designed as gravity walls, allowing limited tension.

17.11.2 Design of Basement Walls

In framed construction of buildings, most of the exterior walls above ground level are generally supported by beams between columns. These beams are also connected to the floor slab. However, the exterior walls of basements below ground level which have to resist lateral pressures are usually designed as free-standing cantilever retaining walls as shown in Fig. 17.8. This procedure is

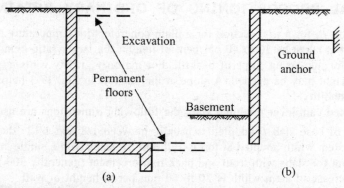

Fig. 17.8 Construction of basement walls as free standing walls: (a) Wall with base; (b) wall with ground anchor.

necessary as the bottom floor of the basements is constructed only in the final stages of work and the foundation slab of walls should not depend on its connection with basement floor slab for its stability. The retaining walls should be stable by themselves. (This practice is followed generally for walls of swimming pools also.) As the earth faces of the basement walls have to be waterproofed, the construction procedures should suit that purpose. The following at rest value of K

$$K_0 = (1 - \sin \phi) > K \text{ active}$$

is usually used for their design.

17.12 LOCATION AND USE OF BASE SLAB KEYS

Keys are usually provided in the base slabs of retaining walls to increase resistance against sliding. As shown in Fig. 17.9, it is preferable to place it at the heel on the earth side as it will be able to mobilize more base resistance than when it is placed at the toe. When placed at the toe, they are likely to be disturbed by rain water, excavations and other causes.

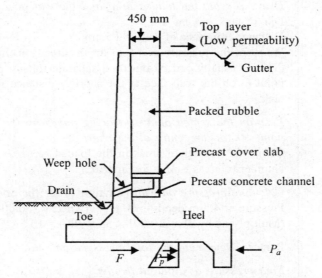

Fig. 17.9 Position of keys in cantilever retaining walls.

EXAMPLE 17.1 **(Pressure on retaining wall due to area load-use of Newmark's chart)**

A rigid retaining wall of reinforced concrete is 7.5 m high. Behind the wall, a water tank of 5.4 m diameter with its front edge at 4.5 m is constructed. If the contact pressure of water tank is 100 kN/m^2: (1) determine the additional pressure at a depth of 4.5 m in front of the load on the wall due to this load using Newmark's diagram, and (2) indicate how the total pressure can be calculated.

Ref.	Step	Calculations
		Part 1: *Use Newmark's horizontal stress diagram with Poisson's ratio.* $\rho = 0.5$ (Fig. 17.4): $AB = 2.5$ cm The scale marked on the chart = AB = Depth of point, where pressure is to be found
Sec. 17.6	1	*Determine the scale for the plan of loaded area* For pressure at 4.5 m depth on the wall, adopt scale so that length 4.5 m = 2.5 cm Dia. of tank in plan $= \dfrac{5.4 \times 2.5}{4.5} = 3$ cm.
	2	*Determine to scale the distance of loaded area from wall* Distance from wall $= \dfrac{4.5 \times 2.5}{4.5} = 2.5$ cm.
	3	*Draw to scale the loaded area and the wall face* Dia. of tank = 3 cm Distance from face of wall = 2.5 cm We want the pressure at 4.5 m depth directly in front of the wall. (This is usually carried out on a separate tracing paper. Mark also point O on the wall face at the shortest distance from the plan of the tank.)
Fig. 17.4	4	*Position the scaled plan on tracing paper on the Newmark chart with point 'O' at the centre of the chart.* Count the number of areas in the loaded area. Number of areas = M = 53 (approx.)
Eq. (17.6)	5	*Calculate pressure on wall* (for rigid walls the effect is twice) Pressure at 4.5 m depth = IMq (where $I = 0.001$) (Multiplying by 2) = 2(0.001 × 53 × 100) = 10.6 kN/m^2
		Part 2: *Determine the total pressure on wall.*
	1	*Find pressure at different depths* Using above method find pressure at depths = 0, 1 m, 3.0 m, 6.0 m and 7.5 m. (The pressures along the depth can be determined.)
	2	*Determine the area of the pressure diagram by splitting into strips and find the total pressure, R*
	3	Determine the centre of pressure by taking moments about the base find $\bar{x}$.
	4	The final effect is a force R acting at $\bar{x}$ from the base.

Note: To find the pressure at, say 5 m, to the left of the centre line of the load, we position point O at a point 5 m (measured to scale) in Fig. 17.4 and find pressures as indicated above [6].

EXAMPLE 17.2 **(Use of empirical formula for point load)**

Estimate the pressure on the wall in Example 17.1 by use of approximate equation 17.2 assuming it is a point load.

Ref.	Step	Calculations
	1	*Data* Assume load is concentrated at centre of circle $P = \dfrac{\pi \times (5.4)^2}{4} \times 100 = 2290 \text{ kN} = Q$ For 4.5 m depth and 4.5 m distance of edge of tank. $m = \dfrac{x}{H} = \dfrac{4.5 + 2.7}{7.5} = 0.96$ $n = \dfrac{z}{H} = \dfrac{4.5}{7.5} = 0.6$
	2	*Find pressure at depth* 4.5 m $p = \dfrac{1.77Q}{H^2} \dfrac{m^2 n^2}{\left(m^2 + n^2\right)^3}$ (for rigid walls) $= \dfrac{1.77 \times 2290}{(7.5)^2} \dfrac{(0.96)^2 (0.6)^2}{(0.92 + 0.36)^3}$ $= 11.4 \text{ kN/m}^2$ This value is higher than that obtained for distributed load.
	3	*Find the total force* Using the above equation, determine the pressure at various depths and draw the pressure diagram. The area of the pressure diagram gives the total pressure. Its C.G is the point of application.

EXAMPLE 17.3 **(Use of Boussinesq's equation for point load)**

Estimate the pressure for a single load in the previous problem by Boussinesq's equation assuming that the load is a concentrated load.

Ref.	Step	Calculations
	1	*Convert the load into a single force* $Q = 100 \times \pi \times (5.4)^2/4 = 2290 \text{ kN}; H = 7.5 \text{ m}$ $x = 4.5 + 2.7 = 6 \text{ m}$ to centre.
Sec. 17.3	2	*Use Boussinesq's equation*
Eq. 17.1		$\sigma_x = \dfrac{3Q}{2\pi}\left(\dfrac{x^2 z}{R^5}\right)$ and $R = 8.4 \text{ m}$ $= \dfrac{3 \times 2290 \times (7.2)^2 \times 4.5}{2 \times \pi \times 44110} = 5.78 \text{ kN/m}^2$ Double the value $= 11.57 \text{ kN/m}^2$ (for rigid walls)

EXAMPLE 17.4   **(Use of empirical formula for line load)**

Determine by Terzaghi's empirical formula the additional thrust on the cantilever wall of a sump, 3 m in height, built for storage of municipal water, if there is a footing running at 2 m away from it along the back of the wall. Assume loading of wall footing is 30 kN/m and it acts at the top level of the fill behind the wall.

Ref.	Step	Calculations
Fig. 17.3 and Sec. 17.4.1	1.	*Estimate magnitude of resultant pressure* Value of $C = 0.29$ for sand with silt (Otherwise use $K_A = \tan^2(45 - \phi/2) \approx 0.3$ when $\phi = 30°$) $p' = Cq'$ $\quad = 0.29 \times 30 = 8.7$ kN/m
	2	*Determine point of application* Distance of point of application from top of wall $= 2 \tan 40 = 1.68$ m from top. *Note:* This method was devised for cantilever walls and its use should be restricted to such walls.

EXAMPLE 17.5   **(Empirical design of retaining walls)**

An ordinary retaining wall 4 m in height is to be constructed with a backfill of type 3 soils (silty sand of Table 17.1) and the slope of the backfill β is 10 degrees. Estimate the horizontal and vertical components of the earth pressure.

Ref.	Step	Calculations
Table 14.1 Fig. 17.5	1	*Read values of K_h and K_v from Fig. 17.5 ($\beta = 10°$)* $K_h = 7.6$ kN/m^2/m $K_v = 1.0$ kN/m^2/m (These factors include weights also)
Sec. 17.7	2	*Calculate P_H* $P_H = \dfrac{1}{2} K_h H^2 = \dfrac{1}{2} \times 7.6 \times 16 = 60.8$ kN/m
	3	*Calculate P_V* $P_V = \dfrac{1}{2} K_v H^2 = \dfrac{1}{2} \times 1 \times 16 = 8.0$ kN/m *Note:* The resultant will be $\sqrt{(P_H)^2 + (P_V)^2}$ acting at an angle θ to the horizontal, i.e., $\tan \theta = \left(\dfrac{P_V}{P_H}\right)$. [We do not assume resultant as parallel to be slope [5].] For calculation of pressures with sloping walls and backfill, use charts available in Ref. [4].

REFERENCES

[1] Bowles, J.E., *Foundation Analysis and Design*, McGraw-Hill, Singapore.

[2] Terzaghi, K., Anchored Bulk Heads, *Transactions ASCE*, Vol. 119, 1954.

[3] Wilun, Z. and Starzewski, *Soil Mechanics and Foundation Engineering*, Vol. II, Surrey University Press, London, 1975.

[4] Terzaghi, K. and Peck, R.B., *Soil Mechanics on Engineering Practice*, John Wiley & Sons, New York, 1948.

[5] Teng, W.C., *Foundation Design*, Prentice-Hall of India, New Delhi, 1995.

[6] Leonards, G.A., *Foundation Engineering*, McGraw-Hill, New York, 1962.

[7] Newmark Nathan, M., Influence Charts for Computation of Stresses in Elastic Foundations, University of Illinois Engineering Experimental Station, *Bulletin* 338, 1942.

[8] Tomlinson, M.J., *Foundation Design and Construction.*, ELBS, Longman, Singapore, 1995.

[9] Singh, N.K. and Ramesh, H., An Engineering Solution for Highway Embankment Protection, *Journal of Indian Concrete Institute*, July–September 2001, Chennai (Madras).

18

Floating Foundations

18.1 INTRODUCTION

Floating foundations are also known by other names such as 'Deep Cellular Rafts', 'Buoyancy Rafts', 'Compensated Foundations'. In theory floating foundations are fully compensated foundations in which an amount is excavated from below the foundation of soil equal to the weight of the building and a basement raft on floating raft is provided to the structure. The weight of excavated earth fully compensates the weight of the building.

The weight of ordinary multi-storeyed buildings can be approximated as follows. The load from basement floor and foundation is about 2.5 t/m^2 and loads from other floors 1.25 t/m^2 to 1.5 t/m^2.

If we excavate 1 m depth, the weight of the soil excavated is about 1.8 t/m^3. Accordingly, for a building with a basement and four floors, the foundation pressure from loads works out to 7.5 t/m^2. If the soil for 7.5/1.8 = 4.2 m depth is excavated and a basement raft is provided, then the building can be placed on very soft and highly compressible clay without any failure of foundation and very little settlement. Such types of basement rafts are also called floating foundations (see Example 18.2). Foundations can also be designed as partially compensated as shown in Example 18.1.

In this chapter, we shall briefly deal with the principles for design of these foundations and also with some of the problems that we meet in the construction of these foundations. (These problems are discussed in detail in Chapters 5 and 18, References [1] and [2], respectively. They should be carefully studied by all those interested in using the method.)

18.2 TYPES OF PROBLEMS TO BE SOLVED

The bearing capacity of clay soils can be expressed as

$q_{ult} = cN_c + D\gamma_1 N_q + 0.5B\gamma_2 N_\gamma$ = (cohesion) + (surcharge) + (strength of soil in foundation).

where $N_c = 5.14$, $N_q = 1$, $N_\gamma = 0$ when $\phi = 0$ (clays)

Now,

$$q_u = 5.14c + D\gamma_1 \text{ for clay foundations} \tag{18.1}$$

As already shown in Fig. 8.1, the increase in bearing capacity due to surcharge will be available only if we adopt a full raft foundation in clay soils. Accordingly, we come across two types of

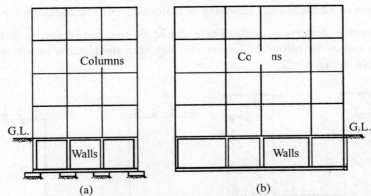

Fig. 18.1 Basement construction: (a) Basement with footings; (b) floating foundation.

problems calling for the use of compensated foundations, for which (a) basement rafts and (b) floating rafts are respectively used.

Type 1: Basement rafts. In situations for which basement rafts are used, we have no difficulty with bearing capacity of soil strata. The bearing capacity is enough to bear the gross load of the building. However the *total settlement and the relative settlement have to be reduced*. In such situations we have two options namely either use a piled raft (see Chapter 15) or excavate the soil so that the net increase in loading on the soil layers will be reduced and the resulting settlement will be small. The foundations can be individual footing or any other type that suits the bearing capacity of the soil. In such cases, the basement floors can be freely planned and made use of for any purpose (see Fig. 18.1a). There is no floatation principle for these types of foundation.

Type 2: Floating rafts. In some situations (as happens in very soft compressible soils), the *bearing capacity is low and, in addition, there can be large settlements also.* In such cases a full *rigid buoyancy raft* (base foundation) has to be used as substructure to make it work like a floating ship in water. Because it is a full raft, the surcharge effect on bearing capacity will also be large. If the weight placed on the foundation is equal to the weight of soil removed, the settlement will also be small. To ensure that the structure acts as one unit, it is important that it has to be made rigid and act as a boxlike structure. Such a layout of the basement floor may not, in many cases, make it suitable for general use (see Fig. 18.1b). In this case even though the net loading on the soil is low or nil the base of the structural foundation must also have enough structural capacity to transmit the full load of the building coming from above to the foundation.

18.2.1 Methods to Prevent Floatation

In buoyancy rafts we should also ensure that the structure does not float in situations where there is a possibility of the ground water rising (as in a water tank below ground level with no water inside the tank). One method is to use an apron slab all around, which will be embedded in the soil. Another method is to use anchor piles, which will be in tension if floatation occurs. However in most multi-storeyed structures, this is not a usual problem.

18.3 EXCAVATION BELOW GROUND WATER LEVEL

If excavation has to be carried out below ground water level, the following two subsoil conditions should be identified.

Case I: Excavation in pervious soil. Lowering of water table will be necessary by suitable means.

Case II: Excavation in impervious soils. There should be two considerations in these situations. First, if pervious soil exists below the impervious soil, then the chances of a blow-out should be examined as shown in Fig. 18.2a.

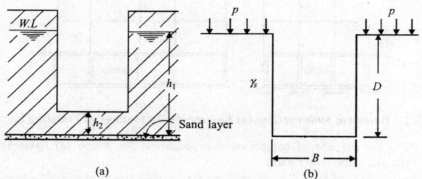

(a)   (b)

Fig. 18.2 Excavations in clay: (a) Blow-out conditions; (b) heave of the bottom due to vertical pressure from sides.

Condition for prevention of blowout is $\gamma_s h_2 > \gamma_w h_1$ (18.2)

where

    γ_s = unit weight of clay soil

    γ_w = unit weight of water.

Secondly, in clays if the shear strength of the soil is low, there is a limit to the depth of excavation that can be made. The heave of the bottom of cut-in soft clays should be examined as shown in Fig. 18.2b. The condition for stability is as follows:

$$\gamma_s D + p = N_c c \quad \text{or} \quad FS = N_c \left(\frac{c}{D \gamma_s + p} \right) \tag{18.3}$$

where

    γ_s = unit weight of clay

    D = depth of excavation

    P = surcharge

    N_c = Skempton's bearing capacity factor

    c = cohesion

    FS = factor of safety.

The critical depth is the maximum depth we can excavate with $FS = 1$. In many cases of floating foundations in soft clays, the full critical depth of excavation may be needed for full compensation and so also, a stiff box-type structure. Hence, the critical depth will have to be increased. This can be accomplished by carrying out the excavation under water or in extreme cases by keeping the excavation in bentonite slurry. Under these conditions, the factor of safety will be as follows:

$$FS = N_c \frac{c}{D(\gamma_s - \gamma_m) + p} \tag{18.4}$$

where γ_m = density of water and mud (bentonite slurry) used in the construction.

18.4 CALCULATION OF BOTTOM ELASTIC HEAVE

The following are the three causes for elastic heave of the foundation, which cannot be fully eliminated, but can be reduced by suitable methods:

1. Elastic upward movement on unloading. This will correspond to the rebound curve of the consolidation tests. This should be calculated and monitored during construction.
2. If the excavation is open for some time, it will gradually absorb water and expand. Hence construction should start along with or immediately after the excavation.
3. As excavation approaches the critical depth, there can be plastic inward movement from surrounding soil. (This should be avoided by proper sheet piling especially when adjacent buildings are present.)

The heave should be always measured during excavations. The first type of heave can be reduced by proceeding with the excavation in stages, by lowering the water table during excavation or using friction piles as detailed in Reference [2] given at the end of this chapter.

18.5 FLOATING FOUNDATION ON PILES

In many cases, piles are also used under floating foundations. They reduce settlements as described in Chapter 15 and also prevent upward movement of structure if the ground water level rises. However, the following points are important in such cases.

* When the piles are founded on an incompressible layer like rock, then the whole weight of the structure will have to be taken by the piles. In such cases, after construction the clay below can settle and as the piles do not settle, the whole weight has to be carried by the pile. Accordingly, only the uplift effect of water will act as compensation.

* When the piles are friction piles in clay, the pile will also sink with the soil so that the piles transfer some load to the clay around the piles. In such cases, full uplift of the soil and also water can be taken into account as compensating the weight of the foundation [2].

18.6 NECESSITY OF USING RAFT FOR FULL FLOATING FOUNDATION

We have already seen that it is not usual to apply the principle of floating foundation to individual footings. Floating foundations are usually rafts or box sections with Veerendeel truss action. If individual foundations are used, the base of the foundation soil must have the full bearing capacity to bear the *gross load* of the building although the *net pressure* applied at the foundation will be much lower. In such a case, it does not act as a floating foundation. However, decrease in settlement will be available due to decrease in soil stresses. A true floating foundation will be a full raft supporting the structure.

In a floating foundation, layout, the walls should also be able to resist the earth pressures with the "earth pressure at rest" condition. Similarly, drainage must be arranged at the lowest corner to keep the base free from water. Ventilation is also necessary to prevent collection of dangerous gases in the basements.

EXAMPLE 18.1   (Design of a partially compensated foundation)

A ten-storey building on a raft foundation (not a floating foundation) is to be constructed in clay with average $m_v = 0.15$ m^2/MN. If the weight of the subsoil is 20 kN/m^3, calculate the depth of the foundation so that the settlement of a raft 10 m in width should be limited to 45 mm. Calculate the required strength of the clay for a full floating foundation.

Ref.	Step	Calculations
Sec. 18.1	1	*Calculate approximate bearing pressure required* Wt. of basement floor @ 25 kN/m^2 = 25 kN/m^2 Load from 10 storeys = 10 × 12.5 = 125 kN/m^2 Total = 150 kN/m^2
	2	*Determine approximate foundation pressure for* 45 mm *settlement* Assume that there will be an increase in stress for a depth equal to width of raft, 10 m. With decreasing stresses, the settlement can be approximated to the settlement of 5 m depth with uniform pressure applied at the foundation level. $\dfrac{\text{Stress}}{\text{Strain}} = E = \dfrac{1}{m_v} = \dfrac{1}{0.15}\dfrac{\text{MN}}{\text{m}^2} = 6.6 \times 10^6 \text{ N/mm}^2$ $\text{Strain} = \dfrac{\Delta L}{L} = \dfrac{0.045}{5000}$ $\text{Stress} = \dfrac{6.6 \times 10^6 \times 4.5 \times 10^{-2}}{5 \times 10^3} = 60 \text{ kN/m}^2$ (We have to reduce stress to 60 kN/m^2) from loading of $\sqrt{150}$ kN/m^2.
	3	*Calculate depth of soil to be excavated* Wt. of soil to be excavated = 150 − 60 = 90 kN/m^2 $\text{Depth} = \dfrac{90}{\text{unit wt. of soil}} = \dfrac{90}{20} = 4.5 \text{ m}$ *Conclusion* 1. The construction of the building with a raft placed at 4.5 m below the ground level will reduce the settlement to the required value.
Eq. (18.1) Table 6.1 Table 1.6	4	*Determine the cohesion required for soil* Required bearing capacity = FS × bearing pressure FS for mat foundation = 1.7 to 2.5 (assume 2.0) Net loading at the level of foundation = 60 kN/m^2 *Ultimate B.C.* = 2 × 60 = 120 kN/m^2 = $cN_c + \bar{q}N_q$ N_c = 5.14 and N_q = 1; $\bar{q}$ = (20 × 4.5) 120 = 5.14c + 20 × 4.5; c = 5.83 kN/m^2 = 0.6 t/m^2 q_u = 2c = 0.6 × 2 = 1.2 t/m^2 Required unconfined strength = 0.12 kg/cm^2 Clay with low SPT value will give this strength.

EXAMPLE 18.2 (Determinate of depth of excavation for a floating foundation)

Estimate the foundation depth required if the foundation in Example 18.1 is to be treated as a floating (or fully compensated) foundation.

Ref.	Step	Calculations
Example 18.2	1	*Find total pressure on the foundation* $p = 150$ kN/m^2
	2	*Find depth of excavation for compensation* Assuming water level is below foundation, $d = \dfrac{150}{20} = 7.5$ m (*Note:* A depth of excavation equal to $2^1/_2$ storeys is necessary for compensating a ten-storey building. As a rough rule, four upper storeys can be built for each storey height in the basement floor.)

EXAMPLE 18.3 (Analysis of stability of vertical cut in plastic clay)

A 4.5 m deep and 2 m wide vertical cut is made for a strip foundation in plastic clay having unit weight of 18 kN/m^3 and undrained shear strength 20 kN/m^2. What is the factor of safety of the cut against heave at the bottom of the cut? What is the effect of the sheet piles used on the sides if they are extended beyond the bottom of the cut? What is meant by critical depth? There is no surcharge on the ground and water level is below the bottom of the cut.

Ref.	Step	Calculations
Chapter 6 Fig. 6.4	1	*Find N_c value for the cut (Use Skempton's values)* For $D/B = \dfrac{4.5}{2} = 2.25$; N_c for strip $= 7.1$
Eq. (18.3)	2	*Determine factor of safety with no surcharge against heave; $p = 0$* $FS = N_c \dfrac{c}{(\gamma_s D + p)} = N_c \dfrac{c}{\gamma_s D}$ $= \dfrac{7.1 \times 20}{18 \times 4.5} = 1.75$
	3	*Effect of extension of sheet piles* Due to the higher stiffness of the sheet piles, there will be an increase in the factor of safety. However, it is difficult to analyse this effect. Excavations using sheet piles have a definite advantage in this respect.
Eq. (18.4)	4	*Critical depth* The maximum depth that can be excavated with *FS* = 1 is called the *critical depth of excavation* in clays. $D = \dfrac{N_c C}{\gamma_s} = \dfrac{7.1 + 20}{18} = 7.9$ m.

REFERENCES

[1] Tomlinson, M.J., *Foundation Design and Construction*, Longman with ELBS, Singapore, 1995.

[2] Winterkon, H.F. and Fang, H.Y., *Foundation Engineering Handbook*, Chapter 18 by H.O. Golder, Van Nostrand Reinhold, New York, 1975.

19

Foundations for Steel Towers and Chimneys

19.1 INTRODUCTION

In this chapter, we will discuss the pad and chimney foundations used for fabricated steel towers and the annular foundations used for structures like concrete chimneys. We will deal only with the general principles and references will be made to available publications for their detailed structural design.

19.2 FOUNDATIONS FOR STEEL TOWERS [1]

Steel towers are very extensively used for transmission line towers, TV towers, and flood lighting towers. As the cost of foundations of these towers can be as much as 10 to 15% of their total cost and as electric transmission requires a large number of towers (as much as 12 towers per kilometre of transmission line) cost of foundation forms a large part of any transmission line project. Transmission line towers are classified according to their angle of deviation from their main direction. When deviation is only up to 2°, they are called tangent towers. Light angled towers deviate 2 to 15°, medium angled over 15 to 30°, and heavy angled ones over 30°. In tower design, there is an optimum base width which gives the minimum cost of tower and foundation. One of the thumb rules used is the Rye's formula [2].

$$B = 0.013\sqrt{m}$$

where
    B = base width in metres
    m = overturning moment at G.L. kg m

The ratio of base width to total height for most towers is generally 1/5 to 1/10t, depending also on the electrical requirements. The foundation design procedures given below are those used in India and described in detail in the Manual on Transmission Towers published by the Central Board of Irrigation and Power [1], IS 4091 [2] and IS 11233 [3].

19.2.1 Loads on Foundations

Structural analysis of a tower gives the following forces shown in Fig. 19.1, for which the foundation has to be designed:

- Downward load
- Uplift load
- Shear forces in transverse and longitudinal directions.

These forces are determined for the normal working conditions (NCs) and also for the broken wire conditions (BWCs). As certain calculations like the lateral analysis of pile use ultimate load analysis, a load factor of 2 is given for NC and 1.5 for BWC.

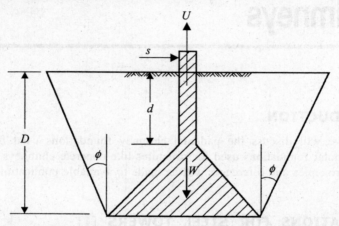

Fig. 19.1   **Chimney and pad foundation for transmission line towers. Forces acting on the foundation.**

19.2.2 Types of Foundations Used

The type of foundation to be selected for steel towers depends on the site and soil condition. As protection against corrosion is very important, modern foundations, as a rule, are exclusively made of reinforced concrete with special precautions for durability. The following are the main types of foundations we can choose from:

1. Concrete block foundation (suitable for small uplift forces)
2. 'Concrete pad and chimney type footing' (with stub angle or in reinforced concrete) shown in Fig. 19.1. (The bottom part is the pad and the shaft is called chimney.)
3. Steel grillage encased in concrete
4. Concrete spread footings
5. Augured foundations
6. Grouted rock anchors
7. Pile foundations
8. Well foundations
9. Concrete mat foundation under the tower
10. Precast foundations.

Of these, the most commonly used type for steel towers is the '*concrete pad and chimney footing*' which we will examine in more detail. Pad and chimney footing foundations isolated foundations relying on the weight of earth to balance the uplift forces. Each leg of the tower is provided with one such foundation. However, when the size of the footing required for the downward forces is small, it may be found cheaper to provide under-reamed piles than a pad and chimney foundation for the uplift forces. When the forces are very large, we adopt R.C. foundations as shown in Fig. 19.2b. Isolated footings should be preferably interconnected at or below the ground level by beams to ensure their unified action.

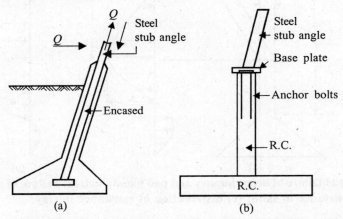

Fig. 19.2   Types of steel tower foundations: (a) Chimney and pad footing; (b) R.C. footing.

19.3 BEHAVIOUR OF PAD AND CHIMNEY FOUNDATIONS

Pad and chimney foundations should withstand the forces given in Section 19.2. As regards the resistance to lateral forces by the shaft or chimney, we can compare its action to that of laterally loaded piles as shown in Fig. 19.3. As in the case of piles, described in Chapter 13, we can classify a pad foundation also as a *shallow foundation* or a *deep foundation* depending on its dimensions.

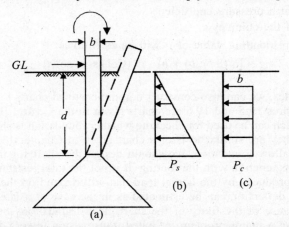

Fig. 19.3   Mode of failure of shallow chimney and pad foundation: (a) Loads resisted by both shaft and footing; (b) distribution of resistance in sand; (c) distribution of resistance in clay.

In a shallow foundation, the lateral resistance that can be mobilised by the chimney part alone will be less than the lateral forces acting on the structure so that the pad has also to come into action. In a deep foundation, the lateral resistance mobilised by the chimney part itself will be larger than the lateral force acting on it. These are indicated in Figs. 19.3 and 19.4.

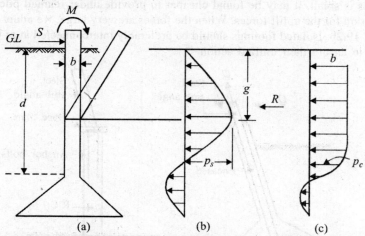

Fig. 19.4   **Mode of failure of deep chimney and pad foundation: (a) Failure of shaft; (b) distribution of resistance in sand; (c) distribution of resistance in clay.**

It is quite obvious that in the case of a shallow foundation, ultimate failure will occur at the junction between the chimney and the pad. The unbalanced moment will then have to be resisted by reaction from the pad which action is absent in the case of a simple shallow piles. In a deep foundation, the failure will take place in the shaft itself. In the case of cohesionless soils, we can prove that the maximum moment will occur at a depth g below the ground level [1], where

$$g = 0.9\sqrt{S/(\gamma K_p b)} \text{ (in cohesionless soils)}$$
S = lateral force
γ = unit weight of soil
K_p = passive earth pressure coefficient
b = breadth of the chimney

In cohesive soils the corresponding value of g will be as follows:

$$g = [S/(8.5c_v b) + b] \quad \text{(Cohesive soils)}$$

where c_v = cohesive soil.

As in the case of piles, we can also construct non-dimensional charts to predict the behaviour of these foundations. Figures 19.5 and 19.6 are charts given in the Central Board of Irrigation and power (CBIP) manual which can be used for checking whether foundation is shallow for cohesionless and cohesive soils [1]. They are similar to Broms chart given in Chapter 13.

In the case of a shallow foundation, we should design the shaft for the maximum moment occurring in the shaft at its junction with the footing. It is not the total resistance, but the deflection of the base of the tower produced by the lateral load that will depend on the modulus of subgrade reaction of the soil. This deflection can be estimated as in the case of a laterally loaded long pile using Broms charts. Because of the fixity of the shaft, deep foundations behave like deep piles. Generally deflection is not a major problem in bolted transmission towers due to large allowable values for deflection for these structures. Deflections are not important for transmission line towers, but they are of some importance in microwave towers.

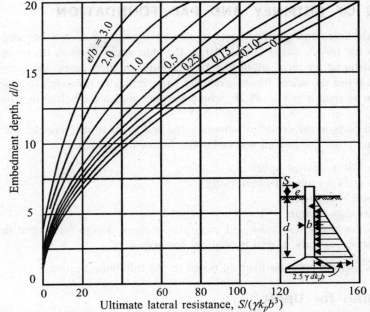

Fig. 19.5 **Chart for estimating the ultimate lateral load resistance capacity of shaft in granular soils.** (If the lateral load resistance capacity S is less than that required for the given problem, the foundation is classified as shallow, see [1]. (Inset figure shows assumed distribution of resistance forces on chimney at failure.)

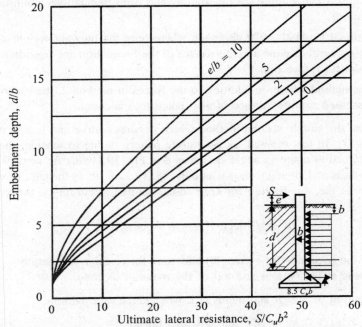

Fig. 19.6 **Chart for estimating the ultimate lateral resistance capacity of shaft in clay soils.** (If the lateral load resistance capacity S is less than that required for the gain problem, the foundation is classified as shallow, see [1]. (Inset figure shows assumed distribution of resistance forces on chimney at failure.)

19.4 DESIGN OF CHIMNEY AND PAD FOUNDATION

As we have already seen, two arrangements as shown in Fig. 19.2, can be adopted for these foundations. When the forces acting are not large, the stub angle is taken inside the shaft to the pad portion and anchored by cleat angle and keying rods. In such cases, the member acts as a composite member. When the lateral forces acting are large, it may be necessary to adopt a reinforced concrete foundation as shown in Fig. 19.2b, where the stub angles are bolted to a base plate fixed in an R.C. shaft.

There are two parts in the design of chimney and pad foundations, namely, stability, analysis and strength design. They are carried out under the following heads:

1. Check the safety against uplift.
2. Check the stability against overturning.
3. Check lateral resistance.
4. Check uprooting of stub.
5. Determine the stress resultants and carry out strength design (structural design).
6. Check bearing capacity of pad in shallow foundation.

The first four aspects only are dealt in detail in the following sections.

19.4.1 Checking for Uplift

The uplift is counter-balanced by the weight of earth that is attached to the structure as shown in Fig. 19.1. Three methods are used to calculate the downward forces that resist the uplift of the foundation [2]:

1. Mayerhof's and Adam's approach for shallow and deep foundations assuming a specified surface of failure.

2. The conventional IS 4191–1979 approach where only the buoyant weight of an inverted frustum of a pyramid or cone and the weight of the foundation are considered as effective in resisting uplift [3] (see Fig. 19.1).

3. The Douglas method where, in addition to the forces in method 2, the shearing resistance along the assumed rupture surface is also taken into account.

We will examine the simple second method which is conservative and is also recommended by the CBIP Manual [1]. In this method, as the failure pattern is due to tension, the sides of the rupture surface is assumed to make an angle shown as ϕ in Fig. 19.1 with the vertical of 20° in the case of non-cohesive soils and an angle shown as ϕ in Fig. 19.1 of 30° in the case of cohesive soils [1]. (Some assume ϕ as the soil friction for cohesionless soils.) Accordingly, the volume of soil resisting uplift is

$$V = (1/3 \text{ depth})\left(A_1 + A_2 + \sqrt{A_1 A_2}\right) \tag{19.1}$$

where

V = volume of the pyramid (for rectangle) and cone for circular foundation
A_1 and A_2 = areas at the bottom and top of the pyramid or cone.

For a square footing of $B \times B$ and depth D it will reduce to a pyramid.

For a pyramid, $V = (D/3)(3B^2 + 4D^3 \tan^2 \phi + 6BD \tan \phi)$ (19.2a)

For a cone, $V = (\pi D/12)(3B^2 + 4D^3 \tan^2 \phi + 6BD \tan \phi)$ (19.2b)

The weight of soil and footings are the downward forces. If they are larger than the design ultimate load obtained by load factor, then the foundation is considered safe against uplift. Alternately there should be a factor safety of more than 1.5 against the maximum uplift force acting on the tower as shown in Example 19.1.

19.4.2 Checking for Stability against Overturning

The stability of the footing against overturning under the forces is checked as follows (see Fig. 19.7):

1. The foundation is assumed to tilt about a point on its base at a distance 1/6 the width from the toe.
2. The weight of footing acts at the centre of the base.
3. We *assume that one-half the weight of soil inside* the "cone of resistance against uplifting" resists the overturning and also that this weight acts through the tip of the heel.

Accordingly, we get the following formula for stability:

$$\left[\frac{W}{2} \times \frac{5B}{6}\right] > \left[(U \times m) + S(D+e) - \frac{W_f B}{3}\right] \tag{19.3}$$

where

W = weight of the soil acting against uplift = (1/2 *wt* of cone resistance)

U = uplift force acting on the member

m = distance of uplift force from tilting point

S = maximum horizontal shear

W_f = weight of foundation (pad and chimney)

B = width of base

D and e are as shown in Fig. 19.7.

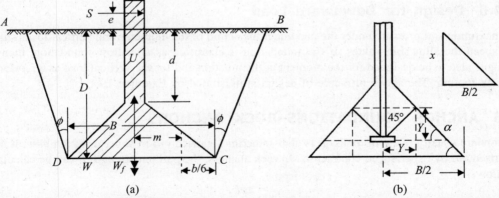

(a)   (b)

Fig. 19.7 **Checks to be made for chimney and pad foundation: (a) Check for stability; (b) check for uprooting of stub.**

19.4.3 Checking for Lateral Resistance

The procedure we use for lateral resistance of piles can be used for these cases also. As already pointed out in Section 19.3, lateral resistance of the deep foundation is provided by the shaft itself and the maximum moment occur as explained in Section 19.2.3 along the shaft. For shallow foundations, because of the large footing at its end, the chimney behaves like a fixed headed laterally loaded pile under the lateral forces. The maximum moment occurs at the junction of footing and shaft. Any moment in excess of what can be resisted by shaft will be transferred to the footing.

Distribution of forces as in Broms method for lateral piles can be assumed for lateral resistance for these cases also. Alignment charts are also available in CBIP manual to determine the maximum moment at the junction for shallow foundations. It can also be worked out roughly by assuming that the whole unit acts as a restrained pile head with redistribution of moments at both ends at ultimate stage (i.e. moments at each end) is one half the cantilever moment. For deep foundations, Broms chart is applicable and the footing at the end of the shaft does not affect the shaft performance.

19.4.4 Checking Uprooting of Stub

Where the stub angle is continued into the shaft, we should check for the strength in pull out of the angle by the uplift force U as shown in Fig. 19.7 using the following formula:

$$A_p f_{ct} \not< U \tag{19.4}$$

where

$A_p = \pi y^2$ with y as in Fig. 19.7.

f_{ct} = tensile strength of concrete $= 0.7 \sqrt{f_{ck}}$

19.4.5 Strength Design of Pad and Shaft

As already stated, if the stub angle is embedded in the shaft to its full depth and anchored to the base slab, the chimney is treated as a composite member. On the other hand, in large towers, the leg of the tower is fixed to the top of the shaft by anchor bolts. In such cases, the shaft is designed and reinforced for tension shear and bending moment as an R.C. member.

19.4.6 Design for Downward Load

The maximum soil pressure under the pad under the action of the moments and vertical loads should not exceed the allowable values. If the foundation is classified as a shallow foundation, then the footing is also to be designed for the moment at the junction and for the vertical load as a reinforced concrete footing. The above principle of design is illustrated by Example 19.1.

19.5 ANCHOR FOUNDATIONS–ROCK ANCHORS

Anchors are usually made in rocks. It is also sometimes carried out in soils, in which case, it must be carried out by experienced contractors. In rock anchors, the pull out strength P can be calculated as follows:

$$P = \pi \phi L \tau \tag{19.5}$$

where

ϕ = diameter of anchor

L = length of anchor

τ = rock grout bond strength

The value of τ depends on the type of rock. The following empirical relation based on SPT value N is generally used:

$$z = 0.07N + 1.24 \text{ kg/cm}^2 \tag{19.6a}$$

The following equation derived from fundamentals of pile foundations is also used in other situations:

$$P = \pi\phi L(Kp \tan \lambda) \text{ for granular soils} \tag{19.6b}$$

where

K = earth pressure coefficients (0.5 to 1.0 for fine sands and sandy silts; 1.4 for dense sand; up to 2.3 for sandy gravel)

p = effective overburden pressure

λ = shaft friction

$$P = \pi\phi L(Fc) \text{ for cohesive soils} \tag{19.6c}$$

with F as the reduction factor on cohesion c.

Anchorage can be carried out as shown in Fig. 19.8.

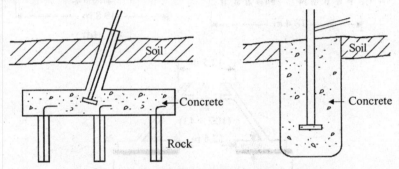

Fig. 19.8 Anchorage of steel towers in rock.

19.6 DESIGN OF FOUNDATIONS FOR CONCRETE TOWERS AND CHIMNEYS

We will now deal with the design of commonly used foundations for structures like concrete T.V. towers and chimneys. These are tall and slender structures. Annular or circular rafts are commonly used as foundation for these structures. The annular shape (with central cutouts) has the advantage that there is more uniform soil reaction at base with loads (vertical loads and moments) and thus, minimum possibility of tilting due to differential settlement in clay soils. It is also more efficient as the contact pressures are more uniform.

The layout of some of the foundations used in TV towers in India is shown in Fig. 19.9. The shaft can be directly supported on the raft or as in the case of water tanks, it may be supported on columns, which in turn, are supported by circular ring beam and slab. In both the cases, the load is assumed to be uniformly applied along a circular ring. The total weight of a 200 m high multiplex chimney may approach 20,000 tons. In such cases, pile foundations for strength or cellular foundation for reduction of dead weight will have to be considered when planning the structure.

Structures like TV towers being tall are wind sensitive. The bending moments produced by wind is more predominant than the effect of gravity loads. Large diameter rafts (as much as 30 m) and thickness of the order of 2 to 3 m may be required in such cases. Some layout may need piles for stability. All these imply a large cost of foundation. As in the case of steel towers, economy in

ht = Apparent height = (height of concrete + height of steel) towers

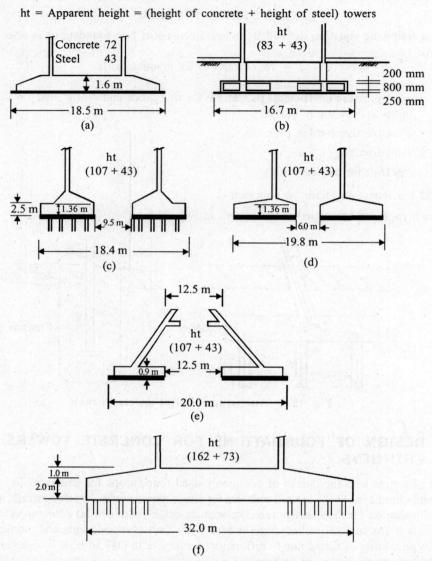

Fig. 19.9 **Foundations of TV towers. Towers at: (a) Kasauli (solid raft); (b) Thiruvananthapuram (cellular raft); (c) Varanasi (annular raft on piles); (d) Ahmedabad (annular raft); (e) Guwahati (annular raft with flare); (f) Delhi (solid raft on piles).**

the construction of these type of structures can be effected only by proper design of their foundations. The superstructure designed by all designers will give more or less the same results and the same cost. However, a suitable layout and proper analysis of the foundation can make a big difference in the cost of the structure.

Cooling towers are also very tall. Ever since 1918, when the Dutch engineer Van Itersen adopted the hyperbolic shell to reduce weight and also to provide stability against gross foundation settlement by the special connection to the foundation, the shape of these structures has remained more or less the same to the present day [5]. In cooling towers, as the main shell is connected to the foundation by a triangulated system of raking support columns, circumferential continuity is provided. The continuous pad foundation may be finally supported on piles as shown in Fig. 19.10.

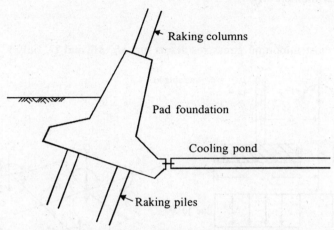

Fig. 19.10   Foundation for cooling towers.

19.6.1 Positioning of Chimney Load on Annular Rafts

When using annular raft, the chimney should be positioned on the raft in such a way that under dead load, the C.G. of the uniform soil pressure from below should coincide with the C.G. of the dead load. For an annular raft, we have the following condition for the C.G. of the uniform pressure (see also Fig. 19.11).

$$\beta a = \frac{\int_{\alpha a}^{a} p r^2 \,(dr)}{\int_{\alpha a}^{a} p r \,(dr)} = \frac{2\left(1 - \alpha^3\right)}{3\left(1 - \alpha^2\right)}$$

where a is the outer radius and αa the inner radius.

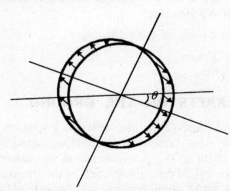

Fig 19.11   Ring load on raft slab due to moments.

The main stress resultants to be found on the annular raft are as shown in Fig. 19.12.

1. The radial moments M_r
2. The tangential moment M_θ
3. The torsional moment $M_{\theta r}$
4. Shear Q_r
5. Shear Q_θ

Of these, the most important stress resultants are M_r, M_θ and Q_r only.)

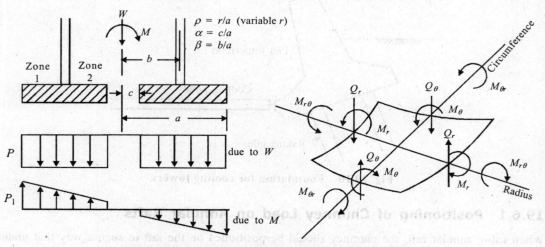

Fig. 19.12 Annular rafts foundation for chimneys.

19.6.2 Forces Acting on the Foundation

The forces acting are the following:

1. *The dead load.* The raft is assumed rigid and the contact pressure is assumed to be uniform.
2. *The moment due to lateral load like wind.* It is transmitted to the raft at the radius where the raft and wall join.
3. *Backfill load.* This is due to the difference in weight of backfill that may exist between the inside and outside of the structure.

The raft foundations can be one of the following:

- Rafts resting on the ground
- Rafts supported on piles

19.7 ANALYSIS OF RAFTS ON THE GROUND

In 1964 Smith and Zar [6] published charts and tables as a solution of the annular raft problem assuming that the slab with the ground reactions is simply supported by the chimney, and the loads are distributed symmetrically about an axis perpendicular to the plane of the slab as well as passing through the centre. They superimposed the uniform load on the slab due to moments with an axially symmetric ring load as in Fig. 19.12. Similar charts and tables based on this method are available in the study by Manohar [7].

In 1966, Chu and Afandi [8] published another procedure for finding M_r, M_θ and Q_r for annular foundation mats as shown in Fig. 19.12. They considered the rafts as simply supported by the walls (there is no transference of moments between zone 1 and zone 2, shown in Fig. 19.12. The maximum pressure distribution due to the vertical load W is denoted by p and the maximum pressure due to moment M produced by lateral loads p_1. The loading due to moment is assumed to vary as shown in the figure. Obviously, this method is not applicable to rafts with resultant tensile contact pressures. The formulae they derived are available in Ref. [9] given at the end of this chapter.

As negative pressures cannot exist in the foundation, the theoretical distribution of pressure in an annular raft will be as shown in Fig 19.13a. Charts are available in Ref. [10] to determine the pressure distribution when tension separations are to be neglected. Design charts based on this type of distribution are also available in Ref. [11]. In actual practice, however, the foundation has some flexibility and exact analysis using finite element analysis by a computer will give the results somewhat as shown in Fig. 19.13b for annular and full rafts. As shown in the figure, elastic analysis gives the most stressed region is a little inside the edges and not at the edges as obtained from conventional analysis. But for exact analysis, no closed form solution is available, and each problem has to be analysed separately by finite element method or by other computer methods. (The finite grid method described by Bowles [12] is more convenient when we are dealing with rectangular plates.)

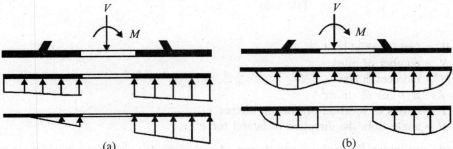

(a) (b)

Fig. 19.13 Difference in base pressures by rigid and elastic analysis: (a) Rigid analysis of annular rafts with base pressure fully in compression and partly in tension; (b) elastic analysis by computer methods for full and annular rafts showing that the stress distribution is not linear.

19.7.1 Influence of Parameters on Stress Resultants

Computer analysis of a large number of rafts has indicated the following:

- The superstructure does not significantly affect the radial moment and the value of maximum soil pressure, except for some redistribution of pressures away from the shaft. However, the tangential moment is changed by superstructure effects as the stiffness of the raft in the tangential direction is increased by its presence.
- Larger modulus of sub-grade reaction reduces the relative stiffness ratio between foundation and ground. This also reduces the maximum value of the stress resultants. Increase of thickness of the raft has the same effect as decreasing the value of the modulus of sub-grade reaction.
- As regards the diameter of a full circular raft, it was found that a raft with 1.43 times the diameter of the shaft is a good first choice for diameter of the raft as it gives a better distribution of soil pressures.

19.8 ANNULAR RAFT ON PILE FOUNDATIONS

Piled foundations on annular rafts are also adopted for very tall towers and we assume the following in their design (see also Chapter 15 on piled rafts).

- The dead load of slab and earth filling over the slab is taken by the soil below the raft slab or if the soil conditions are bad, by the piles.
- All the vertical loads that are assigned to the piles are taken equally by all the piles irrespective of their position.
- The bending moment produced by the shaft moment from the tower produces axial loads in the piles, which are proportional to the distance of the pile from the centroidal axis. (Thus the total load on each pile is the sum of items 2 and 3.)
- The lateral load is also equally shared by the piles if all the piles are vertical. If raked piles are used, the horizontal loads are assigned to the raked piles using principles of structural mechanics.

Piles are usually provided in concentric rings for yielding the maximum moment of inertia. The combined effect of the vertical load and moment on a pile is as follows:

$$\text{Pile load} = \frac{W}{N} \pm \frac{M\,(r\cos\theta)}{I}$$

where

W = vertical axial load
N = number of piles
M = moment in Nm
$I = \Sigma\,(r\cos\theta)^2$ in m^2
r = radius of location of piles in metres
θ = angle from the direction of lateral force.

Charts and tables for analysis and design of such rafts are also given by Manohar [7], and these can be used for their design. A graphical method to find the load in each pile when the lateral loads are to be taken by raked piles is available in Ref. [13]. However, with the availability of reliable methods of design for ensuring strength of vertical piles under horizontal loading, and with the installation of batter piles being difficult, it may be more expedient to use vertical piles for the total lateral resistance also. Modern computer methods are also available for such layouts.

We have already seen that with exact elastic analysis of raft under direct load P and moment M, the most stressed regions are not the ends as shown in Fig 19.13b. For the same reason, we find also image that the most stressed piles will not be the exterior piles but those a little inside the raft [11]. A knowledge of these facts will enable us to adopt a better layout of the piles for these massive structures.

EXAMPLE 19.1   (Analysis of a shallow steel tower foundation)

Analyse the chimney and footing foundation for an electric transmission tower which is subjected to the following forces. Use load factor of 2 for NC and 1.5 for BWC. The foundation is shown in Fig. E.19.1. Assume the soil is clay of $c = 0.15$ kg/cm^2 and unit weight 1.5 t/m^3. There is no likelihood of the foundation getting submerged. Assume the moment acting as each leg = 0.666 t-m.

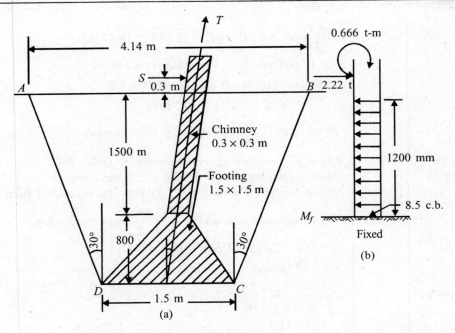

Fig. E.19.1

Nature of load	Working load (tons)		Ultimate load (tons)	
	NC	BWC	NC	BWC
Downward	17.5	24.0	35	36
Uplift	12.8	19.4	25.5	29.1
Shear (transverse)	1.00	1.48	2.0	2.22
Shear (longitudinal)	–	0.64	–	0.96

NC = Normal condition;   BWC = Broken wire condition.

Ref.	Step	Calculations
Sec. 19.3	1	*Check whether foundation is shallow or deep* $d = 1.5$ m; $b = 0.3$ m; $e = 0.3$ m; ultimate $S = 2.22$ tons $\dfrac{d}{b} = 5.0$; $\dfrac{e}{b} = 1.0$; S = ultimate lateral resistance $\dfrac{S}{c_u b^2} = 12.0$; Hence, $S = 12 \times 1.5(0.3)^2 = 1.62 < 2.22$
Fig. 19.6		The foundation to be classified as shallow since the lateral resistance capacity is less than that required in the problem.
Sec. 19.4.1	2	*Check for uplift* For the first approximation, neglect reduction of volume occupied by concrete
Fig. E.19.1		$\phi = 30°$ and vol. of pyramid $= \dfrac{D}{3}\left[A_1 + A_2 + \sqrt{A_1 A_2}\right]$

		$$=\frac{2.3}{3}\left[1.5^2+4.14^2+\sqrt{2.25\times17.14}\right]=19.74\text{ m}^3$$ Vol. of concrete (pad + chimney) = 0.744 m^3 Total wt. = (19.74 − 0.74) 1.5 + 0.74 × 2.3 = 28.5 + 1.71 = 30.2 tons $$FS\text{ on }BWC=\frac{30.2}{19.4}=1.56>1.5\text{ (satisfactory)}$$
Sec. 19.4.2	3	*Check for stability against overturning under BWC* Point of rotation = B/6 = 1500/6 = 250 mm from toe Wt. of concrete foundation = 1.71 tons (as calculated from volume)
		Wt. of soil acting at heel $=\dfrac{W}{2}=\dfrac{28.5}{2}=14.25$ tons $=W_s$
Fig. 19.1		$m = 750 − 250$ mm; Uplift = 19.4 (BWC) $S = 1.48$ (given)
Eq. (19.3)		Condition $W_s\left(\dfrac{5B}{6}\right)>U\times m+S\left(D+e\right)-\dfrac{W_fB}{3}$
		$14.25\left(\dfrac{5\times1.5}{6}\right)>19.4\times0.5+1.48\left(2.4\right)-\dfrac{1.71\times1.5}{3}$
		$17.81 > 9.7 + 3.55 − 0.86$, i.e. = 12.39 (Condition satisfied.)
Sec. 19.4.3 Fig. E.19.1b	4	*Check for lateral resistance (distribution Fig. 19.6)* Consider cantilever action of chimney–Moment acting = 0.666 tm $R = (8.5cb)$ (area) $= 8.5 \times 1.5 \times 0.3(0.3 \times 1.2) = 1.377$ t $M_f = (2.22 \times 1.8) + 0.666 − 1.377 \times 0.6 = 3.836$ mm Assuming redistribution as a restrained pile
		$M_B=\dfrac{M_f}{2}=1.918$ t-m (The CBIP Manual gives design charts for exact calculation of M_B for practical designs) M_B will be acting at the junction of the footing and the chimney and the footing has to transfer this moment and the vertical loads to the ground.
	5	*Structural design of footing* The footing has to be designed for moment M_B and also for the vertical forces due to the weight of footing and soil above the footing using the following equation.
		Pressure $=\dfrac{P}{A}\pm\dfrac{M}{I}y$ The chimney portion above the footing is to be designed as a beam for an ultimate bending moment M_B.

EXAMPLE 19.2 **(Analysis of a deep steel tower foundation)**

With the same data as in Example 19.1, design the foundation if the ultimate shear it has to resist is only 1 ton.

Ref.	Step	Calculations
Fig. 19.5	1	*Check whether the foundation is shallow or deep* $d = 1.5$ m; $b = 0.3$ m; $e = 0.3$ m $\dfrac{d}{b} = 5.0$; $\dfrac{e}{b} = 1.0$ $\dfrac{S}{C_u b^2} = 12.0$; $S = 12 \times 1.5(0.3)^2 = 1.62$ tons (ultimate) Shear capacity = 1.62 tons Actual ultimate shear = 1.00 ton As the chimney part itself can resist the horizontal *load it is taken as a deep foundation.* No moment is transferred to the footing.
	2	*Design as deep foundation* The total horizontal force is resisted by the chimney part. No moment is transferred to the footing. The footing is designed for the vertical load.

REFERENCES

[1] Manual on Transmission Line Towers, Technical Report No. 9, Central Board of Irrigation and Power, New Delhi, 1977.

[2] IS 4091 (1979), *Code of Practice for Design and Construction of Foundations for Transmission Line Towers and Poles,* BIS, New Delhi.

[3] IS 11233 (1986), *Code of Practice for Design and Construction of Radar Antenna*, Microwave and T.V. Tower Foundations, BIS, New Delhi.

[4] Murthy, S.S. and Santhakumar, A.R., *Transmission Line Structures*, McGraw-Hill, Singapore, 1990.

[5] Black, L.S. (Ed.), *Civil Engineer's Handbook*, Butterworth, London, 1975.

[6] Smith, J.W. and Zar, M., Chimney Foundations, *Journal of the American Concrete Institute*, June, 1964.

[7] Manohar, S.M., Tall Chimneys, *Design and Construction*, Tata McGraw-Hill, New Delhi, 1985.

[8] Chu, K.H. and Afandi, D.F., Analysis of Circular or Annular Slabs for Chimney Foundations, *Journal of American Concrete Institute*, Dec. 1966.

[9] Kurien, Nainan P., *Design of Foundation Systems: Principles and Practices*, Narosa Publishing House, New Delhi, 1991.

[10] Fintel, M. (Ed.), *Concrete Engineering Handbook*, Van Nostrand Reinhold, New York, 1974.

[11] Aravindan, P.K., Srinivasa Rao, P., and Krishna, K., *Design Aids for Circular Raft Foundations*, Proc. National Seminar on Tall Reinforced Concrete Chimneys, New Delhi, April 1985.

[12] Bowles, J.E., *Foundation Analysis and Design*, 4th ed., McGraw-Hill, Singapore, 1988.

[13] Bell, B.J. and Smith, M.J., *Reinforced Concrete Foundations*, George Godwin, London, 1981.

20

Well Foundations

20.1 INTRODUCTION

Well foundations were used extensively in India from very early days. Taj Mahal was built on such foundations. Wells are classified as deep foundations. The main difference between a well and a pile is that, while a pile is flexible like a beam under horizontal loads, the well or caisson undergoes rigid body movement under such loads. IS 3955 (1967) Indian Standard Code of Practice of Design and Construction of Well Foundations [1], "the Indian Road Congress publication" IRC 45 (1972) [2] and many other publications [3] give recommendations for design of well foundations for bridges. The layout of a well foundation and its various parts are shown in Fig. 20.1. The basic principles of design of well foundations are dealt with in this chapter.

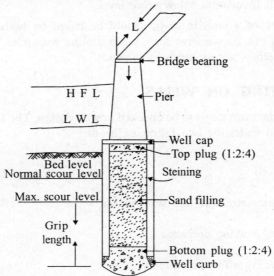

Fig. 20.1   Parts of a well foundation.

359

20.2 HISTORICAL DEVELOPMENT

The first theoretical analysis for computing pressures on rigid bulk heads was presented by Terzaghi in 1943 [1]. In 1947, Pender developed an analysis in which he used the modulus of sub-grade reaction, which increased with depth. On the basis of observations of behaviour of wells and the available literature on the subject, the Bureau of Indian Standards and the Indian Roads Congress published their recommendations, which are extensively used for design of well foundations in India.

20.3 SCOUR DEPTH—MINIMUM DEPTH OF WELLS

For natural streams in alluvial beds, the normal depth of scour below high flood level is important in the design of wells. Similarly, the minimum grip length below scour depth has also to be specified. These are explained in Section 20.6.

20.4 BEARING CAPACITY OF WELLS

As the well is a deep foundation, its bearing capacity requirements can be easily satisfied. However, we should be careful to check the *settlement and stability conditions*. There is considerable increase in bearing capacity if the well is founded in deep cohesionless soils. IS 3955 recommends the following empirical formula for *allowable bearing pressure for sands* based on its N value, for safety against shear failure [see also Eqs. (6.16b) and (8.16)]:

$$q_u = \left[5.4N^2B + 16(100 + N^2)D \right] \times \frac{1}{100} \ (kN/m^2)$$

where

q_u = safe bearing capacity in kN/m^2
N = corrected SPT value
B = smaller dimension of well
D = depth of well foundation below scour level.

The bearing capacity of a well in clays should be based on both its shear strength and settlement (see Section 20.11). As we have seen, when dealing with piles, the increase in bearing capacity of clays with depth is not as much as in sands.

20.5 FORCES ACTING ON WELLS

Stability and strength are the main items to be checked in well design. The forces acting on the well foundation can be grouped under the two following heads:

1. Vertical loads
   - Self-weight of well
   - Buoyancy
   - Dead load of superstructure and substructure
   - Live load
   - Kentledge during sinking operation
2. Horizontal forces
   - Braking and tractive effort of vehicles
   - Forces due to resistance of bearings

– Forces due to water current or waves
– Centrifugal forces for bridges on curves
– Wind forces or seismic forces
– Earth pressures
– Other horizontal or uplift forces like those due to provision of transmission line tower with broken wire condition.

All these effects are converted to resultant vertical and horizontal loads as well as a moment as shown by W, H and M in Fig. 20.2.

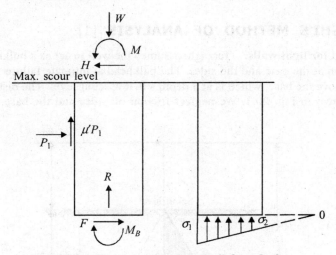

Fig. 20.2   Forces acting on a well foundation.

20.6 METHODS OF ANALYSIS

The external forces acting on a heavy well are the vertical forces W, the horizontal forces, H and a moment M. There can be also transverse forces due to wind. These are resisted by the following forces acting on the well which are also shown in Fig. 20.2.

1. *Net lateral earth pressure* = P_1 acting opposite in direction to H
2. Friction along the embedded height = μP_1
3. Vertical reaction from base = R
4. Moment at base due to unequal distribution of base pressure = M_B
5. Friction at base = F [The friction at base is represented by μ).

The difference between various methods of analysis depends on the assumptions made. For example, the value of P_1 will depend on whether we consider it at the *ultimate state* or the *elastic state* called the *state of incipient failure*. The distribution of the reaction P_1 will be at the Rankine states, if we assume ultimate failure condition. On the other hand, if we assume the elastic state only, then the reaction will depend on the amount of movement of the wall and we use the modulus of sub-grade reaction method to determine the distribution of forces.

Similarly, the point about which we assume the rotation of the well to take place makes large differences in the resisting forces. The magnitude and the directions of frictional forces at the base will depend on the assumed location of the point of rotation of the well. Usually for elastic analysis, we assume that the well tilts about the centre of base and for ultimate failure that the well rotates about a point $0.2D$ above the base.

The accuracy of the method to determine stability depends on whether we take all the above forces into account or neglect some of them. For example, in the first method suggested by Terzaghi, he neglected some of the frictional forces. In this chapter we will examine the method of analysis suggested by Terzaghi and also the method recommended by IRC and BIS.

20.7 TERZAGHI'S METHOD OF ANALYSIS [1]

Terzaghi's method for light walls. Terzaghi assumed the well to act as a bulkhead, which will not develop any friction at the base and the sides. The bulkhead at ultimate failure is assumed to rotate about a point A above the base, which is at a depth y below scour level. The distribution of pressure at failure is as shown in Fig. 20.3. We neglect friction on sides and the base.

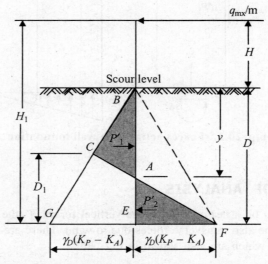

Fig. 20.3 **Terzaghi's analysis for stability of rigid wells on sand as a bulkhead.**

Let q_{max} be the horizontal force per unit length to be resisted as shown in Fig. 20.3. The resistance of the soil is shown in Fig. 20.3. There will be passive pressures and active pressures on the sides depending on the direction of movement of the bulkhead.

$$q_{max} \text{ (per metre)} = (P_1' - P_2') \text{ at point of ultimate failure}$$

$$= \text{area of BGE} - \text{CGF}$$

$$= \gamma D(K_P - K_A) \times \frac{D}{2} - 2\gamma D(K_P - K_A)\frac{D_1}{2}$$

$$= \frac{1}{2}\gamma D(K_P - K_A)(D - 2D_1)$$

Again, taking moments of the forces about the base, we obtain

$$q_{max}(H+D) = P_1' \times \frac{D}{3} - P_2'\frac{D_1}{3} = \text{moment of (BGE - CGF)}$$

Substituting for q_{max} values from above and putting $(H+D=H_1)$, we get

$$(D-2D_1)H_1 = \frac{D^2}{3} - \frac{2D_1^2}{3} \quad \text{or} \quad D_1 = \frac{1}{2}\left[3H_1 \pm \sqrt{9H_1^2 - 2D(3H_1 - D)}\right]$$

After finding D_1, the value of q_{max} can be determined as Q_{max} (total force) $= q_{max} \times L$. For design purposes, we find Q_{max} and assuming a $FS = 2$, check whether the applied force is less than $1/2\ Q_{max}$. For determining the shear and bending forces, we assume that the earth pressures are also reduced by the same FS. With this assumption, find the point where shear force is zero. The moment of forces at that point is the maximum moment to be resisted. For using limit state design, we consider the well to be at the ultimate state conditions. As there is no side friction, the full vertical load is assumed to be acting at the base.

Terzaghi's method for a heavy well. In this case, we assume rotation of the well at the base. If the applied load Q is greater than the allowable load (Q_a) with FS, then the well has to develop a base moment to oppose the balance of the moment at the base. Neglecting frictional forces, we get the base moment required as follows:

$$M_B = (Q - Q_a)(H_1)$$

Assuming that all loads are taken by the base the foundation pressure is:

$$p = \frac{W}{A} \pm \frac{M_B}{Z_B}$$

For safety design, pressure must be less than the allowable pressures.

20.8 IRC AND IS DESIGN RECOMMENDATIONS [2], [3]

The IRC and IS 3955 publications recommend the following procedure for design of well foundations in sand deposits (for clay the expressions should be suitably modified).

1. Check the stability of well under working loads, assuming elastic theory.
2. Find the factor of safety of the well against ultimate failure using ultimate load theory.

These methods are explained below.

20.8.1 A Note on Modulus of Horizontal Sub-grade Reaction

The coefficient modulus of horizontal sub-grade reaction can be expressed in three ways:

Case 1. When it varies with depth, we have the following forms:

(a) Modulus of horizontal sub-grade reaction $= k_h y/D$ (where k_h will be in kg/cm^3)

(b) It is also expressed as $= n_h y$ (where n_h will be in kg/cm^4 and y is the depth below G.L.)

Case 2. When k_h is a function of k_v and the ratio of $k_h/k_v = m$, we have $k_h = mk_v$.

$$\frac{k_h y}{D} = \frac{m k_v y}{D} = n_h y.$$

Therefore,

$$m = \left(\frac{n_h D}{k_v} \right)$$

Case 3. In the third case, k_h is considered as a constant and does not vary with depth.

20.8.2 Checking Stability by Elastic Limit State Theory using Modulus of Sub-grade Reaction

The following assumptions are made:

1. The surrounding soil is elastic, homogeneous and follows Hook's law
2. The ratio of the horizontal to vertical modulus of sub-grade reaction is a constant $m = k_h/k_v$
3. The well tilts about the base as a rigid body, acted by vertical loads and horizontal forces.
4. Stability analysis is to be carried out on the least depth of embedment of the well, but not less than 0.5 times the width of the foundation.

The forces acting on the well are as follows:

W = total downward load
Q = total horizontal force
M = resultant moment of applied forces about the base level.

Let, B = the smaller dimension (diameter or width of well)
L = length of well offering passive resistance (shape factor 0.9 for circle)
D = depth of well below scour level
$m = k_h/k_v$ = ratio of horizontal to vertical modulus of sub-grade reaction.
μ' = tan δ (where δ = wall friction = $2/3 \phi$ but $\not> 22.5°$)
$\beta\mu$ = base friction, where $\beta < 1$ when full friction is not developed.
γ = submerged unit weight of soil.

The well is subjected to the forces as shown in Fig. 20.4. Let the block tilt. For the full passive pressure to act on the body, the tilt should be large. Hence, for elastic stage, the tilt is small and we use the modulus of sub-grade reaction method. Let the value of $m = k_h/k_v$ and variation of k_h with depth be $k_h y/D$ (IRC and IS method).

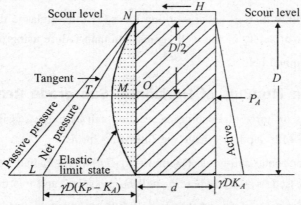

Fig. 20.4   Stability analysis of well foundation at point of incipient failure of soil (elastic analysis).

In deriving the *formulae for various forces (elastic method)*, we assume that the bottom of the well is plugged with concrete and that the top of the well is above the scour depth. The vertical load is taken by the base as well as by friction from the sides of the well while the horizontal load is taken by the reactions from the surrounding soil. For considering lateral earth pressures at elastic stages, we assume that the wall *tilts about the base by a small angle θ*. A large tilt will produce plastic failure conditions, while for a small tilt, the soil will be in elastic stage. We will also designate the maximum elastic condition as *state of incipient failure*. We also assume that only limited base friction $\beta\mu$ (where $\beta < 1$) and not the full friction has to be mobilised at the elastic stage for stability.

Step 1: *Calculation of horizontal pressures P.* With reference to Fig. 20.4, let the lateral pressure at depth y be σ_x = modulus × deflection.

Modulus of horizontal sub-grade reaction = $k_h y/D$.

$$\sigma_x = \frac{k_h y}{D}[D - y]\theta = m k_v \theta y \left(\frac{D - y}{D}\right) \tag{20.1}$$

This relation is a parabolic relation and the maximum value will be at $D/2$. Putting $y = D/2$,

$$\sigma_{max} = \frac{1}{4}(m k_v \theta D) = \frac{1}{4D}(m k_v \theta D^2)$$

Let

P = total pressure developed at elastic limit stage (at stage of incipient failure)

= area of the parabola over depth D and length L.

$$P = \frac{2}{3}\left[\frac{m k_v \theta D^2}{4D}\right]DL = \frac{m k_v \theta D^3 L}{6D} = \frac{2 m k_v \theta I_v}{D} \tag{20.1a}$$

where $I_v = (LD^3/12)$ is the moment of inertia of projected vertical area $L \times D$ about its horizontal centre of gravity. For circle L is taken as equal to 0.9 d.

If we consider the ultimate state of failure by rotation about the base, the active and passive pressure conditions will exist on opposite sides of the well and the pressure distribution will be as shown in Fig. 20.4. The pressures are indicated as active and passive. With reference to this figure, the slope of the *net pressure line along NTL* will be $\gamma(K_P - K_A)$, where K_P and K_A are the passive and active earth pressure coefficients.

At the limit of elastic condition (at incipient failure), the slope of the parabolic distribution at point N should also be along the line NTL corresponding to ultimate failure. Accordingly, from the property of a parabola, we get $OM = MT$ or $OM = (1/2)OT$. Putting $OM = \sigma_{z(max)}$, we get

$$\sigma_{z(max)} = \frac{1}{4}\gamma(K_P - K_A)D$$

This is an important relation as it gives the maximum elastic value that can be mobilized. The area of the parabola will give P_{max} as

$$P_{max} = \frac{\gamma(K_P - K_A)D}{4} \times \frac{2D}{3} \times L = \frac{\gamma(K_P - K_A)LD^2}{6} \tag{20.2}$$

Equating Eqs. (20.1a) and (20.2) in the limiting condition, we have

$$\frac{2 m k_v \theta L D^3}{12D} = \frac{2\gamma(K_P - K_A)LD^3}{12D}$$

Thus we get the magnitude of rotation θ from the following relation:

$$k_v \theta = \frac{\gamma(K_P - K_A)}{m} \qquad (20.2a)$$

Also, the distribution of stress suggested by Eq. (20.1) at any point at elastic limit will be as follows:

$$\sigma_x = \gamma(K_P - K_A)\left(\frac{D-y}{D}\right)y \qquad (20.2b)$$

However, in any given case, it may not be necessary to mobilize this full capacity. This can be investigated as shown below. The magnitude of the external force H that can be applied will also depend on the level at which it is applied. This can be determined by applying equilibrium of forces and the condition that the moments of the external and internal forces about the base should be equal to zero.

Step 2: *Calculation of moment of P about the base of the well.*

$$M_P = P\frac{D}{2} = \frac{2mk_v\theta I_v}{D} \times \frac{D}{2} = mk_v\theta I_v \qquad (20.3)$$

In most cases, P will be less than P_{max}. It is of interest to find the moment of the maximum elastic pressure, P_{max} about base from Eq. (20.2). It will be as follows:

$$M_{P(max)} = P_{max} \times \left(\frac{D}{2}\right) = \gamma(K_P - K_A)LD^3/12 \qquad (20.3a)$$

Step 3: *Calculation of friction on the face or side $D \times L$.*

The friction on the face of wall $= \mu' \times$ resultant pressure $= \mu' P$ (20.4)

where μ' is the coefficient of wall friction.

Assuming uniform distribution of friction around the well, the resultant of the frictional force $\mu' P$ on the surface of the well will act at a distance αD from the vertical axis through the C.G. of the base (for a rectangle α will be equal to $B/2D$ and for a circle it will be diameter/πD. The term a is introduced to make quantity a function of the depth of soil D so that $\alpha D = B/2$, or d/π for the above two cases. (Note that D is the depth of well below scour level.)

Step 4: *Calculation of moment due to $\mu' P$ about the axis through the CG is M_μ.*

$$M_{\mu'} = \mu' P\alpha D = \mu' \times \frac{2mk_v\theta I_v}{D}(\alpha D) = \mu' \alpha 2mk_v\theta I_v \qquad (20.5)$$

Step 5: *Calculation of moment M_B due to base reaction (due to non-uniform pressure as shown in Fig. 20.2.)*

The base also rotates through θ. Considering the stress at the extreme fibre from consideration of modulus of deformation k_v and also from consideration of moment M_B and equating the two, we get

$$k_v \times \left(\frac{B}{2}\theta\right) = \frac{M_B}{I_B}\left(\frac{B}{2}\right) \quad \text{or} \quad M_B = k_v I_B \theta \qquad (20.6)$$

where $I_B = \frac{LB^3}{12}$ and $\pi d^4/64$ for a rectangle and for a circle, respectively.

In the limiting state, substituting from Eq. (20.2a),

$$M_B = \gamma(K_P - K_A)I_B/m \qquad (20.6a)$$

Step 6: *Calculation of friction for F at base.*

Assuming that only a friction $\beta\mu$ and not the full friction is developed at base = μ
Reaction R = vertical load $- \mu'P$ (where μ' is side friction)

$$F = \beta\mu R = \beta\mu(W - \mu'P) = \text{friction developed at base} \qquad (20.7)$$

Step 7: *Equating moments of the applied and resisting moments about the base.* Let M_R represent the moment of all resisting forces about the base line. It should be equal to the moment of the applied forces about the same point. Thus,

$$M = M_R = M_P + M\mu' + M_B + \text{(due to } F \text{ at base} = 0)$$

$$M = mk_v\theta I_v + 2\mu'\alpha mI_v k_v\theta + k_v\theta I_B$$

which reduces to $M = Ik_v\theta$ or $k_v\theta = M/I,\ ...,$ where

$$I = I_B + mI_v(1 + 2\mu'\alpha) \qquad (20.8)$$

Note: I corresponds to M.

Step 8: *Apply the condition of equilibrium (sum of horizontal forces = 0) to check direction of F.*

$$\text{Acting horizontal force} = H = P - F \qquad (20.9)$$

From Eq. (20.7)

$$H = P - \beta_\mu(W - \mu P)$$

or,

$$P = \frac{H + \beta\mu W}{1 + \beta\mu\mu'} = \frac{2mk_v\theta I_v}{D} \quad \text{[From Eq. (20.1a)]} \qquad (20.10)$$

Substituting M/I for $k_v\theta$ from Eq. (20.8), we get

$$P = \frac{2mMI_v}{ID} = \frac{M}{r} \qquad \left(r = \frac{ID}{2mI_v}\right) \qquad (20.11)$$

As $F = P - H = \left(\dfrac{M}{r} - H\right)$ and F = friction at base = $(\beta\mu) \times$ (vertical reaction), we have

$$F = \beta\mu\left(W - \frac{M}{r}\mu'\right) = \left(\frac{M}{r} - H\right) \quad \text{[Eqs. (20.7) and (20.11)]}$$

Thus,

$$\beta = \frac{(M/r) - H}{\mu(W - (M/r)\mu')} \qquad (20.12)$$

The final condition for stability, is that β should be < 1 and it should not be negative. This leads to Eq. (20.13).

20.8.3 Summary of Conditions to be Satisfied by Elastic Method

Finally, summarizing all the above steps, we may conclude that in any given problem that we need to examine only whether the following four conditions are satisfied for equilibrium and safety at the limiting elastic stage.

For this purpose we first calculate the following quantities.

$I_v = LD^3/12$ = moment of projected area Eq. (20.1a)
$I_B = LB^3/12$ for rectangular base and $\pi d^4/64$ for circular base. (20.6)
$\alpha = B/2D$ for rectangular well and $d/\pi D$ for circle. Step 3, Sec. 20.8.2
$I = I_B + mI_v (1 + 2\mu'\alpha)$ Eq. (20.8)
$r = (I\,D)/(2mI_v)$ and $P = M/r$ Eq. (20.11)

Using these values, check the following conditions.

Condition 1: We should check whether the base friction $\beta\mu$ is safe.

The condition is, $\beta < 1$ which when applied to Eq. (20.12) reduces to $\mu\left(W - \dfrac{M}{r}\mu'\right) > \left(\dfrac{M}{r} - H\right)$

or

$$H > \frac{M}{r}(1 + \mu\mu') - \mu W, \qquad r = \frac{ID}{2mI_v} \tag{20.13}$$

Condition 2: It is also necessary that the assumed direction of rotation is correct, that is, β should not be negative.

$$\mu\left(W - \frac{M}{r}\mu'\right) + \frac{M}{r} > H$$

or

$$H < \frac{M}{r}(1 - \mu\mu') + \mu W \tag{20.14}$$

Condition 3: If the soil should remain elastic, the soil reaction at the sides should not exceed the net earth pressures at failure. Hence at depth y taking γ *as the submerged weight in case of a bridge pier*, from the equation to the slope of line *NT*, of Fig. 20.4 we get:

$\sigma_x \ngtr (K_P - K_A)\,\gamma y$. Using Eq. (20.1) this reduces to the following condition:

$$\frac{mk_v\theta}{D}(D - y) \ngtr (K_P - K_A)\gamma \text{ (everywhere)}$$

From Eq. (20.8), $k_v\theta = \dfrac{M}{I}$. Hence the condition to be satisfied can be expressed as follows:

$$\frac{mM}{I} \ngtr \gamma(K_P - K_A) \tag{20.15}$$

Condition 4: The maximum base soil pressure should not exceed the allowable value.

$$\sigma_1, \sigma_2 = \frac{W - \mu'P}{A} \pm K_v\theta \times \frac{B}{2}$$

But M = moment about the base and $k_v\theta = M/I$. Hence

$$\sigma_1, \sigma_2 = \frac{W - \mu'P}{A} \pm \frac{MB}{2I} \tag{20.16}$$

20.8.4 Steps in the Design of Wells for Elastic Conditions

Method 1: In any design calculation for checking the elastic state, we have to check only whether the above four equations Eqs. (20.13) to (20.16) are satisfied.

Method 2: Alternately, we can calculate each component of the forces and find the maximum horizontal load that can be applied with the specified vertical load and moment. We then check whether we have the required safety factor for the horizontal load.

20.9 CHECKING ULTIMATE FAILURE CONDITION OF ABUTMENTS

The load factors to be used for the earth pressures on abutments according to I.R.C. 45–1972 are the following:

- (a) $1.1D + 1.6L$
- (b) $1.1D + B + 1.4(L + C + E)$
- (c) $1.1D + B + 1.4(C + E + W \text{ or } S)$
- (d) $1.1D + B + 1.25(L + C + E + W \text{ or } S)$

where

D = dead load
L = live load
B = buoyancy
C = water current
E = earth pressure
W = wind load
S = seismic load.

20.9.1 Procedure to Check Ultimate Failure Condition of Well Foundations

We assume that at ultimate failure the well rotates about a line 0.2D from the base as in Fig. 20.5. We need only to check the bearing stress and also whether there is enough moment of resistance against rotation. The steps to be followed are now being briefly described. The forces acting are

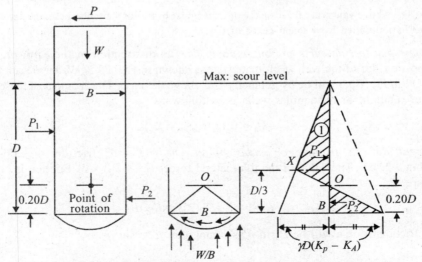

Fig. 20.5 Rotation of well and earth pressures at ultimate failure.

shown in Fig. 20.5. We can prove that point 'X' is at a height $D/3$ from the base if we assume the well to rotate about a point O at $0.2D$ above the base at ultimate failure.

Step 1. The average pressure under maximum load conditions neglecting side friction should not be more than the allowable value. We use the following conservative formula for this purpose:

$$\frac{W}{A} \not> \frac{q_u}{2} \text{ (or allowable bearing capacity)} \tag{20.17}$$

where W = actual load and q_u = ultimate bearing capacity.

Step 2: The well is assumed to rotate about a point of height $0.2D$ from the base and the moment of resistance should be more than the disturbing moment due to the external forces. Three resisting moments are to be considered: (a) moment due to base movement; (b) moment due to earth pressures and (c) moments due to side friction forces. They may be addressed as follows:

Base moment M_b due to frictional force: Assuming a circular surface at the base as shown in Fig. 20.5, we assume full mobilization of friction. Taking moments about the point of rotation, O, the base moment M_b can be expressed as

$$M_b = QB(W \tan \phi) \tag{20.18}$$

where

B = width or diameter of well

Q = constant, depending on the shape of well and ratio of depth to width. Values given by IRC are given in Table 20.1.

(As this is a stabilizing force, we take W = actual load.)

TABLE 20.1   VALUES OF CONSTANT Q

D/B	0.5	1.0	1.5	2.0	2.5
Q	0.41	0.45	0.50	0.56	0.56

Note: The Above values are for a square or rectangular base. For a circular base, the above values are to be multiplied by a shape factor of 0.6.

Moment due to side earth pressures about O: The distribution of the earth pressures acting on the opposite sides of the well at ultimate state is shown in Fig. 20.5. We have seen that the point shown as 'X' in Fig. 20.5 will be by geometry $D/3$ above the base. The moment of these forces about the point of rotation for rectangular wells is as follows:

$$M_s = 0.1 \gamma D^3 (K_P - K_A) L \tag{20.19}$$

Moment due to friction on sides about O: The wall friction is calculated using $\delta = 2/3 \phi$ but $\not> 22.5°$. The value of the total lateral forces $(P_1 + P_2) = P$. Friction is proportional to this pressure, P.

$$P = 1.1/3 \, \gamma D^2 (K_P - K_A) L$$

The frictional force will be $P \sin \delta$ assuming that $\mu' = \sin \delta$.

Case 1: For a rectangular well, the moment of friction force about $O = P \sin \delta \times B/2 = Mf$ ence,

$$M_f = 0.18\gamma(K_P - K_A)LBD^2 \sin \delta \qquad (20.20)$$

where γ = submerged weight of soil.

Case 2: For a circular well of distance from axis = B/π and $L = 0.91B$ (where B is the diameter of the well.)

$$M_f = \frac{1.1}{3}\gamma D^2 (K_P - K_A) \sin \delta \frac{B}{\pi} \times 0.91B$$
$$= 0.11\gamma(K_P - K_A) B^2 D^2 \sin \delta \qquad (20.20a)$$

The final condition for stability at ultimate state reduces to the following.

Total moment of resistance of well M_r should exceed the moment of external forces M. Instead of multiplying the external moment by 1.4 we apply a reduction factor to the resisting moment. With reduction factor $1/1.4 = 0.7$, we get the following condition:

$$M_r = 0.7(M_b + M_s + M_f) \qquad (20.20b)$$

Hence the condition to be satisfied is

$$M_r > M$$

where M = external moment without load factor.

We must note that in this procedure we generally do not apply the load factor to the loads acting on the well. We work with the actual moment acting on the well but reduce the ultimate resisting moment by a factor $1/1.4$.

20.10 BENDING STRENGTH OF THE WELL

From the forces obtained by the above analysis, the axial force, the shear force and the bending moment along the well can be calculated and the strength of the well in bending and shear can be checked.

20.11 CHECKING FOR SETTLEMENT

The settlement of pier foundations was described in Section 4.9. It is very important that the settlement under the applied loads should be within the allowable limits. Settlements in sands take place quickly and are not serious. However, many well foundations which have been built on sands below which there are clay layers, have undergone considerable settlements after construction. Therefore, soil data to a fairly good depth below the foundation strata of the well should always be examined in detail. The procedure used for checking settlements in sand is to calculate the settlement for shallow foundation and then apply corrections as per Fox's curves even though these curves are applicable to flexible foundation in clays (elastic materials) only. The allowable pressures for shallow footing from consideration of settlements in sands with respect to SPT values have already been examined in Chapter 6. According to Terzaghi, we can also assume that the settlement of the base of pier on sand at any depth is not less than about one half the settlement of an equally loaded footing covering the same area on sand of the same characteristics as a shallow footing. Accordingly he recommends the allowable bearing capacity as twice the value that would be normally admissible for footings resting on the same sand [1].

20.12 DEPTH OF SCOUR

The probable maximum scour depth should be estimated considering local conditions. In the case of natural channels flowing in alluvial beds where the width of waterway provided is not less than Lacey's regime width, *the normal depth of scour* (d_s in metres) for a discharge Q_f in m³sec may be estimated from the following formula (Lacey's formula). This is the depth of scour in a river-bed without the well.

$$d_s = 0.473 \left(\frac{Q_f}{f} \right)^{1/3} \tag{20.21}$$

where f = Lacey's silt factor for representative sample of bed material obtained from the scour zone. In the case of constricted waterways, the width will be less than Lacey's regime width and the depth of flow will be large as in the case of incised rivers with sandy bed. The increased scour depth may be estimated by the following formula:

$$d_s = 1.338 \left(\frac{Q_f}{f} \right)^{1/3} \tag{20.22}$$

In Eq. (20.21), the value of f is to be taken as $1.76\sqrt{s}$, where s = weighted mean diameter of particles. Its value for different types of bed materials commonly met with are given in Table 20.2 [6].

TABLE 20.2   VALUES OF SILT FACTOR (IS 3955–1967)

Type of material	Mean diameter (mm)	f
Coarse silt	0.04	0.35
Fine sand	0.08	0.50
Fine sand	0.15	0.68
Medium sand	0.3	0.96
Medium sand	0.5	1.24
Coarse sand	0.7	1.47
Coarse sand	1.0	1.76
Coarse sand	2.0	2.49

20.12.1 Design Depth

The depth as calculated above should be increased as in Table 20.3 to get the local or maximum depth of scour for design of foundations, protection works and river training works.

TABLE 20.3   INCREASE IN SCOUR DEPTH (IS 3955–67)

Nature of river	Depth of scour
In straight reaches	1.25D
At moderate bends as along aprons of guide bend	1.5D
At severe bends	1.75D
At right angle bend or at nose or piers	2.0D
In severe swirls and upstream nose of guide banks	2.5 to 2.75D

20.12.2 Grip Length for Wells in Rivers

According to IS 3955 (1967) and IRC, the depth of foundation should be not less than 1.33 times the deepest scour depth at high flood level. Thus the grip length, which is the height of the well required below the maximum scour level, should be at least one-third the maximum scour depth. Specifications also state that this grip length for piers and abutments should not be less than 2 m when they support arches, and not less than 1.2 m when they support other types of superstructure. The recommendation of the Indian Railways is shown in Fig. 20.6.

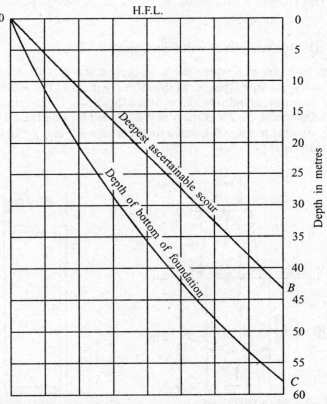

Fig. 20.6   Depth of scour and recommended depth of foundation by Indian Railways.

20.13 MINIMUM THICKNESS OF R.C. WELLS

As per the IRC practice, the minimum thickness of an R.C. well steining should be as follows:

$$t = KD\sqrt{L_D} \tag{20.23}$$

where

t = minimum thickness of well
D = outside diameter of well
L_D = length of foundation (from sill level of bearing) to foundation level
K = constant = 0.033 for single well in clay soils.

For structural design, the B.M. and S.F. diagrams can be drawn and the steel required for the thickness can be calculated.

20.14 CONSTRUCTION OF WELL FOUNDATIONS

Various methods such as manual methods, machine dredging and pneumatic methods are used for well construction. It is of interest to know that the well foundation for Howrah bridge was 24.8 m × 55.3 m in plan with 21 dredge holes and was sunk to a depth of 31.4 m. The well foundation for the bridge across Ganges at Mokamesh was 9.7 m × 16.3 m in plan and was sunk to a depth of 50.3 m.

EXAMPLE 20.1 (Elastic analysis of well foundation)

A well foundation for a pier of a bridge in a sand deposit is 4 m × 10 m in plan and has a vertical load of 15000 kN acting on top of the pier as shown in Fig. E.20.1. The modulus of subgrade reaction values are to be assumed as follows: k_v = 180 MN/m³, k_h is expressed as $n_h y$, the value of n_h = 1.60 MN/m⁴. Determine the FS of the pier if it is acted by a horizontal force of 1000 kN at the top of the bearing. Assume $\mu = \mu' = 0.4$ and ϕ for the sand = 30° and γ = 20 kN/m³. Assume limiting elastic state for analysis [5].

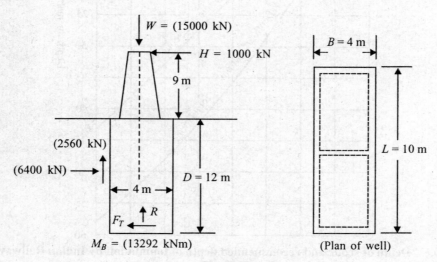

Fig. E.20.1.

Ref.	Step	Calculations
		Procedure: We find the maximum value of horizontal resistance at limiting elastic state and find $FS = H_{max}/H$.
	1	*Find m as in derivation in text*
Sec. 20.8.1		$m = \dfrac{n_h D}{k_v} = \dfrac{1.6 \times 12}{180} = 0.107$

Eq. (20.2)	2	Find P_{max} and μP_{max}; $L = 10$ m; $D = 12$ m

$$P_{max} = \frac{\gamma(K_P - K_A)LD^2}{6}; \quad \gamma \text{ (submerged)} = 10 \text{ kN/m}^3$$

$K_P = \tan^2(45 + \phi/2) = 3.0; \quad K_A = (\tan^2 45 - \phi/2) = 1/3$

$(K_P - K_A) = 8/3$

$$P_{max} = \frac{10 \times 8 \times 10 \times 12 \times 12}{3 \times 6} = 6400 \text{ kN}$$

$\mu \times P_{max} = 0.4 \times 6400 = 2560$ kN

3 — Find M_{Bmax} at base at limiting state (Section 20.5.2, step 5)

Eq. (20.6a)

$$M_{B(max)} = \frac{\gamma(K_P - K_A)I_B}{m}, \qquad I_B = \frac{LB^3}{12}$$

$$= \frac{10 \times 8 \times 10 \times 4 \times 4 \times 4}{3 \times 12 \times 0.107} = 13{,}292 \text{ kNm}$$

4 — *Write the equation of equilibrium*

Two unknown forces are F_T and H

$\Sigma H = 0$; $H = P - F_T = 6400 - F_T$ \hfill (a)

$\Sigma M = 0$ along the scour line and about centre line of well.

$9H = 13.292 - 6400 \times 6 + 2560 \times 2 + 12F_T$ \hfill (b)

Solving (a) and (b), $F_T = 36.94$ kN (direction compatible)

$H = 2706$ kN (max. allowable)

5 — *Find FS for H = 1000 kN*

$$FS = \frac{2706}{1000} = 2.7$$

6 — *Check base pressure with maximum value of H (limiting condition)*

M_{max} at base $= 13{,}292$ kNm (due to base reaction only).

Vertical load at base $= W - \mu P = 15{,}000 - 2560 = 12{,}440$ kN

Step 3 (above)

$$\text{Vertical base pressures} = \frac{P}{A} \pm \frac{M \times y}{I_B}; \quad I_B/y = \frac{10(4)^3}{12 \times 2} = 26.66$$

$$= \frac{12{,}440}{40} \pm \frac{13{,}292}{26.66} = 809$$

(comp.) and 187 (tension) kN/m^2

EXAMPLE 20.2 (Ultimate failure analysis of well foundations)

For the data in Example 20.1, determine the value of H at ultimate failure.

Ref.	Step	Calculations
		Principle: We assume rotation at $0.2D$ above base. The three moments resisting external moment are:
		1. The base moment, M_b
		2. The moment due to earth pressure resistance, M_s
		3. The moment produced by the frictional forces on side of the well, M_f
		$M_{applied} < 0.7 \ (M_b + M_s + M_f)$ (resistance available)
		In the following procedure we do not apply the load factor to the loads, but apply a reduction factor of $1/1.4 = 0.7$ to the resistance moment.
	1	*Calculate M_b at ultimate stage*
		Let us assume W as the actual load $= 15000$ kN
		$M_b = QB(W \tan \phi)$
Table 20.1		$D/B = 12/4 = 3$; $Q = 0.56$ (rectangle)
		$M_b = 0.56 \times 4 \times 15{,}000 \times 0.4 = 13{,}440$ kNm
	2	*Calculate M_s due to earth pressure*
		$M_s = 0.1rD^3 \ (K_P - K_A)L$
		$= 0.1 \times 10 \times (12)^3 \times (8/3) \times 10 = 46{,}080$ kMm
	3	*Calculate M_f due to side friction*
		$M_f = 0.18r \ (K_P - K_A)LBD^2 \sin \delta$
		$M_f = 0.18 \times 10(8/3) \times 10 \times 4 \times (12)^2 = 27{,}648$ kNm
	4	*Equate moments about the centre of rotation*
Sec. 20.9.1		$0.2D = 0.2 \times 12 = 2.4$ m; From top $= (21 - 2.4) = 18.6$ m
Eq. (20.20c)		$M_r = 0.7 \ (M_b + M_s + M_f)$
		$H \times 18.6 = 0.7 \ (13{,}440 + 46{,}080 + 27{,}648)$
		$H = 3281$ kN (ultimate value available)
		With load factor 1.4; $H' = 2294$ kN
		(This compares well with the value of 2706 in Example 20.1.)

EXAMPLE 20.3 (Design of well foundation by IRC method)

A bridge pier in a sand deposit with external diameter $d = 8.5$ and the depth of well below scour level $D = 15$ m is subjected to the following loads: $W = 14{,}000$ kN; $H = 2000$ kN, moment about base level $= 42{,}000$ kN. The value of ϕ of the sand $= 30°$, wall friction $\delta = 20°$, allowable bearing 60 t/m^2; and $k_h/k_v = m = 1$. Check the lateral stability of the well under the above forces according to IRC 45 (1972) recommendations. Assume the weight of soil is 20 kN/m^3 [6].

Ref.	Step	Calculations
Sec. 20.8.3		*Procedure:* In this example, W and H are given and we check the four conditions for stability in the elastic state and also check the ultimate state.
		Part A – Elastic analysis
Eq. (20.13)		(1) $H > (M/r)(1 + \mu\mu') - \mu W$
Eq. (20.14)		(2) $H < (M/r)(1 - \mu\mu') + \mu W$
Eq. (20.15)		(3) $mM/I \not> \gamma(K_P - K_A)$
Eq. (20.16)		(4) $\sigma_1, \sigma_2 = \dfrac{W - \mu'P}{A} \pm \dfrac{MB}{2I_B}$
		$I = I_B + mI_v(1 + 2\mu'\alpha)$
Sec. 20.8.3		$I_v = LD^3/12$ and $I_B = LB^3/12$ or $\pi d^4/64$
		$r = ID/2mI_v; \quad m = 1$
	1	*Determine the parameters*
		$L = 0.9d = 0.9 \times 8.5 = 7.65$ m [L = projected dimension].
		$L_v = LD^3/12 = 7.65 \times 15^3/12 = 2151$ m^4
		$I_B = \pi d^4/64 = \pi(8.5)^4/64 = 256$ m^4 (solid base)
		$\alpha = d/\pi D = 8.5/\pi \times 15 = 0.18$
		$\mu' = \tan \delta = \tan 20 = 0.36$
		$\mu = \tan \phi = \tan 30 = 0.58$
Eq. (20.8)		$I = I_B + mI_v(1 + 2\mu'\alpha)$
		$I = 256 + 2151(1 + 2 \times 0.36 \times 0.18) = 2685.7$
Eq. (20.11)		$r = \dfrac{ID}{2mI_v} = \dfrac{2685.7 \times 15}{2 \times 1 \times 2151} = 9.36$ m
		$K_P = \tan^2(45 + \phi/2) = 3.69; \ K_A = \tan^2(45 + \phi/2) = 0.27$
		M = moment about base = 42000 kNm. [Given]
		H = 2000 kN. [Given]
Eq. (20.13)	2	*Condition 1:* Base friction is less than μ. [$H = 2000$ kN]
		$H > \dfrac{M}{r}(1 + \mu\mu') - \mu W$
		$> \dfrac{42,000}{9.36}(1 + 0.70 \times 0.36) - 0.70 \times 14,000$
		> -4182 kN (satisfied)

Eq. (20.14)	3	*Condition 2:* Direction of rotation is compatible

$$H < \frac{M}{r}(1 - \mu\mu') + \mu W$$

$$< \frac{42,000}{9.36}(1 - 0.70 \times 0.36) + 0.70 \times 14,000$$

$$< 13,156 \text{ kN (satisfied)}$$

Eq. (20.15)	4	*Condition 3:* Soil remains elastic

$$\frac{mM}{I} \not> \gamma(K_P - K_A) \text{ where } \gamma(\text{submerged}) = 10 \text{ kN/m}^3$$

$$\frac{1 \times 42,000}{2685.7} \not> 10(3.69 - 0.27)$$

$$15.6 \not> 34.2 \text{ (satisfied)}$$

Eq. (20.16)	5	*Condition 4:* (M = external moment at base of well)

$$\sigma = \frac{W - \mu P}{A} \pm \frac{MB}{2I}; \quad P = \frac{M}{r}$$

Step 1 — ($I = 2685.7$ and not $\pi d^4/64$)

Step 1

$$P = \frac{42,000}{9.36} = 4487 \text{ kN}; \quad A = \frac{\pi d^2}{4} = 56.72 \text{ m}^2$$

$$\sigma = \frac{14,000 - 0.36 \times 4487}{-56.72} \pm \frac{42,000 \times 8.5}{2 \times 2685.7}$$

$$= 218 \pm 66 = 284 \text{ and } 152 \text{ kN/m}^2$$

Being less than the safe value of 600 kN/m², these values are acceptable.

Part—B Ultimate analysis (Rotation about 0.2*D* above base)

Sec. (20.9.1) — The following two conditions should be satisfied.

Eq. (20.20c)

$$\sigma = \frac{W}{A} \not> q_a; \quad (A = 56.72 \text{ m}^2) \text{ (Condition 1)}$$

Eq. (20.17) — $M_r = 0.7(M_b + M_s + M_f)$ and $M < M_r$ (Condition 2)

M = actual moment acting on the well.

1 — *Calculate stress at base in* kN/m²

$$\frac{W}{A} = \frac{14,000}{56.72} = 246; \quad q_a = 600$$

$246 \not> 600$ (kN/m²) is satisfied.

2 — *Calculate* M_b *(base moment)*

Eq. (20.18) — $M_b = (QB)(W \tan \phi)$

Table 20.1		$D/d = 15/8.5 = 1.76;$ $Q = 0.53 \times 0.6 = 0.32$
		$M_b = 0.32 \times 8.5 \times 14{,}000 \times 0.70 = 26{,}656$ kNm
	3	*Calculate M_s (side earth pressure-moment)*
Eq. (20.19)		$M_s = 0.1\gamma D^3 (K_P - K_A)L$
		$= 0.1 \times 10(15)^3 \times (3.69 - 0.27) \times 0.9 \times 8.5 = 88{,}300$ kNm
	4	*Calculate M_f (side friction moment)* $\delta = 20°$
Eq. (20.20a)		$M_f = 0.11\gamma (K_P - K_A) B^2 D^2 \sin \delta$
		$= 0.11 \times 10 \times 3.42 (8.5)^2 \times (15)^2 \times 0.34 = 20{,}793$ kNm
	5	*Find moment to be resisted at base*
		$M = 42{,}000$ kNm (given value)
		(Instead of multiplying M by load factor, we use the reduction factor for the existing moment.)
	6	*Estimate total resisting moment (with reduction factor $1/1.4 = 0.7$)*
Eq. (20.20b)		$M_r = 0.7(M_b + M_s + M_f)$ Should be more than M applied
		$= 0.7(26{,}656 + 88{,}300 + 20{,}246) = 94{,}641$ kNm $> 42{,}000$ kNm
		$M_r > M$ (Condition 2)
	7	*Final results*
		All conditions are satisfied. Hence safe.

REFERENCES

[1] Terzaghi K. and Peck, R.B., *Soil Mechanics in Engineering Practice*, John Wiley & Sons, New York, 1948.

[2] IRC 45 (1972), *Recommendations for Estimating the Resistance of Soil Below the Maximum Scour Level in the Design of Well Foundation*, IRC, New Delhi.

[3] IS 3955 (1967), *Indian Standard Code of Practice of Design and Construction of Well Foundations*, BIS, New Delhi.

[4] Public Works Department (P.W.D), Govt. of U.P., *Well Foundations for Road Bridges*, Bridge Series No. 1, Lucknow, 1961.

[5] Kurien, N.P., *Design of Foundation System—Principles and Practice*, Narosa Publishing House, New Delhi, 1992.

[6] Gopal Ranjan, and Rao, A.S.R., *Basic and Applied Soil Mechanics*, New Age International, New Delhi, 2000.

[7] Vijay Singh, *Well Foundations*, Nemchand and Brothers, Roorkee, 1981.

21

Foundation on Shrinking (Expansive) Soils

21.1 INTRODUCTION

All clays shrink on drying till the shrinkage limit is reached. They also swell if water is made available to them when they are dry. In addition, there are special clays called *expansive clays* in which this problem is very pronounced. The two main factors to be considered on these swelling soils are firstly the amount of swell and secondly the swelling pressure developed during swelling. These depend on the mineralogical composition and amount of the clay particles present in the soil. It is well known that montmorillonites absorb more moisture than illites, which can absorb more water than kaolinites because of the structural differences. It is also known that montmorillonites can be formed from many types of parent rocks. Thus, the expansive soils of Jordan are formed from the sedimentary limestone whereas the *black cotton soils of India* have been formed from igneous rocks like basalt in alkali environment in the presence of magnesium ions and absence of leaching. The latter conditions are available in climatic regions with seasonal rainfalls and high evaporation with little leaching. They exist in Andhra Pradesh, Maharashtra, Karnataka, Tamil Nadu, Bhopal and some other places. Leaching is present in places which receive heavy rainfall like Kerala or West Bengal and hence expansive soils are rarely found in these places. In actual practice, we find that most of the shrinkage cracking takes place in summer, which indicates that high shrinkage is the main culprit responsible for this problem encountered in expansive soils. We shall study the following aspects of these soils:

- Shrinkage and expansion characteristics of clays
- Methods of identification of expansive soils
- Direct measurement of the swell and the swell pressures
- Classification of damages in light buildings in expansive soils
- Principles of design of foundation in shrinking and expansive soils.

In all these topics, we shall deal with the general principles only and for detailed aspects specialized literature on the subject should be consulted.

21.2 SHRINKAGE AND EXPANSION OF CLAYS

Pores in soils are generally continuous and the size of the pores, to a large extent, depends on the grain size of the soil. The formula for the rise of fluids in capillary tubes H_c is as follows [1]:

$$H_c = \frac{2T \cos \alpha}{R \rho g} = \frac{0.15}{R} \text{ (approx. for water in soil pores)}$$

where

T = surface tension (0.0742 g/cm for water)
R = radius of capillary in cm, which depends on grain size of particle
ρ = density of the liquid
α = contact angle

Taking the value of $R = 0.01$ mm (0.001 cm) for sand and 0.0001 mm (0.00001 cm) for clays (i.e., 100 times less) results in a capillary rise of 150 mm for sands and 15 m for clays respectively. Observed heights in clays are much less, but easily 3 to 4 m. The upward rise of water in a capillary with rising level of water is called *active capillary*, denoted as H_{ca}, and the decreasing level of capillary water with lowering of free water level is called the passive capillary, H_{cp}. It can be seen from Fig. 21.1 that H_{cp} is greater than H_{ca}.

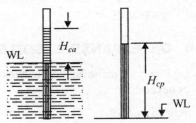

Fig. 21.1   Capillary rise in soils.

21.2.1 Shrinkage of Normal Clays

In partially saturated soils, which are drying from a wet to dry state, the local menisci produce contact stresses between individual particles as shown in Fig. 21.2. The intergranular pressure p_c is given by the following equation [1]:

$$p_c = \frac{\pi T}{2R}$$

where

$R = 0.001$ cm   (sand)
$ = 0.00001$ cm (clay)
$p_c = 0.116$ kg/cm^2
$ = 11.6$ kg/cm^2 (116 t/m^2), which is very high.

The smaller the radius of the particle, the greater will be the contact stress in the soil. Thus, when a clay soil is desiccated due to evaporation of water from the surface of the soil layer, the capillary menisci retreat into the narrowing pores exerting intergranular pressure leading to a decrease in volume and shrinkage. Conversely, when the wetted water reaches the menisci on the surface, it decreases the capillary pressure leading to the reduction of intergranular pressure. The volume of the soil increases and the soil swells. As in consolidation test, the recovery is not fully elastic.

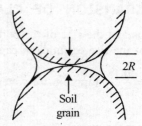

Fig. 21.2 Intergranular pressure in soils due to shrinkage of clays.

21.2.2 Difference between Normal Clays and Expansive Clays

All clays shrink when dried and swell when wetted due to the capillary action described above. However in some clay minerals like montmorillonite, the pore water not only changes the capillary forces, but the clay minerals themselves absorb water into the crystalline lattice and cause swelling. In such cases, the amount of water absorbed can be very high and so also its expansion. These clays are called expansive clays, as their swell can be much more than that of the clay with kaolinite minerals, which may be called as normal clays. Hence our first task is to identify the clay soils we meet and estimate their expansive properties.

21.3 IDENTIFICATION OF EXPANSIVE SOILS

We should consider the following levels of identification of these types of soils, as to whether the effects will be light, moderate or severe:

1. The identification by field inspection
2. The use of simple index properties to classify expansive clays
3. The direct measurement of the amount of free swell and swelling pressures.

21.3.1 Identification by Field Inspection

The major items to be checked by field identification are as listed below:

1. Does the ground crack up during dry seasons?
2. Does the soil become very sticky when wetted with water?
3. Do structures like compound walls and light buildings with shallow foundation around the region show signs of distress like tilting, lifting, cracking etc.?
4. Does the natural vegetation give any indication of expansive type of clay?
5. If there are wells, what is the variation of water level with seasons in them?
6. To the above list, we may add the simple free differential swell field test described in the next section.

21.3.2 Identification by Laboratory Tests

The principal laboratory tests used for identification are the less commonly used mineralogical tests and the more commonly used simple tests.

Mineralogical tests include:

1. Dye absorption tests
2. Differential thermal analysis
3. X-Ray diffraction technique
4. Electron microscopic examination
5. Chemical analysis

Except for the first two, these tests are costly and are more often used for research purposes than for routine analysis.

Simple laboratory tests, as mentioned below, are more commonly used than the above tests. Holtz and Gibbs [2] were the first to work on the identification of expansive soils by laboratory tests. In 1956, during their investigation on construction of linings for canal embankments in expansive soils for the U.S. Bureau of Reclamation (USBR), they proposed the simple free swell tests to forecast the expansion of soils. Their work on natural undisturbed soils indicated that the colloidal content (that is, fraction less than 0.001 mm size) plasticity index, shrinkage limit, and (L.L. – S.L.) (all the four properties taken together as a single criterion) can be used as indicators to predict volume change. Based on their work, USBR recommended Table 21.1 for the identification of expansive soils.

TABLE 21.1   TESTS FOR DEGREE OF EXPANSION OF CLAYS
(Ref. USBR Earth Manual – 1973)

Property of soil	Range of expansion (dry to saturated)			
	Low < 10%	Medium 10–20%	High 20–30%	Very high > 30%
Per cent soil less than 0.001 mm size	< 15	1–23	20–31	> 28
P.I. (%)	< 18	15–28	25–41	> 35
Shrinkage limit (%)	> 15	10–16	7–12	< 11
L.L. – S.L. (%)	0 – 20	20–30	30–60	> 60

Along with these results, other simple laboratory tests given in Table 21.2 should be also used for identification for expansiveness.

TABLE 21.2   TESTS FOR IDENTIFICATION OF EXPANSIVE SOILS

Name of test	Section reference
A. Index tests	
Simple free swell test	21.3.2(i)
Position on Plasticity Chart	21.3.2(ii)
Linear shrinkage (Shrinkage index)	21.3.2(iii)
Position on Activity Chart	21.3.2(iv)
B. Direct tests for swell pressures	
Oedometer free swell test	21.4.1(i)
Oedometer constant volume test	21.4.1(ii)
ASTM tests	21.4.2
Double oedometer tests	21.4.3

These are briefly described below in the order as indicated in the above table.

(i) *The simple free differential swell test:* This test should be distinguished from the oedometer free swell test. (Sec 21.4.1). This is a field test. It is described in IS 2720 (1977) series called *Tests for Soils*, Part 40, *Free swell index of soils*. The test consists of first placing two samples of equal volume of the whole dry soil (say 10 g each) in two identical measuring cylinders of 100 cc capacity. One of the cylinders is then filled with water and the other with kerosene oil up to the 100 cc mark. After stirring with a glass rod, the particles are allowed to settle down completely. The difference in swell expressed as a percentage gives the *swell index*, as the soil in kerosene oil does not swell. Soils are classified as shown in Table 21.3. Soils in which the free swell index is more than 35% are suspects and need to be studied further.

TABLE 21.3 SWELL POTENTIAL FROM SIMPLE DIFFERENTIAL FREE SWELL TESTS
[IS 2911 (1980) Part 3. Under-Reamed Piles, Appendix A]

Differential swell (Swell Index) %	Classification of swell potential
20	Low
20 – 35	Moderate
35 – 50	High
> 50	Very high (soil needs more study)

(*Note:* For test values over 35%, conventional shallow strip footings are not adequate.)

(ii) *Position on plasticity chart:* Casagrande has shown that it is possible to identify different types of clays from its position on the plasticity chart with respect to A-line. It should be remembered that plasticity tests give only the nature of the fine fraction and it is also necessary to examine the amount or percentage of the fines in the soil mass for predicting the behaviour of that sample. The position of expansive soils on the plasticity chart is shown in Fig. 21.3. Soils with less than 15% of fines (< 0.001 m) do not cause much trouble even if it is expansive.

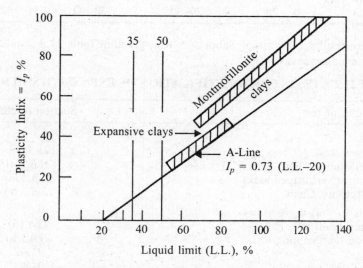

Fig. 21.3 Indentification of expansive clays by plasticity chart.

(iii) *Linear shrinkage*: The Shrinkage Index (L.L. – S.L.) has been used as a means of identification of expansive soils as shown in Table 21.1. A knowledge of the shrinkage limit of the various minerals also allows us to estimate the type of soil we are dealing with. They are as follows:

Montmorillonite — 10 to 15%
Illite — 15 to 18%
Kaolinite — 25 to 30%

(iv) *Position on the activity chart:* Identification on the basis of activity chart was evolved in South Africa and has been found applicable to soils found in India also. Positions of soils as depicted in Fig. 21.4 can be used for such identification. This perhaps is one of the most reliable simple tests and is very much used in practice. Diagrams can be made from case studies for each region. A diagram evolved for places around chennai is shown in Fig. 21.4(b).

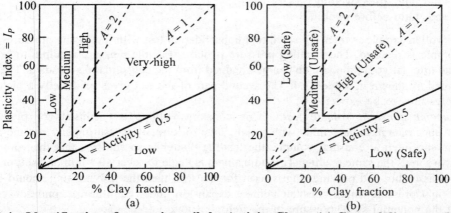

Fig. 21.4   Identification of expansive soils by Activity Chart: (a) General diagram; (b) diagram evolved for Chennai region.

21.4 DIRECT MEASUREMENT OF SWELL AND SWELL PRESSURE

In the third set of methods, we try to directly measure the swelling pressures. A large volume of research has been carried out to estimate the magnitude of swell pressures that will be experienced in the field by means of laboratory tests. As will be explained in Section 21.5, the structural methods adopted to overcome problems with swelling soils consist of either designing the foundation for these uplift pressure or trying to completely isolate these pressures from the foundation. For taking such decision we should know the magnitude of the pressures that can develop in the field. This is best done by direct measurement of these pressures in the laboratory. Only a short account of the IS and ASTM laboratory methods are given here and the original sources should be consulted for detailed procedures of the tests. Generally, a consolidometer (oedometer) is used for conducting these tests. In swell tests for undisturbed soils, the swelling pressure can be defined as the pressure needed to keep the volume of the soil under the lowest natural condition constant. For disturbed samples, the maximum proctor density can be used for the swell test.

21.4.1 IS 2720 (Part 411) 1977 Tests for Swelling Pressures

IS recommends two methods: (a) the oedometer free swell method and (b) the constant volume method. Each uses a consolidation cell for measuring swell pressures. These tests are briefly described below.

Oedometer free swell tests: An undisturbed sample as obtained at the lowest moisture content (taken in the end of summer season—April to June) or a compacted sample compacted to field density and moisture is taken in a consolidation ring (100 mm dia. and 25 mm height). Porous stones boiled in distilled water and in the saturated condition are placed in the cell. An initial seating load of .05, 0.5 or 1.0 kg/cm^2 as required (See Table 21.4) is applied and the sample is inundated by de-aired distilled water with the reservoir kept at the same level as the top of the sample. The sample is allowed to swell till equilibrium is reached, which will take 6 to 7 days. From the dial readings, the free swell can be obtained.

$$\text{Free swell} = \left[\frac{e_1 - e_0}{1 + e_0} \right] \tag{21.1}$$

where

e_1 = void ratio after swelling

e_0 = void ratio before swelling

The swollen sample is then subjected to a consolidation test with increasing pressures till the original volume is reached. The swelling pressure is defined as the pressure required to bring the sample to its original void ratio, which can be obtained from the consolidation test data. The results are interpreted as shown in Table 21.4. The second part of the test gives us directly a measure of the swell pressures to be expected.

Oedometer constant volume test: This constant volume test consists of placing the undisturbed specimen in the assembly with a dial gauge for directly measuring any volume change. To keep the specimen at constant volume, the loading platter is so adjusted that the volume dial gauge always shows the same reading. This adjustment is made for every 0.1 mm of swell or earlier. If a tri-axial assembly and proving ring is used for the test, then the proving ring should be very rigid. The final pressure under constant volume expansion under equilibrium conditions gives a measure of the potential swell pressure in the field.

$$\text{Swelling pressure} = \frac{\text{load for constant volume}}{\text{area of the specimen}}$$

21.4.2 ASTM Methods

Three methods called Methods A, B and C are recommended by ASTM. Like IS methods, they also use the consolidation apparatus for the tests. Tests A and B are similar to the IS consolidometer test except that in Test B, the vertical seating pressure is to be the same as that which exists in the field. Test C is more elaborate and uses a consolidation as well as a rebound curve for the interpretation of results to estimate the pre-consolidation pressures. (Thus, under ASTM we have the following tests.) Tests A and B are as follows:

1. Free Swell (FS) test where the sample is permitted to swell under a load of 0.07 kg/cm^2 and tested as in IS method to get the swell pressure.

2. Swell Overburden test where the initial load is the vertical in-situ overburden pressure.

3. Constant Volume Swell (CVS) test where the sample is allowed to swell but kept under constant volume by application of pressure. After the equilibrium is reached, the sample is unloaded to get rebound characteristics and swell pressure.

21.4.3 Double Oedometer Tests for Prediction of Heave

Jennings and Knight [3] proposed a double oedometer test for prediction of heave under a given water content. The principle of the test is to take two identical undisturbed samples of the same expected moisture content in two oedometers and subject both to a standard loading condition of 0.01 kg/cm^2 for about 30 minutes. Then, to the first oedometer, de-aired water is added and the soil is allowed to swell. At the conclusion of the free swell, a consolidation test is conducted to get the $(e - \log p)$ curve. The second specimen is not subjected to a free swell, but it is loaded with the same loads as used for the consolidation test of the first specimen. Use the two $(e - \log p)$ curves to make the virgin compression curves. For a given applied pressure, note the corresponding water content in saturated and natural water content lines as well as the differences in e, equal to Δe. The potential heave is given by the following expression:

$$\Delta H = \left[\frac{\Delta e}{1 + e_0}\right] H \qquad (21.2)$$

Due to many restraining factors, the heave in the field will be much less than that given by this test but the test is useful to give the magnitude of pressures that can be expected in the field.

21.4.4 Interpretation of Test Results

The following factors affect swelling of clay soils. They should all be taken together in judging the swelling potential of the soil.

1. The mineralogical composition of the clay (in many ordinary clays, the swelling pressures may not be appreciable).
2. The amount of particles less than 0.001 mm in the soil.
3. The initial moisture content or dry state of the soil. Drier the soil, more will be the swell pressure (see Fig. 21.5).
4. Initial dry density of the soil. Swell pressure increases with increasing dry density.
5. The surcharge (or downward load) on the soil. (The influence of this factor is not as much as is usually imagined.)

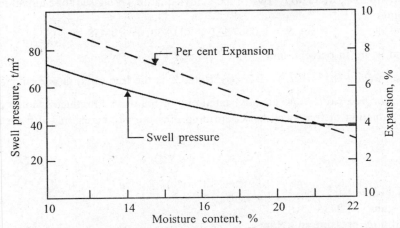

Fig. 21.5 **Variation of swell pressure and percentage expansion with initial moisture content.**

Table 21.4 gives a method of estimating the swell potential of soils from the results of the swell test on undisturbed samples [4]. The term 'free swell of soil' used in literature refers to the free swell obtained in the consolidometer tests and not the simple differential free swell.

TABLE 21.4 ESTIMATION OF SWELL POTENTIAL WITH CONSOLIDOMETER FREE SWELL

Class	Description of soil swelling	Per cent of swell under surcharge 0.05 kg/cm^2	Per cent of swell under surcharge 0.5 kg/cm^2	Estimated swell pressure (kg/cm^2)
1.	Very low	< 2	Nil	< 0.15
2.	Light	2–5	< 2	0.15–0.5
3.	Moderate	5–10	2–4	0.5–1.5
4.	Severe	10–13	4–6	1.5–5.0
5.	Very severe	> 13	> 6	> 5.0

21.4.5 Prediction of Swell Pressure from Index Properties

The following equations giving prediction of swell pressures and percentage swell are useful in preliminary investigation.

Pressure to restrain swell: Komornik and David proposed the following equation as an estimate of the pressure needed to restrain expansion to a 'tolerable' amount [5]:

$$\log P_s = \overline{2}.132 + 2.08(\text{L.L.}) + 0.665(\rho_d) - 2.69(w) \tag{21.3}$$

where

P_s = pressure in kg/cm^2

L.L. = liquid limit in decimal (60% as 0.60)

ρ_d = dry density in g/cm^3

w = water content in decimal

Estimation of free swell (%): Two of the many equations proposed for estimation of free swell are the following:

$$\log S_p = 0.0367(\text{L.L.}) - 0.0833(w) + 0.458 \tag{21.4}$$

where L.L. and w are in percent, and

$$S_p = 2.27 + 0.131(\text{L.L.}) - 0.27(w). \text{ Here, } S_p \text{ is the free swell in percentage.} \tag{21.5}$$

Reduction of free swell: As already stated one of the ways to reduce swell is to apply back pressure. The reduction of free swell by a confining pressure can be estimated from the following equation [5]:

$$S'_p = S_p (1 - A\sqrt{\sigma}) \tag{21.6}$$

where

S'_p = reduced swell

A = constant = 0.0735

σ = confining pressure in kN/m^2

21.5 CLASSIFICATION OF DAMAGES IN BUILDINGS

We will now deal with the fourth aspect, namely, type of damages of building in expansive soils. The scale of damages in buildings is usually classified as shown in Table 21.5.

TABLE 21.5   CLASSFICATION OF DAMAGES IN BUILDINGS

Degree of damage	Approximate crack width	Description
Negligible	≯ 0.1 mm	Hairline cracks
Very slight	≯ 1.0 mm	Cracks visible and can be easily repaired.
Slight	1 – 5 mm	Doors and windows may get affected. Cracks can be repaired.
Moderate	5 – 15 mm	Doors and windows get stuck; water tightness impaired. Repair may need replacement of some bricks in the wall.
Severe	15 – 25 mm	Walls leaning or bulging. Doors and window frames distorted. Section of wall may have to be replaced in repair.
Very severe	> 25 mm	Danger of instability. Needs rebuilding.

21.5.1 Causes and Types of Damages in Buildings on Expansive Clays

The different causes and types of structural damages that take place in expansive soils due to foundation movement can be briefly described as follows:

Case 1:   There is considerable migration of moisture in the soil under buildings. Moisture tends to build up in covered areas under buildings where there is no evaporation due to capillary action. It may take 3 to 4 years after construction to reach equilibrium. As shown in Fig. 21.6, in most places in India, the point of *equilibrium moisture* in the open field (sometimes called the neutral point) is reached at about 3 to 3.5 m depth.

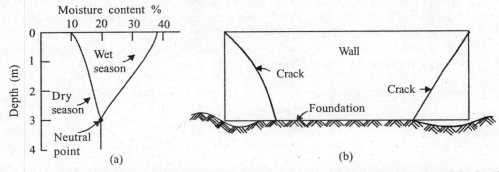

Fig. 21.6   Variation of ground moisture with season: (a) Variation of moisture with depth; (b) cracking of building due to loss of support as most common source of cracking.

Case 2: During dry seasons, the peripheral regions of buildings on clay can undergo large shrinkage compared to the middle of the building. Soil up to a depth of 3 to 3.5 m can be affected. This causes the soil to shrink away from the foundations along the periphery of buildings as shown in Fig. 26(b). If the foundation is rigid and strong, there will be no loss of support along the periphery and it may withstand it. Otherwise, the foundation also goes down with the soil. The soil in the interior does not shrink as much as the soil at the periphery thus causing differential settlements. During unexpected dry weather conditions which usually happen in the tropics, the problem becomes very acute. This is the reason that many buildings show cracks in the summer. Also damages usually occur only where the clay is at least 2 m deep and if the clay depth exceeds 4 m, damages always take place.

Case 3: During the rainy season, the dry soils along the periphery tend to pick up more moisture than the soil inside and swell. In the so-called expansive soils, the soil pressure due to this factor from below may be very high and can exert high pressures at the edges.

Case 4: It is also possible that if the soil in the interior of the building can pick up moisture from any source like leaky water pipes, it can also swell and produce high pressures or heave.

Case 5: Leakage from gully trap chambers (into which the wastewater pipes from bathrooms join the drainage system) usually placed near foundation of extermal walls. Leakage from these on to the foundation is a common cause of cracking of load bearing masonry walls in clay soils.

Thus, in short, in clay soils there is constant movement of the foundations with seasons due to shrinkage and swelling caused by changes in the moisture content. Decrease in moisture causes shrinkage. Access to water increases water content and hence the strength of clays.

21.5.2 Types of Damages and Cracks in Buildings on Expansive Clays

We may now examine the types of cracks that occur in buildings and explain them as follows:

1. If the soil along the exterior walls of the building shrinks away from the building along its periphery, we can expect horizontal cracks and separation of roofs or floors along the exterior due to loss of support as shown in Fig. 21.7(a).
2. If we examine walls running from the interior to the exterior, we will find that because of the settlement of the periphery, severe cracking can occur at the exterior ends as shown in Fig. 21.7(b). The seat of settlement can always be found by drawing a line normal to the line of the visible crack. The seat of settlement is the place where this normal meets the ground.
3. If the ends heave up (so that the middle is lower than the ends), cracks are formed as shown in Fig 21.7(c). The shear cracks at the ends are inclined and the middle cracks are wider at the base and narrower at the top.
4. If the middle part swells up, we can expect cracks as shown in Fig 21.7(d) with the middle cracks wider at the top and narrower at the base.

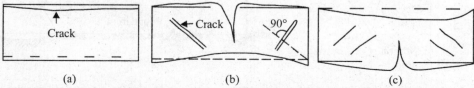

Fig. 21.7 **Pattern of cracks in buildings in expansive soils: (a) Cracking due to settlement along the length of the building; (b) settlement at ends; (c) settlement at the middle.**

5. The most common crack pattern found is the crack, at corners which corresponds to the downward movement of the corners of buildings or the junction of two external walls. These cracks start at the ground level near about the centre of walls, rising diagonally to the top corner of the two walls as in Fig. 21.7(b).
6. Large loss of support can also produce vertical cracks.
7. Cracks can also occur on the floor of the building in conformity with loss of support or uplift of the floor. Floors in expansive soils should be always laid on lime-treated original soil with good sand filling of at least 300 mm. Otherwise, they should be built as suspended floors not supported on the ground.
8. Even in buildings built to produce high foundation pressures to offset expansion, the foundation can go down due to shrinkage. Subsequent saturation, because of the heavy loads, will not be able to lift it up to its original position. However, portions with lighter pressures may swell up, thus causing large differential movements. Such cases occur in columns with footings and filler walls at ground level of multistoreyed buildings. Also differential bearing pressures on different columns can produce differential movement in columns of multistoreyed buildings. These produce corresponding types of cracks.

Thus the common damages observed in ordinary buildings in expansive soils are the following:

- Separation of wall and roof slab
- Uplift of interior footings
- Diagonal cracks near openings
- Separation of interior floorings from exterior walls
- Horizontal cracks on the exterior and interior walls oriented in the long span direction of the top slab
- Vertical and diagonal cracks on exterior walls along short span direction of the top slab
- Longitudinal cracks in roof slab near interior walls due to cantilever action caused by settlement of exterior walls
- Corner cracks as described above.

21.5.3 Loss of Support and Expansive Pressures in Clay Soils

From the above discussion, it is evident that in shallow foundations for ordinary buildings *on all clays* loss of support is the major problem. In most ordinary clays (kaolin and illite clays) providing for loss of support can mitigate many of the problems that may occur due to the foundation movement. On the other hand, with very expansive soils, we have to deal not only with loss of support, but also with the very large upward pressures that can develop due to migration of moisture in different parts of the structure with seasons. The same problems have been found to occur in boiler rooms or other places where there is possibility of heating up the foundations with subsequent loss of moisture from the foundation. *Accumulation of moisture from leaking pipes or other sources of water leakage can also cause severe problem in expansive soils.*

In many regions in the tropics like parts of Chennai city, the soil may be formed by river deposits of alluvial clay. The top layers in many such cases have been subjected to seasonal desiccation in summer. Soil up to 5 m depth consists of stiff, black or brown clay, which shrink in dry summer and expand during rainy season. Below this layer, the deposits remain unconsolidated and soft. Even though pile foundations are the natural choice for the heavy loads in these strata, light buildings can be built on shallow foundations for economy. Under-reamed piles are not applicable in such situations where the soil strength decreases with depth. In these cases, loss of support becomes the major problem in the design of foundations. Rigid foundations at shallow depths are most suitable for ordinary, low cost buildings in these soils.

21.6 PRINCIPLES OF DESIGN OF FOUNDATIONS IN EXPANSIVE SOIL DEPOSITS

Table 21.6 gives a summary of the solutions of problems in expansive soils.

TABLE 21.6 SOLUTION OF PROBLEMS IN EXPANSIVE SOILS

Group No.	Method	Applications
1	Purely structural solution	a. Use heavy foundation pressure to offset expansion pressure
		b. Make structure strong and rigid to resist forces and bridge over lack of contact of foundation due to shrinkage of soil. Use rigid designed rafts. Construction to be done just after rainy season.
		c. Make structure flexible so that settlements and uplifts do not affect them.
		d. Use pile foundation (under reamed for light loads)
		e. Provide basement with foundation below the neutral point.
2.	Purely environmental solution or mitigation of the effects (Zone below 3.5 m depth is not affected by climatic change.)	a. Construct structure with foundation level below active zone or use under reamed piles.
		b. Replace expansive soil up to 3.5 m depth from G.L. below foundation by sand cushion and a *cohesive, non-shrinkable (CNS) layer overfill.*
		c. Stabilize soil by lime slurry injection to 3.5 m depth
3.	Combination of 1 and 2	Mitigate effects by method 2 and design foundation by method 1

The general principles of design of foundation are as follows:

The types of foundations to be used in expansive soils depend on the soil profile at the site. Two types of situation may be envisaged. In the first, the soil strength is constant or increases with depth as in residual soil; and in the second, soft deposits occur below the strong top layers as described in Section 21.5.3. In any case, the shrinkage and swell in the foundation is due to changes in the soil profile caused by moisture. Measurements show that in most places in South India, moisture changes take place for a depth of about 3 to 3.5 m only.

The type of foundation to be adopted should depend obviously on the percentage of *swell and swelling pressures expected.* Thus, for example, if the foundation material is only slightly expansive (made of ordinary illite or kaolinite clays and not expansive clays), only *simple structural solutions* like lime treatment with soil cushion, provision of R.C. foundation with plinth beams and

R.C. bands at lintel levels can lead to a successful solution for the construction of a light building. However, in a very highly expansive soil, the *environmental solutions* (described in the next section) of total replacement of soil up to a depth of 3.5 m below the footings or use of under-reamed piles or regular piles are the only acceptable solutions. Continuous footings at shallow depths are not suitable for such soils.

21.7 ENVIRONMENTAL SOLUTIONS

While dealing with expansive soils, instead of solving the problem structurally we can change the environment to suit the structure.

The following are some of the observations regarding such environmental solutions:

1. The method to be used depends on the potential expansion of the soil, which should be always ascertained by soil investigations.
2. Any new construction on expansive soils should be carried out just after the rainy season so that when covered with slabs or beams the swell will be minimal.
3. Adopt a depth of foundation below zone of climatic change by using under-reamed piles, piers or pads at adequate depth with grade or plinth beams construction at ground level. The grade beams themselves should be isolated from the ground in trenches filled up with suitable soils or sand.
4. Soil replacement is another solution. We may replace the soil in the active zone with good non-expansive soil.
5. Use of lime columns.

21.7.1 Soil Replacement Technique

Replacement (exchange) technique to mitigate the expansion can be classified into two groups: (a) In the first case, all the soils of expansive nature up to the depth of moisture changes are replaced by sand or other suitable material. (b) Replacement of a limited thickness is provided (as in the case of grade beams) and the balance of the heave is provided for by structural strength.

A somewhat ingenious soil replacement method known as compensating sand cushions is shown in Fig. 21.8(a) has been suggested by Russian investigators for heavily loaded foundations [6].

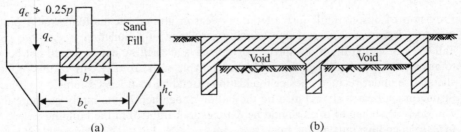

Fig. 21.8 **Remedial measure for shallow foundation in expansive soils: (a) Sand cushion; (b) rigid mat.**

It is designed to reduce the magnitude of non-uniform heave of expansive soils. As can be seen from the figure, when swelling occurs, the sand bed is assumed to heave up at the places where the downward pressure is the least. Due to upward swelling pressure, a hard core is automatically formed in the sand under the footing and this is assumed to assist the sideward movement of the sand. Experiment showed that fine sand acts as a better cushion and increasing the grain size of the sand had a bad or adverse effect on the performance of the cushion. Field observations have also confirmed that when the soil below the foundation heaves, only the lightly loaded part of the sand cushion will heave and the foundation will not undergo significant movement. It is also necessary that the pressure due to backfill q in Fig. 21.8(a) should not exceed 0.25 times the pressure exerted by the footing at the unloaded portions of the sand cushions. For this purpose, the depth of foundation can be kept at minimum as allowed at the site. Because of these requirements the mechanism as described above may not act well with very lightly loaded foundation pressures.

The use of compensating layer is more beneficial under strip footings compared to individual columns footings since the former type is more rigid to withstand sideway expansion and thus assist in the formation of the hard-core mechanism under the foundation. It should be remembered that the exterior sides of a building can have adverse effects due to moisture migration if sand is used as total replacement material. The sand should be covered with a cohesive non-shrinkable (CNS) material like murum, red earth with enough lines, which will not allow rainwater to seep through easily and cause unnecessary expansion of the soil at the interior. Sand allow free flow of water into the foundation, which should be avoided.

21.7.2 Use of Lime Columns

We can alter the nature of soil which causes trouble to the building by lime injection or lime piles. It has been reported that addition of lime drastically reduces the plastic index and increases the shrinkage limit of expansive clayey soils. An addition of about 5 per cent of lime seems to increase the strength considerably (6 to 8 times) and decreases the expansion of soils. Thus, the addition of 2 to 8 per cent of lime by weight of the soil treated can considerably improve the soil. In construction of pavements, in expansine soils lime has been recommended to be mixed with soil and compacted. For treatment of existing foundations of buildings, lime slurry injections can be used with lime in the form of $Ca(OH)_2$. However, in new buildings, *sand lime piles* in a triangular grid in plan has been found to increase strength and decrease the expansion. Ground unslaked lime (CaO) is found to give better results than slaked lime $Ca(OH)_2$ in piles for improving the properties of expansive (shrinkable) clays, perhaps due to the heat generated by it during the chemical reactions.

21.7.3 Other Environmental Protections

1. Provision of aprons built just after rainy season around the buildings help protect the moisture from escaping and thus causing shrinkage of foundation.
2. Tall trees in which the roots spread out sideways at shallow depth should not be allowed to grow very near buildings founded on shrinkable soils. To take care of this problem, we should use under-reamed piles or foundation extending to at least 5 m below ground level. Strong grade beams should also tie the building together. Roots rarely go more than 3 to 4 m deep. Distance of trees should be K times its height from the building where $K = 0.7$ to 2.0 depending on type of trees.
3. It is usually prescribed that foundations on expansive soils should be constructed just after the rains when the soils are fully saturated to the fully expanded condition. Otherwise, the soil should be fully saturated by artificial watering. However, this solution is not fully applicable in the tropics where construction activities may extend over a full year during which the foundation soil may undergo one full cycle of expansion and shrinkage before the full design load is usually applied.

21.8 STRUCTURAL SOLUTIONS

A summary of the structural solutions is given in Table 21.6. Some of the structural solutions are discussed below.

21.8.1 Provide a Rigid Foundation

Some of the types of rigid shallow foundations commonly used with some success in Tamil Nadu in *moderately shrinkable* soils are shown in Fig. 21.9.

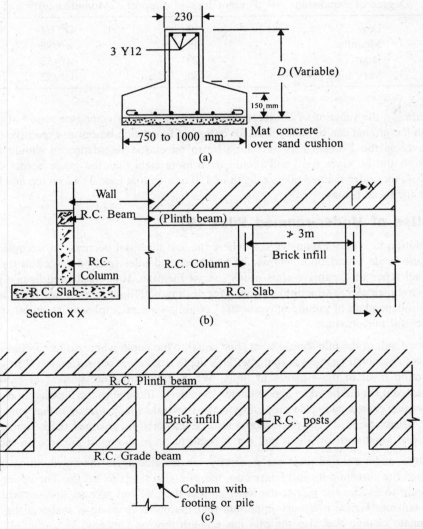

Fig. 21.9 Types of rigid foundations in shrinkable clay soils with increasing stiffness: (a) T beam strip foundation; (b) virendel frame with brick infill acting as becams on elastic foundation; (c) brick infilled virendel girder on piles or stub columns.

21.8.2 T Beams as Strip Footings for Walls

The Building Research Advisory Board [6] and Lytton [7] have recommended slabs and beams on expansive soils to be designed on the basis of loss of support as a beam on elastic foundation. The loss of support and consequent coefficient for maximum moment (as shown in Table 21.7) has been recommended on the basis of research conducted at College of Engineering, Guindy [8] now known as Anna University.

TABLE 21.7   LOSS OF SUPPORT AND MOMENT COEFFICIENT

Degree of expansion	Percent loss of support	Moment coefficient
Low	10	$wl^2/160$
Medium	15	$wl^2/88$
High	20	$wl^2/53$
Very high	30	$wl^2/32$

w = UDL on beam of span L

Accordingly, the value of $wl^2/30$ recommended by IS 2911 for composite action of grade beams supported on the ground can be safely used for design of foundation beams an expansive soil also [9].

However as the T beam acts as a long beam on elastic foundation, it should be properly designed. It should be more rigid and should have more steel than the grade beams described in Section 21.8.4, for under-reamed piles, a depth of 450 mm with at least 3Y12 on top and bottom may be required for these beams.

21.8.3 Use of Under-reamed Piles [9]

The best solution in highly expansive soil where the soil does not decrease in strength with depth is the pile and beam foundation. The use of under-reamed piles (piles enlarged at the base) as a remedy for all types of expansive soils needs special mention. It is considered as one of the most efficient environmental and structural solutions for dealing with light to moderate loads in expansive soils. It acts independent of ground movements. The following principles of its action are important for its successful performance:

1. The depth of the pile should be at least equal to the depth where no loss in moisture occurs due to seasonal changes in that site. This depth is taken as approximately 3 to 3.5 m below ground level in most places in India. Where large trees are present or expected to be planted it should be taken approximately 5 m deep. If the piles are founded in regions where moisture change takes place, the pile will also move along with the soil in that zone. This should be strictly avoided. The piles should also be anchored by enlarged bulbs formed below the neutral point with sufficient pull out strength to offset the uplift pressure on the pile.

2. These under-reamed piles are generally not isolated from the surrounding soil. Hence, when the surrounding soil heaves up, the pile also tends to lift up. The under-reaming is meant to anchor the pile at the base, so that the pile can take up this upward movement in tension. Hence it is very important that the under-reaming is made in the zone of no climate change and also the pile has enough tension capacity.

3. The grade and plinth beams on the top of piles should be tied properly on these piles and the pile reinforcements should be properly anchored into these beams at the pile supports with enough negative steel continuous over the piles.

4. The grade beams themselves should be preferably isolated from the expansive soils by suitable methods. IS 2911 Part 3 on '*Under-reamed Piles*' gives us the details of design and construction of this structural system.

5. It is recommended that in South India, construction of these piles should commence immediately at the end of the principal (N.E.) monsoon i.e. January to February and the full load should be allowed to act before the onset of the next monsoon (July-August). Piles constructed in accordance to this have been found to give good results. The details of under-reamed piles are shown in Fig. 21.10.

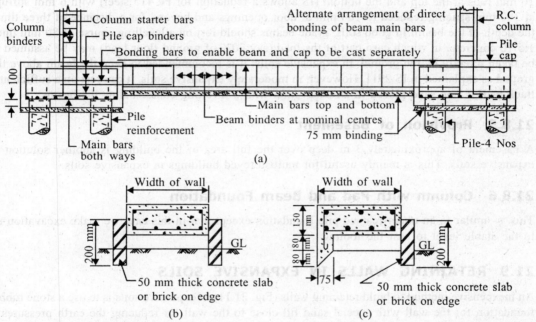

Fig. 21.10   Details of under-reamed piles, pile cap and grade beam: (a) General arrangements; (b) interior plinth beams; (c) exterior plinth beams (IS 2911 Part III).

21.8.4   Design of Grade Beams

Rectangular grade beams are used below walls to support them between columns on footings or between under-reamed piles. Their design can be based on their action:

1. Grade beam between columns on footings supported on the ground. In this case, lintel action can be assumed, with a 60° triangular masonry load, the side loading being transmitted directly to the column by arch action. The load in the triangle is directly transmitted to the ground through the beam. For full action as described above, the wall should be at least 0.86 times the span of the beam.

2. Grade beams connecting under-reamed piles. These beams are constructed as continuous beams directly over the piles with masonry walls above. The piles may or may not project above the beams. The grade beams take the load to the piles. According to IS 2911 Part 3 for considering composite action of grade beam with walls (as deep beams), the minimum height of wall shall be 0.6 times the beam span and the brick strength should be not less

than 3 N/mm². Concentrated loads, and door and window openings disturb this composite action. Considering such composite action. IS recommends the following B.M. coefficients for their design when it supports walls up to a maximum height of two storeys with load bearing walls.

— Beams supported from below, till the wall gains strength: $wl^2/50$.
— Beams not so supported from below: $wl^2/30$

The minimum depth of the grade beam should be 150 mm. There should be a minimum of two 10 mm rods at the top and the bottom (IS allows a reduction for Fe 415 steel) with 6 mm stirrups at 300 mm spacing reduced to 100 mm at door openings and beyond for a distance of three times the depth of the beam. In good soils, grade beams should rest on a levelling course of 80 mm thick 1:5:10 concrete, in which case part of the load (say 20% of ground floor load) may be assumed to be taken directly by the ground. In expansive soils, it is recommended to keep the beam above the ground as explained in IS 2911. However, in moderately expansive soils, it can rest on a sufficiently thick bed of fine sand placed in an excavation with a levelling course below the beams.

21.8.5 Provision of Basement

A basement of approximately 3 m deep over the full area of the building is another solution in expansive soils. This is mainly useful for multistoreyed buildings in expansive soils.

21.8.6 Column with Pad and Beam Foundation

This is similar to an under-reamed pile foundation except that in this case we make excavation up to the stable level to cast the footing.

21.9 RETAINING WALLS IN EXPANSIVE SOILS

An inexpensive method to build retaining walls (Fig. 21.11) in expansive soils is to use a stone rubble foundation for the wall with special sand fill close to the wall for reducing the earth pressures.

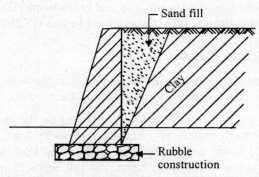

Fig. 21.11   Construction of retaining walls in expansive soils.

21.10 CONSTRUCTION OF NEW FLOOR SLABS IN CLAY SOILS

It will be a good practice to treat the existing clayey ground on which the floors are to be placed with lime spread on the surface or on short lime piles. Fill material under floors should be locally available sand (fine or coarse). The advantage of providing free draining granular base under floors far exceeds its disadvantages. It is also a good practice to isolate the flooring or floor slab from the walls, grade beams, columns etc. Doorframes also should not be supported directly on floor slabs but hung from sides and top if necessary in such a way that expansive forces are not transmitted directly to the upper floors. In extreme cases the floor above the ground should be built as suspended floors not touching the ground at all.

21.11 TREATMENT OF CRACKED BUILDINGS

If an existing building that was constructed without proper planning has cracked, the following remedial measures can be tried. As a first step an examination of the foundation soil should be made to see as to what type of swelling soils (low, medium or high) we are dealing with. In general, the aim should be to treat the soil underneath and also try to prevent change of moisture content to take place during the various seasons. The following remedies are recommended for moderately cracked building in moderately expansive soils:

1. The foundation can be treated by lime injection called *lime slurry pressure injection*. We drill holes 5 to 10 cm dia. at 1.8 to 2.5 m spacing as near the walls as possible and deeper than the foundation level. These holes are filled with 20 to 40% lime solution. The level of lime solution is maintained for some time to allow the lime to seep through. Alternatively, pressure grouting is employed, using 0.3 kg of lime per litre of water at 200–400 psi.

2. To minimize moisture differentials likely to develop in the foundation with time, sand piles 20 mm dia. can be built around the area at about 1.2 m away from the wall and to depths below the foundation of the building. These piles are to be interconnected with a 30 cm wide, 15 cm deep drain filled with sand. This system can be watered in dry season to reduce moisture change in the surrounding soil.

3. Aprons around the outer walls can be built as a slab in lime concrete laid over a well compacted cohesive non-expansive soil (CNS) layer. A CNS layer of about 0.5 m is then laid over the slab, to make it impermeable.

4. All cracks in the building should be closed with lime gauged motor. Large cracks in walls should be stitched with band stones or pre-cast mortar blocks with 8 mm steel rods placed in its centre or with steel rods placed in cement mortar. (Steel should be embedded in mortar and should not touch the bricks for preventing corrosion.)

In very high expansive soils, these remedies may not work and it may be necessary to underpin the building and construct a new, well designed foundation.

21.12 SUMMARY

In constructing foundations on clayey soils, it is always advisable to test the swell potential of the soil as described in this chapter. Depending on the expansion anticipated, potential solutions (environmental, structural or a combination of these) should be prescribed. In most situations— except where the strength of the foundation soil decrease with depth, the use of under-reamed piles as foundation in expansive soils is the best solution for low rise buildings. Where such piles cannot be used, light buildings on low expansive soils may be built on continuous rigid foundations like T beams or Virendel frames combined with lime-treatment of the soil under these structures. Use of suitably designed grade beams and plinth beams greatly reduce cracking of these buildings.

EXAMPLE 21.1 (Prediction of expansion from index test result)

The following values were obtained as index properties of a silty clay from a building site in Anna Nagar in Chennai. Check for the expansive properties of the material.

Plot the values of the samples on (1) the activity chart and (2) the plasticity chart and state whether these soils are likely to be expansive.

Sample No.	Depth (m)	Clay %	L.L. %	P.L. %	P.I. %
1	3.0	56	52	26	26
2	8.0	67	64	32	32
3	2.0	58	48	24	24
4	11.0	69	62	30	32
5	1.5	56	52	26	26
6	4.0	67	62	30	32
7	5.0	59	50	24	26
8	10.0	64	66	30	36

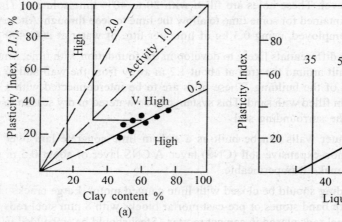
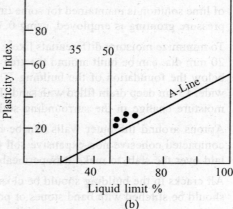

Fig. E.21.1

As can be seen from the figures, the results of all the samples in both the plots are located near the high to very high expansive zones. Hence the soil at the site may be considered as being of the expansive type.

(*Note:* In addition, these samples, when tested for free swell, gave results of 30 to 65% (ref. Table 21.3) confirming the conclusion that the soil is expansive.)

EXAMPLE 21.2 (Calculation of swell pressure)

The following data were obtained for a silty clay with more than 50% fines: L.L. = 52%; natural water content 15% (0.15), and dry density 16 kN/m^3 (1.6 g/cm^3). Estimate the swell pressure, free swell and the possible heave if it is to be loaded by a mat for a four-storeyed building at 15 kN/m^2 per storey [3].

Ref.	Step	Calculations
Sec. 21.4.5 Eq. (21.3) Table 21.4	1	*Calculate expansive pressure* $\log P_s = \overline{2}.132 + 2.08(L.L.) + 0.665(\rho_d) - 2.69(w)$ $\quad = \overline{2}.132 + (2.08 \times 0.52) + (0.665 \times 1.6) - (2.69 \times 0.15)$ $\quad = \text{T}.872$ i.e. $P_s = 0.74$ kg/cm^2 Swell pressure is 74 kN/m^2. The swelling can be described as moderate.
Eq. (21.4) Eq. (21.5)	2	*Calculate free swell* *Method 1.* $\log S_p = 0.0367(L.L.) - 0.083(w_d) + 0.458$ $\quad = 0.0367(52) - 0.083(15) + 0.458$ $\quad = 10.25\%$ *Method 2.* $S_p = 2.27 + 0.132(52) - 0.274(15) = 4.97$ $\quad = 5\%$ approx. Assume average of (1) and (2) = 7.5%
Eq. (21.6)	3	*Estimate swell if we apply a back pressure of 60 kN/m^2* $S'_p = S_p(1 - 0.0735\sqrt{\sigma})$ $\quad = 7.5(1 - 0.0735\sqrt{60})$ $\quad = 3.23\%$ (free swell reduced to = 3.23%) If the depth of swelling soil is 3 m, total swell = 3.23 × 3000/100 = 100 mm (approx.). This assumes that the soil is uniformly dry for the whole depth of 3 m. Even a 50% swell, i.e. 5 cm (2 inches), is very high for the foundation.

EXAMPLE 21.3 (Uplift forces in piles in expansive soils)

Estimate the uplift on the shaft of a pile of 250 mm diameter passing through expansive soil around it for a depth of 3 m. Assume a vertical swelling pressure of 200 kN/m^2 (2 kg/cm^2). (As can be seen from Table 21.4 this soil can be classified as severely expansive.)

Ref.	Step	Calculations
	1	*Assume side uplift* [4] We usually assume side uplift as follows: Side uplift = 15% of vertical uplift pressure is commonly used $\quad = 0.15 \times 200 = 30$ kN/m^2
	2	*Calculate total uplift from side only* $U = \pi DL(f_u) = 3.14 \times 0.25 \times 3 \times 30$ $\quad = 70$ kN. (This amounts to 7 tons.)

REFERENCES

[1] Terzaghi, K. and R.B. Peck, *Soil Mechanics in Engineering Practice*, John Wiley & Sons, New York, 1948.

[2] Holtz, W.G. and H.J. Gibbs, *Engineering Properties of Expansive Clays*, Transaction ASCE, 1956.

[3] Jennings, J.E. and E. Knight, *The Prediction of Heave from Double Oedometer Test*, Symposium on Expansive Soils, South African Institution of Engineers, 1957.

[4] Chen, F.H., *Foundations on Expansive Soils*, Elsevier Science, New York, 1988.

[5] Bowles, J.E., *Foundation Analysis and Design*, International Edition, McGraw-Hill, Singapore, 1988.

[6] *Criteria for Selection and Design of Residential Slabs on Ground*, Research Report Building Research Advisory Board, Washington, 1968.

[7] Lytton, R.L., *Design Criteria for Residential Slab and Gillage Rafts on Reactive Clays*, Research Report, CSIRC, Melbourne, 1970.

[8] Boominathan, S., *On Foundation Practice for Light Structures in Madras City*, Design of Foundations and Detailing, Published by Association of Engineers, Tamil Nadu, Madras, 1992.

[9] IS 2911, 1980, Part 3, *Under-reamed Piles*, Bureau of Indian Standards, New Delhi.

22

Flexible Retaining Structures — Sheet Pile Walls and Braced Excavations

22.1 INTRODUCTION

In Chapters 16 and 17, we dealt with earth pressures on rigid retaining structures. However, for waterfront structures where the upper layers of the soil are weak to support foundations of gravity or other type of rigid walls and also where dewatering of foundation renders construction of foundations difficult, we usually resort to sheet pile walls. They are also used as temporary supports for excavation of earth for construction of foundation. They are called *flexible retaining structures*. Another type of wall for retaining earth is the reinforced earth walls which we will discuss in Chapter 26.

It is also important to note the difference in the modes of failure of rigid and flexible walls. Rigid walls are assumed to fail by sliding or by rotation about the base. On the other hand, sheet piles being flexible and elastic, a wall like an anchored bulk head will fail by rotating about the top anchor or by bulging (or yielding) between the dredge level and the anchor. It can also fail by rotating about its base. In this chapter, we will briefly explain how to estimate the stability conditions of these flexible retaining walls.

22.2 HISTORICAL DEVELOPMENT

Wooden sheet piles (with tongue and groove) were the first to be used from very early days. Later on, reinforced concrete sheet piles were also used. As early as in 1820, cast iron sheet piles were tried but because of their brittleness, the trials were not successful. With the advent of steel rolling techniques, the use of steel sheet piles has become extensive. Today great importance is attached to the shape of their cross section and the strength of the interlocks in tension which allow them to act as continuous walls. They are extensively used for waterfront structures, cofferdams, etc. The classical method of analysis of anchored walls was the elastic line method. In 1931, Blum developed in Germany, the equivalent beam method. Around 1950 large scale tests on sheet piles in sand were made at Princeton in U.S.A for fixed earth support method for sand and by Rowe in U.K. for free earth support method in sand and clay. The simplified methods of analysis are based on these investigations. The most modern methods to solve these problems are based on the finite element methods. However, in this chapter we will deal only with the simple methods of analysis based on statics.

22.3 TYPES OF SHEET PILE WALLS

Though there are many types of flexible walls, we will deal only with the following simple types to illustrate the principles involved in their design:

- Cantilever sheet pile walls
- Anchored sheet pile walls.

In the cantilever type, simple straight sheet piles are driven into the soil to retain earth as shown in Fig. 22.1. When the height of earth to be retained becomes large, we tie back the top of the wall with an anchor and such types are called *anchored sheet pile walls* or *anchored bulk heads*. They can act with hinge at the base or fixed at the base depending on the depth of penetration of these piles. The cantilever walls are assumed to act as simple cantilevers. Anchored sheet pile walls are generally analysed by either the free earth support method or the fixed earth support method explained in Sections 22.6 and 22.7, respectively.

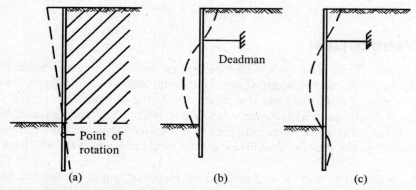

Fig. 22.1 Action of sheet pile walls: (a) Cantilever type; (b) anchored bulkhead driven to shallow depth; (c) anchored bulkheads driven to deeper depths.

22.4 CANTILEVER SHEET PILE WALLS

These piles derive stability from their penetration below the dredge level. They are assumed to fail by rotation about a point at or a little above the lower end of the sheet piles. Regarding the distribution of pressures the back side of the sheet pile is acted on by active earth pressure, and the front side below the dredge line is acted on by passive pressure. The distribution of pressures is commonly assumed to be according to Rankine's theory. We have to determine the required depth of penetration D and the maximum bending moment in the pile. We use the following equations of statics to determine minimum depth of penetration D below the dredge line.

$$\Sigma P = 0$$
$$\Sigma M \text{ (about the base of pile)} = 0.$$

A suitable safety factor is also built into the design by either increasing the value of depth of penetration obtained by theory by 30 to 40% or by assuming that the passive pressure developed in front of the pile is only 50 to 75% of the theoretical value. The bending moment at the point where shear force is zero gives the maximum bending moment.

The approximate depth of penetration needed for cantilever walls in cohesionless soils can be taken as follows (H = height above dredge line) [1]:

Nature of sand deposit	Depth of penetration
1. Dense	$0.75H$
2. Firm	$1.0H$
3. Loose	$1.5H$
4. Very loose	$2.0H$

22.4.1 Analysis of Cantilever Wall in Cohesionless Soils

The cantilever wall is shown in Fig. 22.12(a). The wall is assumed to rotate about a point O above the bottom end of the pile. The theoretical pressure diagram neglecting effect of submergence will be as shown in Fig. 22.2(a). By using $\Sigma P = 0$ and by equating the moment of forces about the base of the pile we can determine D, the needed depth of penetration of the pile.

Simplification for cohesionless soils: Usually in cohesionless soil a simplified pressure diagram as shown in Fig. 22.2(b) is used instead of the theoretical diagram [Fig. 22.2(a)] for analysis. It simpley assumes active pressure on earth side and passive pressure on the dredged side. Without using $\Sigma P = 0$, we get the value of D by taking moment about the base as shown.

$$P_2(D/3) = P_1\left(\frac{H + D}{3}\right)$$

where P_1 is the total active pressure and P_2 is the total passive pressure.

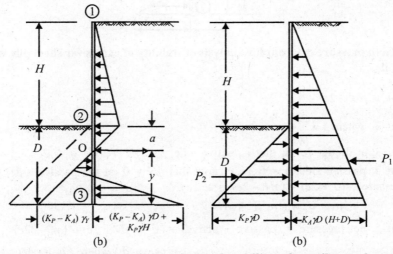

Fig. 22.2   Earth pressure diagrams for analysis of stability of cantilever sheet pile walls in granular soils: (a) Active and passive pressures from theory; (b) simplified pressure diagram for approximate analysis.

The value of D obtained is increased by 30 to 40%. This is illustrated by Example 22.1. The maximum bending moment can be determined by drawing the shear force diagram and finding the bending moment at the point where the shear force is zero.

22.4.2 Analysis of Cantilever Wall in Cohesive Soils

As the cantilever wall is pushed out from the landside, passive pressure develops on the waterside. From Bells earth pressure theory, $p_A = \gamma z K_A - 2c\sqrt{K_A}$. But,

$$\phi = 0 : K_A = 1 = K_P$$
$$p_A = \gamma z - 2c = \bar{q} - 2c$$

Similarly, $p_P = \gamma z + 2c = \bar{q} + 2c$.

With this relationship, we get the pressure diagram shown in Fig. 22.3.

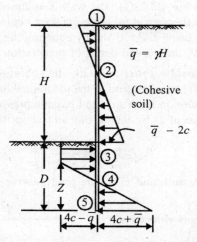

Fig. 22.3 **Earth pressure diagram for analysis of stability of cantilever sheet pile wall in cohesive soils.**

At point 1, $p = -2c$

At point 2, where $z = \dfrac{2c}{\gamma}$, $p = 0$

At point 3, at dredge level, that is, active side, $p = \gamma H - 2c = \bar{q} - 2c$

At point 3, passive side, $p = 0 + 2c$ (note that $\gamma H = 0$ on the passive side)

Net pressure $= (0 + 2c) - (\gamma H - 2c) = 4c - \gamma H$

$$= 4c - \bar{q} \text{ where } \bar{q} = \gamma H$$

At point 5, net pressure $= $ (passive + active) $= (\bar{q} + \gamma D + 2c) - (\gamma D - 2c)$

$$= (4c + \bar{q}) \text{ where } (\bar{q} = \gamma H)$$

After drawing the pressure diagram, we equate the horizontal forces and also the moment of forces *about the base of the wall to zero*. That is,

$$\Sigma P = 0$$

$$\Sigma M \text{ about point 5} = 0 \text{ (i.e. moment about the base of wall)}$$

The value of D obtained is increased by 40% as a safety factor.

22.4.3 Stability Number for Sheet Piles in Cohesive Soils [1]

If the net pressure is zero at dredge level of point 3, there will be no stability. This condition happens when

$$4c - \gamma H = 0 \quad \text{or} \quad H = \frac{4c}{\gamma}$$

This relationship is similar to that of an unsupported cut in clay soil.

The number $c/\gamma H = 0.25 = S$ is called the stability number.

To include the effect of adhesion, c_a between soil and pile S is also expressed as follows:

$$S = \frac{c}{\gamma H} \sqrt{1 + (c_a/c)} \times (F.S.)$$

The value of the expression within the square root works out to 1.25 approximately.

$$S = \frac{c}{\gamma H} \times 1.25, \text{ i.e., } 0.25 \times 1.25 = 0.3 \text{ with } F.S. = 1$$

or

$$H = \frac{c}{0.3\gamma} = \frac{3.3c}{\gamma}$$

This is the limiting value of H (the height above dredge level) for stability of cantilever walls in cohesive soils.

22.5 ANCHORED SHEET PILE WALLS (SHEET PILE BULKHEADS)

When the height of soil to be retained is large, cantilever walls have to be replaced by sheet pile bulkheads, which are walls connected to an anchor or tie back arrangement near its top as shown in Fig. 22.1. For design, we have to find the minimum depth of embedment required as well as the maximum bending moment that occur in the system so that the proper modulus of section can be selected for the pile. Generally, they are analysed by one of the following two methods.

Method 1: ***The free earth support method of design.*** In this case, the depth of penetration is not large and the deflection profile will be as shown in Fig. 22.1(b). The final failure is by rotation of the system about the anchor rod and the pile is assumed to behave as a rigid body with the lower tip of the wall kicking or deflecting outwards. This is also the usual type of failure we can assume in rigid walls like R.C.C. diaphragm walls. Rankine's or Coulomb's earth pressure theory is used to calculate earth pressures. The bending moments produced tends to be larger than in fixed earth condition.

Method 2: ***The fixed earth support method of design.*** In this case the depth of penetration is large and the lower end of the pile driven into the soil is assumed as fixed. The deflected shape is as shown in Fig. 22.1(c).

We will deal only with the general principle of the method as applied to cohesive and cohesionless soils. In real soils, the values should be worked out based on these principles taking into account the water level, the submerged weights and other factors that determine earth pressures.

22.6 STABILITY ANALYSIS OF ANCHORED BULKHEAD BY FREE EARTH SUPPORT METHOD

We will now examine the free earth support method in detail using Rankine's theory of earth pressures for computation of pressures and take the two separate cases of cohesionless and cohesive soil to illustrate the method. In both cases, the usual procedure of analysis is as follows. The method is based on simple static equilibrium of forces as shown in Fig. 22.4 [1]. In free earth support, the lower end is not fixed. Hence we take moments about the anchor point.

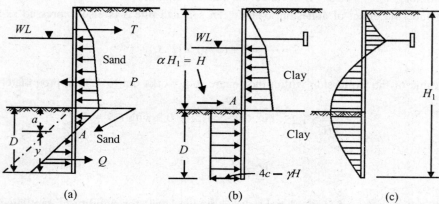

Fig. 22.4 **Earth pressure diagram for analysis of anchored bulkheads by free earth support analysis: (a) Granular soils; (b) cohesive soils; (c) shape of bending moment diagram in free earth support analysis.**

Step 1. Draw the pressure diagram with active pressure acting on back side of the wall and passive pressure in front of the wall where it tends to kick out.

Step 2. Locate the point of zero pressure at a distance a below the dredge line. Let it be called point A.

Step 3. Determine the pressures above A as well as the pressure below A. (We may also work from the basic pressure diagram to get the results.)

Step 4. As the sheet pile is assumed to rotate *about the anchor point near the top of the pile*, for equilibrium, the sum of the moments of the forces about this point should be zero. Determine the value of D, the depth below dredge line required.

Step 5. Determine the required anchor pull using the theory of equilibrium of forces.

Step 6. Determine the maximum bending moment in the pile, by finding the bending moment where shear force is zero.

Step 7. Apply safety factor by increasing the theoretical value of D by 30 to 40% (alternatively reduce the stabilising passive forces in the calculations by 50 to 75%).

Now, we will examine the methods for the two cases of cohesionless and cohesive soils.

Case 1: Free earth support method for cohesionless soil. The assumed active pressures at the back of the wall and the passive pressures at the front of the wall are shown in Fig. 22.4(a). They keep the pile in position. If the water level is high, the submerged weight should be taken in the calculation of pressures. The point of zero pressure will be below the dredge line.

Case 2: *Free earth support method for cohesive soils.* The corresponding pressure diagram without taking tension in clay is shown in Fig. 22.4(b). The point of zero pressure in this case can be taken on the dredge line itself. The pressure at dredge level will be as follows.

Let H be the height above dredge level.

Active pressure at dredge level = $\gamma H - 2c$

Passive pressure ($\gamma H + 2c$) at dredge level = $2c$

Net pressure = $2c - (\gamma H - 2c) = 4c - \gamma H$

This is assumed to be constant with depth.

In both cases mentioned above, the moments of forces are taken about the anchor point to determine equilibrium and the depth of penetration D required.

22.6.1 Rowe's Theory of Moment Reduction in Free Earth Support Method [2], [3], [4]

In the classical theory of free earth support, the pressures on sheet piles are determined by Rankine's theory of rigid walls even though the sheet pile walls are relatively flexible. Experimental work by Rowe around 1950 showed that the actual earth pressures in sheet pile walls differ very much from the assumed hydrostatic distribution. The most significant factors that affect these *pressures in cohesionless soils* are the following [1]:

(a) The relative density of the soil.

(b) The flexibility of the pile called *flexibility number* as expressed by $\rho = H_1^4/EI$ (which is the inverse of rigidity). Here, H_1 is the total length of pile (the length of pile above the dredge line being $\alpha H_1 = H$).

In *cohesive soils, the more significant factors* that affect the pressures are the following:

(a) The flexibility of the pile ρ (as explained above)

(b) The value of α

(c) The stability number $S = \dfrac{1.25c}{\gamma H}$

(where $H = \alpha H_1$, the height of soil retained).

In 1952, Rowe proposed his theory of moment reduction in sheet piles determined by the free earth support method. He showed that the actual values will be less than the values obtained by theoretical calculations. He proposed M/M_{max} ratio which varies with the parameters given above for the cohesionless and cohesive soils. Some of the data for cohesionless soils are given in Fig. 22.5. More details for cohesive soils can be obtained from Ref. [1].

22.7 STABILITY ANALYSIS OF ANCHORED BULKHEAD—FIXED EARTH SUPPORT METHOD

We will now examine the second method of fixed earth support method of design. In the case of free earth support, the lower end was free to move outwards. If the piles are driven deeper, we can

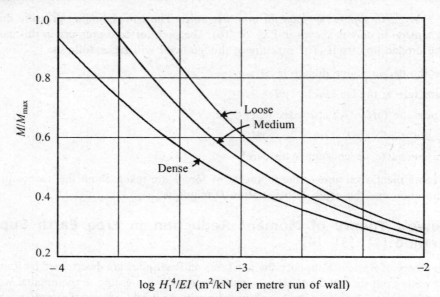

Fig. 22.5 **Rowe's moment reduction curve for free earth support analysis for sheet piles in sand [1].** **(H_1 = total length of sheet pile).**

assume that these piles are fixed at the base as already explained in Section 22.5. There are two approaches possible in this method. They are:

- The elastic line method
- The equivalent beam method which is a simplification of the first method.

The elastic line method is best done as a computer method as explained by Bowles [8], [9]. In this chapter, we will deal only with the simple equivalent beam method to understand the principles involved in the action of these walls. In the elastic line method, the true elastic line of the beam is determined by trial and error. Equivalent beam method is a simplification of this method.

22.7.1 Fixed Earth Support Method—Equivalent Beam Method for Cohesionless Soils

In the equivalent beam method for cohesionless soils, we use a simplification based on the Princeton model tests in sands conducted by Tschebotarioff. *We assume that, for static loading, the point of contraflexure or zero bending moment is located close to the dredge line point f* in Fig. 22.6(c). The value *y* in Fig. 22.6(c) is arbitrarily fixed from the ϕ values as follows [5]:

ϕ	20°	30°	40°
y	0.25h	0.08h	0.007h

Here *h* is the height of the wall above the dredge line. The elastic line of the bulkhead is assumed to be tangent to the vertical at the lowest point. *The part of the bulk head above the hinge can be treated as a separate freely supported beam with an overhanging end.* There will be a reaction

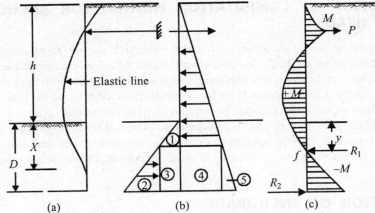

Fig. 22.6　**Earth pressure diagram for analysis of anchored bulkheads in granular soils by fixed earth support: (a) Elastic line; (b) earth pressures; (c) shape of bending moment diagram.**

R_1 at the hinge point which can be determined by taking the moment of all the forces about the anchor point.

　　The bending moment produced in the sheet pile will be as shown in Fig. 22.6(c). Usually, it is sufficient to make the conservative assumption that the point of contraflexure is near the dredge line and that the maximum negative bending moment below the dredge line will be equal to the maximum positive bending moment in the pile above the dredge line. Otherwise, it can be computed from the force diagram. For equilibrium of forces another concentrated force may be assumed to be acting at the bottom of the pile. The method is illustrated by Example 22.3. The effect of the assumption of the point of inflection at various levels is shown in Fig. 22.7.

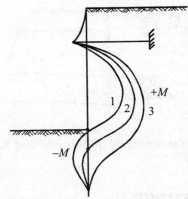

Fig. 22.7　**Variation of bending moment diagram with assumption of points of contraflexure.**

22.7.2　Fixed Earth Support for Cohesive Soils

As data is not available for arbitrarily fixing the point of inflection from actual tests in cohesive soils, it is better to solve these problems by the elastic line method by trial and error.

22.8 SELECTION OF COMPUTATION METHOD FOR ANCHORED BULK HEADS

Anchored *bulkheads in sand are most conveniently analysed by the fixed earth support (also called the equivalent beam method)* based on simple statics of a freely supported equivalent beam. The free earth support and subsequent application of Rowe's procedure to reduce the moments are questionable for sands. The Princeton tests for fixed earth support for sand were based more on real state conditions in the field and can be applied to field conditions.

Anchored sheet piles in clay can be conveniently designed by the free earth support method [5] and Rowe's correction may be applied to the results obtained by this analysis. This correction will considerably reduce the bending moment in the sheet piles and the required modulus of section for these piles.

22.9 POSITION OF ANCHORAGE

It is very important that the anchorage point of these piles is properly placed. Three types of anchorages, as shown in Fig. 22.8, are in use.

Type 1: This is the "deadman" type. The dimensions and depth of embedment of deadman are governed by the pull they have to resist. It should be so placed that the passive wedge of the deadman and the active wedge of the pile in Fig. 22.8 do not interfere.

Type 2: This is the *A* frame anchor type. Such types are adopted when compressible soils are located near the dredge line.

Type 3: This is the battered tension type where *H* piles are installed a inclined up to 40° with the horizontal. They should be used with great care as the junction between *H* and sheet pile requires special attention [5].

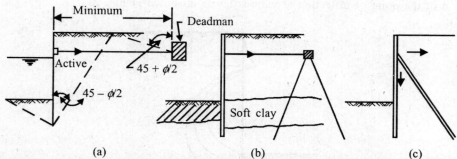

Fig. 22.8 Type of anchorages for anchored bulkheads: (a) By deadman; (b) by a frame; (c) by tension piles.

22.10 BRACED EXCAVATIONS

Earth pressure on bracings of excavations is another subject which developed only after the advent of soil mechanics. Before 1940 bracings of cuts were designed on the assumption that earth pressures acting on them are similar to those on retaining walls and increase with depth. However, a large number of failures of bracings designed by this method happened in subway constructions. It was only after Terzaghi proved that earth pressures depend not only on the nature of the soil, but also on the nature of the movement of the retaining structure that investigations and field measurement were started to find the real nature of pressures on bracings [6]. Near about that time, extensive field measurements were made under Terzaghi, on pressures in struts in an excavation in sand for a subway in Berlin and another set of measurements were made by Peck in U.S.A. in open cuts for the Chicago subway in clay. Many of the present-day empirical recommendations are based on the field results of these tests [6]. Before we go into the details of the present-day designs, we will examine the general field practice in the bracing of excavations.

The types of bracing used depend on the depth of the cut. Cuts less than 5 to 6 m in depth are classified as shallow and cuts deeper than these as deep. The bracings of shallow cuts as that for laying a sewer line or a pipeline is best done by *conventional local practice*. A designed system for these cases will be highly uneconomic. Hence for shallow cuts, we need only make a general soil survey of the sites and use the conventional methods for bracings. For deep cuts, as for a subway or deep sewer, we should properly design the bracing system as the savings and safety achieved in such works will be considerable. Let us first enumerate the methods of bracing used for shallow and deep excavations before we study the modern methods of design of their bracings.

22.10.1 Methods Used for Shallow Open Cuts [7]

The conventional methods used for narrow excavations are shown in Fig. 22.9 (For details see Ref. 7.).

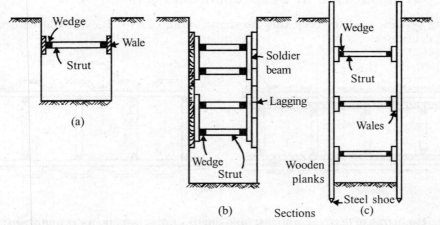

Fig. 22.9 **Timbering of shallow excavations by conventional methods: (a) With simple bracings to prevent tension failure; (b) moderate deepcuts with horizontal laggings soldier beams and struts; (c) cuts in soft soils with vertical poling boards, wales and struts.**

1. Theoretically, no support is necessary for excavations in clay up to the critical height which is in the region of 1.5 m for very soft clays, 1.5 to 3 m in soft clays and 3 to 5 m in medium clays. Stiff clays have joints and the corresponding height will be only about 3 m. Similarly, even though we cannot make vertical cuts in pure sand, in clayey sands the unsupported heights can be up to 3 to 4.5 m.

However, in all the above cases, the upper edge of these cuts are in tension and if left unsupported for a few days, tension cracks can develop. Hence where the excavation does not exceed one half the critical height, *the upper edge of the cut should be braced* against each other. For this purpose we use horizontal wooden planks (called wales) about 75 mm thick along the excavation and braces or struts (called trench braces) at about 2.4 m spacings as shown in Fig. 22.9(a). These struts are tightened by hardwood wedges or by screw arrangements provided at the end of the struts.

2. If the height of the *cut exceeds one half the critical height*, struts are introduced as excavation proceeds. For deeper cuts we use horizontal planks called lagging which are pushed to the soil by short vertical members called soldier beams which in turn are pushed by struts as shown in Fig. 22.9(b). The spacings of wooden struts are about 2.4 m horizontally and 1.2 to 1.4 m vertically. They are 100×150 mm in section for narrow cuts and 150×250 mm for larger cuts (more than 3.6 m) in width.

An alternative arrangement especially in clayey sands, is to drive down vertical timbers called *sheeting* (similar to sheet piles) against the earth in advance of excavation as shown in Fig. 22.9(c). These are supported horizontally by *wales* with *struts* wedged against the wales. The lower one half critical height is left free for people to work. Depths up to 9 m in clayey sands can be excavated by this method.

It should be noted that the struts are placed always after the excavation from top to bottom and this aspect, as explained in Section 22.10.3, is very important in the nature of the pressures developed on the bracing.

22.10.2 Methods Used in Deep Open Cuts [7]

The bracing systems used for deep cuts are shown in Fig. 22.10. They should be designed by structural calculations.

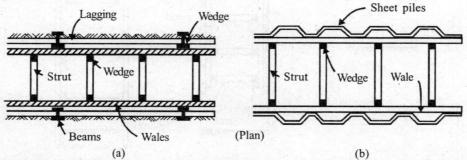

Fig. 22.10 Timbering of deep excavations: (a) Using H beams, lagging, wales and struts; (b) using sheet piles, wales and struts.

1. Deep excavations require *H* piles (as soldier beams) with lagging in between them followed by wales against the soldier beams and struts between the wales.
2. For very deep excavations we can also adopt continuous sheet piles with wales and struts as in Fig. 22.10(b).
3. Wide excavations can be made by using inclined rakes resting on the ground to take the load from timbering to the ground. Similarly for deep open cuts as in basement constructions, the retaining system can be tied back with ground anchors. In extreme cases concrete basement walls made by using slurry trench method can be used instead of bracings to retain the sides of the excavations.

22.10.3 Significance of the Order of Placing Struts in Excavations

We have seen that in all cases of excavation, the strutting is carried from top downwards. Thus, when placing the second series of struts below the first, the horizontal yielding of soil at the top is prevented by the first strut and only inward movement below the strut is possible. The deformation of the bracing will be as shown in Fig. 22.11, inwards at bottom of excavation.

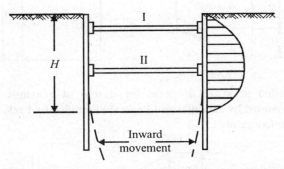

Fig. 22.11 Lateral pressures on timbering of excavations as different from Rankine's pressure distribution.

This movement does not comply with the Rankine state and therefore Rankine's or Coulomb's theory cannot be used to calculate the pressures behind the bracing. From this deformation, we can expect a roughly parabolic distribution of pressure with maximum intensity of pressure near the mid height of the cut. This distribution is quite different from that in retaining walls or in sheet piles.

22.10.4 Differences between Failure Mechanisms of Retaining Walls and Bracings of Cuts

It is also worthwhile to examine the differences in ultimate failure of bracing from that of retaining walls. Firstly retaining walls fail as a unit, local failures do not considerably affect the total failure of the unit. On the other hand, in a strutted excavation, any strut, on failure will throw its load to another unit which may also fail and thus lead *to progressive failure* of the entire bracing. Many such failures have happened in the field. This is why excavation failures are catastrophic.

Secondly, all retaining walls or sheet pile walls can undergo appreciable movement or deformation before failure to bring about active pressure. A strut, being a compression member, cannot yield enough to produce the necessary deformation. *Hence, it is of utmost importance that each strut should be designed for the maximum pressure acting at its location. Local failure should be always avoided.* These aspects are very important in bracings of excavations.

22.10.5 Design Pressures for Bracings of Cuts

The design pressures recommended for bracing of cuts in sands are based on the results of tests in sand conducted in Berlin subway and those recommended for clays are based on the results of tests in clay in Chicago subway. The pressures recommended are shown in Fig. 22.12 and Fig. 22.13 respectively along with the modified diagrams given by Peck, Hansen and Thornburn in 1974. Peck also observed that any settlement of adjacent ground in clays due to deformation of struts

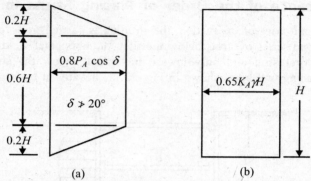

(a)   (b)

Fig. 22.12   **Recommended pressure diagram for design of bracings in open cuts in sand: (a) Recommended by Terzaghi and Peck; (b) modified by Peck, Hansen and Thornburn for moist dense sand.**

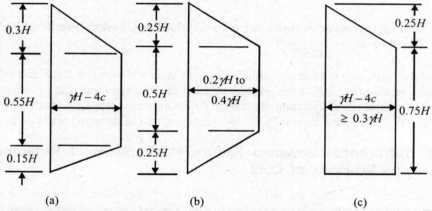

(a)   (b)   (c)

Fig. 22.13   **Recommended pressure diagram for design of bracings in open cuts in clays: (a) Recommended by Terzaghi and Peck for soft and medium clays; (b) recommended by Peck, Hansen and Thornburn for clays when $\gamma H/c \leq 4$; (c) when $\gamma H/c > 4$.**

considerably increased the strut pressures. It was therefore found useful to pre-stress the struts by jacking the opposite wales apart before inserting the strut [7] [8].

For sands, a trapezoidal distribution was recommended by Terzaghi and Peck. Later a rectangular distribution was recommended by Peck, Hansen and Thornburn.

22.10.6 Design Procedure

As already stated, each strut should be designed for the maximum load that can act on it at its location. To estimate this load, first a scaled drawing is made of the vertical distribution of the earth pressure as well as the position of each strut. The load is assumed to be transmitted by beams supporting the load hinged at the locations of the struts. One half load from each adjacent spans can be assumed to be transmitted to the strut. Each strut is designed for the corresponding load or preferably all the struts are designed for the maximum load that can act on the strut with a factor of safety of 2 to prevent buckling. For field operations, it will be more convenient to have all the struts designed for the maximum load.

In a layout with H piles, lagging, wale beams and struts, the laggings and wale beams are designed as simply supported at their ends and carrying the corresponding pressures acting on them. For commonly used wooden members, the following allowable stresses are recommended for elastic design. Direct compression, 6 N/mm^2; bending stress 18 N/mm^2; shear in wale beams, 1.2 N/mm^2; shear in lagging, 1.7 N/mm^2.

22.11 SUMMARY

Flexible retaining walls which are commonly used for waterfront structures are designed by using Rankine's earth pressure theory. However pressures on bracings of excavations do not follow Rankine's theory. The pressures recommended for design are based on the results of actual measurements made in the past on similar structures during construction.

EXAMPLE 22.1 (Excavation in clay)

A vertical cut 2 m wide and 3 m deep is to be made in a clay soil having unit weight 18 kN/m^3 and unconfined strength 40 kN/m^2. Investigate the type of strutting to be used and also examine the factor of safety against base failure.

Ref.	Step	Calculations
Sec. 22.10.1	1	*Find critical height for the clay* The critical depth of vertical cut $= \dfrac{4c}{\gamma}$ $$H_c = \dfrac{4 \times 20}{18} = 4.4 \text{ m}$$ As the depth of excavation exceeds one half the critical depth, we have to provide some sort of bracing for the cut. As the cut is shallow, a conventional system of sheeting wales and struts can be adopted.
	2	*Calculate factor of safety against collapse of bottom of excavation* If we consider the two vertical sides as loaded by its own weight, this weight should not be more than the bearing capacity of the bottom of the cut. Bearing capacity of bottom of cut $= cN_c$ Find N_c from Skempton's curve for $H/B = 4.0/2.0 = 2$ $N_c = 7$; Bearing capacity $= cN_c = 20 \times 7 = 140$ kN/m^2 Weight of soil above $= \gamma H = 18 \times 4 = 72$ kN/m^2 $$F.S. = \dfrac{140}{72} = 1.94 \text{ (Thus, there will be no base failure.)}$$

EXAMPLE 22.2 (Design of struts for bracing of cuts)

A cut 3 m wide and 15 m deep is proposed in cohesionless soil with $\gamma = 20$ kN/m^3, $\phi = 30°$ and $c = 0$. Assuming the struts are placed with the first strut at 0.5 m below ground level and the subsequent struts at every 1.5 m below, find the maximum load on the strut. Assume, the horizontal spacing of strut is 3 m.

Ref.	Step	Calculations
	1	*Find the distribution of pressures vertically and position of struts*
Sec. 22.10.5		$K_A = \dfrac{1 - \sin\phi}{1 + \sin\phi} = \dfrac{1 - 0.5}{1 + 0.5} = \dfrac{1}{3}$
Fig. 22.12		$0.65\,K_A\gamma H = \dfrac{0.65 \times 1 \times 20 \times 15}{3} = 65$ kN/m^2
	2	*Find pressure on a strut spaced* 1.5 m *vertically and* 3 m *horizontally* As the diagram is rectangular, all the struts have to be designed for the maximum load (in compression).
		Max. load $= 65 \times 1.5 \times 3 = 292.5$ kN $= 30$ t (approx.)

EXAMPLE 22.3 (Analysis of cantilever sheet piles in sand by simplified method)

A cantilever sheet pile is to be installed in cohesionless soil of unit weight 2 t/m^3 and $\phi = 30°$. The height above dredge level is 6 m and water level above dredge level is 3 m. Estimate the depth of penetration needed for the sheet pile for stability. Find also the theoretical maximum bending moment in the pile.

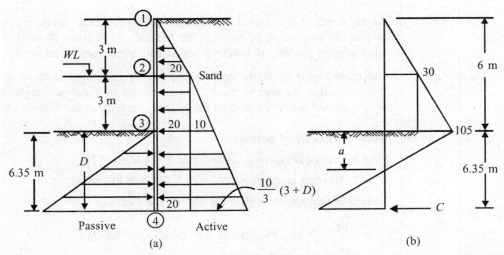

Fig. E.22.3

Ref.	Step	Calculations
	1	[*Note:* We estimate by appropriate method.]
		Find K_A and K_P and draw earth pressure diagram.
Fig. 22.2		For $\phi = 30°$, $K_A = \dfrac{1}{3}$ and $K_P = 3$.
	2	*Calculate pressures at various points*
Sec. 22.4		$\gamma = 20$ and $\gamma' = 10$ kN/m^3

Point	Active	Passive
1	0	0
2	$\dfrac{1}{3}(20 \times 3) = 20$ kN/m^2	0
3	$20 + \dfrac{1}{3}(10 \times 3) = 30$ kN/m^2	0
4	$20 + \dfrac{1}{3} \times 10(3 + D)$	$3 \times 10 \times D$

Ref. for rows: Fig. (22.2), Fig. (E.22.3)

Ref.	Step	Calculations
	3	*Take moment of active forces about point 4*
		Destabilising moment

$$= \frac{20}{2} \times 3 \times (D + 4) + 20 \frac{(D+3)^2}{2} + \frac{10}{3} \times \frac{(D+3)^2}{3}$$

$$= 30D + 120 + 10(D+3)^2 + \frac{10}{9}(3+D)^2$$

$$= 11D^2 + 96.6D + 220$$

4   *Take moment of passive forces about point*

$$\text{Resisting moment} = \left[\frac{3 \times 10 \times D \times D}{2}\right]\left[\frac{D}{3}\right] = 5D^3$$

5   *Equate the two and solve for the required depth of penetration D* (Ref: Steps 3 and 4)

$$5D^3 - 11D^2 - 96.6D - 220 = 0$$

which gives $D = 6.35$ m. Increase by 30%.

Adopt $D = 8.2$ m (approx.)

(*Notes:* (1) The depth required is equal to or more than the height supported. For this reason anchored sheet piles are superior to the cantilever type.)

(2) As we have not considered $\Sigma P = 0$, we may need a concentrated load C at the end of pile for equilibrium as shown in Fig. E.22.3(b).

EXAMPLE 22.4   (**Analysis of anchored bulkhead in sand by free earth support method**)

Estimate the depth of the embedment required for an anchored sheet pile wall retaining 8 m of earth as shown in Fig. E.22.4 in sand. Assume $\phi = 30°$ and $\gamma = 18$ kN/m^3. (Assume no submergence)

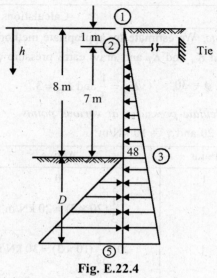

Fig. E.22.4

Ref.	Step	Calculations
Fig. 22.4	1	*Calculate earth pressures* (Fig. E.22.4) $K_A = 1/3$; $K_P = 3$ Pressure at various points: At point 1 = 0 At point 2 = $K_A \gamma h = (1/3 \times 18 \times 1) = 6$ kN/m² At point 3 = $K_A \gamma h = (1/3)\,18 \times 8 = 48$ kN/m² At point 4 = 0 (point of zero pressure) At point 5 = $(K_P - K_A)\,\gamma D = (8/3)(18D) = 48D$ kN/m²
Sec. 22.5	2	*Find depth of point a* (point of zero pressure) $48 = (K_P - K_A)\,\gamma a$ $a = \dfrac{48}{(3 - 1/3)18} = 1$ m (This is below the dredge line).
	3	*Equate moment of forces about point 2 to zero* Moment forces on R.H.S. of pile = $1/2(K_A \gamma h)(h)(2/3 h - 1)$ Moment forces on L.H.S. of pile = $1/2(K_P \gamma D)(D)(2/3D + 7)$ $(1/2)(1/3)18 \times (8 + D) \times (8 + D) \times [(2/3)(8 + D) - 1]$ $\qquad = (1/2)(3 \times 18 \times D) \times D \times (2/3\,D + 7)$ $D^3 + 8.75D^2 - 81.25D - 76 = 0$ gives $D = 6.3$ m. Adopt 1.3 times computed value for safety. $1.3 \times 6.3 = 8.2$ m (for safety). (*Notes:* (i) We find the position of zero shear and the maximum moment to select the required modulus of section of the sheet pile. (ii) Rowe's moment reduction is applicable to analysis by free earth support method.)

EXAMPLE 22.5 **(Analysis of anchored bulkhead in sand by fixed earth support-equivalent beam method)**

Estimate the depth required for Example 22.4 by fixed earth support method.

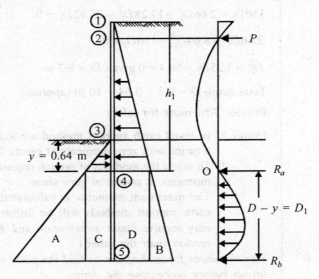

Fig. E.22.5

Ref.	Step	Calculations
Sec. 22.7.1	1	*Assume point of contraflexure from soil data* y below the dredge level for $\phi = 30° = 0.08H$ (from tests) $y = 0.08H = 0.08 \times 8 = 0.64$ m We assume that the B.M. (at $y = 0.64$ m) $= 0$ With a force R acting at 0 for equilibrium
	2	*Find R by taking moments about point 2* $R(7 + 0.64) = \dfrac{1}{3}(18 \times 8.64)\left(\dfrac{8.64}{2}\right)\left(\dfrac{2 \times 8.64}{3}\right) - \left(\dfrac{3 \times 18 \times 0.64}{2}\right) \times$ $(0.64)\left(7 + \dfrac{2 \times 0.64}{3}\right)$ $7.64R = 1290 - 145.7$ or $R = 150$ kN
	3	*Equate moment of forces from 4 to 5 only about 5 to zero to find D_1* Moment of R at $4 = RD_1$ Moment of part $(A + B) = 1/2(K_P - K_A)\gamma D_1(D_1)(D_1/3)$ Moment of part $C = K_P\gamma\, y(D_1)(D_1/2)$ Moment of part $D = K_A\gamma\, h_1(D_1)(D_1/2)$

$150D_1 = 1/2 \,(8/9)(18)(D_1^3/3) + (3 \times 18 \times 0.64 \times D_1^2/2)$

$\qquad -(1/3)(18)(8.64)(D_1^2/2) = 0$

$150D_1 = 2.66D_1^3 + 17.28D_1^2 - 25.92D_1^2 = 0$

$2.66D_1^3 - 8.64D_1^2 - 150D_1 = 0$

$D_1^2 - 3.25D_1 - 56.4 = 0$ given $D_1 = 9.3$ m

Total depth $D = 9.3 + 0.64 = 10$ m (approx.)

Provide 30% more for safety.

(*Notes:* 1. In fixed earth support method we assume the pile to bend as a beam with zero moments at points 2, 4, and 5 (Fig. 22.5).
2. To select the modulus of section required, we find the maximum moments at points of zero shear.
3. The maximum moments as calculated from the free and fixed earth support methods will be different. One of the methods may require *lesser penetration* and *hence larger modulus of section* than the other.)

6   *Plot the shear force diagram to find the point of maximum B.M. on the layout before increasing the depth.*

Total force at dredge level = 105 kN

It then reverses as $(K_P - K_A)rh$

Find the distance of point below dredge line where S.F. is zero as a.

$105 + 30a - (K_P - K_A)\gamma \, a(a/2) = 0$

$105 + 30a - \dfrac{8 \times 10 \times a \times a}{3 \times 2} = 0$

$105 + 30a - 13.33a^2 = 0$

$a^2 - 2.25a - 7.88 = 0$ gives $a = 1.9$ m.

7   *Max. B.M. at 'a' below dredge level*

Put $D = a = 1.9$ m is given by steps 3 and 4

$M_{\max} = 11D^2 + 96.6D + 220 - 5D^3 = 408.3$ kNm.

The modulus of section of the sheet pile to be used should have this capacity.

(*Note:* ΣH will not be equal to zero. Hence, we should assume a concentrated force C acting at the bottom of the pile as shown in Fig. E.22.5.)

REFERENCES

[1] Teng, W.C., *Foundation Design*, Prentice-Hall, Englewood Cliffs, New Jersey, 1965.

[2] Rowe, P.W., *Anchored Sheet Walls, Proceedings*, Institution of Engineers, London, Vol. I, 1952.

[3] Rowe, P.W., *Sheet Piles in Clay, Proceedings*, Institution of Engineers, London, Vol. II, 1957.

[4] Terzaghi, K., *Anchored Bulkheads*, Transactions American Society of Civil Engineers, Vol. 119, 1954.

[5] Leonards, G.A., *Foundation Engineering*, Chapter by G.P. Tschebotarioff on Retaining Structures, McGraw-Hill, New York, 1966.

[6] Terzaghi, K. and R.B. Peck, *Soil Mechanics in Engineering Practice*, John Wiley, New York, 1967.

[7] Tomlinson, M.J., *Foundation Design and Construction*, ELBS, Longman, Singapore, 1995.

[8] Bowles, J.E., *Foundation Analysis and Design*, McGraw-Hill, Singapore, 1988.

[9] Bowles J.E., *Analytical and Computer Methods in Foundation Engineering*, McGraw-Hill, New York, 1974.

REFERENCES

[2] Rowe, P.W., *On the of Sheet Walls, Proceedings*, Institution of Engineers, London.

[3] Rowe, P.W., *Sheet Piles in City, Proceedings*, Institution of Engineers, London.

[9] Bowles, J.E., *Analytical and Computer Methods in Foundation Engineering*, McGraw-Hill, New York, 1974.

23

Design of Machine Foundations

23.1 INTRODUCTION

Design of machine foundations is a vast and specialized subject. Only the basic principles of this subject are discussed in this chapter. Specialized literature from references given at the end of this chapter and IS codes given in Section 2.3.7 should be consulted when one has to undertake detailed design of large machine foundations. Both static and dynamic analyses have to be made when we design machine foundations. In static analysis, the effects of the gravity loads and dynamic loads, converted to static loads are analysed as explained in Section 23.10. In dynamic analysis, we check the adequacy of the foundation with respect to the frequency and amplitude of the oscillation.

23.2 A GENERAL VIEW OF MACHINE VIBRATION

Fortunately most of the problems of machine vibrations can be solved by assuming that they obey the laws of simple harmonic motion, well known to all engineers. An oscillation is said to have only a single degree of freedom when the motion can be described by one coordinate in space. However in general, a machine foundation can have six degrees of freedom, three translational and three rotational as shown in Fig. 23.1.

When an oscillation takes place without any other oscillation affecting it, it is called an *uncoupled oscillation*. On the other hand, if it is affected by one or more other oscillations, it is called a *coupled oscillation*. For example, both the vertical mode and the torsional mode of oscillations of the block foundation shown in Fig. 23.1 can be treated as uncoupled oscillations. But rocking of a block foundation as shown in Fig. 23.1(b) is a coupled oscillation. This is due to the fact that in most cases, the centre of gravity of the foundation is always above the centre of pressure of the horizontal resisting forces on the ground so that rocking motion also has a sliding component inherent in it.

We can also imagine that if we consider the effects of all six degrees of freedom of the foundation by coupling all the effects, the problem will become very complex. Theoretical analysis and experience of actual behaviour of foundation have shown that in most of the practical cases, it is sufficient to consider only one degree of freedom, or at the most, two degrees of freedom of

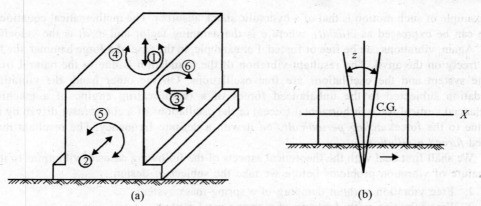

Fig. 23.1 **Types of machine vibrations: (a) Types of uncoupled vibrations: (1) Vertical; (2) longitudinal; (3) lateral; (4) torsional or yawing; (5) rocking; (6) pitching. (b) Coupled vibration rocking and sliding.**

the vibration to be coupled. Thus, in a *block foundation* we generally analyze considering the following modes, two of which are uncoupled:

1. Uncoupled vertical motion
2. Uncoupled torsional motion
3. Coupled sliding and rocking motion.

(Coupled vertical, sliding and rocking motion is very rarely checked.) See also Fig. 23.2.

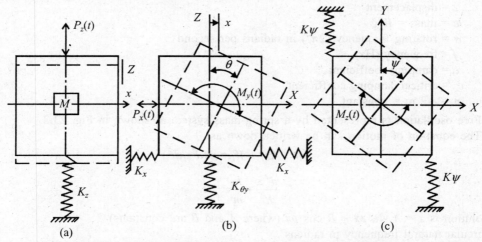

Fig. 23.2 **Modes of vibration of block foundation: (a) Uncoupled vertical mode; (b) coupled rocking and sliding; (c) uncoupled torsion (plan view).**

23.2.1 Types of Uncoupled Oscillation

In all practical cases of vibration, there is a loss of energy with time, which tends to reduce the amplitude. This is called *damping*. One of the common types of damping is defined as viscous damping, where the damping force is directly proportional to the velocity of the oscillating mass.

An example of such motion is that of a hydraulic shock absorber. The mathematical equation for the force can be expressed as $c(dz/dt)$, where c is the damping factor and dz/dt is the velocity.

Again, vibrations can be free or forced. For example, in the case of a forge hammer, the hammer falls freely on the anvil. The resultant vibration of the foundation is due to the natural frequency of the system and the oscillations are free oscillations. On the other hand, the vibration of a foundation subjected to the unbalanced forces of a reciprocating engine of a machine (the unbalanced vertical force or horizontal forces) or the oscillations of a compressor driven by a motor are due to the forces *acting periodically* on it with a definite frequency. The resultant motion is termed *forced oscillations*.

We shall first deal with the theoretical aspects of the following cases of vibrations to illustrate the nature of vibration problems before we take the subject of design:

1. Free vibration without damping of a spring-mass system
2. Free vibration with damping of a spring-mass system
3. Forced vibration with or without damping

23.3 THEORY OF FREE VIBRATION OF SPRING-MASS SYSTEM WITHOUT DAMPING

We will first consider free vibration adopting the following notations:

k = spring constant (force per unit displacement of spring = $C_u A$ (kN/m)
A = area of base of foundation in m^2
C_u = coefficient of elastic compression of ground in kN/m^3
   (Its value can be obtained from tests [1] or taken from Table 23.1)
z = displacement
m = mass = W/g
w = rotating frequency ($2\pi f$) in radians per second
f = frequency (Hz)
c = damping coefficient
c_c = critical damping coefficient
n = $c/2$ m = constant

Free oscillation is represented by a spring-mass system as shown in Fig. 23.2.
The equation of motion can be written down as

$$- (W + kz) + W = m(d^2z/dt^2)$$

or
$$\frac{d^2z}{dt^2} + \frac{k}{m} z = 0$$

The solution is $z = A \sin \omega t + B \cos \omega t$ (where A and B are constants)
ω = circular natural frequency in radians.

Solving, we get

$$\omega_n^2 = 4\pi^2 f_n^2 = \frac{k}{m} \quad \text{or} \quad f_n^2 = \frac{k}{4\pi^2 m} \quad \text{or} \quad f_n = \frac{1}{2\pi} \sqrt{\frac{k}{m}} \tag{23.1}$$

where f_n is the natural frequency of the system.

$$\text{Maximum displacement } z_s = \frac{W}{k} = \text{the displacement under static load} \tag{23.2}$$

We see that the frequency is inversely proportional to $\sqrt{m}$ and directly proportional to $\sqrt{k}$.

23.4 THEORY OF FREE VIBRATION OF SPRING-MASS SYSTEM WITH DAMPING

Next we will consider free vibration with damping.

If c is the damping coefficient, the equation of motion is as follows:

$$-(W + kz) - c\frac{dz}{dt} + W = m\frac{d^2z}{dt^2}$$

$$\frac{d^2z}{dt^2} + \frac{c}{m}\frac{dz}{dt} + \frac{kz}{m} = 0$$

Substituting $z = e^{st}$ the above equation becomes

$$\left(s^2 + \frac{c}{m}s + \frac{k}{m}\right)e^{st} = 0$$

Solving, we get

$$s = \frac{-c}{2m} \pm \sqrt{\left(\frac{c}{2m}\right)^2 - \frac{k}{m}} \quad \text{or} \quad e^{st} = 0$$

There are three cases for the first solution:

Case 1: $\dfrac{k}{m} < \left(\dfrac{c}{2m}\right)^2$ the solution is real

Case 2: $\dfrac{k}{m} > \left(\dfrac{c}{2m}\right)^2$ the solution is imaginary

Case 3: $\dfrac{k}{m} = \left(\dfrac{c}{2m}\right)^2$ then solution is $s = \dfrac{-c}{2m} = -\sqrt{\dfrac{k}{m}}$ (23.3)

The second solution of $z = e^{st} = 0$, which implies no oscillation, defines the *critical damping* value, $c_c = 2\sqrt{mk}$. If the system has a lesser damping c, then the ratio c/c_c is known as *damping ratio*.

Taking again the case of $\dfrac{k}{m} < \left(\dfrac{c}{2m}\right)^2$ when the solutions are real, the value of the amplitude z works out as follows: Let

$c/2m = n$ a constant

ω = circular frequency of damped system

ω_n = circular frequency of undamped system

Then we have

$$z = c^{-nt}(A \sin \omega t + B \cos \omega t)$$

The above equation has the same form as for undamped oscillation except for the term c^{-nt}, which denotes logarithmic decrement with time.

The resultant circular frequency is given by

$$\omega^2 = (\omega_n^2 - n^2)$$ (23.4)

23.5 THEORY OF FORCED VIBRATION WITHOUT DAMPING

We will next examine forced vibration, which has already been defined. Let the forced vibration be represented by the following equation.

$$\text{Exciting force} = P_0 \sin \omega t, \text{ where } P_0 = \text{maximum applied force.}$$

The equilibrium equation will be

$$W - (W + kz) - c\frac{dz}{dt} + P_0 \sin \omega t = m\frac{d^2z}{dt^2}$$

i.e.

$$\frac{d^2z}{dt^2} + \frac{c}{m}\frac{dz}{dt} + \frac{kz}{m} = P_0 \sin \omega t$$

Putting

$$\frac{c}{2m} = n \text{ and } \frac{k}{m} = \omega_n^2 \text{ (natural frequency)},$$

we get

$$\frac{d^2z}{dt^2} + 2n\frac{dz}{dt} + \omega_n^2 z = P_0 \sin \omega t$$

(Without damping, the equation will be $\frac{d^2z}{dt^2} + \omega_n^2 z = P_0 \sin \omega t$)

Solving these equations by parts we get the values. These are very important in design of machine foundations:

1. *Natural frequency is given by the following expressions:*

$$\omega_n^2 = 4\pi^2 f_n^2 = \frac{k}{m} \text{ but } k = C_u A \text{ (Section 23.3)}$$

$$f_n^2 = \frac{k}{4\pi^2 m} = \frac{C_u A}{4\pi^2 m} \tag{23.5}$$

The above equation shows that the natural frequency of the system depends only on k and the mass of *the whole system* as in the case of free oscillation in Eq. (23.1).

2. *Amplitude:* Even though the natural frequency does not change, the resultant amplitude z depends on P_0 and also on the ratio of the exciting frequency f to the natural frequency of the system f_n.

$$\text{For undamped oscillation, } z_0 = \frac{P_0}{k}\frac{f_n}{\left(f_n^2 - f^2\right)} = \frac{P_0}{4\pi^2 m\left(f_n^2 - f^2\right)} \tag{23.6a}$$

$$\text{For damped oscillation, } z_0 = \frac{P_0}{k} \times \frac{f_n}{\left[\left(f_n^2 - f^2\right)^2 + \left(\frac{2cf}{c_c}\right)^2\right]^{1/2}} \tag{23.6b}$$

We can see from the above equation that amplitudes have two parts. The first term P_0/k can be looked upon as deformation under static load. The second term is the magnification factor which depends on the ratio of the natural frequency of the system to the exciting frequency. If $f_n = f$ in an undamped oscillation, z_0 is infinite. The influence of the damping factor c/c_c on the dynamic amplification factor with different frequency ratios of f/f_n (i.e. the ratio of exciting force to the natural frequency of foundation) is usually represented as in Fig. 23.3.

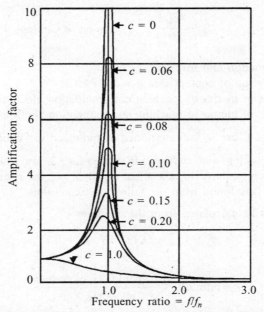

Fig. 23.3 **Magnification factor for frequency ratios and damping factors.**

The above discussions can be summarized as follows:

Type of vibration	Frequency	Amplitude
Free vibration	$f_n = (1/2\pi)\sqrt{k/m}$	$z = W/k$
Free with damping	Not affected	Depends on damping
Forced ($P_0 \sin \omega t$ of frequency f)	Not affected	$z = \dfrac{P_0}{k} \times$ factor
		The amplification factor depends on the ratio, $q = f/f_n$

23.6 FORMULAE FOR NATURAL FREQUENCIES

So far we dealt with vertical oscillation just to illustrate the nature of the formulae we get for computations. Similar expression for *frequency and amplitudes* can be derived for uncoupled sliding, rocking and torsional vibrations as well as for the coupled modes of oscillation like rocking and sliding. Some of these are discussed below.

Uncoupled mode

$$f_{nz}^2 = \frac{C_u A}{4\pi^2 m} \qquad \text{(vertical)} \qquad (23.7a)$$

$$f_{nx}^2 = \frac{C_r A}{4\pi^2 m} \qquad \text{(sliding)} \qquad (23.7b)$$

$$f_{n\phi}^2 = \frac{C_\phi I - Wz}{4\pi^2 M_{m0}} \qquad \text{(rocking)} \qquad (23.7c)$$

$$f_{n\psi}^2 = \frac{C_\psi J_z}{M_{mz}} \qquad \text{(torsion or yawing)} \qquad (23.7\text{d})$$

where

m = mass of foundation and machine

I = moment of inertia of contact area $a \times b = ba^3/12$

M_{m0} = mass moment of inertia of machine and foundation block about the axis of rotation

J_z = polar moment of inertia of machine and foundation about z axis.

The various values of C are to be determined as indicated in Section 23.17.

Coupled mode for rocking and sliding. In Section 23.2, we saw that rocking is always coupled with sliding. Hence we have to take them together and the resultant frequency f_n has to be found from $f_{n\phi}$ and f_{nx}. It is found from the following expression.

Two values of f_n can be calculated from the equation

$$rf_n^4 - \left(f_{nx}^2 + f_{n\phi}^2\right)f_n^2 + f_{nx}^2 f_{n\phi}^2 = 0 \qquad (23.8)$$

where

$$r = \text{ratio of } \frac{\text{M.I. about C.G. of system}}{\text{M.I. about the } Y\text{-axis}}$$

Similarly, expressions for the amplitudes of other coupled motions are also available. Dynamic analysis of foundation consists in determining these *frequencies and amplitudes in the different modes and checking whether they are within allowable limits.* In general, the natural frequencies of the foundation should be well above or well below the operational frequency of the machine if we are to avoid resonance. The amplitudes of vibrations which depend on the magnitudes of the acting forces as described above.

23.7 BASIC PRINCIPLES OF DESIGN OF MACHINE FOUNDATIONS

Rotating machines are generally balanced but reciprocating parts are usually unbalanced. Hence whereas generators and steam turbines are balanced, air compressors and reciprocating pumps are unbalanced. Thus, modern machines are of different types, each with its own peculiar characteristic. Because of this variation, each machine foundation has to be designed with its own characteristics with its own specific requirements. Hence, the Indian Standard Code of Practice for Design of Machine Foundations IS 2974 has been published in five parts. They are the following:

Part 1 COP for reciprocating machines—(1982) revised in 1993

Part 2 COP for impact type of machines like hammers (1980) revised in 1993

Part 3 COP for rotary type machines—medium to high frequency (1992) revised in 1995

Part 4 COP for rotary type machine—low frequency (1989) revised in 1995

Part 5 COP for impact type of machines other than hammers (like forging and stamping press, pig breaks drop crushers etc.) (1987) revised in 1993

Machines are classified as high or low frequency according to their rpm as follows:

0–500 rpm: low frequency machines.

500–1000 rpm: intermediate to high frequency machines.

> 1000 rpm: high frequency machines.

23.7.1 Method of Analysis of Machine Foundations

In general, machine foundations should be analyzed for static and dynamic effects. The general requirements are the following:

1. We make static analysis to see whether the foundation pressures under the static loads and the dynamic forces with suitable overload factors are within safe limits. Usually the specified dynamic loads are multiplied by a factor, 3 to give static values. The settlement due to consolidation and effects of vibration under the static and dynamic loads should also be within limits.

2. We make dynamic analysis to see whether the amplitude of vibration under service condition are within the general prescribed limits as given by the manufacturers or prescribed by the Code. Generally, it is accepted that amplitudes should be less than 0.2 mm (see Section 23.14).

3. We make dynamic analysis also to ensure that there will be no resonance. The natural frequency of the foundation should be high for low speed engines and vice versa. *The general practice is that the natural frequency should be atleast either less than 0.5 times (30–50%) or more than 2.5 times (200–300%) the operating frequency of the machine.* When the natural frequency of the designed foundation is much higher than the operating frequency, the foundation is said to have been *over-tuned*. If the frequency of the designed foundation is much less than the operating frequency the foundation is said to have been *under-tuned*.

23.8 TYPES OF MACHINE FOUNDATIONS

The layout of the foundation depends on the position of the operating floor level, as well as that of the auxiliary equipment and also on many other factors. Considering the structural forms, machine foundations can be classified into the following types (see Fig. 23.4):

1. Block foundation
2. Box type foundation with hollow inside
3. Wall type or pedestal type of foundation with a pair of walls on a base slab supporting the machine on top
4. Framed type foundation consisting of a base slab, vertical columns and top slab
5. Foundations of other shapes to suit the machine.

In general, machines producing impulsive or periodic forces at low frequencies are supported on block foundations while machines working at high speeds like turbines are usually mounted on framed type of foundations. In Fig. 23.4, except for the block type, the machinery is supported on the upper floors and transmits load to soil at the basement levels.

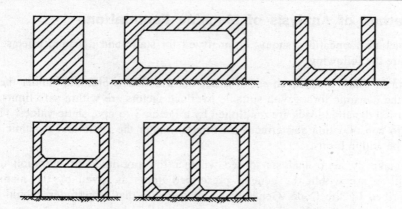

Fig. 23.4   Block and frame types of machine foundations.

23.9 FOUNDATION ANALYSIS

As we have seen, two types of analysis are to be made for machine foundations, namely static analysis and dynamic analysis. *Static analysis deals with foundation pressures and settlements while dynamic analysis deals with resonance and amplitudes of vibration.* However, in many low speed machines only the static analysis may be necessary, though in many other machines like compressors and hammers, where unbalanced forces are high, both analyses are always needed. A list of the usual machines met in practice and the type of analysis to be made with them are given below.

1. Rotary type machines of low frequency.

   (a) Rolling mills—static analysis only
   (b) Crushing mills (jaw and core crushes)—both static and dynamic analysis
   (c) Pumps—both static and dynamic analysis
   (d) Grinding mills— static analysis only
   (e) Motors/generators—both static and dynamic analysis

2. Lathes, milling machines, drilling machines and boring machines generally do not require analysis, but only isolation from other sources of vibration.

3. Impact machines, other than drop hammers, forging and stamping press generally require only static analysis. Dynamic analysis is of very little significance for these machines.

4. Impact machines like drop hammers, forging and stamping press, and drop weight-crushers require both static and dynamic analysis.

5. Fans and blowers require both static and dynamic analysis.

6. Spinning or other looms when installed on the upper floors, it must be ensured that the natural frequency of the floor is not near the operating speed of the loom. Dynamic effects should also be considered in these cases.

The more difficult machines to deal with are those, which run at low frequency of 200–500 cycles per minute. As most *buildings have low natural frequencies*, care should be taken to prevent resonance.

23.10 STATIC ANALYSIS

The forces to be considered in static analysis are, the static loads and the dynamic loads caused by the unbalanced forces. The static forces are easy to be calculated. These are due to the dead weights of the foundation and the machines mounted on it. As far as possible, eccentricity of loads should be avoided. The unbalanced forces are produced by the rotation of the different parts of the machine (as in a multi-cylinder engine). These dynamic forces can be determined from the data supplied by the manufacturers. These forces should be determined in X, Y and Z directions, and the resultant moments about the centre of gravity of the foundation determined. These calculated moments and forces are usually multiplied by a factor called the 'dynamic coefficient' to convert the dynamic effect into static effect. A factor of 3 is usually used.

As already pointed out, in many cases of foundations of machines, only static effect (static loads plus the static effect of dynamic loads) need to be analyzed. Also, empirical values are also used for the dynamic factor. For example, in the design of a tube mill, the dynamic load is generally approximated to a horizontal centrifugal force equal to the weight of the cylinder tube without charge acting at the centre or the axis of the tube.

23.11 DYNAMIC ANALYSIS

Dynamic analysis is the calculation of frequencies and amplitudes. Earlier, machines were usually bolted to the foundation block, which served the function of spreading the load to the soil and increasing the mass of the vibrating system. In cases where fine-tuning of the foundation was to be done after the construction of the foundation, cavities were left to adjust the weight of the foundation and thus adjust its frequency.

23.11.1 Historical Development

In early design of machine foundations, the manufacturer recommended a suitable foundation based on experience and expressed it as weight per horse power of the engine. In 1938, Couzens gave a 'table of recommended weights of foundation' for engine weights for various types of machines without reference to soil types. The ratio of foundation weight to machine weight varied from 2 to 3. However with rapid industrialisation and better knowledge of vibration analysis, the design of machine foundation become a subject of theoretical investigation. The first type to be investigated was the conventional block foundation.

The first to suggest a formula for frequency of vibration of this type of foundation was Alpan who made use of Tschebotarioff's data and gave the following empirical expression for the natural frequency f_n of a block foundation:

$$f_n = \frac{\alpha}{\sqrt{W}} (A_f)^{1/4}$$

where α is a function of the type of the soil, W is the weight of the machine and foundation in kg and A_f is the contact area of the block in m^2.

This formula gave only the probable *natural frequency*, which is inadequate for modern foundation as the values of *amplitudes* are also necessary for proper design of foundations.

Calculations of natural frequency, assuming that a certain mass of the soil (called apparent mass) also acts with the foundation block, was recommended by Pauw in 1952. Accordingly, he suggested the following formula for the natural frequency of the foundation system:

$$f = \frac{1}{2\pi}\sqrt{\frac{k}{m + m_1}} \tag{23.9}$$

where m is the mass of the foundation block and machine, m_1 is the mass of the soil that vibrates with the block and is the spring constant—which is different from the subgrade reaction theory. However, it was found difficult to estimate the mass of the soil vibrating with the machine. Later in 1962, Barkan [4] developed the method of analysis based on linear undamped spring analogy, which is now known as the *modulus of dynamic subgrade reaction method*.

However, many foundation systems such as those supported or piles have quite a lot of damping and Barkan's method is not exactly applicable to such system. In 1962 Richart developed the method based on linear theory of elasticity called the *elastic half-space method* [5] [6]. In this method, the foundation is considered as a semi-infinite elastic solid obeying linear theory of elasticity. The method also uses the results of measurements that should be made to evaluate the soil properties at the given site.

The method using coefficient of elastic compression values and the elastic half-space method for spring constants are the two present-day methods used for the general design of machine foundation. However, special foundations with unconventionally sized (or shaped) beam elements which defy the assumption that are made in the conventional methods have to be solved by model analysis or theoretically by means of more powerful analytical tools like finite element analysis [7] [8]. Only the dynamic subgrade reaction method has been dealt with in detail in this chapter.

As already pointed out, the compressor block foundation and the hammer block foundation are two typical cases of two different types of vibrations. In the case of the compressor, oscillations are produced by *forced vibration* and analysis should follow the theory of such vibrations. On the other hand, in the case of a hammer foundation, the vibrations are produced by the free fall of the hammer and it is a case of *free vibration*. We will examine the foundations for these two types of machines in more detail in Sections 23.13 and 23.14.

23.11.2 Pressure-bulb Concept

As already pointed out, one of the early methods proposed by Pauw to calculate the natural frequency of a block foundation was to assume that a mass of soil below the foundation will vibrate with the system. The soil participating in the system is usually assumed as that enclosed within the bulb of pressure. The depth of the bulb (d_s) is sometimes estimated from the following formula.

$$d_s = \left[\frac{0.477W}{\gamma/g}\right]^{1/2}$$

where W = total (static and dynamic) load.

The suggestion is that the soil participating in the vibration is assumed to be that enclosed within the pressure bulb where γ is the unit weight of the soil. However this is a very crude estimate of the real situation.

Pauw assumed the natural frequency will be as in Eq. (23.9). That is,

$$f = \frac{1}{2\pi}\sqrt{\frac{k}{m + m_1}}$$

where

k = spring constant (different from k of sub-grade reaction theory)

m = mass of machine and block

m_1 = mass of earth vibrating with the block

Charts and diagrams are available to find k and m_1. However, with the advent of the modern concepts of vibrations and availability of field tests to measure soil properties, these methods are no longer in use.

23.11.3 Amplitude of Vibration from Frequency Ratio

Let

$$\frac{f}{f_n} = \frac{\text{frequency of machine}}{\text{natural frequency}} = q = \text{frequency ratio}$$

From Eq. (23.6b),

$$\text{Amplitude } z_0 = \frac{P_0/k}{\left[\left(1 - q^2\right)^2 + \left(\dfrac{2cq}{c_c}\right)^2\right]^{1/2}} \quad \text{for linear oscillation}$$

where P_0 = maximum dynamic force.

23.12 DESIGN OF CONCRETE FOUNDATION

As in many other civil engineering practices, we first fix the type and dimension of the foundation from past experience. Thus, we have typical foundation arrangements for each type of machines. The foundation for a compressor will be different from that for a drop hammer. Easiness in erecting, disbanding, provision of anchor bolts and other details should always be taken care of when detailing. In general, the foundation should extend 15 cm or more beyond the base of the machine. The foundation, where isolation is not required can be cast directly against the soil rather than by using side forms to take advantage of the shear resistance of the soil for vertical motion and rocking. For the latter purpose, the width should be as large as the depth. However, where the amplitudes should not be transmitted to other parts of the building, the foundation has to be isolated by proper methods. The method of analysis of the various types consist of first choosing the design parameters of the soil and then adopting the most appropriate mathematical model for analysis. Depending on the foundation, one degree or two degrees or even three degrees systems may be adopted.

23.13 DESIGN OF A BLOCK FOUNDATION FOR A COMPRESSOR

For compressors, we generally adopt block foundations. Compressors can be the vertical type or horizontal type. The foundation for compressor machines is subjected to *forced vibration with damping*. We make both static and dynamic analysis. In static analysis, we ensure that the foundation pressure and settlement are within their permissible values. In dynamic analysis, we ensure that resonance is avoided and the amplitude of vibration is within limits.

Static analysis

Step 1: From the machine dimensions and data, draw a tentative layout of a suitable type of block foundation based on past experience. In practice, a block approximately 2.5 times the weight (2 to 3 times) of the machine is chosen for this purpose.

Step 2: From the dimensions of the block foundation, find the eccentricities $\bar{x}$, $\bar{y}$ and $\bar{z}$ with the machine founded on it and determine the static pressure and stresses due to moments. In general, eccentricity should always be as small as possible. Soil pressure is calculated as follows:

Soil pressure = $W/A \pm M/Z$

Step 3: From the dimensions of the machine and its characteristics, calculate the following forces and moments depending on whether it is a vertical or horizontal compressor.

- Vertical unbalanced force
- Horizontal unbalanced force
- Unbalanced rocking moments

Determine the additional stresses in the foundation due to these forces. To make these forces into static forces, assume the equivalent static force. This is taken as 3 times the dynamic force. The effect of these loads is added to the forces due to gravity forces.

Dynamic analysis for resonance and amplitudes. Let X be along the length, Y along breadth and Z along the vertical.

Step 1: Find probable frequencies and amplitude in uncoupled modes and check their magnitudes for the following (see Fig. 23.2).

(a) Consider vertical mode and find frequency and amplitude. Use Eq. (23.7a). Values for C_u are taken from test results or from Table 23.1 given in Section 23.17 or from I.S. Code [1].
(b) Consider sliding mode and find its frequency and amplitude using Eq. (23.7b).
(c) Consider rocking mode and find its frequency and amplitude using Eq. (23.7c).
(d) Consider torsional mode and find its frequency and amplitude using Eq. (23.7d).

Step 2: Consider coupled modes (rocking and sliding or vertical, rocking and sliding) and find the frequencies and amplitudes in these modes and ensure that their magnitudes are within limits using Eq. (23.8). The details of the procedure can be obtained from codes and references given at the end of this chapter.

The allowable amplitude in machine foundation depends on the frequency of the machine. For machines up to 1000 rpm an amplitude value of 0.2 mm is considered safe.

23.14 DESIGN OF A BLOCK FOUNDATION FOR A FORGE HAMMER

The foundation for a forge hammer will undergo *free vibration* and the usual requirements are the following:

1. The maximum stresses in soil due to static and equivalent dynamic forces should not exceed the allowable values.

2. For maximum vertical amplitude of vibration of the *foundation block* (due to the impact of hammer) should not exceed 1.2 mm. In the case of foundation in sand below ground water table, the permissible amplitude is limited to 0.8 mm.

3. The permissible amplitude *of anvil depends* on the weight of *falling tup*. It is to be kept as 1 mm for a tup of 1 ton, 2 mm for a tup of 2 tons and 3 to 4 mm for a tup of 3 tons.

Depending on the requirements, the foundation can rest on soil, piles, cork, springs or rubber pads. As shown in Fig. 23.5, the anvil is placed on a suitable insulation layer in the form of timber

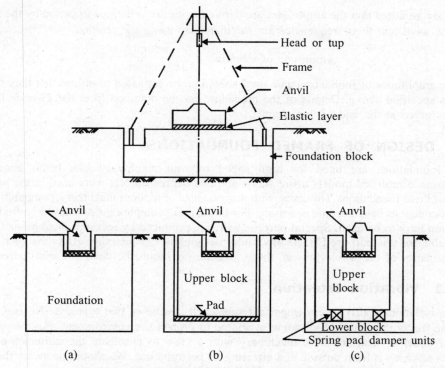

Fig. 23.5 Types of foundations for forge hammers.

grillage or other resilient material. The metal to be forged is placed on the anvil and the tup falls on it repeatedly at regular intervals, the movement of the tup being controlled mechanically by steam or compressed air.

The vertical/horizontal dynamic test is conducted on the foundation for determining their spring constants and the wave propagation test for determining the shear modulus, or else values are assumed for the various parameters. For the dynamic analysis of hammer foundations, it is conventional to assume that the foundation is under free vibration caused by the initial velocity imparted on the anvil by the tup. The hammer foundation can be idealized as shown in Fig. 23.6.

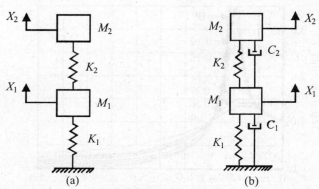

Fig. 23.6 Idealization of hammer foundation: (a) Undamped vibration; (b) damped vibration.

It may be noted that the amplitudes are derived from the velocities imparted by the fall of the tup on the anvil and their frequencies are calculated by using the relation,

$$\text{Amplitude of vibration} = \frac{\text{velocity}}{2\pi(\text{frequency})}$$

The amplitudes of foundation and anvil should be investigated to ensure that they fall within the limits specified above. Details of the procedure can be obtained from the IS code Part 2 and references given at the end of this chapter.

23.15 DESIGN OF FRAMED FOUNDATIONS

Framed foundations are used for high speed rotating machinery like turbo generators in powerhouses. Simplified models using single and two degree models were used in the past for the analysis of these foundations. However, with growing size of modern machinery, comparatively more slender foundations have become necessary. For these, more complex models based on finite element formulation have to be used. Special purpose software produced by research institutions like SERC are available for this purpose [7]. As any faulty design will considerably affect the cost as well as the performance of the whole project, these foundations should be designed with extreme care.

23.15.1 Vibration Isolation

Vibration isolation is also a very important subject. It can be of two types. *Active isolation* is to isolate the machinery induced vibration at source to protect the environment. *Passive isolation* is that used under or near sensitive machinery with a view to eliminate the influence of external vibrations reaching it from outside and affecting its performance. We should be aware that if water level rises above the base, the vibrations will be felt up to a larger distance than otherwise.

The term *transmissibility* is used in isolation. It is defined as follows:

$$\text{In active isolation} = \frac{\text{force transmitted to the foundation}}{\text{vibratory force of the machine}}$$

$$\text{In passive isolation} = \frac{\text{amplitude of the instrument}}{\text{amplitude of the base}}$$

For both cases, a common expression T can be derived which is a function of the frequency ratio of machine to foundation, η, and the damping factor, ξ. The relation is shown in Fig. 23.7.

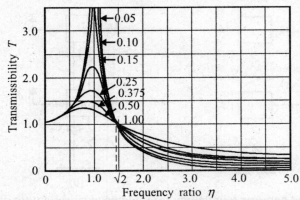

Fig. 23.7 **Variation of transmissibility with frequency ratio and damping factors (frequency ratio to be at least √2 for all cases of vibration isolation).**

It can be seen that with $\eta > \sqrt{2}$ the transmissibility will be small. Thus, the natural frequency of the foundation should be well below $1/\sqrt{2}$ or 0.707 times the disturbing frequency for isolation. Many materials like cork, felt, rubber springs and steel springs are used for isolation. Counter-balancing of frequencies of the machine itself is another method of isolation. Isolation of machines, which have been already installed but needs correction, can be done by increasing the base area of foundation or by stabilizing the soil (thus increasing its stiffness). Digging trenches in the path of the waves also reduces the transmission of waves. The length and depth of the trench required for isolation can be worked out by empirical formulae [9]. Instead of continuous trenches we may adopt a deep wall of hollow piles between the source of vibration and the object to be protected. Theoretical analysis of these situations are available. Sensitive machines should always be isolated according to the manufacturer's specifications by passive isolation.

23.16 CONSTRUCTION DETAILS

Machine foundations should always be constructed with care as it is difficult to rectify any initial defects once they are constructed. Also as any stopping of machines will considerably affect the working of a factory, *the design of these foundations should include a higher factor of safety than adopted for normal structures.* Under no circumstances, should the foundations of important machines like generators, compressors etc. in a factory pose problems.

Block foundations should be cast in horizontal lifts avoiding cold joints. It should be liberally reinforced on all surfaces, around openings. The minimum steel specified is 25 kg/m^3 of concrete (16 to 25 mm rods at 20 to 30 cm spacing in both directions and also on the lateral faces). Concrete cover should be atleast 75 mm for the earth side of concrete and 50 mm for the sides exposed to air.

In the case of a framed foundation, the base slab may be separately cast with a minimum reinforcement of 50 kg/m^3. Around all openings, steel reinforcement equal to 0.5 to 0.7 per cent of the area of the opening should be provided in the form of a cage. Standard detailing practice should be used in all cases. In massive constructions, it may be necessary to reduce the heat of hydration of the concrete by suitable method. It is advisable to cast the whole foundation by continuous casting. Otherwise, liberal steel should be provided at designed construction joints [10].

23.16.1 Machines on Pile Foundations

As f_n^2 varies with k/m, any increase in spring constant k increases the natural frequency of the system. Piles provide additional springs and also damping factors. Piled foundations are used for machines for the following reasons:

1. To increase bearing capacity and reduce settlements under static or dynamic loads.

2. To increase the natural frequency of a foundation by increasing the spring constant (the variation of frequency with rigidity can be seen from Fig. 23.8. A fixed beam is more rigid than a cantilever).

3. To decrease the possible amplitude of natural vibration or the resultant of a forced vibration.

Such designs need special data and analysis for a satisfactory solution [11].

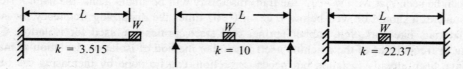

Fig. 23.8 Increase in rigidity with conditions of fixity.

23.17 DETERMINATION OF SOIL PROPERTIES FOR DYNAMIC ANALYSIS [11]

We have seen when dealing with free vibrations from Eq. (23.1) that the natural frequency of a system depends on mass in vibration and the spring constant:

$$f = \frac{1}{2\pi}\sqrt{\frac{g}{\delta_{st}}}$$

where

$$\delta_{st} = \frac{W}{k} = \frac{\text{weight}}{\text{spring constant}} = \text{displacement}$$

Soil spring constant depends on the soil condition which has to be estimated from experience or determined by field tests. IS 5249–1992. "Tests for Determination of Dynamic Properties of Soil" [1] gives details of tests that can be made. The more commonly adopted tests are the *cyclic plate load test* and the *block vibration test*.

Cyclic plate load test. A plate is placed on the ground and it is subjected to increasing loads. As different from ordinary plate load tests, each successive load is maintained till settlement is complete. The load is then reduced to zero and the plate allowed to rebound. The readings for this load will consist of the reading at full load and the settlement at no load. The load is then increased to the next increment and settlements taken at full load and zero load. This cycle of loading and unloading is continued till the required final load is reached. A graph is drawn between load on the Y axis and total elastic settlement for that load on the X axis. The slope of this curve is the coefficient of elastic uniform compression in kN/m^3.

$$C_u = \frac{p}{s}, \text{ kN/m}^3 \tag{23.10a}$$

where p = pressure and s = settlement.

The spring constant $k = C_u \times$ (area of contact) in kN/m $\tag{23.10b}$

The following correction for the actual area A of the real foundation should be used as against the area 'a' of the test when we use the value for a practical problem (A is usually taken as 10 m^2 for expressing C_u):

$$C_u = C_{test}\sqrt{\frac{a}{A}}$$

Block vibration test. For the block vibration test, a concrete block 0.7 m high and 1.5 m × 0.75 m in plan is cast in a pit at the foundation level with the necessary bolts for fixing the oscillator. In the block, the eccentric masses and motor can be set at different angles to produce different vibrations. Accelerator pick ups can be mounted and from the acceleration and known frequency values, the amplitudes can be calculated using the following relation:

$$\text{Amplitude} = \frac{\text{acceleration}}{4\pi^2 \text{ (frequency)}}$$

For vertical oscillation, readings are made to obtain plots with amplitude along Y axis and frequency along X axis. From the plots, the resonant frequency for the given size can be obtained by observing the shape of the curves. The value of k is calculated as follows.

$$k = m\omega_n^2 = (\text{mass of block})(2\pi\, f_n^2)$$

where f_n is the resonant frequency.

We should note that arrangement for similar tests can be made for horizontal vibration also.

Damping factor test. In case of block foundation damping factor is contributed mainly by soil (as for example its embedment). Two tests, one based on free vibration, and the other on forced vibration are available in IS 5249:1992 for this test.

IS recommendations. In the general analysis of machine foundations, we use separate coefficients for each type of vibration. I.S. recommends the following rough correlation between them:

Coefficient of uniform elastic compression C_u

Coefficient of uniform elastic shear $C_\tau = 1/2 C_u$

Coefficient of elastic non-uniform compression $C_\phi = 3.46 C_\tau$

Coefficient of elastic non-uniform shear $C_\psi = 0.75 C_u$

IS also recommends the following values in Table 23.1 for routine design of machine foundations.

TABLE 23.1   RECOMMENDED VALUES OF C_u
(Area of base 10 m²)
As recommended by Barkan [4]

Category	Soil group	Static load pressure (kN/m²)	C_u (kN/m³)
1	Weak soils	Up to 150	Up to 30,000
2	Medium strong	150–350	30–50,000
3	Strong soils	350–500	50–100,000
4	Rocks	> 500	> 100,000

[Note: The following examples are given only to indicate the procedure to be adopted in design of machine foundations. Accordingly they are not worked out fully in detail.]

EXAMPLE 23.1   (Design of a block foundation for a vertical compressor)

A two cylinder *vertical compressor* of weight 10 t is driven by an electric motor weighing 3.5 t working at 600 rpm. The length and breadth of the base of the foundation block are $L_x = 6.6$ and $L_y = 4$ m, and it weighs 54.7 tons. The data of forces generated are as follows:

Unbalanced forces: vertical = 4.24 tons; horizontal = 0 ton
Unbalanced rocking moment = 4.59 t and $\Theta = 78.9°$
Centre of gravity of system; $\bar{x} = 3.3$ m from edge; $\bar{y} = 2.00$ from edge; $\bar{z} = 0.89$ m from base.
M_{m0} = Mass moment of inertia of system = 27.6 t m s^2

Determine the natural frequencies in vertical, sliding, rocking (uncoupled modes) and also in the coupled frequencies of vertical, sliding and rocking mode if $C_u = 4.0 \times 10^3$ t/m^3 and safe bearing capacity 150 kN/m^2.

Ref.	Step	Calculations
	1	*Static Analysis* (Motion is vertical forced vibration)
		Find foundation pressures and settlements.
Sec. 23.13 (Step 1 to 3)		Total vertical weight = $W = 10 + 3.5 + 54.7 = 68.2$ tons
		As eccentricity is 0.33 m in X axis (along 6.6 m), we may neglect it
		Equivalent unbalanced static force = $3 \times 4.24 = 12.72$ tons
		Total vertical load = $68.2 + 12.72 = 81$ tons
		Unit pressure = $\dfrac{81}{6.6 \times 4} = 3.06$ t/m$^2 < 30.6$ kN/m^2 safe
		Assess settlement and assume it is within limits (foundation should not rest on loose sand)
	2	*Dynamic Analysis—Consider vertical mode.*
	2(a)	*Find frequency and amplitude in vertical mode*
		Find frequency
		(Let $C_u = 4.0 \times 10^3$ t/m^3)
Eq. (23.7a)	2(b)	$f_{nz}^2 = \dfrac{C_u A}{4\pi^2 m}$, where m is the mass; $W = 68.2$ tons
		Mass; $\dfrac{W}{g}$; Taking $g = 10$, we have $m = 6.82$ ts^2/m.
		$f_{nz}^2 = \dfrac{4 \times 10^3 \times 26.4}{4 \times \pi^2 \times 6.82}$ (in tons and metres) $f_{nz} = 19.8$ Hz
Sec. 23.7.1 Item 4		Check $\dfrac{\text{disturbing frequency}}{\text{natural frequency}} = \dfrac{10}{19.8} = 0.5$ which is acceptable

Find amplitude

Eq. (23.6a)

$$\text{Amplitude} = \frac{\text{downward load } (P_0)}{4m\pi^2(f_{nz}^2 - f^2)} \text{ for undamped oscillation}$$

P_0 = vertical force = 4.24 tons

f = 600 rpm = 10 Hz

$$z_0 = \frac{4.24}{4 \times 6.82 \times \pi^2 (392 - 100)} = 5.4 \times 10^{-5} \text{ m}$$

Sec. 23.13

= 0.054 mm (is acceptable, being less than 0.2 mm)

3 | *Consider sliding. Find frequency in sliding mode*

Sec. 23.17

$$C_\tau = \frac{1}{2} C_u = 2 \times 10^3 \text{ t/m}^3$$

Eq. (23.7b)

$$f_{nx}^2 = \frac{C_1 A}{4\pi^2 m} = \frac{2 \times 10^3 \times 26.4}{4 \times \pi^2 \times 6.82} = 13.87 \text{ Hz}$$

4 | *Consider rocking. Find frequency in rocking mode*

Eq. (23.7c)

Assume $C_\phi = 8$ t/m^3; $\quad f_{n\phi}^2 = \dfrac{C_\phi I - Wz}{4\pi^2 M_{m0}}$

where

I = moment of inertia about rocking axis
$\quad = 4 \times (6.6)^3/12 = 95.83$ m^4 and $W = 68.2$ tons

z = height of centre of gravity of system from base = 0.89 m

M_{m0} = mass moment of inertia of system about axis of rotation
(Y-axis) = 27.6 t s^2/m

$$f_{n\phi}^2 = \frac{8 \times 10^3 \times 95.83 - 68.2 \times 0.89}{4 \times \pi^2 \times 27.6} = 26.5 \text{ Hz}$$

Eq. (23.8)

5 | *Find coupled sliding and rocking motion (rocking mode)*

Solving equation $rf_n^4 - \left(f_{nx}^2 + f_{n\phi}^2\right)f_n^2 + f_{nx}^2 f_{n\phi}^2 = 0$, we get

$$(f_{n1}^2)(f_{n2}^2) = \frac{1}{2r}\left[\left(f_{nx}^2 + f_{n\phi}^2\right) \pm \sqrt{\left(f_{nx}^2 + f_{n\phi}^2\right)^2 - 4r f_{n\phi}^2 f_{nx}^2}\,\right]$$

where r = ratio of $\left[\dfrac{\text{moment of inertia about C.G. of system}}{\text{moment of inertia about } Y \text{ axis}}\right]$

$$= \frac{M_m}{M_{m0}} = \frac{M_{m0} - m\bar{z}^2}{M_{m0}} = \frac{22.05}{27.60} = 0.80$$

$f_{n1}^2; f_{n2}^2 = S$

$$S = \frac{1}{2 \times 0.8}\left[703 + 192 \pm \sqrt{(703 + 192)^2 - 4 \times 0.8 \times 703 \times 192}\,\right]$$

Sec. 23.13		$f_{n1}^2 = 180$ and $f_{n2}^2 = 941$; $f_{n1} = 13.41$ and $f_{n2} = 30.68$ Hz These are the lower and higher f_n values. Frequency of machine = 600 rpm = 10 per second. Lower f_n is only 1.34 times above the frequency of the machine.
	6	*Check whether amplitudes of oscillations are within limits* The amplitudes can be calculated by standard formula (see Ref. [3]) and check for requirements.

EXAMPLE 23.2   (Design of a block foundation for a horizontal compressor)

Make a dynamic analysis of a block foundation for a *horizontal compressor* with the following data [3] (See Section 4.4.8. Ref [2].)

1 Weight of machines is 36 tons; wt. of foundation is 272 tons
2 Operating speed—150 rpm
3 Horizontal unbalanced force of 12 t acting 0.6 m above foundation level
4 Coefficient of elastic uniform shear $C_t = 2.25 \times 10^3$ t/m^3
5 Base of foundation is 9.5 m × 7.5 m
6 Eccentricity of horizontal force from C.G. of block is 1.56 m
7 Mass moment of inertia about Y axis through C.G. of system perpendicular to plane of vibration (M_m) is 192 t m s^2
8 Mass moment of inertia about Y axis about centroid of base area and perpendicular to vibration (M_{m0}) is 240 t m s^2
9 Common C.G. of machine and foundation: $\bar{x} = 4.745$ m; $\bar{y} = 3.718$ m; $\bar{z} = 1.239$ m

Ref.	Step	Calculations
		Note: This is a case of horizontal vibrations. As the forces are horizontal, the important vibrations are the uncoupled rocking and sliding together with the coupled rocking and sliding. After static analysis, dynamic analysis is made as follows:
	1	*Find frequency of rocking motion (uncoupled)*
Eq. (23.7c)		$f_{n\phi}^2 = \dfrac{C_\phi I - W\bar{z}}{4\pi^2 M_{m0}}$ Let $C_\phi = 9 \times 10^3$ t/m^3 $I = \dfrac{7.5 \times (9.5)^3}{12} = 536$ m^4 $W = (272 + 36) = 308$ t; $m = \dfrac{308}{10} = 30.8$ $f_{n\phi}^2 = \dfrac{9 \times 10^3 \times 536 - 308 \times 1.239}{4 \times \pi^2 \times 240} = 510$ $f_{n\phi} = 22.5$ Hz

Ref.	Step	Calculations
	2	*Find frequency in sliding motion (uncoupled)*
Eq. (23.7b)		$$f_{nx}^2 = \frac{C_\tau A}{4\pi^2 m}$$ Let $C_\tau = 2.25 \times 10^3$ t/m$^3 = \dfrac{2.25 \times 10^3 \times 9.5 \times 7.5}{4 \times \pi^2 \times 30.8}$ $F_{nx} = 11.5$ Hz
Eq. (23.8)	3	*Find coupled natural frequency—rocking and sliding* Solve equation $rf_n^4 - \left(f_{nx}^2 + f_{n\phi}^2\right)f_n^2 + f_{nx}^2\, f_{n\phi}^2$ Gives $f_{n1} = 26$ and $f_{n2} = 11$ Hz These are the higher and lower f_n values.
	4	*Compare with machine frequency* Machine frequency = 150 rpm = 2.5 per second Lower natural frequency = 11 Hz is well above the frequency of the machine. Hence safe.
	5	*Calculate the amplitude of vibration* For details see Ref. [3].

EXAMPLE 23.3 **(Design of a hammer foundation [3])**

Make a dynamic analysis of a hammer foundation with the following data:

Weight of tup = 3.4 t
Weight of anvil = 75 t
Weight of foundation = 163.2 t
Weight of frame = 38.35 t (assumed to be resting on foundation)
Base provided = 7.1 m × 4.7 m (33.37 m^2)
Coefficient of rigidity of pad under anvil = 18.02 × 10^5 t/m (k)
Coefficient of rigidity of base of foundation $C_u = 3.8 \times 10^3$ t/m^3
Area of anvil = 8.32 m^2

[*Note:* This is a case of free vibration. The natural frequencies will be *independent* of the velocity of the tup but the amplitude will depend on the tup velocity. The tup falls on anvil which has pad (timber) under it. We assume foundation shown in Fig. 23.5(a). The timber rests on concrete block which, in turn, rests on soil, (We can have alternate foundation as in Fig. 23.5(b) or 23.5(c).]

Ref.	Step	Calculations
	1	*Find rigidity of timber pad below anvil* $$k = \frac{(\text{modulus of elasticity}) \times (\text{area})}{\text{thickness}}$$ $$= \frac{13 \times 10^3 \times 8.32 \times 10^4}{60} = 18.02 \times 10^6 \text{ kg/cm}$$ $$= 18.02 \times 10^5 \text{ t/m}$$

Eq, (23.1) Eq. (23.7a)	**2** *Find f_n of anvil due to fall of tup (free oscillation)* $$f_n^2 = \frac{k}{4\pi^2 m} = \frac{18.02 \times 10^5}{4 \times \pi^2 \times 7.84} = 5.8 \times 10^3$$ $$\left(m = \frac{(3.4 + 75.0)}{10} = 7.84 \text{ t s/m} \right) \text{ gives } f_n = 76 \text{ Hz}$$ $\omega_a = 2\pi f_n = 477$ radians per second

3   *Find f_n of foundation and frame*

Mass of foundation and frame

$$= m = \frac{163.2 + 38.35}{10} = 20.16 \text{ t s/m}$$

Tup and anvil $m' = \dfrac{78.4}{10} = 7.84$; $C_u = 3.8 \times 10^3$ t/m^3

Eq. (23.7a)

$$f_n^2 = \frac{C_u A}{4\pi^2 m} = \frac{3.8 \times 10^3 \times 33.37}{4 \times \pi^2 \times 28.0} = 114.6$$

$f_f = 10.7$ Hz; $\omega_z = 2\pi f = 67.2$ radians per second

4   As the system, as shown in Fig. 23.1, has two degrees of freedom, the frequencies of combination should be obtained from the following equation as given in Ref. [3].

$$\omega_n^2 - (\omega_a^2 + \omega_z^2)(1 - \alpha)\omega_n^2 + (1 + \alpha)\omega_a^2 \omega_z^2 = 0$$

where $\alpha = \dfrac{\text{mass of anvil}}{\text{(mass of foundation including frame)}}$

5   *Calculate the amplitudes*

The natural frequencies will be independent of the velocity of the tup. But the amplitudes of anvil and foundation will be functions of the velocity of impact. These *amplitudes of the anvil* and *that of the foundations* can be separately calculated by formulae given in Ref. [3]. These should be within safe limits as given in Sec. 23.14.

REFERENCES

[1]   IS 5249–1995, *Tests for Determination of Dynamic Properties of Soils*, Bureau of Indian Standards, New Delhi.

[2]   IS 2974 (Parts 1 to 5), *Codes of Practice for Design and Construction of Machine Foundation*, Bureau of Indian Standards, New Delhi, Part I (1982), Part 2 (1980), Part 3 (1992), Part 4 (1989), Part 5 (1987).

[3]   Srinivasulu, P. and C.V. Vaidyanathan, *Handbook of Machine Foundation*, Tata McGraw-Hill, New Delhi, 1976.

[4]   Barkan, D.D., *Dynamics of Bases and Foundations*, McGraw-Hill, New York, 1962.

[5]   Richart, R.C. (Jr.), *Foundation Vibrations*, Transactions American Society of Civil Engineers, Vol. 127, Part 1, 1962.

[6]   Richart, F.E. (Jr.), J.R. Hall (Jr.), and R.D. Woods, *Vibrations of Soils and Foundations*, Prentice Hall, New Jersey, 1970.

[7]   OSTA 99, *General Purpose Finite Element Software*, User Manual, Part 2, Data Guide, SERC, Chennai, 1999.

[8]   Harris, C.M. and A.G. Piersol, *Shock and Vibration Handbook*, McGraw-Hill, New York, 1976.

[9]   Swami Saran, *Soil Dynamics and Machine Foundations*, Galgotia Publications, New Delhi, 1999.

[10] Major, A., *Vibration Analysis and Design of Foundations for Machines and Turbines*, Collects Holdings, London, 1962.

[11] Bowles, J.E., *Foundation Analysis and Design*, McGraw-Hill International Edition, Singapore, 1988.

24

Stability of Slopes

24.1 INTRODUCTION

Slopes can be natural or man-made. These may be above ground level as embankments or below ground level as in railway cuttings or excavations for construction. Slopes occur naturally along hill slopes and riversides, in which case they are called natural slopes. In all such cases, the forces of gravity tends to move soil from high levels to low levels and the forces that resist this action are on account of the shear strengths of the soil. Presence of water increases weight, reduces shear strength and decreases the stability. Weights of man-made structures constructed on or near slopes tend to increase the destabilizing forces and slope instability. These slope failures are known as slides. In this chapter, we will deal with the fundamentals of the mechanics of stability of homogeneous slopes and describe the limit equilibrium methods used to estimate their factors of safety from a knowledge of the shear strength of the soil constituting them. Failure of non-uniform soil as occurs in natural slopes should be studied individually depending on the environment.

24.2 CLASSIFICATION OF SLOPE FAILURES

Cohesionless soils like sand can easily maintain only a slope equal to its angle of internal friction. It is cohesion combined with friction that allows steeper slopes. Slope failures in soils having cohesion can be classified into the following types as shown in Fig. 24.1.

1. Regular rotational slides
2. Landslides, which may be: (a) Falls, (b) rotational slides, (c) translational slides, (d) flows, (e) compound slides.

Each of these failure modes has its own mechanism and conditions for failure. In this chapter, we shall restrict to the rotational slides only which are common with soils with cohesion. Advanced books on stability of slopes should be referred when dealing with other types of slides and also failure of non-homogeneous slopes such as in earth dams and the naturally occurring slopes. Falls, flows and compound slides are great sources of natural disasters during very heavy rains in mountainous terrains all over the world.

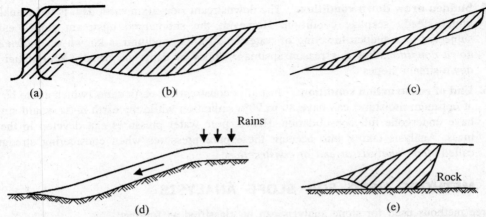

Fig. 24.1 Types of slope failure: (a) Falls; (b) rotational slides; (c) translational slip; (d) flows; (e) compound slides.

24.3 TERMS USED IN SLOPE ANALYSIS

The terms used in slope analysis should be clearly understood. They are generally referred with respect to failure along a circular surface called failure circle (see Fig. 24.2).

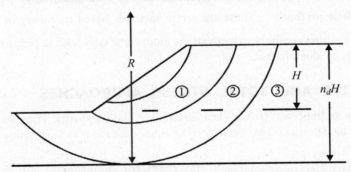

Fig. 24.2 Analysis of slopes assuming failure along a circle: (1) Slope circle failure; (2) toe circle failure; (3) base circle failure.

The terms are now described.

1. **Slope circle failure:** In this case the failure circle intercepts the surface of the slope itself above the toe.

2. **Toe circle failure:** In this case the failure circle passes through the toe of the slope. This occurs in steep slopes of homogeneous soils.

3. **Base or midpoint circle failure:** In this case the failure circle passes below the toe at a depth $n_d H$ from top of the slope of height H. Such cases occur when slopes are flat with weak soil and a stiff stratum occurs below the toe. As their centre is along the middle line of the slope, they are also called midpoint circle failure.

4. **Depth factor:** The ratio of the depth of hard surface to that of the height of the slope is the depth factor n_d, where $n_d > 1$.

5. **Sudden draw down condition:** The downstream side of an earth dam is to be analyzed under steady seepage condition. However, the submerged upstream slopes can be subjected to a sudden lowering of water level. This condition is known as *sudden draw down condition*. For this reason upstream slopes of dams are usually kept flatter than down-stream slopes.

6. **End of construction condition:** Just after construction, earth dams (which are to be built at optimum moisture) can have 80 to 90% saturation while the earth mass would still not have undergone full consolidation. Hence, pore water pressures can develop in the soil mass. Analysis taking into account these pore pressures when considering strength is called *slope analysis at end of construction*.

24.4 METHODS USED FOR SLOPE ANALYSIS

The three methods used for slope analysis can be classified as follows:

1. **Limit equilibrium method:** The basic assumption of this approach is that Coulomb's failure criterion is satisfied along an assumed failure surface, which can be a straight line, an arc of a circle, a logarithmic spiral or any other irregular surface.

2. **Limit analysis solutions:** This method uses the yield criterion and considers the stress-strain relationship. It is based on the lower bound theorem, which pertains to the equilibrium of forces and the upper bound theorem involving work equations.

3. **Probabilistic methods:** These are recent methods based on theory of probability.

However, as the limit equilibrium methods are more commonly used in practice we will deal only with these methods in this chapter.

24.5 EFFECTIVE AND TOTAL STRESS APPROACHES

Pore pressures play an important part in shear strength of clays and silts. The shear strength of soils can be assumed to be determined by the following equation known as Coulomb's equation in terms of total stresses:

$$s = c + p \tan \phi$$

In terms of effective stresses, Terzaghi restated the above equation as follows:

$$\tau = c' + p' \tan \phi'$$

Both of the above equations can be used for stability analysis. The total stress analysis assumes that the pore water pressures developing on the slip surface are similar to those in the laboratory which may not be totally true or that the failure occurs without pore pressure being developed in the soil mass.

The accuracy of effective stress analysis depends on the computation of pore water pressures. However, the total stress analysis is by far the simplest method though with improved methods of predicting of pore pressures that are now available, the effective stress methods are becoming more popular. For slow progressive failures, it has been found that the shear strength as determined by simple box shear apparatus using the total stress analysis method gives us reasonably good results.

24.6 HISTORICAL REVIEW

A short account of historical development of slope analysis helps us to understand the subject more fully [1]. Culman was the first to propose a method for the analysis of stability of slopes in 1866. In his classical solution, he assumed plane surfaces of failure as shown in Fig. 24.3. This type of failure is true for sand without cohesion.

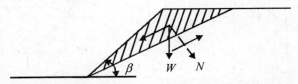

Fig. 24.3 **Culman's assumption of plane surface of failure.**

It was K.E. Petterson of Sweden who in 1915 first suggested that in clays with cohesion, the surface of sliding will be an arc of a circle. He based his proposal on his field observation of the failure of a quay wall at Goeteborg. It has been proved later by Taylor in 1937 [1] that assuming the failure circle to be a circle or a logarithmic spiral does not make much difference though the circle is generally a good approximation of actual conditions in nature for slopes in clay. A large number of actual slides that occurred in railway cuttings in clay soils in Sweden were later examined by the Swedish Geotechnical Commission. They pointed out that the surface of failure of the failed slopes can be approximated to that of the critical failure circle, which had the least factor of safety against rotation about the centre of the circle. It was also borne out in the field that circles may pass through the slope, through the toe or pass below the toe along the base depending on the site conditions and the factor of safety of the slope along these circles. The analysis suggested along these lines is known as the *Swedish Circle Method* (see Fig. 24.4).

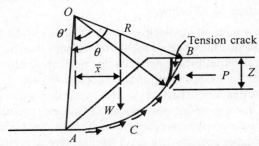

Fig. 24.4 **Swedish circle method of analysis of stability of slopes.**

A number of modifications and refinements of these basic ideas were since then proposed. The more important of them are as follows.

1. **The Fellenius method of slices:** (Fig. 24.5). This method was developed in 1927 (nearly twenty years after Petterson's proposal) by Prof. Fellenius for the Swedish Geotechnical Commission for analysis of slopes in soils with both cohesion and friction. The procedure is described in Section 24.9 below.

2. **The ϕ circle method:** This method is a derivation of the Fellenius method proposed by G. Gilboy and A. Casagrande around 1930. It is a complete graphical solution and is described in Section 24.10 below.

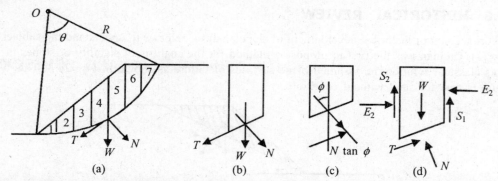

Fig. 24.5 **Fellenius method of slices: (a) Slices 1 to 7; (b) and (c) forces on slices; (d) Bishop's modification of the method taking forces on the sides of the slices also into account.**

3. **Taylor's Charts (Non-dimensional analysis of slopes):** The ϕ circle method suggests that, for a given inclination of slope and value of ϕ, we can represent the required value of c for all heights by using different scales or by introducing the dimensionless function $c/F\gamma H$, where c is the cohesion, F is the factor of safety, γ is the unit weight of soil and H the height of slope. Taylor proposed such a method and called this dimensionless number as *Stability Number*, N. (Terzaghi called the reciprocal of this number as *Stability Factor*, N_s). This is described in Section 24.11.

4. **Terzaghi's Charts [2]:** In 1943, in his book on theoretical soil mechanics, Terzaghi suggested that the reciprocal of Taylor's stability number (which is greater than unity), which he called as stability factor to be used in practice. He represented Taylor's values in two diagrams called Terzaghi's stability charts, which are easier to use. This procedure is described in Section 24.12 below.

5. **Simplified Bishop's method of slices:** For the sake of simplicity, in the Fellenius method of slices, we assume that the effect of the horizontal and shearing forces acting on the sides of the slices are in equilibrium and can be neglected. However this gives us very conservative results. In 1955, Bishop took into consideration the horizontal component of these lateral pressures also (neglecting the vertical components) and gave Bishop's *Simplified Method* for a more accurate analysis of slopes shown as in Fig. 24.5(d). He also based his analysis on effective stress approach. This analysis is more often used nowadays for the analysis of large projects like earth dams where accurate data of the materials are available for design.

6. **Bishop and Morgenstern method [3]:** This is a method proposed in 1960 based on Bishop's method of slices and considers the pore pressure by means of the pore pressure ratio. In 1963 Morgenstern gave a modification of this method for use of analysis of earth slopes during rapid draw down [3]. They introduced the term *stability coefficient* in the analysis of stability of slopes.

Many other improvements on the above methods involving small modifications to get better results have been proposed in recent years. However in this chapter, we shall deal only with the Swedish circle method, the method of slices, the friction circle method and the Taylor's method together with Terzaghi's modification. Details of other methods like Bishop's method and more refined methods can be obtained from advanced text books on the subject [3]. Computer methods and softwares for rapid analysis of slopes are also available.

24.7 STABILITY OF SLOPES IN COHESIONLESS AND COHESIVE SOILS

Sand slopes act like inclined planes. If we take an element of soil, we have the following forces for dry soils. Let β be the angle of slope and ϕ the angle of friction of the soil (see Fig. 24.3).

Weight of soil = W
Component parallel to plane = $W \sin \beta$ (downwards along the plane)
Component of friction = $W \cos \beta \tan \phi$ (upwards along the plane)
For equilibrium $W \cos \beta \tan \phi > W \sin \beta$

Factor of safety (F.S.) against failure = $\dfrac{\tan \phi}{\tan \beta}$.

24.7.1 Stability of Soil with Cohesion and Friction ($c-\phi$ Soils)

We should be aware that it is the effect of cohesion that enables us to have slopes higher than those with only ϕ values. It has also been observed that with cohesion, the surface of failure tends to be the arc of a circle and not an inclined plane. In Chapter 26, where we deal with reinforced earth, we will see how soil reinforcement is like adding cohesion to sand.

24.8 SWEDISH CIRCLE METHOD FOR $\phi = 0$ SOILS (CLAY SLOPES)

The simple Swedish circle method is applicable only to cohesive soils with $\phi = 0$. This was the method proposed by Petterson. It assumes a circular surface of failure and that the resistance is the total cohesion developed along the circle of failure. For safety, the moment of this cohesion about the centre of the circle must be more than the moment of the gravity forces.

The total cohesion resisting rotation failure is as follows (see also Fig. 24.4).

$$C = (\text{length of arc}) \times (\text{cohesion})$$

$$\text{Factor of safety} = \frac{\text{moment of cohesion about the centre}}{\text{moment of the weight about the centre}} = \frac{cR^2\theta}{W\overline{x}} \qquad (24.1)$$

where
c = cohesion in kN/m^2 of the soil
R = radius of trial slip circle in metres
θ = central angle subtended by chord in radians
W = weight of soil mass in kN
$\overline{x}$ = horizontal distance of W from centre of circle in metres.

24.8.1 Effect of Tension Cracks and Water in Tension Cracks

While discussing earth pressures, we saw that in clay soils, tension acts on the soil up to the depth z given by:

$$z = \frac{2c}{\gamma} \sqrt{N_\phi}, \quad \text{where} \quad N_\phi = \tan^2 (45 + \phi/2)$$

$$z = \frac{2c}{\gamma} \quad \text{when} \ \phi = 0 \ \text{(i.e. tension extends to this depth)}$$

(Cuts in clays can theoretically stand vertical for a depth $4c/\gamma$ to balance the tension.)

Thus, cohesive soils up to the depth z, which is in tension can open up. This has two effects. Firstly, the cracks can be filled with water, which will exert a horizontal pressure and increase the disturbing moments. Secondly, only the arc up to the bottom of the tension crack will mobilize shear force to stabilize the potential slip. Thus, the effective angle Θ will be reduced to Θ' as shown in Fig. 24.4.

$$F = \frac{cR^2\Theta'}{W\overline{x} + PL} \tag{24.2}$$

where

Θ' = angle subtended by shear are excluding the tension crack

P = horizontal water pressure acting at vertical distance L from the centre of the circle.

24.9 FELLENIUS METHOD OF SLICES FOR $c-\phi$ SOILS

The basic method of slices proposed by Fellenius is *applicable to soil slopes with both friction and cohesion*. The shear resistance along the slip plane is assumed to vary with the pressure at that point. Accordingly, a possible slip circle is chosen and divided into *strips of equal width* as shown in Fig. 24.5. The problem can be made determinate if we *assume that the interfacial stresses between the strip balance* and that they can be neglected. If we consider an arc strip, the forces to be accounted are only the weight, which can be resolved normally and tangentially, and the shear strength along Δs. The latter has two components: the cohesion, and the friction component, which is proportional to the normal pressure on the surface. Accordingly, we get the following expressions as shown in Fig. 24.5.

Total moment of disturbing forces = tangential component of $W = \Sigma \ TR$

Total moment of resisting forces about the centre of circle

$$= \Sigma \ (c\Delta s + N \tan \phi)R = (cR\theta + \Sigma N \tan \phi)R$$

$$\text{Factor of safety} = \frac{\text{moment of resisting forces}}{\text{moment of disturbing force}}$$

$$= \frac{cR\theta + \Sigma N \tan \phi}{\Sigma T}$$

where

c = cohesion of soil

ϕ = soil friction

R = radius of trial slip circle

θ = central angle subtended by chord

N = component of weight normal to arc of slip in the slice

T = component of weight, tangential to arc of slip in the slice.

24.9.1   Location of Centre of Critical Toe Circle in Homogeneous Slopes

In 1927, Fellenius showed that the location of the centre of the critical circle in homogeneous clayey soils with $\phi = 0$ is independent of the height of the slope. It can be expressed for a specified slope angle β by the angles i and δ as shown in Fig. 24.6. These values for different slope angles β are given in Table 24.1.

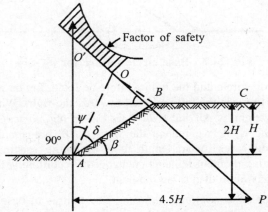

Fig. 24.6   Toe circle failure—location of centre of critical circle for $\phi = 0$ soils by Table 24.1. For $c - \phi$ soils the critical centre O' lies on line PO, its distance increasing from O with increase in ϕ values.

TABLE 24.1   LOCATION OF CENTRE OF TOE CIRCLE FAILURE FOR $\phi = 0$

Slope	Slope angle β degrees	Angle δ degrees	Angle i degrees
1:5	11.3	25	27
1:3	18.4	25	35
1:2	26.6	25	35
1:1.5	33.8	26	35
1.1	45.0	28	37
1:0.58	60.0	29	40

In 1962, Jumik extended the method to locate the *centre of the critical circle to c–ϕ soils.* He showed that these centers O' for various values of ϕ lie along a line joining the point O of the $\phi = 0$ case referred above and another point P fixed at a distance $2H$ below the ground level and $4.5H$ from the toe of the slope as shown in Fig. 24.6. The exact position of the centre of the critical circle O' varies with the ϕ value of the soil, the distance increasing with increasing value of friction. Hence in actual practice one has only to try a few points along OO' and plot the variation of the factor of safety as shown in Fig. 24.6 to find the exact position of the centre of the critical circle.

24.9.2   Base Failure in Cohesive Soils

Fellenius also showed that for base failure in homogeneous cohesive soils, the vertical line through the midpoint of the slope is also the locus of the centre of the circles in which the moment tending to produce sliding is the maximum. (Hence base failure circles are also called midpoint circles.) This theorem can be shown to be valid by use of Fig. 24.7 [4].

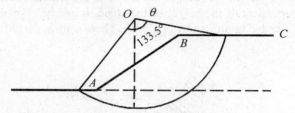

Fig. 24.7   Base circle failure for $n_d = \infty$.

Let the centre O of the circle and the failure circle be fixed. Let us *shift the slope* horizontally through a length ΔL first towards the left and then towards the right. When we move the slope to the left, we increase the weight by ΔW but *reduce the disturbing moment* about O by $(\Delta W)\Delta L/2$. If we move the slope to the right, we reduce the weight ΔW but again *reduce the moment* by $(\Delta W)\Delta L/2$. However, in both cases, the arc length along which the resisting shear forces act remains the same. Hence the resisting moment remains unchanged. Accordingly, the circle along the center line should produce the maximum disturbing moment.

Location of centre of circle for base failure: The centres of base failure circles lie on the midpoint of the slope. The circle also should be tangent to the firm base at $n_d H$ below the top of the slope. Fellenius tabulated the location of these centres with reference to the distance at which the circle meets the ground from the toe at the toe level as given in Section 24.10. According to Fellenius, in flat slopes with low shear strength and very large n_d, the centre of the critical circle subtends an angle of 133.5° and it lies on a vertical line passing through the middle of the sloping face as shown in Fig. 24.7.

24.10   FRICTION CIRCLE METHOD FOR $c-\phi$ SOILS

As already pointed out, this method was proposed by G. Gilboy and A. Casagrande. In the strip method if we assume *full friction is mobilized, then the resultant reaction* ΔP [Fig. 24.8(a)] at the base of each strip will be inclined at ϕ to the normal. This normal passes through the centre of the assumed slip circle of failure. The distance of this reaction from the centre of the circle shown in Fig. 24.8 will be $R \sin \phi$, where R is the *radius of the slip circle*. This circle with radius $R \sin \phi$ is called the *friction circle*. It is evident that the ΔP of various slices will be tangents to this friction circle. Hence, we may assume that the resultant of all ΔP equals is also tangent to the friction circle. This assumption is not strictly correct and P will be, in fact, tangent to a modified friction circle of radius kR, where $k > 1$(k varies from 1.05 for a central angle $\theta = 20$ to 1.20 for $\theta = 110°$) However, for all practical purposes, we may assume P is tangent to the friction circle.

We also assume that the soil is homogeneous and that cohesion is constant along the arc of the circle. Then, the resultant of this cohesion will be acting in the direction of the chord of the circle and the location of its line of action can be determined by taking moments about the centre of the circle as follows [see Fig. 24.8(b)]:

$$c \times L \times a = cR^2 \theta, \quad a = \frac{R^2 \theta}{L}$$

Total cohesion, $C = c \times L$

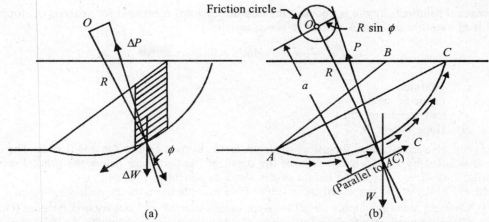

Fig. 24.8 **Friction circle method of analysis of stability of slopes: (a) Equilibrium of forces on a slice; (b) equilibrium of forces along the arc of a circle.**

where

L = length of the chord AC
θ = central angle
a = distance from the centre where resultant cohesion acts.

Thus, the total cohesion C will act a distance a from the centre of the circle and its direction will be that of the chord in equilibrium. The three forces keeping the soil mass in equilibrium can now be drawn. The weight W through the CG, of the sliding mass, the total cohesion C at a distance "a" parallel to the chord, and the resultant P at the point of intersection of W and C, but tangential to the friction circle. Knowing magnitude of W, the total value of C can be computed. The value of cohesion c_m (required) = C/L.

If we denote the factor of safety with respect to cohesion as F_c, then

$$F_c = \frac{c \text{ of soil}}{c_m \text{ (required)}}$$

The minimum factor of safety can be obtained from the critical slip circle. In the above analysis we assume that the full value of ϕ has been mobilized. If we need a factor of safety on friction ϕ also, we use a reduced value of the friction circle $R \sin \phi'$ to find the required cohesion. In such a case,

$$F_\phi = \frac{\tan \phi}{\tan \phi'}$$

The process can be repeated to set $F_c = F_\phi = F_s$.

This method using effective stress analysis is recommended for checking the long-term stability of earth embankments.

24.11 TAYLOR'S METHOD

In 1937, Taylor proposed a non-dimensional analysis of the stability of regular slopes. He based it on the mathematical analysis of the friction circle method. He noted that the friction circle method finally gives a vector of dimension c_1/γ, where c_1 is the unit cohesion required and γ the unit weight of soil. He made it dimensionless by dividing it by H the height of the slope. Thus, in his mathematical solutions, Taylor introduced the non-dimensional parameter for analysis of slopes and called it as *stability number N*, which is given as,

$$N = \frac{c}{F\gamma H} = \text{Taylor's stability number}$$

where

c = cohesion
F = factor of safety
γ = unit weight of soil
H = slope height

Taylor also investigated the effect of depth factor in base failure for $\phi = 0$ soils. The depth factor is denoted by n_d and is the ratio of the depth of the firm base below the ground level on which the clay layer rests to the height of the slope as shown in Fig. 24.2.

In 1937, Taylor [1] presented the results of his investigations in the following form:

1. Chart for stability number $c/F\gamma H$ for slope angles 0 to 90° and soil friction ϕ values 0 to 25°.
2. Chart showing effect of depth limitation $n_d H$ on stability number for $\phi = 0$ soils.
3. Table showing location of critical circle by ϕ circle method (see Ref. 1).

24.12 TERZAGHI'S MODIFICATION AS STABILITY FACTOR

In 1943, Terzaghi substituted the more convenient number, stability factor, N_s in place of Taylor's stability number N. The value of N_s is the reciprocal of N.

$$N_s = \frac{\gamma H}{c} \qquad \text{(stability factor)}$$

He presented Taylor's data with reference to stability factor.

Terzaghi presented Taylor's classical charts corresponding to the following:

(a) For $\phi = 0$ soils, the relation between the *stability factor N_s* slope angle and depth factor. (Refer to Fig. 24.9).

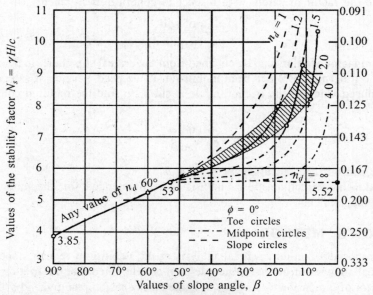

Fig. 24.9 **Terzaghi's modified Taylor curves—Stability factor (reciprocal of Taylor's Stability Number) for slope angle and depth factor for $\phi = 0$ soils.**

(b) For $c - \phi$ soils, the relation between slope angle and *stability factor* N_s (refer to Fig. 24.10).

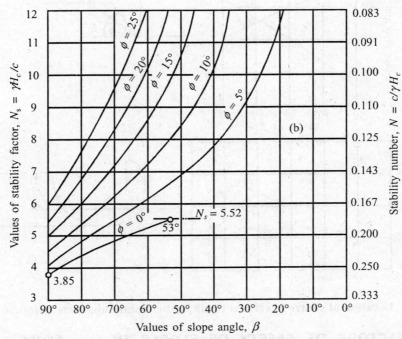

Fig. 24.10 **Taylor's curves for stability analysis of slopes of $c - \phi$ soils.**
(H_c is height of critical slope.)

These charts in Fig. 24.9 for $\phi = 0$ soils indicate the following:

1. Failures of all slopes with slope angle greater than 53° are toe circle failures. The critical value for the stability factor for a 53° slope is 5.52.

2. If the slope angle is less than 53°, the types of failure that can take place depends on N_s and n_d as shown in Fig. 24.9. If n_d is infinite $N_s = \gamma H_c/C = 5.52$. In other words, *for any slope less than 53° and $n_d = \infty$, the critical height will be as follows:*

$$H_c = \frac{5.52c}{\gamma}$$

3. If the slope angle β and the depth factor n_d are given, the value of N_s required can be read off from the figures to determine the critical height of the slope for $\phi = 0$ soils.

4. For a 90° slope or cut and $\phi = 0$, $N_s = 3.85$ which gives the following result. If $\gamma H_c/c = 3.85$, then $H_c = 3.85c/\gamma \approx 4c/\gamma$ obtained from earth pressure theory.

5. The centres of the critical toe failure circles and base failure circles can be obtained from data from Fig. 24.11.

Taylor's curves for slope stability for soils with cohesion and friction are shown in Fig. 24.10.

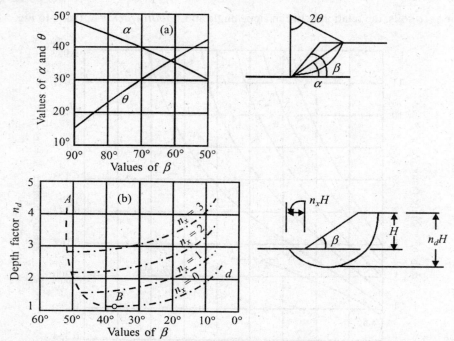

Fig. 24.11 **Location of centre of critical circle for toe failure and base failure in cohesive soils.**

24.13 FACTORS OF SAFETY OF SLOPES IN $c-\phi$ SOILS

Let us assume a soil with $c = 30$ kN/m^2 and $\phi = 30°$. In the slope analysis, when using friction circle method, we assume that full friction is mobilized $\phi = 30°$ and we determine c_m required. If $c_m = 15$ kN/m^2, the factor of safety with respect to cohesion 30/15 = 2.0. This factor of safety is defined as F_c. It is the factor of safety with respect to cohesion.

Now, if we assume *F.S.* = 1.25, for friction,

$$F_\phi = \frac{\tan \phi}{\tan \phi'} = \left(\frac{\tan 30}{\tan 24.8}\right) = 1.25, \qquad \phi' = 24.8°.$$

With this new friction ($\phi' = 24.8°$), we can find a new value of F_c.

Thus, the values of ϕ' can be varied and we get different values of F_c for various F_ϕ for the same slope. Thus, we can prepare a table as shown below.

F_ϕ	1.0	1.25	1.5	2.0	2.5
F_c (calculated)	2.0 (from above)	Values to be calculated			

The unique value $F_c = F_\phi = F_s$ is called the '*True factor of safety*' for the slope. It can also be noted that with $F_\phi = 1$ (full mobilization of friction) the cohesion required for stability is directly proportional to the height of the slope.

$$F_c = F_H = \frac{\text{critical height of slope}}{\text{actual height of slope}}$$

Hence if we find the critical height and divide it by an assumed *F.S.* we get the height of slope with required factor of safety against cohesion.

24.13.1 Suggested Values of Factors of Safety

We should remember that gravity forces are very definite and it is the shear strength parameters which we cannot be sure about. If we can get reasonably correct values of c and ϕ, the following factors of safety can be assumed to be the *minimum required*. (These are much lower than those allowed for steel or concrete construction.)

    1. For earth dams,   *F.S.* = 1.3   at end of construction
                                         F.S. = 1.25 with steady seepage
                                         F.S. = 1.20 for sudden drawdown

    2. For cuttings,   *F.S.* = 1.30 at end of construction
                                         F.S. = 1.20 for long term performance

    3. For embankments, *F.S.* = 1.2   and above.

24.14 SLOPES OF EARTH DAMS AND OTHER EMBANKMENTS

Earth dams usually consist of impervious and relatively permeable materials on either side of the core. (Some classify these materials as impervious, semipervious and pervious.) We have already seen that the upstream slopes of earth dams are kept flatter than the downstream slopes for safety against sudden drawdowns (see Fig. 24.12a).

    Road or railway embankments can be similarly formed with locally available materials with a core of readily available materials along with blankets as shown in Fig. 24.12(b). Such cases of slope analysis require trial circles that cut through the different materials to be examined. The method of slices can be used for such analysis. The safe design of an important dam may require as much as 100 slip circles and the work can be simplified by computer programs.

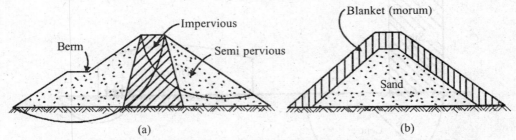

Fig. 24.12   **Composite embankments: (a) Earth dam; (b) railway embankment.**

    In the case of a slope for a dam as shown in Fig. 24.13, we may distinguish four families of probable failure as shown. The factor of safety will depend on mass of the soil displaced, the distance of its centre of mass from the centre of the slip circle, and the magnitude of resistance it can develop along the probable failure line. In a practical case, each family is separately taken for analysis and its factor of safety determined. Subsequently, contours of factors of safety can be drawn to determine the circle with minimum factor of safety. When we make artificial embankments, slope protection by growing turf (as railway embankments) or pitching with stones (as in canal embankments) require special attention. Similarly when making new embankments on a ground which slopes in the direction normal to the length of the embankment, it is recommended to bench the ground to make the base fully integrated with the ground. Such construction details are also important for stability of slopes.

For high embankments and earth dams, we usually provide beams (a level strip at the intermediate height of the slope) for increased stability, as shown in Figs. 24.12 and 24.13. Provision of such beams is very important in the design of high embankments and earth dams.

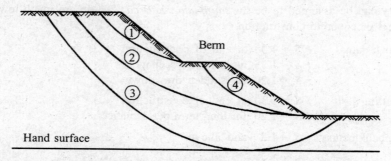

Fig. 24.13   Trial circles for stability analysis of earth dams.

24.15 STABILITY OF FOUNDATIONS

When designing shallow foundations of tall structures like silos and storage tanks especially in clays, their stability against rotational failure should be investigated as shown in Fig. 24.14. Even though such a consideration is made in bearing capacity formulae, special checking is necessary when they are subjected to vertical and horizontal loads. In case of instability, deeper foundations like pile foundations become necessary.

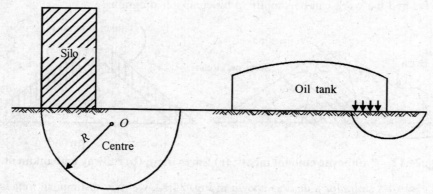

Fig. 24.14   Checking foundation stability of silos and oil tanks.

24.16 LAND SLIDES

Slides in natural slopes may be caused by man-made reasons like undercutting the foot of existing slope and destruction of vegetation cover or it may be caused by natural deterioration of the strength of soils. Such slope failures are most common during heavy rains with temporary increase in pore pressure due to seepage of rainwater. Accumulation of rainwater on top of hills can lead to landslides and mud flows [2], [3].

The shape of landslides will be as shown in Fig. 24.15. In clays of low sensitivity, landslide forms an S-shaped curve in plan. In very sensitive clays, or clays with pockets of sand as well as in clays with rock base at shallow depths, the soil is liable to flow like a liquid when excess pore water due to heavy rainfall is produced inside the mass. We should always make a geological investigation for past slope failure if any at the site when we examine the probability of landslides. Similarly the angle of the existing stable slopes should be also closely examined in detail.

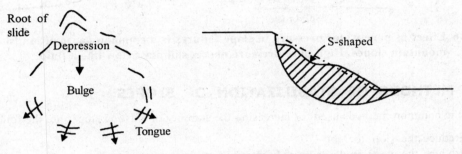

Fig. 24.15   Nature of landslides in natural slopes.

24.17   EMPIRICAL VALUES OF SLOPES

Terzaghi [2] recommends the following empirical values for slope construction:

1. *For embankments*. Slopes less than 6 m in height for railway and highway in good soil: 1 vertical to 1½ to 2 horizontal (33 to 26°). The slopes should be well drained.

2. *For cuttings*. Slopes less than 6 m in depth for railway and highway in good soil: 1 to 2 (26°) to 1 to 3 (18°). (These slopes more than 6 m in depth should be investigated in detail.)

3. *Upstream slopes of dams*: 1 to 3 (18°) to 1 to 2.5 (22°)

4. *Downstream slopes of dams*: 1 to 2.5 (22°) to 1 to 2 (26°)

5. *The standard slope* of cuttings liable to flooding (such as canals)—1 to 2 up to 1:3.

24.18   EFFECT OF PORE PRESSURES

In all the above discussions, we have assumed that there are no seepage and pore pressures in the soil mass. However, downstream and upstream slopes of earth dams, seepage pressures are present. In other situations, pore pressures due to lack of total consolidation or drainage can be present. In all such cases, the strength of soils along the failure surface will be reduced. Similarly submergence of earth under water reduces the weight of the soil and this factor also should be taken into account in our analysis of slopes. In earthquake regions the effect of earthquake forces should also be taken into account. In earth dam analysis, all these factors, even though not dealt with in this chapter, are important and should be considered. In all cases, the basic principles remain the same as those explained in this chapter.

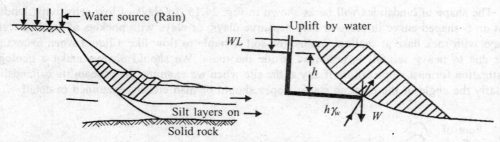

Fig. 24.16 Effect of pore water pressure in slope failures is a common cause of landslides on mountain slopes. High pore pressure makes soil mass flow like a fluid.

24.19 METHODS OF STABILIZATION OF SLOPES

Some of the common methods used for increasing the stability of existing slopes are the following:

1. Reduce the slope height.
2. Reduce the slope angle or provide intermediate beams.
3. Build buttresses with high quality fill so that the slip circle passes through the good material.
4. Employ structural stabilization by retaining walls, soil nailing, tie back anchors, soil reinforcement, etc.
5. Stabilize natural slopes by horizontal drains along the slopes to reduce water level in the slope.
6. Construct drains on top of slope parallel to the length of the slope so that water does not flow on the slope.
7. Grow vegetation (like grass on railway embankments) to reduce erosion and shallow local slides. (It has no effect on deep-seated slides.)

24.20 INSTRUMENTATION IN EMBANKMENTS

The problem of movement of slopes is severe in many parts of India like the hilly regions of Malabar. An inclinometer is the instrument that can be used to monitor this movement. First a vertical boring is made to sufficient depth and it is lined firmly with a special plastic casing, which will deform easily with the movement of the slope earth. The inclinometer measures the inclination of the casing in two perpendicular directions. By lowering the instrument to the bottom and slowly pulling it up to the top, we can measure any movement that has taken place along the plastic casing after the previous measurement and thus detect the movement of the slope in any given direction.

Another method to monitor movements is by installing survey stations at various locations on the ground surface and noting their movement by commonly used survey instruments. Instrumentation to measure the settlement, other movements and pore pressures are also commonly made in earth dams to monitor their safety during and after construction.

EXAMPLE 24.1 **(Analysis of slope)**

The profile of a clay slope 6.5 m in height inclined at 34° is shown in Fig. E.24.1. Determine the factor of safety of the critical circle (1) from fundamentals (2) by using Taylor's stability number.

Assume the unconfined compressive strength of the soil q_u is 50 kN/m² and unit weight of soil q_u is 19 kN/m³.

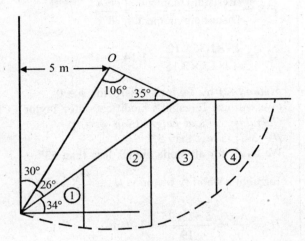

Fig. E.24.1

Ref.	Step	Calculations
Table 24.1	1	***Method (1)*** from fundamentals. *Take unit length of slope and draw to scale the slope (say* 1 *cm* = 2 *m)* *and find the centre of critical circle* For slope angles, $\beta = 34°$ the centre of critical circle lies on $\delta = 26°$ and $i = 35°$ approximately angle $\psi = 30°$. Cohesion $c = q_u/2 = 50/2 = 25$ kN/m²
	2	*Measure the main dimension from the drawing* $R = 10$ m; $\Theta = 106°$ (1.85 radians) Distance of O from vertical through toe = 10.0 sin 30 = 5.0 m
	3	*Cut the soil mass into strips (4 strips) of equal width and find areas of* *each strip.* Total area = Σ (Ht. at middle of each strip × width of each strip) $\qquad$ = 67.5 m² (approx.) Weight $\quad$ = 67.5 × 19 = 1282.5 kN
	4	*Find C.G. of the sliding mass by taking moments about toe* Distance of *C.G.* of *W* from toe $$= \frac{\Sigma \,(\text{area of each strip} \times \text{distance of midpoint from toe})}{\Sigma \,\text{area of each strip}}$$ $\qquad$ = 8.15 m (from the toe) Distance of *C.G.* from centre of rotation *O* $\qquad$ = 8.15 − 5.0 = 3.15 m = $\bar{x}$

5.		*Take moments about O and find F.S.*

$$F.S. = \frac{\text{Resisting moment}}{\text{Disturbing moment}} = \frac{c\Theta R^2}{W\bar{x}}$$

$$= \frac{25 \times 1.85 \times 10^2}{1282.5 \times 3.15} = 1.14$$

Method (2) by Taylor's Chart: for $\phi = 0$
(We will use Terzaghi's modification of Taylor's Chart)

| | 1 | *Calculate critical height (Soil $\phi = 0$)* |

$\beta = 34°$; is less than $53°$
We have, for all slope angles less than $53°$

Terzaghi's stability factor $= N_s = \dfrac{\gamma H}{c} = 5.52$

$$H_c = \frac{N_s c}{\gamma} = \frac{5.52 \times 25}{19} = 7.26 \text{ m}$$

| | 2 | *Determine factor of safety of slope H = 6 m* |

Factor of safety $= \dfrac{H_c}{H} = \dfrac{7.26}{6}$

$F_c = 1.21$
(*Note:* This will also be the factor of safety against cohesive strength.)

EXAMPLE 24.2 (Friction circle method for $c - \phi$ soils)

An embankment made of uniform soil with $c = 30$ kN/m² and $\phi = 15°$ is 8 m in height. Find the factor of safety against failure along a slip circle of central angle $95.5°$ (1.66 radians) passing through the toe of the slope. Assume density of soil is 20 kN/m³. Refer to Fig. 24.8.

Ref.	Step	Calculations
		Note: In this method, we assume that full friction is mobilized and then determine the required cohesion from equilibrium.
Fig. 24.8	1	*Determine total weight of soil mass involved* Draw to scale the slip circle. Determine as follows: Area of mass in slip circle = 79.5 m²/m length (measured) W = weight = 79.5 × 20 = 1590 kN/m Line of action of W = 11.4 m from centre 'O'
	2	*Determine distance 'a' where resultant cohesion acts* (resultant assumed to act along the direction of the chord) Length of chord $L = 21.75$ m

$$a = \frac{R^2 \theta}{L} = \frac{20.25 \times 20.25 \times 1.118}{21.75} = 21.1 \text{ m}$$

Ref.	Step	Calculations
	3	Calculate radius of friction circle $R_\phi = R \sin \phi = 20.25 \times \sin 15° = 5.25$ m
Fig. 24.8	4	*Draw triangle of forces for W, C and P; find C* Draw W to scale acting vertically through the *C.G.* of mass. Draw C at 21.1 m from centre of slip circle and parallel to the chord. Through the intersection of W and C, draw P tangent to friction circle. As W is known and the lines of action of P and C are known, we can draw the triangle of forces and find the magnitude of C required. Thus, $C = 560$ kN
	5	*Find value of cohesion required for equilibrium* $c_m = \dfrac{C}{L} = \dfrac{560}{21.75} = 25.75$ kN/m^2
Sec. 24.3	6	*Determine factor safety with respect to cohesion, assuming full friction is mobilized* Available $c = 30$ kN/m^2 Factor of safety $F_c = \dfrac{30}{25.74} = 1.16$, say, 1.2 *Notes:* 1. The assumed circle of failure above need not be the critical circle. We have to try other circles of failure to get the true *F.S.* using Fig. 24.5 for guidance. 2. Graphical method is not as accurate as using Taylor's (or Terzaghi's) curves.

EXAMPLE 24.3 (Use of Terzaghi's stability factor)

Using Terzaghi's stability factor, find the factor of safety against cohesion of the slope in Example 24.2. State where the critical circle will be located. (Assume full friction can be mobilized.)

Ref.	Step	Calculations
	1	Determine Terzaghi's stability factor mobilizing full friction $\beta = 64°, \qquad \phi = 15°; \qquad N_s = 7.8 = \dfrac{\gamma H}{c_m}; \; c_m = \gamma H / N_c$
	2	*Factor of safety with $c = 30$ kN/m^2* $F.S. = \dfrac{c}{c_m} = \dfrac{cN_c}{\gamma H} = \dfrac{30 \times 7.8}{20 \times 8} = 1.46$
Sec. 24.7.1	3	*Find the position of the critical circle* The critical circle will lie on a line joining point O, the centre of critical circle with $\phi = 0$ and P which is $2H$ below ground level and $4.5H$ distant from toe as in Fig. 24.5.

EXAMPLE 24.4 (**F.S. in cohesion for a given F.S. in friction**)

Find the *F.S.* in cohesion for a *F.S.* = 1.5 in friction in Example 24.3.

Ref.	Step	Calculations
	1	*Soil data* $$\beta = 64; \quad \tan\phi = \frac{\tan 15}{1.5} = 0.179; \quad \phi = 10°$$ $$\gamma = 20 \text{ kN/m}^3$$
	2	*Find Terzaghi's stability factor:* For $\beta = 64°$, $\phi = 10°$; $N_s = \dfrac{\gamma H_c}{c} = 6.8$ Required $c = \dfrac{20 \times 8}{6.8} = 23.5 \text{ kN/m}^2$ *F.S.* against available cohesion $= \dfrac{30}{23.5} = 1.28.$

EXAMPLE 24.5 (**Stability of cuts in $c-\phi$ soils**)

A cut is to be excavated in soil which has cohesion of 12 kN/m², unit weight 12 kN/m³ and $\phi = 10°$. If the angle to be kept for the slope is 60° determine the maximum height of the cut with a factor of safety of 1.5. Use Taylor's chart as interpreted by Terzaghi.

Ref.	Step	Calculations
Sec. 24.12 Fig. 24.8	1	*Stability number for* $\beta = 60°$ *and* $\phi = 10°$ *and* H_c $$N = 0.138 = \frac{c}{\gamma H} \text{ with F.S.} = 1.0; \quad \frac{\gamma H_c}{c} = 7.2;$$ $$H_c = \frac{12 \times 7.2}{19} = 4.55 \text{ m} = \text{critical height}$$
	2	*Excavation height with F.S.* = 1.5 $$H = \frac{H_c}{1.5} = \frac{4.55}{1.5} = 3.03 \text{ m}$$ (This has a *F.S.* 1.5 against cohesion and 1 against friction.)

EXAMPLE 24.6 (**Stability of cuts in soft clay**)

A cut is to be made in a soft clay deposit to a depth of 9 m. Hard stratum lies at a depth of 13.5 m below ground level. If $c = 30$ kN/m² and unit weight of soil is 20 kN/m³ find the slope to be adopted for excavation.

Ref.	Step	Calculations
	1	*Determine depth factor* $n_d = \dfrac{13.5}{9} = 1.5$
Sec. 24.12	2	*For critical height of 9 m, and given γ and c find stability factor* $N_s = \dfrac{\gamma H_c}{c} = \dfrac{20 \times 9}{30} = 6.0$
Fig. 24.9	3	*Find for n_d = 1.5; N_s = 5.7, value of β* From Terzaghi's curves, $\beta = 34°$ The slope should not exceed 34°.

EXAMPLE 24.7 **(Depth of tension crack in $c - \phi$ soil)**

Calculate the depth of tension crack which can occur in a soil with $c = 20$ kN/m^2, $\phi = 8°$ and $\gamma = 17$ kN/m^3. What will be its value when $\phi = 0$?

Ref.	Step	Calculations
	1	*State formula for earth pressure for $c - \phi$ soils* From Bell's equation, $p_a = rzK_A - 2c\sqrt{K_A}$ $K_A = \tan^2 (45 = \phi/2)$ $z = \dfrac{2c}{\gamma\sqrt{K_A}}$ when $\phi = 0$; $z = \dfrac{2c}{\gamma}$
	2	*Find value of z with $\phi = 8°$ and $c = 20$ kN/m^2* $z = \dfrac{20 \times 2}{17 \times \tan 41} = 2.71$ m
	3	*Find value of z of $\phi = 0$* $z = \dfrac{20 \times 2}{17} = 2.35$ m *Note:* With cohesion and friction, the soil is more self-supporting.

REFERENCES

[1] Taylor, D.W., Stability of Earth Slopes, *Journal of Boston Society of Civil Engineers*, Boston, 1937.

[2] Terzaghi, K. and R.B. Peck, *Soil Mechanics in Engineering Practice*, John Wiley & Sons, New York, 1948.

[3] Winterkorn, H.F., and H.Y. Fang Van, *Foundation Engineering Handbook*, Van Nostrand Reinhold, New York, 1975.

[4] Terzaghi, K., *Theoretical Soil Mechanics*, John Wiley & Sons, New York, 1947.

25

Ground Improvement Techniques

25.1 INTRODUCTION

There are many situations where the strength and other properties of the soil have to be improved by ground improvement techniques. In this chapter we will briefly explain the basic principles governing some of the commonly used methods. This also is a very specialized field and for details of the various procedures to be used, published literature on case studies on the subject should be consulted.

25.2 COMMONLY USED METHODS

The following are the commonly used methods:

(i) Pre-loading with or without sand drains

(ii) Soil replacement

(iii) In-place densification by (a) vibrofloatation, (b) compaction piles, (c) simple stone columns, vibrostone columns, and (d) blasting

(iv) Soil stabilization

(v) Grouting and injection methods

(vi) Soil reinforcement.

The details of these methods are given in Tables 25.1 and 25.2.

TABLE 25.1   SOIL IMPROVEMENT TECHNIQUES

Principle	Techniques	
	Commonly used methods	Other possible methods
Consolidation (changing moisture content)	1. Pre-loading by surcharge (with or without drainage)	1. Electro-osmosis 2. Lowering water level
Compaction	1. Falling weights 2. Vibrofloatation 3. Compaction piles (sand piles and lime piles)	1. Use of explosives
Soil stabilization	1. Replacement by good soil 2. Mechanical stabilization 3. Lime piles	1. Using additives like cement bitumen, lime, etc. 2. Calcination
Soil reinforcement	1. Stone column 2. Root piles 3. Micropiles	1. Geofabrics as reinforcement
Grouting, injections	1. Lime slurry 2. Cement	1. Chemicals

TABLE 25.2   TYPE OF SOILS AND METHODS USED

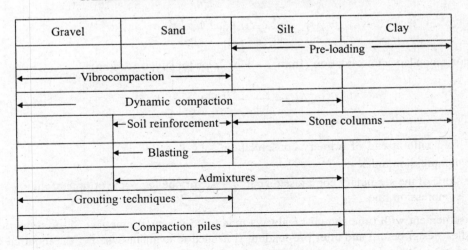

improve shear strength
decrease the water content.
increase the density.

472 *Foundation Engineering*

25.3 PRE-LOADING [1]

This method consists of placing surface loads such as sand fills on the area to be improved before construction. It may also consist of controlled post-loading a structure itself (like an oil tank) after its construction and before it is put to service. Site pre-loading with sand fill is shown in Fig. 25.1. Pre-loading is effective in silty clays and organic deposits.

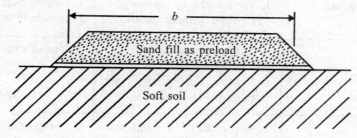

Fig. 25.1 Soil improvement by pre-loading.

The aims of pre-loading are: (a) to eliminate all settlements that otherwise can take place after construction and (b) to improve the shear strength of soil by decreasing its water content and increasing the density. The intensity of pre-loading should be such that it should eliminate all the primary settlement and also very large part of the secondary settlement that can take place in the actual structure. In a pre-compressed soil, it should be higher than the *pre-consolidation pressure* of the soil to be pre-loaded. (This pressure is called as the threshold of high compressibility.) In most cases, the pre-loading surcharge will be more than the estimated weight of the structure to be built at the site so that further secondary compression, can be avoided. The expressions used for calculation of settlements are the following (See Section 11.12).

1. For primary consolidation,

$$\Delta H_p = \frac{C_c}{1+e_0} H \log \frac{p_0 + \Delta p}{p_0} \tag{25.1}$$

2. For secondary consolidation (from $e - \log t$ plot for given loading),

$$\Delta H_s = \frac{C_\infty}{1+e_f} H \log \frac{t_2}{t_1} \tag{25.2}$$

where

e_f = void ratio at end of primary consolidation

C_c = compression index

C_∞ = slope of the secondary compression curve = Δe for one log cycle of time of the secondary compression line.

The settlement with time should be always monitored in actual practice. Shear strength tests (by vane shear tests) before and after pre-loading is needed to evaluate whether the required shear strength has been attained by pre-loading. The special requirements for success are the following:

1. Availability of space. The area to be taken up for pre-loading operation should be always more than the outside perimeter of the proposed structure.

2. Availability of fill material. Although pre-loading can be effected also by water weight or by lowering of water table, heaping of granular fill (so that if does not turn into mud when it rains) is the most desirable method.

25.3.1 Summary of Case Studies

Case studies demonstrate the following:

1. The time taken for completion in most cases of pre-loading is three to eight months.

2. The height of pre-load heap used is generally 3 to 8 m, to be placed above the plan of the structure to be built.

3. The settlements can be 0.3 to 1.0 m depending on the type of soil and loading.

4. The dimensions ($L \times B \times H$) should be large enough for the effect of vertical stresses to be felt over the total thickness of the more compressible soils.

25.3.2 Calculation of Increase in Shear Strength from Settlements

The following theory has been proposed to be used to estimate the increase in shear strength by measuring settlements [1]. Let γ_d the dry weight, w the % water content and G the specific gravity. Their interrelation is as follows (assuming $\gamma_w = 1$ gr/cm^3):

$$\gamma_d = \left(\frac{G}{1 + wG} \right) \qquad \text{(a)}$$

Differentiating this expression and putting Δ values, we obtain

$$\Delta \gamma_d = \frac{G^2 \Delta w}{(1 + wG)^2} \qquad \text{(b)}$$

In a soil deposit of compressible soil as shown in Fig. 25.2(a), the dry weight of the whole soil remains constant so that the change of dry weight is zero. Taking $h\gamma_d$ = weight per sq. metre area, we get

$$\partial(h\gamma_d) = 0$$

so that

$$h\partial \gamma_d + \gamma_d \partial h = 0$$

$$\Delta \gamma_d = -\frac{\gamma_d}{h}(\Delta h) \qquad \text{(c)}$$

Substituting for $\Delta \gamma_d$ and γ_d from (a) and (b), we get the equation

$$\Delta \gamma_d = \frac{G}{(1 + wG)} \frac{\Delta h}{h} = \frac{G^2 \Delta w}{(1 + wG)^2}$$

Hence,

$$\Delta w = \left(w + \frac{1}{G} \right) \frac{\Delta h}{h} \qquad \text{(25.3)}$$

This expression gives the change in water content as a function of settlement.

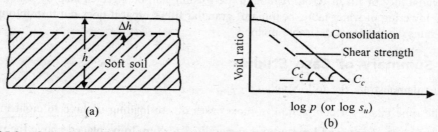

Fig. 25.2 **Calculation of increase of strength of clays with decrease in water content.**

The undrained shear strength of saturated soils is *commonly assumed to vary* with the void ratio as shown in Fig. 25.2(b) as in the case of the consolidation curve. Taking s_u as shear strength.

$$e = -C_c \log s_u + \text{constant}$$

Differentiating the above expression, we get

$$\frac{\partial e}{\partial s_u} = \frac{C_c}{s_u} \log_{10} e = \frac{0.434 C_c}{s_u}$$

$$\Delta e = -0.434 C_c \frac{\Delta s_u}{s_u} \tag{d}$$

In saturated soils, $e = G \times w$ (where w is the natural water content)

$$\Delta e = G \Delta w$$

Substituting for Δe from Eq. (d), we obtain

$$\Delta s_u = \frac{G \Delta w s_u}{0.434 C_c} \quad \text{and} \quad \frac{\Delta s_u}{s_u} = \frac{G \Delta w}{0.434 C_c} \tag{25.4}$$

Substituting for Δw from Eq. (25.3), we get

$$\Delta s_u = \frac{(1 + wG)}{0.434 C_c} s_u \left(\frac{\Delta h}{h} \right) \tag{25.5}$$

(This equation is an attempt to evaluate increase in shear strength with $\Delta h/h$.)

Example. As an example, if $\Delta h = 0.8$ m, $h = 10$ m, $C_c = 0.40$, $s_u = 20$ kN/m^2, with saturated water content $w = 0.55$ and $G = 2.7$ [1].

The increase in strength, $\Delta s_u = \dfrac{(1 + 0.55 \times 2.70)}{0.434 \times 0.40} \times 20 \times \dfrac{0.8}{10.0} = 23$ kN/m^2

The new shear strength $= 20 + 23 = 43$ kN/m^2

Also,

$$\frac{\Delta s_u}{s_u} = \frac{G \Delta w}{0.434 C_c} = \frac{2.7 \times \Delta w}{0.434 \times 0.4} = 15.6 \, \Delta w$$

Thus for every one percent decrease in water content, the strength increases by 15.6%. However, as it is always difficult to get an exact value of *h*, the above derivation should be used only as an estimate of increase in strength. This improvement in strength should be always checked by field measurements as for example, by vane shear tests.

As only 90–95% consolidation will take place in a reasonable time, pre-loading intensity should be greater than the theoretical value. In Salt Lake City in Calcutta 125% of the expected load of buildings and in Haldia 110–115% of the expected load (for a large tank) were used. In the former, no settlement and in the latter 5 to 10 cm settlement took place on construction carried out after pre-loading.

Equation (25.5) can also expressed as follows for a saturated specimen: $e = Gw$:

$$\Delta s_u = 2.3 \left(\frac{1+e}{C_c} \right) s_u \left(\frac{\Delta h}{h} \right) \qquad (25.5a)$$

25.3.3 Use of Sand Drains

Theoretically, the time necessary for the required settlement can be decreased by the use of sand drains. However, field observations show that the real time rate of field consolidation without sand drains can be 10 to 100 times higher than the laboratory predictions due to the presence of natural drainage in most deposits. Accordingly, the decision to install sand drains to speed up consolidation should be based on strong field evidence and field tests, rather than calculations based on parameters obtained from laboratory tests. In most cases of natural deposits, separate sand drains may not be necessary. The drainage system used to hasten consolidation can be any one of the following:

1. Ordinary sand drains
2. Sand wick drains
3. Card board drains
4. Plastic geotextile drains.

Details of design of sand drains can be obtained from specialized literature on the subject. One of the additional use of sand drains is that they reinforce the soft ground in which they are installed and helps to support the fill. Sand drains act also as sand piles. Even though the sand drains replace only 1 to 2% of the volume of the soil, the overall improvement in *bearing capacity* may be more than 10%. From this aspect, the geotextile drains because of its greater strength can be considered to be much superior than the others. However, as in the case of stone columns, there will not be very much reduction in *the magnitude of settlement*, because of the introduction of sand drains.

25.3.4 Cost of Pre-loading

The cost of pre-loading will vary from site to site. The following percentage of total cost can be taken as a rough estimate for each of the operations:

- Provision of sand drains—15%
- Provision of horizontal drainage—15%
- Cost of fill—50%
- Cost of stabilizing berms—15%
- Instrumentation—3 to 5%.

Pre-loading the structure itself is generally used for oil tank foundations, soils, buildings for storage and handling of ores or low rise residential buildings. Preloading of oil tanks in carried out by filling it water and after settlement in completed the water is drained out. The cost ratios of various methods to reduce settlement of a silo for 23,000 tons alumina, 30 m in diameter and 35 m in height on a deposit of medium dense sand to a depth of 18 m but underlain by stiff clay from 18 to 35 m which can cause settlement, was reported as follows [1]:

Method	Cost ratios	Expected settlement (m)
Pre-loading (taken as base)	1.0	0.2
Dynamic compaction	6.0	0.3
Compaction piles 18 m	12.0	0.25
Vibrofloatation to 18 m	13.0	0.25
Stone columns to 18 m	15.0	0.25
Concrete piles to 17 m	26.0	0.25
Concrete piles to 35 m	60.0	0.08

The cost ratio for an oil tank on 27 m soft clay worked out as follows:

1. Pre-loading without drains = 1.0
2. Pre-loading with 28 m deep sand drains = 3.0
3. Piles to a depth of 30 m = 20.0.

These cost ratios show that pre-loading is a very economical method.

25.4 SOIL REPLACEMENT FOR SOIL IMPROVEMENT

Excavation of the original weak soil and replacing it with a better soil compacted to its full density can also be used for improving the bearing capacity. The region of high stress in a shallow foundation is only 1 to 1.5 its breadth and this part can be replaced by selected good soil. This method is useful for construction of light buildings.

In particularly soft soil where the loading is not large, the following method, which is a combination of pre-loading and soil replacement, is commonly used. For this purpose, the fill material of better quality is carefully placed in layers (0.5 to 1 m) using light spreading equipment. The thickness of the fill should be such that if the future foundation to spread the load is 1 vertical to 2 horizontal, the intensity of load on the original soil should be within safe limits. The load is left for about 12 months before construction work of buildings is taken up. We can also monitor whether much of the expected settlement has taken place.

25.5 SOIL IMPROVEMENT BY DENSIFICATION OF SOILS [2]

Densification of in-situ soils can be carried out in many ways. The popular methods are:

1. Vibrofloatation for cohesionless soils
2. Heavy tamping with falling weights for all type of soils
3. Compaction piles for cohesionless soils
4. Stone columns for clayey soils
5. Controlled blasting.

These are described next.

25.5.1 Vibrofloatation

This method, which originated in Germany around 1930, is applicable to cohesionless soils of high permeability (with not more than 20% silt or 10% clay). It is also especially useful to compact loose silt or sea deposits liable to collapse or liquefy under vibratory or earthquake loads.

The method consists of inserting a special vibrator, with a water jet which goes down by its own weight. As compaction due to vibration proceeds, additional cohesionless soil is added which is pushed down by the vibration. By this method, the ground is compacted fully to the depth necessary to carry a shallow foundation.

The effect of the method should be checked by cone penetrometer tests before and after the operation. This procedure can be used to compact soil for a bearing capacity up to 300 kN/m^2. Similarly, loose deposits liable to liquefaction can be compacted to the required density [3]. Densification up to 15 to 18 m depth is possible by using special equipment and techniques.

25.5.2 Dynamic Compaction

The method consists of applying controlled pattern of drops of heavy weights on a grid layout. First a high energy phases followed by low energy impacts called 'ironing' are carried out. After each pass, the depressions are made up by a bulldozer [4]. Field measurements show that the influence of the drop can extend to a depth given by the following formula [4]:

$$\text{Depth in metres} = \frac{\sqrt{WH}}{2} \tag{25.6}$$

where

W = weight of drop in tons

H = height of drop in metres

25.5.3 Compaction Piles and Sand Piles for Densification

Compaction piles are piles driven down solely for the purpose of densifying sand deposits. Bored piles cannot be used for this purpose. Densification results due to the twin effects of: displacement of materials and consequent increase in density and, the effect of vibration during driving. The *composer method* uses vibratory method to install sand piles.

The simplest method of installation of sand piles is to drive a casing with a detachable shoe into the soil and to backfill the resulting hole with granular materials like sand or gravel. For large diameter piles of (say, 400 mm) sand and gravel in the ratio 1:1 can be used. For smaller diameter piles (say, 150 mm) sand and cement or sand lime mixtures are used. These sand piles are spaced 2.5 to 6 times the pile diameter apart. In the ground a relative density up to 70% can be obtained in the pile by this method [3]. These sand piles also act as drainage paths for pre-loading operations in clayey soils.

25.5.4 Stone Columns

We will deal with stone columns under the following heads:

1. Method of installation of stone columns
2. Strength evoluation of the system
3. Settlement of stone column foundations
4. Minimum depth required for stone columns.

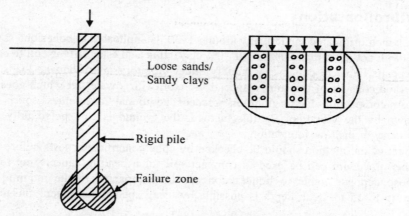

Fig. 25.3   Comparison of action of rigid piles with stone columns.

1. Method of installation of stone columns

The use of vibrofloatation techniques in clays using large size stones led to the development of stone columns. They were first used in 1960. Although they were initially used in cohesionless soils, their present use is mostly in clayey soils. The diameter of the bore that is formed vary from 800 mm to 1100 mm. They can be installed by vibrofloatation machine or by manual labour as in the case of sand piles. We should always remember that stone columns are essentially used to carry loads. It is not a device to reduce settlements. Comparison of their action with rigid piles is shown in Fig. 25.3.

In the manual method, a cased boring is used. The casing can be installed by one of the following methods:

1. Driving the casing with a dispensable shoe in the soft ground by a hammer weighing about 4 tons.
2. Boring with or without bentonite (Boring without bentonite is preferable as presence of clay in stone column tends to reduce its strength).

In either case, the stone columns are installed by the following operations:

(a) After the boring is completed, the bore holes are first partially filled with stone sand mixture up to about 0.5 m/layers.

(b) The material inside the hole is then rammed by a rammer, 1.5 to 2 tons in weight falling through 1 to 1.5 m, with sufficient overlap.

(c) The above steps are repeated till a reasonable height (say 1 m) of stone is compacted. The casing is then lifted up by applying up and down motions.

(d) After lifting the casing for sufficient height to leave an overlap of casing in the stone already rammed, repeat the process of filling in, ramming and lifting in stages, till the stone is heaped about 300 mm above the ground.

(e) The completed stone column is then rammed down by a heavy rammer to make the column compact and bulge outwards.

2. Strength evaluation of the system.

The columns are usually laid out in a 60° triangular grid and the spacing of these stone columns can be varied from 1.5 to 2.5 metres. It is also very important that the treatment by stone columns should be extended beyond the loaded area by at least 2 m all around for continuity effect. As in all structures, there is an increase of contact stresses at edges so that the spacing at edges should also be reduced.

A stone column layout derives its strength from the following three sources:

(a) Strength of the stone column itself.

(b) Strength of the surrounding original soil on which also the load is supported.

(c) *The surcharge effect if the foundation has a surcharge.*

We will briefly deal with each of them.

(a) Evaluation of ultimate strength of stone columns

Method 1: *Strength of stone columns from soil data and ϕ of column.* A very rough approach to predict the ultimate bearing capacity of stone columns surrounded by clay was developed by Greenwood in 1965 as follows [5]. The stone column is considered as a specimen in a triaxial machine with allround pressure. Being flexible, it tries to bulge when vertical pressure is applied, this bulging being resisted by the passive pressure of the surrounding clay as shown in Fig. 25.4.

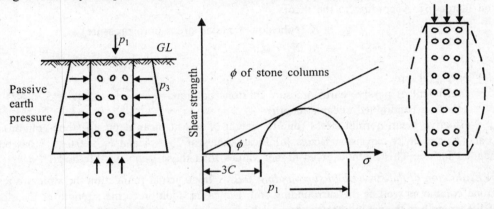

Fig. 25.4 **Theory of calculation of strength of stone columns (Confining pressure p_3 is assumed as $\geq 3c$).**

Accordingly, if we take p_3 as the possible confining pressure, then failure of the stone column will depend on the friction value ϕ, of the material of the stone column.

$$p_1 = p_3 \tan^2 (45 + \phi/2) = p_3 N_\phi \qquad (25.7)$$

If $\phi = 38°$, $N_\phi = 4.2$ and if $\phi = 45°$, $N_\phi = 5.8$

$$p_1 = (4.2 \text{ to } 6.0)p_3 \qquad (25.7a)$$

This means that the ultimate carrying capacity is a function of the passive resistance that the surrounding soil can develop. If we take a purely cohesive soil of clay, the confining pressure can be expressed as a function of the value of the cohesion c of the clay. Hence,

$$\text{Average confining pressure} = p_3 = mc \text{ for clay soils.} \qquad (25.8)$$

where m can be between 3 and 4. Therefore, from Eq. (25.7),

$$p_1 = mcN_\phi \qquad (25.9)$$

(where N_ϕ refers to the material of the stone column.) $= \tan^2 (45 + \phi/2)$ and ϕ can be taken as 45 to 50 degrees).

A factor of safety of 1.5 to 3 depending on the estimate of cohesion should be provided in the calculations. (This is a very rough method of calculation to illustrate the action of stone columns.)

(*Note:* The above formula given conservative values. Hence in method 3 given below we assume that confining pressure should include an additional factor σ_m which is the vertical pressure in the soil at mean depth of the stone column.)

Method 2: *Empirical method of strength evaluation.* The following is an empirical relationship that has also been proposed from the above theory.

$$p_1 = 17 \text{ to } 25 \text{ times cohesion} = q_u = \text{ultimate capacity} \tag{25.10}$$

In all practical applications where large sum of money has to be invested, it is advisable to conduct a field test to determine the actual strength as we do in the case of designing pile foundations. Generally a group of three columns is tested.

Method 3: *Vesic's method for strength evaluation of stone columns:* Another theoretical method to estimate the ultimate capacity q_u of stone column is to use Vesic's cylindrical cavity expansion factor [6]. According to the theory

$$q_u = K (\text{cohesion} + \text{radial stress pore pressure})$$
$$= K(cF_c + \sigma_m F_q - U)$$

where

U = pore pressure

K = coefficient of passive earth pressure of stone column $= \dfrac{1 + \sin \phi}{1 - \sin \phi} = \tan^2 (45 + \phi/2)$

c = cohesion (undrained shear strength)

σ_m = effective mean normal stress (due to weight of soil at mean depth of stone column).

F_c and F_q are cavity expansion factors [6] Mean values of $F_c = 4$ and $F_q = 0.6$ to 1 has been recommended for use. This method gives higher values than those given by Method I.

(b) Evaluation of the strength of surrounding soils. In an actual foundation the structure rests on the stone column as well as the surrounding soil. Hence, in addition to the strength of the stone columns, the strength of the parent material around the stone columns is also available. Its load bearing capacity can be calculated from conventional bearing capacity formula. We use the conventional bearing capacity formula for shallow footing. For clays the ultimate bearing capacity = cN'_c.

(c) Evaluation of surcharge effect. The third component of the strength of the layout is the strength from the surcharge above the foundation level as in the conventional bearing capacity formula. This can also be calculated by the bearing capacity formula.

Now, the total capacity is $\Sigma (a + b + c)$, the sum of above three components.

3. Settlement on stone columns. It is important to remember that stone columns do not eliminate much of the settlements. Assuming that stone columns of diameter d are spaced at $3d$, the area the ratio of space occupied by stone columns would be only 10 per cent. If $E_{col} = 10 \, E_{soil}$ then we can calculate stress taken by column as follows. (Assume unit area of soil.)

$$\text{Equivalent area} = a + \frac{E_s}{E_c}(1 - a) \quad (\text{where } a = \text{area of stone column})$$

$$\text{Stress taken by column} = \frac{q}{a + \dfrac{E_s}{E_c}(1 - a)} = \frac{q}{a + 0.1(1 - a)}$$

$$= 5q \text{ (approx. when } a = 0.1)$$

Accordingly 50% load has to be borne by the top soil directly and 50% by the stone column supported indirectly, again by the soil.

An estimate of the settlement can be made by assuming that the total settlement will be as follows:

$$\delta = \beta\rho_{c_1} + \rho_{c_2}$$

where

δ = settlement of foundation

ρ_{c_1} = settlement of *untreated soil around the stone columns* due to load from structure

β = reduction ratio for stone column treatment

ρ_{c_2} = settlement of *untreated soil below the stone columns* due to pressure transmitted by stone columns

In many field experiments, even though considerable increase has been observed in the bearing capacity, the decrease in settlement has not been substantial. In one case of field tests, with soft clays ($c = 20$ kN/m^2) with 2 m spacing of columns involving 25% replacement the settlement remained at 50% that of untreated soil. With 3 m spacing the settlement was as much as 75 to 80% of the untreated soil (see Fig. 25.5). For this reason stone columns remain useful only for structures that can tolerate high settlements such as oil tanks.

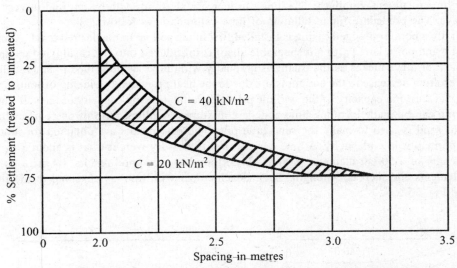

Fig. 25.5   Effect of spacing of stone columns on ground settlement.

3. Minimum depth of stone columns.   There is also a critical depth for stone columns to be active. When the depth of stone column is less than the above, it may fail by punching into the soft ground. Depths very much larger than necessary do not improve the load carrying capacity. Generally a depth not less than six times the diameter is used in practice. The adequacy can be checked by considering the stone column as a rigid pile, as shown in Examples 25.3 and 25.5.

25.5.5 Blasting

Blasting is used mostly in granular soils. It is more effective in submerged sands than sands above water table. Controlled blasting is usually carried out by agencies specialized in such works.

25.6 SOIL STABILIZATION

The methods used for soil stabilization are the following:

1. Mechanical stabilization by soil mixing
2. Admixture stabilization by (a) Cement (soil cement), (b) Bitumen, (c) Resin
3. Lime piles (columns).

Of these, the use of lime piles is the most popular one and it can be briefly described as in the following section [3].

25.6.1 Lime Columns or Lime Piles [7]

Lime columns are more effective in clays and silts than in sands. If we powder calcinated limestone, we get *quicklime* which when slaked with water, we get *slaked lime* which occupies double the volume of quicklime. Generally quicklime with pozzolanic materials are used for lime piles. This mixture is not only hydraulically setting, but also generates much heat during the process (see also Chapter 21). Another basic advantage of lime is the important changes it makes on the properties of the soil. It is well known that in expansive soils, the expansive characteristics are very much reduced by lime treatment. Similarly, 5% lime can increase shear strength by ten fold in very weak reactive clays. The procedure for installation of lime columns is as follows:

Generally a bottom-plugged casing is installed first in the soil up to the desired level. A mixture of quick lime and pozzolana (with a dispensable shoe) is introduced into the casing and compacted by mechanical or other means as the casing is gradually withdrawn as described in stone columns.

The resulting decrease in the soil moisture due to the heat produced by slaking of lime together with the higher carrying capacity of the set lime pile adds to the bearing capacity of the soil. In other cases, the pile can be made of quick lime and sand mixture. Usually a ratio of one part of lime to four parts of sand is used to make the sand lime pile. The best results are obtained for inorganic clays with normal or low plasticity. A lime content of 4 to 6% dry weight (that is about 8 to 12 kg per metre length of a 50 cm diameter pile) has been found to give good results. Its main use is to reduce settlements and increase strength. Their development with time as observed in the field is as shown in Fig. 25.6.

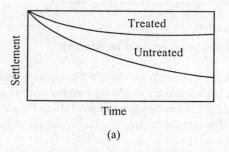

(a)

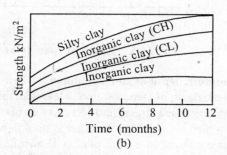

(b)

Fig. 25.6 **Effect of lime treatment on settlement and strength with time: (a) Effect of treatment on settlement; (b) effect on strength on various types of soils.**

25.7 SOIL REINFORCEMENT

The following techniques fall under this head [2]:

1. Root piles
2. Micropiles
3. Reinforced earth and geotextiles.

We will deal with each of these briefly. Uses of 1 and 2 above are shown in Fig. 25.7.

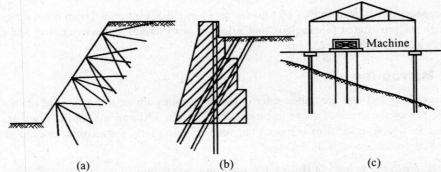

(a)　　　　　　　　　　(b)　　　　　　　　　　(c)

Fig. 25.7　Other methods of soil improvement and foundation treatment: (a) Soil nailing by reticulated root piles for slope protection; (b) micropiles for strengthening of retaining walls; (c) micropiles for supporting heavy machines.

25.7.1 Root Piles (Pali Radice)

A network of root piles is called reticulated root piles (R.R.P). Root piles were invented by the Italian engineer F. Lizzi in 1952 especially for underpinning work [2] [8]. In those days the common diameters allowed for bored cast-in-place piles was 400 mm. Most people were interested in development of piles of as large diameters as possible. Lizzi turned his attention to making smaller diameter (as little as 100 mm) piles with capacities of only 30 to 40 tons which were needed for works like underpinning. This resulted in the development of root piles and micropiles. Root piles are constructed by taking the following steps.

Step 1: Drilling a hole. A hole 10 to 100 dia is first drilled (according to the method which fits the soil environmental conditions best) with or without casing. In one system, a full length pipe with a cutting edge at its end is used. The hole is advanced by rotary drilling and then by direct circulation of water or bentonite. The cutting shoe at the end of the pipe and the fluid discharge are so selected that no core of material is formed. The cuttings along with the fluid come to the surface through the space outside the pipe. For underpinning work the hole is drilled through the structure.

Step 2: Placing the reinforcement. After completing the hole to the required depth, a single reinforcement bar (say 15 mm or more in diameter) as well as a tremie pipe are installed inside the drill pipe which acts as a casing to the hole.

Step 3: Filling with mortar by tremie. The hole is then filled with cement sand mortar (using 600 to 800 kg of cement for one cubic metre of sieved sand which yields a high strength grout.). The mortar is conveyed by the tremie and the hole is filled from bottom to the top.

Step 4: Withdrawing the drilling pipe and applying air pressure. The grouting is performed in repeated stages by dividing the grout length into short sections, so that grout volume and injection pressures can be increased gradually, step by step, to suit the variable soil conditions. At every stage air pressure not exceeding 60 kg/cm^2 is applied at the top as the drill pipe and tremic are gradually withdrawn. Air pressure makes it easy to withdraw the pipe and improves pile soil contact.

Step 5: Completion of pile. After the drill pipe is fully withdrawn, the air pressure is released and the mortar allowed to set.

The capacities can be as low as 10 tons for an 85 mm dia. root pile. These piles are extensively used as single or reticulated (entangled) root piles for works such as underpinning and correction of landslides as shown in Fig. 25.6(a).

25.7.2   Micropiles

Piles not exceeding 250 mm are called micropiles. Micropiles are an improvement of root piles for larger capacities of the order of 100 t to be obtained from a 170 mm micropile. They are pressure grouted piles in which, instead of the steel bar used in root piles, a steel pipe is used in the hole. The method of construction is as follows:

Step 1: Drilling. A hole is drilled by any suitable method.

Step 2: Reinforcement. A steel pipe of suitable diameter is installed in the borehole. This pipe serves the double functions of a reinforcement and a grouting pipe (called tube-a-manchettes) along the grouted length. (It has holes at intervals along its length, so that it can be used for pressure grouting using packers.)

Step 3: Simple grouting. The first stage grouting is simple filling in of the annular space between the pipe and the borehole wall. The grout used is a water-cement mix with additives to prevent segregation.

Step 4: Pressure grouting. Once the first grouting has set, pressure grouting is performed by displacing a grout duct with a double packer along the grout pipe and forcing the grout through holes distributed along the grout pipe at 0.5 m intervals. The high pressure grouting (0.5 MPa) is repeated one or several times, each after the setting of previous stage.

Step 5: Completion. At the end, the pipe will be filled with grout and the pile is allowed to gain in strength.

There are many variations of this technique including use of pre-stressing to anchor the piles and structures together. These are used for repair and renovation of structures.

25.7.3   Reinforced Earth and Geotextiles

Reinforced earth is another technique frequently used in connection with weak soils. The fundamental principles of this type of construction are explained in Chapter 26.

EXAMPLE 25.1 **(Settlement due to extraction of water)**

The subsoil below a building consists of 12 m of sand followed by 6 m of clay lying on a hard rock stratum. The ground water level is at 5 m below ground level. If due to extraction of ground water the ground water level is reduced by 4 m, estimate the probable settlement assuming that the m_v value of the clay is 7.3×10^{-4} m^2/kN.

Ref.	Step	Calculations
	1	*Calculate increase in pressure in clay* Assuming the soils are saturated, the increase in weight will be due to lowering of water level by 4 m. The increase in pressure will be 40 kN/m^2
	2	*Calculate settlement* Δ $\Delta = m_v H \Delta p = 7.3 \times 10^{-4} \times 6 \times 40 = 0.175$ mm *Note:* Very large lowering of water table can produce large settlements.

EXAMPLE 25.2 **(Estimation of secondary consolidation)**

For an expected stress increment of 15 to 40 kN/m^2 in the field, a consolidation test was made in the laboratory. The $e - \log t$ (min) data in a consolidation test for the above increment gave the following results:

- e_f at end of the primary consolidation test = 1.5
- Change of e in one log cycle of the secondary consolidation straight line part = 0.03.

Assuming that this deposit is 6 m in depth, estimate the secondary consolidation expected starting from 10 years and ending in 100 years.

Ref.	Step	Calculations
Sec. 25.3	1	*Substitute data in the formula* $C_\infty = \Delta e$ of one cycle in secondary consolidation part = 0.03 $e_f = 1.5$; $H = 6$ m; $t_2 = 100$; $t_1 = 10$ yrs
Eq. (25.2)		$\Delta H_s = \dfrac{C_a}{He_f} H \log_{10}\left(\dfrac{t_2}{t_1}\right)$ $= \dfrac{0.03 \times 6 \times \log_{10}(100/10)}{(1+1.5)} = 0.072$ m $\Delta H_s = 72$ mm (due to secondary consolidation)

EXAMPLE 25.3 **(Design of stone columns for foundation of an oil tank)**

An oil tank of 79 m diameter exerting a maximum pressure of 130 kN/m^2 is to be founded in a soft clay deposit of 7 m in depth and SPT value 4. If the tank is to be supported on stone columns of 90 cm diameter, estimate, the number of stone columns required and plan their layout. Assume weight of soil is 20 kN/m^3.

Ref.	Step	Calculations
	1	*Estimate cohesion from SPT Value*
Fig. 6.4		$c = \dfrac{N}{20} = \dfrac{2}{10} = 0.2 \text{ kg/cm}^2 = 20 \text{ kN/m}^2; B.C. = cN_c \text{ with } N_c = 6$
		Safe $B.C. = 2c$ (with F.S. = 3) = 40 kN/m^2, < 130 kN/m^2
		Hence, strengthening is required.
	2	*Find a rough estimate of strength of stone column*
		Method 1
Eq. (25.9)		$p_1 = mcN_\phi$ with $m = 3$ to 4
		Assume $\phi = 50°$; $N_\phi = \tan^2\left(45 + \dfrac{50}{2}\right) = 7.55$
		With $m = 4$; $p_1 = 4 \times 20 \times 7.55 = 604$ kg/cm^2
		Assume $F.S. = 1.5$; $q_a = \dfrac{604}{1.5} = 402$ kN/m^2
Step 6		**Method 2** (see Vesic's method)
		σ_m = pressure of mean depth (3 m)
		U = pore pressure at mean depth
		$(\sigma_m F_q - U) = (20 \times 3 \times 0.6 - 10 \times 3) = 6$ kN/m^2
		$p_1 = K [cFc + \sigma_m Fq - U]$
		$\quad = 7.55 [20 \times 4 + 6] = 650$ kN/m^2
		(Increase is small when water level (U) is high.)
		Method 3
	3	*Assuming strength of surrounding clay also takes part, find q_a*
		$q_u = cN_c = 0.2 \times 6 = 1.2$ kg/cm^2
		With $F.S. = 2.0$; $q_a = \dfrac{120}{2.0} = 60$ kN/m^2
	4	*Additional resistance due to surcharge effect is neglected*
	5	*Find number of stone columns required* ($d = 90$ cm)
Step 2		Area per column $= \dfrac{\pi \times 0.9^2}{4} = 0.636$ m^2
		(a) Strength of stone columns only = 0.636 × 402 = 256 kN
		(b) Strength of surrounding soil.
		Assume spacing at 2d in triangular grid
		Spacing = 2d = 1.8 m = s (60° triangle)
		Influence area per column = 0.5s^2 tan 60° s
		$\qquad\qquad = 0.866 \ s^2 = 2.80$ m^2
		Area of column = 0.636 m^2
		Area of soil per column = 2.80 − 0.636 = 2.16 m^2
		Load taken by soil = 2.16 × 60 = 130 kN

Ref.	Step	Calculations
		Total capacity = 256 + 130 = 386 kN (neglect surcharge effects) Total number of stone columns needed $$= \frac{\pi \times 79 \times 79 \times 130}{4 \times 386} = 1650 \text{ stone columns}$$
Step 5	6	*Estimate depth and check capacity as a rigid pile in soft clay.* Assume depth $\nless 6d$, i.e. 6×0.9 or 5.4 m. Adopt 6 m. Q_u of stone column = $604 \times 0.636 = 384$ kN Ultimate capacity as a rigid pile ($N_c = 9$) $= 9\, c\, A_\phi + \pi dLc$ $= (9 \times 20 \times 0.636) + (\pi \times 0.9 \times 6 \times 20) = 453$ kN Hence column will not punch through clay and penetration of 6 d is satisfactory.
	7	*Specify layout of columns* The column should extend beyond the loading point. Assume it should extend at least 3 m beyond end of tank, that is, for a diameter 79 + 6 = 85 m. As the pressures at edges of a rigid footing will be high according to theory, the spacing of stone columns for a diameter of 75 to 85 m should be one half those used for the inside. *Note:* The above example is given to illustrate the general principles involved. In a real situation, field tests should be made to determine the capacities as the quantities of work involved is large and any savings that can be made will be worthwhile.

EXAMPLE 25.4   (Estimate the settlement expected in Example 25.3)

Ref.	Step	Calculations
Example 25.3 Step 5	1	*Estimate amount of replacement* $$\frac{\text{Area of column}}{\text{Area of soil per column}} = \frac{0.636}{2.16} = 0.29 \text{ only}$$ Replacement of about 29% of the soil will not completely eliminate the settlement. E_s of soft clays (Table 1.9) varies from 3 to 30 kg/cm
Table 1.9 (Ch. 1)		Assume $E_s = 15$ kg/cm^2, $\quad m_v = \dfrac{1}{E_s} = 0.07$ cm^2/kg Settlement $\Delta = m_v H \Delta p$ Thickness of compressive layer = 7 m As the diameter of tank is 80 m, there will be very little stress reduction in the clay layer $\Delta p = 130$ kN/m^2 = 1.30 kg/cm^2 assuming uniform loading Settlement $\Delta = 0.07 \times 700 \times 1.30 \doteq 64$ cm (approx.)

		Allowing for rigidity of foundation (0.67)
		We should expect a settlement of the order of $64 \times 0.67 = 43$ cm
		This settlement can be eliminated, by controlled pre-loading of the tank. (*Note:* Provision of stone columns improves bearing capacity but settlements are not much reduced.

EXAMPLE 25.5 (Design of stone columns for a steel storage tank)

A steel storage tank which will exert a pressure of 140 kN/m² is to be built over an area consisting of soft to stiff marine clay deposit to a depth of 10 m below which stiff blue clay exists. The average strength of the soft clay is 40 kN/m². Design a stone column foundation.

Ref.	Step	Calculations
Example 25.3 Step 5	1	*Find area covered by one stone column* Assume 0.5 m stone column on a 60° triangular grid and spacing 1 m Influence area = 0.866 (spacing)² $\qquad = 0.866 \times 1 = 0.866$ m² Area of stone column = $\pi(0.5)^2/4 = 0.2$ m² Area ratio = $(0.2/0.866) \times 100 = 23\%$
	2	*Estimate capacity of stone column* (a) Empirical formula = $25 \times$ cohesion $\qquad q_{ult} = 25 \times 50 = 1250$ kN/m² (b) Empirical formula = $m \times c \times N_\phi$ $\qquad N_\phi = \tan^2(45 + \phi/2) = \tan^2(64°) = 4.2$ $\qquad q_{ult} = mcN_\phi = 4 \times 50 \times 4.2 = 840$ kN/m² Assume mean $q_{ult} = 1000$ kN/m² Safe value = 500 kN/m² (*F.S.* = 2)
Fig. 6.4	3	*Estimate bearing capacity of soil around* $q_{ult} = cN_c = 40 \times 6 = 240$ kN/m² $q_{safe} = 240/2.5 = 96$ kN/m² (*F.S* = 2.5)
	4	*Estimate the surcharge effect* Assume this third component as nil.
	5	*Estimate safe capacity per column with soil around it.* $\qquad$ = (area of column × capacity) + (area of ground × capacity) $\qquad$ = $(0.2 \times 500) + (0.866 - 0.2)(96)$ $\qquad$ = $100 + 64 = 164$ kN per column.
	6	*Estimate depth of stone columns and check safety as a rigid pile* Assume depth = $6d = 6 \times 0.5 = 3$ m Q_u as stone column = $0.2 \times 1000 = 200$ kN

Fig. 6.4		Q_u as a rigid pile $= (\pi dLc) + (cN_cA_p)$
		$= (\pi \times 0.5 \times 3 \times 40) + (40 \times 9 \times 0.2) = 260$ kN
		The strength is enough to prevent punching through the soft clay
	7	*Find bearing capacity of treated ground.*
Step 5		Combined safe $B.C. = \dfrac{164}{0.866} = 190$ kN/m^2
		This is greater than 140 kN/m^2 exerted by the tank.
		In order to improve the situation, disperse the load of tank through a sand fill.
	8	*Calculate settlement*
		Total settlement $= \Delta$ of soil around column $+ \Delta$ of column $+ \Delta$ of soil below column level.
		(The reduction in settlement will not be large).

EXAMPLE 25.6   (Estimation of increased strength of clay due to pre-loading)

Estimate the increase in strength of a clay deposit due to pre-loading with the following data. Height of deposit = 6 m; settlement due to pre-loading = 0.21 m; $C_c/(1 + e_0) = 0.15$; and $s_u = 25$ kN/m^2.

Ref.	Step	Calculations
Eq. (25.5a)	1	*Find Δs_u value*
		$\Delta s_u = 2.3\left(\dfrac{1 + e_0}{C_c}\right)s_u\left(\dfrac{\Delta h}{h}\right)$
		$= 2.3\left(\dfrac{1}{0.15}\right)25\left(\dfrac{0.21}{6}\right)$
		$= 13.4$ kN/m^2
	2	*Estimate increased strength*
		Final strength $= 25 + 13.4 = 38.4$ kN/m^2

REFERENCES

[1] Stamatopoulos, A.C. and P.C. Kotzias, *Soil Improvement by Preloading,* John Wiley & Sons, New York, 1978.

[2] Reinforced Earth and Modern Piling Methods, Symposium on Soil and Rock Improvement Techniques including Geotextiles, Asian Institute of Technology, Bangkok, 29th Nov.–3rd Dec., 1982.

[3] Mitchell, J.K. and R.K. Katti, Soil Improvement, State of the Art Report, *Proc. X International Conference on Soil Mechanics and Foundation,* Stockholm, 1981.

[4] Mitchell, J.K, Stabilisation of Soils for Foundations of Structures, Report—University of California, Berkley, April 1976.

[5] Hughes, J.M. and N.J. Withers, *Reinforcing of Soft Cohesive Soils with Stone Columns,* Ground Engineering, Institution Civil Engineers, London, Vol. 17, No. 3.

[6] Vesic, A.S., Expansion of Cavities in Infinite Soil Mass, *Proc. Journal of Soil Mechanics and Foundation Division*, ASC, 1972.

[7] Broms, B.B and P. Bowmann, Lime Columns. A New Foundation Method, *Journal of the Geotechnical Engineering*, ASCE 1979.

[8] Lizzi, F., Root Pattern Piles Underprinning, Symposium on Bearing Capacity of Piles Building Research Station, Roorkee (UP), 1964.

26

Reinforced or Mechanically Stabilized Earth (MSE)

26.1 INTRODUCTION

The art of stabilizing earth bunds by brushwood, bamboo, straw and other similar materials was practised all over the world from ancient times. In spite of this fact, a French architect and engineer Hentri Vidal was able to obtain a patent for *a general configuration of* using the above principle for embankment construction in 1963. It was quickly accepted on a worldwide basis for retaining walls, bridge abutments and many other projects. The patented general configuration consists of the following three basic components as shown in Fig. 26.1.

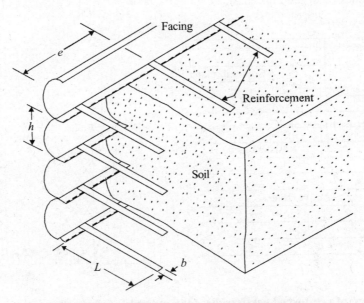

Fig. 26.1   Vidal's concept of reinforced earth.

491

1. The earthfill (usually selected granular materials with less than 15% passing refer US sieve no. 200).

2. Soil reinforcement (this is at present in the form of metal strips, geotextiles or wire grid fastened to the facing unit and extending into the earth backfill for sufficient distance. Special end anchorages can also be provided to decrease the length of anchorage length needed)

3. Facing unit (this is usually made of metal or concrete blocks made to maintain an aesthetic appearance of the structure and prevent soil erosion).

The remarkable features of mechanically stabilized earth (MSE) are the following:

- Strength—It can resist significant earth pressure and seismic force.
- Flexibility. They are flexible gravity structures. It adapts to substandard foundation soils and large settlements. (This is one of its main advantages over rigid walls.)
- Construction—It can be easily constructed by untrained labour.
- Low costs—Costs are low.
- Aesthetic factors—It has good appearance as the facing can be made of attractive designs.

26.2 FUNDAMENTAL CONCEPT OF MSE

The essential component in the mechanism of MSE is the friction mobilized at the soil reinforcement interfaces to prevent the relative motion of soil and reinforcement. The reinforcements restrain the lateral deformation of the reinforced earth mass providing *an apparent cohesion proportional to the density and the tensile resistance of the reinforcement*. The maximum tensile force in the reinforcement occurs at some distance away from the wall and it depends on the type of the structure and the loading conditions. This line of maximum tensile force divides the reinforced earth into the following two zones (also see Fig. 26.2).

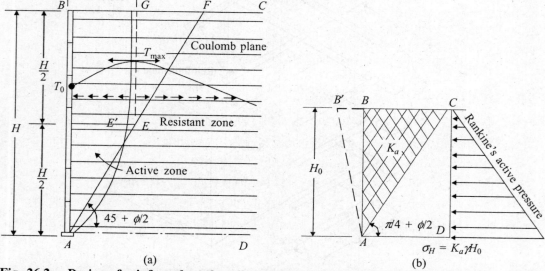

Fig. 26.2 Design of reinforced earth walls: (a) Coulomb's failure plane *AEF* and failure plane observed by tests *AE'G*; (b) usual assumption for calculation of earth pressures using Rankine's theory for conservative design.

1. An *active zone* behind the facing where the shear forces are directed outward giving rise to an increase of tensile forces in the reinforcements.

2. A *resistant zone,* where the shear stresses are mobilized to prevent the sliding of the reinforcement which is directed towards the free end of the reinforcement inside the embankment.

Full scale experiments and observations show that the behaviour of reinforced earth walls is quite different from that of classical retaining walls. The locus of the maximum tensile force in the reinforcement has been found to be different from Coulomb's failure plane.

26.3 HISTORICAL DEVELOPMENT OF THE THEORY OF FAILURE OR REINFORCED EARTH WALLS

Before 1973 it was thought that Rankine's theory is well adapted to the design of reinforced earth walls and that the failure plane corresponds to Coulomb's failure plane. It is quite logical to expect that the apparent cohesion present in the system will produce a different failure plane as in the case of failure of earth slopes with cohesion. Tests at the "Laboratories Central de Pants et Chaussccs" [LCPC] in France conducted from 1968 to 1976 demonstrated that the assumption that the locus of the maximum traction force coincides with the Coulomb's failure plane is too conservative as shown in Fig. 26.2(a). The line of maximum stress is actually a logarithmic spiral, perpendicular to the upper free surface of the wall. This will considerably reduce the length of reinforcement necessary for anchorage of the tension developed in the reinforcements.

Another development that took place was about the nature of backfill. During the first years of construction it was recommended to use only granular materials (clear sand and gravel) to develop friction. Further research has shown that the diameter of the grains that separate the friction soils from purely cohesive soils is about 10 to 20 μ. Accordingly, modern specifications stipulate only that the percentage of grains, of smaller than 0.074 mm (U.S. sieveno 200) in the fill material should not exceed 15% by weight. It has also been shown that we can use cohesive soil if a porous geotextile is used for reinforcement so that drained friction angle ϕ of clays can develop between soil and strip. It has also been found that in actual construction, the backfill soil especially at the faces should be compacted with care. Otherwise if heavy rollers are used for compaction of soil adjacent to the face, the facing units may separate itself from the reinforcement.

26.4 DESIGN OF MSE WALLS

The wall should be designed against the following types of failures:

1. Tension failure of the reinforcement in the earth (internal stability)
2. Bearing capacity failure of the base (external stability)
3. Sliding of the whole block ABCD along the base (external stability)
4. Overturning and tilting under the horizontal earth pressure acting on the mass [2].

Usually, the effect of surcharge in concentrated load is assumed to be distributed using the 2 vertical to 1 horizontal distribution as in Fig. 26.3.

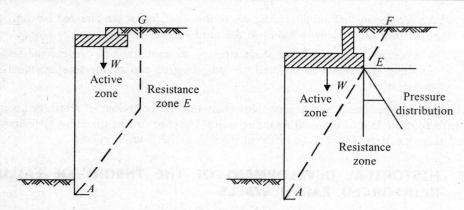

Fig. 26.3 **Assume vertical pressure in soil due to concentrated loads on earth fill.**

The following two types of design methods are used for determining the tension in reinforcements:

- The working stress method
- The failure plane method (limit state method).

In the working stress method, we assume the surface of maximum tension in the reinforcement based on experimental values and work out the necessary anchorage length required for the soil reinforcement. It is used as a general case to deal with all types of reinforced earth walls. In the failure plane method, we consider the equilibrium of several wedges along a potential failure planes and estimate the tension to be developed in the steel reinforcement. We then design for maximum tension. As the working stress method is the more popular and general method, we will discuss only this method in this chapter. The conservative Coulomb's failure surface is also assumed as the surface of failure plane

26.5 DESIGN OF REINFORCEMENT FOR WALLS

The design procedure is as follows for a retaining wall without any surcharge [3]:

Step 1: Adopt a vertical and horizontal spacing of the reinforcement to be used. It may range from 0.2 to 1 m vertically and 0.7 to 1m horizontally.

Step 2: Assume the locus of maximum stress in the soil reinforcements. Different authorities have suggested different locus as shown in Fig. 26.2. The most commonly used is the conservative Coulomb's failure plane (see Section 26.3).

Step 3: Determine the magnitude of horizontal pressure at various depths due to earth pressure as well as due to any superload on the embankment. Usually the active earth pressure distribution is assumed and the *pressure due to superload may be approximately evaluated by using 2 vertical to 1 horizontal distribution.*

Step 4: Take each reinforcement strip and determine the maximum tension that will be developed in it. Let it be T_i. Thus, *take the reinforcement strip at depth z from the top.* The friction f developed will depend on the pressure on the strip and the coefficient of friction $f = \gamma z \tan \delta$.

If b is the width of the strip assuming that friction acts on both faces, the anchorage length L_a required to anchor T_i will be as follows:

$$L_a = T_i/2bf = \frac{T_i}{2b(\gamma z \tan \delta)} \tag{26.1}$$

where

    T_i = tension in soil reinforcement
    b = breadth of the reinforcement
    γz = pressure at depth z
    f = friction developed between soil and reinforcement = $\tan \delta$
    T_i = $(\gamma g K_A) \times$ (area of influence of reinforcing strip). $\tag{26.2}$

For each strip, find L_a, the anchorage length required to develop the corresponding anchorage. The procedure is explained by Example 26.1.

(*Note:* In the field, for easiness of fabrication and installation, all the strips are made of the same length equal to the required maximum anchorage length.)

26.6 OTHER USES OF MSE

The concept of using reinforced earth to improve the strength of soils can be used in many other situations. Figure 26.4 shows an example where it is used to increase the bearing capacity of a foundation. Figure 26.5 shows its use in an earth dam in France. Figure 26.6 is the representation of the slot storage system for coal constructed in the USA [4].

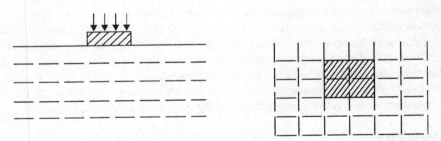

Fig. 26.4 Improvement of bearing capacity by soil reinforcement placed below foundation (section and plan view).

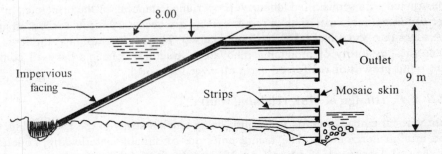

Fig. 26.5 Construction of a low earth dam in France.

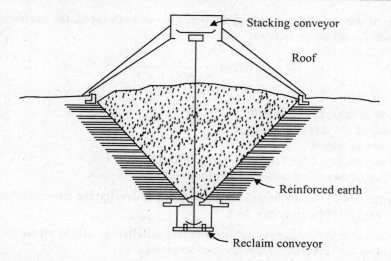

Fig. 26.6   Construction concept of a slot coal storage system in the USA.

26.7 SOIL REINFORCEMENT

The reinforcement used for MSE should be selected with care. Rigid structures like retaining walls require materials with low creep. For embankments that may consolidate with time, materials with some creep may be an advantage.

Metallic reinforcements like galvanized steel and stainless steel (used to reduce corrosion) are stronger than nonmetallics. Plastics have the advantage that they resist corrosion. Plastics are available as fabrics and nonfabrics. Fabrics are textiles manufactured by weaving or knitting. Nonfabrics are in the form of grids and strips, the latter being reinforced sometimes with glass fibre. In any case, the selection of these reinforcements should be made after a study of their strength, creep and durability characteristics. Their selection should be made on the results of laboratory tests furnished by the manufacturer or by approved laboratories.

26.8 SUMMARY

One of most versatile technologies developed in soil mechanics over the recent years is reinforced earth. It can be used in a number of situations to produce an efficient and cheap structure which can be constructed with semiskilled labour. A proper understanding of the principles involved and knowledge of the available materials as reinforcement are necessary for its successful application.

The patent that Vidal had taken has now elapsed. The basic simplicity, the large economic benefits and the possibility of producing innovative structural concepts have all contributed to the present rapid growth of reinforced earth all over the world.

EXAMPLE 26.1   (Design of MSE retaining wall)

A 10 metre vertical embankment is to be built using tension strips in the back filling. The strips are spaced at 1 m horizontally. The facing units are of suitable interlocking concrete blocks. Assuming the soil density $\gamma = 18$ kN/m^3; $\phi = 30°$ and the friction between the strip and soil δ can be taken as 24°, find the length of the soil reinforcement needed. (We plan to use a uniform length of the strip to be placed throughout the height for internal stability). What other checks should be made in the design of this retaining wall? Assume breadth of reinforcement is 100 mm.

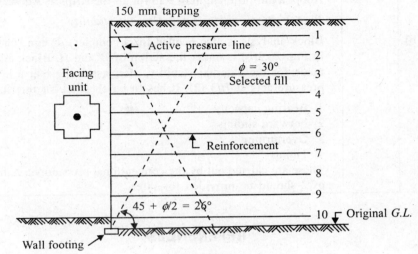

Fig. E.26.1.

Ref.	Step	Calculations
	1	*Part 1. Design for internal stability (length of reinforcements).* *Describe the arrangement of strips.* Let the first strip be placed 0.5 m from top. With uniform vertical spacing at 1 m the 10th strip will be at 0.5 m above the original G.L. as shown. Let the horigontal spacing of strips be also 1 m.
	2	*Find horizontal tension in reinforcement at depth z*
Eq. (26.2)		K_A (for $\phi = 30°$) = 0.3 $T = \gamma z K_A (1 \times 1) = \gamma z \times 0.3$
	3	*Find the length beyond the maximum tension line to resist T.*
Eq. (26.1)		$L_e = \dfrac{T}{2bf} = \dfrac{T}{2b\gamma z \tan \delta}$ $2b\gamma z \tan \delta = 2 \times 0.1 \times \gamma z \times \tan 24 = 0.089\gamma z$ $L_e = \dfrac{0.3\gamma z}{0.089\gamma z}$ 3.37 m beyond Coulomb line Hence L_e is independent of depth.
	4	*Find the distance of the maximum tension surface from face of wall (Adopt uniform length for all strips.)* Assume Coulomb's failure line. Vertical distance of failure line from bottom = 9.5 m Distance of failure plane from face of wall $= H_1 = 9.5 \times \tan 30 = 5.48$ m.

Step 3	5	*Required total length of longest reinforcement.*
		$H_1 + L_{e1} = 5.48 + 3.37 = 8.85$ m
		Adopt a uniform length of 9 m for all the strips as shown in Fig. E.26.1.
Fig. 26.2(b)		*Part 2. Block analysis for external stability*
		Block analysis is also needed for a complete design. The block *ABCD* in Fig. 26.2(b) is under the action of *W* and *H*. Block analysis is to be made for the external stability, after assuming that a horizontal earth pressure acts at *H*/3 [2]. It has to be checked for this following:
		1. Bearing capacity
		2. Forward sliding
		3. Overturning
		4. Tilting.
		These are carried out by the conventional procedures. A factor of safety of 2 should be provided for safety.

REFERENCES

[1] Asian Institute of Technology, Bangkok, Symposium on Soil and Rock Improvement Techniques including Geotextiles, Reinforced Earth and Modern Piling Methods, Bangkok, Dec. 1982.

[2] Colin, J.F.P. Jones, *Earth Reinforcement and Soil Structures*, Butterworth, London, 1988.

[3] Bowles, J.E., *Foundation Analysis and Design*, McGraw-Hill, Singapore, 1988.

[4] Ingold, T.S., Reinforced Earth and Plastics, *Consulting Engineer* (London), Aug. 1980.

27

Soil Exploration—Geological Investigation of Sites

27.1 INTRODUCTION

The first step in any subsoil exploration for a site should be a geological and geomorphological investigation to determine the nature of formation of the site. (Geomorphology means the study of the surface features of the earth. It may also include study of the natural vegetation growing at the site.) The better we know the geology and geomorphology of the site, the more efficient and economical will be the result of the site investigation. Planning the *layout and location* of boreholes to give us the nature and thicknesses of various layers depend on the geology of the site.

27.2 ENGINEERING GEOLOGY APPLIED TO FOUNDATIONS

Engineering geology has many applications in civil engineering. Dam engineers are interested in problems concerning dam stability, seepage, tunnelling, etc. Water supply engineers are interested in ground water problems. Others are interested in geology to check the stability of slopes. Each of them looks at different aspect of engineering geology. However, foundation engineers are interested to know through the study of the geology of the site, *the nature of soil profile that we can expect at the site, the general properties of the foundation materials and also foresee any construction difficulties that can occur.* They are also interested in the problems of weathering of rock and suitability of the rock formation as a foundation material. From experience we also know that sites of the same geological origin show similar soil and rock formations. The problems faced in two sites of the same geologic origin are very similar. Hence we find that we can extend the experience we have gained at an old site to a new similar site having the same geological history.

27.3 TYPES OF SOIL FORMATIONS

Most natural deposits can be classified under one of the following types:

1. River deposits—formed by rivers

2. Shore deposits—formed by sea
3. Glacial deposits
4. Lake or lacustrine deposits—formed by standing water
5. Wind or aeolian deposits—formed by wind
6. In-situ soil or weathered rock or rock modified to soils (laterite).

A brief account of each of these is given below.

27.3.1 River Deposits (Alluvial Deposits)

The deposits occur near the major rivers and can be of various types. They can be further classified into the following categories.

1. River channel deposits
2. Flood-plain deposits
3. Delta deposits
4. Oxbow lake deposits
5. Drowned valleys deposits (paths once traversed by the rivers which due to accidental reasons have been separated and later silted up are called drowned valleys).

Each of these has its own characteristics. For example drowned valley deposits will have fine grained soils on top with coarse grained materials at the bottom. Descriptions of these deposits are available in books on Engineering Geology.

27.3.2 Shore Deposits

These deposits occur all along coastal regions of India. These are deposits formed in the sea by sedimentation left on the shores by waves. Fluctuations in water level over millions of years would have buried or exposed some of the layers. Generally, they consist of sand, gravel, silt, and clay in intricate layers. Fossils of shells and other sea animals may also be present in the clay and sand deposits. In tropics where coral formations are possible, there may exist coral rocks, which should not be mistaken for limestone deposits during soil exploration. In shores, which have shifted with time, we get composite shore deposits.

27.3.3 Glacial Deposits

These are more prevalent in upper latitudes as in North America and UK. They were formed by the action of glaciers. Over consolidated clays, boulders and marl formations are characteristics of these deposits.

27.3.4 Lake Deposits

Lake deposits can be classified into the following:

- Small lake deposits
- Large lake deposits.

In large lakes waves can be formed and due to the turbulence produced, the shore deposits of large lakes can be different from that of small lakes. Similarly, deltas near lakes are not like deltas near seas. Those near lakes are more complex than the latter. There is also difference between fresh water lake deposits and those of seawater lakes. The salts contained in the seawater cause flocculation of the clay particles so that both suspended silt and clay are deposited together in salt water lakes.

27.3.5 Wind Deposits

Wind deposits show remarkable uniformity as found in the deserts. Loess is a uniform cohesive wind blown deposit (particle size 0.01 to 0.05 mm) the cohesion being due to the calcareous binder. On saturation, this bond is removed and the loose structure of loess can collapse into a mass of very little strength.

27.3.6 Weathering of Rock

Rock weathering can be due to mechanical agents or by simple solution of constituents or chemical action. The resulting weathered material depends on the type of rock as well as the climatic conditions of weathering. Some of the black cotton soils found in the Deccan Plateau are in-situ soils formed from rock in *dry conditions*. While the laterite soils found in N.E. part of India and Kerala have been formed from rocks weathered under hot and humid conditions with plenty of rainfall (wet conditions). In igneous rocks, weathering may leave a large number of unweathered boulders, which during boring should not be mistaken for solid rocks (see Section 28.6).

It is well known that in limestone areas, there may be tunnels left under solid rock due to water flow. Similar small tunnels, but of very local nature, have been reported in laterite formations in Kerala also. Footings built on such locations can collapse when they are fully loaded.

Care should be taken when building on rock slopes (like building of penstock foundations) that the foundation material is not on a creeping slope and also that the slopes are stable. Boulders on rock slopes should not be mistaken as solid rock during boring operations.

27.3.7 Formation of Soils by Biological Process

Peat is formed by decay of vegetation. We will find fibrous organic matter in organic clays. Organic deposits are fine-grained clays or silts with a large amount of finely divided organic matter. It is spongy when wet and gives a characteristic odour. Microorganisms form coral reefs and these buried coral deposits may be found under shore deposits also in the tropics, especially in areas where there are coral reefs out in the sea. They should not be mistaken for solid rock as these coral deposits may have sand deposits under them and also above them.

27.4 IMPORTANCE OF MINOR GEOLOGIC FEATURES

Identification of the major geological feature of a site will not give us detailed information regarding the nature and distribution of the soil. For example, we know that in a large riverbed subject to monsoon flows, the main soil types will be sand, clay, silt etc. in intermixed layers. We can only get a rough idea of the characteristics of those soils, as they are river deposits. However the minor geological features like the detailed distribution of soils under the foundation of a given site have to be determined by actual detailed boring and its interpretation with references to the nature of the deposits.

27.5 IMPORTANCE OF OBSERVATION OF WATER LEVELS IN BORINGS

Artician conditions in clays are generally due to continuous silt or sand layers that may exist in the deposit. Generally these silt layers will be missed in ordinary borings. Water level observations can give an indication of artician presence. They are important in open excavations (where lowering of water table is planned) as blowout can occur under certain conditions as shown in Fig. 27.1.

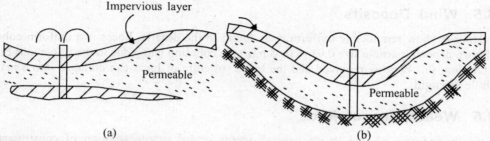

Fig. 27.1 **Artesian conditions and chances of blowout in excavations: (a) In soil deposits; (b) with underlying rock at bottom.**

27.6 IMPORTANCE OF SOIL CRUSTS

In the tropics, the fluctuation of water levels with seasons as well as dissipation due to the heat of the sun produce a hard crust of soil deposits in clayey soils. Soft clay usually exists below the crust where the water level does not change with season. The presence of the crust has very significant impact on (a) settlement of fills placed over the crust (b) bearing capacity of shallow footings (c) differential settlement when its depth varies horizontally. Hence a careful study of the depth of the crust should be made during all soil investigations.

27.7 MATERIALS AND ASSOCIATED LANDFORMS

The type of materials associated with the various landforms are given in Table 27.1.

TABLE 27.1   MATERIALS AND ASSOCIATED LANDFORMS

Type of landform	Texture of soil material developed from or contained in landforms
Sedimentary deposits.	
(a) Sandstone (massive, horizontal or dipping beds).	Sand to sand-clay
(b) Sandstone and shale in alternate layers.	Sand, sand-clay, silty clay
(c) Sandy shale, horizontal or dipping beds.	Sand to sand-clay
(d) Clayey shale, horizontal or dipping beds.	Silty clay
(e) Limestone, horizontal or dipping beds.	Silty clay
Igneous granites and related rocks.	Coarse sand to clay

TABLE 27.1   MATERIALS AND ASSOCIATED LANDFORMS *(Cont.)*

Type of landform	Texture of soil material developed from or contained in landforms
Metamorphic rocks (foliated).	
(a) Slate	Silt
(b) Gneiss and schist	Sand to sandy clay
(c) Quartzite	Sand
Volcanic rocks.	
(a) Lava flows	Silty clay
(b) Basalt sills	Silty clay
(c) Dikes	Silty clay
Glacial (Ice laid) deposits.	
(a) Moraines	A somewhat stratified mixture of sand and silt with scattered gravel and some clay. Heterogeneous mixture.
(b) Till plains	
(c) Eskers, kames	Sand and clay mixture, stratified.
(d) Drumlins	Compact mixture of sand and silt with some gravel and clay
Aeolian (Wind laid) deposits.	
(a) Sand dunes	Sand, fine 80%
(b) Loess	Silt 60 to 90%
Alluvial (Water laid) deposits.	
(a) Outwash plains (also glacial)	Wet stratified sands and silts
(b) Terraces and valley trains	Dry sand and/or gravel, stratified
(c) Alluvial fans	Sand, gravel, silt, complex, stratified
(d) Coastal plains	Sands, silt or clays
Lake and sea deposits	
(a) Lacustrine	Silts and silty clays
(b) Beach lines	Sands and gravels
(c) Recent alluvium	Gravel, sand, silt or clay

27.8 GEOMORPHOLOGY

The study of the surface features of earth like plant growth, drainage patterns etc. is called *geomorphology*. It is possible to guess the nature and origin of the soil system from the geomorphological features and even the nature of plants that grow in the site if it is a virgin site. In large projects remote sensing techniques, air photos and satellite images are also used to study the geological and geomorphological features of the area to be investigated. The geomorphology of the flood plains, lake deposits, wind deposits etc. will be different and can be easily identified if we make keen observation of the site. For example, the identification of the alignment of a fault zone can be seen from the nature of vegetation that grows in the thick layer of soil along the fault.

27.9 EXAMPLES

Most of the complex soil profiles of India exist along the coastal areas only. We shall examine a few of them to illustrate the above descriptions.

EXAMPLE 27.1 (Soil profile at Hazira, Gujarat)

Hazira area is on the mouth of Tapi, on the outer side of the bend of the river. Geologically, it is part of the flood plain of the river in the delta stage of the river near the sea. The soils here would have originated from the Deccan trap and transported by the river. Geologically, the profile should consist of soft to medium stiff silt or clay on the top part with layers of medium to dense silt sand and hard silty clay intermixed below the topsoil. The deeper layers should be deposited during the early years of the formation and consist of coarser sand and gravel. The minor geological features have to be determined by actual boreholes.

EXAMPLE 27.2 (Soil profile of Bombay)

The tail like land mass projecting into the sea has withstood the attack of the sea for a long time. It must have a solid rock base because of its geological formation. In general, the western side which is more often exposed to waves should have more coarse sand deposits while the eastern sheltered areas must have more clay deposits. The minor geologic features have to be determined from boreholes made in the area. In general, there will be the following different types:

Type 1: Hills with rock outcrops and rock at shallow depths.

Type 2: Hill slopes—Deep weathered zone with rock below.

Type 3: Low lands.

Type 4: Shore deposits (The deposits on the west side will be different from those on the east side.)

EXAMPLE 27.3 (Soil profile in Ernakulam–Cochin)

Ernakulam (Cochin) is on the backwaters of Kerala with a large lake (Vembanattu Kayal) extending into the sea. River Periyar empties into the lake. The major geological formation will be lake deposits and shore deposits. We can expect clay and medium fine sand extending to great depths. The minor geological features will vary from place to place depending on the position of the site near the sea and the lake. In most of the areas where fine sand exist at low depths, low-rise buildings on short piles (coconut trunk piles or concrete piles) have been built. A few low-rise buildings with sand piles resting on the top sand layer have also been built. Multistoreyed buildings have been built in clay on very deep bored piles up to 35 m in length.

EXAMPLE 27.4 (Soil profiles of Chennai)

There are no major rivers (except small rivers like Adayar and Coovum) emptying into the sea in Chennai. Rock outcrops are found at St. Thomas Mount (near the airport) and it dips northwards. Near the Chennai harbour, rock is found in some places at about 20 m depth. There have been a large number of marshes behind the seacoast, which have been filled now with soft clay deposits. In areas, which have been raised by subsequent alluvial deposits by flood waters, we get a layer of hard clay on top, which can be mildly expansive in nature. The deposits found are generally shore deposits, marsh deposits and small river deposits depending on the location of the site.

EXAMPLE 27.5   (Geological formation of Kolkata)

Kolkata principally is on the lower reaches of a delta deposit with very deep bed of alluvium. A typical bore data will be that of a delta deposit, mixed sand, silt and clay.

EXAMPLE 27.6

The following are the types of geological problems we come across in soil investigation:

1. A group of factory buildings is to be constructed on the *flood plain of a meandering river*. Show by sketches what type of soil profiles you may expect at such a site. Explain the origin of the strata shown in your sketches.

2. A factory is to be constructed on a valley floor near the foot of the slopes of the valley. The test boring indicate silty sand and soft clay. The soft clay is known to rest on sloping rock surface. The general geology of the site *indicates a drowned valley*. Explain why it is necessary to make core borings into the rock.

3. Test borings were made across a broad ridge between *two river valleys* located at about the same elevation. They disclosed an irregularly stratified deposit consisting of stiff clay, silty sand and clean sand. The water rose at different levels in different holes above the valley floors. Examine by sketches what can you deduct from this observation.

4. In borings along the sea shore (where there are coral formations present act in the sea) calcareous deposits were found at shallow depth. What can we deduce from these findings?

REFERENCES

[1] Legeet, *Geology and Engineering*, McGraw-Hill, New York, 1998.

[2] Krynine and Judd, *Engineering Geology and Geotechniques*, McGraw-Hill, New York, 1990.

[3] Blyth, *Geology for Engineers*, ELBS, London, 1995.

[4] Attewell, P.B. and I.W. Farmer, *Principles of Engineering Geology*, Chapman and Hall, London, 1976.

28

Site and Soil Investigation Reports

28.1 INTRODUCTION

Generally two reports, one called the *Site Investigation Report* and the other called *Soil Investigation Report* are prepared before the start of all construction projects. A brief discussion about these reports and type of field investigations usually carried out are given in this chapter.

28.2 SITE INVESTIGATION REPORT

The first stage of any project is a Site Investigation Report. Foundation investigation work is usually carried out for one of the following purposes:

1. Investigation for undertaking a new work.
2. Investigation for safety of an existing structure.
3. Investigation for a structure that has failed.
4. Investigation for suitability and availability of materials of construction and use of construction methods.

For each of these we use the some general approach, which will be followed by special investigations at a later stage depending on the work.

28.2.1 Details of Site Investigation Report

The site investigation report is a general report and is usually prepared under the following heads:

1. Introduction.
2. Brief description of the work (about the client and the structure).
3. Geographic location of the site with index plan.
4. Topology of the site (description of site with site plan).
5. Climatic data, location on seismic and wind maps.

6. Geological details.

7. Geomorphological features (physical features, plants etc.).

8. Information regarding ground water (report of inspection of wells at site) and tidal features if the site is near the sea coast.

9. Other items.

10. Comments.

Maps indicating these features are also to be attached with the report.

28.3 SOIL EXPLORATION FOR DETAILED FIELD INVESTIGATION REPORT

The general site investigation described above is to be followed by a *detailed field investigation report*. Generally, 0.5 per cent of cost of the project is allotted to site exploration and testing. Based on the geological and other features a detailed soil exploration is planned. Direct soil exploration is made by one of the following two methods:

- By means of test pits and shafts
- By exploratory borings.

28.3.1 Exploration by Test Pits

IS 4453 (1980) deals with pits, trenches, drifts and shafts for soil exploration. Pits are usually 0.8 × 1.8 m in plan dimension. Sampling is carried out as shown in Fig. 28.1. They are used where good soils exist at shallow depths and where we know that there will be no weak layers at lower depths.

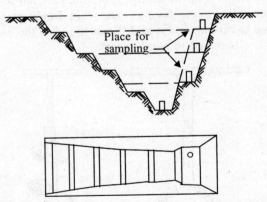

Place for sampling

Fig. 28.1   Method of undisturbed sampling in trenches.

In cohesive soils, cubes of 20 cm (8") can be easily cut out and scaled by first coating them by hot paraffin all over, then wrapping in special paper and insulating with another paraffin coating. They should be properly packed so that they will not be damaged in transport for laboratory testing. Sampling cylinders are also used for sampling undisturbed samples in all soils including sands. They should be at least 100 to 200 mm diameter and 150 to 200 mm height. Sampler is forced into soil by gentle pressure, and advanced by gradual removal of neighbouring material. It must not be driven or rammed into the soil especially with granular soils. The top and bottom are sealed with paraffin to keep the samples from drying out.

28.3.2 Exploration by Boreholes

Exploratory borings are made with the following objectives:

- Determine the stratification of the subsoil.
- Take disturbed or undisturbed soil samples.
- Make field tests to determine the nature of the soils in-situ.

These can be carried by auger boring or by cased boreholes. The internal diameter of casing for simple exploration of stratification should not be less than 50 mm (2 inch). The diameter of boreholes for detailed soil exploration, where undisturbed samples are to be taken ranges from 150 to 300 mm. The outside diameter of SPT (split spoon) sampler is 50 mm and the outside diameter of samplers used for taking out 100 mm (4 inch) laboratory samples will be 106 mm. Most small firms use 150 mm boreholes and take out 100 mm samples. The practice of extending boreholes by bentonite slurry does not yield good results for soil exploration. But many soil exploration companies use this method for cutting down cost.

28.3.3 Auger Borings for Soil Stratification

Simple auger borings can give us the soil stratification. Two types of augers, the posthole augers and the helical augers that are available are shown in Fig. 28.2. Hand-operated augers can be used for study of stratification and for disturbed samples up to about 5 m. Posthole augers give better samples than the helical augers. The smallest helical auger used is 40 mm (1.5 inch). Large machine-operated helical augers are used for larger depths. If the sides are not self-supporting, casing pipes are used. Such borings are called *auger borings*. The main disadvantage of helical augers is that the samples of layers tend to mix up and it is difficult to locate the exact changes in soil strata. In posthole augers, this is eliminated to some extent.

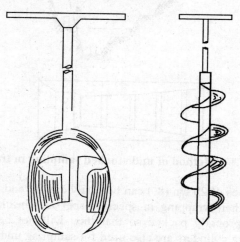

Fig 28.2   Earth augers; posthole and helical augers.

28.3.4 Wash Boring with Sampling

The practice of using wash boring by manual labour or by Calix drill is frequently used in India for soil investigation. An ordinary wash boring pump is used to circulate water through the holes in the drilling bit, the rising water carrying the suspended soil particles to the top. Rotary drilling is another method used in soils and rock.

While drilling, as indicated above, only changes in the colour of the circulating water is usually taken as the change of strata. The water is then turned off and a spoon sampler is used to take a sample. However it is much better to take some sample at every 1.5 metre depth of boring even if there is no change in strata. As Terzaghi and Peck have remarked, "departure from the above procedure should not be tolerated as otherwise we may miss the stratification of the soil."

It is very important to see that while taking sample the water level in the hole is stationary without any hydraulic head. Casings are used for not very deep holes. Some use bentonite for stabilization of boreholes deeper than 15 to 20 m. Under such cases one must be very careful in the identification of change in strata. The SPT spoon samples obtained should be used only for identification of soils and their stratification.

28.3.5 Borings for Detailed Geotechnical Investigations

Borings from 150 mm to 300 mm dia. are used for detailed investigation depending on the importance of the project and the necessity for taking large undisturbed samples. In sandy soils wash borings may have to be used with casings. In deep holes where bentonite slurry is sometimes used instead of full earnings, care must be taken not to mix the samples with bentonite.

When casing is used and the boring is advanced by percussion instruments (shells) and augers the boring is also called *shell and auger borings*. Manually operated shell and auger borings of 150 mm diameter are the standard practice of the small firms dealing geotechnical investigations in India. As far as possible, unlike in pile construction, bentonite mud drilling should be *discouraged for borings in small holes*. Casing pipes should be used throughout the depth in such cases. *If bentonite mud drilling has been carried out, it should be specially recorded in the report.*

In hard or dense soil, the borehole is excavated by a chisel or chopping bit fixed on to the boring rod which is hung by a cable from the top. Below the water table, the loosened soil forms a slurry with the ground water. If the hole is above the water table, water has to be introduced into the borehole to form slurry. Periodically the chisel and rods are removed from the borehole and the slurry is excavated by means of a shell or bailer. Other tools used are the clay cutter and the auger. When samples are to be taken, the boreholes are cleaned and the samples driven in.

28.3.6 Undisturbed Soil Sampling

We can classify sampling into three types:

1. Disturbed samples as obtained from augers
2. In-situ samples for tests on density moisture content etc. as from SPT samples
3. Undisturbed samples for strength and consolidation characteristics.

By convention we assume that clay samples are undisturbed if the area ratio of the sampler is less than 10% (for a split spoon sampler it is as high as 30% and for a Shelby tube sampler (thin walled sampler) it is as low as 6 to 9%). Sampler properties are as defined below:

Area ratio $A_\gamma = 100(D_2^2 - D_1^2)/D_1^2$

Inside clearance $C_i = 100(D_3 - D_1)/D_1$

Outside clearance $C_0 = 100(D_2 - D_4)/D_4$

where D_1, D_2, D_3, D_4 are as shown in Fig. 28.3.

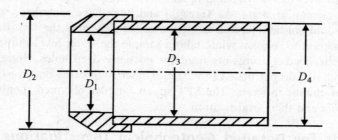

Fig. 28.3   Soil sampling tube with cutting edge.

Quality classification of samples is given in Table 28.1.

TABLE 28.1   SAMPLING AND ITS SUITABILITY FOR TESTS

B.S. Class	Sampling method	Suitability
1.	Special large piston samplers as specified by dry sampling	All tests
2.	Ordinary large samples driven down by hammers from dry holes	Classification, density and moisture tests
3.	Clay cutter or auger from dry holes. Also split spool samples from penetration tests	Classification and moisture determination
4.	As in 3 above but from boreholes with water	Classification only
5.	Pieces from wash borings	Description of stratification only

28.3.7   Spacing and Depth of Boreholes

IS 1892 (1979) Code of practice for subsurface investigation gives us the following guidelines:

1. For a small building one borehole or test pit at the centre can give the necessary data.
2. For a building covering not more than 4000 sq. metres, one borehole or test pit at each corner and one at centre is adequate.
3. For a large project, the number will depend on its geological features and variation of strata. Generally a grid of 50 m spacing should be used with a combination of boreholes and sounding tests. The inexpensive Dynamic Cone Penetration Test is quite suitable for sounding tests.

IS 1892 recommends a *minimum investigation depth* equal to 1.5 times the width of foundation for footings and raft foundations. This depth is also specified as the larger of the following two depths: the depth at which the increase in stress due to the new foundation is 10% of the overburden pressure or, 10% of the applied load. Where piles have to be used, we should explore to find whether there are any good bearing strata and conduct tests as stated in B.S. to a depth that is likely to affect the bearing capacity and settlement of the structure significantly.

28.4 DETAILS AND PRESENTATION OF SOIL INVESTIGATION REPORT

As stated in Section 28.3, in any preliminary preparation of a project, the *site investigation report* described in Section 28.2 is to be followed by a *detailed soil investigation report*. It is also called the *Geotechnical Report*. This report gives the details of the field and laboratory investigations that were carried out and the final recommendations. The usual format used by most agencies for a building site is as follows (It should be suitably modified for other works like an embankment cutting).

Section 1: Introduction giving scope of investigation.

Section 2: Field investigation.

    (a) Description of field investigations

    (b) Data of field investigations (log of boreholes with diagrams and data of in-situ tests)

    (c) Details of ground water observation.

Section 3: Laboratory investigations.

    (a) List of routine laboratory tests conducted (grain size, limits, swell tests, unconfined results of laboratory in standard format) this may be presented as appendix.

    (b) List of special tests conducted. Compression, triaxial test, consolidation test, and test of water with reference to tables in which they are presented.

Section 4: Discussion of subsoil conditions.

This is the heart of the report and should be clear and concise. It is reported under the following subheads:

    (a) Description of soil conditions as evaluated from all field and laboratory results.

    (b) Analysis and discussion of field and laboratory tests results.

    (c) Design criteria like allowable settlements to be used.

    (d) Calculations for determining safe bearing capacity, capacity of pile, slope stability, etc.

    (e) Recommendations on choice of type of foundation, allowable bearing pressures, slope stability, ground improvement, etc.

    (f) Recommendations of soil parameter for structural design.

    (g) Recommendations for safety measures to be taken during construction such as excavation.

Section 5: Conclusions and final recommendations.

This last part of the report should give definite recommendations based on the field and laboratory results.

Note: The format has been recommended by the Indian Geotechnical Society [1].

28.5 IMPORTANCE OF FIELD CLASSIFICATION OF SOILS

It is of utmost importance that the field staff in charge of field investigations should be trained to correctly identify and describe soil and rock samples in the field itself. It is also important that the foundation engineer in the office should be able to understand the description of soil given in the field report. Both of them should have the same method of description of soils. It is for this purpose that A. Casagrande devised his well-known "Descriptive Field Classification of Soils" by examining the soils in the field. It is fully related to the A.C. Classification or Universal Classification and Indian Standard Classification based on the laboratory tests. Field and laboratory classifications, systems even though interrelated are separate from each other. Field classification is based on field tests and laboratory classification is based on laboratory identification tests.

28.5.1 Descriptive (Field) Classification of Soils

Field classification tests are given in IS 1498 (1970) "Classification and Identification of Soils for General Engineering purpose". The main tests used are the following:

1. Visual examination. (If more than 50% of soil particles can be seen by the naked eye, it is classified as coarse-grained. Otherwise, it is fine-grained.)
2. Dilatancy (to distinguish fine sand, silt and clay)
3. Toughness (to distinguish organic soils and soils of low, high plasticity)
4. Dry strength (to distinguish silt and clay with high plasticity)
5. Organic content
6. Other identification tests.

28.5.2 Field Description of Soils

The field engineer should be able to describe the soil properly. For this purpose it should conform to the specified standard format. It should cover the following items:

1. The colour and the in-situ moisture condition. (The base colour is the last in the description. Thus light grey or yellow grey will mean grey soil of light or yellow shading.)
2. Description of its constituents. Example, clay, sand, etc. If it is mixture, adjectives are used. Thus the description of "clayey sand" is more sand than clay as contents of the soil.
3. The structure of the strata (example—loose, dense, hard, soft, etc.)
4. Inclusions or pockets, if any (example—micaceous, calcareous, with shell impurities).
5. For sands, give grain size (coarse, medium, fine, etc.) whether it contains organic matter or cemented and its state of saturation.
6. Natural consistency (for clays give description as hard, soft; and for sands, as loose, firm, dense).
7. An indication of the probable laboratory classification (CH, ML, etc.).

28.5.3 Examples of Visual Classification

The following are examples of the method for describing the field classification of soils:

1. Method of description of coarse-grained soils. Give colour, state of moisture, classification, approximate percentage of fractions of other soils, maximum size, angularity of grains, consistency, local or geologic name, and classification by symbol. Descriptions can be short or it can be detailed as shown in the following examples:

(a) *Example of field classification by short description:* Well compacted, brown, most poorly graded, silty medium, alluvial sand with 10% angular gravel and about 15% nonplastic fines (SM).

(b) *Example of detailed classification:* After the above short description add the following: 10% hard angular gravel, maximum size 10 mm, with 15% fines with low dry strength. Sand is medium and well compacted.

2. Method of description of fine-grained soils. Give colour, soft or hard, descriptive, plasticity, percentage of other soils, and maximum size of coarse grains present, probable geologic origin, other information and classification symbol.

(a) *Example of short description:* Grayish brown, hard in-situ clay of low plasticity with Kankar modulus and coarse particles. In-situ decomposed rock (CL).

(b) *Example of detailed description:* Add the following—about 20% coarse particles and 10% gravel particles of decomposed rock.

28.6 FIELD IDENTIFICATION OF ROCKS

The following adjectives can be used to describe the state of weathering of rocks found at site, in increasing order of weathering. Such classification is also helpful in disputes in payments for excavation in earth work:

1. *In-situ* solid rock.
2. Slightly weathered rock > 90% as rock.
3. Moderately weathered rock > 50% as rock in large pieces, which cannot be broken by hand. (Excavation can be done by explosives only.)
4. Highly weathered rock (large pieces of rock which can be broken by hand, can be excavated by tools and hand with or without addition of water).
5. Decomposed rock (completely weathered rock). Very few pieces of rock present and these can be broken to soil easily.
6. In-situ soil.

28.7 SUMMARY

Site and geotechnical investigations are important documents of all major projects. Sufficient funds must be made available for this purpose in a project budget. It is also important that the field staff engaged in the work are familiar with field identification of soils and rocks.

REFERENCES

[1] Indian Geotechnical Society Committee on Professional Practice, *Message to Owners, Architects and Design Engineers*, Geotechnical Engineering, New Delhi, 2002.

[2] IS 1892–1979, *Code of Practice for Subsurface Investigation for Foundations*, Bureau of Indian Standards, New Delhi.

[3] IS 10042–1981, *Code of Practice for Site Investigation for Foundations in Gravel-Boulder Deposit*, Bureau of Indian Standards, New Delhi.

[4] IS 1498–1970, *Classification and Identification of Soils for General Engineering Purpose—* Bureau of Indian Standards, New Delhi.

APPENDIX A

Determination of Contact Pressure Distribution in Soils and Analysis of Beams on Elastic Foundations by Influence Charts

A.1 INTRODUCTION

The pressure produced by the base of a foundation has to be studied under the following two heads:

1. The pressure at the interface between the foundation and the soil called contact pressure.

2. The pressure produced inside the soil mass i.e. stress distribution inside the soil mass.

The contact pressures are used to determine the shear and bending moments of foundation structures like raft foundations while the stress distribution in the soil mass is used to determine the consolidation or settlement of the foundation. In actual practice, these two forces interact with each other and should be studied together. However, because of the mathematical complexity it is customary to study them as two separate subjects. Accordingly, in this Appendix we will deal in depth with contact pressure distribution. Stress distribution is discussed in Chapter 3. We should also understand the limitations of our present day knowledge of the subject as all our mathematical deductions are in many cases far different from that which exist in the field. Fortunately, even a rough estimate of the magnitudes and distribution of these stresses will enable us to arrive at a satisfactory solution of the problems. Hence it is more important to know about the fundamentals than the mathematical details of the subject.

A.2 RIGID AND FLEXIBLE FOUNDATIONS

A rigid foundation settles uniformly under a load (i.e. the deformation of the foundation is only say less than ten per cent of the total settlement of the soil). A flexible foundation closely follows the theoretical settlement profile of the soil. In reality it is easier to imagine a flexible foundation as one in which the distribution of contact pressure is the same as the foundation loading itself. When dealing with soils, we meet with one of the following situations:

- The soil is homogeneous, elastic, and isotropic such as saturated clay where the simple theory of elasticity applies.

- The soil is homogeneous and elastic but whose rigidity increases with confinement (depth) like sand or gravel, which are single grained in structure.

In the first type of materials, (i.e. clay soils) Boussinesq's equations are applicable for determining contact pressures. This theory gives a concave distribution of contact pressures with very high stress values at the edges as shown in Fig. A.1. However as these high stresses are not sustainable, these regions undergo plastic redistribution as shown in the figure. In granular soils, on the other hand, as there is very little strength at the edges due to lack of confinement (with surface loadings) we can deduce a stress distribution, which is convex (refer Fig. 2.1 of the text 2). As already stated, the settlements in these soils for rigid foundation has to be uniform. With flexible footings and uniform loading, the contact pressures are uniform. However, in the case of settlement for surface loadings, in clayey soils there will be more settlement at the centre. For granular soils, due to lack of confinement, there will be more settlement at the edges then at the centre as shown in Fig. 2.2. However, confinement due to depth of foundation can charge these distributions to some extent in all the cases.

A.3   FORMULAE FOR ELASTIC SETTLEMENTS FOR FLEXIBLE FOOTINGS

As shown in Section 4.2, Boussinesq's analysis can be used directly for calculation of settlements of flexible footings due to a uniform pressure q on an elastic semi-infinite half-space. It gives the following values for settlements:

$$\Delta = s_1 = \frac{qB(1 - \mu^2)}{E_s} I_w \tag{A.1}$$

The settlement of a rigid, square, loaded area on a semi-infinite homogeneous elastic solid can be also derived from complex calculations from the distribution of pressures and it works out to be:

$$s_2 = \frac{0.8qB(1 - \mu^2)}{E_s} \tag{A.2}$$

This uniform settlement as can be seen from the formulae is approximately the average settlement of the flexible footing.

A.4   VARIATION OF CONTACT PRESSURES UNDER RIGID STRIP FOOTINGS WITH INCREASING LOADS TO FAILURE

Prof Schultz [1] has investigated both theoretically and by experimental observation the changes that take place in the distribution of contact pressures under *rigid strip footings* as we load the footing by a line load gradually from a small load to failure load. He assumed soils having c and ϕ values and cohesionless soils with only ϕ values. He further assumed that the soil behaves elastically in the initial stages but plastically at the final stages. In the intermediate stages certain parts of the foundation becomes plastic and the remaining parts behave elastically.

Figure A.1 shows a rigid strip footing under increasing concentrated load W in a $c - \phi$ soil. Schultz obtained the following changes in distribution of the contact pressures as we slowly increase the load from a small value to failure load.

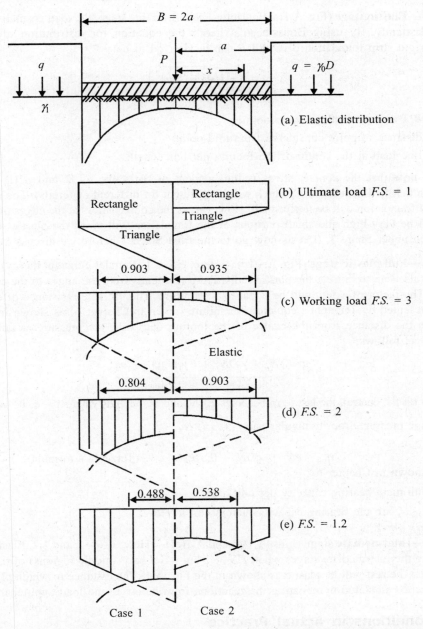

(a) Elastic distribution

(b) Ultimate load *F.S.* = 1

(c) Working load *F.S.* = 3

(d) *F.S.* = 2

(e) *F.S.* = 1.2

Fig. A.1 **Contact pressure distributions beneath a rigid footing on loading gradually up to ultimate bearing capacity of the soil: Case 1, Granular soil** $\phi = 30°$, $c = 0$; **case 2, Soil** $c = 10$ kN/m^2 **and** $\phi = 15°$.

(a) Stage 1—Elastic stage (Fig. A.1(a)).   Here, *F.S.* = 3. In this stage, the load is small and the soil behaves elastically. By using Boussinesq's theory the equation for distribution of pressure p beneath a rigid strip foundation of width B can be derived to be:

$$p = \frac{W}{\pi a}\left(1/\sqrt{1-(x/a)^2}\right) \tag{A.3}$$

where

a = $B/2$ = half-width of strip footing

x = distance of point considered from mid-point

W = line load at the centre of the footing per unit length.

We should note that the contact stress is independent of the value of E_s and μ (It is only the deformation that will depend on E_s which will be different for different materials). The influence of the depth of foundation will be fairly small. However, as the contact stress at the edges of the footing ($x = a$) will be very high and small portions of the foundation will reach the plastic stage as will be explained under Stage 3. (Let us now go to the final Stage 3 before we discuss Stage 2.)

(b) Stage 3—Full plastic stage (Fig. A.1(b)).   Here, *F.S.* = 1 (Prandel Terzaghi theory). If the load is steadily raised up to failure, the plastic redistribution extends from the edges to the centre of the soil mass. The factor of safety will be equal to 1 at failure. The ultimate resistance offered by soil can be represented by Terzaghi's equation for failure (given in Chapter 6) as shown in Fig. A.1b. Taking x as the distance from the centre of the footing outwards, the pressure at failure can be represented as follows:

$$p = \underbrace{cN_c + \gamma DN_q}_{\text{Rectangle}} + \underbrace{B\gamma_1 N_\gamma(1-x/a)}_{\text{Triangle}} \tag{A.4}$$

When $x = 0$ (at the centre), the last term becomes $\beta\gamma_1 N_\gamma$ and at the ends where $x = a$, its value is zero.

Average pressure from triangular part = $0.5\beta\gamma_1 N_\gamma$.
Hence,

$$q_{\text{ult}} = cN_c + \gamma_0 DN_q + 0.5\beta\gamma_1 N_\gamma \qquad \text{(Terzaghi's formula)}$$

where (as shown in Chapter 6)

q_{ult} = ultimate bearing capacity per unit area

N_c, N_q, N_r are the bearing capacity factors and $a = B/2$

(c) Stage 2—Intermediate stage (Figs. A.1(d) and A.1(e)).   Here, *F.S.* = 2 and 1.2. Elastic – Plastic state. During the intermediate stages when *F.S.* > 1 but < 3 a part (middle regions) of the base will be elastic and the rest will be plastic as shown in the Fig. A.1. The distance to which plasticity has reached can be calculated by equating the reactions from below to the load applied from above.

A.4.1 Conditions in Actual Practice

The above discussion shows that in field situations we usually assume a factor of safety of 2 to 3 so that contact pressures in these situations can be assumed to be distributed as for the elastic stage with concentration of stresses at the edges. Prof. Schultz has also made laboratory studies, field measurements and also analysis of past records, which agreed with these predictions. In view of these findings, some German designers assume a contact pressure distribution with higher pressures at the edges as shown in Fig. A.2 for routine design of rigid footings.

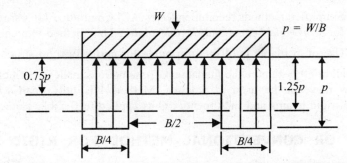

Fig. A.2 **Recommended contact pressure distribution for design of footings in cohesive soils.**

A.5 CALCULATION OF PRESSURES UNDER BEAMS ON ELASTIC FOUNDATION

In elemental analysis of raft foundation, we cut the raft into beams and consider them as beams on elastic foundation. Hence, we will next consider contact pressures of elastic beams on elastic foundation. Consider a beam resting as an elastic base. We make the following assumptions to simplify the calculation of contact pressures:

- The loading on a foundation depends on the rate of construction and the settlement of the structure, which are nonlinear as well as time dependent. We neglect latter in the calculation of contact pressures.

- In spite of the fact that the nature of column connections to the foundation and the rigidity of the superstructure are important factors that affect the final effect on the foundation, we neglect both of them in the first phase of calculation of contact pressures. However, in each problem, the designer should examine (apart from contact pressure) the effect of transfer of moment from column to foundation on the bending moment and shear force of the foundation even though we may neglect them for calculation of contact pressures during the first stage.

- Many other factors like adhesion between soil and foundation, depth below ground level, nonhomogeneity of soil below foundation level are all neglected in our theoretical calculation of contact pressures.

A.6 METHODS FOR CALCULATION OF CONTACT PRESSURES UNDER BEAMS ON ELASTIC FOUNDATIONS

In spite of the complexity of the problem, we have to estimate the contact pressures by simple internationally accepted methods. The following methods are generally used:

Method 1. The rigid or conventional (also called the simple) method of uniform distribution of contact pressure under symmetric loading and linearly varying distribution under eccentric load.

Method 2. The elastic method of using modulus of subgrade reaction or coefficient of subgrade reaction method using Winkler model.

Method 3. The elastic method using modulus of Compressibility or stiffness coefficients. It is also known as the *general method* or the *elastic half space method*.

Method 4. Simplified methods recommended by ACI Committee 436 using the Winkler model for *semi rigid beams* and *flexible plates*. This method is recommend by IS 2950.

Method 5. Use of available published formulae for perfectly rigid structures.

Here, we shall briefly examine the fundamental assumptions made in each of the above methods and examine how they can be used in practice. Method 4 is fully dealt with in Appendix B as applied to semi-rigid beams and in Appendix C as applied to flexible plates.

A.7 SIMPLE OR CONVENTIONAL METHOD FOR RIGID BEAMS

For rigid beams we use the well-known simple equation given below for a raft foundation, $B \times L$. This equation is given in IS 2950-1981 [2].

Taking p = stress at a given point x, y, and W = resultant load on beam, we get

$$p = \frac{W}{A} \pm \frac{(We_y)y}{I_x} \pm \frac{(We_x)x}{I_y} \tag{A.5}$$

For a rectangular raft this reduces to

$$p = \frac{W}{A}\left[1 \pm \frac{12e_y y}{B^2} \pm \frac{12e_x x}{L^2}\right] \tag{A.5a}$$

where

L = dimension of raft in the X-direction
B = dimension of raft in the Y-direction
A = area = $L \times B$

IS 2950 Part I (1973) gives readymade chart for the above formula [2]. If the resultant load happens to be outside the middle third, adjustments have to be made for tension and consequent loss of contact of foundation with the ground. However, such situations should be avoided in clayey soils liable to consolidate with time as this may lead to progressive failures due to unequal loading on soils. This simple method is easy to operate and has been found to work satisfactorily in rigid foundations. However it leads to over-dimensioning of long foundations (of increasing flexibility) and under-designing of short rigid foundations where the contact pressures can be high. Because of this under-estimation, we found that a stress distribution as shown in Fig. A.2 is sometimes recommended for clay soils.

A.8 METHOD USING WINKLER MODEL

Winkler published his paper on Laws of Elasticity and Strength in 1867 where he introduced the concept of elastic springs in which the reaction from the spring is taken as being proportional to the deflection of the spring. This is known as the Winkler model. The term coefficient of subgrade reaction was however first proposed by Zimmermann later in 1888 to represent the proportionality between load on a railway sleeper and its settlement into the subgrade due to a load. We should note that this law of proportionality refers only *for a small region of loading,* the rail being considered as a deformable beam of infinite length resting on elastic supports. In later years, structural engineers took this concept to *beams supported continuously* on an elastic foundation also by assuming that the contact pressure will be proportional to the deflection of the beam all along its length. Thus the subsoil has been replaced by a system of springs independent of each other. The stiffness of the spring is assumed as constant throughout its length. If necessary, it can be also varied to represent weaker spots in the foundation. It is noteworthy that Westergard in his classic paper on design of rigid pavements has taken the pavement to rest on a liquid subgrade instead of springs.

A.9   WINKLER SOLUTION FOR A CONTINUOUS BEAM ON ELASTIC FOUNDATION

A continuous beam means a beam of infinite length like the rails of a railway line. Hetenyi proposed the use of Winkler Model for such a beam in 1945 [3] [4] and [5]. The differential equation for an ordinary beam of width B, with a downward load q/m^2 can be written as

$$EId^4y/dx^4 = qB$$

where
  $q \times B$ = load per unit length of the beam (kg/m)
    y = deflection

For a beam resting on springs with an upward reaction proportional to the deflection, this equation reduces to the following:

$$EId^4y/dx^4 = qB - (KB)y \tag{A.6}$$

where
  K = modulus of subgrade reaction in (kg/m^3)
  B = breadth of beam; KB = load per unit length for unit deflection (kN/m^2)

A.9.1   Solution for a Column Load P on a Beam

For a beam of width B as in Fig. A.3, if we consider a point P at the origin and for the positive values of x away from P,

$$EId^4y/dx^4 = -KBy$$

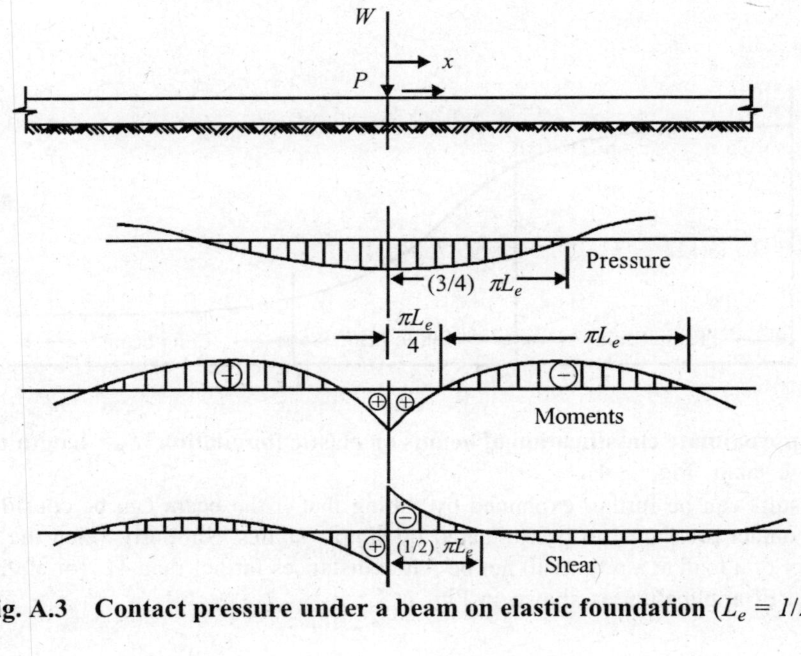

Fig. A.3   Contact pressure under a beam on elastic foundation ($L_e = 1/\lambda$).

$$d^4 y / dx^4 = -KBy/EI \qquad \text{(A.6a)}$$

We can see that in the above equation, if EI is very large (i.e. for a rigid beam) the pressure distribution can be taken as uniform as deflection is constant. This can be considered as a particular case of the general equation. Equation (A.6a) is a homogeneous linear differential equation and the general solution will give four terms. However when we consider a very long beam two of its terms will become zeros and we get the final solution for positive values of x with only two constants as

$$y = e^{-\lambda x}[c_1 \cos \lambda x + c_2 \sin \lambda x] \qquad \text{(A.7)}$$

(Because of symmetry the same solution can be used in the negative side also.)
In Eq. (A.7),

λ = "characteristic coefficient"

$\lambda = \sqrt[4]{KB/(4EI)}$ which has a dimension L^{-1} so that λx is dimensionless and taken as radians

The quantity $(1/\lambda) = (4EI/KB)^{1/4}$ is a length and can be called L_e, the *characteristic length* or *elastic length* of the system. If we designate L_B as the length of the real beams, then $\lambda L_B = L_B/L_e$ is a number. [Usually the expression is derived for B = unity]

Vesic [6] has suggested that this quantity λL_B can be taken as an indication of the relative rigidity of the beam foundation system. Hence if we consider $\lambda = 1/L$ and relate it to the actual length of the beam L_B, then we get the following relations:

$\lambda L_B = 1.75$ (the beam acts in short rigid beams)

$\lambda L_B > 1.75 \le \dfrac{3\pi}{2}$ or 4.7 (the beam is a finite beam i.e., a short beam)

$\lambda L_B > 3\pi/2$ (the beam is a long beam)

See Fig. A.4.

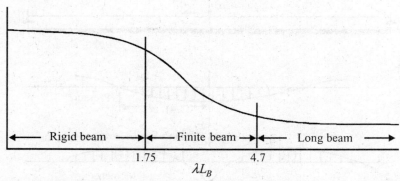

λL_B

Fig. A.4   Approximate classification of beams on elastic foundation (L_B = length of the beam) (see also Fig. 8.4).

The above results can be further explained by stating that if the beam can be considered as rigid, variation of contact pressure can be estimated by simple statics. Similarly when the beam is very long, the effect of a load at a point will not be felt at distances farther than $4L_e$ (or at the most $4.5L_e$) from the point of application as shown in Fig. A.3.

A.9.2 Winkler Solution for Short Beam on Elastic Foundation

Figure A.5 shows a short beam subjected to a concentrated load. As distinct from a long beam, the solution for a short beam will have all the four constants. A closed form solution is rather complex and it is easier to handle the problem by influence coefficients. Different investigators have used different methods to solve the problem and some of these can be briefly described below.

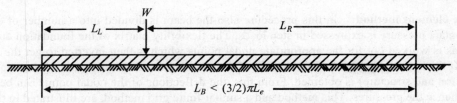

Fig. A.5 Finite beam on elastic foundation.

1. Successive approximation method: In this method, an arbitrary pressure distribution is assumed and the deflection is determined by the moment area method. From the deflections, the pressures are determined using the Winkler model. These are corrected so that the C.G. of loads and reactions coincide. Based on the adjusted reactions, the deflection line is recalculated till convergence takes place. Such a method was first proposed by Ohde in 1942 [7].

2. Finite difference method: In 1957 K.C. Ray used finite difference method to solve this problem [8], [9]. The equation to the beam with load can be written as

$$EI(d^4y/dx^4) + KBy = qB$$

$$(d^4y/dx^4) + \frac{KBy}{EI} = \frac{qB}{EI} \tag{A.8}$$

The beam is cut into 20 intervals of length δ and the above differential equation is reduced to the finite differential form

$$\frac{1}{\delta^4}(y_{n+2} + 4y_{n+1} + 6y_n - 4y_{n-1} + y_{n-2}) + \frac{KB}{EI}y_n = \frac{q_n B}{EI}$$

or

$$y_{n+2} - 4y_{n+1} + y_n\left(6 + \frac{KB\delta^4}{EI}\right) = \frac{(q_n B)\delta^4}{EI} = \frac{S\delta^4}{EI}$$

Assuming load P is distributed over length δ, we get $P = S\delta$, and hence,

$$y_{n+2} - 4y_{n+1} + y_n\left(6 + \frac{KB\delta^4}{EI}\right) = \frac{(q_n B)\delta^4}{EI} = \frac{P\delta^3}{EI} \tag{A.8a}$$

In order to find the influence line for a load $W = 1$, the position of point $W = 1$ is varied through the length of the beam and each case is solved as an independent problem. The term,

$$\frac{KB\delta^4}{EI} = \frac{KB}{EI}\left(\frac{L_B}{20}\right)^4 \tag{A.9}$$

is designated m. value of m can be varied from 0.0001 to 0.50 to represent the various cases of relative rigidity of the foundation with respect to the beam. Influence coefficients for bending moments shear and pressures have beam given by Ray in his publications [8], [9].

3. Finite element method: In this procedure also the beam is divided into a number of elements and a contact pressure is expressed in step loads. The flexibility matrix of the foundation due to this step loads is worked out for the appropriate nodal points which is then inverted to get the stiffness matrix. If this is added to the stiffness matrix of the structure the stiffness matrix of the total system (foundation and structure) is obtained. From this, the deflections of the nodal points can be worked out and hence the pressures. This method and a similar finite grid method, are illustrated in the book, *Foundation Analysis and Design* by J.F. Bowles.

4. By use of simultaneous equations: Another method used to solve the problem is to match the deflections of foundation and the beam at nodal points using simultaneous equations. The pressures at the nodal points can be determined. The advantage of the method over finite element method is that it requires less computation.

5. Iyengar's tables using series method: Iyengar and Raman [10] have published influence coefficients for beams on elastic foundations by developing a solution to the differential equation in the form of a series as follows.

They assumed the solution for a short beam as containing the following four terms (mRHS):

$$y = [c_1 \sin \lambda x \sinh \lambda x + c_2 \sin \lambda x \cosh \lambda x + c_3 \cos \lambda x \sinh \lambda x + c_4 \cos \lambda x \cosh \lambda x] \tag{A.10}$$

The solution is put in series form as

$$y(x) = \sum_{m=1}^{d} A_m \phi_m(x) \tag{A.11}$$

in which A_m is a constant and $\phi_m(x)$ are characteristic functions representing the normal mode shapes of a freely vibrating beam, which represents the real beam. Influence coefficients are available for beams with $\lambda L = 0.10$ to 9.0 in increments of 0.20 and these can be directly used for design calculations. In Iyengar's table, X denotes the position of load and Y denotes the distance from the left end of the point where the B.M., S.F. and pressure are required.

6. Wolfer tables using series method [11]: In this method, the problem of a beam on elastic foundation is represented in terms of the bending moment M.

$$EI(d^2y/dx^2) = -M \tag{A.12}$$

Also,
$$(d^2M/dx^2) = q = BKy$$

$$y = \left(\frac{1}{BK}\right)(d^2M/dx^2) \tag{A.13}$$

We have

$$\frac{1}{\lambda} = L_e = \left[\frac{4EI}{BK}\right]^{1/4}$$

which is called the elastic or characteristic length. Therefore,

$$(1/BK) = (L_e^4/4EI)$$

From Eq. (A.13), we have

$$y = (L_e^4/4EI)(d^2M/dx^2)$$

Differentiating twice,

$$EI\,(d^2y/dx^2) = (L_e^4/4)(d^4M/dx^4)$$

or

$$\left(\frac{L_e^4}{4}\right)\left(\frac{d^4M}{dx^4}\right) + M = 0 \qquad \text{(A.14)}$$

Putting back $1/L_e = \lambda$, we get the solution for unit load as:

$$M = [c_1 \cos \lambda x \cosh \lambda x + c_2 \sin \lambda x \sinh \lambda x + c_3 \cos \lambda x \sinh \lambda x + c_4 \sin \lambda x \cosh \lambda x] \quad \text{(A.15)}$$

These are solved for various positions of load indicated as $\lambda_L = 0$ to 0.5 and $\lambda_R = 0$ to 0.5 in the Wolfer tables. In these tables,

$$\lambda_L = \frac{\text{length of beam to the left of load}}{\text{elastic length}}$$

$$\lambda_R = \frac{\text{length of beam to the right of load}}{\text{elastic length}} \qquad \text{(A.15)}$$

Wolfer tables give the coefficients for bending moment, shear and contact pressures for various cases. With this publication very detailed results can be obtained.

7. Tables by Timoshenko and Gere [12]: Similar tables have been published by Timoshenko and Gere, which can be used for designing beams on elastic foundation using the Winkler model.

The problem of beams on elastic foundation can be solved by the use of these tables very easily. Otherwise, if a computer and the necessary software are available, the solution can be easily read off. In any case it is advisable to have a background of the theory if the results are to be applied intelligently.

8. By computer Saftware: Readymade computer software for these calculations are also available.

A.9.3   Limitations of Winkler Model and its Improvement

As we have already seen, the springs in Winkler model act independent of each other so that there is no continuity at the ends of foundation. As shown in Fig. A.6, in the real settlement of a foundation, there is always continuity and settlement extends beyond the ends of the beam.

A number of other spring models called *coupled models* have been suggested to improve the simple model. But these only increase the complexity of the problem. It is generally felt that such improvements in methods of computation are not warranted when our knowledge of the homogeneity of the soil as well as the modulus of subgrade reaction cannot be accurate. What we can arrive at in any case is only a fair estimate and never the exact values. Further more, the effect of settlements of the beam due to causes like consolidation of soil is very large and these are to be further estimated

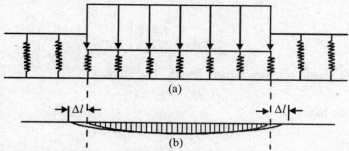

Fig. A.6   Winkler model for beams on elastic foundation (Note discrepancy in deflection at the ends).

for the final solution of the problem. Hence if we want a more accurate solution, it is wiser to solve the problem by the recently developed and more realistic elastic half space model than to use improved spring models.

A.10   ELASTIC HALF-SPACE OR MODULUS OF COMPRESSIBILITY METHOD FOR BEAMS ON ELASTIC FOUNDATION

The third method used to determine contact pressure is the elastic half space method which is also known as the stiffness coefficient method. We have, in theory of consolidation, the equations

$$a_v = \Delta e / \Delta \sigma$$

$$E_s = \text{stress/strain} = \frac{\Delta \sigma}{(\Delta e / 1 + e)} = \frac{(1 + e)}{a_v} = \frac{1}{m_v} \tag{A.16}$$

The quantity m_v is called the *modulus of compressibility* (or *coefficient of volume compressibility*). The reciprocal of the above modulus is called the *stiffness coefficient E_s*. In our usual analysis E_s is considered as a constant along the depth of the soil. However, if necessary, improvements can be also made by assuming it as varying with depth.

If we imagine a three dimensional space divided into two by an imaginary horizontal infinite plate out of which the upper half is empty and the lower half is filled with an elastic homogeneous material which behaves elastic in all directions, such a model is the elastic half space model which is closer to reality. Fundamental deformation equations have been derived by Boussinesq and Schleicher for deformation of such a space in terms of the stiffness coefficient E_s.

For a beam of reinforced concrete, the problem reduces to a beam of length L_1 width B and thickness t, flexural stiffness D, Young's modulus E_1 and Poisson's ratio μ_1. For the soil the properties are E_2 and μ_2. Many cases of loading can be assumed and for closed form solution, the easiest will be the case of a uniformly loaded strip load. The basis of the analysis is to match the displaced shape of the beam and the surface of the half space under the action of the applied loading.

Even though closed form solutions for beams on elastic half space are available, the popularity of computers have made solution of these problems by numerical methods more easy and popular. The method frequently used is to cut the beam into a number of elements (say, 10) as shown in Fig. A.7. Each part is connected to the foundation below by a rigid bar through which the unknown contact pressure acts. The vertical deflection of each segment is affected by the contact pressure

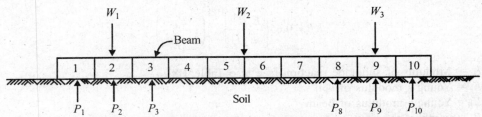

Fig. A.7   Determination of contact pressure under beams on elastic half-space.

of the adjacent element also and its magnitude can be worked out by the influence coefficient method.

We establish compatibility conditions of deflection of external load and contact pressure as well as equilibrium condition between external load and contact pressures by equating the loads. From a series of equations the contact pressures can be determined. The book *Numerical Methods in Geotechnical Engineering* by Desai and Christian [13] covers this subject with examples and can be used as a reference.

In Europe, the work along these lines was started by Ohde, Kany and others around 1955. The publication by Kany [14] gives a clear account of the method used. The procedure can be also extended to rafts as a plate as explained in one of the recent books by Hemsley *Elastic Analysis of Raft Foundations* [15]. Another recent method (1965) for beams and plates on elastic foundation is the stiffness method of analysis by Cheung [16], [17] using methods of matrix analysis of structures.

A.11   SIMPLIFIED ACI METHOD

Fritz Kramrisch and Paul Rogers described in 1961 [18] a procedure for design of a certain category of beams (that we normally meet in practice) that are supported on Winkler foundation. This method has been recommended by ACI [19] and also included in IS 2950 (Part I) 1981 (Second revision) [2]. It is to be noted that in this method, the total length of the beam between exterior columns should be at least $(3 \times 1.75)/\lambda = 5.25/\lambda$. Such beams are long and the end conditions do not influence each other. This method is described in detail in Appendix B.

A.12   FORMULAE FOR CONTACT PRESSURES UNDER PERFECT RIGID STRUCTURES

IS 2950 (Part I) 1973 First revision Appendix E gives a number of formulae derived from Boussinesq's equation for contact pressure distribution below rigid foundations, on elastic isotropic half space of depth not less than the width of the rigid structure. If the stresses are large, the calculated maximum values, should be rounded off to the bearing capacity values and redistributed to maintain equilibrium conditions as shown in Section A.4.

A.13   SELECTION OF SUITABLE MODEL FOR BEAMS ON ELASTIC FOUNDATIONS

Vesic [6] has shown that for a long beam on an infinite depth of soil with a constant modulus of soil, E_s and apparent modulus of subgrade reaction K, the value of KB is given by the following formula (see also Eq. (1.14) of the text). This value is recommended by IS 2950 (Part) 1981 Clause B-3.3 also.

$$KB = 0.65 \left[\frac{E_s B^4}{E_B I} \right]^{1/12} \left(\frac{E_s}{1 - \mu^2} \right) \tag{A.17}$$

where

K = Modulus of subgrade reaction [see also Table 1.8]
E_s = Young's modulus of soil
E_B = Young's modulus of beam
B = width of the beam
I = M.I. of beam cross-section
μ = Poisson's ratio of soil
k = modulus of subgrade reaction in kN/m^3

The theoretical work by Gibson [21], as well as by Carrier and Christian [22] have shown that, when the E_s value is assumed to increase with depth, the settlement of the beam behaves according to Winkler theory. Massalskii [23] and Ward et. al. [24] give experimental evidence for such behaviour. These investigations show that improvements in the mathematical model is not as important as the difficult problem of choosing the value of the soil parameters for the modulus and also the procedure to include the right rigidity of the structure in the analysis. A more recent approach to the problem is to use finite element methods to model the soil to obtain an apparent spring constant, which can then be used for easy structural analysis. Actual field measurements and comparison with analysis by the two methods (Winkler model and Elastic half space model) have revealed the following:

1. Both models give fairly good results, which are conservative.
2. The superstructure in many cases give more stiffness to the foundation than usually assumed in the analysis.
3. The highly indeterminate foundation is not as much stressed as indicated by both types of analysis.

These results confirm that regardless of how the foundation is modelled, the important and difficult problem is the selection of the soil parameters.

A.14 ANALYSIS BY COMPUTERS

The modulus of subgrade reaction method has been popular till recently because of its simplicity and availability of published values of influence coefficients. However with the availability of computers, the elastic half space method has also now become popular. Many large organizations use computer aided design programmes based on the elastic theory. Any complex foundations system can now be modelled by finite element methods to give the resultant contact pressures and other design parameters. Such analysis are needed for complex cases but for ordinary cases, and regular layouts, approximate solutions give satisfactory results.

A.15 EFFECT OF CONSOLIDATION SETTLEMENT

When the foundation is on clayey soils, the effect of consolidation settlements, which is nonlinear as well as time dependent character, should be also taken into account in our designs. Terzaghi's theory, or a modified form of his theory, is used for calculation of the consolidation effects. We should remember that it is most important that we must represent the ultimate deformability of the soil somehow in our calculations. All the methods of soil structure interaction finally reduces to the problem as to how to represent the soil deformation and how to represent the structure. Because of the consolidation effects in clayey soils, all the present representation of the stiffness of the soil is only very approximate imitations of the reality. Similarly, the superstructure structure has rigidity and its rigidity has also to be represented. Thus, we should be aware that very sophisticated improvements in analysis of a raft foundation as a structure, are not warranted unless equal improvements are made in modelling the soil also.

A.16 RELATIVE RIGIDITY OF STRUCTURE

The formulae given in Chapter 8 Section 8.7.1 can be used to determine approximately the relative rigidity (stiffness) of the foundation structure compared to the soil below the foundation.

A.17 LIMITATIONS OF THE THEORY

Footings can be solved as beams on elastic foundations. However rafts are treated as plates on elastic foundations. Cutting them into beams and solving them as beams on elastic foundation is an approximation that is applicable only to design of rafts with a regular layout of columns. For irregular layout of rafts computer methods have to be resorted to.

A.18 SUMMARY

In this chapter we have dealt only with beams on elastic foundations. The concepts discussed are applicable to rafts when we can use the elemental analysis. A more accurate method of analysis of rafts, especially of irregular layout is to treat them as plates supported on elastic foundation. There are many computer methods available to solve such problems [15].

REFERENCES

[1] Schultz, E., *Distribution of Stress Beneath a Rigid Foundation*, Technische Hochschule, Achen, Germany, 1971.

[2] IS–2950, Part I, 1973, *Code of Practice for Design and Construction of Raft Foundations, First Revision*, Also, Second Revision in 1981, Bureau of Indian Standards, New Delhi.

[3] Hetenyi, M., *Beams on Elastic Foundation*, University of Michigan Press, 1945.

[4] Hetenyi, M.A., General Solution for the Bending of Beams on Elastic Foundations by Arbitrary Continuity, *Journal of Applied Physics*, Vol. 21, 1950.

[5] Seeley, F.B. and J.O. Smith, *Advanced Mechanics of Materials*, John Wiley & Sons, London, 1952.

[6] Vesic, Alexander, Beams on Elastic Sub-grade and Winkler Hypothesis, Proceedings, 5th International Conference on Soil Mechanics and Foundation Engineering, Paris, 1961.

[7] Ohde, *Calculation of Soil Pressure Distribution under Foundations* (in German), Der Bawingenicur, Bawng, Berlin, 1942.

[8] Ray, K.C., Finite Beams on Elastic Soils Influence Lines, *Journal of Institution of Engineers* (India), Vol. 38, Oct. 1957.

[9] Ray, K.C., Influence Lines for Pressure Distribution under a Finite Beam on Elastic Foundation, *Journal of the American Concrete Institute*, Detroit, Dec. 1958.

[10] Iyengar, K.T.S. and Raman S. Anantha, *Design Tables for Beams on Elastic Foundations*, Applied Science Publishers, London, 1979.

[11] Wolfer, K.H., *Beams on Elastic Foundation, Influence Tables* (English Edition), Bauverlag, GMBH Wiesbaden and Berlin, 1978.

[12] Timoshenko and M. Gere, *Beams on Elastic Foundation, Charts and Tables of Coefficients*, McGraw-Hill, New York, 1961.

[13] Desai, C.S. and T.T. Christin, *Numerical Methods in Geotechnical Engineering*, McGraw-Hill, New York, 1977.

[14] Kany, *Calculation of Raft Foundation* (in German), Verlag W. Ernst and Sohn, Berlin, 1959.

[15] Hemsley, J.A., *Elastic Analysis of Raft Foundations*, Thomson Teltord, London, 1998.

[16] Cheung, Y.K. and O.C. Zienkiewiez, Plates and Tanks on Elastic Foundations, An Application of Finite Element Method, *International Journal of Solids and Structures*, 1965.

[17] Cheung, Y.K. and D.K. Nag, Plates and Beams on Elastic Foundations: Linear and nonlinear behaviour, *Geotechnique*, 1968.

[18] Kramrisch, F. and Paul Rogers, Simplified Design of Combined Footings, *Journal of the Soil Mechanics and Foundation Division*, SM 5, ASCE, Oct. 1961.

[19] ACI Committee 436, Suggested Design Procedures for Combined Footings and Mats, *Journal ACI*, Oct. 1966.

[20] Bowles, J.E., *Analytical and Computer Methods in Foundation Engineering*, McGraw-Hill, New York, 1974.

[21] Gibson, R.E., Some Results Governing Displacements on a Nonhomogeneous Elastic Half Space, *Geotechnique*, Vol. 17, 1967.

[22] Carrier W.D. and J.T. Christian, Analysis of an inhomogeneous Elastic Half Space. *Journal of Soil Mechanics and Foundation Division*, ASCE, March 1973.

[23] Massalskii, E.K., Experimental Study of Flexible Beam on Sand Foundation, *Soil Mechanics and Foundation Engineering*, No. 6, ASCE, 1964.

[24] Ward, et al., Geotechnical Assessment of a Site at Mudford Nortolk for a Large Proton Accelerator, *Geotechnique*, Vol. 18, 1968.

APPENDIX B

ACI Method for Analysis of Beams and Grids on Elastic Foundations

B.1 INTRODUCTION

IS 2950 Part I 1981 [1] and ACI Committee 436 [2] recommend the use of a simplified method for solving beams on the Winkler foundation obeying the following conditions:

1. There should be a minimum of three bays.
2. Variation of adjacent span lengths should not be more than 20%.
3. The average column spacing should be such that the value of λL_B should not be less than 1.75 and should not be more than 3.50 (see Fig. A.4). (L_B = average spanlength.)
4. The column loads should not vary by more than 20%.

Rafts with regular column layouts can be cut into beams and analysed by this method.

B.2 DERIVATION OF THE METHOD

We will briefly derive the formulae and study an example to see how it is applied to determine the pressures and moments in a beam on elastic foundation. The full derivation is available in Ref. [3] given at the end of this Appendix.

(a) Formula for value of negative moment below load point: Set $1/\lambda = L_e$. We found from Eq. (A.7)

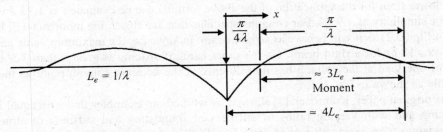

Fig. B.1 Length of influence of loads on a beam resting on an elastic foundation (see also Figs. A.3 and C.1).

531

in Appendix A that the bending moment is an infinitely long beam on elastic foundation due to a column load W_1 at point C can be written in the following form and represented by Fig. B.1.

$$M_x = \frac{W_1}{4\lambda} C_{\lambda x}$$

where

$$C_{\lambda x} = e^{-\lambda x}(\cos \lambda x - \sin \lambda x)$$

Hence if there are several loads W_1, W_2, ..., the influence of the various loads for a point C can be represented as follows:

$$M_c = \frac{W_1}{4\lambda} C_{\lambda x_1} + \frac{W_2}{4\lambda} C_{\lambda x_2} + \frac{W_3}{4\lambda} C_{\lambda x_3} \tag{B.1}$$

where x_1, x_2, x_3 are the distances of loads W_1, W_2, W_3 from point C.

Now, if we restrict the spacing of the loads between $1.75/\lambda$ and $3.50/\lambda$ the trigonometric function for $C_{\lambda x}$ can be approximated to a straight line. Again if the loads are more or less equal, then the negative moment under an internal column M_i as shown in Fig. B.2 can be written down as follows [3]:

$$M_i = -\frac{W_i}{4\lambda}(0.24\lambda L_A + 0.16) \not> -\frac{W_i L_A}{12} \tag{B.2}$$

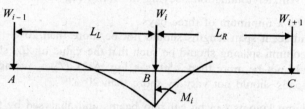

Fig. B.2   Negative moment under the load in a beam on elastic foundation.

where

W_i = column load at point
L_A = average length of the adjacent spans
λ = characteristic length

The right-hand side of the equation shows that the *negative bending moment* at the support can not be greater than the value for a continuous beam with uniform reaction as in a rigid beam.

The lower limit for the application of the above formula can be evaluated as $1.78/\lambda$ which can be taken for simplicity as $1.75/\lambda$. For columns spacings that are closer, the moments will be greater than that in Eq. (B.2) as it will behave as a rigid beam. In any case, the maximum value can be only less than $WL_A/12$ as for a rigid beam. On the other hand, if spacing is greater than $3.5/\lambda$ then the influence of one load at the column has no influence at the adjacent column point as the beam is very flexible as shown in Fig. B.1.

In his original paper, Kramrisch [3] showed by worked out examples that with equal loads and equal spacing and with varying ratios of stiffness of foundation and stiffness of structure, the greatest deviation from exact value of M_i from Eq. (B.2) is only about 3.5%. Even with a deviation of 20% in the column spacing as well as column loads, a variation within 16% with considerably smaller average deviation was obtained. These variations are well within the range of redistribution of moments possible in reinforced concrete and are acceptable for design.

(b) Contact pressures in interior spans: Our next aim is to determine the contact pressures in the interior span so that we can calculate the total span moment M_0 due to the contact pressures. For this purpose we assume a linear distribution of the soil pressure with a maximum value below the load point (columns) and a minimum at the centre of adjacent spans as shown in Fig. B.3.

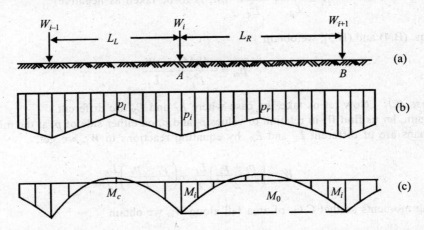

Fig. B.3 Beam subjected to concentrated loads resting on an elastic foundation: (a) Beam; (b) contact pressure diagram; (c) bending moments.

We also assume that the negative moment M_i is not affected much by the additional loads beyond the adjacent columns and remain as given by Eq. (B.2). Let

p_i = contact pressure below column i

p_l = contact pressure at centre of span left of i where we consider load W_i

p_r = contact pressure at centre of span right of $i - 1$ when we consider load W_{i-1}

$P_m = (p_l + p_r)/2$

L_L = length of left span from column i

L_R = length of right span from column i

$L_A = (L_L + L_R)/2$

Case (i): Let us first take the case of equal spans and equal loads.

$$p_l = p_r = p_m$$

We can obtain the magnitude of the negative moment by considering AB and BC in Fig. B.3 as fixed beams.

$$M_i = \frac{p_m L_A^2}{12} + \frac{(p_i - p_m)L_A^2}{32} = \frac{L_A^2}{96}(3p_i + 5p_m) \tag{B.3}$$

We can see from Fig. B.4 that

$$W_i = L_A(p_m + p_i)/2 \quad \text{or} \quad p_m = \frac{2W_i}{L_A} - p_i \tag{B.4}$$

From Eqs. (B.3) and (B.4), we get the value of p_i the pressure under W_i as

$$p_i = \frac{5W_i}{L_A} + \frac{48M_i}{L_A^2} \quad (M_i \text{ is to be taken as negative}) \tag{B.5}$$

From Eqs. (B.4) and (B.5), we obtain

$$p_m = \frac{-48M_i}{L_A^2} - \frac{3W}{L_A} \tag{B.5a}$$

Case (ii):   Now let us take the case where L_L and L_R are different.

Again, let us find W_i in relation to values p_l and p_r on either side of p_i at the mid span points. When spans are of different L_L and L_R, by equating reactions to W_i, we get

$$W_i = \left(\frac{p_l + p_i}{2}\right)\frac{L_L}{2} + \left(\frac{p_i + p_r}{2}\right)\frac{L_R}{2} \tag{B.6}$$

By taking moments so that C.G. of area fall along W_i, we obtain

$$p_l = \frac{2W_i}{L_A}\left(\frac{L_R}{L_L}\right) - p_i\left(\frac{L_A}{L_L}\right) \tag{B.6a}$$

$$p_r = \frac{2W_i}{L_A}\left(\frac{L_L}{L_R}\right) - p_i\left(\frac{L_A}{L_R}\right) \tag{B.6b}$$

When the spans are equal,

$$p_l = p_r = p_m = \frac{p_l + p_r}{2} = (2W_i/L_A) - p_i \tag{B.6c}$$

$$p_m = -3W_i - (48M_i/L_A^2) = \frac{-48M_i}{L_A^2} - \frac{3W_i}{L_A} \tag{B.6d}$$

Equations (B.8a) and (B.8b) give the required pressure distribution when L_L and L_R are different.

In actual practice, if there is variation in either the load or the span length, we find the mid-point pressure in a span first as caused by the load on the right and then as caused by the load on the left. The mean of the two values is then assigned to the mid point for our calculation of M_0 in the span.

(c) Total positive moment in interior spans: When we have the ordinates of the pressure diagram in a span L_1 (as shown in Fig. B.4 with ordinates p_1, p_c and p_2) the value of the total span moment can be calculated as M_0 and will reduce to the following:

$$M_0 = \frac{L_1^2}{48}(p_1 + 4p_c + p_2) \qquad \text{(B.7)}$$

where

    L_1 = span

    p_1 = pressure ordinate on the left of span

    p_2 = pressure ordinate on the right of span

    p_c = pressure ordinate at centre of span

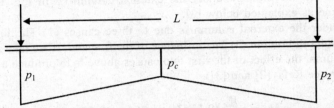

Fig. B.4   Calculation of total span moment M_o from contact pressure in the span.

The positive moment M_c at the centre of the beam as shown in Fig. B.3 is obtained from the following relation:

$$M_0 = M_c + M_i \qquad \text{(B.8)}$$

where

    M_0 is the simply supported moment at the centre

    M_i is the average negative moment under the columns at each end of the bay shown in the figure

    $M_i = (M_{il} + M_{ir})/2$

(d) Moments in exterior span of beam: For determining the distribution of contact pressure under the external column we make the following two assumptions:

   1. The load of the exterior column is equal to the resultant of the subgrade reaction starting from the centre of the first bay to the end of the beam i.e., to the tip of the projection as in Fig. B.5.

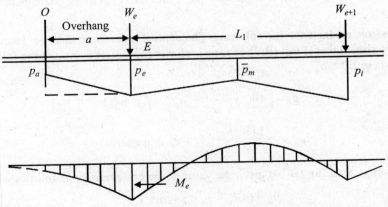

Fig. B.5   Behaviour of end span of a beam on elastic foundation loaded with concentrated loads.

2. The contact pressure from the edge to the centre of the adjacent span will have a maximum value under the external column load and a minimum at the tip of the projections and also another minimum at the centre of first bay as shown in Fig. B.5. The distribution is assumed linear. The contact pressure at the tip of the projection cannot exceed this value under the exterior column.

Let us now take the exterior span which is different from the interior spans. We also assume the projection is less than the elastic length L_e. Using procedure a similar to that explained above, Kramrisch has shown that the moment under the external column (E in Fig. B.5), which has a projection can be found as explained below [3].

The moment under the external column is due to three causes (1) The load itself (2). The influence of the next interior column (3) The influence of the free end. If we take M_e as the moment under the exterior column, the effect of the first two causes above is to produce a moment as given below. (For derivation see Refs. [2] and [3]):

$$M_e = -\frac{W_e}{4\lambda}(0.13\lambda L_1 + 1.06\lambda a - 0.50) \tag{B.9}$$

where a is the length of the projection and L_1 is the length of the exterior span. If we again assume that the length of projection is very small, it may require high subgrade reaction to produce the above value of moment. However, the maximum value of p_a can be only equal to the pressure under the external column. By equating the load and pressure we get the maximum value of p_e as follows:

$$W_e = p_e a + \frac{1}{2}(p_e + \bar{p}_m)(L_1/2)$$

Hence,

$$p_e = (4W_e - \bar{p}_m L_1)/(4a + L_1) \tag{B.10}$$

where $\bar{p}_m$ is as shown in Fig. B.5 and is the pressure at the mid point of the first interior span. Using the above value of p_e the maximum possible value of M_e will be given by the following equation:

$$M_e = -p_e(a^2/2) = \frac{(4W_e - \bar{p}_m L_1)}{(4a + L_1)}\left(\frac{a^2}{2}\right) \tag{B.11}$$

The lesser of the two values obtained from Eqs. (B.9) and (B.11) is to be taken as the design value for M_e.

(e) Contact pressure under exterior columns. The contact pressure in *external span* works out as follows. It can be shown that if Eq. (B.9) governs, referring to Fig. B.5, we get the following values for p_e and p_a, where $p_e > p_a$.

$$p_e = \left(4W_e + \frac{6M_e}{a} - p_m L_1\right)\bigg/(a + L_1) \tag{B.12}$$

$$p_a = -\frac{(3M_e)}{a^2} - \frac{p_e}{2} \quad (M_e \text{ is negative}) \tag{B.12a}$$

If Eq. (B.11) governs, then Eq. (B.10) gives the value of the end pressure as follows when $(p_e = p_a)$.

$$p_e = (4W_e - p_m L_1)/(4a + L_1) \tag{B.12b}$$

The procedure using the above method is illustrated by Example B.1.

B.3 SUMMARY OF THE METHOD

The following steps as given in IS 2950 (1981) Appendix E are recommended in the design of beams on elastic foundation by the above ACI method.

(a) Consider interior spans

Step 1. Calculate λ and the elastic length L_e and *check whether the four conditions for ACI method* given in B.1 are applicable

$$\lambda = \left(\frac{kB}{4EI} \right)^{1/4} = \frac{1}{L_e}$$

Step 2. Calculate negative moment of interior span using Eq. (B.2).

$$M_i = -\frac{W_i}{4\lambda}[0.24\lambda L_A + 0.16] \not> -\frac{W_i L_A}{12}$$

Step 3. Determine the *maximum contact pressure p_i* under load. Use Eq. (B.5), where M_i is negative

$$p_i = \frac{5W_i}{L_A} + \frac{48M_i}{L_A^2}$$

Step 4. Determine the minimum contact pressures at the centres of the left and right spans (interior spans) from Eqs. (B.6a) and (B.6b), respectively.

$$p_l = \frac{2W_i}{L_A}\left(\frac{L_R}{L_L}\right) - p_i\left(\frac{L_A}{L_L}\right)$$

$$p_r = \frac{2W_i}{L_A}\left(\frac{L_L}{L_R}\right) - p_i\left(\frac{L_A}{L_R}\right)$$

When spans are equal, using Eq. (B.6d), we get

$$p_m = \frac{2W_i}{L_A} - p_i = \frac{-48M_i}{L_A^2} - \frac{3W_i}{L_A}$$

In practice, if the column loads are different, we first find the values of the pressure for the point first as obtained from the load situated on the right of the point and then find the value from the load situated on the left of the point and take the mean value as the real value.

$$P_m = (p_{mr} + p_{ml})/2$$

Step 5. Calculate M_0 using Eq. (B.7).

$$M_0 = (L_A^2/48)\,(p_l + 4p_c + p_r)$$

Step 6. Determine the central moment M_c using Eq. (B.8).

$$M_c = M_0 - M_i$$

(b) Consider exterior span

Step 7. Find moment under exterior column.

$$M_e = -\frac{W_e}{4\lambda}(0.13\lambda L_1 + 1.06\lambda a - 0.50)$$

Step 8. Find pressure p_e under exterior load using Eq. (B.12) (M_e to be taken as $-ve$).

$$p_e = \left(4W_e + \frac{6M_e}{a} - p_m L_1\right) \Big/ (a + L_1)$$

Find also pressure p_a at exterior load using Eq. (B.12a) (M_e to be taken as $-ve$).

$$P_a = (3M_e/a^2) - (p_e/2)$$

Step 9. Find M_e assuming $p_a = p_e$ in Eq. (B.12b) to get

$$P_a = p_e = (4W_e - p_m L_1)/(4a + L_1)$$

$$M_e = -\frac{p_e a^2}{2} \text{ from Eq. (B.11)}$$

Take the lesser value from Steps 7 and 9 for design.

Step 10. Determine the positive moment in exterior spans.

M_e and M_i are known. From Eq. (B.7), we get the following:

$$M_0 = \frac{L^2}{48}(p_e + 4p_c + p_i)$$

$$M_{ce} + ve = M_0 - (\text{average moment below of 2 adjacent supports})$$

Step 11. Sketch the pressure and moment diagrams.

These steps are illustrated in Example B.1.

B.4   ANALYSIS OF GRID FOUNDATIONS

In cases where the foundations are a system of intersecting strip foundations as shown in Fig. B.4, we get a grid foundation. In most such cases, an inverted T beam type of foundation with slab below will be found to be more rigid and easy to construct.

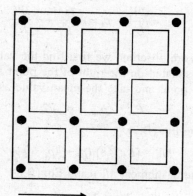

Fig. B.6   Layout of grid foundation.

The report of ACI Committee 436 Recommends '*grid foundations to be analysed as independent strips using column loads proportional in direct ratio to the stiffness of the strips acting in each direction*' [2]. In this method each column load will be proportioned in each direction in the inverse proportion to the distance to the next column point. The strips need to be designed only with these assigned column loads. It is claimed that this grid action occurs in grid arrangement occupying even up to 70% of the plan area [4].

However, in the example worked out by Fritz Kramrisch and Rogers in their paper [3] from which the above simplified ACI method was evolved, the authors have analysed a grid foundation using the full load in each column taken in both directions for illustration of this method. This is an extension of the method of raft design as an inverted floor in which the raft is divided into strips in *X* and *Y* directions and each strip designed for full column loads in both directions. The second method gives a good conservative design of the grid system.

EXAMPLE B.1

A slab 450 mm thick and 5.4 m breadth supports four column loads at a spacing of 5.4 m and overlong of 1.5 m as shown in Fig. E.4.1. Assuming a coefficient of subgrade reaction of 3.7 kg/cm^3 (3700 t/m^3) and *E* of concrete as 20×10^4 kg/cm^2, find the B.M. and pressure distribution using the ACI method.

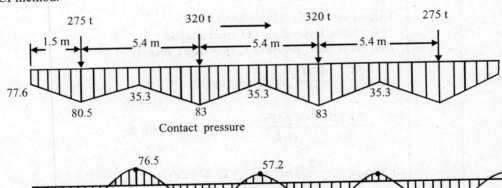

Contact pressure

Bending moment (tm)

Fig. E.B.1

Ref.	Step	Calculations
Summary	1	*Calculate elastic length*
		L_e = elastic length $= \left(\dfrac{4EI}{KB} \right)^{1/4}$
Sec. B.3		Span length $L_A = 5.4$ m and $B = 5.4$ m
		$I = \dfrac{5.4(0.45)^3}{12} = 0.041 \, \text{m}^4$

Ref.	Step	Calculations

$K = 3700$ t/m^3; $E_c = 20 \times 10^4$ kg/cm^2 (20×10^5 t/m^2)

$$\frac{1}{\lambda} = L_e = \left[\frac{4 \times 20 \times 10^5 \times 0.041}{5.4 \times 3700}\right]^{1/4} = 2.01 \text{ m}; \qquad \lambda = \frac{1}{2.01}$$

$$\frac{L_A}{L_e} = 5.4/2.01 = 2.68$$

Sec. B.1

$2.68 > 1.75$ and < 3.5 ACI method is valid as all the necessary four conditions are satisfied.

(a) Consider interior spans

Step 2

Calculate M_i negative moment for interior span (load 320 t)

Eq. (B.2)

$$M_i = -\frac{W_i}{4\lambda}[0.24\lambda L_A + 0.16]$$

$$= \frac{320 \times (2.01)}{4}\left[\frac{0.24 \times 5.4}{2.0} + 0.16\right] = -129.4 \text{ t m}$$

Largest value $(W_i L/12) = -144$ t m
129.4 being lesser than 144 is admissible

Step 3

Determine max. pressure p_i (per metre length)

Eq. (B.5)

$$p_i = \frac{5W_i}{L_A} + \frac{48M_i}{L_A^2} \quad (M_i \text{ is negative})$$

$$= \frac{5 \times 320}{5.4} - \frac{48 \times 129.4}{(5.4)^2} = 83 \text{ t/m for width } B$$

$$\text{Pressure} = \frac{83}{B \times 1} \text{ t/m}^2 = \frac{83}{5.4} = 15.37 \text{ t/m}^2$$

(Add to this the self weight of slab as U.D.L.)
Self weight $= 0.450 \times 2.4 = 1.08$ t/m^2
Total pressure $p_i = 16.45$ t/m^2

Step 4

Determine the minimum pressure at centre span

Eq. (B.6d)

$$p_l = p_r = p_m = -\frac{48M_i}{L_A^2} - \frac{3W}{L_A} \quad (\text{as spans are equal})$$

$$(\text{As } M_i \text{ is negative}) = \frac{48M_i}{L_A^2} - \frac{3W}{L_A}$$

$$= \frac{48 \times 129.4}{(5.4)^2} - \frac{3 \times 320}{5.4} \quad (\text{Interior spans load 320 t})$$

$$= 35.3 \text{ t/m (for width } B)$$

$$\text{With self wt.} = \frac{35.3}{5.4} + 1.08 = 7.62 \text{ t/m}^2$$

Ref.	Step	Calculations
Eq. (B.7)	5	Calculate M_0 $M_0 = (L^2/48)(p_l + 4p_c + p_R)$ (where p is to be in t/m) $= \dfrac{(5.4)^2}{48}(83 + (4 \times 35.3) + 83)$ $= 186.6$ t/m
Eq. (B.8)	6	Determine M_c *(positive moment)* $M_c = 186.6 - 129.4 = +57.2$ t/m (Step 2. The largest value of $M_1 = M_2 = 144$ t m)
		(b) Consider exterior spans
Eq. (B.9)	7	Find M_e under exterior column by Eq. (B.9) Load = 275 t; over hang = a = 1.5 m s, Interior span = L_1 = 5.4 m. $M_e = -\dfrac{W_e}{4}(L_e)[0.13(L_1/L_e) + 1.06(a/L_e) - 0.50]$ where $L_e = 1/\lambda$ characteristic length = 2.01 m $= -\left(\dfrac{275 \times 2.01}{4}\right)\left[\dfrac{0.13 \times 5.4}{2.01} + \dfrac{1.06 \times 1.5}{2.01} - 0.50\right]$ $= -88.44$ t/m (first value)
Eq. (B.12)	8	Find pressure at exterior load using Eq. (B.12) $p_e = \left(4W_e + \dfrac{6M_c}{a} - p_m L_1\right)\Big/(a + L_1)$ (with sign as M_c negative) $= \left(4 \times 225 - \dfrac{6 \times 88.44}{15} - 35.3 \times 5.4\right)\Big/(0.5 + 5.4)$ $p_e = 80.55$ t/m (for width B) Pressure $= \dfrac{80.55}{5.4} + 1.08 = 15.99$ t/m^2 Find also pressure at exterior end (with M_e as negative)
Eq. (B.12a)		$P_a = -(3M_e/a^2) - (p_e/2)$ $= \dfrac{3 \times 88.44}{(1.5)^2} - \dfrac{80.55}{2} = 77.66$ t/m Pressure $= \dfrac{77.66}{5.4} - 1.08 = 15.46$ t/m^2
	9	Again find M_e by Eq. (B.12b) assuming $p_a = p_c$ $p_a = p_e = (4W_e - p_m L_1)/(4a + L_1)$ (p_m in Step 4 = 35.3 t/m)

Ref.	Step	Calculations
Eq. (B.12b)		$p_e = \dfrac{(4 \times 275 - 35.3 \times 5.4)}{(4 \times 1.5 + 5.4)} = 79.79 \text{ t/m}$
Eq. (B.11)		$M_e = -\dfrac{p_e a^2}{2} = -\dfrac{79.79 \times (1.5)^2}{2} = -89.76 \text{ t m}$ (second value)
		M_e is lesser of Eq. (B.9) and (B.11) L_e Steps 7 and 9
		$= -88.4 \text{ t m}$
(Step 2)	10	*Determine positive moments in the exterior spans*
		$M_e = -88.44$ and $M_i = -129.4$ (for exterior span)
Eq. (B.7)		$M_0 = \dfrac{L^2}{48}(p_e + 4p_c + p_i)$
		$= \dfrac{(5.4)^2 \times [80.55 + (4 \times 35.3) + 83]}{48}$
		$= 185.4 \text{ tm}$
As in Eq. (B.8)	11	$M_c = 185.4 - \left(\dfrac{88.44 + 129.4}{2}\right) = 76.5 \text{ t m}$. (+ve moment external span).
		Sketch the contact pressure B.M. and S.F. diagrams
		These are drawn as Fig. E.B.1.
		(*Note:* Design of footing to be based on moment at face of column only and not at the centre of column.)

Notes 1. This problem can be worked out by using Tables in Refs. [6] or [7] with much more ease and accuracy. No lengthy calculations are necessary and restrictions of Sec. B.1 do not apply to these tables.

2. Even though we carry out the analysis using centre-to-centre distances for detailing of steel we need to consider only the moments at the face of the columns.

REFERENCES

[1] IS 2950 Part 1981, *Code of Practice for Design and Construction of Raft Foundation*, Bureau of Indian Standards, New Delhi.

[2] American Concrete Institute, *Suggested Design Procedure for Combined Footings and Mats*, Report of ACI Committee 436, Detroit, Michigan, 1966.

[3] Kramrisch, F. and P. Rogers, Simplified Design of Combined Footings, *Journal of the Soil Mechanics and Foundation Division, Proc. ASCE*, Oct. 1961.

[4] Kurien, N.P., *Design of Foundation System: Principles and Practice*, Narosa Publishing House, New Delhi, 1992.

[5] Iyengar K.T.S. and S.A. Raman, *Design Tables for Beams on Elastic Foundations*, Applied Science Publishers, London. 1979.

[6] Wolter K.H., *Beams on Elastic Foundations*, Influence Tables (English Edition), Bauverlag, GMBH. Wiesladen and Berlin 1978.

[7] Timoshenko and M. Gere, *Beams on Elastie Foundation—Charts and Tables of Coefficients*, McGraw-Hill, New York, 1961.

APPENDIX C

Analysis of Flexible Plate on Elastic Foundations

C.1 INTRODUCTION

We have found that an approximate analysis of beams on elastic foundation can be made by one of the following methods depending its relative rigidity K (as shown in section A.14) and column spacing L_B.

1. As a rigid beam when column spacing L_B is such that λL_B is less than 1.75.

2. Using influence tables if $\lambda L_B > 1.75 < 4.7$ (Appendix A)

3. By ACI approximate method if λL_B is between 1.5 and 3.5 (Appendix B).

In this chapter we will deal *with the fourth approximate flexible method* of analysing a very flexible elastic plate on elastic foundation using Hetenyi's solutions as given by ACI Committee 436[1] and also IC 2950 (Part I), [2]. In this method we find the radial and tangential moments (M_r and M_t) and the shear produced by a concentrated load at a radial distance r.

C.2 DESCRIPTION OF PROCEDURE

The following is the procedure usually followed:

· *Step 1*. Determine the minimum raft depth for maximum punching shear. Let the depth adopted be t.

Step 2. Determine the flexural rigidity D of the foundation per unit width.

$$D = E_c t^3/12(1 - \mu^2) \text{ (in kN/m)} \tag{C.1}$$

where

E_c = modulus of elasticity of concrete (20 to 25 $\times$ 10^6 kN/m^2)

μ = Poisson's ratio of concrete ≈ 0.15

Step 3. Determine the *radius of effective stiffness* L_e which gives us a measure of the flexibility of the raft.

$$L_e = \left(\frac{D}{K_{soil}}\right)^{1/4} \text{ (Note the definition of } L_e \text{ which will be in metres.)} \quad (C.2)$$

where K_{soil} = coefficient of subgrade reaction adjusted for mat size in kN/m^3.

The radius of influence of the column load is approximately $4L$ only as shown in Fig. C.1.

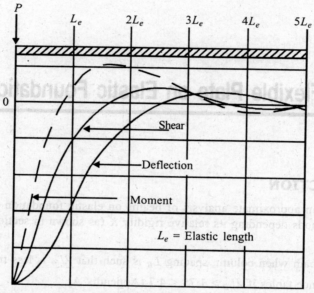

Fig. C.1 **Distance affected by moment, shear and deflection of a beam on elastic foundation subjected to a concentrated load.**

Step 4. From Hetenyi's solution, M_r and M_t, per unit width due to a load P can be determined for any point distant $x = r/L_e$ by using Z factors from the following equations [1], [2]:

$$\text{Radial moment, } M_r = -\frac{P}{4}\left[Z_4 - \frac{(1-\mu)}{x}Z_3'\right] \quad (C.3)$$

$$\text{Tangential moment, } M_t = -\frac{P}{4}\left[pZ_4 + \frac{(1-\mu)}{x}Z_3'\right] \quad (C.4)$$

$$\text{Shear, } V = -\frac{P}{4L}Z_4' \quad (C.5)$$

$$\text{Deflection, } \Delta = \frac{PL^2}{4D}Z_3 \quad (C.6)$$

where the Z values are obtained from Fig. C.2.

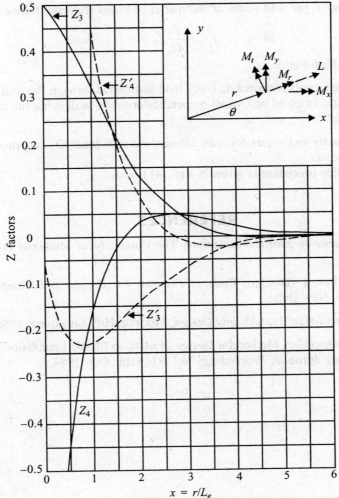

Fig. C.2 **Hetenyi's Z factors for calculating deflection moments and shears in a flexible plate.**

$$\text{The deflection under the load, } \Delta H = \frac{PL^3}{8D} \quad \text{(when } r/L_e = 0) \tag{C.7}$$

Step 5. Convert radial M_r and M_t into rectangular M_X and M_Y by the following transformation (see Fig. C.2):

$$M_X = M_r \cos^2 \theta + M_t \sin^2 \theta \tag{C.8}$$

$$M_Y = M_r \sin^2 \theta + M_t \cos^2 \theta \tag{C.9}$$

where θ is the angle as defined in Fig. C.2. The value of $x = r/L$ and L is as defined in Eq. (C.2).

At points where more than one load is effective, add their effects. When the edge of the mat is within the radius of influence, we first calculate the moments and shear perpendicular to the edge of the mat assuming the mat is infinitely large. Then we apply these as edge loads with opposite sign to satisfy the edge condition. For this purpose we use the method as applied for beams on elastic foundation.

Step 6. The shear *V per unit width* of the mat is obtained from the following equation:

$$V = -\frac{P}{4L}Z_4'$$

(C.10)

where Z_4' is obtained from Fig. C.2.

Step 7. A stiff deep wall is treated as a line load distributed through the wall to the mat. The mat may be divided into strips of unit width perpendicular to the wall using the method of beams on elastic foundations.

Step 8. All moments and shears for each column and wall loads are superimposed to get the final moments and shears.

An example of this procedure is given in Ref. [4] below.

REFERENCES

[1] Hetenyi, M., *Beams on Elastic Foundation*, The University of Michigan Press, Ann Arbor, 1946.

[2] IS 2950–1198: Part 1 (Design), *Code of Practice for Design and Construction of Raft Foundations* BIS, New Delhi.

[3] Bowles, J.E., *Foundation Analysis and Design*, McGraw-Hill, Singapore, 1988.

[4] Skukla, S.N., A Simplified Method for Design of Mats on Elastic Foundations, *Journal of the American Concrete Institute, Proceedings,* Vol. 81, Sept.–Oct. 1984.

APPENDIX D

Cyclic Load Tests and Estimation of Settlement in Piles

D.1 INTRODUCTION

In this appendix we will deal with the following topics to get an understanding of the type of settlements that taken place in single piles under vertical loads.

1. Cyclic load tests
2. Estimation of settlement of a single pile under vertical loads from soil data.

(The methods of estimation of the settlement of a group of piles is given in Chapter 4.)

D.2 CYCLIC LOAD TESTS ON PILES

This test was proposed by Van Weele in 1957. The aim is to evolve a test to separate the strength in friction and in bearing of a single pile. It is generally used as an initial test where the pile is loaded to its ultimate capacity (generally assumed as 2.5 times working load or settlement of 10% diameter of the pile). The allowable load on pile is defined as follows:

$$Q_{\text{allowable}} = \frac{Q_{U \text{ friction}}}{1.5} + \frac{Q_{U \text{ bearing}}}{3} \qquad (D.1)$$

where Q_U are the ultimate values.

The difference in factors of safety given above is due to the fact that whereas very little movement is needed to mobilize friction, larger movement is necessary to mobilize bearing resistance.

D.2.1 Cyclic Load Test Procedure

The *cyclic load test* should be conducted as detailed in IS 2911 (Part 4) 1985. Appendix A [1]. A plot of the elastic recovery at each unloading cycle versus load applied at that cycle is used for separating bearing and friction. The elastic recovery curve becomes linear after a few cycles. A graphical method used for this purpose is as follows:

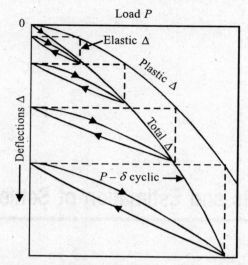

Fig. D.1 **Separation of elastic and plastic settlement in a cyclic load-settlement diagram.**

Step 1. Apply increments of 20% *of the calculated safe load.* At each loading the pile is unloaded to zero load and the loading and unloading curves are obtained as in Fig. D.1. By deducting plastic or permanent deformation from total deflection at each stage we get the elastic recovery for each load (Fig. D.1).

Step 2. Draw the load elastic recovery curve C_1 shown in Fig. D.2. The elastic recovery curve is made up of the elastic deformation (a) for mobilizing friction, (b) for mobilising bearing and (c) due to the deformation of the pile itself (Fig. D.2).

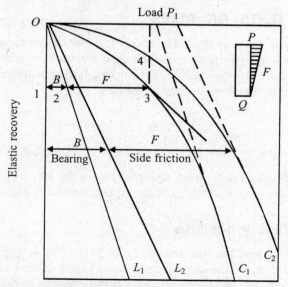

Fig. D.2 **Separation of point bearing and skin friction resisting using load-elastic compression curve got from cyclic load test.**

The elastic deformation of the pile $= (P - 1/2Q_{f/2})\dfrac{L}{AE} = \Delta L$. (D.2)

where

P = load on top of the pile

Q_f = friction resistance assumed as varying linearly from the top to the bottom as shown in Fig. D.2. Hence we apply factor 1/2 for calculating deformation.

E_p = modulus of elasticity of pile material.

L and A are respectively the length and area of cross-section respectively of pile. (We assume that the deformation is similar to that of a column under a load P at the top and subjected to frictional resistance linearly varying from top to bottom. The total frictional resistance being Q_f).

Step 3. We assume that only after full friction is mobilized bearing comes into play and *that the load settlement relation for bearing* will be linear. The last straight line part of the elastic recovery diagram can then be taken as representing the part due to bearing resistance.

Assuming that the elastic shortening of the pile $\Delta L = 0$, we draw a line parallel to the last straight line portion of load elastic recovery curve through the origin represented by straight line C_1 in Fig. D.2. We can assume roughly that under a load P_1, point 1 to 2 represents bearing and 2 to 3 represents friction Q_f.

So far we have not separated the pile deformation ΔL. We can now determine $(P - Q_{f2})(L/AE)$ as its first approximation. This is deducted from curve C_1 to get a new curve C_2. In Fig. D.2 for load P_1, $\Delta L = 3$ to 4, so that point 4 is on the curve C_2.

Step 4. The above operation is repeated to get new values of Q_f and Q_b till by successive approximation we get the final curve where there is not much difference between the two C curves.

Step 5. After deriving the final curve, a line parallel to the last linear part through the origin is drawn. The value of Q_b and Q_c corresponding to the failure load is read off and the safe load is calculated as follow.

$$Q_{safe} = Q_b/3.0 + Q_f/1.5$$

Notes:

(1) If we assume that the deformation of the pile is negligible, we may apply the principle explained above to the load total settlement curve of a conventional pile test loaded to its ultimate load also, to get approximate values of friction and bearing. By drawing a line parallel to the last linear part of the load settlement curve through the origin we can separate the capacity in bearing and capacity in friction. To these we can apply the factor of safety.

(2) It is obvious that the load elastic recovery curve we use in cyclic load test does not give the total settlement at various loads. To find the total settlement expected, we should use the load total settlement curve.

D.3 SETTLEMENT ANALYSIS OF SINGLE PILES

There is no accepted method for the estimation of the load settlement curve of a single pile under vertical load from soil data. Poulos and Davis [2] deals with this subject in great detail in their book on 'Pile Foundations Analysis and Design'. The following are some of the findings by various research workers.

1. Terzaghi's consolidation theory which is applicable for settlement of a group of piles is not applicable for calculating the settlement of a single pile.

2. Rate of settlement is of minor importance in a single pile. At loads well below the ultimate load, there is only a relatively small amount of time-dependent settlement for a single pile [3].

3. Large number of tests have shown that for all types of single piles up to 600 mm even in cohesive soils, the final settlement under working load will not exceed 10 mm more than that obtained in a pile test if we have a factor of safety of at least 2.5 on ultimate load based on codal provisions.

4. Reducing pile load by increasing the number of piles of the same length may reduce the settlement of one pile but will not decrease the total settlement.

5. The load is carried initially by friction which is fully mobilized by a settlement as little as 0.5% of shaft diameter in sand and about 1% of shaft diameter in clay (a settlement less than that specified at working load in many codes). Full mobilization of base resistance requires a movement as much as 10% tip diameter for driven piles and 20 to 30% base diameter for bored piles. Hence in the usual range of working loads the principal load carrying mechanism is the skin resistance except in the case of very soft soils.

D.3.1 Approximate Method for Drawing Load Settlement Curve

The following method based on the suggestion of Burland, Butler and Dunican [2] can be used to draw a very rough load settlement curve of a pile. We assume the relation is bilinear, the first part is due to friction and the second part due to bearing. The strength in bearing comes into play only after friction is exhausted. Friction is fully mobilized at 0.5% diameter of pile in sand and 1% of the diameter of the pile in clay depending on the type of soil. Thus we have the first part $0A$ in Fig. D.3 representing friction. The second part corresponding to strength in bearing can be assumed to be fully mobilized at a total settlement 10 to 20 percent of the diameter of the pile depending on the type of the soil. This represents part BC of the figure. A smooth curve between these boundaries is assumed to give a fair idea of the P–Δ curve.

D.3.2 Basis of the Theoretical Methods of Estimation of Load Settlement Curve of Single Piles by Paulos and Davis

Poulos and Davis [3] deal with many theoretical as well as a simplified method of estimation of load settlement of piles. We shall deal with only the basis of the simplified method. As it is based on a number of charts prepared for this purpose, we will not go into the details of the method.

The basic principle is to separate the load carried by friction and bearing for the floating piles and the bearing piles. In a floating pile the tip load will be a function of the L/D ratio, the larger its value the lesser will be the load transmitted to the tip. If β is the load transferred to the

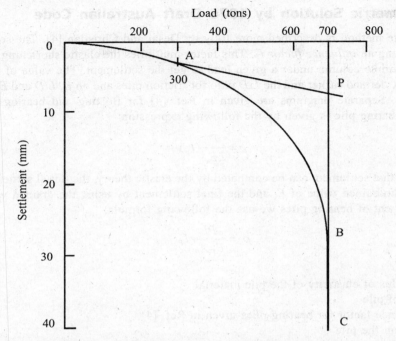

Fig. D.3 **Estimation of load-settlement curve of a pile from soil data.** [Also, see Fig. D.2]

base, then the load on the shaft will be $P(1 - \beta)$. Having separated the loads carried by the pile in friction and bearing we estimate the load settlement due to these separate effects and combine them to get the total effect. We also assume that most of the base settlement takes place only after the full frictional resistance has been mobilized.

One of the important factors thought of as affecting transfer of loads to the tip of end bearing piles is the *pile stiffness factor K* which is a messure of the relative compressibility of pile and the soil.

$$K = \frac{E_p R_A}{E_s} \tag{D.3}$$

where E_p and E_s are the modulus of elasticity of pile and the soil and R_A = area ratio = actual area of pile $\div$ $(\pi d^2/4)$, which for a solid pile, is equal to unity.

Typical values of K for solid concrete piles are as follows [3]:

Dense sand—500
Stiff clay—300
Loose sand—1500
Medium clay—2000
Soft clay—6000

The lesser the value of K, the lesser will be load carried by the tip and greater will be load carried by friction. For details, Reference 3 should be consulted.

D.3.3 Parametric Solution by 1976 Draft Australian Code

This approximate method is described more fully by Desai and Christian [4]. The settlement is calculated by using an *influence factor* I_P. This factor multiplies the elastic shortening of the pile as if it were a simple column under a given load to get the settlement. The value of I_P depends on the value of K defined earlier and the L/D ratio for friction piles and on K, L/D and E_p/E_s values for bearing pile. Separate diagrams are given in Ref. [4] for floating and bearing piles. The settlement for floating pile is given by the following expression:

$$\rho = \frac{P}{LE_s}(I_p) \tag{D.4}$$

We also assume that settlement can be computed by the elastic theory, the initial settlement being given by using undrained value of E_s and the final settlement by using the drained value of E_s.

For settlement of bearing piles we use the following formula:

$$\rho = \frac{PL}{E_P A_P} I_P \tag{D.5}$$

where

E_P = modulus of elasticity of the pile material
A_P = area of pile
I_P = influence factor for bearing piles given in Ref. [4].
P = load on the pile

One of the important uses of the above theory is to determine the value of the modulus of elasticity E of the given site by pile load test. The immediate settlement of the pile gives the undrained and the final settlement the drained values.

EXAMPLE D.1   (Cyclic load test on piles)

The following data was obtained in a cyclic load test on concrete piles. Determine the bearing and skin friction values at a load of 78 tons. Assume D(pile) = 400 mm; L = 10 m and f_{ck} = 25 N/mm^2.

No.	Load = P (tons)	Deflections (mm)			Diff. in recovery
		End of loading	End of unloading	Elastic recovery (R)	
1	40	2.50	1.50	1.00	
					1.3
2	80	5.50	3.20	2.30	
					3.2
3	120	10.50	5.00	5.50	
					4.1
4	160	24.00	14.40	9.60	
					4.1
5	200	29.70	16.00	13.70	

(*Note:* As the difference in elastic recovery towards end of test is almost linear last part is linear.)

Ref.	Step	Calculations
	1	*Plot the load elastic recovery diagram OAB* – Curve C_1
Fig. D.1		(*Note:* It is not the load total settlement diagram.) There should be a linear part *AB* towards the end of loading. Draw a line *OC* parallel to *AB*.
	2	*Find correction for Δl and draw modified diagram* Curve C_2 First assume $\Delta l = 0$ and find bearing (Q_b) and friction (Q_f). Find $\Delta l = (P - Q_f/2)(L/AE_c)$ using the following values:

$$E_c = \left(5000\sqrt{f_{ck}}\right) = 25 \times 10^6 \ \text{kN/m}^2$$

$$A = \pi(0.4)^2/4 = 0.126 \ \text{m}^2$$

$$L/AE_c = \frac{10 \times 1000}{0.126 \times 25 \times 10^6} = 3.17 \times 10^{-3} \ \text{mm/kN}$$

Example $P = 40$; $Q_f = 22$

$\Delta l = (40 - 22/2) \times 3.17 \times 10^{-3} = 0.092$ mm

For $P = 40$; $(R - \Delta l) = (1.0 - 0.092) = 0.91$

Repeat for all other values of for cycle 1. Plot the curve.

| | 3 | *Plot new values of load versus elastic recovery.* Repeat the process till the curve obtained is nearly the same. |

P tons	Δ mm	Trial 1			Trial 2			Q_{f3}	$(P - Q_f)$ $= Q_b$
		Q_{f1}	Δl	$R - \Delta l$	Q_{f2}	Δl	$R - \Delta l$		
40	1.00	22	0.092	0.91	28	0.082	0.918	28	12
80	2.30	40	0.290	2.11	54	0.168	2.132	54	26
120	5.50	58	0.190	5.21	66	0.276	5.220	66	54
160	9.60	66	0.400	9.20	70	0.396	9.204	70	90
200	14.00	68	0.520	13.48	70	0.523	13.47	70	130

As $Q_{f2} \approx Q_{f3}$, the trials can be stopped and the final values obtained.

| | | In this problem the second trial itself gives reasonable values. Generally, not more than three cycles will be required. |
| | 3 | *Find components of load at 75 tons* Components at $P = 75$ tons (50 tons in friction and 25 tons in bearing) (*Note:* Most of loads at lower intensity of loads are carried by friction). |

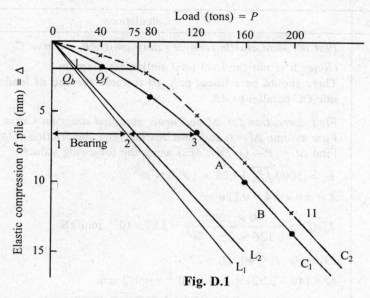

Fig. D.1

EXAMPLE D.2 (Estimation of load settlement curve)

The estimated frictional capacity of a pile as estimated from soil properties is 300 kN and its end bearing capacity is 400 kN. If the pile is 300 mm diameter and is installed in a medium sand deposit, estimate its probable load settlement curve.

Ref.	Step	Calculations
Sec. D.3 Item 4	1	*Find settlement to mobilize friction in full* For medium sand deposit, assume that full friction will be mobilized at settlement of 1% diameter of pile = 3 mm. Load for 3 mm settlement = 300 kN
Sec. D.3 Item 4	2	*Find settlement to mobilise bearing in full* Assume 10% dia. = 30 mm Load for 30 mm settlement = 300 + 400 = 700 kN
	3	*Sketch the load settlement curve* Draw a smooth curve from origin passing through the following points (assume scale 1" = 200 t and 1" = 20 mm) $P = 300$ kN; settlement = 3 mm $P = 700$ kN; settlement = 30 mm. A very approximate load settlement curve is as shown in Fig. D.2.

EXAMPLE D.3 (Separation of friction and bearing in pile load test)

The load settlement curve from test of a concrete bearing pile is shown by Fig. D.3. Estimate the approximate point resistance and skin resistance of the pile at the allowable load as per IS code on the pile. Assume M.20 concrete.

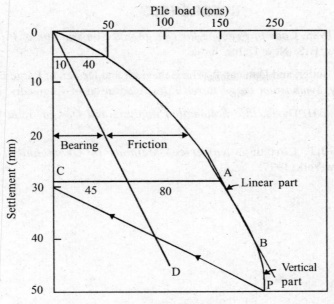

Fig. D.3

Ref.	Step	Calculations
IS 2911 (Part 4) 1985	1	*Determine the allowable load* It should be the lesser of the following. (a) 2/3 load for 12 mm settlement = 76 × 2/3 = 50 tons (b) 50% of load for settlement at 10% dia. of pile (400 × 0.10 = 40 mm) = 176/2 = 86 tons (c) Safe structural capacity = $(\pi D^2/4)(0.25\, f_{ck})$ = $[\pi \times (400)^2/4](0.25 \times 20)$ = 62.8 tons say 65 tons Hence allowable load = 50 tons (least of the three).
Sec. D.2	2	*Find approximate bearing and friction at allowable load* Assume settlement of the concrete pile in negligible. Draw a line *OD* parallel to *AB* the straight line portion of the pile load test curve. At 50 tons we have the following: Bearing value = 10 tons Friction value = 40 tons
Eq. (D.1)	3	*Find the bearing and friction from ultimate load* 2.5 × 50 = 125 tons (Assumed as ultimate capacity) Bearing capacity = 45 tons Friction value = 80 tons Check *F.S.* in friction and bearing $$\frac{80}{1.5} + \frac{45}{3} = 68 \text{ tons}$$ There is enough *F.S.* against bearing and friction.

REFERENCES

[1] IS 2911 (Part 4), 1985, *Code of Practice for Design and Construction of Pile Foundations, Load Test on Piles,* BIS, New Delhi, India.

[2] Burland, J.B, F.G. Butler, and Dunican P., The Behaviour and Design of Large Diameter, Bored Piles in Stiff Clay, *Symposium Large Bored Piles*, Institution of Engineers, London, 1966.

[3] Poulos, H.G. and E.H. Davis, *Pile Foundation Analysis and Design*, John Wiley & Sons, New York, 1980.

[4] Desai, C.S. and J.T. Christian, *Numerical Methods in Geotechnical Engineering*, McGraw- Hill, New York, 1977.

APPENDIX E

Building Foundations in Theory and Practice

Extracts of a PAPER BY KARL TERZAGHI*

E.1 INTRODUCTION

This paper deals with the influence of scientific reasoning on foundation engineering. Foundations can appropriately be described as a necessary evil. If a building is to be constructed on sound rock, no foundations are required. Hence, in contrast to the building itself which satisfied specific needs, appeals to the aesthetic sense and fills its makers with pride, the foundations merely serve as the support of the structure at the site which has been selected.

On account of the fact that there is no glory attached to the foundations, and that the sources of success or failure are hidden deep in the ground, building foundations have always been treated as stepchildren; but their acts of revenge for the lack of attention can be very embarrassing.

The Egyptian temples still arouse our admiration, three or four thousand years after they were built. Yet the design of the foundations was amateurish, and the performance of the foundations is a prolific source of concern for the engineers in charge of maintenance.

In the sixth century A.D. the engineers and architects of the Byzantine emperor Justinian amazed their contemporaries by the construction of the masonry dome of St. Sophia in Constantinople, which has a diameter of one hundred feet. To design this dome without the assistance of applied mechanics was an extraordinary accomplishment of engineering intuition. The dome was neither too weak nor too strong, and if the foundations of the supporting pillars had been adequate, the dome would have stood forever. However, when it came to design of the foundations, intuition did not operate properly and the dome collapsed repeatedly, during the first centuries of its existence, on account of a progressive outward tilt of the supporting piers. The buttresses which have been added to the piers to stop the movement deface the structure.

---

*This paper was presented by Prof. Terzaghi around 1950. Since then, a lot of progress has been made in Geotechnical Engineering. The above extracts are reproduced here only to indicate the approach Prof. Terzaghi recommended to engineers in their practice of Foundation Engineering.

Modern counterparts to the inadequate foundations of the Egyptians temples and St. Sophia are numerous and impressive: Railroad Terminal in Le Havre (about 1930), Palais de Justice in Cairo (about 1935), Charity Hospital in New Orleans (1938), Office Building Compania Paulista di Seguro, Sao Paulo (1945), and, quite recently, the Normal School of Mexico City. This structure was completed recently at an expense of about two million U.S. dollars. From an architectural point of view the building is a masterpiece. The walls are decorated by murals by one of the greatest modern painters of Mexico. Immediately after the building was completed an International Engineering Congress was inaugurated in its auditorium, and the members of the congress were impressed by both the architecture and the workmanship. Two years after the completion of the structure, the walls had already cracked up to such an extent, on account of unequal settlements, that it was necessary to evacuate the structure. It could not be reoccupied until the underpinning operations were completed and the defective structural members repaired.

Most of the members of this congress are primarily interested in the design and the construction of buildings and not of foundations. Hence in their practice they may try to assign the unglamorous occupation of foundation design to somebody else, reducing their own share to the request that the foundation "should not settle". However, the assignment may pass into the hands of a bungler, as it has so many times before. Therefore, the "Superstructure-man" should at least be informed on the hazards involved and on the progress which has been made in foundation engineering for reducing the hazards.

E.2   HISTORICAL REVIEW

The design of foundations is a branch of civil engineering. Experience has shown that most of these branches have passed in succession through two stages, the *empirical and the scientific stage*, before they reached the present and final one, which may be called the *state of maturity*.

In the *empirical stage*, results are obtained by trial and error at the price of occasional failures. The most important prerequisite for signal success is intuition, and, unfortunately, intuition is not hereditary. Hence progress is intermittent and slow.

In the *scientific stage*, an attempt is made to predict results by mathematical reasoning on the basis of test data and a few fundamental relationships. At the outset of this stage, the prospects for success appear to be unlimited, because it takes time until first disappointments and setbacks are the fore-runners of the third stage.

In the *third semi-empirical stage*, the ardour of the scientist is already tempered by bitter experience. The restrictions which nature has imposed upon the theoretical approach to engineering problems are clearly realised, and further progress is made on a *semi-empirical basis. A store of knowledge is accumulated which supplements and qualifies the conclusions based on analysis, whereby the status of analysis is gradually reduced from that of a Caesar to that of a member of an advisory committee.*

In the empirical stage of foundation engineering the relations between cause and consequence received no attention whatsoever. As a matter of fact, *in the middle ages*, the foundation was not even recognised as a specific part of the buildings. The lowest part of every wall was flared out as a matter of routine, and the base of the flared-out part was established on the bottom of a trench with a depth of several feet. If the earth exposed on the bottom of the trench inspired confidence it was not touched at all, and if it appeared to be weak it was reinforced by driving wooden piles into it.

It was towards the end of the nineteenth century, when science began to invade the various branches of engineering that it was realised by some advanced members of the profession that the width of the footings should be adapted in some fashion to the nature of the soil exposed on the bottom of the trench. This was accomplished by assigning to the principal types of soils 'allowable bearing values,' but no attempt was made to correlate the unit load with settlements. It was simply claimed—in the spirit of the empirical stage—that a building does not settle at all unless the unit load on the base of the footings is greater than the allowable bearing value, and the others believed the claim. The capacity for faith, in the empirical stage, is almost unlimited.

The transition of foundation engineering from the empirical stage into the scientific stage lagged far behind the corresponding transition in all the other branches of civil engineering, for the simple reason that foundations are a means and not an end. The transition started about 1900. It was prompted by increasing evidence that the gospel of the 'allowable soil pressures' does not live up to its promises.

The scientific stage of foundation engineering came into existence as soon as it was realised by a foundation engineer (and not by a physicist) that every load produces settlement, regardless of what the 'allowable bearing value' of the subsoil may be. The settlement depends on many factors other than the contact pressure on the base of the footings and the type of soil in contact with the base. These factors include the soil profile to a considerable depth below the base, and the dimensions of the loaded area. Therefore, a foundation cannot adequately be designed unless the relation between unit load and settlement is taken into consideration. Once this obvious fact was recognised, the artificial concept of the *allowable bearing value* was replaced by the concept of 'allowable settlement', and the efforts of a whole generation of engineers were concentrated on the development of reliable methods for predicting settlement on the bias of the results of laboratory tests.

Boussinesq published his equations for stresses in elastic media in 1885. As a result of such research activities, the relations between surface loads and the corresponding stresses and strains in the loaded soil were determined. The causes of the progressive settlement of building above clay strata became known through theory of consolidation published in 1922. Satisfactory techniques for sampling and testing were developed, and the theoretical problems involved in settlement forecasts were solved.

All this was accomplished within a quarter of a century, between about 1915 and 1940. During the same period, the first attempts were made to apply the findings to the design of foundations. Thus it was realised that the costs of accurate settlement forecasts are commonly out of proportion to the practical value of the results. *In most cases a crude estimate is all that is needed*. Therefore, the efforts of the research workers gradually turned from the exploration of the fundamental .relationships to the task of correlating settlement in a semi-empirical manner with the results of simple laboratory or field tests, such as penetration tests in drill holes. The next step was to verify the conclusions based on the test results by observations on full-sized structures, and to determine the errors involved in the use of the semi-empirical procedures. Investigations of this kind are symptomatic for the last or mature stage in the development of an engineering discipline. The indications of growing maturity can be recognised in every one of the different branches of foundation engineering.

E.3 SPREAD FOOTINGS

As a result of theoretical and experimental investigations covering a period of several decades, it is now known that the settlement of a footing due to a given load per unit of area of its base is a complex function of the dimensions of the base and of the compressibility, permeability and Poisson's number of all the soil strata located between the base and *a depth which is at least equal to three times the width of the base.* In other words, the relationship between unit load and settlement is very complicated. An accurate forecast of the settlement of a single footing supported by natural ground, on the basis of the results of soil tests, would be a full-time job for an exceptionally competent research engineer, backed by a sponsor who does not count the costs. On a foundation job involving the design of many footings with different sizes, it would be necessary to assign one such engineer, together with his sponsor, to each one of the footings, because as a rule the mechanical properties of the subsoil change from point to point, at least in a vertical direction.

On account of the complexity of the relations involved, scientific research in the realm of spread footings did not yield any results of immediate practical usefulness. However, it cleared the field of deep-rooted superstitions, and disclosed the type and relative importance of the factors which determine the settlement of the footings. Expedient and yet adequate procedures for footing design were subsequently developed by radical simplification of the real relationships, and by adapting the methods of subsoil exploration to suit the different types of soil.

The design of the footings for the Shamrock Hotel, a 22-storey reinforced concrete structure in Houston, Texas, is an example of a technique which can be used, if the subsoil consists of stiff, but non-homogeneous clay. The building covers an area of 275 by 200 ft. and it rests on 250 spread footings. The subsoil consists to a depth of at last several hundred feet of stiff Pleistocene clay with sandy layers and a few layers of fine, silty sand. The test borings furnished continuous, undisturbed samples to a depth of 50 ft. below the surface. The base of the footings is located at about 13 ft. below the surface. The liquid limit of the clay varied between 26 and 60, the natural water content between 17 and 29 and the unconfined compressive strength between 2.2 and 3.3 tons/sq.ft. It was obviously impracticable to find out which ones of the 250 footings are located on the least compressible parts and which ones on the most compressible parts of the clay deposit. Therefore, it was arbitrarily assumed that the largest footings rest on the most compressible parts of the clay stratum. The structure could be damaged by differential settlement only. An upper limiting value for the differential settlement was obtained on the basis of the fact that the difference between the settlement of any two adjacent columns will hardly be greater than the settlement of the heaviest footings. The design load was chosen such *that the computed settlement of this one footing does not exceed 3/4 inch.* The settlement computation was made on the basis of the results of soil tests which were performed many years ago in connection with another job in the proximity of the site of the new hotel.

If the subsoil of a footing foundation is cohesionless, the costs of securing undisturbed samples in adequate number are likely to be prohibitive, and the soil tests on such samples require very elaborate equipment. Therefore, several methods have been developed for securing information on the compressibility of cohesionless soils by means of penetration tests in the drill hole. Without such tests or equivalent subsoil investigations, the real settlement of the footings may be many times greater than the anticipated ones. The following incident is an example.

The footings for the columns of a one-storey factory building in Denver, Colorado, were designed on the assumption that the 'allowable bearing value' for the underlying sand is 2 tons/sq.ft. The unit pressure on the sand due to dead load was only 0.95 tons/sq.ft. When the total unit load increased for the first time on account of a heavy snowfall to 1.4 tons/sq.ft., which was still well below the "allowable bearing value", the columns settled by amounts ranging between 1/2 and $3^1/_2$ in.

At a later date, R.B. Peck *made penetration tests* in the same sand stratum preparatory to the design of the footing foundation of another structure. He found that the structure of the sand ranged between *loose* and *very loose*, and that it varied erratically in both vertical and horizontal directions. This observation explained the unsatisfactory performance of the foundation of the older structures, and furnished the data for the rational design of the footings of the new one.

In the humid tropics, crystalline rocks like granite or metamorphic schists are likely to *be decomposed* to great depth and transformed into a clay-like substance. Proceeding from the surface in a downward direction three different layers are encountered, a layer of topsoil or *creep material*, a layer of *soft decomposed rock*, and a layer of *hard decomposed rock*. Below the layer of topsoil, the original structure of liquid limit may be as high as 50 and the porosity as high as 35 per cent. The base of the footings is customarily established on the surface of the hard decomposed rock or, if this surface is located at great depth, on the surface of the soft decomposed rock. The boundary between the layers is commonly very uneven. In Brazil, the position of the boundaries is ascertained by measuring the rate of progress of wash borings. Each layer corresponds to a definite range of the rate. The method is satisfactory, provided the wash borings are made in strict compliance with standard specifications concerning the water pressure and the manipulation of the wash pipe.

If footings are to be constructed on cohesive soil, it is necessary to determine whether or not the properties of the soil located beneath the level of the base of the footings are subject to seasonal variations. Fortunately, significant variations below a depth of four or five feet are rather rare, but there are exceptions. Some twenty-five years ago, a Middle Western institute of higher learning decided to investigate the influence of the size of loaded areas on the settlement of footings. The project was sponsored by a government agency. The footings were established at a depth of several feet below the original ground surface on a gentle ridge during the winter months, and the loads were applied. In the spring it was found that some of the largest footings, carrying heavy loads, were located above the level which they occupied before the load was applied. This observation indicated that the clay soil composing the hill was subject to seasonal volume changes to considerable depth.

The most conspicuous seasonal variations of soil properties to considerable depth were observed in loess regions, and in areas located above highly colloidal and heavily pre-compressed clays in regions with marked contrasts between dry and wet seasons.

The strength of loess decreases rapidly with increasing moisture content. Hence, during the rainy season the bearing capacity of loess may be very much smaller than during the dry season. Some twenty years ago a large coal bin was built near Bobriki, south of Moscow in U.S.S.R. The footings rested on loess, and they were designed on the basis of an 'allowable bearing value' of 3 tons per sq.ft. This value was obtained by means of a loading test performed during the summer. In the fall, when the autumn rains started, the bin had not yet exceed a small fraction of the design load. Nevertheless, the structure was so severely damaged by unequal settlement that it had to be abandoned. Examples of the settlement of structures on loess due to leakage into the loess from sources located within the buildings were described by O.K. Peck in the proceedings of the Second International Conference on Soil Mechanics.

In order to avoid miscalculation of the bearing capacity of loess, the material should be tested at the highest water content which it may acquire after the structure has been erected, and provision must be made that the water content will never exceed this value on account of leakage from defective pipe lines or other manmade sources.

In regions with well-defined dry and wet seasons such as central Texas, parts of South Africa and the central plains of Burma, buildings with spread footings on highly colloidal and heavily precompressed clay are likely to be damaged by differential swelling to the accumulation of moisture beneath the areas covered by the buildings, or by differential shrinkage in exceptionally dry seasons. *Damage of this kind can be avoided by carrying the foundations to the lower boundary of the zone subject to seasonal variations, or else by maintaining free circulation of air between the ground surface and the base of the building.* Both procedures have been successfully used in Texas. It may also be possible in some cases to prevent, or at least to reduce differential heave, by giving to the base of the footings such dimensions that the pressure on the soil under dead load alone is equal to or greater than the swelling pressure of the clay.

These examples illustrate the present status of our methods for coping with the problem of footing design. The 'fundamental research' concerning the factors which determine the settlement of spread footings was practically completed many years ago, but the procedures for adapting our theoretical knowledge to the practical requirements are still in an experimental stage. The development work can only be carried out in the field in connection with foundation jobs, and the relative value of the results obtained can be judged only on the basis of well-documented case records accompanied by the records of reliable settlement observations.

E.4   RAFT FOUNDATIONS

Once the mechanics of settlement were revealed by soil mechanics research, it became evident that the settlement of a raft foundation does not depend on the weight of the building which is supported by the raft. It depends only on the difference between this weight and the weight of the soil, solid and water combined, which was removed prior to the construction of the raft, provided the heave produced by the excavation was inconsequential.

A few engineers gifted with exceptional common sense knew this fact long before soil mechanics came into existence. The design of the foundations of the Albion Mills in London by John Rennie, towards the end of the eighteenth century, and that of a few other old structures resting on very soft ground were based on the principle of keeping the structure "afloat." Yet, the number of engineers who grasped this principle and dared to take advantage of it was very small. As late as 1926 the writer met stubborn resistance when he tried to persuade one of his clients, the president of a prominent firm of consulting engineers, to omit the piles beneath a raft-supported structure, the weight of which was almost exactly equal to that of the displaced mass of water and soil.

The settlement of a raft-supported structure with a weight equal to that of the displaced materials, is roughly equal to that distance through which the soil rises. The level of the base of excavation should not be carried beyond the depth at which the weight of the surrounding soil may produce an upward heave movement of the soil located beneath the excavation. The methods for estimating heave in advance of excavation on the basis of the results of soil tests are rather inaccurate. *Therefore, it has become customary to verify the results of the estimates during the excavation operations by periodic levels on a set of underground observation.* The results of such heave observations are documents of general interest and should be published.

If the weight of excavated materials is smaller than the weight of the structures, the difference between the two weights can be assigned either to the soil or to piles. By driving the piles prior to excavation, the heave of the bottom of the excavation can be considerably reduced.

Outstanding examples of skilful utilisation of the principle of 'floating' and 'semi-floating' foundations can be found in Mexico City. The subsoil of this city, down to a depth of about 200 ft., contains thick layers of highly colloidal clay with water contents up to 300 per cent, of the dry weight. By systematic soil investigation, it was found that these clays do not start to consolidate unless the unit load on the strata is increased by very roughly 0.5 tons/sq.ft. beyond the overburden pressure. This critical load is referred to as the *breaking point* of the structure of the clay. On account of the relatively important difference between breaking point and overburden pressure, tall and heavy buildings can be constructed in Mexico City without the risk of important settlement. This is done by giving to the sub-basements such a depth that the ultimate load on the subsoil of the raft is slightly smaller than the load corresponding to the breaking point. The breaking point is determined prior to construction by standard consolidation tests on undisturbed samples.

The subsoil to Mexico City contains several layers of water-bearing sand. If the excavation for a sub-basement is made, the water table must be lowered to a level below the bottom of the excavation. Otherwise the heave may be excessive. Both soil mechanics and experience have shown that the process of drainage causes a bowl shaped settlement of the ground surface surrounding the seat of the pumping operations. The settlement at the centre of the bowl depends on the thickness and compressibility of the silt or distance through which the water level is lowered. In Mexico these strata are very compressible. Therefore, the settlement may be important enough to damage existing structures located in the proximity of the drained area.

An original and successful method for preventing such damage has recently been used by L. Zeevaert in Mexico City, in connection with the excavation of the sub-basement for a 44-storey office building. The depth of the excavation was about 40 ft. and the base of the footings of the adjacent buildings is located at a considerable height above the bottom of the excavation. In order to prevent settlement due to the consolidation of the highly compressible subsoil of the existing footings by drainage, the water which is pumped out from beneath the excavation is injected under pressure into the subsoil of the footings.

All these important and original applications of soil mechanics to the solution of exceptionally difficult foundation problems were conceived and put into practice by Mexican engineers, after their interest in the young science had been aroused. Yet, at the same time, and at the very seat of their activities, spectacular failures like the differential settlement of the Normal School have occurred, because from time to time even the foundations of important structures are still designed without taking advantage of what the best informed local engineers have known for many years. Similar incongruities may be encountered in almost every part of the world. They are due to the fact that it takes time for newly acquired knowledge to percolate from the points of origin within the individual engineering communities to the outlying districts and to rise, by capillarity, to the peaks of administration.

E.5 PILE FOUNDATIONS

During the empirical stage of foundation engineering it was sincerely believed that the settlement of a pile foundation depends exclusively on the load per pile. Hence the settlement of the pile foundation was assumed to be equal to the settlement of the test pile under the design load.

When the other branches of civil engineering entered, the scientific stage one by one, foundation engineers made pseudo-scientific attempt to simplify and improve the methods of pile foundations by the derivation of the so-called pile-formulae. These equations represent the relation between the penetration of the last blows of the hammer and the ultimate bearing capacity of the pile.

The design of pile foundations did not enter a truly scientific stage until it was realised *that the ratio between the settlement of a pile foundation and that of a simple pile acted upon by the design load can have almost any value.* This is due to the fact that the settlement of an individual pile depends only on the nature of the soil in direct contact with the pile, whereas the settlement of a pile foundation also depends on the number of piles and on the compressibility of the strata located between the level of the points of the piles and the surface of the bedrock. If a single pile is loaded with one half of its ultimate bearing capacity, its settlement never exceeds half an inch. Commonly it is very much smaller. However, if each one of five hundred piles is assigned a load equal to one half of its ultimate bearing capacity, the settlement of the foundation may have any value between half an inch and several feet, depending on the nature of the soil strata located beneath the points of the piles.

Modern methods for the design of pile foundations take into consideration all the factors which determine the settlement of pile foundations, *including the compressibility of the soil located below the points of the piles.* Hence these methods can be considered reliable, provided the subsoil of the proposed foundation has been adequately explored. On the other hand, if the subsoil conditions have been misjudged, for instance, on account of inadequate sampling operations, erroneous interpolation between anticipated and real settlement can be distressingly important in spite of our advanced knowledge of the mechanics of the settlement of pile foundation. This is due to the fact that the *correct interpretation of erroneous data* has no advantage over the *erroneous interpretation of accurate data* which has been practised so extensively during the empirical stage of foundation engineering. The consequences of misjudging the soil conditions are illustrated by the following incident.

A few years ago an important structure was erected on the gentle slope of a shallow valley in one of the suburbs of New York. The site was investigated by means of 120 standard exploratory borings to bedrocks. The drill holes were spaced 50 feet both ways. According to the boring records, the rock bottom of the valley was covered with a thick layer of sand and gravel which, in turn, was overlaid in succession by soft clay, peat and recent fill. Therefore, it was decided to establish the foundation on point-bearing concrete piles to be driven into the sand and gravel stratum. The piles were driven with a heavy steam hammer, and driving was continued until the penetration under the last eight blows became less than one inch. The design load was 30 tons per pile.

During the pile driving operations it was noticed that the elevations at which the piles of the same cluster met refusal varied by amounts up to thirteen feet. This fact did not receive any attention because it was reasoned that it does not make any difference how deep the piles go provided they penetrate the gravel stratum and meet refusal. However, when the building was almost completed the first settlement cracks appeared, and during the next four years the middle part of the south wall, oriented at right angles to the axis of the valley, had gone down by about ten inches with reference to its ends. The maximum differential settlement of the south wall amounted to about three inches.

The owner claimed that the settlement was due to inadequate bearing capacity of the piles. In order to find out whether this accusation was justified, the heads of the piles supporting one of the largest footings were exposed by excavation. Some of the piles were cut off and loading tests were performed by inserting hydraulic jacks between the base of the footing and the upper ends of the several piles. The loading tests furnished the following result: None of the piles moved with reference to the base of the footing under a pressure of less than 100 tons, and two of the piles could not even be moved by a pressure of 200 tons. Prior to the test, none of the piles had carried a load of more than 25 tons. Yet the cluster had settled eight inches and it continued to settle during the loading tests.

The test results, combined with various other indications, led to the conclusion that the homogeneous sand and gravel stratum shown in the official boring records did not exist. Its place was *occupied by a very much thicker layer of clay*, interspersed with lenses of sand and gravel. The clay located between the lenses of sand and gravel had escaped the attention of the man in charge of the soil exploration. Very few, if any, of the piles had approached the base of this stratum. *Most of them had met refusal in the gravel pockets close to the upper boundary*. This was shown by the driving records of the different piles in each cluster. The longest piles had crossed in succession two of three hard 'layers' separated from each other by soft material, whereas the shortest ones met refusal in the first gravel pocket they met. The progressive settlement was due to the gradual consolidation of the layers of clay located between the gravel pockets which contained the points of the piles.

As long as the prevalent standards of boring, sampling and testing still permit such flagrant oversights, occasional failures of pile foundations will occur, in spite of the fact that the mechanics of the settlement of pile foundations are already clearly understood.

The only important controversial issue connected with pile foundations is the effect on the consistency of the clay of driving piles into clay. Some engineers claim that the effect is inconsequential. Others maintain that the penetration of the pile, combined with the vibrations set up by the falling hammer, destroy the structure of the clay completely and inaugurate a new process of consolidation which drags the piles in a downward direction. Hence, it is said, once the piles are driven into the clay, they would settle on account of their contact with the 'remoulded' mass of clay even if they are not loaded at all.

Experience indicates that some clays behave in accordance with the opinion of the first group of engineers, whereas others oblige the second group. *The soft glacial clays of Detroit*, Michigan, appear to be almost unaffected by pile driving operations. On the other hand, the soft organic clay of Abbots inch, West of Glasgow in Scotland, was practically liquefied to a distance of many feet from the seat of pile driving operations. When the driving of the second cluster of piles was started, at the site for a pile foundation, the piles of the first cluster started to rise. To prevent the rise it was necessary to load them. However, we do not yet know whether the re-consolidation of this or of similar clays is associated with a significant volume decrease. This important question can be answered only by systematic levels of the ground surface during and after pile driving operations or by settlement observations on groups of piles which have been driven but not loaded. Such investigations have not yet been made.

E-6 CONCLUSIONS

The preceding review of the interaction between soil mechanics and foundation engineering has shown that foundation engineering has definitely passed from the scientific state into that of maturity. *The time is gone when contributions of great practical importance could still be made by pure reasoning at the desk or by small-scale laboratory tests.* As a matter of fact, perusing the field, one gets the impression that research has outdistanced practical application, and that the cap between theory and practice still widens.

Intricate mathematical investigation are still being performed on the subject of the influence of elastic anisotropy on the stress distribution in the subsoil of loaded footings. The errors due to neglecting this influence can hardly exceed thirty per cent. On the other hand, we learn from time to time about recently constructed, expensive buildings which must be underpinned on account of excessive settlement. The necessity for underpinning indicates that the settlement is *at least ten times greater than the designer anticipated.* The investigations of the relation between the pile penetration under blow and the ultimate bearing capacity of the individual pile have reached an unprecedented level of refinement; but on the job, few engineers are inquisitive enough to attempt correlation between the *boring and the pile-penetration records.* If the piles of an individual cluster meet refusal at very different depths, they hardly care about the cause unless it is explained to them, at a later date, by the expert witness of the owners before the courts.

If the soil conditions are clear and simple, an elementary knowledge of soil mechanics, combined with the most primitive methods of dry-sample borings, is nowadays sufficient to prevent flagrantly erroneous forecasts. Such conditions prevail, for instance, if the site for a structure is located above continuous layers of soft clay with well-defined upper and lower boundaries. During the empirical stage of foundation engineering, subsoil conditions of this type were responsible for some of the most spectacular cases of settlement on record, including most of the cases listed at the outset of this paper. The recurrence of foundation defects under simple conditions in recent years is due merely to the fact that some foundation engineers are still in the empirical stage. The advancement into the higher stages is a voluntary and not a compulsory act.

Unfortunately, in practice, clear and simple soil conditions are rather uncommon; and if the soil conditions are complex, the advanced state of soil mechanics is of no avail. The engineer in charge of the soil exploration should be fully aware of the virtues and deficiencies of the different techniques, and capable of adapting these techniques to the local soil conditions and the exigencies of the job.

Since there is an infinite variety of subsoil patterns and conditions of saturation, the use of the different methods of subsoil exploration cannot be standardized, but the methods themselves still leave a wide margin for improvement, as far as expediency and reliability are concerned. Hence it appears that the development of these techniques and the comparison between forecast and actual performance of the foundation constitutes for the present, and for many years to come, one of the most important subjects of research in the realm of building foundations. These methods include penetration tests in the drill hole, vane tests and unconfined compression tests on the job by means of portable apparatus. Other equally important topics for further research are the effect of pile penetration on the consistency of clays, the 'breaking point' of the structure of soft clays, and the laws which determine the rate of settlement of structures above clay due to secondary time-effects. All these investigations can be performed only in the field, at appropriately selected sites. The journal Geotechnique and the proceedings of the International Conferences on Soil Mechanics and Foundation Engineering serve as clearing houses for these findings.

Index